Asian American Religious

Asian American Religious Cultures

Jonathan H. X. Lee, Fumitaka Matsuoka, Edmond Yee, and Ronald Y. Nakasone, Editors

Volume 2

Entries I–Z

American Religious Cultures

ABC-CLIO™

An Imprint of ABC-CLIO, LLC
Santa Barbara, California • Denver, Colorado

Library of Congress Cataloging-in-Publication Data

Asian American religious cultures / Jonathan H.X. Lee, Fumitaka Matsuoka, Edmond Yee, and Ronald Y. Nakasone, editors.

    volumes cm .– (American Religious Cultures)

  Includes bibliographical references and index.

  ISBN 978-1-59884-330-9 (alk. paper) – ISBN 978-1-59884-331-6 (ebook)

1. Asian Americans–Religion–Encyclopedias. 2. Asian Americans–Social life and customs–Encyclopedias. 3. United States–Religion–Encyclopedias. I. Lee, Jonathan H. X., editor. II. Matsuoka, Fumitaka, editor. III. Yee, Edmond, 1938- editor. IV. Nakasone, Ronald Y., editor.

  BL2525.A845   2015

  200.89′95073–dc23   2014046610

ISBN: 978-1-59884-330-9
EISBN: 978-1-59884-331-6

19 18 17 16 15   1 2 3 4 5

This book is also available on the World Wide Web as an eBook.
Visit www.abc-clio.com for details.

ABC-CLIO, LLC
130 Cremona Drive, P.O. Box 1911
Santa Barbara, California 93116-1911

This book is printed on acid-free paper ∞

Manufactured in the United States of America

Contents

VOLUME 2

PART 2: Entries

Guide to Related Topics

ESSAYS

Arts and Cultural Production
Bible and Asian Americans
Care and Service
Catholics
Christian Fellowships
Gender and Sexuality
Immigration
Interpretation
Islamophobia
Jews
LGBT Asian Americans and Christianity
Muslims
Panethnic Religious Institutions
Politics and Religion
Religion and Law
Religion, Race, and Orientalism
Secularization and Asian Americans
Spirituality
Theological Construction

ENTRIES

Canonical Literature

Confucian Canon
Daoist Canon
Hindu Canon
Islamic Canon
Sikh Canon
Tripiṭaka (Buddhist Canon)

Ethnic Religious Communities

Afghan American Religions
Burmese Americans
Cambodian American Religions
Cambodian Americans and
    Mormonism
Cham Americans
Cham Muslims
Chamorro Spirituality
Chinese American Religions
Filipino Protestants
Hawaiian Religion
Hezhen (Nānai) Shamanism
Hmong American Religions
Hmong Shamanism
Indian American Christians
Indian American Muslims
Indian American Sikhs
Indonesian American Muslims
Indonesian American Religions
Iu Mien
Japanese American Christianity
Japanese American Internment,
    Remembrance and Redress

Japanese American Mortuary and
  Memorial Rituals
Japanese American Religions
Korean American Religions
Korean Buddhism
Korean Shamanism
Laotian American Religions
Marshall Islands, Religion in
Micronesian and Polynesian Traditional
  Religions
Mongolian American Religions
Nepali American Religions
Okinawan (Ryūkyūan) Spiritual
  Culture
Pacific Islander Religious Cultures
Pakistani American Religions
Samoan Spirituality
Taiwanese American Religions
Thai American Religions
Thai Buddhist Immigrant Culture
Thai Buddhist Immigrant Spirituality
Tibetan American Religions
Tongan Spirituality
Vietnamese American Buddhists
Vietnamese American Catholics
Vietnamese American Religions
Yamato Colony

Religious Arts and Music

Aikidō
Arabic (Islamic) Calligraphy
Buddha Image
Butoh
Chanoyu
Chinese Drama and Religion
Classical Indian Dance
Hindustani Classical Music
Japanese Gardens
Shin Buddhist Music
Sho, Calligraphy

Religious Concepts, Deities, Ideas, and Symbols

Aloha Spirit
Dragons
Guangong
Guanyin
Han
Kava
Lotus Flower
Nāga
Reincarnation in Dharmic Religions
Sikh Gurus
Sovereignty
Swastika
Tianhou, Empress of Heaven
Yinyang

Religious Denominations, Sects, and Traditions

Asiamericans in the Episcopal Church
Caodaism
Confucianism
Daoism
El Shaddai
Falun Dafa/Falun Gong
Filipino Protestants
Gedatsu-kai
Higashi Honganji
Hoa Hao Buddhism
Iglesia Ni Cristo (INC)
Ijun
Jainism
Jehovah's Witnesses
Jōdo Shū (Pure Land Sect)
Konkōkyō/The Konko Faith
Lutherans
Mahikari (True Light)
Malaysian American Religions
Mormons

Nichiren Shōshū
Nichiren Shū
North American Pacific/Asian Disciples (NAPAD)
Presbyterian Churches of Japanese Heritage
Reiyūkai
Rinzai Zen
Risshō Kōsei-kai (RKK)
Santo Niño
Seichō no Ie (SNI)
Sekai Kyūsei-kyō Izunome (Church of World Messianity)
Selma (California) Japanese Mission Church
Seventh-day Adventist Church
Shamanism, Modern
Shingon
Shinnyo-en
Shinrankai
Shintō
Soka Gakkai
Sōtō Zen
Tendai Shū
Tenrikyō
Theravāda Buddhism
United Church of Christ (UCC)
United Methodism

Religious Festivals

Chinese New Year
Duanwu Festival
Eid al-Adha, Festival of Sacrifice
Ghost Festival/Zhongyuan Festival
Indian Festivals
Matsuri
Mid-Autumn Festival
Obon (Urabon)
Qingming Festival
Ramadan
Songkran

Ullambana Assembly
Vesākha (Vesak)

Religious Figures

Aglipay, Gregorio (1860–1940)
Bhante Dharmawara (Bellong Mahathera) (1889–1999)
Chan, Wing-tsit (1901–1994)
Choy, Wilbur W. Y. (1918–)
Estrella, Julia Keiko Higa Matsui (1940–)
Henepola Gunaratana (1927–)
Hsuan Hua (1918–1995)
Imamura, Yemyō (1867–1932)
Kagiwada, David (1929–1985)
Kubose, Gyomay (1905–2000)
Mahā Ghosananda (1929–2007)
Matsushita, Eiichi (1930–1984)
Morikawa, Jitsuo (1912–1987)
Nakamura, Paul T. (1926–)
Rajan, Frederick E. N. (1949–)
Ratanasara, Havanpola (1920–2000)
Sano, Roy I. (1931–)
Shunryū Suzuki (1904–1971)
Swami Prabhavananda (1893–1976)
Swami Vivekananda (1863–1902)
Tarthang Tulku (1935–)
Thich Duc Niem (1937–2003)
Thich Thien An (1926–1980)
Trungpa, Chögyam (1939–1987)
Tu Weiming (1940–)
Wake, Lloyd K. (1922–)
Wangyal, Ngawang (1901–1983)
Yee, James J. (1968–)

Religious Institutions and Organizations

Bala Vihar
Berkeley Buddhist Monastery

Religious Rituals and Practices

Part 2

Entries

I

Iglesia Ni Cristo (INC)

Iglesia Ni Cristo (INC), translated as "Church of Christ," is a religion indigenous to the Philippines. Felix Y. Manalo, a charismatic jack-of-all-trades turned preacher and proselytizer at age 28, founded the INC on July 27, 1914. It celebrated its centennial year in 2014 with a flurry of construction projects, the most notable of which is the Philippine Arena, the world's largest domed indoor arena with a capacity of 55,000.

Early in its growth, Manalo saw the importance of a distinct architecture to mark the INC. Its churches in the Philippines, which it officially calls chapels, are in the modern Gothic style, with lancet windows, pinpoint spires, towers, and minarets. Its building aspirations are realized through its own Engineering and Construction Department, whose staff consists of church members. INC churches are now regular features of the Philippine landscape.

From 12 converts in Punta, Santa Ana, the INC has expanded to more than 70 countries and territories, with large congregations in places with concentrations of Filipino diaspora. As the leading home and destination of Filipino immigrants and transnationals, the United States hosts the highest number of INC believers outside the Philippines, with most residing in California. The states in which the INC has not been able to establish a congregation are Delaware, Louisiana, Maine, North and South Dakota, Vermont, West Virginia, Wisconsin, and Wyoming. However, if the INC's astonishing growth continues, it will extend its reach to all 50 states.

The Iglesia Ni Cristo now permeates the globe. In North America, aside from the United States, the INC is also thriving in Canada and Mexico. INC believers are scattered throughout Africa, Europe, the Pacific Islands, the Caribbean, the Middle East, and Central and South America. Other countries with a significant number of "locales," as INC congregations with resident ministers are called, include Australia, New Zealand, Italy, Germany, the United Kingdom, Japan, Malaysia, and Taiwan. Although still a predominantly Philippine religion, INC members and ministers are no longer limited to Filipinos. Its media website claims that the INC comprises 110 nationalities. It is a far cry from its beginnings when the only non-Filipinos on its membership rolls were military spouses stationed at U.S. bases in the Philippines. The INC does not allow interreligious marriages. Conversion into the INC is required for all spouses of INC members.

In spite of the INC's perceptible global reach, the precise number of INC believers is not available. The INC does not publish statistics on its total membership numbers and the overall number of ordained ministers.

Thousands of followers of the Christian sect Iglesia Ni Cristo (Church of God) listen to speakers during a religious rally, February 28, 2012, in Manila, Philippines. The gathering was one of the biggest religious gatherings to rival the mammoth crowd during Pope John Paul II's visit in 1995. (AP Photo/Pat Roque)

In the Philippines, 2.3 percent of the population identifies as belonging to the Iglesia Ni Cristo. Islam, a non-Christian religion that is firmly rooted in the Philippines, accounts for 5 percent of the population. In 2013, 80 percent of the population was affiliated with Roman Catholicism. The Philippine population was estimated at around 107 million in 2014. Many speculate that the continuing success of the INC in the Philippines is due to their use of local dialects, particularly Tagalog, from its inception, instead of English. Like many indigenous Philippine religions still thriving in Central Luzon, the INC emphasizes the importance of brotherhood among its members by enjoining them to be generous and helpful to each other in practice. Members also call each other *Kapatid* (brother/sister).

The INC's unprecedented growth in the Philippines and abroad can be attributed to its successful recruitment of members of Catholic and Protestant denominations. Although its name invokes a Christian identity, the INC preaches distinct differences between its beliefs and those of other Christians, particularly Catholicism. The fundamental difference between the INC and other Christian churches is the INC's teaching that Christ is not God but man. Christians consider Christ true God and true man. For the INC, there is the one true God, the Creator, and it is not Jesus Christ. Although Christ is not God, neither is he an ordinary man because God has exalted him above other men and sent him to save mankind from sin. With the absolute oneness of God and the humanity of Christ, the Catholic doctrine of the Trinity loses its value in the eyes of the INC.

According to the INC, faith in Jesus is not enough for salvation. One must be a member of the Iglesia Ni Cristo to be saved on Judgment Day. INC theology maintains that the Iglesia and Christ's body are one, and if a person enters Christ's body by becoming an INC member, then the person shall be free from condemnation and shall be saved. Those outside the Church of Christ, who are separated from his body, will face eternal damnation.

The INC also strongly rejects the Catholic tradition of the veneration of saints and the worship of images, which it calls idolatry. It claims that image worship is a pagan practice, and that the Catholic Church appropriated many pagan beliefs into its theology. It also repudiates the Catholic practices of confession of sins to priests, the Mass, and the notion of purgatory.

INC's denunciation of Catholicism is a result of the charge that Catholic teachings are replete with man-made doctrines, and therefore have strayed from the true gospel. On the other hand, INC claims that their beliefs are strictly based on the Bible, with its ministers as true teachers of the scriptures. Felix Manalo's own journey of faith may have influenced the INC's total adherence to the Bible. He allegedly attained enlightenment after locking himself up without

food and water for three days and three nights, with only the Bible as his company and reference. For 49 years Manalo guided the INC, training ministers on the Bible instruction and evangelization.

The INC's absolute faith in the Bible is reflected in its worship services, which are offered twice a week on Thursdays and Sundays. Lasting approximately an hour, worship service consists primarily of Bible studies, using the Socratic method of teaching, and hymn singing led by a choir. A minister leads the service by asking theological questions, which can be answered by quoting passages from the Bible.

Grand Evangelical Missions (GEMS), which introduce nonmembers to the INC, are also organized around a Bible lesson. For about an hour every month, a group within the church sponsors a GEM by inviting newcomers and preparing a reception following the Bible lesson.

Similar in format to a GEM, Bible expositions occur once or twice a year. After the Bible lesson, an elaborate program follows, where attendees are treated to a generous buffet, musical performances by the church members, and an introductory video or slide presentation.

At Manalo's death in 1963 at the age of 77, he became more than the first executive minister of the INC. Members viewed him as the "Last Messenger of God." INC leadership passed on to his son, Eraño Manalo, also known as *Ka* Erdy (Brother Erdy), until his death in 2009. The current INC executive minister is Eraño's son, Eduardo.

Under Ka Erdy's leadership, the INC expanded to the "Far West." Its first mission outside the Philippines was in Hawai'i in

Ewa Beach, Honolulu. The establishment of the Honolulu locale on July 27, 1968, was seen by the INC as the fulfillment of God's prophecy in Isaiah 43:5, "From the far east will I bring your offspring, and from the far west I will gather you." The prophecy was confirmed with the organization of the first INC congregation on the U.S. mainland. In August of the same year, the INC formed the San Francisco, California, locale. Aside from San Francisco, some of the INC's largest congregations are in Northern California. Today, the INC church in Daly City, where Filipino Americans are the majority of the population, serves as the Northern California District Office.

Under the tutelage of the Manalos, the INC has established itself as a civic-minded religious institution. It classifies its social projects into four areas: employment and livelihood; housing and rural settlement; health services and disease prevention; and environmental protection and disaster relief. Daly City has recognized the INC's civic engagement by twice declaring a week in July as Iglesia Ni Cristo Week. INC members have been actively involved in community service events such as blood drives, beautification projects, and food distribution programs. In February 2014, the INC launched a massive charity walk in Manila for victims of the super typhoon known locally as Yolanda, which devastated the city of Tacloban in the province of Leyte. This INC event set the Guinness world record for most number of participants in a charity walk.

Ofelia O. Villero

See also: Entries: Aglipay, Gregorio; El Shaddai; Filipino Protestants

Further Reading

Elesterio, Fernando G. *The Iglesia ni Kristo: Its Christology and Ecclesiology.* Quezon City, Philippines: Ateneo de Manila University Press, 1977.

Gonzalez, Joaquin Jay, III. *Filipino American Faith in Action: Immigration, Religion, and Civic Engagement.* New York: New York University Press, 2009.

Santiago, Bienvenido, ed. *75 Blessed Years of Iglesia ni Cristo: 1914–1989.* Quezon City, Philippines: Iglesia ni Cristo, 1989.

Ijun

In 1972, Takayasu Ryūsen (aka Rokurō) was inspired by traditional Ryūkyūan (Okinawan) shamanic beliefs and culture to found Ijun, which was recognized in 1980 as a new religion under the Japanese Religious Corporations Law (Shūkyō Hōjinhō). As soon as it received official sanction, Ijun joined the Shinshūren (Federation of Japanese New Religions) and began its overseas activities.

Ijun is devoted to the worship of Kinmanmon, the supreme cosmic deity of the Ryūkyūs, who is mentioned in *Ryūkyū shintōki* (*A record of the deities of Ryūkyū*) by the Jōdo Shū Buddhist cleric Taichū Ryutei (1552?–1639). After an absence of 360 years, Kinmamon appeared to Takayasu in the early 1970s and convinced him of the need to systematize Ryūkyūan spirituality and create a new world religion. The absence of Kinmamon from the world corresponds to the Japanese domination of the Ryūkyūs that commenced with Satsuma's 1609 invasion and the pending return of the Ryūkyūs to Japan in 1974.

Takayasu understood Kinmamon to be a mysterious universal life force that people must awaken to; this life force is accessible to everyone, regardless of his or her faith tradition. He identified the power that possessed him to be "*Uchinaa* or Ryūkyū Power." Ordinarily, *uchinaa* is an expression that the Ryūkyūans (Okinawans) have used to refer to their island homeland. Even today Okinawans refer to themselves as *Uchinaanchu*, people of Uchinaa, vis-à-vis the Japanese.

Born in Naha on the island of Okinawa, Takayasu exhibited from an early age the classical signs of a Ryūkyūan *yuta* (shaman). His community recognized that he possessed *saadakaumari* (inborn capacity) for *kamidaari* (spirit possession, shamanic trance). Cognizant of his shamanic propensities, his mother introduced him to Seicho no Ie, a spiritual movement founded by Taniguchi Masaharu (1893–1985) in 1930. As a result of his spiritual capacity Takayasu was appointed to lead the Okinawan branch of the organization at the age of 36. Takayasu attracted many devotees because of his ability to access and channel the energy of the Ryūkyūan and ancestral spirits to healing. However, since shamanic healing was not part of the Seicho no Ie program, he was expelled from the organization. Shortly thereafter, he experienced *kamidaari* that resulted in sleep disorders, psychosomatic disturbances, and visions. Takayasu's shamanic journey corresponds to the pattern of the Ryūkyūan *yuta*, except for one important difference: the office has been traditionally reserved for women.

After leaving Seicho no Ie, he started the magazine *Ijun*. The expression *ijun* means "artesian well" or "spring" in the vernacular; it is rendered by the Sino-Japanese characters for *ryū*, "dragon" and *sen*, "artesian well." By associating the characters for "dragon," a most auspicious creature, with "artesian spring," the ancient Ryūkyūans articulated their profound appreciation for life-giving water and its mysterious source and power. Water sources are designated as *ugwanju*, sacred places worthy of devotion.

Ijun established its headquarters at Ginowan City in 1983. At that time it had approximately 1,000 devotees. Three years later, the organization was severely criticized for wanting to erect a large image of Kannon (Avalokiteśvara) at an ancient grave site. Shortly thereafter several members of the leadership absconded with the organization's money, leaving it in disarray. Two months later Ijun left its Ginowan headquarters, which is now a dormitory. After this event Takayasu received a revelation of employing a "power card" to receive spiritual energy from Kinmanmon.

The teachings of Ijun have been in Hawai'i since the early 1980s; at that time it had a membership of about 30 persons, mostly Okinawan Americans. The group met on the 1st and 15th of each month at a private home. Unable to attract new members, the group gradually declined as members passed away. According to a 2012 update posted on "Ijun: Shinshūkyōkenkyū sito" (Ijun: New religions research site), Ijun is no longer active as an organization; but devotees still pay homage to Kinmamon. As of 2014 Takayasu was still living in Okinawa.

Ronald Y. Nakasone

See also: Entries: Okinawan (Ryūkyūan) Spiritual Culture; Seicho no Ie

Further Reading

Ijun: Shinshukyokenkyu Website. http://new religions.ldblog.jp/archives/19688917 .html. Accessed June 13, 2014.

Lebra, William P. *Okinawan Religion, Belief, Ritual, and Social Structure.* Honolulu: University of Hawai'i Press, 1966.

Nakasone, Ronald Y. ed. *Okinawa Diaspora.* Honolulu: University of Hawai'i Press, 2000.

Reichl, Christopher Albert. "Transplantation of a Ryūkyūan New Religion Overseas: Hawaiian Ijun." *Japanese Religions* 30, nos. 1 & 2 (2005): 55–68.

Reichl, Christopher Albert. "Ijun in Hawai'i: The Political Economic Dimension of an Okinawan New Religion Overseas." *Nova Religio* 7, no. 2 (2003): 42–54. *ATLA Religion Database with ATLASerials,* EBSCO*host.* Accessed May 11, 2014.

Takayasu, Rokuro. *Beyond Eternity, The Spiritual World of Ryūkyū.* Michigan City, IN: Reichl Press, 1993.

Imamura, Yemyō (1867–1932)

Imamura Yemyō led the Jōdo Shinshū Hongwanji Buddhist community in Hawai'i for 32 years. He was born at Sentokuji, the family temple in the village of Todo, Asawa-gun, now a suburb of Fukui City. His birth mother, Mitsue, died in 1870; he was just three years old. Shortly thereafter his father, Imamura Yejitsu, married Satomi Misao. As was customary, the firstborn Yemyō was expected to inherit the family temple and carry out its clerical responsibilities. At nine he received the *tokudo* or basic ordination. At 17 Imamura continued his education in Kyoto and later Tokyo during the period of Japan's modernization.

While in Kyoto, the young Imamura attended Bungakuryō, an innovative Hong-wanji high school that was established to respond to changing educational needs. He majored in English. Imamura involved himself with the Hanseikai (Review Society) and Kaigai Senkyōkai (Association for Overseas Spiritual Propagation). In 1886 the association started a monthly publication, *Hanseikai Zasshi,* forerunner of *Chuo Koron* that reported on the overseas Buddhist groups and the current condition of Buddhism. In an essay, "*Bukkyō seinen no shugo-tai yosu*" (The need for an assembly of young Buddhists), Imamura called for restructuring of the status quo by soliciting fresh ideas from young priests, *monto* (parishioners), and *shintō* (believers) to give life to Buddhism and its institutions. Further, Buddhist institutions should be open to the views of the secular disciplines. In short, he believed that everyone must contribute to the propagation of Buddhism. Imamura advocated for the democratization of the tradition and the institution.

Imamura subsequently enrolled at Keio University in Tokyo in the Department of Literature, which exposed him to a wide range of disciplines and where he came under the influence of Fukuzawa Yukichi (1835–1901). In the 18 volumes of *Gakumon no susume* (*On Study*), Fukuzawa outlined the principle of equality of opportunity and the importance of education as the key to greatness. Fukuzawa also advocated "national independence through personal independence" in response to the pressures of European imperialism. To this end, Japanese education needed to foster individualism (independence), competition, and the exchange of ideas. These ideas would guide Imamura's work in

Hawai'i. After graduating from Keio in 1893, Imamura went first to Tokushima and later to Fukui Prefectures as a public school teacher.

In 1899, Imamura arrived in Hawai'i with Rev. Satomi Honi (1853–1922). Shortly thereafter Satomi returned to Japan and in 1900 Imamura became *kantoku* or superintendent) of the fledging Honpa Hongwanji Mission of Hawai'i. In 1906 he was named *sochō* or bishop when the mission became a *betsuin* or branch headquarters. During his 32-year tenure Imamura would test his ideas and give new life to Buddhism. Imamura pursued two objectives: propagation in English and democratization of the Hawaiian mission. But his more immediate task was to support the many young contract agricultural laborers. In 1900, soon after his arrival, Imamura established the Hawai'i Young Men's Association. In addition to offering night classes, where young men could learn English or take courses to complete their Japanese education, the association sponsored parties, baseball teams, and tennis tournaments. The association also organized classes in citizenship and first aid and offered assistance in employment placement in addition to spiritual instruction. He also played a crucial role in settling the 1904 strike against the sugar plantation companies; most of the strikers were Japanese contract laborers. In 1908 he received a license to perform marriages, the first issued to an American Buddhist cleric. In traditional Japan, Buddhist priests did not perform marriages.

Imamura understood that for Buddhism to be meaningful in the West, creative transformations were needed. Firmly convinced that English was the language in which to propagate Buddhism among the Hawai'i-born second generation Japanese and non-Japanese, he founded the English Department of Honpa Hongwanji in 1918. Rev. M. T. Kirby (dates unknown), the first director of the English department, was succeeded by Rev. Ernest Hunt (1876–1967) in 1927. Hunt, a British national who moved to Hawai'i after he converted to Buddhism, advocated for a nonsectarian approach to Buddhism. In 1929 after a visit and being urged by the eminent Chinese modernist cleric Taixu (1890–1947), Hunt and Imamura formed a branch of the International Buddhist Institute (IBI), a worldwide organization dedicated to breaking down sectarian barriers, uniting all Buddhists, and fostering understanding of the faith among the Hawaiian-born Japanese. A month after Taixu's visit, the Hongwanji hosted the Indian polymath and poet Rabindranath Tagore (1861–1941).

At the time when the *sūtras* were rendered by linguists, Imamura called for English translations by Buddhists who could also transfer the spirit of the Buddha-Dharma (Buddhist teachings). The first English Buddhist *gathas* (hymns) were composed and published in 1924. But since they sounded like Christian hymns, the composer and conductor Yamada Kosaku (1886–1965) was invited to revise these *gathas* for a more genuinely Buddhist flavor.

One of the most visible reminders of Imamura's constructive changes is the present Honpa Hongwanji temple building at 1727 Pāli Highway in Honolulu, built on land donated by Mary E. Foster (1884–1930). Imamura insisted that the new building not follow the traditional Japanese Pure

Land temple style. The result is a blend of Indian, East Asian, and Western architectural motifs that are consistent with the Japanese push to establish a pan-Asian Buddhism. The building was completed in 1918.

Imamura believed that Buddhism had a place in the community and that Buddhists could integrate into American life. He worked to support democracy and separated himself from any meaningful support for Japanese nationalist ambitions. To this end he worked to involve all of the members into running the mission. The Hawaiian mission adopted the Giseikai (Legislative Assembly), a legislative body of ministers and representatives from the respective temples, who at their annual meeting decide on the budget and policies. The mission convened its 101st session in 2013. It must be noted that Imamura and the Japanese community faced considerable racial discrimination and resistance by Christian denominations due in part to the rise of Japanese imperialist activities in Asia and the South Pacific.

On December 22, 1932, during a meeting with Hunt, Imamura suddenly excused himself and retreated to his residence. Shortly thereafter, he was discovered by a parishioner stretched on his bed, dead of a heart attack. He was 65.

In October 1933, Ashigaka Zuigi (1872–1944) was appointed to succeed Imamura. He carried on Imamura's broad nonsectarian vision of Buddhism. Hunt continued the English department until 1935, when a new bishop, Kuchiba Gikyo (1883–1955), assumed leadership of the Honpa Hongwanji Mission. An ardent nationalist, Kuchiba opposed Imamura's vision and rescinded most of his policies; he developed programs focused almost exclusively on the Japanese community and fostered close ties to Japan. He fired Hunt and closed the English department. After World War II the Hawai'i Hongwanji community returned to Imamura's vision of an American-style Buddhism. His son, Kanmo Imamura (1905–1986), would later assume leadership of the Hawaiian mission between 1967 and 1974.

Ronald Y. Nakasone

Further Reading

Aloha Buddha Documentary. Produced by Lorraine Minatoishi and directed by Bill Ferehawk and Dylan Robertson. 72 min. Radiant Features. DVD. 2011.

Hunter, Louise H. *Buddhism in Hawai'i, Its Impact on a Yankee Community*. Honolulu: University of Hawai'i Press, 1979.

Moriya, Tomoe. *Yemyo Imamura: Pioneer American Buddhist*. Honolulu: Buddhist Studies Center, 2000.

Tabrah, Ruth M. *A Grateful Past, A Promising Future, the First 100 Years of Honpa Hongwanji in Hawai'i*. Honolulu: Centennial Publication Committee, 1989.

Indian American Christians

At least 110 countries of the world today have each become home for a minimum of 100,000 Indians. Asian Indians in today's United States amount to 1 percent of the population, the third largest immigrant group next only to those of Chinese and Filipino descent. Religions travel with people—as do people of other religious traditions, Christians from India bring their faith and traditions along as they travel to and find their home in another country. After a brief historical survey, this entry will address the topic of Asian Indian Christians in the United States, their history, and the ways in which they maintain their own identity and impact life and service in their new home.

The two adjectives in the title of this entry beg for specific identification. What do we mean when we say "Indian" and "American"? The question applies to the third word in this title too, considering the variety of Christians, Christian denominations, and Christian teachings that span the globe today. To distinguish this group of people from the Native American Indians, we call these new immigrants to the United States Indian Americans. They are identified as Indian Americans as they have been Americanized through generations, yet without compromising the values and mores that initially shaped them and their parents primarily on the Indian subcontinent and have been preserved even as they have been living long-term as citizens and immigrants in the United States. The appellation "Christian" also deserves recognition as India, their country of origin, has been famously identified as the traditional home of Hindus, approximately 15 percent of the world's population.

Indian culture is among the world's oldest, dating back about 5,000 years, having evolved from two major groups of people known as the Arians and the Dravidians. Over millennia, India has been the homeland of numerous diverse peoples speaking separate languages, practicing various religions, and embracing a miscellany of worldviews. Diversity in all aspects of life is the imprint of India's makeup. The different regions of the country have their own unique and discrete cultures, each with their own distinctive expressions in languages, religion, food, art, and architecture. Hinduism, Buddhism, and Sikhism are among the major world spiritual traditions that originated in India. There are about 22 official languages and nearly 400 living languages spoken in various parts of the country. Although Hindi is the nation's official language, English works as the most helpful linguistic link between the various peoples and communities within India, thanks to two centuries of British occupation of this Asian subcontinent.

Innately philosophical, practical, inclusive, and pluralistic, ongoing reforms within Hinduism have enabled this tradition of the vast majority of Indians to hold its ground solidly amidst other religions and spiritual traditions that mushroomed within the country as well as the incoming major religions of Christianity and Islam. Hinduism has traveled successfully with its followers throughout the world. Islam entered the subcontinent mainly through the Arab (711 CE) and Turkish (ca. 1000 CE) invasions beginning with the northwest (what is now Pakistan), and established its strongholds throughout the country through politics, commerce, and conversion. For several centuries, Islamic empires thrived throughout the country, contributing also to the growth of Islam as the second largest religion of India and making the Indian Republic the home of the world's fourth largest Islamic population.

Christians of India trace their origins as far back as the apostle St. Thomas. Following up on Thomas's apostolic mission, Christians from Persia and Syria immigrated en masse to India's Malabar Coast, especially since the fourth and sixth centuries. From this formative band of Christians, in due course, the Knanaya, Nestorian, Orthodox, and much later the Mar Thoma and numerous other traditions emerged. The immigrants also intermarried with the local people, sharing their values and cultures, thus creating indigenous communities of Christians, yet preserving Syrian forms of worship, liturgy, and an assortment of other ecclesiastical traditions and expressions. Although the least in numerical strength, the Knanaya Christians of India claim their lineage to the Jews as far back as King David, having come to south India through Syria and Babylon. While this community is greatly entrepreneurial and wholly engages the culture, even today they practice endogamy and make every effort at preserving racial purity. In the 16th century the Jesuits introduced Roman Catholicism in India especially with the arrival of Francis Xavier in Goa in 1542. The Catholic Church in India has grown 20 million strong as the second largest of its kind in Asia, after the Philippines.

On July 9, 1706, Bartholomäus Ziegenbalg and his colleague Heinrich Plütschau arrived at the Danish Colony in Tranquebar in India's southeast shore, marking the inauguration of the Protestant mission. At least a dozen Lutheran denominations exist today throughout the nation, together having founded the United Evangelical Lutheran Churches of India. Eight decades later in 1793 British Baptist missionary William Carey (1761–1834) and colleagues disembarked in Calcutta in the northeast, marking another breakthrough in the Protestant mission. Numerous other missionary ventures ensued, with the result that every Christian agency in the world has connected with India through its own mission service. Indian Christians have spearheaded historic conferences and pioneered attempts at uniting major Protestant denominations, resulting in the formation of the Church of South India in 1947 and the Church of North India in 1970.

Secularism and pluralism are lived realities in India. Indian Christians have found it unreasonable to distinguish religion and politics. Religious leaders and leaders of political parties of even atheistic presuppositions share the platform in public affairs and foster sociocultural activities reciprocating patronage of one another. Modern Indian Christians perceive their homeland as a laboratory of theological experiments. The above brief, selective sketch of India's demography is helpful to understand the people of Indian descent settled in the rest of the world. Also known as *Desi* Indians, Indian Americans constitute one of the most diverse communities in the United States. They are comprised of people from a variety of cultural backgrounds and varying socioeconomic status, education, values, worldviews, and lifestyles. A community survey conducted in 2005 by the American Census Bureau showed that Indians comprise 16.4 percent of the Asian American community, ranking as the third largest, next to the Chinese and the Filipinos, in the nation. Since the year 2000, among all immigrants to the United States, Asian Indian Americans have achieved a 130 percent growth rate, 10 times the national average of 13 percent. A 2012 Pew survey showed that the United States is now home to 2.8 million Asian Indians.

It is said that the first Indian came to the United States in the 1700s. Several waves of immigrants from India have followed since. During the early decades of the 20th century, a large number of people, especially from the Punjab region, arrived in groups in the state of California. Another significant influx took place at midcentury, when professionals in various disciplines, mainly in nursing and medicine, and university students from India kept coming wherever employment opportunities were available. A further substantial surge has been occurring since the 1990s resulting from the technology boom that increased business and employment opportunities internationally. Multinational companies and businesses based in the United States have in them today people of Indian descent at all levels of the corporate ladder.

Indian immigrants have in the last two decades founded more companies in engineering and technology than immigrants from the United Kingdom, China, Japan, and Taiwan combined, according to joint research from Duke University and the University of California, Berkeley. Immigrants from India have demonstrated versatility in all aspects of American life. Asian Indians in the thousands have made significant newsworthy contributions in society, politics, religion, art, science, technology, and business. One-third of the Silicon Valley engineers are of Indian descent, and 7 percent of the valley's high-tech firms have Indian CEOs. Among the famous Indian immigrants are two state governors, several state senators and congressmen, Nobel Prize winners, a NASA astronaut, the co-founder of Hotmail, athletes, performers, authors, and political commentators.

Immigrants from India are one of the fastest growing populations in the United States. Indian Americans remain more in the metropolitan areas of the country as a vast majority of them are professionals and their dependents. The number of Asian Indians living in the United States accelerated, benefiting from the Immigration Act of 1965 that put an end to favoring European nations and opened the door for people globally to immigrate to this land of freedom and opportunity. This act accelerated the arrival of millions of skilled workers with their families from all over the world to come and settle in America.

Asian Indians are scattered throughout the United States. They have settled in towns and cities of more than 20 states, including California, New York, New Jersey, Texas, and Illinois. Their presence in the major metropolitan areas is so remarkable that, for example, in New York alone there about 20 enclaves of Asian Indians that are celebrated as "Little India." Everything Indian such as designer clothing, fashion jewelry, home goods, food, groceries, eateries, and entertainment with their own Indian ethnic specificity is in ample supply in these locations. Indian Americans either own businesses or are partners with others who run major corporations and businesses like hotels, gas stations, and other enterprises.

Most Asian Indian immigrants are well educated and many are highly accomplished professionals. More than 65 percent have college degrees; 43 percent have graduate or professional degrees. Indian

Americans lead all other groups by a significant margin in their levels of income and education. Seven in 10 Indian American adults ages 25 and older have a college degree. Asian Americans are the highest-income, best-educated, and fastest-growing racial group in the United States. They are more satisfied than the general public with their lives, finances, and the direction of the country, and they place more value than other Americans do on marriage, parenthood, hard work, and career success, according to a comprehensive new nationwide survey by the Pew Research Center.

They constitute one of the most diverse communities in the nation, yet maintaining at all levels the identities, cultures, values, and religions they inherited from their country of origin. Indian American subgroups have a preference for their native Indian tongues like Hindi, Punjabi, Marathi, Malayalam, and Tamil, and many other regional languages representing different communities. About 75 percent of Asian Indians are familiar with English and speak at least one other Indian language. Even after becoming residents and citizens of the United States, 50 percent of Indian Americans read daily newspapers in the vernacular and 25 percent subscribe to Indian publications on a regular basis. Indian Americans publish newsweeklies, poetry, and literature in the vernacular, targeting especially future generations to help preserve their cultural heritage.

Throughout the United States, Indian immigrants have established indigenous religious and cultural organizations, especially in cities and towns where Asian Indians live in clusters. Temples, *mosques*, and churches are erected mirroring the original Indian art and architecture that embody particular religious traditions. They preserve at all costs their core beliefs and conventions, and spiritual and cultural identities in the new home. Parent organizations deploy Indian religious leaders such as priests, imams, and *gurus* to serve the immigrant population, without compromising their distinctiveness in the places where their members have relocated. As is true of most diaspora, immigrants create their own sacred ground and sacred space in their new dwelling place, invoking the god(s) of their traditions and performing sacred rites in customary ways. Indian American Muslims and Jews likewise maintain their own institutions and associations upholding their specific values and worldviews. At the same time, immigrants more readily become involved in interfaith activities for defending religious freedom, approaching other religions professionally, and advancing their own core beliefs and values. Faith and culture overlap among immigrant communities as they jointly observe festivals of various religions and celebrate India's national and regional holidays, discounting conflicts and distinguishing church and state least.

Hinduism firmly established its religious roots in America with the inaugural address Swami Vivekananda gave at the Parliament of the World's Religions in Chicago in 1893. Two decades later, in 1912, the first Sikh *gurdwara* was established in Stockton, California. Communities of Hindus, Muslims, Christians, Sikhs, Jains, Buddhists, Parsis, and Jews from India have founded their religions and hierarchies in the United States, all entering this country first through immigrants.

Today there are plentiful Sikh *gurdwaras*, and Hindu, Buddhist, and Jain temples in all 50 states. In urban areas the same edifice will house icons and hold ceremonies of Hinduism, Buddhism, and Jainism all under one roof, signifying plurality of cultures and spiritualities. The Vedanta Society and *yoga* practices of the Hindu religion have over the years attracted more than 20 million Americans. Hindu Americans have formed the Hindu American Foundation, which represents American Hindus and aims to educate others about Hinduism. All religions publish catechetical materials for their preservation and promotion in the new world, including in languages they inherited from India. As in their country of origin, Hinduism is the religion of the vast majority of Indian immigrants. Data from a Pew Research Center survey gathered in 2012 showed that 51 percent of Indian Americans are practicing Hindus, 18 percent are Christians, 10 percent are Muslims, 5 percent are Sikhs, and 2 percent are Jains. About 10 percent of immigrants do not identify themselves with any specific religion. Among Indian immigrant Christians, the number of Protestants is double the size of the Catholics. About 15 percent of immigrant Christians are nondenominational, although participating intermittently in the rituals of a variety of Christian denominations.

All the mainline Christian churches in India have formed their corresponding group-specific congregations and, in some cases, bishoprics and dioceses in the United States, depending on sustainability. Christian churches in India deploy Indian clergy and other spiritual leaders to minister to the diaspora, enabling membership to preserve their distinctive ethnic identities even when they settle in other countries. Mainline churches set term limits for their clergy's overseas service. Clergy return to India as their terms end and new ones are deployed for their designated terms of service. Bishops and their emissaries make frequent visits to their overseas membership and supply them with liturgical and catechetical materials in their respective vernaculars. The membership will in turn send their dues to their home congregations in India and underwrite projects for the sake of their mother churches, churches that have a centuries-old institutional history in India and are naturally well resourced, keeping such ties strong, solid, and constantly interacting with their international counterparts. The Orthodox, Knanaya, Syro-Malankara, the Mar Thoma Church, the Church of South India, and the Church of North India have excelled in such partnerships.

Indian Christian Americans have formed the Federation of Indian American Christian Organizations of North America (FIACONA) to represent a network of Indian Christian organizations in the United States and Canada. Protestant and Evangelical Christians from India immigrate to America as they are connected with the American churches and mission agencies of kindred spirit, resulting from the modern missionary movement. Indian American Protestants share similar values with their American counterparts such as contemporary worship, gospel music, small group ministry, and Bible study and prayer partner fellowships. Every year, close to 100, 000 students come from India to the United States for study and research.

American seminaries are an attraction for Indian Christians for global theological education, research, and publication. Similar opportunities enable Indian Christians to gather in groups and fellowships transcending denominational affiliations. These groups also support Christian missionaries within India, indigenous to India's native culture. Those who have not yet found a church home in the United States and those Indian Christians whom multinational companies deploy in the different regions of the nation are by and large transient as they move frequently from place to place. They do not establish sustainable local congregations that maintain a denominational identity. For congregational worship, they join other Christians in the neighborhood who share similar values and customs ecumenically.

Indian American Christians have forged a certain trajectory for global mission and ministry. New immigrants are welcomed as members of communities their predecessors have already formed. Like-minded Christian immigrants congregate locally in small groups, initially overseeing denominational allegiance. Denominational identities are preserved as opportunities arise, nevertheless. Clergy and church officials make periodic visits to wherever their congregants cluster to perform religious rites for members and families consonant with their distinctive ecclesiastical tradition. Evangelical Christian immigrants join mostly nearby English-speaking congregations that share traditions akin to their personal faith and lifestyle. They participate regularly in interdenominational fellowships and Christian volunteer service organizations. Language-specific congregations are formed wherever immigrants who speak the same mother tongue live together in large communities. They train spiritual leaders from among their ranks to minister indigenously until they are able to afford official clergy. Prayer groups and bible study fellowships eventually grow into steady congregations and affiliate with the national council of immigrant churches.

Immigrants bring with them families and dependents wherever possible. Research analysts estimate that about 700,000 Indian-born older adults live in the United States. Most of the older immigrants have come to the United States under the sponsorship of their adult children to live with and to be supported by them. Multigenerational households are maintained with pride and honor among immigrants from Asia. Heeding the traditional culture and worldview, most immigrants from India live in the United States as extended families, adult children taking care of senior parents and senior parents nurturing grandchildren especially in matters of faith and patterns of behavior that the native cultures dictate. Children provide for parents in every bodily need. Families serve as the best nurseries for religion, spirituality, and the moral and ethical formation of children. Household conversations in the mother tongue keep the vernacular alive intergenerationally among immigrants. Ministry activities in the vernacular are inevitable, especially for the sake of the seniors whose English competency ordinarily is at a minimum.

English-speaking Christian churches in America have been reaching out to the new immigrants with due diligence. Many communities that are sensitive to the needs of newcomers invite them with open arms to join their new spiritual home. Some congregations make available for the immigrants church facilities for community gatherings and worshipping in their native tongue. They proceed with caution to circumvent cultural barriers such as sharing a common kitchen, promoting language, music, and art forms that may be foreign to the host congregation. Immigrants, albeit with restraint, adapt well to the new environment without having to give up their core values and identities. Adapting fully to a new culture has been burdensome for new immigrants, especially as their personal formation took place in an altogether different context than that to which they have transferred. While many bridges are being built between cultures, many are also burned, sadly, by the passing of generations. Sharing a common faith and confession helps curb tensions and alleviate pressures as believers together acknowledge the lordship of Christ over all people.

The younger adults and children of immigrants adapt to the American culture and lifestyle at a faster pace than their senior counterparts. The vast majority of these have studied in English-medium schools and colleges operated by Christian churches and mission agencies. Already in India, these students may have experienced English-style worship and church life, participating in Bible studies and small group activities also conducted in English. They would be familiar with the latest worship styles and contemporary Christian music, thanks to technology and Internet access availability that is shrinking the world into a global village.

Younger immigrants conversant in English naturally are drawn to English-speaking congregations. They and their families make every effort at blending well with the new culture in which they live. They also break away from the traditional sociocultural boundaries their native culture has maintained. Intercaste and interfaith marriages are gaining momentum among new immigrants, while causing concerns for seniors who consider such practices off-limits.

Recent immigrant Christians from India are changing the face of American Christianity and shaping its future. In living, religion, and community, Asian Indian Christians are making a difference in their new home. Diversity of cultures and pluralism of religions have already become an integral part of American life. As the land of opportunity, this nation fosters mobility, communication, success, and transnational religious experiences. New ethnic groups, new religions, new lifestyles are inhabiting America's neighborhoods. Asian Indian Christians are transforming the face of American Christianity.

Victor Raj

See also: Entries: Indian American Muslims; Indian American Sikhs

Further Reading

Bergunder, Michael. *The South Indian Pentecostal Movement in the Twentieth Century.* Studies in the History of Christian Missions. Grand Rapids, MI: Wm. B. Eerdmans, 2008.

Hudson, D. Dennis. *Protestant Origins in India: Tamil Evangelical Christians, 1706–1835.* Studies in the History of Christian Missions. Grand Rapids, MI: Wm. B. Eerdmans, 2000.

Korahthomas, Anthony. *The Christians of Kerala: A Brief Profile for the Evolution of All Major Churches in Kerala*. 2nd ed. Kottayam: DC Press, 2001.

Pew Research Center. "Pew Research Center Charitable." 2013. http://www.pewresearch .org/. Accessed November 27, 2013.

Williams, Raymond Brady. *Christian Pluralism in the United States: The Indian Immigrant Experience*. Cambridge Studies in Religious Traditions. New York: Cambridge University Press, 1996.

Indian American Muslims

The term "Indian American Muslim" acknowledges the sending country and the practiced or claimed systems of belief of a segment of migrants from South Asia. By classifying all Muslims within a homogeneous category, the nomenclature "Muslim" essentializes similar cultural practices and overlooks divergences within the practiced traditions of Islamic jurisprudence and thought. Thus, members of Sunni, Shia, and Ahmadiyya communities are lumped together in a broad classificatory regime, in a manner that may be seen as problematic to many leaders of the organizations that adhere to these traditions. The establishment of the Al Sadiq *Mosque* in Bronzeville, Chicago, by Mufti Muhammad Sadiq, the first missionary of the Ahmadiyya movement in 1922, may be overlooked in many narratives of Indian American Muslims or even Muslim immigration from South Asia, due

Muslim American women settle in for the first service at the Islamic Society of Orange County's newest *mosque*, Masjid Al-Rahman, November 2, 2001, in Garden Grove, California. (AP Photo/Kim D. Johnson)

to the legal and political status of the Ahmadiyya movement. Nonetheless it is safe to mention that the contemporary presence of Indian Americans who practice various traditions of Islam can be traced to the aftermath of the immigration regime (i.e., the Immigration and Naturalization Act) that was put in place in 1965. Indian Muslim immigration was also precipitated by the partition of India in 1947 and the breakup of Pakistan in 1971. While many earlier Muslim migrants were from the erstwhile princely state of Hyderabad in south India, many recent arrivals hail from the western state of Gujarat.

Among foreign-born and first-generation Muslims, immigrants from South Asia are numerically significant. While they usually have high median incomes, advanced degrees, and are prominent in health care, many espouse conservative positions on family, religiosity, and other social issues. The experiences of Muslim migrants from India are, in many ways, different from those hailing from the Islamic majority South Asian states of Pakistan, Bangladesh, and the Maldives. Indian Muslims were subjected to the institutions and politics of a constitutionally secular democracy. This also shaped their outlook and attitudes toward, and expectations arising from, democratic processes in the host nation. Accustomed to being a religious minority in India, where electoral choices preclude quotas for minority religionists (quotas are reserved on caste-based considerations), for many Indian American Muslims, the transition to the expectations and experiences of another secular democracy may be relatively smooth. While familiarity with democratic

processes is occasionally reflected in localized political participation, empirical data indicate that in general, they are less likely to participate in rallies, follow politics, or send petitions.

In the United States, religion is often seen as the most nonthreatening basis of group formation. For many immigrant Indian American Muslims, the physical transplantation to an alien milieu, coupled with the need to educate their children in the nuances of the culture and values of the sending society, makes many of them send their children and youth to weekend schools for religious instruction called *fiqh*. Apart from being places of religious services, local *mosques* are also used as community centers and for propagating culture. Many of these have large community halls with raised platforms, public address systems, and kitchen facilities. While religious instruction may be imparted in English, knowledge of Arabic and Urdu languages is emphasized. Along with the larger local Muslim community, the religious occasions of Eid and Ramadan are meticulously observed. While a *mosque* may be nominally accessible to any Muslim, the leadership and participation in many immigrant chapters tend to be determined by place of origin. Thus, in a given setting, although Indians, Pakistanis, and Bangladeshis may join hands in formal service and participation, the country-specific organizations or local associations address their needs better.

It has been argued that for many South Asian Muslims, religious identity transcends national identity. Cross-border family ties in the subcontinent and divided national loyalties (visible during cricket matches between India and Pakistan) as immigrants may further complicate relations. For Indian American Muslims, the choice is often between ardent opposition to Hindu right-wing assertiveness, and claims to secularism espoused by the Indian state, and not so much radical transnational Islam. While events like the demolition of the Babri *mosque* in 1992, the Gujarat anti-Muslim pogrom in 2002, and the 2008 Mumbai terrorist bombings may anger the expatriate Muslim community or even create solidarity with other oppressed groups in India, notably Dalits, for many there exists a conscious association with the nominal secularism of the Indian state (as opposed to theocratic claims on many immigrants from Pakistan or Bangladesh). Interestingly, ethnographic evidence suggests that people speaking a common language may overlook religious or political differences in choosing company. In the face of discrimination, South Asians, irrespective of citizenship or belief, tend to support each other.

Organizations that cater to the needs of Indian Muslims play pivotal roles in negotiating many of these transitions. With a membership of around 200,000, the American Federation of Muslims from India (ca. 1989) is comprised largely of male professionals and physicians. It promotes secularism and looks after the prospects for Muslims in education and employment in India. They publish the *Muslim Observer*, a widely subscribed weekly for Indian Muslims in the United States. They collaborate with similar organizations like the Indian Muslim Relief Council, and even support marginalized groups, like Dalits. By liaising with national Muslim organizations like the Muslim Public Affairs Council and the Council on American Islamic Relations, they also seek to politically mobilize American Muslims. In the aftermath of the 2002 Gujarat killings, the Indian American Muslim Council was formed in reaction to the sway of Hindu right politics in India and its overseas supporters. With 13 chapters in the United States (as of August 2012), it is the largest advocacy group of Indian American Muslims.

Other Muslim organizations for Indian immigrants cater to sectarian needs, like the Ithna'Asharis, the Hussaini Associations, the Dawoodi Bohra Jamaats, and the Nizari Ismailis. Subregional associations like the Gujarati Muslim Association (ca. 1990) emphasize the social and economic improvement of Muslims, both among migrant Gujarati Muslims and those (specifically riot victims and indigent students) in Gujarat State in India. Apart from these, the Consultative Committee of Indian Muslims in the United States and Canada is an umbrella group that promotes amity between Indian Muslims and other Indians by celebrating Indian secular public events (like Independence Day, Republic Day, and the birthday of Mahatma Gandhi), by facilitating the exchange of secular ideals, and by creating greater awareness of communal violence in India and possible discrimination in the United States due to religion or skin color.

In the aftermath of 9/11 and the ascendancy of the Hindu right in Indian politics, the larger Indian Muslim organizations in the United States have espoused a secular agenda and have worked with Indian Christian organizations and Dalit groups in opposing hate campaigns (across campuses, online, and in professional forums) by

Hindu right-wing groups (among others) and their followers, and also by participating in interfaith events. By showcasing the secular claims of India, as opposed to that of Hindu nationalism or Islamic extremism, Indian Muslim groups in the United States have mostly trodden a middle ground between religious extremist narratives and the need for greater participation in the improvement of India's Muslims, who are largely victimized and neglected in India's developmental narrative of economic improvement and social empowerment. In so doing, Indian American Muslims have charted their own course.

Amitava Ray

See also: Essays: Islamophobia; Muslims; *Entries:* Indian American Christians; Indian American Sikhs; Islamic Canon

Further Reading

Jalalzai, Farida. "The Politics of Muslims in America." *Politics and Religion* 2 (2009).

Khandelwal, Madhulika. *Becoming American, Becoming Indian: An Immigrant Community in New York City.* Ithaca, NY: Cornell University Press, 2002.

Kurien, Prema. "Religion, Ethnicity and Politics: Hindu and Muslim Indian Immigrants in the United States." *Ethnic and Racial Studies* 24, no. 2 (2001).

Kurien, Prema. "Who Speaks for Indian Americans? Religion, Ethnicity, and Political Formation." *American Quarterly* 59, no. 3 (2007).

Leonard, Karen. *The South Asian Americans.* Westport, CT: Greenwood Press, 1997.

Mohammad-Arif, Aminah. *Salaam America: South Asian Muslims in New York.* London: Anthem, 2002.

Rangaswamy, Padma. *Namaste America: Indian Immigrants in an American Metropolis.* University Park: The Pennsylvania State University Press, 2000.

Indian American Sikhs

The Sikh faith is the fifth largest in the world and the majority of its adherents emanate from Punjab, literally "the land of the five rivers." Historic Punjab, where Punjabi is spoken, is presently divided between the modern nations of Pakistan and India. The region is remarkably fertile and agriculturally productive, and includes the site of the ancient Indus Valley civilization. Punjabi farmers help feed the entire Indian subcontinent with a wide variety of crops, including wheat, rice, cotton, sugarcane, and numerous fruits and vegetables. Due to its agricultural productivity, Indian Punjab, "the breadbasket of India," is the wealthiest Indian state. Similarly, Pakistani Punjab has historically accounted for over half of that nation's GDP.

Punjab sits immediately south of the precipitous mountain ranges that divide South Asia from the areas to the north, making it the site of numerous invasions and battles since ancient times. With this long history of conflict, Punjabis have been widely recognized for their fighting skill and valor. They were particular favorites of the British, who viewed them as one of the "martial races" of the subcontinent. This martial ethos merged well with the concept of the saint/soldier introduced by the sixth of 10 human Sikh gurus, or prophet/teachers.

Sikhs, adherents of the world's fifth largest religion, have a particular affinity toward Punjab and Punjabi, and are widely

The United Sikh Mission float, A Sikh American Journey, featuring a replica of their 100-year-old place of worship in Stockton, California, appears during the 126th Rose Parade in Pasadena, California, January 1, 2015. (AP Photo/Ringo H.W. Chiu)

associated with both. This is due not only to Punjab being the birthplace of their faith, but because their religious scriptures, the *Guru Granth Sahib*, are written in Punjabi in the *gurmukhi* script. In addition, most Sikhs are from, and reside in, Indian Punjab—where they represent a slight majority of the state's population.

The Punjabi language belongs to the Indo-Aryan family and dates back to at least the 11th century. The language has numerous dialects, which can vary considerably by region, and may be written in different scripts. Large diasporic Sikh and Punjabi communities exist throughout the world, particularly in major cities in the United States, the United Kingdom, Canada, and throughout various regions of southeast Asia, Europe, and Africa.

Decision to Migrate

By the late 1800s, economic conditions in Punjab deteriorated to the point where migration represented a viable option for many young men, especially the younger sons in families. Their departure provided the extended family a valuable remittance from abroad and prevented the division of family land, which was split equally among the sons. The exorbitant price of land in Punjab, inflated partially because of the foreign remittances of departed Punjabi men, combined with changes in the land tenure system instituted by the British to leave small landowners in a financially vulnerable position. These stark financial circumstances in Punjab, beginning in the late 1800s, were further exacerbated by a population explosion, followed by droughts, starvation, and widespread disease.

After weighing the other choices—enlisting in the army or moving to an arid and unpopulated area of Punjab—many Sikh men opted to go overseas to make their fortunes. During this time, Punjabis of all faiths began to view North America as a place where they could earn a living if they worked hard. As they began their journey abroad, surely not a few also hoped to somehow strike it rich. They were drawn to North America not only by the promise of higher wages in the developing economies and population centers of the Pacific Coast, but by the promise that they would labor as free men, not indentured servants, or "coolies."

Sikh migrants, like others coming to the United States from throughout Asia, rarely had the money to pay for the expensive passage to North America. With the possible exception of army veterans, most consequently had to borrow money, sell precious goods, or most commonly, mortgage their share of the family's land. Thus, the looming threat of losing a portion of the treasured family land undergirded the migration experience for up to 80 percent of these early migrants. The migrants were mostly younger sons from peasant backgrounds, in their twenties, with little education. Some were married and left their wives and children to live with their parents. Almost all of those who left Punjab at this time intended to eventually return home wealthy and prosperous.

Most of the early Sikh American migrants came from the Doaba region of Punjab, north of the Sutlej River and east of the Beas River. Groups of several men from a village would often plan the trip together, sometimes joining with relatives from elsewhere in Punjab. These village and kinship ties were the glue that held together the pioneer Sikh migrant communities in the difficult times they would face in North America. They formed an almost entirely male community, because of laws aimed at preventing the formation of a second generation of Sikh Americans who would be citizens by birth. The members of the close-knit community helped each other to survive in a land hostile and forbidding to their skin color, language, and religious heritage.

Arrival and Reception in North America

Sikhs in the army played an important role in the early migration to North America. As the economic strife in Punjab deepened, enlistments in the army rose and Sikh soldiers were sent to places such as Hong Kong and Singapore. Some settled in these regions after their enlistments ended. Hong Kong was a particularly important site for many early Punjabi migrants because of its *gurdwara* (Sikh temple), which served as a place to stay for migrants waiting to get on a ship to North America. In keeping with Sikh tradition, travelers, regardless of religious belief, could stay in the *gurdwara*, as well as receive free food.

Through their army networks, Sikh veterans convinced others to migrate as well. In 1897, Sikh soldiers visited Canada on their return to Hong Kong from Queen Victoria's Diamond Jubilee in London. Many enjoyed the visit and noted British Columbia's possibilities for employment. In addition, a significant number of Sikhs became alienated from the British Army, particularly over the lack of respect white officers accorded Indian officers. Many resigned in protest. These officers, along with others who migrated after their enlistment period ended, were among the first South Asians to settle in North America.

The voyage itself was long and difficult, with crowded, unsanitary living conditions, and food that was unfamiliar and often inedible to the Punjabi migrants. The journey for most went from Punjab to Calcutta, then to Hong Kong, and finally to North America. Punjabis began to enter Canada and the United States in noticeable numbers in the early 1900s through the ports of Vancouver, Seattle, San Francisco, and Astoria. Approximately 85 percent of these Punjabi American pioneers identified themselves as Sikhs, 13 percent as Muslim, and the rest Hindu. For those who went to Angel Island in San Francisco Bay, the conditions of detention there—while the state ascertained if it determined them fit to enter the United States—were equally wretched and depressing. Angel Island was a site from which many thousands of would-be migrants from South Asia were denied entry, after the rise of racist, exclusionary pressures from white workers, media, and politicians.

First for cultural and economic reasons, and later because of racist and gendered

U.S. laws restricting the migration of women from Asia, the overwhelming majority of migrants from South Asia at this time were men. This racialized legal restriction was in sharp contrast to laws applying to European migrants, who were allowed to bring their wives into the United States on a nonquota basis. The results of these legal barriers were especially effective on immigrants from South Asia, as women comprised far less than 1 percent of California's South Asian immigrant population in 1914. This curtailed the ability of the community to regenerate itself, as many South Asian men either stayed single or married women of Mexican descent. While U.S. capitalism desperately needed their labor for the rapidly expanding economies and communities in the western part of the continent, the nation did not want to bear the social costs of these racially and economically exploited workers having normal family and social lives. Thus, it was not until 1952 that the reunification of some long-separated South Asian families occurred.

In the absence of women in their community, Punjabis formed small groups in which they worked, lived, ate, traveled, and socialized. These democratic groupings—consisting of members who shared a common language, values, heritage, and sense of purpose—served as surrogate families for the lonely Punjabi men far from home, security, and loved ones. The leader of each group was often the one with the best command of English, and he served as a mediator and agent for the others in employment and other representational matters.

Sikh American Migration

Sikh American migration can be divided into six periods: (1) 1898–1907, a time of open migration; (2) 1908–1924, when legal barriers were put in place to prevent the migration of South Asians and other Asian groups, including numerous racialized laws; (3) 1924–1945, the exclusion era, when migration was illegal due to race and national origin, but approximately 3,000 Punjabis migrated nonetheless; (4) 1946–1964, when Asian American immigrants were finally allowed to naturalize, ending a racist legal prohibition dating to 1790, and reunification of pioneer migrants' families began; (5) 1965–1980, when racial restrictions removed from U.S. immigration policy led to a large influx of professionals, as stipulated in the preferences in the 1965 Immigration Act; (6) 1980–present, when Punjabi migrants, while still containing a significant number of professionals, increasingly consist of less educated and less affluent family members of previous migrants. This final migration includes a significant number of migrants who sought the protection of U.S. asylum law, as they fled massive human rights violations by the Indian state against its Sikh minority.

The time of unrestricted migration was short, and only about 6,000 migrants came in the first decade of the 20th century. Even including the undocumented migrants who came through Mexico or Canada, the total number of all South Asians who came to the United States in the first half of the 20th century was likely less than 10,000, so the community was much smaller than that of Chinese or Japanese Americans.

Sikhs represented the distinct majority of the migration throughout this period.

Faced with such a harsh reception from the host society and its leaders, many South Asians returned voluntarily, including about 3,000 between 1920 and 1940. Others were deported, ensuring that the numbers for the community remained very small until the 1970s. Because of exclusionary pressures, nearly 3,500 South Asians were denied entry into the United States between 1908 and 1920. The most common pretext for denial by immigration officials was likelihood of becoming a "public charge," a common refrain in the case files of Sikh men who sought admission to the United States through Angel Island Immigration Station.

Entering the Labor Economy and the Rise of White Supremacist Sentiment

The wages men received in Punjab, around 5 to 15 cents a day, paled in comparison to reports in Indian journals that claimed that a man could earn as much as two dollars a day in America. The dire need of U.S. farmers for cheap field labor for the rapidly expanding California agricultural economy was another significant factor that drew Punjabis to the United States. The Western Pacific Railway also attracted a number of South Asian laborers. By 1907, there were as many as 2,000 South Asians at work on the railroad, completing a large number of bridges, tunnels, and section work in northern California between 1907 and 1909. However, the end of railroad construction necessitated finding other means of employment.

The lumber industry provided jobs for several hundred Sikh and Punjabi migrants. Owners of the lumber mills in Oregon, Washington, and as far south as Chico, California, cared less about the race and religion of the immigrants than their ability to deliver consistent labor. The arrival of the Sikhs worsened an already tense situation between workers and employers on the West Coast, producing a lethal mixture of economic insecurity and white supremacy. From their arrival, Sikh Americans were clearly distinct from the majority of Americans because of their race, language, religion, culture, and, of course, their distinctive turbans. These visible markers made them easily identifiable targets for racist sentiment from white workers. Not only did they suffer discrimination in everything from housing, to employment, to political rights, but they were described by nativists as unassimilable and undesirable.

Like other migrants from Asia, Sikh Americans were manipulated by employers to prevent all workers from demanding better wages. Forced to work for lower wages than whites—despite being viewed as better workers by employers—they endured because they had so much at stake in an alien, hostile land, with family at home waiting for money from their earnings. As they became increasingly proficient in their work, white capitalists began to replace white workers with Punjabis, sometimes asking the Indian migrants to work double shifts. The loss of white jobs led to an angry reaction against the hard-working Punjabi Americans who were working to ensure the survival of their families in India, instead of the mill owners who pitted the workers against each other to depress the wages of all.

Augmenting the racist sentiment among whites of all classes, local and national media publications produced alarmist articles that raised the specter of a "Hindoo Invasion," or a "Tide of Turbans" supposedly inundating the country. In town after town—from California, to Washington, to Alaska—South Asian Americans were driven from the mills by frenzied mobs of white workers. The workers were often themselves immigrants from Europe, but nonetheless considered themselves defenders of the national tradition of white supremacy.

The worst of these racial expulsions occurred in September 1907 in Bellingham, Washington, when a mob of around 500 white men stormed the area of town where the South Asian Americans lived. Battering down doors, the mob threw the belongings of the residents into the street, while the looters also pocketed any valuables such as jewelry and money. They dragged terrified brown men from their beds, forcing them to flee town in their nightclothes. Some were injured when they jumped from buildings to escape the rampaging mob. Those who could not escape in time were beaten and threatened with their lives if they did not leave town. Faced with such outrage from their white workers, the mill owners, who had been profiting handsomely from paying lower wages for better work to the Punjabis, turned against their South Asian employees. They openly called them undesirable workers and discharged them all, fearing damage to their property. The South Asian migrants quickly left town.

Along with those workers who had been driven from the lumber mills, many of the workers who had worked on the railroad joined their brethren already working in agriculture. The majority of the Punjabi immigrants had come from farming backgrounds and naturally gravitated toward agriculture. Perhaps more importantly, working in rural areas allowed the immigrants to distance themselves from the anti-Asian sentiment so prevalent in highly populated urban areas with large concentrations of white workers. Working in the fields allowed South Asian Americans to work where there was little competition for jobs from whites, thus garnering relief from the ever-present threat of racial violence. Furthermore, agricultural expansion in California had created competition for labor in the state, raising wages and making it more profitable to work on farms than lumber mills.

Sikh Americans fit into California's regional economies at many levels. They helped initiate rice cultivation in northern California, grew grapes and other crops in central California, and moved to the southern Imperial Valley to help establish cotton as a crop in the region. Several South Asian Americans began to move up the agricultural ladder despite the racist sentiments dominating society at the time. This white supremacy was often encoded in the law to preserve the racial privilege of white Americans. These laws included California's Alien Land Laws, which prevented immigrant nonwhites from owning land and was targeted primarily at successful Japanese and South Asian American farmers.

Working initially as laborers, several South Asian immigrants were able to amass enough capital to eventually lease or even purchase their own land, usually in partnership with friends or relatives. By pooling the resources of two or more men and cleverly evading the state Alien Land Law by putting land in the name of their U.S.-born children or an agent, South Asians were able to acquire over 88,000 acres of land in California by the 1920s. Some became spectacularly successful, including Jawala Singh, a Sikh who earned the moniker "the Potato King" for his efforts. An activist at heart, he helped found the Ghadar Party and the Stockton *gurdwara*, and was eventually arrested and imprisoned by the British for attempting to foment revolution in India.

Revolutionary Political Activity

Also migrating at this time were a group of political refugees from British India. They sought a place where they could freely organize to liberate their homeland from British imperialism. The nationalist movement these exiles created took the name *Ghadar* (revolution), and it found tremendous support within the ranks of the Punjabi and Sikh American migrants, who daily struggled under the oppressive conditions of white supremacy. The Ghadar Party assumed the formidable task of trying to set India free from the colonial rule of the British Empire, while operating on the other side of the globe. It disseminated its revolutionary ideas through a weekly newspaper, and actually engaged in an attempt to militarily dislodge the English.

The pervasive racism faced by the early Punjabi Americans made them more reliant on their countrymen and co-religionists, creating powerful community bonds. It also made them more open to supporting a radical organization like the Ghadar Party.

Much of the group's activity emanated from the first *gurdwara* (Sikh house of worship) built in the United States, founded in 1912 in Stockton, California. Serving not only the spiritual needs of the community—Sikhs and non-Sikhs alike—the Stockton *gurdwara* also served as a social and political center for the entire Pacific Coast Punjabi community. Political discussions, including those on the liberation of India, were often held there, making it a gathering point for the entire community. Consequently, it is widely considered the most important organization formed by early South Asian American immigrants.

Jaideep Singh

See also: Essays: Islamophobia; *Entries: Gurdwara*; Indian American Christians; Sikh American Legal Defense and Education Fund (SALDEF); The Sikh Foundation

Further Reading

Grewal, J. S. *The Sikhs of the Punjab*. New York: Cambridge University Press, 2008.

Jensen, Joan. *Passage from India*. New Haven, CT: Yale University Press, 1988.

LaBrack, Bruce. *The Sikhs of Northern California: 1904–1975*. New York: AMS Press, 1988.

Leonard, Karen Isaksen. *The South Asian Americans*. Westport, CT: Greenwood Press, 1997.

Indian Festivals

Indians affirm and celebrate their tradition through a series of annual festivals that mostly commemorate events and personalities from their mythology. Coinciding with the traditional agricultural cycle, India's lunar calendar has six seasons, each of which is approximately two months; because of the lunar calendar shifts, lunar months vacillates over three solar months. The year begins with *vasantha* (spring, March-April-May); *grīsma* (hot season, May-June-July); *ketu* (rainy season, July-August-September); *śarad* (autumn, September-October-November); *hemānta* (late autumn, November-December-January); *śiśira* (end of winter, January-February-March). In contrast to the solar Georgian calendar that is used today, the festival dates shift with the lunar calendar. The different regions celebrate these festivals differently and often on different days. This entry highlights the most important festivals, beginning with Holi that marks the beginning of the annual calendar.

Holi is celebrated at the end of the winter season on the last full moon day of the lunar month Phalguna that usually falls in late February or early March. While Holi is linked to the devotion of Krishna and his consort Rādhā, it originally celebrated the spring harvest and the New Year. Holi is the occasion for purging the accumulated emotional impurities of the past year. The night before the New Year, bonfires are lit in a ceremony known as Holikādahan (burning of Holikā); it is an occasion for singing and dancing. In anticipation of the colors of spring, children and youth sprinkle *gulal* (colored powder solutions) on each other; elders in turn smear *abir* (dry colored powder) on each other's faces. The hosts tease visitors to their homes by first smearing them with colors, before they are served special Holi delicacies, desserts, and drinks. After playing with colors, cleaning up, and bathing, people put on new clean clothes to visit friends and family. In southern India, the women will clean the area in front of their homes and create *rangoli*, elaborate patterns made from white, usually rice, flour. This ritual is intended to welcome Lakṣmī, the goddess of wealth and the consort of Vishnu. However, should there be a death in the family, *rangoli* is delayed until funeral rites are completed.

Kṛṣṇa-Janmaṣtami celebrates the birthday of Krishna (Kṛṣṇa), who was born during the Varsha (rainy) season, which fell on August 17 in 2014. According to legend, Vishnu decided to be born as Krishna to destroy Kaṁsa, the cruel ruler of Mathura. A prophecy warned the king of the pending birth. Kaṁsa imprisoned Krishna's parents and killed the first six of their children. His mother feigned a miscarriage and immediately after his birth spirited the newborn Krishna across the Yamuna River to be raised by foster parents. Upon reaching adulthood, Krishna returned to Mathura with his elder brother Balarāma to kill Kaṁsa. Kṛṣṇa-Janmashtami is celebrated mostly in and around the Mathura region and northern India.

Indians celebrate Gaṇeśa-chthurtī, the birthday of the elephant-headed Gaṇeśa, during the Sharada (autumn) period, which fell on August 29 in 2014. Gaṇeśa, the patron of learning and the remover of obstacles, is one of the most popular deities in the Indian pantheon. Gaṇeśa is invoked before every undertaking; his image appears in most homes and graces every wedding invitation. Indians of Mahārāṣtra are especially fond of Gaṇeśa and celebrate his birthday in a big way.

The Navrātrī festival is the most auspicious devotional *ṣaḍāna* directed to *Śakti*, the primordial cosmic energy that moves through and supports the universe; it is also the agent for change. During the second half of Sharada that began on October 3 in 2014, Indians expressed their devotion to the goddesses Durgā, Lakṣmī, and Sarasvatī over nine days; on the 10th day they celebrated Vijayadasami or victory day. This series of festivals can be traced to Vedic times. Durgā, Lakṣmī, and Sarasvatī are personifications of *Śakti*, who is associated most closely with female fertility and the ability to bring forth life.

The first three days of the Navrātrī festival are dedicated to Durgā, "the inaccessible" or "the invincible," who is the most popular incarnation of *Śakti*. She is celebrated for her power to vanquish evil, and her color is red. Lakṣmī, the consort of Vishnu, is the patron of wealth and prosperity, and her color is yellow. Sarasvatī, the consort of Brahma, is the patron of knowledge and the arts, and her color is white. On the 10th day, Vijayadaṣami, the completion of the rituals, is celebrated. In northern India it commemorates Rama's defeat of Rāvaṇa. In southern India, devotees dress dolls and display them on their doorsteps. Visitors are offered *prasādam*, traditional dishes and sweets. This is also an occasion to wear festive clothes and ornaments. The last three days of Navratrī are official national holidays.

Divālī, popularly known as the Festival of Lights, is celebrated in autumn. Like many festivals, Divālī recalls events special to different parts of India. In the north it celebrates Krishna's return to Ayodhya and his coronation as king; it also honors Lakṣmī, the goddess of wealth. Devotees celebrate the victory by setting off sparklers and fireworks, displaying candles, wearing new clothes, and sharing sweets. In the western states of Gujarat and Maharashtra, the merchant community celebrates Divālī by opening new accounts and by participating in *pūjā* (ritual worship) of Lakṣmī. In southern India, devotees dress dolls and display them on their doorsteps; it is also an occasion to wear festive clothes and ornaments. Visitors are offered *prasādam*. Most of the festivities take place at home and center on family and friends.

Makarasmakranti marks the end of winter, and the day at which the sun is farthest from the earth. It heralds the arrival of spring as the sun approaches closer to earth with each passing day. Makarasamkranti falls on January 14; it is one of the few Indian festivals that coincides with the solar Gregorian calendar.

These festivals are celebrated communally at ashram-sponsored rituals and at home. Each festival is accompanied by the chanting of appropriate devotional hymns. Domestic rituals are much simpler and the chants shorter. Most Hindu families have a family shrine, which is the focus of their worship. They frequently light a candle, or more recently, turn on a light each morning before offering a chant. The family shrine is richly decorated on special festival days. Families will offer flowers and *prasādam*, and gather to chant. Indians in the United States try to retain and transmit their spiritual traditions through visits to a nearby ashram, but mostly continue the daily worship at their family shrine. The following are a few mantras (sacred chants) that are commonly recited. The first is chanted before any project is undertaken in the hope that it will proceed without trouble and be carried out to completion.

(Salutations to Śrī Vighna Vinayaka [Gaṇeśa])

Muussika-vaahana modaka-hasta	Whose vehicle is the mouse and who grasps the *modaka* (a traditional sweet delicacy);
Caamara-karnna vilambita-suutra |	Whose large ears are like fans, and who wears a long sacred thread;
Vaamana-ruupa mahesvara-putra	Who is short in stature and is the son of Śrī Māheśwara (Shiva);
Vighna-vinaayaka paada namaste ||	Prostrations at the feet of Śrī Vighna Vinayaka, the Remover of the Obstacles.

The second mantra is a traditional aspiration that is chanted immediately after waking in morning. Though it appeals to the great *devis* (goddesses), it is recited by women and men. Sarasvatī, the consort of Brahma, is associated with knowledge, wisdom, and the arts; Lakṣmī, the consort of Vishnu, is the patron of wealth, love, prosperity (both material and spiritual), and the embodiment of beauty; Gouri (Pārvatī), the consort of Vishnu, is the source of all power.

Karāgrē vasatē Lakṣmī	Lakṣmī dwells on the top of the hand (palms);
Kara madhyē Sarasvatī	Sarasvatī resides in the middle of the hand;
Karamūlētu Gouri (Pārvatī)	Gouri dwells at the base of the hand.
Prabhātē karadarśanam	We see them in our hands when we awake in the morning

The following Santi mantra is recited on any occasion when one wishes for protection for one's self and for friends and family.

Om sarve bhavantu sukhinā	Om, may all become happy
Sarve santu nirāmayā	May all be free from illness.
Sarve bhadrāṇi paśyantu	May all see what is auspicious
Mā kashcid-duḥkha-bhābhavet	May no one suffer.
Om śāntī, śāntī, śāntī	Peace, peace, peace.

Amba Raghavan and Ronald Y. Nakasone

See also: Entries: Classical Indian Dance, Hindu Canon

Further Reading

Basham, A. L. *The Wonder That Was India.* New York: Grove Press, 1959.

Klostermaier, Klaus K. *A Survey of Hinduism.* Albany: State University of New York Press, 1989.

Radhakrishnan, Sarvepalli. *The Bhagavadgītā.* New Delhi: HarperCollins India, 1993.

Radhakrishnan, Sarvepalli. *The Hindu View of Life.* New Delhi: HarperCollins India, 2009.

Rinehart, Robin, ed. *Contemporary Hinduism, Ritual, Culture, and Practice.* Santa Barbara, CA: ABC CLIO, 2004.

Indonesian American Muslims

The Indonesian diaspora in the United States constitutes a small fraction of the 242 million population of Indonesia. The 2010 U.S. Census data show about 95,270 people having Indonesian ancestry. On its *Congress of Indonesian Diaspora 2012* website, the Indonesian Embassy states that more than 150,000 Indonesian Americans reside within the U.S. borders. Indonesian Americans likely share the religious affiliations of other Asian Americans, wherein Catholics and other Christians exceed Muslim by five times. The number of

Indonesian American women pass a police checkpoint at Yankee Stadium to attend a memorial service called A Prayer For America, September 23, 2001, in the Bronx borough of New York. The service was held in remembrance of those who were lost in the September 11th attack on the World Trade Center. The women wore the chador, a traditional Muslim headdress. (AP Photo/Mark Lennihan)

houses of worship supports these data. Indonesian Americans own and run more than 120 churches of various denominations in 25 states (Newsantara) while there are only two *mosques* on the East Coast. These Indonesian Muslims are among the six million American Muslims of diverse cultural and racial backgrounds. Despite their small number, Indonesian Muslims practice and preserve their religious and cultural traditions and continue engaging in interfaith efforts to relive the interfaith harmony common in Indonesia. In addition, they join the existing Muslim communities or establish their own organizations, Islamic centers, or *mosques* to fulfill their religious duties, hold religious gatherings, and educate their children about their religion and cultural heritage.

Religions in Indonesia

The proportion of Muslims in the Indonesian American population contrasts sharply with that in their homeland. The Republic of Indonesia's philosophical foundation, *Pancasila* (Five State Principles), serves as the blueprint for its nation building. The first principle, *Ketuhanan yang MahaEsa* (Belief in one God), translates into requiring Indonesian citizens to indicate their religious affiliation on their official documents. Recognizing Buddhism, Christianity (Catholicism and Protestantism), Confucianism, Hinduism, and Islam as the official religions, the country observes the major holidays of all these religions. The majority of 240 million Indonesians are Muslims, making Indonesia the country with the largest Muslim population. Being the dominant religion, Islam affects the social, economic, and political life in Indonesia. Most public buildings, such as schools, offices, airports, and shopping malls, have a prayer area to enable Muslims to perform their five obligatory daily prayers. In addition, government offices have a longer lunch break on Fridays to allow the male Muslims to perform the Friday noon congregation prayer and have lunch before going back to work.

Indonesian Muslims establish numerous organizations for economic, social, political, and educational reasons. The largest social-educational organizations include Muhammadiyah, a reform group founded in 1912 that has about 30 million members, and Nahdatul Ulama, a traditionalist group founded in 1926 that has about 40 million members. Numerous other organizations and political parties incorporate Islam in their philosophy and participate at different levels of social, economic, and political activities in Indonesia.

Mosques

Mosques are an important institution to Muslims, including Indonesian Muslims. Being the heart and locus of the implementation of Islam, a *mosque* plays a central role in Muslims' life. Millions of *mosques* exist throughout Indonesia. About 239,497

of them are registered as either the landmarks of a region, historically notable, or having authentic architecture features. In these *mosques* and their communities, Indonesian Muslims perform their religious rituals, education, and celebrations, which include the following:

- Prayers: the five daily prayers, Friday congregation prayers, night prayers during the fasting month of Ramadan, and the two celebrations (Eid) prayers.
- Education: *Qur'an* recitation, the sayings and traditions of the Prophet Muhammad (*hadith* and *sunnah*), and other topics such as Islamic history, law (*syariah*), jurisprudence (*fiqh*), and mannerism.
- Celebrations: *Eid al-Fitr* (at the end of Ramadan fasting), *Eid al-Adha* (commemorating Prophet Abraham's sacrifice of his son), *Isra* (Prophet Muhammad's night visit to Al-Aqsa *mosque* in Jerusalem), and *Mi'raj* (Prophet Muhammad's ascension to heaven from Al-Aqsa *mosque*).
- Rites of passage: birth of a child (*aqiqah*), circumcision (*khitan*), wedding (*nikah*), care, prayers, and burial of the deceased (*janaiz*).

In addition, many Muslim communities, groups, or organizations regularly hold *pengajian*, which is a gathering where some verses from the *Qur'an* are recited and explained using the sayings (*hadith*) and traditions (*sunnah*) of the Prophet Muhammad. *Pengajian* sessions usually feature guest speakers, which can be an imam (clergy or religious leader), a scholar of Islam, or experts in nonreligious fields deemed important for the community and who will deliver a talk, lecture, or sermon and answer the audience's questions about the topic of the lecture.

Indonesian Muslims in the United States

Most of the 150,000 Indonesian Americans live in the cities where Indonesian government offices are located: Chicago, Houston, Los Angeles, and San Francisco (consulate general), New York (consulate general, Indonesian Central Bank, and permanent mission to the UN), Washington, D.C. (embassy), and Atlanta (Indonesian American Chamber of Commerce). Since 1998, many Indonesian Americans have started to form an enclave in south Philadelphia. The Indonesian American Muslim population likely spread together with the larger Indonesian American population. Those who live near the Indonesian government offices benefit not only from having access to more Indonesian Americans in the area, but also from other supports provided by the offices including the Friday congregation prayers and the Eid prayers and celebrations. Those who live near an Indonesian *mosque* generally join the religious activities and celebrations organized by the *mosque*, while others who live in areas with only a few Indonesian Muslims usually join the existing Islamic centers and *mosques*. In the event that they live in areas where no *mosques*, Islamic center, or other Muslims live, many Indonesian Muslims perform their religious duties at home, and possibly join a telephone or online *pengajian* group.

The Indonesian Muslim student population applies a similar strategy. In the 1970s, when their number was still small, the Indonesian Muslim students joined the Malaysian Islamic Student Group (MISG). As their numbers grew, and prompted by the reform movement in Indonesia following the fall of Soeharto, in 1998 they decided to establish their own organization, the Indonesian Muslim Student Association (IMSA). IMSA continues to collaborate with the MISG in organizing a joint annual conference. In 2006, IMSA changed its name to Indonesian Muslim Society in America to include any Indonesian Muslims interested in joining. In addition, many Islamic organizations from Indonesia, such as the Ikatan Cendikiawan Muslim Indonesia (ICMI or Indonesian Association of Muslim Intellectuals), have established a branch in North America and often invite scholars from Indonesia.

Like the *mosques* and Muslim communities in Indonesia, Indonesian Muslims in America continue the *pengajian* tradition, either in face-to-face gatherings, by telephone, or via the Internet. Some *pengajian* groups use social media such as Yahoo! Group and Facebook to facilitate communication among members. As of 2012, Yahoo! Group listed at least 17 *pengajian* groups in various states that have existed for two to 15 years, with six to 147 members. Similar to the *pengajian* activities in Indonesia, these groups organize weekly or monthly sessions as well as sessions in conjunction with the Eid celebrations.

These *pengajian* sessions often occur informally in private residences, and as the number of participants grows, they find larger spaces such as rooms in the

Indonesian government offices, local churches, rental halls, or parks. When scholars from Indonesia visit the United States, different *mosques*, organizations, or groups will invite them to speak at their *pengajian* gatherings. *Pengajian* groups also help community members to network and organize. Members coordinate activities related to the rites of passages or provide assistance to those in need. When the membership grows to include second-generation Indonesian Americans, many *pengajian* groups and *mosques* develop education programs to teach the basic tenets of Islam and Indonesian traditions to their offspring. Moreover, these *pengajian* groups often become the impetus for a more formal organization. When the membership outgrows the space, the community establishes a formal organization, an Islamic center or a *mosque*.

In the early 1980s the Indonesian Muslims in New York City held their *pengajian* activities in the Indonesian consulate general building. In 1989 the community founded the Indonesian Muslim Community, Inc. (IMCI) to realize their dream of having a *mosque*. After collecting donations from members, the permanent mission to the UN, and Bank Indonesia, the IMCI was able to purchase a building in Long Island City, Queens, on August 17, 1995. After a complete renovation of the building, supported by a substantial donation from the late President Soeharto, the IMCI established Masjid Al-Hikmah, the first Indonesian *mosque* in the United States. Masjid Al Hikmah holds five daily prayers, Friday congregation prayers, Eid prayers and celebrations, educational activities for adults, youth, and children, as well as cultural and interfaith activities.

Similarly, Indonesian Muslims living in Philadelphia established the Indonesian Community of Greater Philadelphia, Inc. (ICGP) after organizing *pengajian* in different locations since the 1990s. In 2007, the ICGP collected enough funds to make a down payment for a two-story apartment that they later converted into a *mosque*, named Masjid Al-Falah, its office, as well as four rental rooms. Masjid Al-Falah is the second Indonesian *mosque* in America. The activities of Masjid Al-Falah include five daily prayers, Friday congregation prayers, weekly *pengajian* sessions, weekend education for children and youth, as well as interfaith activities.

The Indonesian Muslim families living around Washington, D.C. established the Indonesian Muslim Association in America (IMAAM), Inc. in 1993. With donations from the community, IMAAM purchased two residential houses on adjacent lots in 2001 and 2006 in Rockville, Maryland. IMAAM, Inc. is still in the process of building IMAAM Center, which will become the third Indonesian *mosque* in America. At present, the community uses the houses to hold *pengajian* sessions, their educational and interfaith activities, but they still borrow different halls for their congregation prayers and Eid celebrations.

Key Figures

Syamsi Ali serves as the director of the Jamaica Muslim Center, chair of the Masjid Al-Hikmah Board of Trustees, and the *imam* of Islamic Cultural Center of New York. Imam Ali is a well-known figure in the Indonesian Muslim community and a public face of Islam and American Muslims. He arrived in New York City in 1995 to become the *imam* of the newly established Indonesian *mosque*. He received a BA in *Tafseer* and an MA in comparative studies of religions from the International Islamic University in Islamabad, Pakistan. Imam Ali dedicates his time to interfaith activities and has received recognition and numerous awards for his interfaith activities, including appointment as the Ambassador for Peace by the International Religious Federation (2002), an interfaith discussion on Religions and Sustainable Development at the White House (2007), the ICLI Interfaith Award (2008), and the Ellis Island Medal of Honor Award (2009). Imam Ali was recognized as one of the seven most influential religious leaders in New York City, and one of the 500 most influential Muslims in the world (by the Royal Islamic Strategic Studies Center in Jordan and Georgetown University, 2009).

Muhammad A. Joban has served as the imam of Masjid Ar-Rahmah since its founding in 2006. The *mosque* is run by the Muslim Association of Puget Sound (MAPS). He arrived in America in 1989 to become the *imam* of Masjid An-Nur in Olympia, Washington, which is owned and run by the Cham community who relocated there from Cambodia in the 1980s. Masjid Ar-Rahmah activities include education programs for children, teens, and adults. Imam Joban has a BA in Arabic from the Islamic University in Jakarta, Indonesia, a BA in Theology, Islamic Call and Culture, and an MA in Islamic Studies from Al-Azhar University in Cairo, Egypt. In addition to serving as the *imam* of Masjid Ar-Rahmah, Imam Joban is the Muslim chaplain for the Department of Corrections in the state of Washington, an instructor for the Online Islamic University, and an active interfaith speaker.

Lahmuddin serves as the *imam* of the Islamic Society of Joplin, Missouri, which opened in 2007. He came to the United States in 1995 on a Fulbright scholarship and got a master's degree from the University of Arkansas in 1997. He returned to the University of Arkansas in 1998 and received his PhD in History in 2004. He spent a few years in New York City before returning to Indonesia. In 2008, he became the *imam* of the Islamic Society of Joplin (ISJ), serving about 50 families, none of whom, except his own, are Indonesians. Imam Lahmuddin is active in interfaith activities in Joplin in addition to his other activities and responsibilities at the Islamic Society of Joplin. The *mosque* of ISJ was burned on August 6, 2012, during the Ramadan fasting month, which posed a serious challenge to the community. Receiving interfaith support from various organizations in the United States and other countries, the society will build their new *mosque* at a different location.

Conclusion

Even though their number is small and their existence scattered, Indonesian Muslims continue practicing their religion, preserving their culture, and engaging in interfaith efforts to connect with other Indonesian Muslims, Muslims from other backgrounds, and with the larger American population. They fulfill their religious duties and educate their offspring about their religion and culture by participating in the activities of the existing Muslim communities or their own organizations, Islamic centers, or *mosques*. They preserve their *pengajian* tradition to connect with other Indonesian Muslims and their home country, while also engaging in interfaith efforts to transition into being a part of the larger American society.

Trikartikaningsih Byas

See also: Essays: Islamophobia; Muslims; *Entries:* Indonesian American Religions

Further Reading

Byas, Trikartikaningsih."Gamelan to Dangdut: Indonesian American Performing Arts That Foster Rukun (Harmony) in Pluralistic America." In Jonathan H. X. Lee and Roger V. Chung, eds. *Contemporary Issues in Southeast Asian Americans Studies*. San Diego: Cognella Academic, 2011, pp. 87–96.

Grim, Brian J., and Mehtab S. Karim. *The Future of the Global Muslim Population: Projection for 2010–2030*. New York: Pew Research Center, 2011.

IMAAM Center. http://www.imaam.org/. Accessed July 14, 2014.

Indonesian Diaspora. http://www.diaspora indonesia.org/about.php. Accessed July 14, 2014.

Kosmin, Barry A., and Ariela Keysar. *The American Religious Identification Survey (ARIS 2008): Summary Report*. Hartford, CT: Institute for the Study of Secularism in Society & Culture, 2009.

Masjid Al-Falah. http://www.facebook.com /groups/347890055292921/. Accessed July 14, 2014.

Masjid Al Hikmah. http://www.masjidalhik mahnewyork.org/. Accessed July 14, 2014.

Newsantara. http://www.newsantara.com/usa /GerejaDiArCa.html. Accessed July 14, 2014.

Setiyawan, Dahlia G. "Indonesian American Religion." In Jonathan H. X. Lee and Kathleen Nadeau, eds. *Encyclopedia of Asian American Folklore and Folklife*. Santa Barbara, CA: ABC-CLIO, 2010, pp. 554–57.

Indonesian American Religions

With a population of around 240 million in 2010, Indonesia is the fourth largest nation in the world after the People's Republic of China, India, and the United States. However, Indonesians are very poorly represented in the United States. With only 30,085 among the 6,876,394 Asians living in the United States, Indonesians or Indonesian Americans are the 15th among all minorities.

Indonesians came to the United States when in 1953 ICA (now USAID) provided scholarships for the faculty members of the medical school of the University of Indonesia to study at the University of California at Berkeley. This opportunity was later widened when in 1956 scholarships were also offered to faculty members of the Bandung Institute of Technology to study at the University of Kentucky.

At about the same time Christian church leaders also began to undertake further study in the United States. It started when Prof. Elmer D. Homrighausen of Princeton Theological Seminary came to Indonesia in 1955 to give a series of lectures on Christian education. This was a new discipline in theological studies for Indonesian Christians then. His visit was followed by an offer to study for several Indonesian church leaders at Princeton Theological Seminary and some other seminaries.

Most of these young church leaders returned to Indonesia and taught at various seminaries.

In the mid-1960s, when Indonesia's economy turned from bad to worse and the persecution of the Chinese minority intensified, many Chinese Indonesians opted to leave their country and settle down elsewhere. Some went to the Netherlands, Germany, and Australia, others came to the United States, while a few decided to go to Brazil, which was a growing economy at that time.

After the May 1998 tragedy when hundreds of Chinese Indonesian girls and young women were raped, killed, and burned, many Chinese Indonesians once again fled their country and applied for asylum in other countries. According to Damai Sukmana, since 1998, more than 20,000 asylum cases have been filed by Indonesians. Until 2007, 7,359 asylum cases involving Chinese Indonesians were approved, 5,848 were denied. Many cases were also filed by Christian Ambonese after the interreligious conflict in 1999–2001 in the Mollucan archipelago.

In the United States, Indonesians tend to live in the areas where jobs are widely available and the climate is friendly. They prefer big cities where there is a high concentration of Asians, especially Chinese, Vietnamese, Filipinos, Malaysians, and so on. This is important because it is easier for them to find familiar foods. Therefore, Indonesians tend to live in Los Angeles, the San Francisco Bay Area, Houston, Chicago, Philadelphia, New York City, Washington, DC, New Hampshire, and so on. However, since Indonesians are a heterogeneous group, they tend to live among their own ethnic groups. For example, most Minahasans flock together in Los Angeles, Loma Linda, Philadelphia, New York City, and New Hampshire. The Chinese Indonesians, however, are more widely spread because they themselves do not form a homogeneous community.

The division among the Indonesian community in the United States is more clearly seen from their publications. Two Indonesian magazines are published in Los Angeles: *Indonesian Media* is run by the Chinese Indonesian community, while *Indonesian Journal* is published by the Minahasan community. Their contents reflect their differences. *Indonesian Media* contain news about the Chinese Indonesian community and issues related to this community both in the United States and in Indonesia as well. *Indonesian Journal* contains more news about the Minahasans in the United States. Another magazine, *Kabari*, is a monthly publication by a small group of Chinese Indonesians in San Francisco, on paper as well as online. It regularly publishes articles about immigration issues of interest to Indonesians living in the United States.

Other than by ethnic divisions, the Indonesian community in the United States is also divided along religious lines. Although Indonesia is the largest Muslim community in the world, nevertheless Christians form the largest group since most Minahasans and many Chinese Indonesians are Christian. There are also many Moluccans in the United States, most of whom are Christian. Muslim Indonesians consist of Javanese, Sundanese,

Minangkabau, Makassarese, Acehnese, and so on.

Faith Communities

In the early 1970s, some faith communities, especially Christian churches, began to develop. The first one was a Seventh Day Adventist church in the Loma Linda area of California. This area is known for its big Adventist community. Many Indonesian Adventists came to this area and lived there. The second Indonesian Christian church was opened in the San Francisco Bay Area. It was started by a Chinese Indonesian Baptist pastor who came to the United States for further study. He initiated this church to serve the members of his home church in Jakarta who migrated to the United States. Today the church is one of the few Indonesian churches that own their own church buildings.

Today there are a lot of Christian churches from many different denominations: Presbyterian, Lutheran, Roman Catholic, Adventist, Baptist, evangelical, Pentecostal, and Charismatic as well. Most of them are found in the areas where there are high concentrations of Indonesians. Many of these Indonesian churches are Pentecostal or Charismatic. They are served by pastors who were brought to the United States and came with a religious worker visa. Since this visa enables them to later apply for green cards, many of them decided not to return to Indonesia. Many of these pastors serve several congregations, some three to four at the same time. Thus, services are held on Friday evenings, as well as Saturday and Sunday mornings and evenings in different places.

Indonesian Muslims are supported by the Indonesian government through its embassy and consulate general offices. These offices also sanction imams who serve the community, especially by giving religious instruction to the members of the community, performing religious events, and so on.

Relationships among Indonesians of different faiths are casual. Indonesians of any religion would usually come to the embassy or the consulate general offices for the Ramadan as well as the Eid al-Adha celebrations, especially for the food and the fellowship.

Other than that, relationships between Christians and Muslims are usually rather lukewarm. In February 2007, after Aceh was hit by the tsunami in 2006, an interfaith prayer was organized in Cupertino in Northern California. However, not one Indonesian Christian came.

Cultural Organizations

Americans became familiar with Indonesia, its people, and its culture mainly through their contacts with the people of Indonesia and their cultural programs that are introduced in the United States. Several American universities offer courses on Bahasa Indonesia, Indonesian studies, gamelan music, and so on. Some *pencak silat* groups and gamelan orchestra groups are also found in some big cities. Many of their members are Caucasians.

From time to time several Indonesian communities in Los Angeles, San Francisco, New York City, and so on also organize bazaars where Indonesian food and snacks are sold and cultural events are shown.

Employment

Many Indonesians who overstayed their visas cannot work legally. Therefore they usually take odd jobs that do not pay them well. Those who take odd jobs are forced to do so because they lack fluency in English. Many of these people do not have health insurance because they cannot afford it. Those who stay legally usually have good-paying jobs. Some Indonesians even hold high positions in society. Nelson Tansu is a Chinese Indonesian who teaches at Lehigh University in Pennsylvania. There are quite a number of other Indonesians who teach in other American universities and colleges, such as Sylvia Tiwon, Ninik Lunde, George Anwar, Marina Liem, and so on. A few Indonesian Christians live and work in the United States. Rev. Dr. David Wu is a Chinese Indonesian pastor serving as a board staff executive of the United Methodist Church, and Rev. Max Surjadinata, a Chinese Indonesian pastor of the United Church of Christ, has been active on human rights and social justice issues from the Vietnam War to the East Timor and Palestinian struggles for self-determination.

Some other famous Indonesian Americans are Cynthia Gouw, a 1984 Miss Chinatown USA, a TV journalist and a three-time Emmy Award–winning reporter; Tania Gunadi, a Chinese Indonesian American actress who performed in *Pixel Perfect* and *Go Figure*; and Li-young Lee, a Chinese Indonesian American writer whose memoir, *The Winged Seed*, won the American Book Award from the Before Columbus Foundation. Many people may not be aware that the Van Halen brothers of the Van Halen band were born of an Indonesian Dutch mother. Perhaps the most famous Indonesian American today is Maya Soetoro-Ng, the half-sister of President Barack Obama.

9/11 and the Indonesian Community

The September 11 tragedy brought about very deep fear among Indonesians living in the United States. Many Indonesians chose to stay in the United States illegally after their visas expired. They believe in the American dream, that if they stay and work very hard, they will be able to make it. Their American dream tells them that no matter what, the situation in the United States would be better. In the past overstaying would not be too much of a problem. However, after the 9/11 attack the U.S. government took some harsh measures. In January 2002, people holding passports from Middle Eastern countries were required to register at the INS offices. On February 2002, Indonesians were included among those who were called to register at the INS offices.

Many Indonesians felt threatened when they saw this measure was made to relate to the Islamic faith. Chinese Indonesians were also surprised when they registered themselves at the INS offices and were suspected of being Muslims. This was due to their names that no longer sounded Chinese. In 1966 Chinese Indonesians were urged by the New Order government under President Soeharto to change their names into those sounding more "Indonesian." Some of them took names that sounded more like Islamic or Middle Eastern names to make them more acceptable and adaptable to the natives. Therefore some of them took names such as Rachman, Hamzah, Ismail, even though they were not Muslim. Deportation and its consequence that deportees cannot return to the United States within 10 years has made many Indonesians decide to return to their homeland and forgo their "American Dream."

Stephen Suleeman

See also: Entries: Indonesian American Muslims

Further Reading

"Prof. Nelson Tansu, Ph.D. Usia 25 Tahun Mengajar S-3." http://www.tokohindonesia .com/ensiklopedi/n/nelson-tansu/index .shtml. Accessed July 14, 2014.

Sukmana, Damai. "Game of Chance: Chinese Indonesians Play Asylum Roulette in the United States." *Inside Indonesia* 95 (January –March 2009). http://www.insideindonesia .org/edition-95/game-of-chance. Accessed July 14, 2014.

Institute for Leadership Development and Study of Pacific and Asian North American Religion (PANA Institute)

Established in 2000 as a center of the Pacific School of Religion (PSR), and closed by the action of the PSR faculty in September 2009, the Institute for Leadership Development and Study of Pacific and Asian North American Religion (PANA Institute) grew out of eight years of consultation among Asian American and Pacific Islander (API) scholars and national leaders in the church and in theological education. During its existence PANA gained national recognition as a unique and important resource for leadership development and networking, study and research, advocacy, and public information on matters pertaining to Asian and Pacific Americans' (API) religious practices and perspectives in North America. Unique among theological centers with an Asian American focus, PANA's orientation and design was ecumenical, interfaith, and cross-cultural from the institute's inception. Its programming invited participants from a myriad of cultures and faith traditions to discover the differences and commonalities in their approaches to theology, ministry, and civic life.

The stated mission of the PANA Institute was "to provide educational resources and opportunities for Pacific and Asian North American faith communities and individuals to develop leadership and strengthen their contributions to a wider community with the foci on

- Leadership development for faith communities
- Intellectual tradition-building among scholars and leaders in [the] faith community
- Public discourse on issues of religion and societal concern."

PANA's First Five Years (2000–2005)

PANA's most noteworthy accomplishments during its first five years of operation include the following:

- Launching Represent to Witness (R2W), a leadership development project involving Asian and Pacific Islander youth from Seattle, the San Francisco Bay Area, Southern California, and Hawai'i.

- Organizing the annual conference of the Asian Pacific Americans and Religion Research Initiative (APARRI), which convenes pastors, community leaders, and scholars to explore important themes and developments in the Asian Pacific American religious experience.

- Completing the first phase of the Historical Documentation (HDoc) Project, a unique collaboration between PANA, UC Berkeley's Bancroft Library, and the Presbyterian Church in San Francisco's Chinatown, which is the oldest Asian American church in the United States.

- Sponsoring public lectures and roundtable discussions that support social justice and advocacy efforts focused on such topics as the Japanese American internment, the Wen Ho Lee trial, and the impact of the events of September 11, 2001, on Asian Americans.

- The first Senior Fellow program: Bishop Roy Sano of the United Methodist Church (2000–2001); Dr. Rudigir Busto, then teaching religious studies at Stanford University (2001–2002); and Dr. Donna Maeda of Occidental College (2002–2003).

- Raising almost $4.5 million in endowment gifts and pledges, foundation grants, and individual contributions.

Why was there such an urgent need for an institute like PANA? There are now more than 12.5 million Asian Americans and Pacific Islanders living in the United States, approximately half of them on the West Coast. In California alone, the Asian American and Pacific Islander population grew by 40 percent over the 10 years from 1990 to 2000, so that Cambodian, Chinese, Filipino, Japanese, Korean, Samoan, Tongan, Vietnamese, and other APIs now comprise more than 12 percent of California's total population. According to the 2001 American Religious Identification Survey, a significant percentage of this growing API population—43 percent—identifies as Christian. In other words, churches and religious institutions exercise considerable influence over this rapidly growing population, yet many Asian American and Pacific Islander faith communities—with the possible exception of Korean Americans—face a critical shortage of leaders. PANA predicted continued growth of the API population over the next 10 years, along with an expanding need for effective religious leadership, engaged scholarship, and prophetic witness, the very priorities to which the PANA Institute committed itself.

The PANA Institute was designed to embody a faith that is visionary, compassionate, and nondivisive at a time when polarization and defensiveness are the prevailing postures of far too many Christian communities in the United States. It provides educational experiences that build leadership for a trustworthy and credible future for faith communities. It offers programs that reflect the interfaith and pluralistic nature of our contemporary context while also affirming our ecumenical Christian heritage.

PANA's Later Goals and Objectives (2005–2009)

The PANA Institute identified three overarching goals in the areas of leadership development, intellectual tradition, and public voice. Each goal statement is accompanied below by three key objectives for the period 2005–2009.

Leadership Development. To cultivate religious, academic, and civic leadership shaped by the lived experiences, spirituality, and culture of Asian American and Pacific Islander communities in North America.

- Increase API leadership in faith communities (clergy and lay leaders) and in academic settings (scholars and students).
- Recruit and guide the formation of coming generations (high school, college, and seminary-age groups) of API leadership in North American churches, agencies, denominational judicatories, and theological and academic institutions.
- Facilitate partnerships of churches, seminaries, and denominational judicatories in leadership development efforts.

Intellectual Tradition. To develop supportive spaces in which members of Pacific and Asian North American faith and scholarly communities can bring all of their commitments—be these religious, cultural, intellectual, or political—to the exercises of reflection and theorizing on issues of shared concern.

- Facilitate the sharing, critique, extension, and dissemination of emerging scholarship on API religion.
- Sponsor research projects made possible by the PANA Institute's unique position as a multiethnic and nondenominational faith-based organization.
- Support the networking of individuals and organizations engaged in critical reflection on issues of religious and theological concern to the API community.

Public Voice. To cultivate Pacific and Asian North American religious voices on social, political, and community issues.

- Promote the public sharing of critical religious reflection and ethical perspectives on current social, political, and community issues.
- Cultivate a network of API spokespeople available for speaking engagements and media interviews, including voices on API theologies and social justice advocacy.
- Assemble an archive of lectures, sermons, materials, and resources of notable API clergy, scholars, and community leaders.

Accomplishments (2005–2009)

Leadership Development Projects and Program Strategies

- Represent to Witness: Supported by the Lilly Endowment through Represent to Witness (R2W), the PANA Institute was nurturing a new generation of

Asian and Pacific Islander pastors, public theologians, religious scholars, and other faith leaders. Established in 2003 with funding from the Lilly Endowment, R2W involves Asian and Pacific Islander youth from four regions: Seattle, the San Francisco Bay Area, Southern California, and Hawai'i. These high school and college-aged youth participated in an intensive, two-week summer institute at PSR, followed by year-round regional workshops emphasizing leadership development, cultural consciousness, social justice, and engaged spirituality.

- Vocational Discernment Support: API students training for the ministry at PSR and other seminaries at the Graduate Theological Union are often faced by questions not directly addressed by seminary curricula. What does it mean to bring the gifts of being Asian American or Pacific Islander to the work of professional ministry? How is the process for discerning a Christian calling affected by the particularities of race and ethnicity? One of the four priorities in the recently approved PSR Strategic Plan is "dismantling racism and building cross-cultural competence." Yet for API seminarians, this is simply the beginning of a process that equips the seminary community to reach beyond removing barriers to actually creating conditions that allow future church leaders to flourish. To support this work, PANA assumed an active role in designing new curricula and educational programs, as well as helping to strengthen support networks

for API students and other students of color at PSR and the GTU.

Intellectual Tradition Projects and Program Strategies

- HDoc: PANA's Historical Documentation (HDoc) Project brought to light the memories and narratives of several generations of Asian Americans. A unique collaboration between PANA, UC Berkeley's Bancroft Library, and the Presbyterian Church in San Francisco's Chinatown (the oldest Asian American church in the United States), HDoc has archived more than 8,000 photographs, oral histories, microfilm, and other historical records. This material was exhibited at PSR's Badè Museum and the Presbyterian Church in Chinatown, providing an important precedent for collaboration between a seminary, congregation, and research institution. During the period 2005–2010, PANA undertook a second phase of HDoc, focusing on the faith experiences of Japanese Americans interned during World War II. The project was funded by the Rockefeller Foundation.

- APARRI Conference: With funding from the E. Rhodes and Leona B. Carpenter Foundation, PANA co-sponsored the annual Asian Pacific Americans and Religion Research Initiative (APARRI) Conference, which explored important themes and developments in the Asian Pacific American religious experience. APARRI 2005, hosted by McCormick Theological Seminary in Chicago, featured workshops on such topics as

"Present-Day Dynamics of Being Muslim in America," "Negotiating Hybridity: Being Asian and Being American," and "Speaking Truth to Power: The How's and Why's of Asian American Social Criticism." Over several years, APARRI has become one of the most important networks for emerging Asian American religious scholars—people who first attended APARRI conferences as doctoral students now return as assistant professors and program administrators.

- Website: To better support such activities as HDoc and APARRI, and the various leadership development and public voice activities envisioned for the coming five years, PANA upgraded and improved its website. PANA focused on expanding its Web-based resources for API religious scholars and graduate students, clergy and lay leaders, and community leaders engaged at the intersection of faith and social justice work.

Public Voice Projects and Program Strategies

- Lectures and Local Advocacy Program: Supported by the grants of the Henry Luce Foundation, PANA's Public Voice lectures and roundtable discussions helped to support emerging voices in public theology—not only pastors and religious scholars, but community-based social activists and grassroots leaders who recognize the role that faith institutions have played in the cultivation of justice, diversity, and ethnic consciousness. Lectures and gatherings addressed such topics as

"Civil Rights and Civil Marriage" and "Racial and Religious Dimensions of September 11th and the War on Terror." During the period 2005–2010, PANA formalized these lectures and roundtable discussions as short courses, workshops, and other activities offered through PSR's expanding Community Education Program.

- Civil Liberty & Faith Project: With support from the Henry Luce Foundation, PANA undertook a major new initiative during the period 2005–2010, the Civil Liberty & Faith Project, a leadership development program for API religious leaders and community leaders committed to two important goals: (1) creating greater interreligious and interethnic understanding, and (2) promoting civil liberty, social equality, and economic justice for all human beings.

PANA's Core Operations, Infrastructure, Staffing, and Oversight

Included in the costs for core operations and infrastructure development were a portion of the salaries for PANA's three senior staff members (executive director, program director, and director of research programs), as well as secretarial/administrative support, rent and utilities, office equipment and supplies, telephone, copying, and postage/shipping. PANA's core operations provided the flexibility required to take on new issues and challenges as they arose, such as providing organizational support for the annual conference of

PANAAWTM (Pacific, Asian, and North American Asian Women in Theology and Ministry), a leadership development organization for API women in theology and ministry in the United States.

Staffing. The PANA Institute was staffed by seven people with a total staff capacity of 4.35 FTE (exclusive of student workers). To support the expanded volume of work anticipated for the period 2005–2010, PANA intended to increase its staffing capacity by a modest 7 percent to 4.65 FTE. The PANA executive director was a senior PSR faculty member selected by the PSR faculty, president, and trustees in consultation with the PANA Oversight Committee. Fumitaka Matsuoka, former dean, professor of theology, and an ordained minister in the Church of the Brethren, served as PANA's founding executive director.

Oversight. The PANA Institute was advised by an Oversight Committee comprised of API faculty members from PSR and other seminaries belonging to the Graduate Theological Union. Through its various efforts to cultivate new leadership and a strong intellectual tradition among API scholars and clergy, PANA helped to ensure a continuing stream of API students, professors, pastors, and community leaders equipped to sustain and expand the good work.

The Advisory Committee was charged with three areas of responsibility: (1) advising the PANA staff and Oversight Committee on the development of new projects and programs; (2) assisting with national fundraising efforts; and (3) offering policy recommendations to PSR's president and trustees to advance PANA's work and the seminary's overall support for API faculty, students, and staff.

Fumitaka Matsuoka

Further Reading

Pacific School of Religion, Brochure. "PANA Institute," 2001.

Pacific School of Religion Website. psr.edu /pana-institute. Accessed July 15, 2014.

International Society of Krishna Consciousness (ISKCON)

Among the religious movements that originated in the United States during the 1960s, the International Society for Krishna Consciousness (ISKCON) is unique for its solicitation practices. Informally referred to as the Hare Krishna movement, its organizational form took shape due to the efforts of the Bengali Hindu religious leader A. C. Bhaktivedanta Swami Prabhupada in 1966 in New York City. Born Abhay Charan De in Calcutta in 1896, the future Prabhupada was inspired by the revival of the 16th-century bhakti or devotional tradition of the followers of Vishnu in medieval Bengal (followers of the Hindu deity Vishnu are called Vaishnavas). Influenced deeply by the Gaudiya Vaishnava religious tradition (literally the form of Vaishnava devotion that originated from Gaur in medieval Bengal), he disseminated the theological and cultural practices in India and in the West. Along with his organization's followers, he played a pivotal role in initiating thousands of young Americans into an alternative counterculture. In so doing, they were

Parade goers and participants march down the walkway near the beach in Santa Monica, California, August 4, 1996, to celebrate the International Society for Krishna Consciousness's 20th annual Festival of Chariots. The parade, featuring four-story high chariot-style floats, was followed by a festival at Venice Beach with a vegetarian meal and theatrical performances. (AP Photo/Arindam Shivaani/NurPhoto/Sipa USA)

often in conflict with the legal and social mores of the day.

The Prabupada called his theological doctrine "Krishna consciousness" to differentiate it from those of other Vaishnava groups and also from other Indic traditions that were broadly defined as Hindu. Like other immigrant religious traditions, Gaudiya Vaishnava rituals and practices were either modified or maintained, keeping in view the contemporary needs of the given society. Among the maintained practices, devotees commit themselves to an ascetic regimen, share collective responsibilities, and adhere to a vegetarian diet. Part of the ascetic regimen includes, but is not limited

to, the avoidance of gambling, alcohol abuse, drug abuse or even the consumption of caffeine, and limiting sexual activity to connubial procreation. While "congregational" devotees adhere to normal lifestyles and career choices, "temple-based" or full-time devotees have semimonastic lives in the temples. The latter's primary task is to spread awareness of Krishna (the Hindu deity Vishnu in his earthly embodiment as Krishna) by active outreach directed at members of the general public. In this, they are guided by Prabhupada's reading of Caitanya Mahaprabhu's doctrine that irrespective of birth, *bhakti* or devotion alone conferred the right to practice

Vaishnavism. The easiest way of attaining this state of spiritual attainment was by devoutly chanting the Hare Krishna mantra, which was crucial to the original Vaishnava ritual of *sankirtan*.

Although *sankirtan* was originally understood as a hortative expression of religious passion involving dancing and singing praises of Krishna, for Prabhupada and his acolytes, this included chanting and singing the mantra, distributing the voluminous body of Krishna consciousness literature written by the Prabhupada, preaching, garnering recruits, and soliciting donations in publicly accessible spaces. While ISKCON's nascent communities were sustained by devotees' *sankirtan* efforts, after 1972, followers began selling consumer goods like candles, record albums, candy, and cookies. Following the Prabhupada's instructions, *sankirtan* efforts were extended to shopping malls and parking lots. Funds thus collected were considered communal property and crucially supported their communities. Many communities currently administer schools, restaurants, and farms. ISKCON's Food for Life program is a coordinated scheme that freely distributes vegetarian food to the needy.

Public spaces have been critical in ISKCON's evolution. While *sankirtan*-related activities are more notable, another example of the use of public space is the chariot festival or *Rath Yatra* that was started in 1968. This was inspired by the festival at Puri Jagannatha Temple in the eastern Indian state of Orissa, where the idols of the deities Jagannatha (another name of Vishnu in his earthly embodiment as Krishna), his sister Subhadra, and elder brother Balarama are carried on three gigantic chariots, each with 12 wheels, and are pulled over ropes by thousands of devotees. Unlike the festival at Puri, where the route and itinerary has remained unchanged for centuries, ISKCON's adaptations across North American urban public spaces has kept various constraints under consideration, like existing municipal restrictions, width of the thoroughfares and their availability, and local sensibilities. ISKCON's chariot festival is organized during the summer. Unlike other public occasions of religious or cultural significance, like, for example, a Saint Patrick's Day parade or a Cinco de Mayo parade, the timings, dates, and locations of ISKCON's *Rath Yatra* are by and large flexible, and keep in view local sensibilities about public solicitation and proselytization, and local awareness of the ritual of *sankirtan*.

While the ritual of *sankirtan* had its fair share of detractors and critics, with some taking recourse to the law and others writing or campaigning against it, it was in many ways crucial to the initial evolution of the movement and set the foundations for ISKCON's later growth and revival. Apart from ensuring resources, many of the public contacts crystallized into memberships, or even informal bases of support. The constitutional protection of the First Amendment facilitated *sankirtan* in public spaces like airport lounges, national parks, and state fairs. In the United States, immigrant religious groups have traditionally had better legal standing as compared to those of homogeneous white converts. Also, as public evaluation and response critically determine resource mobilization, recruitment strategies, and the movement's overall prospects, ISKCON had since the 1970s successfully sought support from immigrant Asian Indians to avoid being stereotyped as a conversion-dependent group.

During the mid-1970s, ISKCON's missionary activities were widely seen as having a pecuniary intent, and this often led to public backlash. Many followers concealed their identities as Hare Krishna devotees during solicitation. The decline of the 1970s counterculture made public spaces less conducive to recruitment and solicitation. As counterculture-oriented youth communities left areas like the Haight-Ashbury district in San Francisco and the Bowery on the Lower East Side of New York City, places traditionally frequented by Hare Krishna followers, solicitation and recruitment efforts dwindled. To counter this and approach inaccessible groups, *sankirtan* and solicitation were extended to airports, state fairs, and bus terminuses.

With these efforts increasingly identified as pecuniary, anticultist groups portrayed them as deviant and coercive, and guided primarily by material concerns. The association of a religious organization with material objectives made for a convincing case of misuse of the First Amendment, which further diminished public goodwill. Not surprisingly, by the mid-1970s, ISKCON devotees were avoided or even targeted in public spaces. In many state fairs, legal rulings restricted their soliciting practices to booths and stalls, thereby denying them potential patrons. State courts also prohibited ISKCON's solicitation in airport facilities (in Los An-geles, Seattle, and Chicago), public zoos, and county fairs (in California and New York). By 1978, the O'Hare International Airport was closed to ISKCON. In 1981, the Minnesota Supreme Court ruled that devotees were not legally entitled to solicit donations and distribute literature at county fairs. In 1992, the U.S. Supreme Court restricted the interior of airport terminals from solicitation efforts. Due to legal rulings, ISKCON had to restrict its peripatetic activities to fewer sites.

While the charismatic persona (following the definition of Max Weber) of the Prabhupada was instrumental in ISKCON's initial growth, it was his creation of the Governing Body Commission (GBC) in 1970 as his de facto spiritual successor (after his death in 1977) that enabled ISKCON to survive well into the succeeding century. Guiding this was the need to improve temple management, spread Krishna consciousness, distribute literature, open centers, and educate followers. Today, an enhanced and self-elected GBC takes consensual decisions on the movement's functioning and its future. These have involved changes to the group's identity and purpose, and relevant adaptations by keeping the social context in view. Notwithstanding its largely democratic approach to decision making, internal dissension among Prabhupada's disciples, including latter-day adherents, made many followers leave the fold altogether or even start rival organizations. Notable among them is the ISKCON Revival Movement, whose premise of initiating disciples through ceremonial priests has been rejected by the GBC.

Within the decade of the passing of the Prabhupada, ISKCON faced serious internal problems. In the run-up to a 1976 case of "brainwashing" of a minor, the U.S. Supreme Court fined the organization substantially. In the 1980s, following media reports and a disclaimer in an official publication, ISKCON was sued by 95 former pupils for physical, emotional, and sexual abuse. To protect itself, ISKCON formed teams for child protection, screening abusers, educating children and adults on child abuse, and encouraging vigilance. Also for bringing forth greater accountability, ISKCON created an ombudsman organization, ISKCON Resolve. With allegations of murder and fraud linked to the movement, and some former members being convicted, the GBC distanced itself from the offenders and assumed a more proactive role.

While ISKCON's transformative phases and organizational growth have not always been coterminous with the spirit of the Hare Krishna movement as generally understood, it stands that energies and ideals that have spurred either, even if at odds occasionally, have reinforced and supported each other at crucial stages, and in doing so eased the passage into the next millennium. Whether this synergy is upheld till the next is an answer that the Prabhupada might have loved to contemplate.

Amitava Ray

See also: Entries: Hindu Temples in America

Further Reading

Brooks, Charles. *The Hare Krishnas in India.* Princeton, NJ: Princeton University Press, 1989.

Bryant, Edwin, and Maria Ekstrand, eds. *The Hare Krishna Movement: The Postcharis-matic Fate of a Religious Transplant.* New York: Columbia University Press, 2004.

Nye, Malory. *Multiculturalism and Minority Religions in Britain: Krishna Consciousness, Religious Freedom, and the Politics of Location.* Surrey, UK: Curzon Press, 2001.

Rochford, E. Burke. *Hare Krishna in America.* New Brunswick, NJ: Rutgers University Press, 1985.

Rochford, E. Burke. *Hare Krishna Transformed.* New York: New York University Press, 2007.

Islamic Canon

Expressed most simply, the religion of Islam as a whole rests on but two authoritative scriptural bases. Above all else it is the *Qur'an* that plays the most central role in defining Islamic thought, norms, and metaphysics, being considered as divinely revealed text and the ultimate guide for all monotheists. The recipient and transmitter of this revelation was the Prophet Muhammad, in whose person we find the source for the secondary Islamic scriptural authority: the narrative accounts of words and deeds attributed to him, collectively known as hadith, which were recorded, compiled, and thenceforth considered as a model for exemplary human behavior (inasmuch as they were deemed authentic).

The *Qur'an*

History. The *Qur'an* (that which is [to be] recited, recitation) is the name given to a collection of Arabic verses that are understood to have been divinely revealed to Muhammad (ca. 570–632 CE), a merchant of the city of Mecca on the western

Arabian peninsula. These revelatory verses or *āyāt* (plural of *āya*, sign, revelation, verse) were received by Muhammad only gradually, beginning in his 40th year in 609 CE and continuing until the year of his death in 632.

Although it has always been considered a book, within Muhammad's lifetime the *Qur'an* was chiefly preserved and transmitted not through writing but rather in being committed to memory by Muhammad himself, his closest companions, and reciters who took it upon themselves to become living repositories of this revelation—not unusual in the context of the strong oral literary tradition of the time. At the same time, the verses and chapters of the *Qur'an* were also preserved in writing during Muhammad's lifetime (using media such as parchment, the wide stalks of palm leaves, and thin rocks), and after his death a compiled physical copy became ever more important as the emergent political and religious movement of Islam expanded rapidly through the Near East, encompassing an ever greater variety of native cultures and languages. One event in particular underscored the urgent necessity of recording the *Qur'an* in writing: In 633, the year after the Prophet's death, the lives of many reciters were lost in the battle of Yamama, among them Sālim, one of the few people authorized by the Prophet himself to teach the *Qur'an*.

Thereupon Muhammad's first successor (*khalīfa*, regent) as guardian of the fledgling Muslim community, Abu Bakr, ordered the compilation of all the extant Qur'anic material—whether from written sources or from those who had memorized the revelations—into one volume. Upon Abu Bakr's death Muhammad's widow Hafsa bint Umar became the guardian of this book until the third *khalīfa*, 'Uthmān, having become aware of differences in pronunciation among the diverse converts to Islam, around 650 decided to canonize the *Qur'an*, such that it would thenceforth be recited in one standardized dialect. In this process, all personal copies or codices of the *Qur'an* were ordered destroyed. The *Qur'an* used today is based on 'Uthmān's recension, which was in turn based on the material gathered by Abu Bakr. Although minute discrepancies in pronunciation still exist due to divergent use of diacritical marks (most notably between the two recitative traditions, *Hafs* and *Warsh*), the content of the *Qur'an* remains fundamentally unchanged through these differences.

Content. The *Qur'an*, comparable in length to the Christian New Testament, consists of 114 chapters or *suras* (Ar. *sūra*, pl. *suwar*), which are arrayed more or less from the longest in the beginning to the shortest at the end of the book, with the notable exception of the first *sura*, Al-Fātiha (The Opening); this chapter, which represents a distillation of the *Qur'an*'s message as a whole, consists of the seven short verses repeated by Muslims with every prayer:

- In the name of God, the Infinitely Merciful, the Compassionate:
- Praise be to God, the Lord and Sustainer of the worlds,
- The Infinitely Merciful, the Compassionate,

- Master of the Day of Judgment.
- To You alone do we turn in worship, to You alone do we turn for help.
- Lead us upon the direct path, the path of the Upright:
- The path of those upon whom You have bestowed your favor, not of those whose lot is wrath, nor of those who wander in delusion.

The *Qur'an* refers to itself as the latest, indeed the final and most perfect, expression of the monotheist message that runs through the Semitic traditions of the Near East, and posits Muhammad as the final and most perfect prophet in the long line of Biblical prophets leading back to Adam, the first human being. The ever-repeated admonition to the worship of one God alone thus comes not only as a response to the Arabian polytheistic traditions of Muhammad's time, but as a confirmation and renewal of the age-old message of God's oneness and indivisibility seen in Judaism and Christianity, whose prophets are at the same time those of Islam. At the same time, both of the earlier traditions are in part criticized, directly or indirectly, for having strayed from the essential monotheistic impulse. For example, although Jesus is held in high esteem as a prophet of the Abrahamic tradition, Christianity's view of him as "son of God" or member of a divine trinity is seen as an aberration. One short *sura* in particular, known as Al-Ikhlās, is often recited for its succinct expression of the monotheistic doctrine, as opposed to such views:

"Say: it is God, who is One; God, the Eternal, the Self-Subsistent, who neither begets nor is born; and nothing compares to Him."

The *Qur'an*'s principal message of the remembrance of God is interwoven throughout with fundamental articles of Muslim belief. Most notably, the *Qur'an* refers to the destiny of the human soul in the afterlife (*ākhira*) following a resurrection of human souls and a Day of Judgment in which it is decided, based on one's actions and inner attitude in this world, whether one's destiny is the refreshing paradise of the Garden or the tormenting hell of the Fire. Belief in this proposition alone is seen as a condition for achieving the more salutary outcome, in addition to belief in the existence of angels and in the various divinely inspired messengers together with the revelatory "book" that they bring to their respective peoples.

The admonition to believe in the afterlife naturally plays an important role in reinforcing the legal and ethical norms set forth in the *Qur'an*, norms that encompass the entire spectrum of human activity, from the personal to the political. The *Qur'an* pays particular attention to the rights of those who in Muhammad's time enjoyed the least legal protection, such as women, orphans, the needy, thus enlarging the understanding of harmony within the community and overall social stability, which forms the basis of ethics in the *Qur'an*.

Both the practical aspects of worldly life and the metaphysical explanations of the nature of reality, together with elucidation of the spiritual attitudes and practices meant to connect these two sides of human existence, are richly illustrated throughout the *Qur'an* through the use of metaphors, parables, and stories of earlier peoples, prophets, and religious communities, many of whose themes would be immediately familiar to Jews and Christians. Moses, for example, is the most oft-mentioned prophet in the *Qur'an*, while Mary, the mother of Jesus, is the most frequently mentioned female figure.

At the same time, the *Qur'an* repeatedly makes reference to events contemporary to its own revelation in Muhammad's lifetime. Thus, despite the timeless aspect of much of the *Qur'an*'s wisdom, one must acknowledge that some of the ethical norms and injunctions that were articulated in response to specific situations (for example, the tension between the emerging Muslim community and the hostile resistance that confronted them from the Meccan population) might need to be given special treatment in their interpretation and significance for other times and other cultures.

The fundamental message of the *Qur'an*, one that is repeated in the most diverse ways, is attentiveness. Attentiveness means seeing things as they really are, with the eyes of faith; it means discerning in creation and in oneself, as well as in the revealed scripture, the signs of the Creator and Revealer. Without that mindfulness and heedfulness no divine-human relationship is possible.

Hadith

History. The collected statements pertaining to the Prophet Muhammad's exemplary way of life (*sunna*), expressed through his utterances and deeds as well as the impressions he left on his companions, form the secondary basis for the legal and ethical norms of Islam, as well as for enhanced understanding of the *Qur'an*'s metaphysical and ontological message. Unlike the *Qur'an*, however, the corpus of prophetic hadith literature (*hadīth*, report, narrative, pl. *ahādīth*) did not emerge unambiguously as a single complete work in the way the *Qur'an* did, nor did it arise contemporary to Muhammad himself; rather, it resulted from an effort spanning centuries to gather and record any material that could be traced back to contemporaries of the Prophet who had witnessed him and recorded—whether in memory or in writing—what they had seen and heard.

The systematic codification of hadith began toward the beginning of the eighth century as an effort to create an authoritative standard for behavioral norms in the Muslim community, which by then had expanded to include territories from the Iberian peninsula to Central Asia and thus encompassed a tremendous variety of cultures with their own distinctly non-Arabian ways of thinking and behaving. Even though the message of the *Qur'an* naturally accompanied the advent of Islam in these lands, in itself it could not communicate the way its message was understood and put into practice by the Prophet, his companions, and those who had lived within their immediate sphere of influence; therefore a great need was felt to seek all available reports about Muhammad's way of life, through which the faithful of a far-flung empire could enjoy the conviction that they were living, as nearly as possible, according to the model of their beloved Prophet.

Through the effort of numerous scholars who searched the farthest corners of the Muslim world for these reports (which had by then been transmitted for generations, both orally and in written form) and then assiduously sifted through and systematized them, by the end of the ninth century the bulk of the material in use today had been gathered. To lend credibility to the entire recension process and thereby the content of the transmitted material, criteria had to be developed that justified the adoption or the rejection of the hadith material; thus a kind of scientific method for determining the authenticity of these accounts arose over time, according to which the moral character and reliability of any given member of a chain (*isnād*) of transmission played an important role, as did missing links in the chain's continuity on the one hand, and the number of simultaneous transmitters at each stage of transmission on the other. Depending on such criteria, hadith were assigned varying categories of trustworthiness: those deemed to be sound or genuine (*sahīh*) had the strongest evidence for their authenticity, while others were judged to be, for example, "fair," "weak," or "fabricated."

Ultimately, the collections of six scholars (known as the Six Sound Hadith Collections) were taken as the accepted hadith canon of Sunni Islam, although two in particular enjoy the greatest respect and thus popularity as reference works. Above all it is the *Sahīh* of Muhammad ibn Ismā'il al Bukhārī (810–70) that is generally acknowledged as the masterpiece of this field, second only to the *Qur'an* in its authority; the other is the *Sahīh* of Muslim ibn al-Hajjāj (d. 875). The remaining four collections are those of Abū Dāwūd (d. 888), al-Tirmidhi (d. 892), al-Nasā'ī (d. 916), and Ibn Māja (d. 886).

Shi'i Islam, while not rejecting these collections outright, relies on different hadith collections, most notably the "Four Books": *Kitāb al-Kāfī* of Kulaini (d. 941), *Man la yahduruhu al-Faqīh* of Ibn Bābawayh (d. 992), and the *Tahdhīb al-Ahkām* and *Al-Istibsār* of al-Tūsī (d. 1067).

Content. The subject matter of the hadith ranges from Muhammad's responses to the circumstances of his day, his elucidations of the *Qur'an*, and his opinions on legal, ethical, and general religious points to descriptions of mystical experience, including divine revelations that stand apart from those in the *Qur'an*. However, despite the important role of hadith literature in complementing the information provided in the *Qur'an*, in the case of any apparent conflict on a particular issue, the *Qur'an* must necessarily take precedence as the definitive authority.

In each of the hadith collections, which because of their vast content (the *Sahīh* of Bukhārī includes over 7,000 entries) are generally divided into several volumes, the transmitted reports are organized into "books" according to a general topic; within these books the entries are divided into chapters dealing with more specific subtopics. Each entry comprises two parts: first, a formal introduction providing the *isnad* leading from that contemporary of Muhammad who first related the *hadith* (in English translations often abridged to mention that person alone), followed by the body of text itself, a document of the event—whether an utterance, an action, a general practice of the Prophet, or commentary from one of his companions—observed by that person. For example (with parentheses indicating the nontranslated *isnad* in its entirety):

(Ya'qūb narrated that Ibrahim ibn Sa'd narrated, on the authority of his father, on the authority of al-Qāsim ibn Muhammad, that) 'Ā'isha—may God be pleased with her—said that:
Allah's Messenger . . . said, "If somebody innovates something which is not in harmony with the principles of our religion, that thing is rejected." (Bukhārī)

Beside the prophetic hadith literature that informs the way of life and religious practices of both the Sunni and Shi'i traditions, Shi'i Islam (most prevalent among Iranians, though also found in Iraq, Syria, and Turkey, among others) also relies on a body of reports attributed to the Imams, those descendants of the Prophet's family whom the Shi'i (as opposed to Sunni Islam) recognize as his legitimate successors.

Reflecting the broad spectrum of Muslim communities living in the United States, the respective preferred *hadith* collections of both the Sunni and Shi'i traditions are represented in this country. The *Qur'an*, however, as the undisputed authority for all adherents of Islam, is universally accepted in its entirety, despite any dogmatic differences between sects.

Neal Kenji Koga

See also: Essays: Muslims

Further Reading

Brown, Daniel. *A New Introduction to Islam.* Oxford: Blackwell, 2004.

Burton, John. *An Introduction to the Hadith.* Edinburgh: Edinburgh University Press, 1994.

Esposito, John. *The Oxford Dictionary of Islam.* New York: Oxford University Press, 2003.

Muhammad Asad, trans and ed. *The Message of the Qur'ān.* Rev. ed. London: The Book Foundation, 2008.

Murata, Sachiko, and William C. Chittick. *The Vision of Islam.* St. Paul, MN: Paragon House, 1994.

Rahman, Fazlur. *Islam.* London: Weidenfeld and Nicolson, 1966.

Renard, John. *Seven Doors to Islam.* Berkeley: University of California Press, 1996.

Schimmel, Annemarie. *Islam: An Introduction,* Albany: State University of New York Press, 1992.

Iu Mien

The Iu Mien are an ethnic group that have lived in the mountain regions of Laos for centuries and practice a distinctive form of shamanism and ancestor veneration. Due to political events in the 1960s and 1970s the Iu Mien have dispersed as refugees to many nations. As of 2012 it was estimated that approximately 50,000 Iu Mien live in the United States with the largest communities residing in Sacramento—15,000—and the San Francisco Bay Area—13,000.

History

Originally coming from China, for centuries the Iu Mien people practiced a basic subsistence farming life in the mountains of Laos. During the so-called "Secret War" conducted by the Central Intelligence Agency in Laos in conjunction with the war in Vietnam, many of the young Iu Mien males were enlisted in support of the United States. As a result, after the U.S. withdrawal the Iu Mien were targeted by the Communist government and many fled to refugee camps in Thailand. During the 1980s, the United States allowed many to migrate, creating significant Iu Mien communities especially on the West Coast in Portland, Seattle, Sacramento, and the San Francisco Bay Area. Currently there are many grassroots attempts to support the nascent communities and to preserve traditional practices and perspectives. One such example is the Lao Iu Mien Culture Association (LIMCA) in Oakland, California.

Beliefs and Practices

The Iu Mien worldview contains a rich vision of the interrelation of the physical and spiritual worlds, which are structured in similar ways. The physical world consists of relations between nature, family, and neighbors, and the broader political arena. Likewise, the spirit world consists of relations between evil spirits, spirits in nature, one's close ancestors, and a high spiritual realm based on Taoist and Buddhist deities. This fusion forms a layered spiritual outlook and practice.

A central practice is paying reverence to one's ancestors, which are remembered back for nine generations. Offerings of food and money at a household altar support the departed soul in the next life. Ignoring one's filial duties can bring physi-

cal, emotional, and material problems in the present life by angering departed spirits. Indeed, physical illness is seen as a manifestation of spiritual illness caused by some disturbance in the spiritual realm and healing may require a shaman as much as a medical doctor. However, ancestral respect serves more than just placating anger; by maintaining constant contact with one's ancestors the departed can be aware of what is going on and thereby help since humans cannot totally solve their own problems without this assistance.

The most important spiritual figure for the community is the shaman, who performs many roles that support the harmonious coexistence of physical and spiritual worlds. Viewed as a community leader, the shaman is responsible for solving people's problems by divining which spirit is upset and why. He must then prescribe the proper ceremony to address the situation, checking astrological calendars for an auspicious date to hold the ceremony. Most important, the shaman must perform the ceremony, which involves intricate rituals that have been committed to memory through years of training. Among the more outstanding activities required of the shaman is ritual slaughter of a pig or chicken to bring balance to the spiritual world. Shamans can only be male and the process of becoming one requires intensive apprenticeship that involves mastering ceremonial texts written in a form of Chinese. While many of the ritual practices are done in individual residences as required, there are also community ceremonies performed during the year.

Assimilation into the United States has presented various challenges to Iu Mien traditional spiritual practices. For example, animal sacrifice is an essential practice, yet many Iu Mien members rent housing where such practices may not be permitted. Also, the close connection of physical and spiritual illness may create difficult situations regarding health care since spiritual healing performed by a shaman is equally, if not more, essential than medical care. Likewise, the purification ceremony after death that is necessary for the spirit to move on to the next world must be done at home and therefore elders "may not call an ambulance at the end to ensure that this happens." A final challenge to traditional spiritual practices is the conversion of many Iu Mien to Christianity, in part due to the sponsorship of many Christian groups that helped enable migration to the United States.

Peter L. Doebler

See also: Entries: Hmong American Religions; Hmong Shamanism; Laotian American Religions

Further Reading

Fadiman, Anne. *The Spirit Catches You and You Fall Down: A Hmong Child, Her American Doctors, and the Collision of Two Cultures.* New York: Farrar, Straus and Giroux, 1997.

Giacchino-Baker, Rosalie, ed. *Stories from Laos: Folktales and Cultures of the Lao, Hmong, Khammu, and Iu-Mien.* Translated by Charlie Chue Chang-Hmong, et al. El Monte, CA: Pacific Asia Press, 1995.

Gross, Miriam. "Community Portrait: Lao Iu Mien." http://www.wildflowers.org/community/IuMien/portrait.shtml. Accessed May 7, 2014.

Hall, Richard, and Fahm Fong Saeyang. *Death of a Shaman.* DVD. Seattle: Indie Flix, 2000.

Lao Iu Mien Culture Association. "Study 2000." http://www.limcacenter.org/?q=node/6. Accessed May 7, 2014.

MacDonald, Jeffrey L. *Transnational Aspects of Iu-Mien Refugee Identity.* New York: Garland, 1997.

Velazquez, Elaine. *Moving Mountains: The Story of the Yiu Mien.* DVD. Portland, OR: Feather & Fin Productions, 1989. Online at http://www.folkstreams.net/film,149.

Young, Bernice. "The Shaman's Apprentice." *San Francisco Weekly*, September 5, 2001. http://www.sfweekly.com/2001-09-05/news/the-shaman-s-apprentice/full/. Accessed May 7, 2014.

J

Jain Temples

Jains are followers of an Indian religion known as Jainism. Jainism developed contemporaneously with Buddhism in India; thus, it shares some basic fundamental religious principles with Hinduism and Buddhism such as the relationship between *karma* and the cycles of reincarnation (*saṃsāra*) and rebirth. Together with Buddhism, Jainism stresses compassion (*metta*) and nonharming (*ahimsa*). The principle of nonharming in Jain is so great that it informs nearly all aspects of Jain lifeways, such as observing vegetarianism and not doing any type of work that harms any other sentient beings. There are two major schools of Jainism: Digambara (Sky-Clad) and Svetambara (White-Clad). The Digambara practice complete nudity and have two material possessions: a peacock feather broom and a gourd for water. The peacock feather broom is used to delicately sweep the floor while walking or before sitting to remove any creature that may be accidentally harmed. The Svetambara wear white and cover their nose to avoid accidentally killing a sentient creature while breathing or speaking. There are about 10 to 12 million Jains in the world today. It is also considered the smallest world religion. Although it is small in numbers, its teachings, especially on nonharming and compassion, have had a great impact on world civilization. Mahatma Gandhi was known to be inspired by Jain teachings.

In the early 1970s, the Jains started arriving in significant numbers in the United States. At the moment, there are nearly 100 Jain temples and centers in the United States and about 100,000 Jain Americans. Two events before the 1970s anticipated the arrival of the Jains. First, there was the construction of a Jain temple at the St. Louis World's Fair in 1904–1905. At that time, there were no Jains in the United States. After the fair, it was dismantled and rebuilt in Las Vegas, only to be taken down in the 1960s. Now that Jains live in the United States, the remains of the building have been acquired by the Jain Society of Los Angeles. The second event was the arrival of Virachand Gandhi, who is considered the father of American Jainism. Today, there are more Jain temples and communities in the United States than in any country outside India.

As a group, the Jains are more affluent than other people in India and also in the United States as most of them are in white-collar professions that do not harm other living creatures. In India, Jains go to the market and purchase animals such as pigs, chickens, and goats and give them sanctuary in a "zoo" near the temple. They also house and nurse injured animals in their temple-zoo. This is not the case in the

The top of the historic 1904 wooden Jain Temple structure, originally built for the 1904 St. Louis World's Fair, being reassembled and restored at the Jain Center of Southern California (JCSC) in Buena Park, California, August 16, 2013. The ancient Indian religion of Jainism, a close cousin of Buddhism, has a strict adherence to nonviolence that forbids eating meat, encourages days of fasting and places value on even the smallest of insects. In India, Jains account for about 1 percent of the population and the community in the U.S. counts about 150,000 followers. (AP Photo/Nick Ut/Corbis)

United States. However, many Jain Americans volunteer at the Humane Society and foster dogs and cats for adoption.

Some of the basic features of Jain temples in the United States are the use of marble, which reflects the medieval western Indian architecture of Rajasthan; the emphasis on the arches found in Rajasthan vernacular architecture; the curtain at the entrances; and the spacious main hall combined with the sanctum. Marble statues of Mahavira (founder of Jainism), Parsvanatha, Rishabadeva, and modern saints (e.g., Acharya Sushil Kumar Ji) are enshrined as objects of worship in the *mandapas*, or halls. Similar to Jain temples in India, Jain temples in the United States are sites of religious festival celebrations, daily worship, the ritual tradition of *darshan* (divine seeing), and distribution of *prasada*, or ritual offerings.

Because of the Jain tradition of complete compassion and nonharming, Jain temples in the United States have attracted many non-Indians. Jain temples are located in roughly 19 states, including New York, New Jersey, California, Massachusetts, Maryland, and Wisconsin. Jain temples and the Jain communities in the United States will continue to inspire others to create a world free from suffering and violence.

Jonathan H. X. Lee

See also: Entries: Jainism

Further Reading

Federation of Jain Associations in North American (JAINA): http://www.jaina.org/. Accessed July 16, 2014.

Rangaswamy, Padma. *Namaste America: Indian Immigrants in an American Metropolis.* University Park: The Pennsylvania State University Press, 2000.

Young Jains of America: http://www.yja.org/. Accessed July 16, 2014.

Jainism

Who Are the Jains?

Jains are followers of one of the most ancient *Dharmic* (religious) traditions of India; the others being Hindu, Buddhist, and Sikh. Jains are followers of the Shramana tradition, the oldest of the non-Aryan traditions. Etymologically Jain comes from the word *Jaina* meaning conqueror; not conqueror of the world or master over others but conqueror of self, that is, one who has conquered his or her passions.

Historically, Jain tradition can be traced back about 3,000 years but some historians have speculated that its roots go much deeper, prior to the so-called Indo-Aryan migration into India. Jaina tradition believes in 24 *Tirthankaras* (ford-makers or teachers) of the current cosmic cycle; Mahavira (the Great Hero) being the last of them, living about the same time as the Buddha in the sixth century BCE.

Jains form a very small minority of India, less than one-half of 1 percent, but their influence on Indian culture has been considerable. Jain *Dharma* (erroneously called Jainism but used here for the sake of convenience) is the least known religious tradition of India outside India. Jains did not venture outside India for a variety of reasons. It was, for them, *Kala Pani* (literally, black water or forbidden lands). Travel to foreign lands, across the oceans, was not encouraged, if not taboo as in the Hindu system called the *Samudrolanghana*, meaning the offense of crossing the sea, which would entail the loss of one's *Varna* status (one of the four traditional social classes of India). *Sadhus* (mendicants) and "holy men" were not permitted to cross the seas or go abroad. For lay Jains it was discouraged by custom and tradition to travel abroad, as much as by religious considerations, chief among them being food. Jains are vegetarian, some more than others. Their faith is based on ahimsa (nonviolence, noninjury) to any living being.

Jains in North America

Hence it was rare to find Jains in any significant numbers in the United States (also in Canada) before the mid-1960s, as was the case for other East Indians, when immigration laws for entry of Asians were relaxed, repealing the Asian Exclusion Act (enacted May 26, 1924). The Chinese Exclusion Act (1882) was repealed in 1943. The Immigration Act of 1917 excluded Asian Indians. However, a law passed by the U.S. Congress in 1965 changed all that, giving preference to immigrants with skills needed in the United States.

The most significant time of Jain immigration began in the early 1970s, though there are a few isolated cases of some Jains visiting the United States for conferences or lectures or to study before the sixties. The first Jain of some note to visit America was Virchand Gandhi (1864–1901) who represented Jain Dharma at the first Parliament of World Religions in 1893. Some 40 years later he was followed by a Jain citizen-scholar, Champat Rai Jain, who came to deliver an address to the World Fellowship of Faiths at Chicago in 1933. It would be nearly another 40 years until another Jain of some significance, Chitrabhanu, a former *sadhu* (monk), came to the United States to deliver a series of lectures at Harvard Divinity School in 1971. He had to give up his monkhood and take off his monastic robes before being allowed to travel abroad in ordinary householder garb. Gurudev, as he is belovedly called, established the Jain Meditation Center of New York and the Jain Society of Toronto in 1973.

The first practicing Jain monk to visit the United States was Sushil Muni (1926–1994), later Acharya Sushil Kumar, in 1975. He is lovingly called a founding father of American Jainism because of the effort he made in establishing an ashram (monastery, hermitage, or retreat) at Blairstown, New Jersey, in 1983, known as Siddhachalam. In this case it was the first Jain *Tirtha* (pilgrimage site) in North America. Acharya Sushil Kumar also established multiple Jain centers throughout North America. He was instrumental in founding the federation of Jain associations in North America (JAINA) in the 1980s. It has been a very successful organization representing Jains of both the Svetambara and Digambara sects, and holding biennial conferences. It has promoted Jain *Dharma* among the Jains and the larger community by publishing books and a magazine.

Jains are now firmly established in North America, numbering over 100,000. They have their own national and local organizations. They have established temples coast to coast, so much so that the United States has the most Jain temples outside India, including one called the Hindu-Jain Temple of Pittsburgh. Many Jains are in white-collar jobs, in professions or self-employed businesses.

University Courses

The University of Toronto was one of the earliest in North America to offer a course on Jainism (1989). It also hosted the first International Conference on Jaina Studies (1995) and was the first to establish an annual public lecture on Jainism named the Roop Lal Jain Lectures, which have been delivered by some well-known scholars of the world, beginning with Padmanabh Jaini. There are now several American universities and colleges that are offering courses in Jainism. In addition, JAINA has been offering a summer school on Jaina Studies (ISSJS) in India since 2005, attended by students and teachers from all over the world.

Jain Beliefs

Jain beliefs can be summarized as the 3As: (1) *ahimsa* (noninjury, nonharm to any living being); (2) *aparigraha* (nonattachment to worldly things); and (3) *anekantavad*, referring to the principles of pluralism and multiplicity of viewpoints, one of the most unique doctrines of Jainism, aptly suited to a multicultural society. One of the great proponents of nonviolence in India in modern times was Mohandas Gandhi, who was greatly influenced by Jainism. Being a *dharmic* religion, Jainism shares many of its features with Hinduism, for example, belief in *saṃsāra* (the continuous cycle of life, death), reincarnation, *karma* ("action," past beneficial or harmful actions are reciprocated in future births), and *moksha* (liberation). The aim of Jain life is to achieve liberation of the soul.

Jains do not believe in a God who is the creator or the destroyer of the universe. In that matter they are atheists. However, they do believe in the divinity of God as a perfect being, and that every human has the capacity to be a perfect being, a liberated soul, through self-purification and renunciation, when he or she obtains infinite knowledge, infinite vision, infinite power. This is in accordance with their three jewels: right faith, right knowledge, and right conduct. Jain scriptures tell us that this universe has no beginning or end with respect to time, and that this and other universes are eternal as are their substances. The universe has its own cosmic laws and runs on its own accord without any intervention by any God or Supreme Being.

Social System

Jains have a fourfold order made up of ascetics, mendicants, *sadhus*, and *sadhvis* (monks and nuns), who follow the five great vows (*mahā-vrats*). The latter have given up all earthly possessions and worldly desires but have become spiritual and inspirational leaders of the *Sangha* (community), which is made up of *Shravaks* and *Shravikas* (male and female householders or lay followers).

Sushil Jain

See also: Entries: Jain Temples

Further Reading

Jain Digest: Magazine of the Federation of Jain Associations in North America. 1985–. http://www.jaina.org/?page=JD_Publi cation. Accessed July 14, 2014.

Jain, Prakash C. *Jains in India and Abroad.* New Delhi: International School for Jain Studies, 2011.

Jain, S. K. "Gaining Academic Recognition for Jainism." *Jain Journal: A Quarterly on Jainology* XXVII, no. 3 (January 1993): 129–10.

Kumar, Bhuvanendra. *Jainism in North America.* Mississauga, Ontario: Jain Humanities Press, 1996.

O'Connell, Joseph T., ed. *Jain Doctrine and Practice: Academic Perspectives: An Anthology of Nine Roop Lal Jain Lectures at the University of Toronto.* Reviewed in *Studies in Religion/Sciences Religieuses* 30 (2001): 3–4.

Shah, Nathubhai. "The Western Order of Jainism." *Jain Journal* XXX1, no 1 (July 1996).

Tweed, Thomas A., and Steven Prothero, eds. *Asian Religions in America: A Documentary History.* New York: Oxford University Press, 1999.

Wagle, N. K., and Olle Qvarnstrom, eds. *Approaches to Jaina Studies: Philosophy, Logic, Rituals and Symbols.* Select Papers presented at the First International Conference on Jaina Studies, held at the University of Toronto, March 31–April 2, 1995. Toronto: Centre for South Asian Studies, University of Toronto, 1999.

Japanese American Christianity

In 1885, the Meiji government of Japan began to allow large-scale emigration of laborers to Hawai'i and the United States. These immigrants, who were raised with a combination of Buddhist and Shintō teachings from their homeland, encountered a new society where Christianity was the dominant religion. For many of the Isseis that were struggling in their new surroundings, the practical lessons offered by Christian churches became especially appealing. Within the next decade, several Japanese American Christian churches had been established throughout the West Coast and Hawai'i. In fact, it was not until 1899 that the first Japanese American Buddhist temple was built. For this earliest wave of Japanese immigrants, Christian organizations played a pivotal role in their acculturation to the United States.

However, setting foot on American soil was not necessarily the immigrants' first encounter with Christianity. Christianity in Japan can actually trace its history back to the 16th century, when Jesuit and Franciscan missionaries reached Japan and converted up to an estimated 10 percent of the population to Catholicism. However, in the early 17th century, the Tokugawa shogunate expelled all foreign missionaries, and what little Christianity remained was forced underground into what are now referred to as *Kakure Kirishitan*, or "Hidden Christian" communities.

Early Japanese America and the Christian Church

On March 31, 1854, Commodore Matthew C. Perry sailed to Japan and, by 1858, coerced the ruling Tokugawa shogunate to sign the Treaty of Kanagawa, thus ending Japan's three centuries of seclusion. This moment marked the beginning of trade between Japan and the United States, and also enabled Christian missionaries to proselytize within Japanese borders. By the start of the Meiji era in 1868, American and Canadian missionaries from several Protestant denominations had established a number of mission schools throughout Japan. Many of the earliest students at these mission schools were *shizoku*, or members of the former samurai class, which had previously been abolished by the Meiji emperor.

In the early 1870s, a *shizoku* student from Yamaguchi Prefecture named Kanichi Miyama made his way to Tokyo, where he opened a clothing store. During these early years of the Meiji era, the Japanese government encouraged wealthy young men to travel abroad to Europe and the United States to learn and bring back skills to help modernize Japan. Miyama was a perfect candidate to heed this call, and he would eventually move to San Francisco in 1875 at the age of 27. Before departing, he met Rev. George Cochrane, who was one of the earliest Canadian Methodist missionaries to Japan. Rev. Cochrane wrote Miyama a letter of introduction to his Methodist colleague in San Francisco, Rev. Thomas Guard.

Soon after arriving in San Francisco, Miyama and two other young Japanese men visited Rev. Guard at the Powell Street Methodist Episcopal Church. Apparently unsure of what to do with these Japanese immigrants, he instead directed them to the nearby Methodist Episcopal Chinese Mission, just about one mile away in Chinatown. Christian missionaries such as Rev. Otis Gibson had been in Chinatown since at least 1852 in response to the over 25,000 Chinese laborers living and working there. Despite the large Chinese population, there were likely only about 200 Japanese in San Francisco at the time.

Rev. Gibson of the Methodist Episcopal Chinese Mission allowed these young Japanese men to study English and have regular Bible study sessions in the basement of his Chinatown church. On February 22, 1877, Kanichi Miyama became the first legal Japanese immigrant to the United States to be baptized, and soon he was instrumental in creating the Fukuinkai (Gospel Society), which was the first voluntary Japanese organization in the United States. In addition to promoting Christian teachings and values, the Fukuinkai also hosted English lessons and several secular workshops to help the Japanese immigrants settle into their new surroundings.

The Initial Growth of Japanese American Christianity

By 1881, the Fukuinkai had split into two different factions, with one remaining under the guidance of Rev. Gibson and the Methodist Episcopal Church, while the other moved under the influence of the Presbyterian Church. In 1885, this Presbyterian group, known as the Tyler Fukuinkai, organized the earliest Japanese American church, the First Japanese Church of San Francisco (present-day Christ United Presbyterian Church). That same year, the Methodist Episcopal Church California Conference officially allocated a budget of $2,100 for a Japanese mission in San Francisco, which led to the establishment of the Japanese Methodist Episcopal Church (present-day Pine United Methodist Church) under the leadership of Bishop Merriman Colbert Harris and his now ordained assistant, Rev. Kanichi Miyama. In 1887, the Methodist Episcopal Church California Conference became aware of the large masses of Japanese laborers immigrating to Hawai'i (which at the time was still an independent kingdom). Rev. Miyama joined with Congregationalist minister Dr. C. M. Hyde of the Hawai'i Evangelical Association and created the Japanese Methodist Church in Hawai'i (present-day Harris United Methodist Church) and Nu'uanu Congregational Church.

By the 1890s, Japanese American communities throughout California, Hawai'i, and several other western and Rocky Mountain states had their own Christian churches. While the Methodists and Presbyterians were the earliest denominations to specifically reach out to the Japanese immigrant community, several other groups soon followed, such as the Congregationalists, Baptists, and Episcopalians. In fact, some of the different denominations even worked with one another to focus on specific geographic areas for practical reasons. For example, in 1901, Methodist bishop M. C. Harris and Presbyterian superintendent Dr. Earnest Sturge created an agreement so that the Methodists would focus on Santa Clara County, while the Presbyterians would take care of Santa Cruz and Monterey Counties. This led to certain churches changing their denominational affiliations, such as Westview Church in Watsonville, California, which switched from Methodist to Presbyterian.

Throughout the early decades of the 20th century, Japanese American Christianity continued to grow, especially as increasing numbers of Japanese laborers married and started their own families. During this period, it is estimated that 15–20 percent of all Isseis were Christians, with even higher numbers for their Nisei children, who greatly contributed to the exploding new church memberships. In 1920, many of the different Japanese American Christian churches began to work together to host a conference for high school and college-aged Niseis. The Young People's Christian Conference (YPCC) became extremely popular, and would eventually bring upwards of 500 young Japanese Americans together from various churches to socialize as Japanese American Christians. Although YPCC stopped due to World War II, several subsequent Japanese American Christian youth summer camps such as the Lake Sequoia Retreat, Japanese Evangelical Missionary Society (JEMS) Mt. Hermon Conference, and the United Methodist Asian American Summer Camp trace their roots to these early annual meetings.

Japanese American Churches and World War II

On December 7, 1941, Pearl Harbor was bombed by the Imperial Japanese Navy. Due in part to the combination of war hysteria and a general distrust of Japanese Americans, President Franklin D. Roosevelt signed Executive Order 9066, which led to the forced incarceration of over 110,000 individuals of Japanese descent living on the West Coast into concentration camps scattered throughout the United States. The Japanese American churches in the affected regions, some of which were now over 50 years old, were forced to shut their doors for the duration of the war.

Even though the churches closed, Japanese American Christians continued to actively practice their faith throughout their stay in temporary assembly centers and more permanent concentration camps. The Pacific Japanese Provisional Conference of the Methodist Episcopal Church, which had just been formed in 1940, was forced to hold their annual meeting in 1942 at the Santa Anita racetrack assembly center under armed supervision. All 10 of the concentration camps had regularly scheduled Christian worship services, as well as Sunday schools for the children. In many cases throughout the different camps, Christians received preferential treatment over Buddhists, who were viewed as "less American."

In the years immediately following World War II, Japanese Americans resettled throughout the country. While many would eventually return to their former West Coast hometowns such as San Francisco and Los Angeles, a significant number chose to start over in cities such as Chicago and Minneapolis. As new Japanese American communities sprouted in these cities, Japanese American Christian churches were also formed there during the late 1940s and early 1950s.

For the Japanese American Christians that chose to reopen their churches on the West Coast, a series of new issues began to affect the direction of their respective congregations. During World War II, Japan was clearly the enemy of the United States. In response to constant villainization of Japan by the American media, it is understandable that many of the young Japanese Americans (who were most likely born and raised in the United States) began to distance themselves from culturally Japanese signifiers such as language and customs. Instead, many Japanese Americans chose to adopt a much more patriotic identity, as can be seen in the thousands of Japanese Americans who volunteered for the highly decorated 100th Battalion and 442nd Regimental Combat Team.

By the 1950s, Niseis began to take senior leadership roles in many of the Japanese American Christian churches. For the first time, the ethnically Japanese leaders of these churches were native English speakers who could better serve their increasingly English-speaking congregations. As the Sansei generation was generally born during and immediately following World War II, it is possible that many were raised in households that chose to ignore much of their Japanese heritage. Perhaps not coincidentally, these years line up chronologically with the dissolution of the Methodist Pacific Japanese Provisional Conference in 1964. This dissolution, which sought to create a more "colorblind" church, caused all Japanese American Methodist churches to be removed from an ethnic grouping and instead be placed under the supervision of geographic-based leadership. This is particularly significant since it occurred during the civil rights movement when many ethnic minority groups took the opposite route and instead chose to proudly embrace their heritage.

Recent Developments of Japanese American Christianity

By the 1980s and 1990s, most of the original Issei founders had passed away, and Japanese American Christian churches encountered an entirely new set of issues to face. Some of the churches have disappeared, and many have distanced themselves from their historically Japanese American identity to different degrees. Ontario Community United Methodist Church in eastern Oregon, for example, currently has an aging Nisei and Sansei population, while the younger church members are almost exclusively white. Meanwhile, some churches such as Buena Vista United Methodist Church in the San Francisco Bay Area now have an increasingly panethnic congregation, which reflects its local neighborhood. In 1990, the Japanese Congregationalist and United Methodist churches in Fresno, California, merged to create the United Japanese Christian Church. Evergreen Baptist Church in Los Angeles, which is now one of the largest and most well known pan-Asian congregations, developed from a specifically Japanese congregation. At the other end of the spectrum, Wesley United Methodist Church in San Jose Japantown is one of the last remaining Japanese American churches to employ a full-time Japanese-speaking minister, specifically to serve the significant Shin-Issei community.

A recent survey has estimated that 43 percent of all Japanese Americans claim a Christian identity. While this number is less than the nearly 80 percent of all Americans that identify as Christian, it is significantly larger than the 1 percent Christian population in Japan. Although it is true that many Japanese American Christians have since joined mainline Christian congregations and are no longer members of Japanese American churches, the historical significance of Japanese American Christian churches remains. In fact, only a couple of generations prior, it would have been impossible for Japanese Americans to worship anywhere else. From their humble roots inside a Chinatown basement, Japanese American Christian churches have persevered in the face of injustice and are now well into their second century of ministry. Today, they lead the way for the next generation of church members that are increasingly diverse ethnically, generationally, and geographically.

Dean Ryuta Adachi

See also: Entries: Fujinkai (Buddhist Women's Association); Japanese American Religions; Japanese American Religious Federation (JARF); Japanese Evangelical Missionary Society (JEMS); Presbyterian Churches of Japanese Heritage

Further Reading

Hayashi, Brian Masaru. *For the Sake of Our Japanese Brethren: Assimilation, Nationalism, and Protestantism among the Japanese of Los Angeles, 1895–1942.* Stanford, CA: Stanford University Press, 1995.

Jeung, Russell. *Faithful Generations: Race and New Asian American Churches.* New Brunswick, NJ: Rutgers University Press, 2005.

Spickard, Paul. *Japanese Americans: The Formation and Transformations of an Ethnic Group.* New York: Twayne, 1996.

Suzuki, Lester. *Ministry in the Assembly and Relocation Centers of World War II.* Berkeley, CA: Yardbird, 1979.

Yoo, David. "A Religious History of Japanese Americans in California." In Pyong Gap Min and Jung Ha Kim, eds. *Religions in Asian America: Building Faith Communities.* Walnut Creek, CA: Altamira Press, 2002, pp. 121–42.

Yoshida, Ryo. "Japanese Immigrants and Their Christian Communities in North America: A Case Study of the Fukuinkai, 1877–1896." *Japanese Journal of Religious Studies* 34, no. 1 (2007): 229–44.

Japanese American Internment, Remembrance, and Redress

On July 31, 1980, U.S. president Jimmy Carter signed the bill to create the Commission on Wartime Relocation and Internment of Civilians (CWRIC) with the purpose of reviewing Executive Order 9066 of February 19, 1942, and its consequences. E.O. 9066 set in motion the evacuation and detention of 120,000 Japanese and Japanese Americans living in the designated Military Areas 1 and 2 on the West Coast during World War II to 10 concentration camps located in isolated areas across the country. They were Manzanar in eastern California, Tule Lake (Newell) near the California-Oregon border, Minidoka (Hunt) in Idaho, Topaz in central Utah, Poston

(Colorado River) and Gila River in Arizona, Amache in Colorado, Heart Mountain in Wyoming, Jerome (Denson) and Rohwer in Arkansas. Two-thirds of those interned were U.S. citizens and more than half were children. In late March 1942, a series of 108 "Civilian Evacuation Orders" began the removal initially to 16 hastily organized Assembly Centers located at fairgrounds, racetracks, and similar facilities where overcrowding, communal showers and outhouses, and former horse stables were the prevailing conditions while awaiting the construction of the 10 "relocation centers" or concentration camps. Limited to the standard two suitcases per person, only what they could carry, many lost what took a lifetime to build. By October 1942, the transfer to the 10 "camps" was completed, yet the dislocation was only beginning.

On February 19, 1976, President Gerald R. Ford revoked E.O. 9066 due to an organized effort led by the Seattle Japanese American Citizens League (JACL) Evacuation Redress Committee, sparked by the realization that it was still in existence. The first of 10 public hearings of the CWRIC opened in Washington, D.C. and 750 witnesses eventually testified. Although the WRA (War Relocation Authority) had attempted to create a semblance of normalcy with schools, churches, hospitals, newspapers, some degree of self-government, and activities such as baseball and social dances, guard towers and barbed wire outlined the perimeters. The open latrines and public showers, constant lineups for meals at the mess hall, the lack of privacy in the barracks, lack of insulation from the extremes of climate in high desert areas, and

uncertainty about their fate amidst the forced confinement created a tense existence. A loyalty review aggravated divisions and conflicts within the population; a segregation camp for "disloyals" was created at Tule Lake in September 1943 that also contained a stockade, a prison within a prison. Earlier that year, President Roosevelt had announced the formation of an all-Nisei military unit, the 442nd Regimental Combat Team, and the ironic call for volunteers went out to all 10 concentration camps.

In 1983, the CWRIC released its findings, which concluded that the exclusion, expulsion, and incarceration were not justified by military necessity, that the decision was based on racial prejudice, war hysteria, and a failure of political leadership. It recommended that Congress pass a joint resolution to recognize the grave injustice done and offer the nation's apologies and a one-time per capita symbolic compensation payment of $20,000 to each of the approximately 80,000 surviving persons or their heirs at that time. On August 10, President Reagan signed the Civil Liberties Act of 1988 that granted such redress, which also included provisions for a public education fund, later known as the Civil Liberties Education Fund, and the authorization of the construction of a National Japanese American Memorial in Washington, D.C., which had its inauguration ceremony in November 2000. On October 9, 1990, the first redress payments were made with the apology letter signed by President George H. W. Bush. The complete text of the apology sent to the surviving Japanese Americans who were interned reads as follows:

A monetary sum and words alone cannot restore lost years or erase painful memories; neither can they fully convey our Nation's resolve to rectify injustice and to uphold the rights of individuals. But we can take a clear stand for justice and recognize that serious injustices were done to Japanese Americans during World War II.

In enacting a law calling for restitution and offering a sincere apology, your fellow Americans have, in a very real sense, renewed their traditional commitment to the ideals of freedom, equality and justice. You and your family have our best wishes for the future.

Sincerely, George H. W. Bush (signed)

The commission hearings and redress marked a significant moment in the process of healing the pain and suffering that had been shrouded in silence and shame for over 40 years. It continued the process that had begun years before with the pilgrimage to Manzanar in 1969 and the Days of Remembrance (DOR).

The first DOR was held in 1978 at the Puyallup Fairgrounds near Seattle, Washington, and was a turning point in the redress movement, which until that point involved only a fraction of the overall Japanese American community. In response to a request for a news story for ABC's *20/20* program, Chinese American playwright Frank Chin, together with Frank Abe, a Sansei actor, approached the Seattle Evacuation Redress Committee with the idea of a reenactment of the evacuation and internment. During Thanksgiving weekend on November 25, more than 2,000 Japanese Americans and their friends gathered for the Day of Remembrance; it would be the first time for many participants to confront this painful part of their history that shame had urged them to forget, "to relive something, we knew [we] didn't want to relive." After being given yellow name tags similar to those during evacuation, "shipping tags" filled out with their identification numbers from World War II, the participants "drove in procession" in a caravan of about 300 cars and buses with military escorts to the site of the former assembly center at Puyallup, ironically called Camp Harmony, where they entered through a barbed-wire fence. This reenactment induced vivid memories of that time, at the same time giving release from them. For the Sansei, the reenactment provided one of the first opportunities to experience a taste of the evacuation, together with their parents and collectively with other Japanese Americans. This first Day of Remembrance highlighted the essence of the redress movement, which was "the healing of the wounds through confronting the injustice," not simply about monetary payment. This and similar events were a catalyst for the Japanese American community to come to terms with long-buried emotions and to realize that a great injustice had been done by the U.S. government. Through the DORs, the community garnered the emotional commitment to engage in the campaign for redress.

Yet after the passage of the Civil Liberties Act of 1988, the Days of Remembrance and pilgrimages continue to this day in response to the continued spiritual need for the healing of the wounds of both persons and communities. Hidden meanings and stories begin to emerge. Joy Kogawa writes that "to a people for whom community was the essence of life, destruction of community was the destruction of life." Internment was an attack not merely on persons and their possessions but on their collective and therefore spiritual existences, as it meant the termination of their communities on the West Coast. The DOR and pilgrimages opened up the deeper layers where resilience and hope reside amidst the suffering. And where only meaningless pain remained, these collective spaces began to break down isolation and offered the possibility to bear that pain together. These aspects of the ordeal affected both the Issei (first) and Nisei (second) generations, who lived through the experience, and the Sansei, who inherited a legacy of painfulness and injustice that was left unexplained due to the silence of their parents and the U.S. history books. As Sansei (third generation), it is part of our generational task to acknowledge the pain, honor and listen to both the suffering and hope that emerges, move with the release of energy for the common good, and transmit the rediscovered wisdom and collective memory together with the subsequent generations (Yonsei, fourth; Gosei, fifth, etc.) and the broader diverse American and global community. There is an ongoing redress struggle for Japanese Latin Americans who did not qualify for the 1988 Redress provisions, categorized as "illegal aliens" when in fact they were forcibly brought to the United States from their countries, stripped of their documents, and detained in Department of Justice camps.

Events are regularly planned across the country on what is now a National Day of Remembrance, February 19, the date in 1942 on which President Roosevelt signed Executive Order 9066 that set in motion the evacuation and internment. This ongoing process of remembrance, which also includes the pilgrimages to various former sites of detention, denotes practices of collective memory, healing, and hope. There have been pilgrimages to the 10 concentration camp sites, with regularly scheduled and organized pilgrimages of sizable participation occurring at Tule Lake (biannually) and Manzanar (annually). In the context of a community of interreligious faith, the legacy of injustice transforms into a legacy of suffering and hope that forms a people and informs a compassionate vision for the future.

Joanne Doi

See also: Entries: Tule Lake

Further Reading

Burton, Jeffery, Mary M. Farrell, Florence B. Lord, and Richard W. Lord. *Confinement and Ethnicity: An Overview of World War II Japanese American Relocation Sites.* With a foreward by Tetsuden Kashima. Seattle: University of Washington Press, 2002.

Daniels, Roger. "Redress Achieved, 1983–1990." In Roger Daniels, Sandra C. Taylor, and Harry H. L. Kitano, eds. *Japanese Americans: From Relocation to Redress.* Seattle: University of Washington Press, 1986, 1991.

Drinnon, Richard. *Keeper of Concentration Camps: Dillon S. Myer and American Racism.* Berkeley: University of California Press, 1989.

Hatamiya, Leslie T. *Righting a Wrong: Japanese Americans and the Passage of the Civil Liberties Act of 1988.* Stanford, CA: Stanford University Press, 1993.

Hohri, William Minoru. *Repairing America: An Account of the Movement for Japanese-*

American Redress. Foreword by John Toland. Pullman: Washington State University Press, 1988.

Ina, Satsuki. *Children of the Camps: The Documentary*. Produced by Satsuki Ina. Directed and edited by Stephen Holsapple. 57 minutes. National PBS Broadcast, 1999, DVD.

Ishizuka, Karen L. *Lost and Found: Reclaiming the Japanese American Incarceration*. Forewords by John Kuo Wei Tchen and Roger Daniels. Urbana: University of Illinois Press, 2006.

"The Japanese American Cases, 1942–2004: A Social History." *Law and Contemporary Problems* 68, no. 2 (Spring 2005): 168.

Kinoshita, Cherry, Carole Hayashino, and William Yoshino, producers. *Redress: The JACL Campaign for Justice*. San Francisco: Visual Communications, 1991. Film.

Maki, Mitchell T., Harry H. L. Kitano, and S. Megan Berthold. *Achieving the Impossible Dream: How Japanese Americans Obtained Redress*. Forewords by Representative Robert T. Matsui and Roger Daniels. Urbana: University of Illinois Press, 1999.

Nagata, Donna K. "Intergenerational Effects of the Japanese American Internment." In Yael Danieli, ed. *International Handbook of Multi-Generational Legacies of Trauma*. London: Plenum Press, 1998, pp. 125–39.

Niiya, Brian, ed. *Encyclopedia of Japanese American History*. Foreword by Senator Daniel K. Inouye. Introductory essay by Gary Y. Okihiro. New York: Facts on File, Inc., 2000.

Personal Justice Denied. Report of the Commission on Wartime Relocation and Internment of Civilians (CWRIC). Foreword by Tetsuden Kashima. Washington, DC: The Civil Liberties Public Education Fund; Seattle: University of Washington Press, 1997.

"Redress for War Internees Ended." *New York Times*, Feb. 15, 1999, as cited in Roger Daniels.

Takezawa, Yasuko I. *Breaking the Silence: Redress and Japanese American Ethnicity*. Ithaca, NY: Cornell University Press, 1995.

Japanese American Mortuary and Memorial Rituals

The Japanese American community observes a series of late life celebrations, mortuary rituals, and memorial rituals that chart a person's progress from elderhood, the transition from corporal to spiritual being, and maturation into ancestorhood. These rituals are rooted in archaic Japanese beliefs in the continuum of life and death, and the reciprocity between the corporeal and disembodied or spiritual worlds, Confucian ideas of filiality, and Buddhist notions of *karma*. This entry provides an overview of the late life, mortuary, and memorial rituals and funerals that Japanese Americans observe.

Late Life Celebrations

Late life celebrations begin with the 60th birthday or *kanreki* that marks, according to the Chinese zodiac, the completion of one life cycle and the beginning of another. For reasons I have yet to uncover, the 70th, 77th, 80th, 88th, 90th, and 99th birthdays are designated as important milestones.

Kanreki is an occasion for great joy. The elder is dressed in red, a color that represents birth (a newborn is referred to as *akachan*; *aka* means "red" and *chan* is a diminutive), and honored with a gala party. The 70th year is *koki* or "rare age" celebration; it consists of two Chinese ideograms: "ancient" and "rare." In the past when life expectancy was approximately 50 years, a life of 70 years was indeed a rare event. The 77th year or *kiju* is another joyous milestone. The 80th-year celebration is *sanju*. *Beiju* marks the 88th year. *Bei* or rice is combined with the ideogram *ju* or longevity, or *beiju*. The 90th year is *sotsuju*. The 99th year is *hakuju*. *Haku* is a play on graphs. *Haku* is the graph for 100; when the uppermost horizontal that forms the graph is excised, *haku* is formed. One hundred minus one is 99.

In addition to giving elders milestones to look forward to, late celebrations are didactic. Grandchildren learn to respect and care for their parents by observing their parents caring for their elders. These celebrations are public expression of filiality and to repay, albeit only partially, parents for their sacrifices, and to honor them. Late life celebrations are observed throughout the community, regardless of the family's faith affiliation.

Buddhist Mortuary Rituals

The archaic beliefs in the continuum of life and death and related beliefs in the transformation from the corporal to spiritual being, and the reciprocity between the living and dead are given form in Buddhist

Little Tokyo center in Los Angeles, August 6, 2013, as a memorial to those lost when atomic bombs were dropped on the Japanese cities of Hiroshima and Nagasaki in 1945. (AP Photo/Nick Ut)

mortuary rituals and memorial observances. The living help the deceased to prepare for his or her spiritual life by providing for a proper funeral and assisting the passage toward ancestorhood by sponsoring a series of memorial observances.

Preparing the deceased for the afterlife begins with *makuragyō* (pillow-service) and is followed by *yukan* (washing), *otsuya* (wake), and *sōgi* (funeral) services. Today, *yukan* (washing) and *otsuya* (wake) are rarely performed. When death approaches, a priest is summoned to perform the *makuragyō* at the bedside and in the presence of the family. In Jōdo Shin or Pure Land tradition, the predominant Japanese sect in the United States, the priest chants the *Amidakyō* or *Smaller Sukhāvatīvyūha-Sūtra* that describes the beauty of *Sukhāvatī* or Pure Land. Pastorally, the *makuragyō* service is the last opportunity for the dying person to hear the teaching of the Buddha and surrender to its truth. Existentially, it is meant to calm the mind and ready the dying person for the life to come. However, this service is usually performed at the bedside after a person has passed away, or more commonly at the mortuary. It is rarely performed as it is intended.

The funeral is a community event. Anyone who had any connection with the deceased is expected to be present and offer *okōden*, literally "incense offering." This practice, that first appeared in Tang China (618–907), is a form of funeral insurance. In reality *okōden* is money that the family uses to defray the cost of the funeral; the giver expects to be reciprocated at his or her funeral. Those who cannot attend will visit the family to offer their condolences.

Traditionally after the funeral the family sponsors a memorial service every 7th day until the 49th day (these first seven services are based on Indian Buddhist ideas of *karma* and successive lives); thereafter there are the 100th day, 1st, 3rd (these three are based on Confucian ideas of filiality), 7th, 13th, 17th, 23rd or 25th, and 33rd anniversaries of death. Unless the person is especially noteworthy, the 33rd- or 50th-year memorial service is the last service dedicated specifically to the memory of an individual. In Okinawa and some of the rural locales in Japan proper, the final service marks the complete transition of the individual to an ancestral spirit, or *kami*. After the completion of the service, the memorial plaque on which an individual's name is inscribed is ritualistically burned and is moved to the ancestral altar with other more distant and long-forgotten ancestors.

Memorial Observances

The rationale and format for the memorial cycle observed by many Japanese American Buddhist families have their roots in mediaeval China. By the late Tang period the Chinese had seamlessly integrated Indian Buddhist notions of *karma* and successive lives with the Confucian emphasis on ancestral veneration. In pre-Buddhist China, the Chinese believed that at death one passed from this world to the realm of the ancestors. However, the introduction of Buddhism sometime during the beginning of the Common Era complicated the passage from death to rebirth. Buddhism brought with it the idea of a continual existence through successive rebirths and the idea of an intermediate state that commences immediately after death and continues until one is reborn in another physical form. The first chance of rebirth occurs seven days after death. Should that moment not be opportune, the prospect for rebirth occurs at the beginning of any subsequent seven-day cycle. The 49th-day service is especially important, because it marks the last opportunity for rebirth. While the rationale for the 100th-day and first-year observances is not clear, the third-year service corresponds to the Confucian dictum that a child is weaned from his or her parent between two and two and a half years. A filial child thus should mourn the death of a parent at least as long. The third-year memorial service is observed on the second anniversary of death, because it marks the beginning of the third year of mourning.

Even today the living descendants demonstrate their filiality during this confusing and unsettled intermediate stage by commissioning clerics to perform rites to assist the ancestral spirit pass through each of the 10 realms. These observances together with their accompanying sacrificial offerings and donations to the celebrant priests and their temple transfer merit to the deceased to mitigate past misdeeds, alleviate punishments, ease the passage through the 10 realms of purgatory, and result in a favorable rebirth. The ritual observances expand the notion of *karma*, which originally had been confined to an individual's action, to include the efficacy of actions dedicated on behalf of another. The Chinese concern for filial piety is melded with the Buddhist ideas of karma, successive births, and the accumulation and transference of merit.

To the 10 Chinese observances, the Japanese added the 7th-, 13th-, 25th-, 33rd-, and 50th-year services. The origins and significance of these particular years are unclear; however, the long memorial ritual cycle that marks the stages of an individual's transformation from a physical being to a *kami* or ancestorhood reveals the nature of our memories. As years pass, our recollections of the deceased become less and less distinct and he or she gradually loses his or her individuality. The deceased becomes, in our memories, increasingly vague.

The present Japanese American community has modified the traditional 33-year memorial cycle to reflect the practical realities of U.S. society. In traditional Japan, where families lived in close proximity to one another and to the temple, it was possible to faithfully observe the full complement of the mortuary and memorial cycle. The current custom observes the first 7th-day, 49th-day, and the first-, third-, and seventh-year memorial service. The first seventh-day service is often observed the day after the funeral, coinciding with a committal service at the cemetery, even though it may not fall exactly on the seventh day. The next five services are skipped and the family and close friends gather for the 49th-day service.

Memorial services are normally held at the temple, but can be observed at home in front of the *butsudan* (Buddhist altar). At either site the service is dedicated to the deceased whose presence is signified by the *ihai* or spirit tablet on which the *hōmyō* or Buddhist name of the deceased is inscribed. The *hōmyō* is presented at the time a person makes a decision to become a devotee of the Buddha, or if a person has not received one, by the priest who officiates at the funeral. Memorial or spiritual tablets were adopted from the Chinese custom that believes an individual possesses two spirits: *hun* and *po*. At death the *hun* leaves the body and ascends to heaven. The *po* remains with or near by the body. Since the spirit has no place to reside, the spiritual tablet inscribed with the name of the deceased becomes its place of abode. While few believe that the spirit of the deceased resides in the *ihai*, it serves as a focus of grief and memories.

The intergenerational relationship between the living child and the deceased ancestor is further reinforced by the midsummer Obon observance, which is based on the belief that the deceased ancestors return to their earthly homes. It is a time of great festivity and joy, because the entire family is together again. Memorial rites and the Obon reveal a reciprocal and unbroken relationship between the living and the dead. Additionally, the local temple observes an annual *eitaikyō* or perpetual memorial service, normally in November, for any and all persons who may no longer have descendants or anyone to remember them.

Japanese American families continue to transform the late life celebrations, mortuary, and memorial rituals of their ancestral homeland. The memory and significance of rituals, however, dims with each passing generation and through intermarriage with non-Japanese and non-Buddhist spouses. In the past, the temple played a prominent role in these observances; however, families now frequently conduct these services outside its orbit. Other transformations include the almost exclusive use of English and the abbreviated "informality" of the rituals. Another notable change is the type of offerings that families bring. Tradition-

ally families brought *manju* (rice bean cakes) and white or yellow chrysanthemums, but more recently Western-style pastries and more colorful flowers are brought as offerings for family services.

Ronald Y. Nakasone

See also: Essays: Care and Service

Further Reading

Confucius. *The Analects* (*Lun yü*). Translated by D. C. Lau. London: Penguin Books, 1979.

Heishiki, Yoshiharu. "Okinawa no ihai saishi." In *Tōtōmē to sosensūhai—hisashi ajiya ni okeru ihaisaishi no hikau* (*Memorial Tablets and Ancestral Veneration—A Comparative Study of Memorial Tablets and Services in East Asia*). Naha, Okinawa: Okinawa Times, 1994.

Matsudo, Kōdō. *Butsuji, hōyō no subete* (*Everything about Buddhist Services and Memorials*). Tokyo: Nihon bungei sha, 1991.

McLaren, Ronald. "*Kawaiso*: Justice and Reciprocity: Themes in Japanese and Western Ethics." In Jackson H. Bailey, ed. *Aesthetic and Ethical Values in Japanese Culture.* Richmond, IN: Earlham College, 1990.

Nakasone, Ronald Y. 2003. "Late Life, Mortuary, and Memorial Rituals in the Japanese Community." *Journal of Religious Gerontology* 15, no. 4 (2003): 3–14.

Namihira, Emiko. "The Characteristics of Japanese Concepts and Attitudes with Regard to Human Remains." In *Japanese and Western Bioethics, Studies in Moral Diversity.* Dordrecht: Kluwer Academic, 1997.

Teiser, Stephen F. "The Growth of Purgatory." In *Religion and Society in T'ang and Sung China.* Honolulu: University of Hawai'i Press, 1993.

Yanagawa, Keiichi. *Japanese Religions in California, a Report on Research within and without the Japanese-American Community.* Tokyo: Department of Religious Studies, 1983.

Japanese American Religions

The religious history of the Japanese American community has been shaped by the experience of migration, adaptation to a foreign environment, resistance to bigotry and discrimination, and social interaction with other religious and ethnic groups. As with other immigrant communities, the first generation of Japanese in Hawai'i and North America suffered from poverty, social instability, and political alienation. And, as with other immigrant communities, they brought their customs, cultures, and religious traditions. But Japanese religious practices were harshly scrutinized. As non-Christians, Japanese Americans were doubly marginalized, for their race and for their religious faith.

Buddhism dominates Japanese American religious history. The majority of Japanese immigrants who arrived in Hawai'i and North America came from rural prefectures in Japan where Jōdo Shinshū Buddhism prevailed. Of the two branches—Nishi and Higashi Hongwanji—Nishi Hongwanji established the most missionary branches in Hawai'i, Canada, and the continental United

Members of the Japanese Independent Congregational Church of Oakland, California, attend an Easter service in April 1942 prior to evacuation of all persons of Japanese ancestry from certain West Coast areas to War relocation authority centers for the duration of the war. (U.S. War Relocation Authority/Corbis)

States. Other Buddhist sects—Shingon, Nichiren, Tendai, and Sōtō Zen—were also established by the first generation of Japanese immigrants (Issei). A minority of immigrants were Christians, converted by Presbyterian, Congregational, Methodist, and Baptist missionaries.

It is estimated that prior to World War II, more than 50 percent of Japanese Americans were members of a Buddhist sect; nearly 30 percent were affiliated with a Christian denomination. Three overseas districts—the Buddhist Churches of America, Hongpa Hongwanji Mission of Hawai'i, and the Jōdo Shinshū Buddhist Temples of Canada—claim over 100 temples in their jurisdiction. These are still the largest Buddhist denominations in North America, representing more than 30 percent of those who claim Buddhist affiliation.

The religious culture of Japanese American communities is adaptive, creative, and syncretic. Japanese American congregants and congregations adjusted to a hostile social atmosphere by consolidating resources to protect the community. They made imaginative use of space and location, acculturating without conceding to wholesale assimilation. And they collaborated across denominational, generational, and ethnic boundaries, innovating syncretic and lively spiritual traditions that helped to sustain and strengthen their communities.

Issei Adjustment

Issei immigrants were, by and large, agricultural workers who labored on sugar and pineapple plantations in Hawai'i and in the farming and fishing industries along the Pacific Coast of North America. Jōdo Shinshū ministers and missionaries arrived first in Hawai'i and San Francisco, responding to requests by Japanese immigrants for help in coping with their hardships.

Kagahi Sōryū i (1865–1917), a Jōdo Shinshū priest who arrived in Hawai'i in 1889, conducted the first Buddhist service there and subsequently established the Great Imperial Japan Hongwanji Denomination, Hawai'i Branch (Dai Nippon Teikoku Hongwanji-ha, Hawai'i), Kagahi was not an official representative of Nishi Hongwanji; he took it upon himself to investigate the social and spiritual conditions of Japanese plantation workers. As a result of his efforts, several small Buddhist temples were erected in plantation camps and served by itinerant priests. In 1897, an official representative of Nishi Hongwanji, Miyamoto Ejun (1853–1919), was sent to Hawai'i and Yamada Shoi (1879–1945) was made the first *kaikyoshi* or missionary priest. By 1899, six official temples were established; within five years there were 14 more throughout the islands.

Miyamoto was later dispatched to California on a similar mission, arriving in San Francisco in July 1898. He was met by the small community of Issei men who had already formed a Young Men's Buddhist Association (YMBA). One year later, two priests, Sonoda Shuye (1863–1922) and Nishijima Kakuryo (1873–1942), arrived in San Francisco and founded the North American Buddhist Mission, later to be known as the Buddhist Churches of America (BCA).

Hawai'i's Japanese population grew rapidly, requiring extensive outreach by Buddhist ministers. Japanese workers were the largest ethnic group in Hawai'i from 1900 to 1942, ultimately representing over 40 percent of the island's population by World War II. Imamura Yemyō (1867–1932) arrived in Hawai'i in 1899 and served there until his death in 1932. During his tenure, he built nearly one temple a year on every island, often in and around plantation camps rather than in nearby towns and villages. Because of their isolation, Buddhist temples became an essential link between Japanese workers throughout the islands, acting as a social and communication network.

Christianity was an important part of the religious life of the Issei generation as well, especially for those early immigrants who came to the United States as students between 1868 and 1880. Although some had converted to Christianity before leaving Japan, many others became members of Protestant congregations through the efforts of missionaries in California. Methodists, Baptists, Presbyterians, and Congregationalists reached out to Japanese immigrants, offering housing, food, language instruction, and help securing employment. A small group of San Francisco Issei Christians founded their own Bible study group, the Fukuinkai ("Gospel Society") in 1877 and, a year later, the Presbyterian Japanese Gospel Society. These groups formed the basis of Japanese American Christian congregations such as the First Japanese Presbyterian Church in San Francisco in 1885. Christianity spread rapidly in California, which had the largest Japanese population outside of Hawai'i. Between 1885 and 1942, 46 Japanese congregations were founded in Southern California alone. In Northern California, 30 congregations and as many as 6,000 members comprised the Northern California Japanese Christian Church Federation.

There were far fewer Japanese Christian churches in Hawai'i. With some exceptions such as the Reverend Takie Okumura's Makiki Christian Church (1904), there were few large Japanese Christian congregations. Okumura (1865–1951) established the first Japanese-language school in Hawai'i and opened his home to students who traveled to Honolulu to further their education or to take jobs. But in communities where Buddhism was strong, Christian conversion was much less prevalent.

Other religious organizations were brought to Hawai'i and North America by Issei. In Hawai'i where the Japanese population was more than twice the size it was in North America there was greater religious diversity. Temples and shrines were built by Sōtō Zen, Nichiren, Tendai, and Shingon Buddhists and followers of Shintō Shintō, Tenrikyō, and Konkōkyō. The greatest number of temples and shrines were built in California and Hawai'i. Forty-eight Shintō shrines were built in this era, indicating the importance of indigenous cultural practices and traditions for the Issei.

Religious groups utilized many adaptive strategies as they integrated into the American religious landscape. Japanese Christians formed their own churches, responding to the racial hostility of white Americans. Buddhists adopted the denominational structures and English terminology such as "church" and "bishop." They created a Sunday worship schedule, installed pews, and sang hymns. Architectural forms represented an attempt to find a balance between tradition and modernity.

Congregations sometimes opted for a traditional Western façade with signage in kanji and English. Takie Okumura's Makiki Christian Church was built to resemble Kochi Castle in Japan, symbolizing Christianity as a refuge. Yemyō Imamura's Hawai'i Hongwanji headquarters resembles a traditional Indian Buddhist *stūpa*, suggesting the universalism of Buddhism.

Buddhist leaders also responded to the challenge of establishing a new religion in a Christian country by making explicit outreach to white Americans. Within a year of his arrival, Kakuryo Nishijima began publishing *Light of Dharma*, which featured writing by prominent Japanese Buddhists. Yemyō Imamura invited the public to services and celebrations and created an "English Department" to oversee these efforts. He, too, published and distributed English-language materials on Buddhism. In both cases, Buddhist ministers found it necessary and advantageous to cultivate the curiosity and goodwill of white Americans. Through these efforts, Jōdo Shinshū institutions became incubators for American Buddhism.

For the Issei, religious institutions provided a needed connection to home. In many towns, a church or temple was the only site available for community gatherings. Churches and temples hosted religious services, but also cooperated in staging seasonal celebrations that in Japan would have involved an entire village. New Year's celebrations, which involved symbolic representations of Shintō and Buddhist customs, were not restricted to specific faith traditions. Denominational affiliations were less important than a sense of common ethnic identity and ancestry. In that way, Japanese religious communities were far more syncretic than was common in the United States.

Nisei Adaptation

For the Nisei generation, religious faith played the paradoxical role of encouraging their independence as Americans and reinforcing their ties to their families. Buddhist and Christian religious leaders were challenged by the demands placed on the Nisei whose status as American citizens did not protect them from bigotry and institutional discrimination. Nisei relied on their association with religious organizations to help them negotiate the border between adapting and assimilating.

Churches and temples often functioned as a bridge between Issei and Nisei. The Nisei generation, who possessed American citizenship, were under much greater pressure to assimilate. As noncitizens, their parents had little incentive to abandon their language and customs. The Nisei, however, were often forced to choose between the false dichotomy of loyalty to their country and devotion to their families. Buddhist and Christian ministers recognized the precarious position Nisei were placed in. As Japanese, they were obliged to offer respectful obedience to their parents. But as Americans, they were encouraged to express themselves as individuals. Religious institutions were a space where Japanese values and filial bonds were reinforced through religious idioms and the shared experience of worship.

Christianity and Buddhism offered Nisei opportunities to socialize, organize, and develop leadership skills. Individual churches had youth organizations, but the YMCA and YBA (Young Buddhist Association) were the largest religious confederations for Nisei. These religious organizations provided important opportunities for Nisei men and women to meet and socialize, opportunities that did not exist anywhere else, particularly in places where Japanese Americans were a visible minority. Attending youth conferences, participating in sports leagues, organizing fundraisers and dances were opportunities to socialize and make friends, but also a chance to exercise their leadership skills, opportunities that might not have been available to them in typical white American high schools or colleges. These organizations provided a sense of solidarity and a way to share their common faith and their common struggles.

World War II Incarceration

The mass incarceration of the entire Japanese community was an egregious betrayal of the constitutional rights of Nisei citizens and the human rights of their Issei parents. Although the evacuation, resettlement, and incarceration were traumatic experiences, it forced Issei and Nisei, Buddhist and Christian to reevaluate their religious faith and national loyalty. Christians who may have assumed their faith might protect them from suspicion were no less vulnerable than Buddhists.

In the years leading up to the war, federal agencies engaged in surveillance of Japanese American communities. Issei leaders—religious clergy and language school teachers—were suspected of being

agents of the Japanese government. Buddhist priests and institutions were targeted because Americans did not understand the differences between Buddhism and Shintō, nor did they make any clear distinction between state Shintō propagated by the Japanese government and Shintō as the religion that was indigenous to Japan. Therefore, in the days and weeks following the bombing of Pearl Harbor, Buddhists priests were immediately rounded up by agents of the U.S. government. As noncitizens, they were classified as "enemy aliens." They were incarcerated by the Department of Justice and many were later deported. Those who remained in the United States were isolated from the rest of the Japanese American community.

Consequently, Christian ministers outnumbered Buddhist priests in War Relocation Authority (WRA) camps. Buddhists consolidated their congregations, working together to sustain Buddhist practices across sectarian lines. Christians and Buddhists also worked together in camps, cooperating in efforts to run schools and social programs. Religious activity in the camps was limited and proscribed. Because use of Japanese was prohibited, Buddhists texts, prayers, and songs had to be translated into English. With no altars, statues, or other material manifestations of faith, internees improvised, fashioning religious objects from locally available materials. However, religious institutions became all the more important because they helped to preserve community values. In spite of efforts to more fully Americanize the Nisei, incarceration strengthened their ties to their parents, reinforcing filial values. Religious faith supported rather than undermined community cohesion.

The internment has shaped subsequent generations of the Japanese American community. Some have sought to recover the experiences of their parents and grandparents, imbuing these painful events with spiritual meaning. The Tule Lake Pilgrimage, for example, brings together survivors and their families and supporters to embark upon a sacred journey of return. The pilgrimages, which began in 1969, return to several internment sites where participants gather, listen, teach, learn, and reflect. Similarly, the annual Day of Remembrance, which commemorates the signing of Executive Order 9066, has become a sacred occasion and catalyst for community cohesion and celebration.

Postwar Developments

The postwar years saw both expansion and retraction for Japanese American congregations. Newly established branches of the Buddhist Churches of America were opened in Cleveland and Chicago in 1944. Nisei who left the camps to return to college established Young Buddhist Associations providing a seed for the growth of future temples. The reestablishment of temples that had been closed before the war was an important milestone for many communities, but in several cases, new temples were built to replace those that had been lost or to serve congregations in new locations.

The postwar years also witnessed an increased interaction between Japanese Americans and white Americans who became interested in Buddhism. Conversion to Buddhism was limited before World War II, but many of those who did convert became affiliated with the BCA. After the war, Buddhist temples hosted Dharma study and meditation groups for the growing number of Americans who had been introduced to Buddhism while serving in Japan or who were attracted by visiting monks such as D. T. Suzuki. When the Berkeley Buddhist Church reopened in 1946, Kanmo Imamura (1904–1986) (the son of Yemyō Imamura) and his wife Jane Matsuura Imamura (1920–2011) provided dormitory space and other services to students from the University of California. They reached out to Nisei and Sansei, reviving the Young Buddhist Association, but also to white students who were curious about Buddhist practice. The poet Gary Snyder, who would go on to intensive Buddhist study in Japan, began his education with the Imamuras. They also helped to launch a long-running series of lectures by religious leaders, which came to be known as the Pacific Seminar. The activities of the Berkeley Buddhist Church signal the importance of the already established institutions like the BCA in launching a new phase of American Buddhism.

In the late 20th century, the expansion of religious choices and religious diversity in the United States has affected Japanese American religious culture. The introduction of new religious movements from Japan such as Soka Gakkai have influenced how Japanese and Japanese American religious traditions are perceived. Buddhism has spread and become more diverse as Japanese Americans intermarry at greater rates and as more non-Japanese join the church and become ministers. Internet access has also vastly influenced the shape and direction of religious organizations, promoting interreligious dialogue and facilitating virtual links between faith communities. As Buddhism has become more mainstream and accessible, Japanese American religious culture is exposed to greater and more diverse influences, adapting to new demands and challenges.

Lori Pierce

See also: Entries: Japanese American Christianity; Japanese American Internment, Remembrance, and Redress; Japanese American Religious Federation (JARF)

Further Reading

Kashima, Tetsuden. *Buddhism in America.* Westport, CT: Greenwood Press, 1977.

Smith, Buster. "Variety in the Saṇgha: A Survey of Buddhist Organizations in America." *Review of Religious Research* 48, no. 3 (2007): 308–12.

Williams, Duncan Ryuken. "Complex Loyalties: Issei Buddhist Ministers during the Wartime Incarceration." *Pacific World: Journal of the Institute of Buddhist Studies* 3, no. 5 (2003): 255–74.

Yoo, David. *Growing Up Nisei: Race, Generation, and Culture among Japanese Americans of California.* Urbana: University of Illinois Press, 1997.

Yoshida, Ryo. "Japanese Immigrants and Their Christian Communities in North America: A Case Study of the Fukuinkai, 1877–1896." *Japanese Journal of Religious Studies* 43, no. 1 (2007): 229–44.

Japanese American Religious Federation (JARF)

The Japanese American Religious Federation (JARF) is an interfaith consortium of Buddhist, Christian, and independent faith traditions. Its origins date to 1948 when leaders of Japanese faith congregations in the city of San Francisco established the Shukyōka kondankai (religious leader's discussion group) to coordinate the immediate housing needs of Japanese Americans returning from the internment camps. The churches and temples served as hostels until 1954. This informal gathering incorporated in 1968 as Nichibei shukyō renmei (Japanese American Religious Federation) as a nonprofit entity.

This early experience of providing housing for the Japanese community galvanized JARF to incorporate the Japanese American Religious Federation Housing (JARF Housing) in 1975 to partner with the Department of Housing and Urban Development (HUD) to build and operate Nihonmachi Terrace and Hinode Towers, a 245-unit low-income housing facility for low-income seniors. The housing needs of frail low-income elders prompted members of the Pine Street Methodist Church to explore the possibility of securing a suitable facility. JARF took up the cause and incorporated the JARF Assisted Living Facility (JALFI) in 1996. The San Francisco Redevelopment Agency awarded JALFI a contract in 1977 to develop the 54-unit Kokoro Assisted Living Facility for moderate- to low-income seniors on the former site of Ohabai Shalom Synagogue on 1881 Bush Street. JARF and JALFI launched a capital campaign in 1999, broke ground in 2001, and welcomed its first residents two years later.

Interestingly, the clerical and lay leadership of JARF insisted that spiritual and cultural components be integral to the design of the Kokoro facility, staff training, services, and administrative policy, not an afterthought. This insistence was the result of years of experience with the cultural and spiritual insensitivity of the American health care system toward Japanese cultural and spiritual values. Such sensitivity is particularly critical during a resident's later and last stages of life, and in helping families cope with grief and mourning. To this end JARF commissioned the Stanford University Geriatric Education Center and the Graduate Theological Union to offer a six-unit graduate course, Aging and Spirituality in the Japanese Experience, during the 1999–2000 academic year to heighten awareness of the cultural and spiritual needs of Kokoro's intended residents. The year-long course also helped to galvanize community support for the project and for raising funds.

In addition to its housing projects, JARF sponsors the annual interfaith community-wide Memorial Day, Thanksgiving, and Atomic Bombing Commemorative services. JARF also sponsors a monthly interfaith radio program, *Kurashi no shirabe* (Wisdom of living), provides monthly services at Kokoro Assisted Living Facility, Kimochi Home, and participates in other community-wide activities.

The founding congregations of JARF were the Buddhist Church of San Francisco, Christ Episcopal Church, Gedatsu Buddhist Church of America, Christ United Presbyterian Church, Konkōkyō Church of San Francisco, Nichiren Buddhist Church of America, Pine United Methodist Church, St. Francis Xavier Catholic Church, San Francisco Independent Church, Seventh-Day Adventist Japanese Church, and Sōkōji Zen Temple of San Francisco. The

Gedatsu Buddhist Church, Seventh-Day Adventist Church, and the San Francisco Independent Church are no longer part of JARF. Hokkeshū Hon'nōji Buddhist Temple, Risshō Kōsei Kai Buddhist Church, and Tenrikyō–America West are now part of the organization. The membership roster is current as of 2011.

Ronald Y. Nakasone

See also: Entries: Japanese American Christianity; Japanese American Religions

Further Reading

Drummond, Donald C. "The Creation of JALFI: A Senior Assisted Living Project of the Japanese American Community." Unpublished study submitted to the University of San Francisco's Executive Certificate Program for Non-Profit Management. 1998.

JALFI Services Committee. *The JALFI Survey of Assisted Living for Japanese American Seniors in the San Francisco Bay Area.* San Francisco: American Religious Federation Assisted Living Facility, 1998.

Japanese American Religious Federation Assisted Living Facility. *Japanese American Religious Federation Assisted Living Facility, Inc. By-laws.* San Francisco: American Religious Federation Assisted Living Facility, 1998.

Nakasone, Ronald Y. "Teaching Religion and Healing: Spirituality and Aging in the San Francisco Japanese Community." In Linda Barnes and Inez Talamantez, eds. *Teaching Religion and Healing.* Oxford: Oxford University Press, 2006, pp. 277–91.

Japanese Evangelical Missionary Society (JEMS)

On February 19, 1942, President Franklin Roosevelt signed Executive Order 9066, which sent over 120,000 Japanese Americans to 10 concentration camps in the western United States. About 73 percent of the internees were American citizens, and many were the parents of citizens, who were not able to become citizens by law. Much has been written about the dilemma of the Japanese Americans, the injustice of the government, and the later admissions by successive presidents that the internment was a "mistake." When peace was declared in August 1945, the camps were closed, and the imprisoned Japanese Americans were released, JEMS, the Japanese Evangelical Missionary Society, was initiated because of the need for fellowship, their common experience of internment, and seeking their prewar status of equality and justice in resettlement. For the Christian leaders this was the challenge for the future. It was hoped that the victimization, injustice, racism, poverty, and suffering would work together for good. Two urgent missions confronted the Japanese Americans: one was the strengthening of bonds within our Japanese American community; and the other was salvation—salvation meaning finding peace, purpose, security, and hope for the future, as well as faith in God.

Rev. Dr. Paul Nagano was called by Rev. Dr. Ralph L. Mayberry of the Los Angeles Baptist City Mission Society in the autumn of 1945 even before the camps were officially closed and the captives released, to come to Los Angeles and help the bewildered Japanese Americans to settle into civilian life after their captivity of two to four years. Rev. Nagano was able to develop an ecumenical worship service in East Los Angeles (Boyle Heights) and help people get resettled and find places to live and jobs. In February 1946 he was able to initiate the Nisei Baptist Church (conveniently named "Nisei" to encourage the English-speaking, second-generation Japanese Americans to find a place of refuge, fellowship, and support) located on East Second Street and Evergreen Avenue. Soon afterward, the Japanese Free Methodist Church began a church nearby and the pastor for that church was Rev. Hideo Aoki. Being lonely and in need of companionship and prayer, Rev. Aoki and Rev. Nagano met together for prayer once a week. It was not long after that the prayer meeting grew and became a breakfast-prayer fellowship with over 20 Japanese American ministers attending. The spirit of these prayer meetings and breakfasts was great! The longing for mutual strength and affirmation was something to behold! A similar group was developed in Central and Northern California. For more fellowship and prayers the combined groups met together at Mount Hermon in the Santa Cruz Mountains where eventually the JEMS Mount Hermon Conference, the largest Japanese American Conference, was developed (now approximately 1,500 people of all ages meet together each year).

The founding of JEMS came at the Wee Boys' Lodge in Palos Verdes, California, in 1950. Ernest Ono, a dedicated Los Angeles schoolteacher and counselor, was editor of *Vision and Faith*, the publication of JEMS. In 1985, the issue that celebrated the 35th anniversary of JEMS remembered the steps in the inspired experience of the birth of JEMS:

The group was in its second day of its retreat, spending much time in deep, earnest prayers. The requirements for leadership had been thoroughly altered; a person with vision, enthusiastic [sic], dedication, an initiator, an innovator, a polished speaker, a capable organizer, and administrator, one with a flare and zeal for evangelizing. Seeking guidance from God in selecting their first leader. The prayers finally ended. Silence followed. Then came what the Vision of Faith calls "The electric moment": Breaking the agonizing silence, Rev. Paul Nagano addressed the group. "If the Evergreen Baptist Church feels with me that this is the direction of our Lord, and after discussing this with my family, we feel this is the direction of God for our lives, and if you feel that I am the person of God's choice, I will be willing to give myself to this ministry."

The ministers confirmed that God had called Rev. Paul Nagano to be their first executive secretary. They supported the first executive secretary of JEMS by pledging ten dollars per month from their limited salaries. Looking back over the years, the Vision of Faith could not identify with certainty who the 21 members of that prayer meeting were, but the best attempt at such identification yielded the following: Hideo Aoki, Llewellyn Davis, Harry Hashimoto, Eishi Hirose, George Hirose, Roy Ishihara, Ren Kimura, William Kobayashi, Akira Kuroda, John Miyabe, Harry Murakami, Paul Nagano, John Nagayama,

Harumi Nishimoto, Harper Sakauye. Dan Shinoda, Joseph Sakakibara, George Takaya, Roy Takaya, Howard Toriiumi, and Paul Waterhouse. Having experienced imprisonment in the concentration camps, there was a deep unity and love among the Japanese American ministers. The mission of JEMS was shared throughout California and other parts of the United States, as well as Canada, Japan, and South America. On May 1, 1953, Dr. Hideo Aoki was officially appointed as the JEMS radio missionary. He broadcast the Gospel in the United States and Canada, with one broadcast going to Japan via the Philippines.

During 1951, Gospel teams composed primarily of college students traveled over 10,000 miles ministering at churches, camps, conferences, retreats, and special rallies. One year the team conducted its summer schedule by traveling to Palacio, Texas, to minister and have fellowship with Nisei Christians there. Those who traveled for JEMS included David Shigekawa, Hiro Yoshida, Saburo Masada, Roy Sano, George Inadomi, and in time, Ray Narusawa. Five of the Gospel team members became ministers in Japanese American churches. Roy Sano became a bishop of the United Methodist Church and Hiro Yoshida became an administrator of a Christian enterprise in the Midwest. Rev. Akira Hatori, the first missionary JEMS staff member from Japan, took over the radio ministry of Hideo Aoki and the Japanese-language ministry, first in the United States and later in Japan as part of the Pacific Broadcasting Association (PBA). A JEMS Gospel team went to New York, Chicago, and Texas. Later two teams went to Hawai'i. The Hawai'i teams consisted of Masumi Toyotome, Bill Tamagi, Art Tsuneishi, and Herbert Murata. After one of these trips in 1952, He was asked to consider the pastorate of the Makiki Christian Church of Honolulu. He left word with the Makiki Christian Church that He would ask the JEMS Board, as well as my family, if they believed this was the will of God, the same process as when He accepted the position as the executive secretary of JEMS in 1950. With the consent of the JEMS board and his family, in March 1954 He left the position with JEMS and became the English-speaking pastor of the Makiki Christian Church in Honolulu, where He served from March 1954 until August 1962. Executive directors of JEMS that followed him from January 1954 included Hideo Aoki, Roy Takaya, Ray Narusawa, and Masumi Toyotome. Upon his return from Hawai'i in September 1962, Dr. Nagano was asked to resume as executive director and served until 1971. Sam Tonomura, who originally was from Canada and served as associate pastor of the Gardena Valley Baptist Church, became the executive director in September of that year (1970) and has served until his recent retirement after 30 years, but continues to serve under the present leadership of Rev. Richard "Rick" Chuman, former pastor of the English section of the Los Angeles Holiness Church.

JEMS is one of the truly indigenous organizations that is not sponsored by any particular Christian denomination, but has existed primarily with the Japanese American churches and has a three-story building near Little Tokyo, Los Angeles. Its primary ministry has been among Japanese Americans since 1950. It is amazing that the Jap-anese American Christian community has initiated and has continued to serve our mostly Japanese churches, missionaries, and community for over 64 years at this writing! The question is asked, why was it started and what motivated its long ministry? JEMS was formed in 1950 mostly by the Japanese American ministers and Christians who had a special vision and mission for the Japanese community in the United States and, as the result of years of consistent prayer, concern for Japanese everywhere. Most of the Japanese Christians in the United States were influenced by the popular conservative evangelical Christianity that was prevalent in the establishment of the first Japanese American churches; for that matter, most churches were evangelical and conservative. The zeal and initiative of the evangelical churches were popular and growing. It was this zeal that brought the first JEMS ministers together. As the result of much prayer the affirmation was to save the lost by sharing the Gospel (good news) of God's saving grace. At the early prayer-breakfast meetings and earnest prayer meetings, the emphasis was predominately evangelism, "winning the lost," especially the Japanese. The burden of prayer was for Japan, presumably a non-Christian nation that was in need of the Gospel of Jesus Christ. In time, the burden of prayer led to the salvation of Japanese everywhere, including South America. The major denominations were not sending Japanese American missionaries to Japan or where the Japanese were moving and settling. Some independent Japanese Americans took the initiative to go to Japan as missionaries and shared their vision with members of JEMS.

With this zeal, JEMS caught the vision to share the Gospel with Japanese everywhere. Thus the identity of JEMS— Japanese Evangelical Missionary Society. This evangelistic motivation led JEMS to develop groups on university campuses, in athletics, Japanese immigrants, Japanese language ministries, sponsoring conferences, mission tours, retreats, evangelistic meetings, musicals, and sponsoring missionaries to other countries. Of course, the Mount Hermon Conference for all ages is one of the annual events of JEMS. It was the initiative of JEMS that brought about a closer relationship with Hawai'i, with several becoming pastors of the churches in Hawai'i, and the intimate relationship that have been developed through the years.

JEMS was unique as it gave the executive secretary the opportunity to freely visit all the churches ministering to Japanese of their communities. He was able to get to know the various congregations and the pastors. This is not available to those who are settled in a church or for committed pastors. Today, fifty years later, JEMS now involves all Asians through its ministries with the local church, on college campuses, through conferences and retreats, and many other programs and ministries. Sharing the gospel overseas has also expanded with the development of many programs and the inclusion of South America as another mission field. Headquartered in Los Angeles, JEMS is a non-profit, para-church organization. It is supported by an inter-denominational network of Japanese and Asian American churches and especially by individual supporters who share a faith in Jesus.

Paul M. Nagano

See also: Entries: Japanese American Christianity; Japanese American Internment, Remembrance, and Redress

Further Reading

"Educating & Empowering Ministry." www.ministrywatch.com. Accessed July 11, 2014.

"Japanese Evangelical Ministry Society in Los Angeles, California (CA)." www.nonprofitfacts.com. Accessed July 11, 2014.

"JEMS' Ministry." www.jems.org. Accessed July 11, 2014.

Japanese Gardens

The Japanese garden is predicated upon the idea of an experience wherein art and nature merge seamlessly. Soteriologically the concept of the garden extends out of the temple complex, as it does historically from the courtly palaces. The interplay between Pure Land and Zen traditions in and around medieval Kyoto produced a number of landscape gardens that were not only formulative, but are to this day exemplary—as with the renowned Saihō-ji temple gardens, which were altered to fit the more meditative aspects of Zen in the Muromachi period (1336–1573). From that time especially, the idea of the garden has generally taken the aspect of an aid to contemplation (and enlightenment); and it is often attached to other cultural practices, such as the tea ceremony (*chanoyū*). While they are preeminently physical and experiential, the image of the garden is also important—occupying as it does the main subject of many

Japanese Gardens | 569

Pagodas in the Japanese Tea Garden at Golden Gate Park in San Francisco, California. (Celso Diniz/ Dreamstime.com)

works of art due to the associations with nature, beauty, and spiritual experience. While certain core aspects may be found in different gardens—landscape in miniature, suggestions of rustication, concepts of transience, as well as the strategic use of stones and plant life—there are seven types of gardens that are commonly distinguished:

- *chisen-shoyū-teien* (pond garden, also as *shinden-zukuri-teien*)
- *jōdo-teien* (the Paradise Garden)
- *kare sansui* (dry landscape, literally, dry mountain water)
- *cha niwa* (the tea garden, also as *roji niwa*—dewy ground garden)
- *kaiyū-shiki-teien* (the stroll garden)
- *tsubo niwa* (the courtyard garden; miniature versions are known as *hakoniwa*, small boxed garden)
- the hermitage garden

The first of these, introduced from China, suggests the excursions that take place from the main building (the *shinden*) across the lake by boat ride. The next four (*jōdo-teien*, *kare sansui*, *cha niwa*, and *kaiyū-shiki-teien*) are mentioned below. *Tsubo niwa*, known for their small size and enclosed space, were developed from inner courtyard gardens and today form the basis for many urban architectural gardens found in temples and businesses alike. Bamboo and stone lanterns are commonly used, and the emphasis is on an immaculate area of natural, calming respite that is, however, not usually entered. Finally, the hermitage garden was typically created around an architectural work for the purpose of inspiration. Here, also, the emphasis is on a microcosm of the (natural) world. By far the most prominent of these is Shisen-dō (now a temple), built by the Confucian scholar and landscape architect Jozen Ishikawa (1583–1672)—known also for its main hall, Shizen-no-ma (Poets' Room), which houses the work and images of 36 classical Chinese poets.

There are perhaps more contemporary American and global adaptations of the Japanese garden than can be counted or classified, though the prevalence of domestic examples—especially along the West Coast of the United States—should be mentioned. Journals, books, video, and new media (including the Internet) have prolonged the intellectual and practical life of the Japanese garden in recent years, especially as seen in the upsurge in demand for practical skills and knowledge for their private creation. The contemporary rendition typically shares something of the traditional East Asian notion that sustained looking at beautified nature is of inherent spiritual value.

Early Japanese gardens were inspired by contact with the Chinese, and certainly the indigenous Shintō belief system—which saw in natural objects (such as stones) a profound spiritual significance—was also a major factor. The Hindu-Buddhist tradition of mythical mountains and the Daoist legend of the Isles of the Eight Immortals were also significant. Though few early structures are extant for study, the two eighth-century imperial gardens uncovered at Nara are important—one a *chisen-shoyū-teien* (pond garden), another a stream garden. By the Heian period (794–1185), the architectural *shinden* develop, as does the practice of setting stones "upright" (*ishi wo tateru*). As the aristocracy became more concerned with internal concerns and religious thought, the Buddhist associations become more entrenched, and many of the formulaic design principles can be seen at this time. The imperial gardens are famously described by Murasaki Shikibu's (ca. 978–1014 or 1025) *Tale of Genji* (*Genji Monogatari*, ca. 1005), where they are the setting for courtly life. Illustrated hand scrolls of the book from this period suggest some of the composition of the gardens. Toward the end of the Heian period, Pure Land Buddhism begins to proliferate, and with it the Paradise Garden comes into fashion as a suggestion of Amida's Paradise of the West. Among the foremost examples of these gardens is at Byōdō-in in Kyoto.

The warring of clans of the late 12th century resulted in a weakened emperor, resulting in the establishment of the Kamakura shogunate in 1185 by Minamoto no Yoritomo (1147–1199). The *shogun* reestablished relations with China, and the renewed contact resulted in not only newfound interest in Song Dynasty culture but a revival in Japanese garden design. Kinkaku-ji (Rokuon-ji), erected by the third Ashikaga shogun in ca. 1398, stands as a key example of this legacy, as well as of Muromachi (1336–1573) design in general. Likely developed from a preexisting *shinden*, rocks and islands were apparently added in an elicitation of cosmology. Minimalist principles are even more apparent in the Japanese Zen rock gardens developed at this time, most famously at Ryōan-ji in Kyoto. This dry rock garden (*karesansui)* consists only of 15 stones and raked gravel (*shirakawa-suna*, white river sand), emphasizing simplicity and meditative looking from a fixed point of view. While theoretical and symbolic interpretations abound (e.g., the gravel as a sea or the rocks as the star constellation Cassiopeia), they perhaps risk missing the emphasis on abstraction and the space. Musō Soseki (1275–1351) was the Zen (Rinzai) monk who created Saihō-ji (Kōinzan Saihō-ji), known not only for its lower moss garden but also for its upper garden of (dry) rocks and "pools."

Powerful daimyos expanded their power with the 1573 overthrow of the Ashikaga shogunate; they built new castles with gardens, such as Tokushima in Shikoku. It and Sanbō-in in Kyoto share the Momoyama (1573–1615) aspect of a view from a distance with a perspective from above—as from a castle or certain view from within a building. They also feature large ponds and several paths as aspects of the stroll garden (*kaiyū-shiki-teien*). At Sanbō-in, the cherry blossom festival was also a prime motivation. The tea ceremony (*chanoyu*), profoundly influenced by Sen no Rikyū (1522–1592) and the emphasis on the quality of *wabi*, called for a small garden (*cha niwa*) of a reserved, sober quality with a winding path

and soft elements of color (cherry blossoms). Kobori Masakazu's (Kobori Enshū, 1579–1647) design innovations, such as the use of *O-Karikomi* (trimming shrubs in topiary fashion), beginning at this time are also noteworthy.

In the Edo period (1615–1868), the *Sukiya-zukuri* style, reflecting the tea ceremony, predominated in architecture, as at Katsura Imperial Villa where the style extended into the gardens. The architectural views opening up into the garden are important, as is the placement of the palace facing southeast (rather than the traditional south) to better view the rising moon relative to the garden plan. The references to actual (Ama no hashidate) and legendary sites are key to understanding the design. The Meiji period of the late 19th and early 20th centuries (1868–1912) saw the importation of Western ideas, such as the development of public parks and private lawns.

Contemporary versions range from the traditional, to blends of traditional and contemporary design (e.g., Shumyō Masuno), to the more dramatic—as with Tado Ando's (b. 1941) Awaji Yumebutai. This "environment creation" served to restore a devastated landscape where earth was once removed to create artificial islands in Osaka Bay. The site is a part of the larger Awaji Island International Park City, which hosts a conference center and resort. The sprawling hillside gardens replace the landscape that was stripped for soil for the Kansai Airport and features strong geometric design, reflecting pools, and the spartan concrete architectural elements he is most known for.

It is difficult to generalize about all Japanese gardens, given the variety of types (as listed). Still, there are some common threads that may be gleaned in terms of artistic and philosophical concepts governing their creation. Behind the notion of the garden is an idealized vision of the natural world, and it may also be seen as a condensed experience of some aspect of the cosmos or mythological legend. These concise reproductions of greater aspects of the world lend to the garden its sense of contemplation and spiritual experience, whether it is part of a sacred site or not. Idealized nature, however, is decidedly according to East Asian conception—either as adaptation from China or in distinctly Japanese thought. Hence, plans are not laid out in a grid of predictable symmetry but are rather meant to coordinate with the irregularity of nature, as well as its element of surprise. To that end, and especially with the advent of the tea garden, the aesthetics of the Japanese garden often parallels that of *wabi-sabi*—privileging transience, imperfection, rustication, economy, and (philosophical) emptiness. Unlike so many Western gardens, the Japanese garden is at once a succinct elicitation of a larger world or truth and at the same time a continuation of it, wherein boundaries and perimeters are less distinct. Treatises on the artistic design of gardens are known from the Heian period.

With regard to garden elements, there are some common features. Water is a key element, whether it comes as a surrounding pond or running stream. For early Japanese gardens, especially, boating across the pond to experience the garden was important. Bodies of water have an important religious significance, extending to Hinduism, Shintōism, and Buddhism alike. There is also a keen distinction between wet landscape and dry landscape, even as the rock formations in a dry landscape are often orchestrated to suggest water. Stones, rocks, and gravel are another main constituent of the garden, owing also to ancient spiritual practices. The arrangement of stones in a garden is important in evoking not only harmony, but also symbolism and irregularity. Sand is also used at times, and sand or gravel may be used to suggest the idea of water. Architecture is often significant not only as a setting (e.g., hermitage garden), but also in terms of a framing and contrasting element for the garden. Sometimes, as at Katsura, interior views of the outside garden are central to the design, whereas other times (such as with many tea gardens), the interior and exterior do not significantly penetrate. Architectural adornments (gates, lanterns [*tōrō*], basins [*chōzubachi*], bridges) are present relative to the specificity of the site and typically utilize natural materials, such as bamboo, wood, or stone. Certain gardens emphasize elaborate pathways and movement (e.g., *kaiyū-shiki-teien*), while rock gardens may be situated for contemplation only, from a fixed point of view (e.g., Ryōan-ji). The level of greenery and color, as well as borrowed scenery (*shakkei*), will vary significantly with respect to the type of garden.

Japanese Gardens in the United States and Canada

Japanese gardens can be found throughout the United States, even in regions known for long or harsh winters (e.g., Normandale Japanese Garden, Bloomington, Minnesota), and they are particularly frequent along the West Coast. Some of the more well-known American examples include the Hagiwara Japanese Tea Garden in San Francisco's Golden Gate Park (the oldest public example in the United States); Hakone Gardens (Saratoga, California); Hayward Japanese Gardens (Hayward, California); Seiwa-en at the Missouri Botanical Garden (St. Louis); Shofuso Japanese Garden (Philadelphia); Anderson Japanese Gardens (Rockford, Illinois); Japanese Hill-and-Pond Garden, Brooklyn Botanical Garden (Brooklyn, New York); Nitobe Inazo Garden (Vancouver, British Columbia). Elements that are commonly found in the gardens of Japan can be found in these American iterations—such as stone lanterns, ponds, and winding pathways. Moreover, these gardens help to articulate to American audiences some of the aesthetic principles that have informed their Japanese forbearers: asymmetry, naturalness, and austerity.

In addition to the above public spaces, Japanese garden design is ubiquitous in Hawai'i, the West Coast states, and other locales with a Japanese community. The liberal use of stone and sand, manicured pine trees, maples, azaleas, camellias, and moss are popular features in the front yards of many homes. The impact of Japanese garden design can be attributed in large part to the lack of employment opportunities to Japanese immediately after the end of World War II. Unable to secure employment, many earned a living tending lawns and designing gardens.

Larry M. Taylor

See also: Essays: Arts and Cultural Production

Further Reading

Addiss, Stephen. *Japan and the West: The Filled Void.* Wolfsburg: Kunstmuseum Wolfsburg; Köln: DuMont, 2007.

Fujioka, Michio. *Japanese Residences and Gardens: A Tradition of Integration.* Tokyo: Kodansha International, 1982.

Hibi, Sadao. *A Celebration of Japanese Gardens: Photographs by Sadao Hibi.* Tokyo: Graphic-sha, 1994.

Kuitert, Wybe. *Themes in the History of Japanese Garden Art.* Honolulu: University of Hawai'i Press, 2002.

Levick, Melba. *Japanese-style Gardens of the Pacific West Coast.* New York: Rizzoli, 1999.

Locher, Mira. *Zen Gardens: The Complete Works of Shunmyo Masuno, Japan's Leading Garden Designer.* Rutland, VT: Tuttle, 2012.

Mansfield, Stephen. *Japan's Master Gardens: Lessons in Space and Environment.* Rutland, VT: Tuttle, 2011.

Mansfield, Stephen. *Japanese Stone Gardens: Origins, Meaning, Form.* Rutland, VT: Tuttle, 2009.

Masuno, Sunmyo. *The Modern Japanese Garden.* Rutland, VT: Tuttle, 2002.

Murase, Miyeko, and Pierre-Emmanuel Dauzat. *L'Art du Japon.* Paris: Librairie Générale Française, 1996.

Oster, Maggie. *Reflections of the Spirit: Japanese Gardens in America.* New York: Dutton Studio Books, 1993.

Jehovah's Witnesses

Founded in the late 1870s by Charles Taze Russell (1852–1916), the Jehovah's Witnesses are a nontrinitarian, millenialist Christian denomination with strong restorationist and evangelical aspects. At just under eight million adherents worldwide today, this Brooklyn-based sect is known for the distribution of its publications (e.g., *The Watchtower*), restricted fellowship, and various cultural declinations, such as the refusal to salute the national flag. The group originally formed in Pittsburgh, Pennsylvania, as part of the larger Bible study movement, before Russell established the organization in New York, where it is run today (from a complex known as Bethel). With Nelson H. Barbour (1824–1905), he published *Three Worlds* in 1876, which prophesied that Christ had begun his return two years prior to that, and that 40 years from then would consummate the end of the "Gentile Times" (cf. Lk 21:24). At the end of the decade Russell initiated publication of *Zion's Watchtower and Herald of Christ's Presence*, and congregations began to form ("Russellites") to study the Bible. His successor, Joseph F. Rutherford (1869–1942), took an oppositional stance to World War I and the various Christian churches that supported it, and he later (1931) would advance the name of the group as it is known today. He was arrested and imprisoned for sedition in 1919 for refusal to participate in military service. During the 1960s, a number of Witnesses (based on *Watchtower* publications) suggested that the millennium might begin in 1975, a proposition that was not official teaching but did serve to cause a temporary influx of new memberships. When that expectation was not met, however, it initiated an overhaul of the organization, restraining its president's powers and reassigning more of them to the Governing Body, which administers the organization today. Governing Body statements carry much authority, though the Protestant canon of the Bible is ostensibly viewed as the ultimate authority. Modern leaders of the Watchtower Society have included Nathan H. Knorr (1905–1977), Frederick W. Franz (1893–1992), Milton G. Henschel (1920–2003), and Don A. Adams (b. 1925).

Jehovah's Witnesses do believe in Jesus, his divine origin and status as Messiah and "a god," his atoning sacrifice, as well as in the idea that faith in Christ leads to eternal life. However, Christ's statement that "the Father is greater than I am" (Jn 14:28) is taken to mean that there is an essential cleavage between Jesus (not seen as eternal) and the Father, barring belief in a Trinity and refusing the worship of Christ as God. While this belief differentiates Witnesses from mainstream Christianity, they consider themselves followers of Jesus and pray in his name. (The Holy Spirit is interpreted as Jehovah's "active force.") They do not consider themselves Protestants, nor do they see themselves as actively protesting or reforming the Catholic Church. Certain holidays, such as Christmas, are not celebrated due to concerns over the actual date of Christ's birth, as well as association with pagan holidays. God is seen as the Creator, but the biblical act of creation need not be taken literally (i.e., not as fulfilled in six literal days but perhaps thousands of years), thus inviting a measure of compatibility with modern science. Witnesses believe that when Jesus spoke of his "kingdom" he was not limiting the idea to a suggestion of the heart or to celestial matters, but in fact aimed to point to a real world government—even to the removal of all earthly dominions (since the "world system" is currently viewed as under satanic control). Based on Ecclesiastes (9:5), the soul is viewed not as immortal but rather as dying with the body, wherein the dead simply "know nothing," and thus do not suffer punishing torments.

Worship is notably conducted in distinctive structures known as Kingdom Halls, a name first given to these rather functional buildings by Rutherford regarding a structure in Hawai'i. Iconography is not part of the worship space, which is given over to the dissemination of the "good news of the Kingdom." (Witnesses also do not believe Jesus was martyred on a cross but rather a "torture stake," and thus cross imagery does not appear elsewhere.) Membership surpassing 200 prompts the construction of a new hall and formulation of a new congregation. One communion service is held annually on the eve of the Jewish Passover, the most significant observance of the year, known as the "Lord's Evening Meal" or "The Memorial [of Christ's Death]." Beliefs generally follow conservative Christian traditions, as with the views that procurement of an abortion or homosexual activity are serious sins. Another distinctive trait is the refusal of blood transfusions, which is based on an interpretation of the Book of Acts (15:28–29). The Bible is the inspired word of God, and their New World Translation (first published in 1960) is typically used, though other translations are not forbidden. Evangelization is a formulative part of belief, conducted at doorsteps under a mandate that requires a monthly quota ("Field Service Report").

Refusal to participate in wartime activities, especially, has historically garnered the Jehovah's Witnesses a significant amount of government oppression and persecution, as well as suspicion from other religious groups. European Witnesses were imprisoned during World War II, and in Germany they were marked with purple triangles in the concentration camps, where 250 are known to have been executed. About 6,000 Witnesses had been imprisoned or moved to camps by the year 1939, four years after the Reich ordered local officials to disband the Watchtower Society. They were also interred in Canada, where they had already faced censorship in World War I. The religion has come under criticism during postwar years for the eschewal of independent thought, insularity, and failed predictions about the end of the age. Social and cultural isolation sometimes further stems from their nonparticipation in holidays and certain cultural and political activities.

The resistance to saluting the flag caused a considerable amount of problems for its members during the first part of the 20th century in the United States, when such public salutations were mandatory. Suspicions about the group meant that *The Watchtower* was forbidden for a time in Canada. Politically, contemporary Witnesses tend to ally with conservatism and the Republican Party. The largest concentrations are found in the western and southern regions of the United States. A large majority (63 percent) do not have children—a figure comparable to American Evangelicals and Catholics, but significantly higher than Mormons or Muslims. The belief that Christ will soon establish a millennial kingdom wherein all ethnic groups will live in peace may have a certain appeal to Asian Americans and other cultural minorities. Though it is one of the few religious movements that began in the United States, most Witnesses (over 80 percent) live abroad—though Canada and Latin America have high numbers. In legal battles over religious freedom, they have often pursued cases to the highest level with much success (e.g., *West Virginia Board of Education v. Barnette*, 1943). Famous former Witnesses include Michael Jackson, Patti Smith, the Filipino actress Carmina Villaroel, and the Japanese singer Hinano Yoshikawa. Among other groups, Jehovah's Witnesses have conducted some of the most recent missionary work in the Pacific Islands, and there has been rapid growth recently in certain Asian nations, as in Japan after 1970. Asian Americans are adherents to this religion in numbers less than 0.5 percent, according to a 2008 Pew Research Institute Forum on Religion and Public Life.

Larry M. Taylor

Further Reading

Bergman, Jerry, ed. *Jehovah's Witnesses: A Comprehensive and Selectively Annotated Bibliography*. Westport, CT: Greenwood Press, 1999.

Chryssides, George D. *Historical Dictionary of Jehovah's Witnesses*. Historical Dictionaries of Religions, Philosophies, and Movements no. 85. Lanham, MD: Scarecrow Press, 2008.

Holden, Andrew. *Jehovah's Witnesses: A Portrait of a Contemporary Religious Movement*. London, New York: Routledge, 2002.

Penton, M. James. *Jehovah's Witnesses in Canada: Champions of Freedom of Speech and Worship*. Toronto: Macmillan of Canada, 1976.

Peters, Shawn Francis. *Judging Jehovah's Witnesses: Religious Persecution and the Dawn of the Rights Revolution*. Lawrence: University of Kansas Press, 2000.

Rabinowitz, Harold, and Greg Tobin, eds. *Religion in America: A Comprehensive Guide to Faith, History and Tradition*. New York: Sterling, 2011.

Jikei Kai: Japanese Benevolent Society

Responding to the need to care for the destitute, sick, and injured migrant Japanese and to secure a proper burial site for those who died, the Japanese community that included business and religious leaders in the San Francisco Bay Area established the Kashu Nihonjin Jikei Kai (Japanese Benevolent Society of California) on February 1, 1901. On August 2 the state of California granted Jikei Kai, as it is commonly known, its nonprofit status and by the end of the year it was able to raise more than the $1,400 needed to purchase two acres of land in Colma, California, for a cemetery. Exactly one year to the day after the property was acquired, on March 17, 1903, the Jōdo Shinshū cleric, Rev. Nishijima Kakuryo (1873–1942), officiated at the opening of the cemetery.

The need for a permanent cemetery dates to 1879 when the Lone Mountain

(Laurel Hills) and Masonic cemeteries refused to accept the remains of three Japanese nationals (names unknown). In 1890 Japanese physicians Kurosawa Kakusaburo (dates unknown), Abiko Kyūtaro (1865–1936), and others representing the Japanese community approached the city of San Francisco for land to establish a permanent resting place. City officials offered three possible sites and asked the physicians to select one. They selected a site, now occupied by the Sutro Heights Park parking lot, just north of Point Lobos Avenue. However, in 1898 the city rezoned the entire area, including the land on which the Japanese cemetery was located, and banned burials within city limits after August 1, 1901. In the meantime in 1896 officials agreed to allocate a portion of the Chinese section of Masonic Cemetery for Japanese burials. However, the caretakers refused to allow the internment of the remains of Takagi Shima, Ikeda Miyo, and Inaki Mine, who succumbed to bubonic plague in July 1901. The women from the Tohoku region resided at 845 Washington Street in the red light district and were in all likelihood sex workers. This incident highlighted the need for an independent Japanese cemetery.

In 1914 Jikei Kai began to reinter the 207 remains of Japanese buried in the public cemeteries in the city in Colma. The project was completed in 1940. Jikei Kai built a columbarium in 1968 and purchased in 1969 an adjacent property for $1,000,000 to meet the community's growing needs. Jikei Kai sponsors an annual interfaith Memorial Day ceremony in memory of those who are buried in the cemetery. It also serves as a rallying force for the Japanese American community by spearheading historical, cultural, and other events that honor the Japanese heritage in the United States. In 2010 Jikei Kai commemorated the arrival of the Japanese naval ship *Kanrin Maru* captained by Katsu Kaishū (1823–1899) and John Manjirō Whitfield (1827–1898) to San Francisco 150 years earlier.

The work of the Jikei Kai is supported by donations and monies from fees from the sale of burial plots and niches. Reports of the April 18, 1906, Great Earthquake of San Francisco prompted the Japanese emperor Meiji (1852–1912) to allocate $50,000 to Jikei Kai's relief efforts; he also donated $5,000,000 to the city of San Francisco. In 1937 the Japanese emperor Showa (1901–1989) donated $25,000 to support Jikei Kai's work.

Ronald Y. Nakasone

See also: Entries: Fujinkai (Buddhist Women's Association)

Further Reading

Jikei Kai Website. http://www.jikei-kai.org/. Accessed July 14, 2014.

Jōdo Shinshū Buddhist Temples of Canada (JSBTC)

The first Jōdo Shinshū Buddhist temple in Canada was founded in 1905 with the assignment of Rev. Senju Sasaki to Vancouver, British Columbia. As the number of Japanese immigrants to Canada increased, so did the demand for Jōdo Shinshū temples, leading to the eventual founding of the Buddhist Churches of Canada (now

The Buddhist Church of San Francisco with a view of the stūpa that was specially built to house a portion of the corporeal remains of Siddhārta Gautama, the Buddha. In 1935, Masuyama Kenjū (1887–1968), together with Noboru Tsunoda Noboru (1913–2005), traveled to Siam (present day Thailand) to the remains that were discovered in Piprahwa, India in 1898. (Photography by Ronald Y. Nakasone, April 22, 2015.)

the Jōdo Shinshū Buddhist Temples of Canada, or JSBTC) in 1933. With World War II came the internment of Japanese immigrants to Canada and as such, the closing down of all official operations of the organization. After the war JSBTC was never fully restored but slowly began to reform as an institution. In 1967 the JS-BTC was placed under the supervision of the Buddhist Churches of America in the United States, a relationship that lasted only until 1968 when the Canadian tem-

ples broke off to reestablish as a distinct entity. At present JSBTC has over 1,750 members, 12 temples, and 9 official overseas ministers and is slowly branching out beyond the Japanese community and attempting to reach the greater Canadian population.

Christina R. Yanko

See also: Entries: Buddhist Churches of America; Higashi Honganji; Honpa Hongwanji Mission of Hawai'i; Shin Buddhist Music

Further Reading

Buddhist Churches of America: Volume 1, 75 Year History, 1899–1974. Chicago: Nobart, 1974.

Watada, Terry. *Bukkyo Tozen: A History of Jōdo Shinshū Buddhism in Canada 1905–1995.* Toronto: HpF Press and the Toronto Buddhist Church, 1996.

Jōdo Shū (Pure Land Sect)

Jōdo Shū traces its beginnings as the first independent school of Pure Land Buddhism in Japan to when its founder Hōnen (also known as Hōnen-bō Genkū, 1133–1212) left the Tendai monastic center of Mount Hiei in 1175 to spread his teachings to the general populace. The Pure Land denomination known today as Jōdo Shū was established by one of Hōnen's main disciples, Shōkō-bō Benchō (1162–1238), who founded the Chinzei branch in Kyushu in the south, and his disciple Ryōchū (1199–1287), who formed the branch in the Kanto (present-day Tokyo) region. The sect welcomed a period of great prosperity under the patronage of the shogun Tokugawa Ieyasu (1543–1616), who in 1590 selected

Jōdo Shū sect Buddhists pray during the memorial service to commemorate the 800th anniversary of the death of monk Hōnen at Chion-in Temple on October 2, 2011, in Kyoto, Japan. Hōnen, the founder of Jōdo Shū passed away on January 25, 1212. (Sankei/Getty Images)

Chion-in in Kyoto and Zōjō-ji in Edo (present-day Tokyo) to be the family's temples. Today, Jōdo Shū has approximately 7,000 temples, of which Chion-in is the grand head temple (*sōhonzan*). The head temples (*daihonzan*) are Zōjō-ji (Tokyo), Kurodani Konkaikōmyō-ji (Kyoto), Hyakumanben Chion-ji (Kyoto), Shōjōke-in (Kyoto), Zendō-ji (Kurume), Kōmyō-ji (Kamakura), and Zenkō-ji Daihongan (Nagano).

Life and Teachings of Hōnen

Hōnen was born in Mimasaka Province (now Okayama Prefecture) in 1133 as the only child of the provincial lord Uruma no Tokikuni. According to the official 48-volume illustrated biography, *Hōnen Shōnin gyōjō ezu* (translated by Coates and Ishizuka as *Hōnen, the Buddhist Saint: His Life and Teaching*, 1925), compiled by Shunjō in 1141, when Hōnen was nine, his father Tokikuni was assassinated by a political rival, Akashi no Sadaakira. On his deathbed, Tokikuni was said to have told his son not to avenge his death, but to become a monk and pray for his and his enemy's deliverance. The Daigo-edition Hōnen biography, however, mentions that Hōnen had already left for Enryaku-ji Temple on Mount Hiei before his father passed away. In either case, Hōnen was ordained in 1147 and devoted himself to the study of the Tendai teachings. In 1175, at the age of 43, Hōnen abandoned other forms of practice and devoted himself exclusively to repeating the *nembutsu*—"*Namu Amida Butsu*" (Homage to Amida Buddha). In 1198, at the request of his patron and disciple, the former regent Kujō Kanezane (1149–1207), Hōnen composed *Senchaku hongan nembutsu shū* (Passages on the Selection of the Nembutsu in the Original Vow), in which he systematically laid out the teaching of *nembutsu* and established the basis for Jōdo Shū.

Hōnen taught that the Pure Land path (*Jōdo mon*) was the most expedient means for attaining enlightenment in the age of *mappō* (degenerate or latter Dharma). To this end, he emphasized the importance of faith in Amida (Skt. Amitābha) Buddha and continuously chanting the *nembutsu*. The accessibility of the *nembutsu* teaching attracted people from all walks of life, regardless of gender, social class, or education level. The popularity of Hōnen's teaching, however, alarmed the entrenched Buddhist orthodoxy and eventually led to his expulsion from Kyoto. In 1207, at the age of 75, Hōnen accepted his exile to Shikoku as a way to spread his teaching. Though pardoned later that same year, he was not permitted to return to the capital until 1211. On the 23rd day of the first month of 1212, Hōnen authored his final testament, *Ichimai kishōmon* (The One-Page Document), which stated the essence of his *nembutsu* teaching. Two days later, on the 25th day, Hōnen passed away at the age of 80.

Hōnen's teachings had a major impact on Japanese Buddhism. Over his lifetime, Hōnen had some 200 disciples and many more followers of all classes and walks of life. Among the most prominent of his disciples were Shōkū (1177–1247), whose followers established the Seizan branch of Jōdo-shū, and Shinran (1173–1263), whose descendants founded Jōdo Shinshū. Also, as the leading figure advocating exclusive adherence, Hōnen greatly influenced subsequent Buddhist reformers during the Kamakura period such as Nichiren (1222–1282), who promoted the exclusive recitation of the title of the *Lotus Sūtra* (*Namu Myōhōrengekyō*), and Dōgen (1200–1253), who promoted the sole practice of Zen meditation.

Jōdo Shū in Hawai'i

Overseas activity for Jōdo Shū started in the late 19th century with the rise of Japanese immigration to Hawai'i. Learning of the hardships of the immigrant workers in the sugar plantations, Rev. Ikawa Takuzen (n.d.) expressed an interest in establishing an overseas mission and solicited the help of the chief abbot Hino Reizui (1818–1896) and other influential leaders of the sect in 1893. In the same year, Rev. Shiraishi Gyōkai (1854–1927) led the effort to raise funds for the Hawai'i Missionary Group (*Hawai'i senkyō kai*) through the head temple Zōjō-ji in Tokyo. In March 1894, Rev. Matsuo Taijō (1868–1898) arrived in Hawai'i, followed by Rev. Okabe Gakuō (1866–1922) in May of that year. The two pioneering ministers traveled throughout the islands offering spiritual solace. In November 1896, Okabe began raising funds to build the first Japanese Buddhist temple in the Hamakua area on the island of Hawai'i. Rev. Tanaka Makaen

(1893–1905) arrived in March 1898 and led the effort to build a second Jōdo Shū temple, the Laupahoehoe Jōdo Buddhist Assembly Hall, to serve its congregation of 662 members in the following year.

By the early 20th century, Jōdo Shū had quickly established 16 temples (eight on the island of Hawai'i, three on Maui, three on O'ahu, and two on Kaua'i). In 1902, temples were established in Olaa (present-day Kurtistown) and Kapaau (present-day Kohala) on the island of Hawai'i. The Kohala temple built the first and only *sūtra* repository—an architectural feature of the traditional Japanese temple complex—in the entire state for the *Shukusatsu Daizōkyō*, an unabridged, reduced-sized set of the complete *sūtra* collection. In 1903, the Laupahoehoe temple became the headquarters for the Hawai'i Overseas Mission. Rev. Shimizu Shinjun (d. 1919), later the first bishop, recognized the need for the headquarters to be in the burgeoning capital of Honolulu and had a new temple constructed at South and King Streets in 1907. The current head temple, the Jōdo Mission of Hawai'i (also known as the Betsuin, or branch headquarters), located at 1429 Makiki Street, Honolulu, was built in 1936.

Three more temples were established on the island of Hawai'i in the towns of Hakalau and Wainaku in 1905, and another in Hawi in 1909. In 1910, Koloa Jōdo Mission became the first Jōdo Shū temple on the island of Kaua'i, and Puunene Jodo Mission (relocated to Kahului in 1969) became the first on Maui. The following year, Hilo Meisho-in was established on the island of Hawai'i. Temples were also founded in Haleiwa, O'ahu; in

Lahaina, Maui; and in Kapaa, Kaua'i, in 1912. The community in Wailuku, Maui, built their temple in 1914. The devotees of Ewa, O'ahu, formed a worship community in 1916 and met at a temporary facility until building a temple in the following year. The Ookala community on the island of Hawai'i founded a missionary center and Japanese school in 1920.

In addition to the temples, these communities established 18 Japanese-language schools and various Buddhist associations such as Seinenkai (youth group) and Fujinkai (women's group). The temples also served as a community gathering place for social and cultural programs. With the outbreak of World War II, the priests were interned and the mission was temporarily suspended. The U.S. Army requisitioned some of the temple buildings and shuttered others. Services were also prohibited since no more than five people of Japanese ancestry were allowed to gather.

In December 1945, the interned priests returned to Hawai'i, where they resumed their activities in spite of the significant challenges in rebuilding their community due to the scattering and loss of members. In the 1970s, several temples disbanded due to the loss of employment of many of their members who worked in sugar cane and pineapple plantations.

Today, the Hawai'i Council of Jōdo Missions consists of 13 temples with approximately 1,000 families. Although membership has greatly declined, members continue to enjoy fellowship at various temple functions including Sunday services and in statewide organizations, such as the Laypersons' Association, Fujinkai (Women's Association), and YBA (Young Buddhists' Association). The different temples and organizations each contribute to the community in their own way such as *imon* (visitations to elderly homes and centers), participating in community cleanup, and cooperating in community service work programs for juveniles.

Jōdo Shū in North America

The history of Jōdo Shū in North America began in 1936 with the arrival of the Rev. Nozaki Reikai Nozaki (1901–1978) in Los Angeles from Honolulu. However, the outbreak of World War II disrupted his ministry. After the end of the war, in October 1950, the community established a temple at 2003 Jefferson Boulevard. Archbishop Shiio Benkyō (1876–1971), abbot of Zōjō-ji, led the celebration for the dedication service. In 1972, Chief Abbot Kishi Shinkō (1889–1979) was the lead celebrant for the 35th anniversary of the establishment of the North American ministry in tandem with the 800th anniversary of the founding of Jōdo-shū.

In the late 1980s, Jōdo Shū North America Buddhist Missions relocated to Little Tokyo in Los Angeles into a newly built facility with the support of the Jōdo Shū–affiliated Bukkyō University in Kyoto. The first floor houses the Bukkyō University–LA Extension, while the temple is located on the second floor. The Japanese artist Koiwai Shūhō (1920–2007) created and donated the paintings of the state flowers of the United States and the national flower of Japan that adorn the ceiling of the second-floor sanctuary. On June 28, 1992, Chief Abbot Nakamura Koryu (1906–2008) led the dedication celebration of the new temple.

The Jōdo Shū North America Buddhist Missions facility is a center of worship, learning, research, and publication. In 1995, the temple instituted the Los Angeles Seminar, a program to nurture Jōdo Shū ministers for the 21st century. The continuing focus of the seminar is to familiarize participants to the religious and cultural pulse of the United States by visits to churches and social welfare facilities and through home stays. Eight seminars have been held thus far. Of the 40 participants, five have elected to become overseas missionaries. In autumn of 1996, Jōdo Shū North America Buddhist Missions together with Bukkyō University–LA Extension hosted the first joint seminar of the three Jōdo Shū overseas ministerial districts—Hawai'i, United States, and Brazil. In 2007, Jōdo Shū North America Buddhist Missions celebrated its 70th anniversary in conjunction with the 15th anniversary of the construction of its current facility in Little Tokyo. That same year, Bukkyō University–LA Extension published *Teachings of Hōnen*, an English translation of *Hōnen Shōnin gohōgo* (*Hōnen Shōnin sayings*). In 2012, the Los Angles temple hosted the 800th Grand Memorial Service of Hōnen Shōnin, which was officiated by Chief Abbot Itō Yuishin (1931–) from Chion-in. During the winter of 2012, the Los Angles Temple held *Gojū sōden*, a three-day Fivefold Transmission retreat, in which 50 participants received certificates of completion issued by Chion-in temple.

Beliefs

[R]ecite single-heartedly and exclusively the name of Amida Buddha while walking, standing, sitting, or lying down, without regard for length of time, and to engage in the recitation of nembutsu without cessation throughout one's life. This is called the rightly established practice because it is in accordance with the essential vow of Amida Buddha.

Inspired by the above passage from *Guan wuliang shou jing zhuo* (*Kanmuryōjukyō sho*; *Commentary on the Meditation Sūtra*) by Shandao (Zendō, 613–681), Hōnen laid the foundations for the single practice of *nembutsu* recitation (*shōmyō nembutsu*) and exclusive devotion to Amida Buddha. In his *magnum opus*, *Senchaku hongan nembutsu shū*, Hōnen systematized the basis for an independent Pure Land, Jōdo Shū tradition, by drawing upon the Indian and Chinese Pure Land patriarchs. Indian patriarchs Nāgārjuna (ca. 150–250 CE) and Vasubandu (ca. 400–500 CE) provided buddhological justification for single-practice recitation of the *nembutsu* and single-minded devotion to Amida Buddha; and his Chinese predecessors clarified such key notions as Original Vow, the nature of Amida Buddha, Other Power, and recitation of the *nembutsu*. From Shandao, Hōnen identified the Three Pure Land *Sūtras* (*Jōdo sanbukyō*).

The Three Pure Land *Sūtras* refer to three independent works: *Daimuryōkyō* (*Larger Sukhāvatīvyūha-sūtra* or *Larger Pure Land Sūtra*), *Amidakyō* (*Smaller Sukhāvatīvyūha-sūtra* or the *Smaller Pure Land Sūtra*, also known as the *Amida Sūtra*), and *Kanmuryōju kyō* (*Amitāyurdhyāna-sūtra*, commonly known as the *Meditation Sūtra*). Regarded as the principal canonical text, the *Larger Pure Land Sūtra* narrates the story of Dharmākara Bodhisattva (Hōzō Bosatsu), who pledges that he will not become Amida Buddha nor establish his Pure Land, Sukhāvatī, until he fulfills 48 vows. Of these Original Vows, Jōdo Shū considers the 18th, 19th, and 20th vows to be the most important. In the 18th vow, Amida Buddha promises to accept all beings who repeat his name and wholeheartedly and sincerely place their trust in him. In the 19th vow, Amida Buddha promises to personally welcome, at the moment of death, the devotee who performs meritorious deeds. With the 20th vow, Amida Buddha promises to receive anyone who repeats his name with the goal of birth into the Pure Land. The *Amida Sūtra* is regarded as the concluding text of the *Larger Pure Land Sūtra*; it describes the Pure Land and its inhabitants, by clarifying their spiritual nature, and attainment of the Pure Land and virtues of Amida Buddha.

Since there is no Sanskrit original, scholars speculate that the *Meditation Sūtra* was composed in China or possibly Central Asia. The drama unfolds in a cell in Bimbisāra Prison, where Śākyamuni Buddha miraculously appears before Queen Vaidehī, who had early appealed to him to reveal a land without suffering where she might be born. Śākyamuni proceeds to instruct her on 13 meditations through which she can calm her mind to overcome her anguish as a mother and as a spouse. Her son, Prince Ajātaśatru, had imprisoned his mother Vaidehī, because she had smuggled food to her spouse King Bimbisāra, who happens to be Ajātaśatru's father. Learning of his mother's ruse, the enraged prince drew his sword to strike his mother. Persuaded against such rashness by his ministers, he imprisons her instead.

Hōnen drew upon Shandao's conclusions from the *Daśabhūmikavibhāṣa Śāstra*, in which Nāgārjuna asserted that, in addition to long years of discipline and study (Path of the Sages), faith (Easy Path, also known as the Pure Land) is a legitimate *upāya* (expedient means) method for attaining enlightenment. Vasubandhu provided additional support for Pure Land devotion in the *Sukhāvatīvyūhopadeśa*, where he listed chanting the name Amida among four other forms of meditation. Hōnen looked to the Chinese Dharma master Danluan, who in his commentary on Vasubandhu's *Sukhāvatīvyūhopadeśa* (Ch. *Wangsheng lun chu*, Jpn. *Jōdo ronchū*), equated the name of Amida with ultimate reality, thus attributing to it the power to break through ignorance that bound sentient beings to *saṃsāra*. This, in turn, lends support to the efficacy of Amida Buddha's Vow or Other Power to embrace all beings who recite his name to effectively transcend the duality between the devotee and the goal of *Nirvāṇa* or enlightenment.

Shandao and his spiritual mentor Daozhuo were active when the idea of *mofa* (Jpn. *mappō*, the degenerate or latter Dharma) had gained currency in China and Japan. *Mappō* refers to the last era of a Buddhist millennium theory that states the further we move from the time of the historical Buddha, the less sincere devotees become and the less authentic the Dharma becomes. The first 500 years are referred to

as the age of the true Dharma; the second 500 years are the age of the counterfeit Dharma. According to Chinese reckoning 611 CE was exactly 1,001 years after the death of Śhakamuni Buddha. In *Anlo chi* (Jpn. *Anraku shū*, *Essays on the Pure Land*), Daozhuo clarifies the distinction between the Path of the Sages and the Easy Path of the Pure Land, first articulated by Nāgārjuna. The former outlines the means to realizing enlightenment through the investigation of truth through discipline and study. The latter or Path of Faith, in contrast, asks the devotee to reflect on the inadequacy of human effort and to accept the Original Vow of Amida. Similarly the Japanese scholar monk Genshin (942–1017) champions the idea that in the age of *mappō*, the only hope for spiritual release resides in the Other Power of Amida in *Ōjōyōshu* (Essentials of Birth [in the Pure Land]).

Drawing from these spiritual predecessors, Hōnen advocated the simple practice of vocalizing the *nembutsu* or reciting "*Namu Amida Butsu*" to save all beings in the age of *mappō*. By chanting *nembutsu*, the devotee would be welcomed by Amida Buddha at death to the Pure Land, where enlightenment could be most effectively realized. Thus, Hōnen encouraged the development of deep faith in Amida and the continual recitation of *nembutsu* until one's last moment.

Practices

The central practice of Jōdo Shū devotees is *shōmyō nembutsu* or the continuous recitation of Amida Buddha's name, "*Namu Amida Butsu*." Services at most temples include the traditional form of chanting (see http://english.jodoshuna.org/prayer/daily-prayer/), followed by the recitation of the Golden Chain and the Eightfold Path and the singing of Hōnen's poem *Tsukikage* (Moonlight) and English *gathas* or hymns. Sermons are offered in Japanese and/or English, or both. Some temples also hold monthly *obetsuji* or special *nembutsu* chanting sessions. Like most other Japanese Buddhist sects in the United States, Jōdo Shū has adopted the practice of Sunday services and installation of pews.

Jōdo Shū temples serve as spiritual centers as well as places of cultural and community gatherings. Annual observances include New Year's service, Gyokie (Hōnen's memorial service), Nehan-e (Nirvana Day service), Ohigan-e (spring and autumn equinox services), Hanamatsuri (Buddha's birthday service; "Buddha Day" in Hawai'i), Mother's and Father's Day services, Obon (commemoration for the deceased), Ojūya (literally, 10 night [chanting of *nembutsu*]), Jōdo-e (Buddha's Enlightenment service), and Joya-e (New Year's Eve service).

Maya Hara and Jodo Tanaka

See also: Entries: Buddhist Churches of America; Higashi Honganji; Honpa Hongwanji Mission of Hawai'i

Further Reading

Andrews, Allan A. "Hōnen and Popular Pure Land Piety: Assimilation and Transformation." *Journal of the International Association of Buddhist Studies* 17, no. 1 (1994): 96–110.

Andrews, Allan A. "Pure Land Buddhist Hermeneutics: Hōnen's Interpretation of Nembutsu." In Alfred Bloom, ed. *Living in Amida's Universal Vow: Essays in Shin Buddhism*. Bloomington: World Wisdom, 2004, pp. 231–246.

Atone, Jōji, and Yoko Hayashi, trans. *The Promise of Amida Buddha: Hōnen's Path to Pure Land Bliss*. Boston: Wisdom, 2011.

Blum, Mark L. *The Origins and Development of Pure Land Buddhism: A Study and Translation of Gyōnen's* Jōdo Hōmon Genrushō. New York: Oxford University Press, 2002.

Coates, Harper Havelock, and Ryūgaku Ishizuka, trans. *Hōnen, the Buddhist Saint: His Life and Teaching*. Translation of *Hōnen Shōnin gyōjō ezu* by Shunjō. Kyoto: Chion-in, 1925.

Fitzgerald, Joseph A., ed. *Hōnen the Buddhist Saint: Essential Writings and Official Biography*. Bloomington, IN: World Wisdom, 2006.

Inagaki, Hisao, trans. *The Three Pure Land Sūtras*. Revised 2nd ed. BDK Tripiṭaka Series. Berkeley, CA: Numata Center for Buddhist Translation and Research, 2003.

Jōdo Shū North America Buddhist Missions. "Daily Prayer." http://english.jodoshuna.org/prayer/daily-prayer/. Accessed July 14, 2014.

Jōdo Shū Research Institute. "Hōnen's View of Senchaku (Selection) & the Nembutsu." Jōdo Shū Research Institute Website. http://jsri.jp/English/Hōnen/TEACHINGS/senchaku.html. Accessed July 14, 2014.

Urakami, Kenjō S. *Amida Buddha and His Pure Land: Three Sūtras and One Treatise*. n.p.: Kenjo S. Urakami, 1997.

Watts, Jonathan, and Yoshiharu Tomatsu, eds. *Traversing the Pure Land Path: A Lifetime of Encounter with Hōnen Shonin*. Tokyo: Jōdo Shū Press, 2005.

K

Kagiwada, David (1929–1985)

In 1929, David Kagiwada was born into the Christian Church (Disciples of Christ), which was often prone to the prejudices, discrimination, and biases of the dominant culture. In the early history of the Christian Church this was demonstrated by the structure inherent in the Asian Disciple communities of which Kagiwada's parents, Frank and Sachiko Kagiwada, were members. The early Christian Church congregations for Chinese, Japanese, and Filipino Christians were missions of agencies such as the United Christian Missionary Society and the Christian Women's Board of Missions or local churches. These churches were not autonomous communities responsible for their own communal existence, so Asian American Disciples remained marginalized by a power structure that saw them as the recipients of the mission. At the same time, these churches acted as important cultural centers that fed members spiritually, provided care for those in need, and educated children. Prior to the establishment of these local American communities, the Disciples had missionaries working in Japan. As part of their mission, Disciples opened the Margaret K. Long School (Joshi Sei Gakuin) in Tokyo. There, Japanese women, such as Sachiko Togasaki (1905–2002), were taught. Togasaki was also trained as a Bible Woman by the Disciples missionaries. As a result of this work, Togasaki became a Bible teacher in Akita, Japan, where Disciples had established a kindergarten, and then she was sent to teach Japanese immigrants in Los Angeles, California. She met and married Frank Eiho Kagiwada (1895–1995) during her time in Los Angeles.

Unfortunately, most of the Christian Church (Disciples of Christ) mission congregations that had developed on the West Coast for Asian Disciples closed due to factors such as decreases in attendance, prejudice, and funding shortages. In particular, the Japanese churches were closed after Pearl Harbor due to Executive Order 9066 issued by Franklin D. Roosevelt that created the Japanese internment camps. David Kagiwada was 12 when Executive Order 9066 was issued and his family was sent to the Poston, Arizona, internment camp. It was probably because of his parents' own Christian faith that Kagiwada connected with the church activities led by Christians during the family's internment in Arizona.

The experience of internment and being a Nisei (second-generation Japanese American) led Kagiwada to pursue a life encouraging and empowering not only Asian Americans but also women and other minorities. While working on his bachelor's degree at Ohio Wesleyan University, Kagiwada worked with diverse people and sought to reconcile historically antagonistic groups and individuals. After college he started training in social work but was advised to go to divinity school instead, based on the questions he was asking. Kagiwada graduated from the University of Chicago School of Divinity (Disciples Divinity House) in 1954 and was ordained by the Illinois Region of the Christian Church (Disciples of Christ), having maintained his mother's connection with the denomination.

In his 1954 ordination statement, Kagiwada stated, "I want to bear witness to the goodness which finds its source in the God of our Lord Jesus Christ. . . . It is a ministry which involves judgment as well as healing. It is to this task that I commit my energies, talents, vision, and life." After ordination, Kagiwada served as Minister of Education at Central Christian Church in Pasadena, California (now Memorial Drive Christian Church). He served four other churches after Central Christian: in California, Coachella Valley Christian Church (Indio), First Christian Church (Visalia), and San Lorenzo Community Church (UCC, San Lorenzo); and in Indiana, Crestview Christian Church (Indianapolis), where he was serving when he died on July 10, 1985, at the age of 55. While at Coachella Valley, Kagiwada provided opportunities for pastors and their wives to come together across theological and denominational lines in response to the needs of the small community at a time when friendships with parishioners were discouraged. Hospitality was an important part of his ministry at First Christian Visalia where he was very active in local community and justice issues, most especially for the Chicano children (known as "Brown Berets") in the neighborhood and farmworkers who were marching for fair wages and better working conditions. Kagi-

wada's wife JoAnne, whom he met at a conference during his time in Pasadena, started law school in Berkeley, which was the catalyst for Kagiwada's move to San Lorenzo. This church shared Kagiwada's own dedication to supporting women in leadership, a pattern that continued during his ministry at Crestview Christian Church. There, he actively supported at least 10 women who chose to enter ordained ministry.

Kagiwada's ministry extended beyond the walls of these individual congregations. He also saw his ministry as a tool to persuade historically antagonistic Asians to work together in the name of Christ. He was able to work toward this goal within the larger general church structure of the Christian Church (Disciples of Christ). Only two distinctly Asian congregations from before World War II existed after 1945, and it was not until the 1970s that new Asian Disciples congregations began to come about as part of an effort to create an Asian and Pacific Islander community that would be integrated into the mainstream of the denomination instead of being kept on the margins. Official attempts to develop an Asian Disciples community began with Harold Johnson (b. 1921), executive for evangelism of the Disciples Division of Homeland Ministries (DHM). The first consultation on Asian ministries took place in July 1978 and established the Fellowship of Asian American Disciples (FAAD). The second consultation in 1979 was attended by David Kagiwada, who was named one of the two inaugural editors of the newsletter for the group. At this time FAAD also changed its name to American Asian Disciples (AAD) to be inclusive of Asian Disciples in Canada and Latin America as well as the United States.

It is through these efforts that together Harold Johnson, David Kagiwada, and Soongook Choi (1933–2002) helped Asian Disciples to integrate, not just assimilate, into the Disciples. This was demonstrated in a significant way when the Asian Disciples were recognized informally at the 1979 General Assembly in St. Louis. Kagiwada's particular leadership in this continued effort was recognized when he was elected convener at the inaugural convocation of the American Asian Disciples' Executive Council, held in Indianapolis in October 1980. The next convocation was held in California in 1982, in conjunction with Pacific Asian American Ministries of the United Church of Christ (PAAM). Though his time as convener was limited to a two-year term, Kagiwada continued to be an important voice for the AAD. At the third convocation, in August 1984, Kagiwada spoke on the theme "From Strangers to Christ's Company." This was Kagiwada's last convocation before his death in 1985.

Kagiwada's legacy, built on his work on behalf of ecumenism and reconciliation, is celebrated by the Christian Church (Disciples of Christ) on the second Sunday of September, which was named Kagiwada Sunday in 1993. The week following is dedicated to honoring and drawing attention to the work of North American/Pacific Asian Disciples (NAPAD, previously AAD). Also developed in his honor is a named scholarship for Asian/Pacific Islander seminarians. The work Kagiwada began has continued in the years since his death, in part through the continued dedication of his wife JoAnne, who is considered by many to be the godmother of NAPAD. Throughout his life, Kagiwada's work was a true reflection of his belief, stated in his January 1985 Ministerial Profile "Statement of Ministry," that his ministry was "rooted in the Beloved Community of which every manifestation of church is increasingly called to more fully embody. Faithfulness is expressed in 'being on the road' toward that fullness." Kagiwada touched every manifestation of the Christian Church (Disciples of Christ)—local, regional, and general—and helped many find the road toward recognizing the fullness of the Body of Christ.

Sarah Kingsbery

See also: Entries: North American Pacific/ Asian Disciples (NAPAD)

Further Reading

Graves, Robyn. "NAPAD Congregations Celebrate Life of Kagiwada." *Disciples World*, September 9, 2006.

Hill, Nathan J. "NAPAD Celebrates Past, Looks to the Future." *Disciples World*, July 31, 2009.

Hunnicutt, Loretta. "Pivotal Role: How Women Shaped Japanese and Indian Churches." *Disciples History Magazine* 72, no.1 (Spring 2013): 8–13, 28–31.

Jha, Sandhya. *Room at the Table: Struggle for Unity and Equality in Disciples History.* St. Louis: Chalice Press, 2009.

Lee, Timothy S. "From Coerced Liminality to In-Beyond the Margin: A Theological Reflection on the History of Asian-American Disciples." Brite Divinity School (Texas Christian University). http://ccu.disciples .org/Portals/CCU/pdf/NAPAD%20 paper%20-%20Tim%20Lee.pdf. Accessed July 9, 2014.

Lee, Timothy S. "In View of Existing Conditions: A Brief History of the North American Pacific/Asian Disciples, 1891–2010 (From the Margins to the Mainstream)." *Discipliana: A Journal of Stone-Campbell History* 71, no. 1 (Spring 2012).

North American Pacific/Asian Disciples. "David Tamotsu Kagiwada: A Compassionate Healer." http://www.napad.net/Portals/napad/pdf/david%20tamotsu%20kagiwada%20a%20compassionate%20healer.pdf. Accessed July 9, 2014.

Yu, Geunhee. "Asian American Disciples." In Douglas A. Foster, et al., eds. *The Encyclopedia of the Stone-Campbell Movement.* Grand Rapids, MI: William B. Eerdmans, 2004, pp. 40–41.

Kava

Historical Developments

Among the most notable cultural practices of Polynesia in particular, and Melanesia and Micronesia in specific locations, is the consumption of *kava*. Explorers, anthropologists, colonial administrators, and other visitors to the Pacific Islands made regular mention of its role in the cultural life of the islands. *Kava* is a drink taken from the roots of the plant *Piper methysticum*, a plant found natively throughout many of the islands. The plant is a member

Participants taste *kava* at a traditional drinking ceremony at the Kava Festival in Honolulu, October 7, 2006. Resembling dishwater and tasting like mud, *kava* is an unlikely hit drink. But to devotees, *kava*, or "awa" in Hawaiian, is a treasured elixir that can calm nerves and deepen sleep. Islanders from Fiji to Hawai'i have been drinking *kava* for centuries to cement bonds among friends and strangers. Priests and elders offered *kava* to the gods in religious ceremonies. (AP Photo/Lucy Pemoni)

of the same family as the tree that produces betel nut, another commonly consumed plant throughout the Pacific Islands. The plant is a member of the pepper family and is found and widely consumed throughout central Polynesia, as well as parts of Melanesia and Micronesia, as a social and ceremonial drink. Some Australian Aboriginal communities have also been known to use *kava*, but it has not been integrated as a part of their traditional cultural systems as in other parts of the Pacific Islands. Known primarily by the name *kava*, it is also referred to as *yaqono, grog, kava-kava, kawa, kawa-kawa, ava, ava-ava, awa*, or *sakau*.

The significance, meaning, and history of *kava* drinking varies from island to island and from culture to culture throughout the islands. A true understanding of *kava* as it relates to culture and religion would require one to focus explicitly on one or another island to understand the vast significance of the *kava* drinking ritual relative to that island community. Each community developed its own rituals, practices, and meanings related to *kava* drinking, so that an overall description such as this entry will leave much out.

The preparation of *kava* begins with cutting the roots and the extreme base of the stem of the *Piper methysticum* (*Piper* being Latin for pepper and *methysticum* being Latinized Greek for intoxicating) plant. These were then beaten on a stone and reduced to fragments. Once the fragments were small enough, they typically were given to young men or young women (because of their usually good teeth and strong jaws) who chewed on them until they were soft and ground into even smaller pieces. These fragments would then be spit into a large bowl, after which the mashed mass would be mixed with water or coconut milk until it reached a certain color and consistency. The liquid would finally be filtered through a strainer of fibers from either local plants or coconut husks and kneaded until finally it was squeezed into cups to be consumed.

The chewing of the fragments has generally been replaced by placing the fragments in a mortar and pounding them into small shreds, which can then be added to the bowl and mixed with water or coconut milk. The subsequent preparation of the *kava* is the same. E. F. Steinmetz (1973) argues that there is a difference in chemical effect when the method of preparation changed from chewing to pounding in a mortar, but this did not seem to impact the practice of drinking *kava* nor its role in rituals and cultural practices. This drink is often served in a special ritualized ceremony as it is an integral part of the religious and social life of many of the cultures throughout the Pacific. Drinking *kava* is essential on occasions of hospitality and feasting, but one will find a wide range of rituals and a considerably variation in the customs of the various islands or groups of islands.

Kava has historically been central to ceremonial and religious rites in the islands where it is consumed. With the introduction of Christianity and changes in traditional patterns of life, *kava* has become more commonly associated with festivals and socializing, though it has been adapted to certain religious practices in the introduced religions.

There is a clear physiological effect arising from the consumption of *kava*. Immediately upon consuming *kava*, a sense of relaxation begins to take over. Drinkers of *kava* often remark the immediate sense of numbness found in the lips or face. It affects the sensory system and has a relaxing effect on the muscles. Observers and consumers of *kava* note that a small quantity initially manifests a short euphoric state followed by a relaxed feeling. There is none of the excitement that is associated with alcohol, and because the mental alertness of the person is not adversely affected, relaxed conversation often results from drinking *kava*. Many note that the drinker of *kava* is tranquil and friendly, and generally seems difficult to annoy or bother.

The physiological effect of tranquility and relaxation led to its being associated with divine inspiration and openness to the transcendent. It was seen as a way for recently dead chiefs, gods, or other significant ancestors to communicate through a priest or chief who had consumed *kava*. *Kava* would also be used to invoke the gods to identify one committing a transgression if there was little chance of identifying the transgressor. A small amount of *kava* would be poured out prior to consumption with a prayer asking for the *kava* to be filled with *mana* (a certain power believed to come from a deity or an ancestor) to identify the transgressor. A small knot would be placed in the *kava* with the belief that the culprit would end up with the knot in his *kava* cup.

Many of the religious beliefs associated with *kava* have changed with the introduction of other religious traditions, primarily Christianity. The conversion of many islanders to Christianity has brought with it a different framework for articulating and relating to the divine. As a result, many of the religious beliefs linked with *kava* have changed. The result is a transition from the original religious meaning of *kava* drinking to more of a "socioreligious" or "politico-religious" ritual.

Beyond the changes in the consumption of *kava* as a link to the divine, some islands have lost touch with their traditional practice of *kava* drinking altogether. This decline in *kava* drinking is often linked with missionaries who brought Christianity to the islands and found drinking *kava* to be improper behavior for Christians. These were often religions that associated *kava* drinking with alcohol consumption and found them equally inconsistent with a holy life. For example, in Micronesia, this was particularly true of Kosrae, which shared a tradition of *sakau* drinking with neighboring Pohnpei, but eventually disavowed the practice owing to the Christianization of the island.

In more recent years, one of the more significant changes has been brought about by the migration of Pacific Islanders to other parts of the Pacific and the world, and the transformation of many island economies from subsistence to cash economies. One of the impacts of migration is an increase in the amount of *kava* produced for export to be brought to islands or nations where *kava* is not normally consumed. The transformation to cash economies has resulted in many *kava* bars opening on islands alongside typical alcohol bars for businessmen, politicians, and others to spend time after work or in the evenings to discuss important matters over a few glasses of one of the favorite drinks of the islands. These bars have even begun to spring up in locations far from the Pacific Islands where either there are concentrations of immigrant populations from *kava*-drinking peoples, or where someone has introduced *kava* as a drink for socializing or medicinal purposes.

Beliefs and Practices

Kava is a central part of the cultural practices of many Polynesian, Micronesian, and Melanesian island communities. At its most informal, it is shared by groups of people in the evenings as they sit around and talk. *Kava* was traditionally consumed only by men, although this has begun to change in recent decades with women participating more freely in the drinking of *kava*. *Kava* drinking is a central symbol of community and signifies a link to the cultural past of the community. In many cultures, the meaning of the ceremonies has begun to change or be lost, but they are still practiced.

Kava often represents a gift presented to the person being called on when one visits a neighbor, friend, or relative. Here the *kava* root is presented by the visitor and prepared by those being visited. If no *kava* root is brought, it is usually offered by those being visited, and if none is available, profuse apologies are given for not being able to provide *kava* for the guest. *Kava* is thus part of even the most basic level of relationships among members of the community.

Beyond the informal interactions during which *kava* is often consumed, it is also used for formalizing relationships or contracts, including during celebratory occasions. Engagements, weddings, funerals, winning prizes, giving titles all involve formal *kava* ceremonies. It would also be offered as a gift or peace offering when a crime or violation has been committed against another person, family, tribe, or chief, and even as a an act of begging forgiveness or to remove curses believed to result from violating supernatural prohibitions.

The traditional religious uses for *kava* were related to the presence of the spirit or gods. The first was to make an offering to the gods as a part of the ceremony or appeasement. The pouring out of the first cup of *kava* onto the ground is a sign of respect, often after a prayer or a word of officially offering the cup to the gods. The pouring of the *kava* onto the ground could be understood as an act of acknowledging the presence of and the people's respect for the spirit or gods.

Acknowledging the presence of the spirit or gods led to a desire to be connected to the spirit or gods. Connecting involved a spiritual openness, which was associated with the consumption of *kava*. Typically, drinking *kava* was seen as a preliminary to inspiration. Since the *kava* ceremony was often linked with communication with the sacred, the feeling of relaxation brought about by *kava* consumption without inhibiting one's mental awareness allowed one to commune with the gods and communicate their messages to the community.

In several of the Polynesian Islands, a particular structure of the ritual expresses its social and religious dimensions. The community would sit in an oval with the chief at one of the oblong ends and the *kava* table opposite the chief. The individual who mixes the *kava* occupies an important role in the community and sits with the *kava* table opposite the chief. The chief usually does not speak, but rather has another person who sits to his right who speaks for him. If the chief wishes to say something, he shares it with his speaker, who then relays the message to the community.

The serving of the *kava* drink begins with the chief and then proceeds around the table; it is usually served by several women. In some instances, the passing of *kava* follows very rigid guidelines and procedures. This was particularly important because the chief was believed to represent the ancestors and gods of the community, and thus he was the manifestation of the spirit world. As the presence of the spirit being at a ceremony, the chief was also the mediator of communication and the one through whom those at the ceremony would communicate with ancestors or the gods. Following the ritual was thus essential for ensuring communication with the sacred. Thus, the use of the speaker instead of the chief speaking himself helped to ensure and symbolize the chief as the mediator of spirits and the ancestors.

The physiological effect of tranquility and relaxation led to *kava* drinking's association with divine inspiration and openness to the transcendent. It was seen as a way for recently dead chiefs, gods, or other significant ancestors to communicate through a priest or chief who had consumed *kava*. *Kava* would also be used to invoke the gods to identify one committing a transgression if there was little chance of identifying the transgressor. A small amount of *kava* would be poured out prior to consumption with a prayer asking for the *kava* to identify the transgressor. A small knot would be placed in the *kava* with the belief that the culprit would end up with the knot in his *kava* cup.

In several Polynesian islands, *kava* was always included in food brought to the graves of those who passed away, a ritual often maintained for several years with a cup poured onto the location of the grave every six months. However, others would only pour it until such time as they determined the spirit had moved on from the area of the grave. In both instances, *kava* was seen as a gift to be brought to ancestors and the world of the spirits.

Kava remains closely aligned with reconciliation and festival ceremonies, as well as traditional rites and ceremonials. Some of these have been incorporated into the ever-changing political and social systems and as a result have become increasingly social in function. However, many of the traditional ceremonies have been modified or Christianized and integrated with the foreign practices and systems to help the changes maintain a connection to the indigenous culture. Thomas McGrath provides an insight into the relationship between the traditional function of *kava* in seeking forgiveness with the Roman Catholic tradition of penance or reconciliation in Pohnpei, Micronesia.

The traditional request for reconciliation to the *Nanmwarki* (traditional chief along one line of authority in Pohnpei) involves asking the *Nankin* (the chief along the other line of authority in Pohnpei) or one of his kin to intercede. When the person is identified, the *kava* plant is picked. The *kava* is then prepared, placed in a cup, and presented to the *Nanmwarki*. He will ask what the cup is for, and the intercessor will explain. If the *Nanmwarki* drinks the cup, forgiveness is given. If not, another cup of *kava* will be prepared and presented. This continues until the *Nanmwarki* forgives the transgressor.

The process for reconciling with the *Nanmwarki* in Pohnpei has been adapted to communal reconciliation with the Roman Catholic tradition. The ritual involves 10 individuals—four men to pound the *kava*, a cup bearer, a *kava* bearer (who carries the plant), a cross bearer, two candle bearers, and the priest—as part of the procession with the community already seated in the church. All but the *kava* bearer proceed into the church. After some initial prayers and a reading, the *kava* bearer is led into the church. The *kava* is then prepared and a cup presented to the priest. Here the priest, like the *Nanmwarki*, asks what the cup is for. Upon being told, the priest turns to the altar, prays to God for forgiveness, and then he consumes the *kava* as a sign that God extends his forgiveness to the community. The cross bearer then consumes a cup in the name of the whole community. The community then recites prayers of penance and prayers of absolution are offered. Through this ritual, the traditional role of *kava* in reconciliation has been adapted to reconciliation within the Roman Catholic tradition.

Michael J. Liberatore

See also: Entries: Aloha Spirit; Pacific Islander Religious Cultures; Tongan Spirituality

Further Reading

Deihl, Joseph. "*Kava* and *Kava* Drinking." *Anthropological Quarterly* 5, no. 1 (1932): 61–68. Online at http://kavaroot.com/History/Deihl_AnthroQ.htm.

Feldman, Harry. "Informal *Kava* Drinking in Tonga." *Journal of Polynesian Society* 89, no. 1 (March 1980): 101–103. Online at http://kavaroot.com/Geography/Tonga/FeldmanTonga.html.

Harrison, Tom. *Savage Civilisation*. London: Victor Gollancz, 1937.

Leach, Edmund. "The Structure of Symbolism." In J. S. LaFontaine, ed. *The Interpretation of Ritual*. London: Tavistock, 1972, pp. 239–75.

Lemert, Edwin. "Secular Use of *Kava* in Tonga." *Quarterly Journal of Studies on Alcohol* 28 (1967): 328–41.

Lester, R. H. "*Kava* Drinking in Vitilevu, Fiji." *Oceania* 12 (1941): 97–121.

Lester, R. H. "*Kava* Drinking in Vitilevu, Fiji." *Oceania* 12 (1942): 226–254.

McGrath, Thomas B. "Sakau in Towm. Sarawi in Towm." *Oceania* 44, no. 1 (September 1973): 64–67.

Newell, W. H. "*Kava* Ceremony in Tonga." *The Journal of the Polynesian Society* 56, no. 4 (1947): 364–417.

Peterson, Glenn. "The Complexity of Power, the Subtlety of *Kava*: Pohnpei's Sakau." *Canberra Anthropology* 18 (1995): 34–60.

Pratt, M. A. Rugby. "A *Kava* Ceremony in Tonga." *The Journal of the Polynesian Society* 31, no. 124 (1922): 198–201.

Steinmetz, E. F. *Kava-Kava: Famous Drug Plant of the South Sea Islands*. San Francisco: High Times, Level Press, 1973.

Tomlinson, Matt. "Perpetual Lament: *Kava*-Drinking, Christianity and Sensations of Historical Decline in Fiji." *Journal of the Royal Anthropological Institute* 10 (2004): 653–73.

Turner, James W. "'The Water of Life': *Kava* Ritual and the Logic of Sacrifice." *Ethnology* 25, no. 3 (July 1986): 203–14.

Konkōkyō/The Konko Faith

Konkōkyō (the Konko faith) is a belief system characterized by an accepting and nonjudgmental view of humanity. It teaches belief in a divine parent (called *Tenchi Kane No Kami*) who is the life and energy of the universe—indeed *is* the universe—as well as a loving parent who wishes only the happiness and well-being of all human beings, the children. "Kami" is the term most frequently used for this entity. A core teaching of Konkōkyō is that Kami and humans exist in a relationship of interdependence or "mutual fulfillment" known as *aiyokakeyo*: Kami fulfills humanity and humanity fulfills Kami. In this relationship, humans are exhorted to cultivate an attitude of sincere gratitude for Kami's blessings received daily, both large and small. This principle of *aiyokakeyo* encompasses the fundamental nature and workings of the universe, which includes the dynamic, synergistic, and loving relationship between Kami and humanity.

By extension, human beings also exist in relationships of mutual dependence with each other and with the larger social and natural world. They are therefore encouraged to help each other and take care of the world they live in. Other notable features of Konkōkyō include respect for and appreciation of other belief systems, an absence of rigid dogma, and a personalized, customized approach to advising individuals and ministering to believers. Realizing happiness, peace of mind, and divine blessings by living in harmony with Kami, as well as helping others to do so—these are important spiritual goals for a Konko believer.

Historical Developments

Konkōkyō was founded in rural Japan in 1859, a decade before the Meiji Restoration that launched Japan into the modern world. Its founder was a farmer named Kawate Bunji (1814–1883) who lived in what is now Okayama Prefecture, located approximately 200 kilometers west of Osaka. (*Note:* Names in this entry are in customary Japanese order, family name first.) He is described as having been devout even as a child, visiting shrines and temples and praying to the myriad deities, buddhas, and guardian spirits that populated the religious landscape of mid-19th-century Japan. He was not in the best of health growing up, but he survived a number of ailments and succeeded to the headship of his adoptive family in his early twenties. He had always been a hard worker, and the farm prospered; he ranked among the 10 most prosperous landowners in a village of 130 households. However, he also encountered a succession of tragedies—the deaths of three children in their infancy, the loss of two oxen (critical for farming), and, at age 42, a life-threatening illness that affected his throat and left him unable to speak or take nourishment.

Religious beliefs in Japan at that time consisted of a syncretic mixture of Buddhism (various sects), "shrine Shintō" (festivals and rituals centered on local shrines, local deities, and the cycle of the seasons), and a wide range of folk beliefs and superstitions that had come to Japan from the Asian continent and become rooted in the daily lives of the people. Prominent among them was the belief in various calendar and directional taboos referred to as the "Days and Directions": certain days and directions were not good for certain activities because of the presence of a deity of misfortune called Konjin. Bunji followed accepted practices of the day to maneuver around these taboos but was still plagued by misfortunes.

When Bunji fell ill, some around him thought that his difficulties stemmed from Konjin's anger at a violation of these taboos; others protested that he had followed the applicable rules. Listening to this exchange as he lay ill and unable to speak, Bunji was struck by the realization that he might indeed have behaved irreverently toward Konjin, even if unintentionally. In that instant, according to his memoirs, he felt his throat clear and he apologized wholeheartedly. He then heard the voice of the deity saying that he would be saved because of the depth of his sincerity and faith. Bunji recovered.

Through this experience and many other encounters with the divine, Bunji came to learn that Konjin was not a fearsome deity of misfortune, but rather a benevolent one—a far cry from prevailing beliefs. After this revelation, Bunji began to refer to the deity as Kane No Kami, a different reading of the same kanji characters as for "Konjin." Later, this was further changed to Tenchi Kane No Kami. (The Konkōkyō crest is the single character *kon* or *kane* in a circle surrounded by eight stylized waves.)

We are told that through direct communication with Kami, Bunji received instructions and advice for farming and myriad other activities. Following these instructions, which often went against prevailing wisdom, resulted in many blessings for Bunji and his family, for which he expressed even greater gratitude. As his relationship with Kami deepened, he also received a succession of religious titles from the deity. The last of these is the basis for the name by which he is known today, Konkō Daijin.

People soon noticed Bunji's pious attitude and good fortune and started coming to him for guidance. He would listen with compassion, pray intently, relay their problems and requests to Kami, then communicate Kami's message back. This was the start of *toritsugi* mediation, a central practice in Konkōkyō that continues today (see Practices section).

As more and more people were helped by this *toritsugi* mediation, the number of visitors coming to seek guidance increased, making it necessary for Bunji to constantly interrupt his farming to go back to his house and pray for them. Finally, it is said, Kami asked that Bunji give up farming altogether and devote himself full time to helping both people and Kami through *toritsugi* mediation. The day Bunji received this "divine call" to start a new life as intermediary between Kami and humanity is considered the founding date of Konkōkyō: November 15, 1859. Thereafter, the founder sat next to the simple altar he had constructed in the front room of his house and received seekers individually. So many people were helped by this *toritsugi* mediation that Konkō Daijin soon gained a large following, with his house becoming a worship hall.

Such activities were bound to attract notice; and the founder and early believers were plagued by unfounded rumors and friction with other religious groups, in particular the so-called mountain priests (*yamabushi*) who on several occasions attacked the worship hall and destroyed property. There was also the problem of a farmer—Bunji—not farming and instead behaving like a priest or monk and dispensing spiritual advice without formal credentials. In the strictly controlled and hierarchical society that was Tokugawa Japan, this was not allowed. To avoid persecution and suppression by the authorities, Konkō Daijin applied for and received certification as a "shrine Shintō" priest in 1867. However, in the very next year, 1868, the old Tokugawa *shogunate* came to an end, the new Meiji government was established, and all such certifications were revoked.

From the beginning, the Meiji government sought to use Shintō to unify the country under the rule of the emperor. Thus was born "state Shintō" (as opposed to "shrine Shintō"), an institution that fostered nationalism, was used to justify Japan's imperialism, and held sway until the country's defeat in World War II. Konkō Daijin had an opportunity to obtain certification again as a Shintō priest under this new structure, but he refused, because he would have had to preach the tenets of state Shintō. In 1873, the Meiji government passed a law suppressing what it considered superstitious practices. Konkō Daijin was ordered to take down the altar in his Worship Hall and stop teaching his followers, because he was not officially recognized as a member of the Shintō priesthood.

This was a particularly dark time for Konkōkyō and its early believers. Unable to seek guidance from their beloved founder or to pray at the altar, and forbidden to propagate their faith, they were sustained by a revelation received by Konkō Daijin on April 11, 1873: the *Tenchi Kakitsuke*. Konkō Daijin wrote down the words of the revelation, as directed by Kami, and gave copies to his followers.

This revelation served as a reminder to the faithful that, even if they were deprived of the presence of Konkō Daijin, of the Worship Hall, and of the comfort of *toritsugi* mediation, they would not be deprived of Kami's blessings, for these were to be found in their own hearts and attitudes. As the core revelation of the faith, the *Tenchi Kakitsuke* continues to hold a central place in Konkōkyō faith practice, services, and prayer. With the easing of some government restrictions shortly after these events, Konkō Daijin was able to resume his activities in the worship hall, praying, performing *toritsugi* mediation, and ministering to seekers.

Konkō Daijin passed away on October 10, 1883, and was succeeded by his fifth son Ieyoshi, known as Konkō Shijin. The faith continued to spread in Japan during the 10 years of his headship, south to Kyushu and north to Hokkaido. In 1885, Konkōkyō gained official recognition as a sect of Shintō. In 1893 began the long, 70-year stewardship of the third spiritual leader, Konkō Setsutane, who was the grandson of the founder. He succeeded at the age of 13 and spent his entire life ministering to believers who flocked to the main Worship Hall, conducting *toritsugi* mediation for each. The year 1900 saw the official independence of Konkōkyō as an organization, though it was still registered as one of 13 "official" sects of Shintō.

The seven decades under Setsutane's headship, 1893 through 1963, were years of tremendous change and turmoil in Japanese society as well as the world. It was also the period during which Konkōkyō experienced its greatest growth. By the time of Setsutane's death in 1963, there were over 1,600 churches and nearly 4,000 ministers. At its peak, its followers were estimated to have numbered nearly two million in Japan. While many factors no doubt contributed to this growth, many attribute it to the character, personality, and deeply compelling spirituality of Konkō Setsutane himself. He was succeeded by his son Konkō Kagamitarō, who was followed in turn by his son Konkō Heiki in 1991.

Overseas propagation of Konkōkyō had also started under Setsutane; 1919 saw the formation of the first two associations of Konko believers in Seattle, followed by the establishment of the Konko Church of Seattle in 1928—the first Konko church in North America. Propagation in Hawai'i and in Los Angeles started in 1926 with the formation of believers' groups. By the start of World War II there were seven churches on the west coast of the United States and two in Hawai'i. The ministers of the churches in the continental United States, viewed as leaders of the Japanese American community, were all detained by the U.S. government as enemy aliens during World War II. Most spent the war years in federal detention separated from their families, who were themselves interned in 10 War Relocation Centers/concentration camps for the duration of the war.

After the war, Japanese American churches and temples of all faiths gradually re-established themselves in their prewar communities as well as in new locations. Four more Konko churches were established in Hawai'i, and two more in the continental United States. Two churches were established in Canada as well. Finally, the churches on the continent were incorporated as the Konko Churches of North America (KCNA) in 1969, and 1971 saw the incorporation of the Konko Missions in Hawai'i (KMH). Four more churches have been added in recent years for a total of 15 in North America.

Konkōkyō is also found in other parts of the world. Brazil has seven churches and a propagation hall, and there has been a Konkōkyō Activities Center in Asunción, Paraguay, since 1996. There is also a Konkōkyō Seoul Activity Center and faith gatherings in Europe. It is estimated that followers of Konkōkyō currently number approximately 400,000 worldwide.

Beliefs

Konkōkyō is a belief system that focuses on helping individuals to attain happiness and peace of mind in their daily lives through an appreciation of their relationship with Kami. It does not attempt to answer such questions as how or why the universe was created, what are the details of the afterlife, or the "problem of evil." Konkōkyō is concerned with this life and with helping people to find solutions for their problems through the teachings of the founder. Principal beliefs are described below.

As mentioned in the Introduction, Konkōkyō teaches belief in a deity called Tenchi Kane No Kami (or Kami), who is described somewhat impersonally as "the universe," its life, forms, and energy. At the same time, Kami is also described as a loving parent whose earnest wish is for everyone's happiness and well-being. This is one of several profound mysteries at the heart of the Konko faith. Believers are encouraged to develop an intimate, personal relationship with this divine parent, always looking to Kami, conversing with Kami through prayer and *toritsugi* mediation, becoming "one with Kami." The divinity that is worshipped in Konkōkyō is therefore both the impersonal universe—earth, the heavenly bodies, the forces of nature, physical laws both known and as yet undiscovered—as well as a very personal, caring, and nonjudgmental deity who is the ideal loving parent, both mother and father.

The parent-child model may help explain another mystery of Konkōkyō, the teaching that humans exist in a relationship of interdependence or "mutual fulfillment" (*aiyokakeyo*) with Kami, as already mentioned. Believers are taught that human beings certainly need Kami, as children need their parents, but Kami needs them as well and is dependent on their happiness and well-being to be fulfilled as Kami, as the divine parent. The analogy—though imperfect—is that, in an ideal familial relationship, human parents are emotionally and psychologically fulfilled as parents by the happiness, well-being, and love of their children.

There is an important corollary to this principle of *aiyokakeyo*, namely, that human beings also exist in a relationship of interdependence with each other and also with nature. People are therefore called upon to look after one another and care for the human and natural world around them.

Furthermore, the personal, parental deity of Konkōkyō is not an "other" who is external to and separate from the individual. All humans are born with a part of Kami within them, and one of the goals of followers of Konkōkyō is to bring to life this divinity within. The goal of believers is not to "go to heaven" or to be otherwise rewarded in the afterlife. Rather, it is to awaken the *kami* or divinity that is already within them and to live a life consistent with their mutually dependent relationship with the divine parent and with the human and natural world.

An important manifestation of the divine parent's love for humanity is the concept of *okage*, or blessings. There are grand blessings on a large scale, such as the very fact of life itself; others may seem mundane and often taken for granted, such as being able to eat when hungry. Some may seem small at first but turn out to be quite significant; others may not seem to be blessings at first—quite the contrary, in fact—yet turn out to be life-changing. Believers are encouraged to cultivate an "attitude of gratitude," to realize blessings in every aspect of life. They are also taught to pray earnestly and sincerely to Kami in gratitude for blessings and to ask for continuing divine favors.

Belief in the power of prayer to realize blessings—provided it is based on the right attitude—is fundamental to Konkōkyō. Believers are taught that if they pray selflessly, with gratitude, humility, and sincerity, the prayer will be answered and blessings granted, though maybe not in the manner requested. There are also stories told of miraculous cures of illness after sincere, intense prayer by the minister and/or the believer. A less dramatic, though no less important, benefit of prayer is the peace of mind that believers report when they pray wholeheartedly, do their best, and then trust the outcome to Kami. Ultimately, the goal of prayer is said to be a state of mind in which the believer is in a continuous conversation with Kami—constantly aware of Kami, grateful for even the smallest blessing, and becoming one with Kami.

As to the source of these blessings, Kami is of course the ultimate source. Yet, paradoxically, blessings are also to be found within people's own hearts. This is the profound message of the *Tenchi Kakitsuke*, the revelation that encapsulates the core teachings of Konkōkyō. The *Tenchi Kakitsuke* exhorts believers to "Pray sincerely, with all your heart" to Tenchi Kane No Kami; at the same time, "Kami's blessings begin within / Hearts grateful and caring, in harmony and joy." That is, blessings both come from Kami and already reside within the believer's heart, a heart that is joyful and grateful, cares about others, and exists in harmony with Kami and the world.

While the focus of Konkōkyō is more on this life than on the details of the afterlife, it does teach that the spirit lives on after death. Humans are born with bodies from nature and spirits from Kami. Upon death, the body returns to nature and the spirit to Kami. The spirits of those who have passed away are called *mitama*, and they continue to intercede with Kami on behalf of those who call on them. For many believers, the idea that a beloved relative or friend who has died is still with them, though unseen, and will help them navigate the many vicissitudes of life—this is a most comforting teaching. Those who have small altars at home will often display photographs of such loved ones and pray to and for their *mitama* spirits as part of their daily prayer routine. This honoring of and looking to the deceased is a characteristic shared by many belief systems in the world. The founder's *mitama*, his "eternal spirit" called Ikigami Konkō Daijin, holds a special place in the faith, second only to that of Tenchi Kane No Kami. In fact, many believers pray to Tenchi Kane No Kami through Ikigami Konkō Daijin.

Another feature of the Konko faith is a great tolerance of other belief systems. This is not unusual in Japan, which has not had the history of religious strife that has plagued many other parts of the world. But given the world we live in today, Konkōkyō's welcoming stance toward other faiths is a characteristic worth mentioning.

Konkōkyō also has few specific, absolute rules. Believers are exhorted to pray with true sincerity, to apologize for irreverences, and to give thanks for blessings. They are further encouraged to be continuously aware of Kami, of the workings of Kami in their daily lives, and of what is expected of them in their mutually dependent relationships with Kami and the human and natural world around them. Beyond that, however, if asked specific questions about appropriate behavior, a minister may give very different, even seemingly contradictory, advice to two people with similar problems. This absence of dogmatism and absolutes—a positive characteristic for many believers—also makes it challenging to explain Konkōkyō succinctly and, by extension, to propagate it. For some believers, it is frustrating that a faith that in their view is so open-minded, inclusive, and positive in its approach and teachings also has difficulty expanding its reach precisely because of these qualities.

Practices

Central to the practice of the Konko faith is *toritsugi* mediation, in which a believer asks a minister to intercede with Tenchi Kane No Kami on his or her behalf, to act as a kind of "go-between." The request may be related to something consequential, such as a serious illness or a difficult personal relationship. It may be more mundane, such as a request for prayers for a safe journey. Some requests for *toritsugi* mediation may be to give thanks for the positive outcome of a previous request. In every case, the minister's duty is to listen compassionately, pray on the believer's behalf, and provide guidance and/or comfort, as appropriate. In doing so, the minister calls on his or her understanding of the teachings as well as on the support of the eternal spirit of the founder, Ikigami Konkō Daijin.

This very individualized way of ministering to people extends to the head of the Konko faith. Thousands of believers travel to Konkōkyō headquarters annually and are able to access directly the spiritual leader of the faith, referred to as Konkō-sama. The current leader is the great-great-grandson of the founder. Most, though not all, Konko churches in Japan are also handed down within the minister's family.

While this was also the practice earlier in North America, it is less so today.

Although individual *toritsugi* mediation is at the heart of Konko faith practice, churches also hold regular services, generally followed by fellowship and the sharing of a meal. In spring and autumn, there are special memorial services dedicated to *mitama*, the spirits of those who have died. Another service in spring is designated the Tenchi Kane No Kami Grand Ceremony honoring Kami; in fall, the Ikigami Konkō Daijin Grand Ceremony honors the eternal spirit of the founder.

Believers make offerings to express gratitude for *toritsugi* mediation or for blessings received, as well as on the occasion of a service. In the case of monetary offerings, there is no designated amount, not even a "suggested donation." It is entirely up to the individual and what she or he feels moved to give.

Many external elements of Konkōkyō reflect its early association with Shintō. For example, the vestments and headgear worn by ministers during services, as well as the wooden staff they hold, are very similar to those used by Shintō priests. In other respects, Shintō elements have been modified or adapted for use in Konkōkyō ritual. In the Konkō faith, the start and end of prayers is marked by four hand claps; visitors to Shintō shrines typically clap twice. For every service, the Konkōkyō minister prepares a special written prayer that is read aloud in solemn tones. This is similar to Shintō practice.

Since the postwar years, Konkōkyō has been shedding the external trappings of Shintō. One of the most important of such changes has been the replacement of the old prayers, which had been taken verbatim from Shintō ritual and echoed passages from ancient Japanese texts. They did not convey Konkōkyō teachings or beliefs very well. The new prayers, which are more closely aligned with Konkōkyō beliefs, came into common use in North American churches in the 1980s. Some North American churches include the older prayers to this day. New, original prayers and practices continue to be created to reflect the needs of a heterogeneous North American society.

Conclusion

Konkōkyō was one of several belief systems that were founded in mid-19th-century Japan and whose early, formative years coincided with the turbulent decades of the late Tokugawa and early Meiji periods. Being a relatively young belief system, it has not yet had the kind of thoroughgoing discussion and debate about its teachings and role in the world that older religious traditions have had. It has also been bound geographically and culturally to Japan for most of its first hundred years. Nevertheless, it continues to evolve as an institution and faith community in Japan, North America, and elsewhere, its goal being to expand beyond its ethnic roots and serve the spiritual needs of all. It will be interesting to see how the Konko faith navigates its way beyond the Japanese immigrant and Japanese American communities and adapts its messages to a very different culture from that of its birthplace.

Material Resource Committee
Konko Churches of North America

Further Reading

Fukuda, Yoshiaki. *Live with Faith: Being a Konko Believer*. San Francisco: Konko Church of San Francisco, 2007. English translation; originally published in Japanese as *Shinja no Kokoroe*, 1958.

Konko Daijin: A Biography. San Francisco: Konko Churches of America, 1981.

Konko Kyo's 50 Years in America. San Francisco: Konko Churches of America and Konko Missions in Hawai'i, 1976.

Konkōkyō Kyōten [Konkōkyō Scriptures]. 5 vols. Tokyo: Konkōkyō Headquarters, 1987.

Konkōkyō Website. www.konkokyo.or.jp/eng. Accessed July 14, 2014.

Prayer Book. Tokyo: Konkōkyō Headquarters, 2010.

Shine from Within. Tokyo: Konkōkyō, n.d.

Voice of the Universe: Selected Teachings of Konkōkyō. Tokyo: Konkōkyō Headquarters, 1996.

Korean American Religions

Korean Americans number approximately 1.5 million persons for whom religion, primarily Protestant Christianity, arguably has been the most salient feature of their experience as a community. Korean Americans have been in the United States for over a century, and their history is marked by three waves of migration: Labor, Picture Brides, and Independence (1903–1945); Post–World War II Period (1945–1965); and Post-1965 Period (1965–present). Throughout their history, Korean Americans have experienced migration within a transnational context marked by colonialism and exile. Religion, as it has manifested itself through institutions, ideas, and practices, has been

Korean American members of the Korean Evangelical Church pose for a picture, May 26, 2014, at the start of the 96th Staten Island Memorial Day parade in Staten Island, New York. (Robert Nickelsberg/Getty Images)

a critical framework by which Korean Americans have given shape to their times. The structures and sensibilities of religion have provided its adherents with vital social services, racial-ethnic spaces, and a source of faith and meaning. Survey data suggest that there are over 3,000 Korean Protestant churches, 154 Roman Catholic parishes, and 89 Buddhist temples in the United States. While figures vary, 80 percent of Korean Americans are affiliated with Protestant ethnic churches, 11 percent with Roman Catholicism, 5 percent with Buddhism, and 4 percent with other or no religion. Koreans in the United States—past and present—have been deeply influenced by the dominance, di-versity, and at times, divisiveness of religious experience.

Labor and Independence (1903–1945)

The first wave of Korean men and women, numbering approximately 10,000 persons, entered the United States beginning in 1903 largely as a labor force for sugar cane plantations. Religion played an important role from the very start as recruiters for American companies in Korea called upon Protestant missionaries in Korea to persuade those in their care to make the journey to the islands. As a result, Protestant Christians were among the first

Korean Americans to venture to the United States, and approximately 40 percent of the early community claimed to be Christian. Congregations on the plantations, in Honolulu as well as on the mainland, quickly became the gathering place for Korean Americans, serving as clearinghouses of information and social services. Churches also provided spaces, under the umbrella of religion, to explore a wide range of issues, including their status as racial-ethnic minorities in the United States and their role in the transnational independence movement to free Korea from Japanese colonial rule. Key immigrant/expatriate leaders such as Ahn Chang-ho (1886–1939) and Syngman Rhee (1875–1965) all were influenced by the reform-minded ideas based in the Christian institutions (schools, hospitals, churches) that had helped form their worldviews. Moreover, Korean Americans looked to religion for a sense of meaning amidst the often harsh realities of life and labor that they encountered. At the same time, religion could also be the source of division as churches and religious organizations were enmeshed in the politics of community. For better and worse, religion, represented in the mix of the theological, cultural, political, and social, infused the lives of the majority of Korean Americans.

Postwar Period (1945–1965)

Approximately 14,000 persons—Korean wives of American servicemen and their children, adoptees, and professional workers and students—arrived during the second wave of migration, marked by the end of World War II and Japanese colonialism and Cold War politics that resulted in the Korean War (1950–1953) and a divided peninsula. Ties to the United States via the military and educational and church-related institutions provided some Koreans a means of starting new lives in America. The presence of immigrant churches established during the first wave of migration offered students an opportunity to find a form of community even as Korean military wives and adoptees represented a different trajectory of migration and settlement.

1965–Present

The passage of new immigration legislation by the United States in 1965 removed restrictive and discriminatory measures that had been firmly in place for close to five decades. Korean immigrants, along with others from Asia as well as Latin America, entered the United States in increasingly larger numbers, and at the peak in the mid-1980s, figures for Korean Americans topped 30,000 persons per year. This influx transformed smaller, historic Korean American communities in urban settings such as Los Angeles and New York, and these newer immigrants make up the majority of the million or so Korean Americans in the country today. The boom in the population has been accompanied by a literal explosion of immigrant churches, temples, and other religious organizations. This largely Protestant phenomenon in part reflects the growth and spread of Protestant Christianity in Korea, but it is also clear that many men and women have affiliated with churches after their arrival in the United States.

Religion continues to be the heart of this racial-ethnic community, informing the daily lives of men and women in the midst of the pressures of economic survival and sociocultural adjustments set into motion by the migration and settlement process. At the same time, religion has also been part of a transnationalism aided by communication and transportation technologies that have facilitated the movement of people, goods, and ideas. Religion has been very much part of this exchange, and institutions range from small, house-based groups to mega-churches that rival any religious organization in the country in terms of membership, programming, and resources. Religion has continued to play a critical social service function for Korean Americans, creating webs of relationships that attend to a host of needs that immigrants face. That religious and racial-ethnic space has been intertwined has also been important for Korean Americans, as it has been for so many other immigrant groups throughout our collective history. Religious institutions have offered psychic and physical space within which individuals and communities can affirm traditions and customs from the home country, even while wrestling with the changes and conflict that can be engendered by new settings. As a source of faith and meaning and as a locus of ritual and spiritual practice, religion is a powerful and enduring influence in the lives of the diversity that is Korean America—from attending services in churches and temples to the less institu-tional, more popular forms of devotion and ritual activities.

Perhaps the defining moment of the post-1965 period was the 1992 Los Angeles riots/uprising. The ways that this event and its related issues have been refracted through the religious landscape of Korean America—from joint services with African American congregations to community assistance programs to apathy, denial, and neglect—suggest that while religion has been and continues to be at the core of this community, its nature is by no means uniform. Second-generation, English-speaking Korean American, pan-Asian American, and multiracial/ethnic institutions signal the maturation and diversification of a post-1965 community.

David K. Yoo

See also: Entries: Han; Korean Buddhism; Korean Shamanism

Further Reading

Choy, Bong-Youn. *Koreans in America*. Chicago: Nelson-Hall, 1979.

Hurh, Won Moo. *The Korean Americans*. Westport, CT: Greenwood Press, 1998.

Kim, Elaine. *Sa-I-Gu*. 1993. Film.

Lee, Mary Paik. *Quiet Odyssey: A Pioneer Korean Woman in America*. Seattle: University of Washington Press, 1990.

Yoo, David K., and Ruth H. Chung, eds. *Religion and Spirituality in Korean America*. Chicago: University of Illinois Press, 2008.

Korean Buddhism

The first Korean immigrants—56 men, 21 women, and 25 children—arrived in the territory of Hawai'i on the RMS *Gaelic* on

January 13, 1903. By 1905 the Korean immigrant population had swelled to 7,843. Unlike the Chinese, Japanese, and Okinawans, who were farmers, most of the Koreans were urbanites from seaport towns. The men were recruited as strike breakers against the plantation agricultural workers who were demanding higher wages and better working conditions. Like their East Asian cohorts, most did not intend to settle permanently, but to return after earning their fortunes. Immigration slowed with the informal Gentlemen's Agreement of 1907 between the United States and the empire of Japan, the latter of which then declared Korea a protectorate in 1907 and annexed the country in 1910. In the meantime, until the U.S. government passed and implemented the 1924 Oriental Exclusion Act, approximately 800 Korean picture brides made their way to Hawai'i. Immigration resumed in mid-century with the arrival of Korean brides of American servicemen and orphans as a result of the Korean War (1950–1953). Immigration accelerated with the passage of the Immigration Act of 1965. The experiences of the descendants of pre-1924 immigrants and their American-born descendants are markedly different from the more recent immigrants, especially those arriving after the mid-1960s. The 2010 U.S. Census reported 1.7 million persons who self-identify themselves as Koreans.

History: Korea

Buddhism entered the Korean peninsula during the period when three kingdoms—Koguryŏ, Paekche, and Silla— contested for power. Koguryŏ officially recognized Buddhism in 372 and Paekche in 384. Silla embraced Buddhism in 529, only after some aristocrats were convinced of its power by witnessing the miraculous outflowing of white, not red, blood from a beheaded Buddhist supporter. The ancient Koreans were impressed with Buddhism's comprehensive and rational explanation of the world, the vast store of new knowledge possessed by its clerics, and the pantheon of deities who wielded potent powers that could protect the state. The succeeding Unified Silla (668–935) and Koryŏ (918–1392) dynasties adopted Buddhism as a state ideology. During this time Korean Buddhism modeled itself after the comprehensive and syncretistic vision of Chinese Huayan and Tiantai.

A review of the treatises produced by Korean scholar-monks reveals that they were actively participating in the doctrinal developments of the many strands of Buddhist thought current during the Tang dynasty (618–907) and Song dynasty (970–1279). Among these were Samnon (Ch. Sanlun), Kyeyul (Skt. Vinaya), and Yŏlban (Skt. *Nirvāṇa*). Korean monks and intellectuals were particularly interested in Huayan and Chan. Most notable was Wŏnhyo (617–686), who composed more than 100 treatises and commentaries, of which about 20 remain. He is perhaps one of the most prolific and profound thinkers of Korean Buddhism. His commentaries on the *Taesŭng Kisillon* (*Awakening of Faith in Mahāyāna*), *Taesŭng Kisillon-so* (*Commentary on the Awakening of Faith in Mahāyāna*), and *Taesŭng Kisillon Pyŏlki* (*Special Commentary on the Awakening of Faith in Mahāyāna*) are of such importance that they greatly influenced Fazang's

Dasheng qixin lunyi ji (*Notes on the Significance of the Awakening of Faith*). His friend and colleague, Ŭisang (625–702), went to China to study with Zhiyan (602–668), the second Chinese Huayan patriarch and a senior colleague of Fazang (643–712), the third Huayan patriarch. Ŭisang's *Hwaŏm ilsŭng pŏpkye to* (*Diagram of the Avataṃsaka Single Vehicle Dharmadhātu*), drafted in the form of a *maṇḍala* consisting of 210 characters, gives form to his understanding of Huayan doctrine. On his return from China, he founded the Hwaŏm (Ch. Huayan) school.

Korean Sŏn tradition credits Pŏmnang (632–647), a student of Daoxin (580–651), with the introduction of Sŏn (Ch. Chan), and its popularization to Sinhaeng (704–779) and Toŭi (d. 825). Many others traveled to China for study. As a result, nine Sŏn schools were established, eight of which carried on the lineage of Mazu Daoyi (709–788). The Sumi-san school founded by Iŏm (869–936) was based on the Caodong (Jpn. Sōtō) school.

The scholarly study of Buddhism enjoyed great popularity during the Unified Silla period. Scholar-monks pursued Yusik (Ch. Weishi; Skt. Yogācāra) and Chŏngt'o (Pure Land). Wŏnhyo taught the Pure Land practice of *yŏmbul* (Ch. *nianfo*; Jpn. *nembutsu*) that still persists, especially among the laity. During the following Koryŏ dynasty, Pojo Chinul (1158–1210), inspired by a series of spiritual epiphanies and his study of the Buddhist canon, founded the Songgwangsa Monastery at Mt. Chogye, the namesake of the Jogye (Chogye) order. This new order taught a comprehensive approach to Buddhism that included meditation, chanting, lectures, and study of doctrine. Chinul was thus able to bridge the chasm between those who avoided the study of doctrine and those who rejected practice. Chinul also established lay meditation and scripture study societies that offered an alternative to the ritualism, geomancy, prognostication, and magic that had infiltrated Koryŏ Buddhism.

One of the most significant events during the Koryŏ period was the publication of the two woodblock editions of the Tripiṭika. The first edition, completed in 1029, was destroyed by Mongol invaders in 1232. The second edition that was published between 1214 and 1259 is extant in Haein-sa Monastery; it served as the model for subsequent editions of the Tripiṭika.

The fortunes of Buddhism changed dramatically with the establishment of the Chosŏn dynasty (1392–1910), whose leaders adopted neo-Confucian thought inspired by Zhu Xi (1130–1200) as a state ideology. An Hyang (1243–1306), who visited Yuan China (1271–1368) and was struck by the rationality of Zhu Xi's thought, brought back copies of his writings. Neo-Confucianism offered Koreans an alternative worldview. Zhu Xi maintained that all things are brought into being by the union of *qi*, vital (or material) force; and *li* (rational principle). Every material object and person possesses *li* and is thus part of the *Taiji* or Great Ultimate, the creative principle that is embedded in the human spirit or mind and works its way through the person. *Li* and *qi* are mutually dependent and are present in all existences.

In contrast with Buddhism that posited a transient and nonsubstantial illusionary world, neo-Confucianism stated that change is real. Instead of attempting to escape and transcend change as advocated by Buddhism, neo-Confucianism asserted a need to conform to the patterns of change. Moreover, neo-Confucianism charged that the "Buddha-nature" and "*Nirvāṇa*" pursued by Buddhists are illusionary. Moreover, chasing after such illusions is a waste of time and ultimately self-indulgent; personal salvation, putting one's need ahead of society, is selfish. Such selfishness places an unfair burden of taxes and *corvée* labor on those who choose not to enter the monastery. When a person enters the monastery or nunnery, he or she renounces responsibilities to the family. Moreover, Korean intellectuals were disgusted with the corruption of Buddhist clergy and their supporters. These developments led to the eventual overthrow of the Koryŏ dynasty by Yi Sŏngye (1335–1408) in 1392.

As a consequence of this shift, the court slashed its patronage of Buddhism and promulgated measures to diminish the status and power of its clerics. Buddhist temples were banished from the urban areas to the remote mountains. By the middle of the Chosŏn period, Buddhism was completely delegitimized. Clerics were seen as no better than beggars and outcasts. It was only after Sŏsan Taesa Hyujŏng (1520–1604) organized and led militias comprised primarily of Buddhist monks, which helped to repel the Japanese invasion in the Imjin War (1592–1598) at the end of the 16th century, that the Chosŏn leaders eased their persecution of the faith. Ironically, Buddhist monks were assigned to build defensive fortifications and to train in the martial arts in exchange for "legitimizing" their clerical standing.

Buddhist clerics and temples responded first by countering their neo-Confucian critics and later by educating their monks. Tŭkt'ong Kihwa (Hamhŏ, 1376–1433) attempted to reconcile Buddhism and Confucianism by arguing that the Buddhist path to enlightenment is identical to Confucian sagehood, that the five Buddhist precepts are synonymous with Confucian moral directives, and that both doctrines support the calming of the mind as the way to quell evil and support the country. Kihwa's efforts did not mollify the Confucian ideologues. Consequently, a century later the guerilla monk Hyujŏng believed that if Buddhism were to survive, the monks would need to have a better understanding of Buddhism as well as the dominant Confucian ideology under which they lived. In the meantime temples continued to receive support from sympathetic aristocrats and the common people who turned to the temples for spiritual support during times of personal crisis and to memorialize their ancestors. Temples received money for upkeep and renovation; they also secured farmland on which the monks grew produce to feed themselves and to sell. Temples earned income by functioning as state archives, retreats, and entertainment centers. The common people for their part supported the temples with the fruits of their labor and with money.

Buddhism's fortunes picked up somewhat during reforms in the late 19th century and with the coming of the Japanese. The 500-year ban on clerics entering the cities was lifted in 1895. During the Japanese occupation, which began in 1910 and lasted until 1945, the Japanese began to refashion Korean Buddhism by abolishing celibacy and by transforming the traditional communal administration of temples by appointing their abbots.

Since 1945 the Korean Peninsula has been divided into the Republic of Korea (South Korea) in the south and the Democratic People's Republic of Korea (North Korea) in the north. After World War II the Sŏn school of Korean Buddhism once again gained acceptance. In 1954, President Yi Sŭng-man (Syngman Rhee, 1875–1965), allied with a number of monks, ordered a separation of the Jogye order into two orders, one composed of celibate monks and the other of those who had families; the latter came to be known as the Taego (T'aego) order. The Communist North has suppressed most religious and spiritual activity and has instead promoted the ideology of *Juche* (Chuch'e) or "self-reliance" that has overtones of neo-Confucian and Marxist thought. By way of contrast, the South has experienced a growth of Buddhist and Christian communities, new spiritual traditions, and traditional shamanism. Today Korea is the home of many Buddhist sects, including Wŏn, a new Buddhist movement.

History

The Korean Buddhist experience falls into two broad categories: centers catering to Euro-Americans who are interested in meditation, and temples that serve the Korean émigrés and their children for whom Buddhism is a devotional exercise and a family tradition. Interest in Korean Sŏn began in 1964 when Seo Kyongbo (Sŏ, Kyŏngbo) Sunim (1914–1996) spoke in the New York area; he returned six years

later to serve as dean of the Buddhist College at Dongguk (Tongguk) University. Later, in 1972, Sung Sahn (Sungsan) Sunim (1927–2004) arrived in Providence, Rhode Island. He went on to establish the Dharma Zen Center in Los Angeles in 1974, the Chogye International Zen Center in New York City in 1975, and Empty Gate Zen Center in Berkeley, California, in 1977. In 1983 he founded the Kwan Um Zen School to train married Western devotees and lay Dharma teachers.

Kosun Sunim, a disciple of Seo Kyongbo Sunim, arrived in 1969; active on the East Coast, he established Hankook Sa (temple) in the Washington, D.C. area and in 1976 founded the Seneca Zen Center and American Zen College in Germantown, Maryland. Samu Sunim came to the United States in 1967 and in 1968 established the Zen Lotus Society of New York. He later moved to Toronto, Canada, and went on to found temples in Ontario, Canada; Ann Arbor, Michigan; and Mexico City.

Devotional temples are primarily located in areas with sizable Korean populations. Koreatown in Los Angles emerged as a major center of the Korean American community in the 1990s. In the aftermath of the 1992 Los Angeles riots, many Koreans moved to the San Francisco Bay Area, first to downtown Oakland and subsequently to other parts of the Bay Area. The greater New York and Baltimore-Washington metropolitan areas also have large Korean populations. Plans for constructing the first Buddhist Korean temple in the United States began in 1970 by Han Sang Lee, a lay Buddhist from Korea in Carmel Valley to serve Koreans in the city of San Jose and the larger San Francisco Bay Area. The temple, Sambosa, was completed in 1973.

The recent arrival of Korean Buddhists contrasts with more than a century of the Korean Christian experience. About half of those Koreans who arrived in Hawai'i were members of the Inchŏn church of Rev. George Heber Jones (1867–1919). Subsequent arrivals were predominantly Christians. Since Sunday worship and other church-sponsored activities were an almost universal feature of Korean plantation life, eventually almost everyone converted to the faith. The Korean Christian church, like the Japanese Shintō shrine and Buddhist temple, was a purveyor of Korean culture and a venue for community activities. A similar pattern occurred with the post-1965 immigrant experience. It is estimated that 70 to 80 percent of Korean Americans identify with Christianity, and 40 percent of this number converted after arriving in the United States. Currently, there are approximately 3,000 Korean Christian churches throughout the United States and 90 Buddhist temples.

Beliefs

The images and symbols that populate a temple offer a glimpse of the beliefs and practices of the Korean Buddhist devotees in the United States. Among the many buddhas and bodhisattvas of the Buddhist pantheon the most popular are the historical Sŏkkamoni Pul (Śākyamuni Buddha), Amit'a Pul (Amitābha Buddha), Kwanseŭm Posal (Avalokiteśvara Bodhisattva), Chijang Posal (Kṣitigarbha Bodhisattva), and Mirŭk Posal (Maitreya Bodhisattva). An image of Śākyamuni, the historical Bud-

dha, is a constant reminder that anyone can attain Enlightenment through spiritual exercise and the observance of the precepts. The other celestial spiritual heroes personify the highest ideals of the tradition; these personalities and the sacred texts that are used in rituals offer insight into the practice of Buddhism in the immigrant Korean community.

The image of Sŏkkamoni Pul is that of a seated Buddha with the left hand, palms open and up, resting on the lap, and right hand hanging over the knee, palms inward, pointing to the earth. This hand gesture is the *bhūmisparśa mūdrā*; it represents the moment the Buddha-to-be responded to Māra's query: Who vouches that you are worthy of becoming the Buddha? Siddhārtha responds by touching the ground and summons the earth to be his witness. This image is popular in the Theravāda tradition.

Amit'a Pul and Kwaseŭm Posal, prominent in the devotional lives of devotees, are personifications of compassion. According to the *Larger Sukhāvatīvyūha*, the principal document of the Pure Land tradition, Amitābha Buddha possesses an immeasurable store of merits. This store was earned over the five *kalpas* (eons), while Amitābha, as the Bodhisattva Dharmākara, resolved to fulfill 48 vows to create a Pure Land in which he would reside to welcome all beings. Of these 48, the 18th vow states that any being desiring to be born in the Pure Land will be guaranteed a place by sincerely calling Amitābha's name, even as few as 10 times. The 19th vow states that he, Amitābha Buddha, together with a retinue of Bodhisattvas will appear and welcome those who call his name at the moment of death. The "ease" and "openness" in which Amitābha Buddha accepts anyone who calls his name is most appealing. The *Smaller Sukhāvatīvyūha Sūtra*, commonly chanted at funerals, describes the beauty of the Pure Land and the beings who reside there. The *Vajracchedikā prajñāpāramita* or *Diamond Sūtra* is also used.

"Kwan[se]ŭm" is the Korean pronunciation of "Guanyin," the Chinese translation of "Avalokiteśvara." The 25th chapter, "The Gateway to Everywhere of the Bodhisattva He Who Observes the Sounds of the World" of the *Saddharmapundarīka Sūtra* (*Lotus Sūtra*) describes Avalokiteśvara as a compassionate bodhisattva who hears the cries of sentient beings and who tirelessly works to help those who call his name. The bodhisattva appears in 33 different guises, including a feminine incarnation, to accommodate the various needs of those who call to him. Although I have been referring to Avalokiteśvara as masculine in gender, Avalokiteśvara, like other celestial Buddhist personalities, is androgynous. Chun-fan Yu argues that Avalokiteśvara was transformed into Guanyin, the goddess of mercy, because Buddhism and neo-Confucianism lacked feminine symbols with whom women could identify. The model for a feminine savior can be found in the image of Lady He (Ho Xiangu), one of the Eight Daoist Immortals, and the Chinese deification of the historical Princess Miaoshan. The feminization of Guanyin, who was not associated with other Buddhist personalities or their aristocratic sponsors at the time, appealed to women.

Kwanseŭm is frequently pictured with a vase in one hand and a willow spray in the other. The vase contains *amrita*, the nectar of compassion; the willow represents her ability and willingness to liberally sprinkle "sweet dew" on the afflicted to relieve their suffering. The willow, long considered to have medicinal value, symbolizes her role as a healer.

Another popular image is the 1,000-armed Avalokiteśvara. The 1,000 arms represent the innumerable ways Avalokiteśvara helps. There are many legends relating the origins of the 1,000-armed Avalokiteśvara. The most popular is attributed to Amitābha Buddha who, seeing his protégé's head split into 11 pieces while struggling to comprehend the needs of so many, gives the bodhisattva 11 heads with which to hear the cries of the suffering. Upon hearing these cries, Avalokiteśvara reaches out with two arms, which also shatter into pieces because of the great need. Once more, Amitābha Buddha comes to his aid and invests him with 1,000 arms with which to aid the suffering multitudes. According to Chinese lore, on the other hand, the 1,000-armed Avalokiteśvara is an incarnation of Miaoshan, who selflessly gave up her sight and arms to be used as ingredients to concoct a medicine to cure her father. After the father learned of his daughter's sacrifice, Miaoshan was transformed into the 1,000-armed Guanyin.

Having accomplished all that is needed to enter *Nirvāṇa*, Chijang Bosal is the spiritual peer of Sŏkkamoni Pul. However, seeing that there is still so much need in the world, Sŏkkamoni Pul asks Chijang Posal to remain in this world until Miruk Posal appears sometime in the distant future. Thus charged, Chijang Posal tirelessly traverses the six realms assisting where he can to relive suffering. He is especially active in hell, where his wisdom and compassion is most needed. He is typically represented as a bald monk, holding an iron staff in his right hand and cradling a "wish-fulfilling jewel" in his left palm; the jewel grants all selfless requests.

With the exception of Sŏkkamoni Pul, the selection of these celestial heroes project the deep yearning of the Korean people to be released from suffering and their aspirations for a better life. Amit'a Pul, Kwaseŭm Posal, and Chijang Posal are beloved for their compassion. Mirŭk Posal personifies their aspirations that better things await. The images and symbols differ in different temples, an indication of the nonsectarian nature of Korean Buddhism. Images of protector deities are also common.

Practices

The yearnings and aspirations of the Korean people and their immigrant brethren are also revealed in their communal and private Buddhist and traditional rituals. While Sŏkkamoni Pul may occupy the revered central position on the altar, the Koreans have a special affection for Avalokiteśvara as evidenced by the *Panya simgyŏng* (*Prajñāpāramitā Hṛdaya* or *Heart Sūtra*) and portions of the *Ch'ŏnsugyŏng* (*Dabei Zhoujing*; *Thousand-hand Sūtra*) that are chanted daily. In the *Panya simgyŏng* Avalokiteśvara instructs Śāriputra that through *prajñāpāramita* (perfection of wisdom), sentient beings will understand their true nature, which is the key to Enlightenment. The bodhisattva goes on to say that *prajñāpāramita* is the great spell (*mantra*),

the spell of great knowledge, the utmost spell, the unequalled spell, the allayer of all suffering.

In the *Ch'ŏnsugyŏng*, Avalokiteśvara spells out the conditions that quicken the efficacy of the Great Compassion Heart Dharani (*mantra*) before an assembly of Buddhist spiritual heroes, *devas* (deities) from the 10 directions, the dragon king, and other auspicious creatures. In the beginning the bodhisattva declares to the Buddha and the multitudes that he wishes to share the mantra of Great Compassion Heart Dharani that propelled him to his present spiritual level. First, those who wish to practice this mantra must first quicken great compassion for all beings and commit to observing 10 vows that include obtaining the Wisdom Eye, ferrying all beings to spiritual liberation, and mastering skillful means to teach. Thereafter the devotee must recite the name Namo Avalokiteśvara Bodhisattva with a deep-felt sincere heart, and also recite single-mindedly the name of his teacher—Amitābha Tathāgata (Namo Amitābha Buddha). Then the devotee must recite this mantra five times or more a day to be removed from the weighty sins of births and deaths accumulated in hundreds of thousands of billions of *kalpas*.

Subsequently in the *Ch'ŏnsugyŏng*, Avalokiteśvara enumerates the benefits to those who believe and recite the Great Compassion Heart Dharani. These benefits include curing 84,000 kinds of diseases, extending one's lifespan, vanquishing demons, eliminating personal misfortune, and guaranteeing a good death; it even restores harmony between husband and wife. The king who chants this holy

Dharani will bring prosperity and peace to his people and country. Avalokiteśvara also promises to protect those who quicken a merciful and compassionate heart toward all living beings. In short, the *Ch'ŏnsugyŏng* articulates the deepest yearnings to be free from any and all manner of suffering. The quickening of a compassionate heart expresses a profound sentiment for the happiness of others, a prime Buddhist virtue. Because of the great Korean love for this *Sūtra*, Korean Buddhism is often referred to as Buddhism of the *Thousand-Hand Sūtra*.

The thrust of these two *Sūtras* is Avalokiteśvara's compassion. The bodhisattva offers the believer a means to practice and realize wisdom through the chanting of *mantras*. The *Heart Sūtra* is in its entirety a *mantra*; and is in its being, *prajñāpāramitā*, the perfection of wisdom. It unlocks great wisdom and in so doing allays suffering. A *mantra* (spell) is a "magical" incantation, a formula that has wondrous effects. The *Sūtra* as mantra is "magical" and efficacious, because it crystallizes the spiritual truth of *prajñāpāramitā*. Through the constant and repetitive chanting, the believer fills or enters into the life and spirit of the *Sūtra*, becomes one with it, and quickens *prajñā*, transcendental wisdom.

To the nonbeliever the efficacy of reciting a mantra is at best self-hypnosis and the goal of *prajñā* or transcendental wisdom, a delusion. But the idea of identifying with the truth and life and spirit of the *Heart Sūtra* can be understood by appealing to Indian and Japanese aesthetics. A cardinal tenet in ancient Indian aesthetics holds that the artisan can only sculpt an image of Buddha (or any other image) when that image is fully present in his or her mind and being. To render an object with any authority the artisan must be fully absorbed in it. Such absorption occurs when the knower and the known, the seer and the seen meet in an act transcending distinction. This idea is recapitulated by the Japanese poet Bashō (1644–1694), who discoursing on capturing the essence of the pine tree or the bamboo plant, said that the poet must "enter into the life of the object, perceive its delicate life, and feel its feeling, whereupon a poem forms itself." The aesthetic exercise of identifying with and entering into the life of the object is precisely what occurs through mantra recitation.

Celebrations

Buddhism survived 500 years of active suppression because during the 1,000 years before the establishment of the Chosŏn period, its teachings and rituals had become part of the annual rhythm of the people. Not all festivals are of Buddhist origin, but are closely associated with the tradition. The most important festivals are Yŏndŭng-hoe, Ch'op'ail, and Paekchung. Yŏndŭng-hoe, the Festival of Lotus Lanterns, the first major ceremony offered to the Buddha in the New Year, is observed on the 15th day of the first lunar month. Ch'op'ail celebrates the birth of the historical Buddha; it is observed on the eighth day of the fourth month. Celebrated on the 15th day of the seventh lunar month, Paekchung, also called Uranbunjŏl (Skt. *Ullambane*) is dedicated to spirits of the ancestors and corresponds to the Japanese

Buddhist Obon and the Vietnamese Vu Lan ritual. Other festivals such as Tano, celebrated on the fifth day of the fifth lunar month; Yudu, observed on the 15th day of the sixth lunar month; and P'algwan-hoe, celebrated on the 15th day of the 11th lunar month, are seasonal celebrations with archaic origins in the seasonal rhythms.

Unlike Japanese families who have a *butsudan* or Buddhist altar that often doubles as an ancestral shrine, Korean temples have a separate altar that is populated with memorial plaques inscribed with the names of the deceased. Such altars are reminders of the Chosŏn rulers who, guided by neo-Confucian ideology, urged commoners to engage in more regular and systematic worship of their ancestors. Five centuries of neo-Confucian rule has left a strong imprint on Korean society. Such Confucian values as filiality, loyalty, and sincerity are embodied in the Buddhist rituals and national rites. Confucian values that guide Korean behavior and social interaction, especially toward parents, elders, and teachers, are evident in the Buddhist rituals, especially in mortuary and memorial services. Services honoring and remembering the ancestors are also performed on lunar New Year and Chusŏk (Autumn Moon Festival), celebrated on the 15th day of the eighth lunar month. In addition to these communal rites, families sponsor *chesa* or memorial rites at the temple that mark the 49th and 100th days of passing; and the first- and third-year anniversaries of death. Thereafter memorial rites are observed annually, often at home, to mark the anniversary of death.

Conclusion

With a relatively brief experience in the United States, Korean Buddhists still observe the practices and traditions of the homeland; and Korean is the *lingua franca* in all aspects of services. Some temples have begun programs to accommodate their English-speaking children and to be more welcoming to non-Koreans. In the homeland, devotees attend services on the first and 15th days of the lunar calendar that correspond to the new and full moon respectively; but many of the services are now observed on weekends to accommodate the American work schedule. Like other immigrant faith institutions, the immigrant American Buddhist temple serves as purveyor of the faith, as a community resource, as well as a cultural center.

Ronald Y. Nakasone

See also: Entries: Han; Korean American Religions; Korean Shamanism

Further Reading

Buswell, Robert E., ed. *Religions of Korea in Practice.* Princeton, NJ: Princeton University Press, 2007.

Cho, Eun-su. "Going Beyond Tradition and Striving for the Future: Challenges and Tasks Faced by the Korean Buddhist Community in American Society." *Pacific World: Journal of the Institute of Buddhist Studies*, no. 5 (October 2003).

Conze, Edward. *Buddhist Wisdom Books, Containing the Diamond Sūtra and the Heart Sūtra.* London: George Allen & Unwin, 1958.

Coomaraswamy, Ananda K. *The Transformation of Nature in Art.* New York: Dover Publications, 1934.

Grayson, James Huntley. *Korea—a Religious History*. London: Routledge/Curzon, 1989.

Great Compassion Dharani Sūtra. http://huntingtonarchive.osu.edu/resources/downloads/sutras/05bodhisattvaYana/Great%20Compassion%20Dharani%20Sūtra.doc.pdf. Accessed September 11, 2013.

Harvey, Young Sook Kim, and Soon-Hyung Chun. "The Koreans." In John F. McDermott. *People and Cultures of Hawai'i, a Psychocultural Profile*. Honolulu: University of Hawai'i Press, 1980.

Kim, Hwansoo Ilmee. *Empire of the Dharma, Korean and Japanese Buddhism, 1877–1912*. Cambridge, MA: Harvard University Asia Center, 2012.

Korean Buddhist News USA, ed. *The Sangha Book of Korean Buddhism*. Fairfax, VA: Korean Buddhist News, 2012.

Samu Sunim (Kim, Sam-Woo). "Turing the Wheel of Dharma in the West—Korea Sŏn Buddhism in North America." In Ho Youn Kwon, Kwang Chung Kim, and R. Stephen Warner, eds. *Korean Americans and Their Religions: Pilgrims and Missionaries from a Different Shore*. University Park: Pennsylvania State University Press, 2001.

Satomichi, Norio. "Chōsen hantō no Bukkyō (Buddhism of the Korean peninsula)." In *Higashi ajia shochi'iki no Bukkyō* [Buddhism of the different regions of East Asia]. Tokyo: Kosei Shuppan, 1976, pp. 13–126.

Scripture of the Lotus Blossom of the Fine Dharma (The Lotus Sūtra). Translated by Leon Hurvitz. New York: Columbia University Press, 1976.

Shim, Jae-ryong. *Korean Buddhism, Tradition and Transformation*. Soeul: Jimoondang, 1999.

Suh, Sharon A. *Being Buddhist in a Christian World: Gender and Community in a Korean American Temple*. Seattle: University of Washington Press, 2004.

Ueda, Makoto. *Literary and Art Theories in Japan*. Ann Arbor, MI: Center for Japanese Studies, 1967.

Yang, Eun Sik. "Koreans in America, 1903–1945." In Hyung-Chan Kim, ed. *The Korean Diaspora: Historical and Sociological Studies of Korean Immigration and Assimilation in North America*. Santa Barbara, CA: ABC-CLIO, 1977.

Yu, Chun-fang. *Kuan-yin: The Chinese Transformation of Avalokiteśvara*. New York: Columbia University Press, 2001.

Yu, Eui-Young. "The Growth of Korean Buddhism in the United States, with Special Reference to Southern California." *Pacific World: Journal of the Institute of Buddhist Studies*, New Series (1988): 82–93.

Korean Shamanism

Korean shamanism is an indigenous religion of the Korean peninsula. Some scholars believe that Korean shamanism's origins reach all the way back to 6000 to 5000 BCE (Lee, 186–198). It was and is a monotheistic belief system centered around a divine figure called Ha-nuel-nim or the Heavenly Emperor with strong ties to eco-spirituality. Korean shamans were and are mainly women. Early in Korean history, shamans were revered and held seats of religio-political power. With the rise of Confucianism's influence, shamans became less influential in the political world of Korea and were relegated to a household folk religion practiced behind closed doors. With the growing influence of Confucianism, female shamans, who were once at the height of power, were now considered atypical women who functioned outside the commonly accepted Confucian paradigm of gender.

Christianity's arrival on the Korean peninsula contributed to the colonization of Korean culture and Korean indigenous religion. Korean shamanism, which was already perceived as a lower-class form of religion and belief system, became even more sacrilegious as Korean Christians began to adopt Western Christianity as their own.

Today's contemporary Korean Shamanism is still predominantly facilitated by female shamans called *Mansin* or *Mudang* (the later being a somewhat derogatory term). Shamans commune with the spirit world on behalf of their clients, both individuals and entire households. A *Mansin* is "called" to this profession through the process of *Shin-byung*, or "god disease," which can become instigated through personal trauma. *Shin-byung* can include refusal to consume food or drink, fever, depression, and hallucination.

A *Mansin*'s major task in contemporary Korean society is to perform household cleansings called *Kuts*, or *Chasu Kuts*, which placate unsettled or angry spirits, chasing away bad luck. Their role in the community is to reinstate balance or harmony by carrying out *han-puri*, or the releasing of suffering and inner turmoil, for the living and the dead. *Mansin* use Korean folk songs and folklore, which they sing and chant as part of cleansing rituals. Through their work, *Mansin* have the potential to earn a substantial living.

Through the process of immigration to the United States, those belonging to the Korean diaspora, like other immigrants before them, brought with them their religious traditions. Some of these religious traditions have been more pronounced than others such as Christianity and Korean Buddhism. Others have become so inherently part of Korean and Korean American culture that they are no longer religions but ways of life. Among the latter are both Confucianism and shamanism. Though shamanism is no longer called thus in Korean American culture, some would argue that remnants of Korean shamanism are embedded into parts of Korean American Christianity and also broader Korean American cultural transmission. Folklore attributed to shamanism's origins, particularly stories related to filial and self-sacrificial women such as *Simcheong the Blindman's Daughter, Princess Pari, Arang*, and *Kkong-Ji Patzi* are still transmitted to American-born generations of Korean Americans. Often from mother to daughter or grandmother to daughter, this transmission echoes the shaman's role of educating the community, especially women, through the singing and telling of folklore and folksongs.

Remnants of shamanism, particularly its acknowledgement of a unique female spirituality and spiritual ability, can also be found in Korean American immigrant churches. It can be argued that the *kwonsah*, a title given to mainly older Korean immigrant women who have proven themselves faithful to Christian values, share qualities of the traditional Korean shaman. The typical *kwonsah* in the Korean immigrant church is considered a woman of prayer and deep faith. She is an individual who has the ear of God. Congregants and even ministers may seek her out for intercessory prayer during particularly difficult times in their lives, for healing, and in some charismatic Christian contexts even for prophecy.

Much like the *Mansin*, the *kwonsah* is "called" or chosen for this particular role through her spiritual perseverance, especially through personal trials. As part of her spiritual duties she may fast on behalf of those in her community as a way of pleading with God, memorize scripture, speak prophetically, and perform other duties on behalf of her community members. She plays a role similar to the traditional Korean shaman, a bridge between the spirit world and the temporal world. Though Korean shamanism has not been explicitly transmitted to the Korean American diaspora, attributes of shamanism, especially the shaman's role within her community as a healer, educator, and mediator, still thrive in hidden ways.

Christine J. Hong

See also: Entries: Korean American Religions

Further Reading

Lee, Jonghyun. "Shamanism and Its Emancipatory Power for Korean Women." *Affilia: Journal of Women & Social Work* 24, no. 2 (2009): 186–98.

Kubose, Gyomay (1905–2000)

Gyomay Kubose was born in San Francisco, California. He was taken to Japan as an infant, then returned to the United States as a young man. Rev. Hata Taigan (1889–1968) of the Oakland Buddhist Church introduced him to the Jōdo Shinshū teachings of Akegarasu Haya (1877–1954). Inspired, Kubose studied at Akegarasu's temple for five years from 1936 to 1941; he returned in July 1941 on the next to last ship to leave Japan for America before the outbreak of World War II. Following Akegarasu's advice, he founded an independent temple that would be free from sectarianism and petty intra-denominational squabbles, and from which he could creatively give form to the Buddhist message. After a stay in World War II internment camps, he relocated to Chicago where he founded the Buddhist Temple of Chicago in 1944. Kubose retired from active ministry in 1988 and passed away at the age of 95.

Kubose preserved much of the material culture and ritual format of the Jōdo Shinshū sect; but he felt that the manner in which the leaders of the sect presented Amida Buddha in the United States was dualistic and lent to its objectification as a "savior." Instead he understood Amida Buddha to be Universal Life that underlies individual lives. At his Chicago temple's 30th anniversary, he summarized his vision:

I have always dreamed of establishing an American Buddhism—different from Indian, Chinese, or Japanese Buddhism—a uniquely American Buddhism that could be easily understood and practiced by Americans and that would contribute to American life and culture. This Buddhism can be explained in simple, everyday language and practiced in every aspect of our daily life. Yet, it is a unique Buddhist life-way—non-dichotomized and non-dualistic—that will bring about a peaceful, meaningful, creative life, both individually and collectively.

Kubose's simple, down-to-earth, and easy to understand explications of Buddhism draw inspiration from the life and teachings of Gautama Buddha and their expression in Japanese Mahāyāna, especially Shin (Pure Land) and Zen. From these he draws a universal message for everyday living for people of all backgrounds. His approach to the Dharma is contained in his *Everyday Suchness* and *The Center Within.*

Kubose's teachings and approach continue through the work of his son, the Rev. Koyo S. Kubose, who upon retiring from temple ministry in 1995 established Bright Dawn Center of Oneness Buddhism. "Bright Dawn" is the English rendering of "Gyomay." Since 1996, the center has continued the elder Kubose's pioneering work of Americanizing Buddhism. In addition to hosting a variety of resources for cultivating individual spirituality through its website, the Bright Dawn Center offers a three-year, nonresidential lay ministry program. The thrust of the program, the application of Buddhist thought and practice to daily life, is known as the Way of Oneness. Bright Dawn graduates are active across the country.

Koyo S. Kubose

See also: Entries: Japanese American Religions; Jōdo Shū (Pure Land Sect)

Further Reading

Bright Dawn Center of Oneness Buddhism. www.brightdawn.org. Accessed July 10, 2014.

Buddhist Temple of Chicago. *The Buddhist Temple of Chicago 30th Anniversary Album, 1944–1974.* Chicago: The Buddhist Temple of Chicago, 1974.

Kubose, Gyomay M. *The Center Within.* Coarsegold, CA: Dharma House, 1986.

Kubose, Gyomay M. *Everyday Suchness.* Coarsegold, CA: Dharma House, 1967.

Remembering Sensei. Coarsegold, CA: Bright Dawn Center, 2000.

L

Laotian American Religions

History of Religious Influences on Laos

Among the more than 6.8 million people who live in the central Southeast Asian country of Laos, well over half are ethnic Lao. Because of their most frequent habitation and rice paddy production along the river valleys and low-altitude towns of Laos, the politically and culturally dominant Lao have historically been referred to as Lao Loum (sometimes Lao Leum) or Lowland Lao. They are distinguished from the many tribal highlander populations of the mountaintops and upper slopes designated as Lao Soung (such as Hmong, Mien, Akha, and Lahu), and from the mid-altitude populations called Lao Theung (including principally the Khmu), who were perhaps the original inhabitants of Laos.

The Lao are perhaps descended from Ai Lao ethnic groups found in southern China's Yunan Province, which included tribes categorized as Tai that speak tonal languages from the Tai-Kadai family. Religiously, many of the early Tai practiced animism as their traditional religion. Ancestors of Lowland Lao began to migrate from southeastern China into what is now Laos during the first millennium. Movements of substantial numbers of Tai from China occurred between the 7th and 13th centuries CE during times of Han Chinese growth and Mongol invasions that impacted Tai treatment and agricultural opportunities.

Upon arrival, the Tai-Lao peoples encountered a religiously and culturally mixed environment. Numerous indigenous Austroasiatic tribes held strong animistic beliefs, which were adapted by many Lao with similar worldviews. They also found heavy Mon and Khmer influences from peoples who also had been migrating into Southeast Asia from northeast India and southwest China since perhaps 2000 BCE. Ancient Khmer Hindu empires filtered influences northward into the region. Indian trading in the Mekong River basin area led to widespread imprints of Indian notions of kingship, literature, art, writing, and religion throughout the territory. Mon influence, which had established a significant city-state west of Bangkok as early as the third century, continued to spread northward and eventually brought a Buddhist presence into central and northern Laos in the eighth century. Such expansion set the stage for the practice of Theravāda-style Buddhism by an overwhelming majority of Lao in later centuries and prepared for Buddhism's role as the state religion beginning in the time of the first king of Laos, Fa Ngum, when in 1353 he founded the Lao Empire of Lan Xang, or the Kingdom of a Million Elephants, in Luang

Maly Khanthaphixay poses for a portrait at the Lao Buddhist Temple of Colorado in Westminster, which was destroyed by fire on January 12, 2012. The Buddha, at right, is used in outdoor New Years ceremonies and was not damaged. "We hope to rebuild for our children, our elders and the students—we have a lot of students that come to understand the meaning of life," Khanthaphixay said. (Craig F. Walker/The Denver Post/Getty Images)

Prabang. The monarchical form of government was to last for 600 years in Laos until its takeover by Communist leadership in 1975.

Historical Religious Beliefs and Practices, Daily Life in Laos

Theravāda Buddhism. Theravāda Buddhism, also common in Cambodia, Thailand, Myanmar/Burma, and Sri Lanka, is scripturally linked with the Pāli canon that is thought to contain the original teachings of the Buddha. Also known as Southern Buddhism or the "teaching of the elders," and sometimes referred to pejoratively as "The Lesser Vehicle" (or Hīnayāna Buddhism), Theravāda Buddhism encourages believers to revere the historic Buddha, uphold his four fundamental teachings of nature (*Dharma*) called the Four Noble Truths to eliminate suffering, and support the order of monks that Buddha founded (*Sangha*). Together, these form the "three jewels" (or Triratna) of Buddhism. Adherents seek to gain merit (in Lao, *het bun*) toward salvation by following Buddha's Noble Eightfold Path of right view, right resolve, right speech, right action, right livelihood, right effort, rightmindedness, and right concentration to eliminate suffering.

Beyond the spiritual cohesion that Theravāda Buddhism has offered Laos, it has likewise supported the economic viability and social well-being of the Lao. Throughout the centuries, the Buddhist temple (called *wat*) has served as the focal point of Lowland Lao life in every village and town. Followers are allowed to earn merit in the next life by supporting temple life and its monks. Most Laotian men and a lesser number of women have served as monks or nuns for brief or longer periods of time, wearing saffron (and for women, white) robes and upholding vows of poverty, celibacy, and inoffensiveness, and committing to not "destroy life of any kind, steal, commit adultery, tell a falsehood, use intoxicating drink, eat at forbidden times, attend worldly amusements, use perfume or ornaments, sleep on high beds, or accept money." *Wats* also have assumed important educational leadership roles in villages by providing residents their only formal education previous to French colonialism and the establishment of state schools.

Politically, Buddhism served for centuries to legitimate the Lao kingship and prevailing social structure of the country's leadership, and thus has been given official encouragement and protection by traditional Lao kingdoms. Since the days of Fa Ngum, a social hierarchy existed in the ancient capital comprised in descending rank of the king, royal clan members in the capital, an aristocracy of powerful provincial families, lowland Lao peasantry, and the Lao Theung and Lao Soung. Power was administered at all levels on behalf of the king, who was thought to be semidi-vine. This social structure for the Lao monarchy and Lao social standing was legitimated by a world view in which Lao creation myths establishing both territorial claims and social origins were set within the framework of Buddhist conceptions of kingship, merit, and *karma*. Annual New Year celebrations focused on rituals that at once revered the Buddha, reiterated the authority of the Buddhist clergy called *saṇgha*, and reinforced the king's legitimate right to rule.

During the later French colonial occupation of Laos from the end of the 19th century until 1950, Buddhism functioned to preserve Lao culture and to generate nationalist resistance to colonial authority. Under the Communist takeover of Laos in 1975, the Lao monarchy ended and the new government at first banned almsgiving. This policy damaged the ability of monks to survive and led large numbers to flee to Thailand or leave behind the monkhood, until public criticism led to the elimination of the ban. Currently, it is mandatory for all monks to study Marxist/Leninist theory, and reforms have again rebuilt the numbers of monks to those before the revolution. Article 9 of the Lao PDR Constitution states: "The state respects and protects legitimate activities of Buddhists and believers of any religion, and . . . prohibits any affairs that discriminate against religions." In 2005, the government claimed 4,937 Buddhist temples and 75 percent of the population practicing Theravāda Buddhism in the Lao PDR.

Animism. Spirit worship, also called animism or shamanism, has simultaneously influenced the historical religious world of the Lowland Lao perhaps more strongly than in other countries practicing Theravāda Buddhism. Animism predominates among the religious practices of Lao Soung and Lao Theung tribes, and predated Buddhism in the country. But also for Lowland Lao, local and guardian spirits are believed to intersect with Buddhism to provide protection and well-being by clearing potentially dangerous spirits from the "civilized" Buddhist social order. The Lao affirm 32 spirits called *khwan*, which are believed to protect the body. Ceremonies called *basi* are undertaken to call back the spirits at important times of transition, anxiety, or during holidays, as a departure of the spirits is thought to bring harm. Malevolent spirits are also called *phi* and are often given offerings of rice wine and chicken to ensure prosperity and protection against them. Many of these spirits are rooted in Hindu heritage.

Hinduism/P'aam, Islam, and Baha'i Faith. Hinduism was introduced into central and southern Laos as early as the first century CE, likely as a result of Indian trading influences on Khmer Angkor dynasties at that time. Wat Phou in Champasack Province near Laos's southern border with Cambodia dates from the 6th to 12th centuries, and still holds annual rituals that depict Hindu images of gods such as Shiva, Ganesh, Indra, and Brahma. The royal Lao icon of the three-headed elephant, depicted on Lao coins and currency before the revolution and Communist takeover in 1975, was the form of a Hindu deity, Airavata. Hindu-style snake images, called *Nāgas*, are shown reverence and believed to rule the waters. Spiritual practices called P'aam

that relate to appeasement of the spirits also have roots in Hinduism and have been followed by Lao for generations.

Islamic worshippers are located especially in Vientiane, where a *mosque* is near the capital city's historic Nam Phou fountain. Hinduism mixes comfortably in Laos with Buddhist and Hindu influences, and 2005 government estimates indicated that approximately 400 Lao have practiced Islam under the current regime. The Baha'i faith was introduced to Laos by Iranian language teachers in 1957 and has approximately 8,500 adherents.

Christianity. The initial Catholic presence in Laos was reported as early as 1642, when Father Jean Marie DeLeria from Italy entered to spend five years in Vientiane. After 1880, Catholic missions expanded their work into the northern provinces of Houaphan and into the southern areas of Done Don, Kengsadoc, and Paksane. The Protestant presence entered when Presbyterian Dr. Daniel McGilvary crossed on an elephant from North Siam on explorations in the early 1870s. Swiss Brethren arrived in Laos in 1902, and the Christian Missionary Alliance church became active in 1928 when G. E. Roffe became the first resident Protestant missionary in north Laos. Christianity took hold most especially among tribal, poor, and outcast populations. The Royal Lao government often received Christianity with tolerance, while French colonial rule from 1887 to 1945 met Christianity with a mix of tolerance and resistance.

Christianity grew under indigenous influences of leaders like the Khmu villager Kheng in the 1950s and under Khmu pastor

Moum Douangmala, who worked in later years especially in Sayaboury and Xieng Khouang provinces. Some Lowland Lao leaders from the south, such as Rev. Saly Khounthapanya, received training and traveled extensively along the rivers of the north to train others. In 1957, Rev. Saly was elected to serve as the Lowland Lao representative in a multiethnic leadership structure in the first indigenous Laotian church coordinating organization, called the Lao Evangelical Church (LEC). In 2005, the Lao government reported 95 Roman Catholic churches with 41,746 followers and 221 Lao Evangelical churches with 60,000 followers spread in 17 provinces.

Lao Religious Cultures in Refugee Camps

After the Royal Lao king relinquished his throne on December 2, 1975, and the Communist Lao People's Democratic Republic was established at the hands of the Pathet Lao, an estimated 10 percent of the population of Laos escaped from the deteriorating conditions, reeducation camps, and punishment enacted upon them because of their service as America's allies during the U.S. "secret war" in Laos. Of these, nearly 120,000 Lowland Lao entered the United States as refugees under the provisions of the Refugee Act of 1980 between the years of 1975 to 1996. The United States was the largest receiving country for Laotion refugees. But before arrival into the United States, tens of thousands of Lowland Lao languished in refugee camps such as Ban Napho, Ban Nong Saeng, Ubon, Nong Khai, Phanat Nikhom, and others, which stretched along the Lao border in

Thailand. Life in the camps was simple and harsh. Families stayed for months or years before being processed out as refugees to other countries. At the end of 1990, 22,000 lowland Lao refugees still remained in the Ban Napho camp.

In all the camps, many families held small Buddhas in hopes of protection, some monks engaged in chanting, and the minority of Christians present prayed amidst the dislocations of camp life. Animistic and P'aam rituals were common, including practices to pacify the *pi* (spirits) through feeding, decorations, or dancing. At Nong Khai, refugees reported watching Christian baptisms in a pond just outside the fence. Residents could be issued a card to travel out of the camp to church. Thai monks and Mormons were allowed to visit and share resources inside the camp at Ubon. Simplified Buddhist *basi* practices were visible during special life occasions within the camp. In Nong Seng, a temple and a church each had small buildings. In 1980, founders of what would later become the Buddhist Relief Mission visited Indochinese refugees in Thai camps and reported they found few Buddhist activities and little to no external support for Buddhist temples in the camps. But by 1988 in Camp Ban Napho, Lao refugee monks opened a new temple, and Thai and Lao Christians developed a church with a baptismal pond.

With few occupying activities and great human needs, faith-based presence and nongovernmental organizations emerged to offer healing, training, and hope. The Committee for the Coordination of Services to Displaced Persons in Thailand (CCSDPT) identified 40 groups at work in

Thailand's camps in 1988, of which 1 was Zen Buddhist and 21 were Christian. As examples, the Christian and Missionary Alliance denomination expanded upon its historical commitments in Southeast Asia to form Compassion and Mercy Associates (CAMA). CAMA began in 1972 to reach out to refugees fleeing Laos, Vietnam, and Cambodia to "flesh out the good news of God's love for people—body and soul" by providing food, clothing, job training, medical care, and witness of their faith. Theravādan master Somdet Phra Mahā Ghosananda of Cambodia shared tracts of Buddha's love with refugees and established Buddhist temples in the Thai-Cambodian refugee camps by as early as 1978. The Catholic Bishops' Conference of Thailand established the Catholic Office for Emergency Relief and Refugees (COERR) in December 1978 to provide assistance to Laotian and other refugees in border camps. For over 15 years, COERR's local and international staff met basic needs and offered education, vocational training, care for the elderly and disabled, agricultural training, health care, and shelter assistance to the Lao.

Lao Religious Cultures in the United States

Disjunctions from traditional religious practices as experienced in the Thai refugee camps heightened further within the challenges of third-country resettlement in the United States. A majority of Lowland Lao Americans live in California, Texas, Minnesota, Washington, and North Carolina. Seventeen percent of Lao families live below the poverty level. Laotians have

educational levels that are among the lowest in the nation, with only 49 percent graduating high school. Fifty-two percent of Lao adults are limited in English proficiency, more than one-third live in overcrowded housing, and less than half have yet received citizenship.

In this context, animists and Buddhists alike often continue to pray for protection from evil spirits, and family elders may reward spirits with rice wine and chicken. Traditional healing herbs and remedies are accessed and shared through elders at home and in community settings. More formal refugee religious institutions are also indicators of cultural preservation and identity formation. One source records nearly 90 Lao temples in existence in the United States. Temples offer psychological encouragement for resiliency, and their construction symbolizes economic stability and acuity in accessing resources and navigating local permits and policies. Religious gatherings strengthen internal Lao communities and function as cultural teaching and networking centers between Lao and mainstream populations that build increased social power, access to resources, and contacts for health, housing, education, and employment. The Lao congregation (*wat*) in New Iberia, Louisiana, is one case in point. There, Lao pipe fitters and welders gradually gained economic standing and improved their housing during the early 1980s, then formed a Temple Corporation to build a Lao temple with adjacent housing. Job referrals frequently occurred through the temple, and elders gathered daily for lunch. The design and festivals of the temple helped maintain Lao culture.

Beyond their social functions, Lao religious communities must overcome leadership challenges and transformed rituals to support the monks and temples in ways essential for individual and community practices. One midwestern temple contacted a national monks association to help select Lao and Thai leadership. Donations from both community members and resettlement program grants have supported the temple's development. A lay Buddhist association and maintenance workers offer volunteer support, and dance, language, and cultural arts programs are offered on site. Traditional customs, such as monks walking local streets to gather alms, have been altered due to weather and vicinity of neighbors, and alms are brought directly to the temple. Other temples report community festivals and healing rituals have been greatly abbreviated in time due to attendees' work schedules. Monks preside over funerals and weddings, offerings for ancestors, merit-making and transfer of merit rituals, and meditation instruction. Temple leaders face needs to introduce and redesign practices for youth and young adult generations born outside of Laos or within it since Communist restrictions of Buddhist practices after 1975.

Lowland Lao Protestant Christian communities have continued a unified spirit similar to the Lao Evangelical Church structure within Laos by founding the Lao Conference of Churches (LCC) in 1981. It serves Laotian churches by making resources available that will maximize their effectiveness for God's service in North America. An emphasis is placed on leadership development and training conferences for its 42 member churches in the United States and 2 in Canada. Up to 150 individual Lao churches exist within the United States, and local churches of various denominations also develop unifying networks for gender support and congregational events, such as the Lao Christian Women's Ministry in Fresno. The Laotian Catholic National Pastoral Center formed in the early 1980s to serve Lao Catholics, visit the sick, celebrate sacraments, and support families in the midst of intergenerational and cultural transitions in the United States. Conferences are held every two years for Catholic churches in the United States and Canada to address pastoral and community concerns.

Christian churches emphasize Bible study, practices of justice and mercy, healing and visitations for the sick, and worship and music. Many highlight Lao dancing, language, clothing, and community meals centered around Lao food. Despite religious differences, many church leaders demonstrate unity through participation in aspects of cultural celebrations at local temples, such as during Lao New Year festivals.

Like temples, Christian churches create social networks between Lao groups and with mainline populations, which strengthen family, community, economic, emotional, and employment support. Faith-based organizations such as FIRM (Fresno Interdenominational Refugee Ministries) serve Lowland Lao of various faiths through citizenship and English classes, community gardens, preschool programs, employment assistance, physical and mental health resources, and community organizing for neighborhood improvements. Laotian Christian communities have also developed networks such as the Lao American Ministry Partnership and Laos Partners to offer medical supplies, English training, and water purification projects that offer Lao in diaspora new connections with their former homeland of Laos.

Sharon Stanley-Rea

See also: Entries: Hmong American Religions; Hmong Shamanism; Iu Mien

Further Reading

Kounthapanya, John. "History of Lao Christians: From Laos to America." Unpublished. University of California, 1992.

Stanley, Sharon. *Bamboo, Borders, and Bricks: Theology Building for Housing Improvements with Lao Refugees in Fresno, California.* Decatur, GA.: Columbia Theological Seminary, 2008.

Van Esterik, Penny. *Taking Refuge: Lao Buddhists in North America.* Tempe: Program for Southeast Asian Studies, Arizona State University, 1992.

Lotus Flower

The lotus flower, a plant in the *Nelumbonaceae* family, is an aquatic perennial that is commonly mistaken for a water lily. For many Asian Americans whose religious traditions originate from Asia, such as Hinduism, Buddhism, and Jainism, the lotus flower is a sign of purity and the potential for humans to overcome mundane existence. The lotus is so popular in Asia

The lotus flower is a symbol of purity and the human potential to raise up and out of pollution. It is a symbol of spiritual perfection and purity in dharmic traditions: Buddhism, Jainism, Hinduism. It is popular in folk and religious arts and architectural design. (Haiyuelou/Dreamstime.com)

that it is the national flower of India and Vietnam. It is also the inspiration for great deal of folk art in all of Asia.

In Hinduism, Hindu gods and goddesses are imagined as sitting on lotus thrones. Images of Hindu gods and goddesses will always have a lotus as a symbol of their purity versus the population associated with the human world. In Buddhism, when the Buddha was born, he walked on lotus that suddenly grew from the ground. This communicates his supreme purity. The same is true for Jainism and its founders, or *tirthankaras*.

The lotus is an aquatic plant growing in swampy environments. This represents the people and vices of the physical world. However, as the lotus flower blooms, there is no mud or dirt on its petals, because it has a waxy layer. This is interpreted as the human potential to transcend material existence and the vices of the world—greed, anger, hate, lust, and so on—to become clean and pure, like the lotus flower that grows from the swamp and mud. Each tradition—Hinduism, Buddhism, and Jainism—employs the metaphor of the lotus as a way to communicate its teaching's potential to bring one out of the mundane world. The lotus is so central to Mahāyāna Buddhism that one of the greatest *Sūtras* is named after it: the *Lotus Sūtra*.

In Chinese folk art, the lotus becomes a sign of immortality. In Buddhist Asia, the folk arts and crafts depicting the lotus may indicate that one is Buddhist. Among Hindus, Buddhists, and Jains in the United States, the lotus is a reminder of their religious goals. The lotus is also popular in jewelry design, wood crafts, and clothing. Since it is edible, it is a common ingredient in various traditional medicines in ethnic Asian enclave communities in the United States.

Jonathan H. X. Lee

See also: Entries: Dragons; *Nāga*; Swastika

Further Reading

Billing, Kelly, and Paula Biles. *The Lotus: Know It and Grow It*. Churchville, NY: International Waterlily & Water Gardening Society, 2007.

Watson, Burton, trans. *The Lotus Sūtra*. New York: Columbia University Press, 1993.

Lutherans

The Protestant Reformation, the biggest schism in the history of Christianity in Europe, was set off by the German monk Martin Luther (1483–1546) when on October 31, 1517, he nailed the 95 theses on the door of the Castle Church of Wittenberg, resulting in the formation of the Lutheran church. The year 1619 marked the time when the first European Lutheran set foot on American soil. Two hundred and twenty-nine years later the first group of Chinese laborers arrived in California in 1848. But the Euro-American Lutherans were too busy with their own affairs to pay attention to the newcomers from the other side of the Pacific. It was not until 1896 that the California-Nevada District of the Evangelical Lutheran Synod of Missouri, Ohio, and Other States (the predecessor body of the now Lutheran Church–Missouri Synod) thought of ministering to the Chinese in San Francisco, California, but there was no evidence indicating that further concrete actions were actually taken by this church.

A refugee is given seedlings by other refugees working in the Reclamation Garden Project organized by the Lutheran World Federation (LWF) and funded by the World Food Programme (WFP) in Beldangi 2 refugee camp on March 13, 2015, in Beldangi, Nepal. More than 22,000 Bhutanese refugees still reside in the refugee camps set up in Nepal in the 1990s, after hundreds of thousands of Bhutanese fled the country following a campaign of ethnic cleansing by the Bhutanese Government against the country's ethnic Nepali population. After more than 20 years in Nepal, over 90% of the refugees have been successfully resettled in third countries, thanks to programs by UNHCR and IOM. Those remaining in the camps are supported by several organizations that undertake a wide variety of projects. Helped by remittances sent back to Nepal by families already resettled in other countries, the refugees still in the camps have set up their own small businesses in the camps and the roads near them, roads which are also replete with Nepali-owned businesses. (Omar Havana/Getty Images)

Beginnings

In 1935, a group of Chinese Americans in New York City left the Church of All Nations, a Methodist Episcopal congregation, to form its own ministry. These Chinese American Christians organized a Sunday school named *Lingguang* (True Light) in New York's Chinatown. In the following year they approached the English District of the now Lutheran Church–Missouri Synod for support. After a series of negotiations and conferences, support was granted, giving birth to True Light Lutheran Church. This was the first formal Asian American affiliation with Lutheranism. By the mid-1950s this church had become the largest Protestant Chinese church in America, with a membership of more than 800.

World War II and the establishment of the People's Republic of China in 1949 brought numerous missionaries to Japan and China back to the United States. Missionaries returning from Japan tried to initiate ministry with the Japanese around Fresno, California, but to no avail. In the meantime, a lay Caucasian couple from Minnesota had befriended some former Japanese internees (more than 100,000 Japanese were put into concentration camps across America during WWII) and through them a ministry was established in Los Angeles, California. This ministry too eventually disappeared.

The United Lutheran Church in America at the urging of the Japanese Lutherans in Japan also attempted a ministry to the Japanese in Los Angeles, using the leadership of a retired missionary couple who had served in Japan and Paul T. Nakamura, a seminarian intern. This too was not successful.

In 1963, Wilbert Holt, a former missionary to China from the Lutheran Church–Missouri Synod, began a ministry to the Chinese in San Francisco's Chinatown. With the help of Amy Hau Mui, a parish worker originally from Hong Kong, Holt was able to birth the Lutheran Church of the Holy Spirit.

Subsequently Wilson Wu, originally from China, and the native-born Paul T. Nakamura of the Lutheran Church in America were able to organize Chinese and Japanese congregations respectively in Southern California. The American Lutheran Church by the mid-1970s also had a Chinese ministry in Hawai'i. Moreover, the Lutheran Church–Missouri Synod also attempted a ministry to the Filipinos in

that state. But the Filipino response was not positive and the ministry was later closed.

The initial phase of Asian American Lutheran ministry was initiated mainly by Asian Americans themselves or at the urging of Asian Lutherans from abroad and by missionaries who had returned from Japan and China.

Turning Point

American society in the 1960s was in tumult: the civil rights movement was in high gear; the assassinations of President John F. Kennedy and his brother Robert and key civil rights leader Martin Luther King Jr. shocked the nation; the escalation of the war in Vietnam caused nationwide protests and riots; and the equalization of immigration policy of the Lyndon B. Johnson administration brought tremendous changes to the demographic landscape. West Coast Lutheran leaders of the various denominations, recognizing the rapid demographic change among the Asian communities and the decline of their own Euro-American membership, urged their respective denominations to seriously consider ministry to Asian Americans.

The Lutheran Church in America accepted the challenge in 1977 by appointing a Chinese American with a newly acquired PhD degree from the University of California, Berkeley, to teach at Pacific Lutheran Theological Seminary, Berkeley, California, and to serve as a consultant/resource developer for Asian ministry, beginning on January 1, 1978. Other Lutheran denominations too followed suit by appointing Asians to staff positions with responsibility for Asian ministries.

Thus, from 1936 to 1977, Asian Lutheran ministries in America were not institutionalized, but self-initiated mainly by or with the help of Asian Americans. However, beginning in 1978 Asian American Lutheran ministries in America became the formal responsibility of some Lutheran denominations. The number of Asian American Lutherans in America in 1978 was about 4,000, with most of them scattered in English-speaking congregations.

Progress

During the last 35 years progress has been made. Today Asian American Lutheran ministries are primarily undertaken by the Lutheran Church–Missouri Synod and the Evangelical Lutheran Church in America. (This church was born in 1988 from a merger of the American Lutheran Church, the Association of Lutheran Churches, and the Lutheran Church in America.) As of 2010 these two denominations reported a combined membership of about 50,000 (most of them members of English-speaking congregations), and a total of 320 ethnic-specific congregations and/or preaching stations, with the majority if not all being served by Asian ministers from overseas.

Asian American Lutheran congregations are smaller than the average-sized white congregations within their denominations. They also have a higher attendance record and a slightly lower financial contribution rate than their counterparts.

Even though progress is being made, these Asian American Lutheran churches are in the main isolated within their denominations, like small drops of tea floating on top of a bucket of milk, unable to penetrate its depth or to spread across its surface. They operate on the periphery of the denominations with little power or influence. Thus they tend to form their own organizations within the institutions for the sake of fellowship and spiritual support.

Contributions and Functions

Be that as it may, some individual Asian American Lutherans have been able to break through institutional and racial barriers to become contributing members in theological and general education and national/regional/synodical/district staff members. But socially the gap in many cases is still wide between Asian American Lutherans and others. Sometimes it is by institutional design and at other times it is due to difficulties in crossing language, cultural, theological, class, and racial lines.

As a group Asian American Lutherans have added color and texture to the nearly all-white institutions. Furthermore Asian American Lutherans, with an infusion of their members into the rank and file of the major Lutheran denominations in America, have also statistically helped the institutions to stop their memberships from slipping away even faster than they are.

Identity

Asian American Lutherans have no historical link or emotional tie to the Reformation heritage of the Euro-American

Lutherans. Asian American Lutherans became Lutherans initially either in Asia or in America as the result of historical and sociological accidents or influenced by friends who were already Lutherans and families. But now there are also second- and third-generation Asian American Lutherans. Their Lutheran identity is framed within the larger context of the Christian community, though liturgically to a certain extent some do adhere to the traditions of their denominations. Moreover, they do not have a pan-Asian American Lutheran identity. Each ethnic group tends to form either a caucus or something similar of its own. This is not to say that there have not been pan-Asian American gatherings, but forging a pan-Asian American Lutheran identity has not been easy.

Challenges

The Asian American community is rich, complex, and diverse with many languages being spoken, cultures practiced, and issues faced. Asian American Lutherans in general share these rich opportunities and challenges as well. And Asian American Lutheran professional workers, as a distinct minority within their own denominations in the United States, face additional challenges. As clergy coming from overseas to serve congregations in the United States, they encounter numerous problems in dealing with ministry and their respective denominations, especially in the areas of polity, communication, language, culture, theology, and racial and social issues.

Within their parishes the ministers are overwhelmingly engaged in helping to guide parishioners through the maze of American society, language issues, and cultural gaps within families between immigrant older generations and younger American-born ones. And when interacting with their own colleagues, Asian American immigrant and native-born professionals must weave their way through a host of issues stemming from different languages, cultures, styles of communication, worldviews, and perspectives on issues.

Yet these challenges can also be turned into opportunities for mutual enrichment. To a certain degree this has happened within Asian American Lutheran circles through formal and informal gatherings and conferences. But it has not taken place within the larger denominations, which continue to marginalize or exclude them, intentionally or not.

Conclusion

Asian American Lutheran ministries at the beginning were initiated by Asian Americans themselves with little institutional recognition. With the return of missionaries from Japan during World War II, these former missionaries also attempted to minister with the Japanese Americans but to no avail. However, one returned missionary to China succeeded in organizing a thriving congregation in San Francisco's Chinatown (the congregation was relocated out of Chinatown some years ago).

With the rapid demographic changes in America beginning in the 1970s, intentional ministry with Asian Americans by Lutheran denominations began in 1978. Today Asian American Lutheran ministry has taken root in the periphery of American Lutheran soil. The growth has been slow but steady, helping to boost the continuous decline of memberships in Lutheran denominations since 1963.

Edmond Yee

See also: Entries: Matsushita, Eiichi; Nakamura, Paul T.; Rajan, Frederick E. N.

Further Reading

Yee, Edmond. *The Soaring Crane: Stories of Asian Lutherans in North America.* Minneapolis: Augsburg Fortress, 2002.

Yee, Edmond, and J. Paul Rajashekar, eds. *Abundant Harvest: Stories of Asian Lutherans in North America.* Minneapolis: Lutheran University Press, 2012.

M

Mahā Ghosananda (1929–2007)

Samdech Preah Mahā Ghosananda, a Theravāda monk who played a key role in rebuilding Buddhism in Cambodia after the fall of the Khmer Rouge, died on March 12, 2007, at the age of 81 in Northampton, Massachusetts. Mahā Ghosananda moved to the United States in the late 1980s at the invitation of the Nipponzan Myohōji Buddhist order in Leverett, Massachusetts.

Mahā Ghosananda was born in Takeo Province, Cambodia. He studied Pāli scriptures in the local temple high school and was ordained at 19. He trained at monastic universities in Phonm Penh and Battambang before attending Nālanda University in India, where he received a doctoral degree in 1957. In 1965, Mahā Ghosananda went to Thailand to study with Bhikkhu Buddhadasa (1906–1993); subsequently he began a nine-year meditation forest retreat under the Achaan Dhammadaro (1913–2005). In 1975, during his forest retreat, the Khmer Rouge gained power and began targeting Buddhist clerics. Mahā Ghosananda lost his entire family, including 16 siblings. After the Vietnamese toppled the Khmer Rouge in 1979, he returned to Cambodia to train a new generation of monks and to advocate for peace; he was one of a handful of remaining senior clerics. His activism culminated in the famous *Dhammayietras*, peace walks through war-torn, landmine-infested regions of Cambodia. In 1989 together with Peter Pond (1906–2000), he returned to Cambodia to establish the Inter-religious Mission for Peace, a Bangkok-based project designed to bring monks and refugees together from all the refugee camps on the Thai-Cambodian border, including those run by the Khmer Rouge, to teach peace and nonviolence through Buddhism.

Mahā Ghosananda publicized the plight of the Cambodian people at any number of international forums and established a number of temples in the United States. He was nominated for the Nobel Peace Prize three times in the 1990s.

Ronald Y. Nakasone

See also: Entries: Cambodian American Religions

Further Reading

Harvey, Peter. *An Introduction to Buddhist Ethics*. Cambridge: Cambridge University Press, 2000.

Hunt, Scott A. *The Future of Peace: On the Front Lines with the World's Great Peacemakers*. San Francisco: HarperSanFrancisco, 2002.

Mahā Ghosananda. *Step by Step: Meditations on Wisdom and Compassion*. Berkeley: Parallax Press, 1991.

Marston, John Amos, and Elizabeth Guthrie. *History, Buddhism, and New Religious Movements in Cambodia*. Honolulu: University of Hawai'i Press, 2004.

Supreme Cambodian Buddhist Patriarch Mahā Ghosananda in 1998, leading a peace march in Phnom Penh, Cambodia's capital. Ghosananda, who lived in Leverett, Massachusetts, and Providence, Rhode Island, was believed to be in his late 70s at the time of his death in 2007. (AP Photo/Heng Sinith)

Mahikari (True Light)

Established in 1959 by Okada Yoshikazu (1901–1974), Mahikari (True Light) is a spiritual organization that, after a split in 1978, exists as two separate groups, Sekai Mahikari Bunmei Kyōdan (Church of the World True-Light Civilization) and Sūkyō Mahikari (Sūkyō True Light). Despite the separation, the groups largely share the belief and practice established by Okada, which teaches that certain spiritual principles underlie the world and humans can attain greater happiness by attuning themselves to these principles. The core practice for connecting with these spiritual principles is giving and receiving Divine Light energy, transmitted through the palm, which produces physical, psychological, and spiritual benefits. While the primary focus of light-giving is to help others and foster one's own personal growth, it is not restricted to humans. Light may be given to any sentient or nonsentient being and overall increases the connection of humans to their environment.

The North American headquarters of Sūkyō Mahikari are in Rancho Santa Margarita, California. It operates 23 centers in major U.S. cities as well as Canada and Puerto Rico. Current membership for the North American Region is 10,000. Sekai

Mahikari Bunmei Kyōdan's main centers are in California, New York, and Kentucky. It also operates a traveling minister system where leaders visit remote locations.

History

In August 1959, Okada Yoshikazu established a group called Yōkōshi Tomo no Kai (Sunlight Children Friends Association) and then, in 1963, registered it as a religion with the name Sekai Mahikari Bunmei Kyōdan. Okada formed Yōkōshi Tomo no Kai based on what he claimed was divine revelation he received in February 1959 from Mioya Motosu Mahikari Ōmikami (Great Parent, Original Lord, God of True Light), also called Sushin or Su God (Creator God). Subsequent revelations occurred through 1967 and they are collected in the *Goseigen* (holy words), a key text for Mahikari teachings. Previously, Okada had been active in Sekai Kyūseikyō (Church of World Messianity). Okada later changed his name to Okada Kōtama (jewel of light) and took the honorific title *Sukuinushisama* (lord savior).

After Okada's death in 1974 there was a struggle for power between Okada Sachiko, Okada's adopted daughter who took the name Keiju, and Sakiguchi Sakae. In 1978 the organization split. Sakiguchi's group retained the name Sekai Mahikari Bunmei Kyōdan while Okada's took the name Sūkyō Mahikari.

Mahikari's presence in the United States has been relatively small. Regarding Sekai Mahikari Bunmei Kyōdan, in 1988 the United States authorized it as an incorporated religious organization and it is primarily located in California and New York. The second leader was Sakae Sekiguchi (1909–1994). Under his leadership the construction of the Su-za World Main Shrine in Amagi, Japan, was completed in 1987. Sekiguchi Katsutoshi (1939–), Sakae's son, is the current leader and one of his achievements was implementing a study-abroad program for Japanese students in 1990, particularly to the University of California, Irvine.

Sūkyō Mahikari's current leader is Okada Koya (1947–). While Sekai Mahikari Bunmei Kyōdan's activities have largely remained focused on the spiritual practice described below, Sūkyō Mahikari has expanded its activities, giving particular attention to environmental issues. These include environmental cleanup and tree planting and advocating for organic gardening as a spiritual practice. Sūkyō Mahikari also operates a research center, the Yoko Civilization Research Institute, which conducts conferences and other activities, investigating how Mahikari relates to modern science, medicine, and other fields. It is also an affiliate member of the United Religious Initiative of North America.

Belief and Practice

In his writings, Okada presented a cosmology that consisted of a supreme god, Su God, which created everything and shared its spirit with the creation. Su God is the head of a group of gods related to the sun. This group withdrew and placed the world under the rule of lesser gods related to the moon. During this time the world became more materialistic, ignoring spiritual realities, and various problems arose until ultimately a time would come when "Su God would reveal himself and return the world to its pristine form, ushering in a new civilization of spirit characterized by health, peace, and prosperity. To prepare humankind for the advent of this radical change, Su God chose Okada Kōtama as the *Sakigake no meshia* . . . the harbinger Messiah of the new age who urges people to undergo the great 'cleaning' and so become the *tanebito* . . . the 'seed people,' of the new civilization."

This cosmological-eschatological vision of the need for universal purification grounds Mahikari's core notion of the importance of *mihikari* or "Divine Light" that proceeds from Su God and purifies and eliminates problems, including physical and spiritual illnesses, moral and relational problems, or material and financial wants. It is also referred to as *mahikari* or "True Light." The significance of True Light motivates the core practice of Mahikari, *okiyome*, the activity of dispensing Divine Light through one's hand onto any object that needs healing. This light is believed to purify the body from possessing spirits and from "toxins," poisonous material accumulated in the body. The whole world is seen as needing purification, so the ritual can be performed on any object, sentient or nonsentient. Essential to effective *okiyome* is wearing a special amulet called an *omitama* that is given to new members at the end of the initiatory three-day course. After the basic three-day course, intermediate and advanced courses are offered to deepen one's understanding and practice. While *okiyome* is what Ma-

hikari is best known for, the practice of transmitting divine energy through the hand is not unique to it. The activity also exists in the spiritual traditions of Sekai Kyūseikyō and Oomoto. The extent to which these earlier groups influenced the formation of Mahikari is debated.

For Mahikari, then, all physical, psychic, emotional, and social problems are rooted in conflict in the spiritual realm. In addition to Su God and the lesser spirits under it, there are other personal spirits and impersonal forces. Ancestral spirits play an important role and maintaining a good relationship with them through daily offerings is emphasized. Impersonal forces include the notion of *ki*, which can refer to a feeling in a place, a psychological or bodily state, or a vital essence that permeates and unites the cosmos, as well as *kotodama*, the spiritual power of words, *reihasen*, "cords of spiritual vibrations," and *reiha* or *hinami*, "spirit waves." Mahikari also endorses a view of reincarnation.

Organizationally, Mahikari maintains a hierarchical system of leadership and locations, including *dojos* (training centers) of various sizes, *okiyomechō* (centers for the transmission of light), and *han* (home centers) led by *dōjōchō* (president of a *dojo*), *dōshi* (ministers), and *honcho* (leaders of a squadron or of a small center). When a group is large enough they may form an *okiyomechō* center. An *okiyomechō* will have an altar in the front, called the *goshinden*, containing the *goshintai*, a scroll inscribed with the characters for the word *mahikari* and a *chon*, or comma-shaped mark, on a gold disc on a cross. The *chon* is described as the shape or physiognomy of the spirit and the supreme divinity and is also the first sound of the 48 sounds of Japanese, and thus of all existence. In addition, there is a statue of Izunomesama, the god who represents the materialization of spiritual energy and who is worshipped and thanked for material benefits.

Rather than seeing itself as exclusive of other religions or spiritual traditions, Mahikari is quite inclusive, claiming to be the fulfillment of what other religious traditions pointed to. Okada Yoshikazu insists that "all religions are basically one, belief is basically one, mankind is basically one, and the earth is originally one," but adds that the importance of the historical religions lies only in their function as "breaks" to prevent mankind's total deviation from God's plan. They will be superseded in due time by the *sūkyō*. In this way, Mahikari does not require that new members reject their previous beliefs or practices. But while Mahikari sees itself as universally relevant and more than just a local Japanese spiritual tradition, this has presented challenges. While Mahikari's emphasis on solving immediate, practical problems has been very attractive to Western audiences, other features resist adaptation to new contexts and inevitably produce a certain foreignness. It is the correct performance of the ritual and the exact pronunciation of the prayers that brings about the desired results. Both the teachings and the rituals are, moreover, believed to be divinely revealed, and thus not subject to change. The ways both Sūkyō Mahikari and Sekai Mahikari Bunmei Kyōdan negotiate this balance between cultural particularity and global adaptation will certainly impact their continued relevance in the future.

Peter L. Doebler

Further Reading

Broder, Anne. "Mahikari in Context: Kamigakari, Chinkon kishin, and Psychical Investigation in Ōmoto-lineage Religions." *Japanese Journal of Religious Studies* 35, no. 2 (2008): 331–62.

Cornille, Catherine. "Mahikari." In Peter B. Clarke, ed. *Encyclopedia of New Religious Movements*. New York: Routledge, 2006, pp. 383–85.

Cornille, Catherine. "The Phoenix Flies West: The Dynamics of the Inculturation of Mahikari in Western Europe." *Japanese Journal of Religious Studies* 18, nos. 2–3 (1991): 265–85.

Davis, Winston. *Dojo: Magic and Exorcism in Modern Japan*. Stanford, CA: Stanford University Press, 1982.

Hurbon, La Ennec. "Mahikari in the Caribbean." *Japanese Journal of Religious Studies* 18, nos. 2–3 (1991): 243–64.

Knecht, Peter. "The Crux of the Cross: Mahikari's Core Symbol." *Japanese Journal of Religious Studies* 22, nos. 3–4 (1995): 321–40.

McFarland, H. Neill. *The Rush Hour of the Gods: A Study of New Religious Movements in Japan*. New York: Macmillan, 1967.

McVeigh, Brian. *Spirits, Selves and Subjectivity in a Japanese New Religion*. New York: Edwin Mellen Press, 1997.

McVeigh, Brian. "The Vitalistic Conception of Salvation as Expressed in Sukyo Mahikari." *Japanese Journal of Religious Studies* 19, no. 1 (1992): 41–68.

Melton, J. Gordon, and Jones, C. A. (1994). "New Japanese Religions in the United States." In Peter B. Clarke and Jeffrey Somers, eds. *Japanese New Religions in the West*. Sandgate, UK: Japan Library/Curzon Press, 1994, pp. 33–53.

Seiō (Okada Kōtama*). Goseigen: The Holy Words*. Tujunga, CA: Sekai Mahikari Bunmei Kyōdan, 1982.

Sūkyō Mahikari. *Holy Words: Goseigen.* Second English edition. Rancho Santa Margarita, CA: Bishop of North American Region of Sūkyō Mahikari, 2002.

Tsushima, Michihito, Shigeru Nishiyama, Susumu Shimazono, and Hiroko Shiramizu. "The Vitalistic Conception of Salvation in Japanese New Religions: An Aspect of Modern Religious Consciousness." *Japanese Journal of Religious Studies* 6, nos. 1–2 (1979): 138–61.

Weston, Erin Leigh. "Transcultural Possessions in/of Mahikari: Religious Syncretism in Martinique." *Japanese Studies Review* 6, no. 1 (2002): 45–62.

Young, Richard Fox. "Magic and Morality in Modern Japanese Exorcistic Technologies—The Study of Mahikari." *Japanese Journal of Religious Studies* 17, no. 1 (1990): 29–48.

Malaysian American Religions

Rev. Ouyang Wen Feng addresses the audience of the Malaysian Church Community's gathering in Kuala Lumpur, Malaysia. The gay Malaysian pastor who plans to marry his American partner in New York has pledged to throw a wedding banquet in his home country despite stern criticism by Muslim politicians. (AP Photo/Alex Wan)

Religion in Malaysian America is a deep mosaic reflecting on its surface an ancient encounter and dialogue with many indigenous and world religions, fed by a continuing underground spring of indigenous Malay-Polynesian (Bhumiputra) culture and sacred geomantic perspectives that unite the cosmos into a unified, organic manifesting and nonmanifesting whole. This highly complex culture is alive in an equally complicated American fabric pervaded by the persistent pan-Asian geomancy that is definitive in both Daoism and sacred agrarian Malay religious cultures. For Malaysian Americans, ancient and modern political realities go hand in hand with religious culture and beliefs spread across Malaysian varieties of Hindu, Buddhist, Daoist, Confucian, Muslim, and Christian cultures where world religions merge thematically into the ever-present indigenous primal Malay (Bhumiputran) base.

The complex indigenous tradition is itself forged from many ancient southward-moving migrations of Tibetan and Yunnan peoples into the Irrawady, Menam, and Mekong valleys and into the Malay Peninsula, spilling over into Indonesia, displacing primal Negrito populations and further fusing with Polynesian influences. As part of Farther India, anciently compatible Hindu traditions following Vaisnavite,

Saivite, and Tantric lines paved the way for an acceptance of later Indian Buddhist pilgrims who were attempting to reform the Hinduism of their time back to its Vedic roots. Significant *yoga*-samkhya meditative techniques loosely following Patanjali, and used by the historical Buddha, interacted profoundly throughout all of Farther India, influencing pervasive indigenous meditative and ritual trance practices. As nearly as anyone can tell, the complex Malay-Polynesian family draws from ancient Central Asian Pyus, Indian Bhils-Gonds, Mon-Khmers, and Malays whose combined presence sets a profoundly unbroken psychological tone expressive of an indigenous primal Malaysian religious perspective very much alive today as Bhumiputra culture. Modern religio-cultural fractures along the many fault lines of these ancient civilizations have in recent history ceded parts of Burma (Myanmar) to Malaysia proper, while others have been folded back into India surrounding Bangladesh, territorially carving out the current kite-with-a-tail shape of modern Burma (Myanmar) and the long peninsular tail of Thailand dipping into the Malay Peninsula. An island portion of Malaysia lies across the sea on the northern half of the large Indonesian island of Kalimantan (Borneo), placing many Malaysian religio-cultural perspectives closer to revitalizing Hinduized primal traditions of this and other Indonesian islands, with nearby Indonesian Bali and India itself acting as the current hub exporting spiritual meditative and ritual expertise to wider Indonesian and Malaysian regions. A long blueprint for tolerance of multiple blended perspectives follows at least politely into the American diaspora, where Malaysian Americans are practicing new communication skills that have the potential to reverberate back into Malaysia.

With more than 60 modern ethnically differentiated peoples, the critical Malaysian politico-religious distinction is that between indigenous Bhumiputran and non-Bhumiputran cultures and ancestry. This tension is expressed in America in subtle ethnic appraisals everywhere, even in American food blogs where latent ethnic hostility contends that Bhumiputra alone in all its dimensions is the only authentic Malaysia. Tendentious Malaysian struggles toward political unity and modern statehood mask powerful Bhumiputra perspectives carried to America that are not sympathetically shared by the Straits Chinese Malaysian minority. The Malaysian mosaic of perspective includes the tiny but thriving close-by island nation of Singapore, not technically part of Malaysia, but reflective of the many strands of intense and radical religio-ethnic pluralism of Malaysia, as well as the large nearby island of ancient trade and gold, Sumatra, thought by some archaeologists to contain a cradle of indigenous Malay civilization near Palembang and Sri Vijaya. The American diaspora, if anything, continues to refract and even separate Malaysian Americans further from each other, ceding the cultural integration role to American higher education courses, faculty, and multicultural student associations, which provide expressive vehicles and antidotes for latent fracturing and fomenting hostilities. The legal umbrella of freedom of religion and expression encourages opportunities for Malays and Malay minorities to at least partially recover and research ancient cultural and religious influences and underlying unities.

The vast geographical American expanse absorbs and disperses a comparatively small number of Malaysian Americans into mixed marriages and the ready-made streams of institutionalized major world religions. Islam and Christianity each give broad accessible shelter to Malaysians stemming from centuries of missionary work by Catholic and Protestant missionaries, colonial forces, and Muslim traders who established Muslim communities and *mosques* along the Straits and deeper inland. Indian and Straits Chinese Malaysian Americans, Christianized or not, find numerous Indians Abroad organizations, Buddhist, Daoist, Confucian, and successor societies of secret Chinese aid organizations in America, inviting them to degrees of instant affiliation, an experience only too familiar to Malaysians accustomed to the prismatic pluralism of the comparatively tiny Malaysian homeland. Malaysian Americans recognize the recurring need to band together, often against other ethnic and religious groups, to survive interethnic competitions. In the United States, they can do so across multiple hereditary and mixed-marriage lines while privately cherishing a persistent Daoist-like unified geomantic and spirit attitude, which may be better understood as pan-Asian, and whose voice is louder in indigenous Malay primal religious traditions. Some Malaysian Americans are reverting to better-understood Hindu and meditative practices, once freed to swim in the vast anonymity of the American democracy.

Extending a hand, the Buddhist Churches of America (BCA), Zen practice centers,

and the Nichiren Shōshū of America (NSA) have expanded beyond coastal California immigrant landing platforms to East Coast and scattered inland locations, along with Sufi and *yoga* centers for Indian and Muslim Malaysians. Peninsular Chinese Christian Malaysian Americans, mostly strict Roman Catholics, verbally disavow primal, Daoist, and Confucian practices in favor of a Catholicism that keeps close to American church-sponsored schools and universities, notably Jesuit and Methodist institutions and state institutions with strong multicultural programs. Muslim Malaysian Americans, hailing from a 60 percent Muslim state, find immediate acceptance within growing American Islamic communities where an instant *ummah* (community) welcomes them through an American door to a global community as diverse and familiar as Malaysia itself. Younger Malaysian immigrants of all stripes are stepping out of narrow missionary and official molds into mixed marriages and higher-education explorations of traditional South Asian meditative traditions, recovering religious roots systematically with a Malaysian ease. Malaysian Americans, attracted to meditative traditions, relate well to meditative and mystical aspects of the Westernized Middle Eastern traditions of Christianity and Islam (Sufi) with an accent on the contemplative dimensions of Asian Christianity and Islam.

American higher education institutions assume new cultural roles for Malaysian Americans who are curious about religion and interested in meditative-leaning traditions. By creating and consolidating comparative information and international student associations, new awareness and opportunities abound for Malaysian Americans as they move toward rebuilding a comprehensive Malaysian ethnic and religious consciousness and enter advanced academic study leading to original research opportunities in Malaysian and South and Southeast Asian studies. Courses in world religions, Oriental philosophies, anthropology, and historical and comparative studies focused on South Asia attract intellectually curious and empowered Malaysians who can acquire the necessary extra research languages needed to excel. It is difficult to predict where the new systematic study of beliefs and philosophico-religious systems, replacing on-the-ground cultural encounters, will lead Malaysian Americans in the full recovery of their own deeper senses of ritual meanings and comparative understandings. Important reframes of Daoist geomantic practices, once passing out of context as mere disjointed superstition, are already occurring in the revitalized Malaysian American communities that are blossoming in American higher education forums.

Straits Chinese Malaysian Americans, including Chinese Malaysian Christians, affiliate with secret aid societies in the United States following symbolic Daoist and Confucian geomantic perspectives, rituals, lunar agricultural calendars, animist beliefs, degrees of meditation, spirit trance, and spirit medium practices that connect them to each other, to mutual success, propitiation of ancestors, Daoist anthropomorphic gods and goddesses, festivals, seasons, stars, and ghost chasing, despite all changes in latitude or longitude. Confucian social concerns and bonds create a secular religious humanism that persists in the underlying nature mysticism inside Daoist and Malay rituals. Ancestor and spirit propitiation for success and protection persist in America in symbolic ritual activities connecting living persons to the sacred ancestral spirit stream flowing from the Yellow (Heavenly) Emperor through his Daoist title as the Jade Emperor and beyond into matriarchal and patriarchal deifications of the vast Ultimate Dao, a Dao that never shows itself completely, remaining mostly invisible to the physical senses. Chinese American enclaves quietly yield contacts for numerous serious ritual activities found by discreet word of mouth. Contacts can be made inside Chinese secret aid societies, American Taoist and *qigong* centers, favored Malaysian restaurants, Chinese American pharmacies, and Chinese Buddhist and Tibetan Tantric Buddhist centers.

Promotion of Malay as a national unifying culture and language in the modern Malaysian political state remains especially sensitive for Straits Chinese Malaysian Americans who perceive the policy as discriminatory. Many wonder aloud where the Malays are, disputing hereditary distinctness and citing prejudice against Straits Chinese financial success, sacred and secular religious geomantic perspectives. Such disputes are, in their view, buried in the official promotion of the Malay language and primal Malaysian religions. Chinese-language schools in America, as in Malaysia, remain central expressive vehicles for this essentially religious dispute, and central to full invitation into Chinese American cultural and aid societies. Financial struggles of many Malaysian Chinese-language schools are assisted financially by Straits Chinese Malaysian Americans, who are increasingly looked on as less Chinese and more simply Malaysian (or Indonesian) by global Chinese communities if they do not speak or read Chinese, a fact noted almost immediately by all Southeast Asians.

Barbara A. Amodio

Further Reading

Church, Peter, ed. *A Short History of South-East Asia.* 5th ed. Singapore: John Wiley and Sons (Asia), 2009.

Coomaraswamy, Ananda K. *History of Indian and Indonesian Art.* New Delhi: Munshiram Manoharlal, 1972.

Debernardi, Jean. *Rites of Belonging: Memory, Modernity, and Identity in a Malaysian Chinese Community.* Stanford, CA: Stanford University Press, 2004.

Geertz, Clifford. *Negara: The Theatre State in Nineteenth-Century Bali.* Princeton, NJ: Princeton University Press, 1991.

Mahathir bin Mohamad. *The Malay Dilemma.* Singapore: Times Books International, 1970.

Smith, Huston. *The World's Religion: Our Great Wisdom Traditions.* Revised and updated ed. San Francisco: HarperCollins, 1991.

Marshall Islands, Religion in

The Marshall Islands, composed of two chains of coral atolls running generally north-south, are located in the western Pacific just above the equator. Formerly governed by Germany, Japan, and the United States, the Marshalls became an independent nation as of 1986 and have a population of about 55,000.

Historical Developments

The seafarers who settled the small atolls of the Marshalls are thought to have first arrived there in the century or two before the time of Christ. During this period voyagers had sailed from northern Melanesia in their ocean-going canoes to make their home throughout eastern Micronesia. Even today the languages of the peoples in this area are closely related and the customs similar.

We know very little of the development of the Marshallese people until the onset of European contact in the 16th century. The chiefly system in the Marshalls, surprisingly elaborate for small communities on coral atolls, suggests that at some point Polynesian influence reached the islands. For the rest, Marshallese culture retained its distinctive features: people relied heavily on pandanus as a staple food, traveled extensively from one island to another in their single-outrigger sailing canoes, and honored their traditional religious beliefs.

In the late 16th century, the Marshall Islands had their first contact with the West when a few of the atolls were visited by Spanish ships crossing the Pacific on their search for the treasures of the East. It wasn't until the mid-19th century, however, that extensive contact with Westerners began. U.S. whaleships occasionally visited the islands during the 1840s and 1850s, but most of these contacts were fleeting and ended with hostility between the islanders and the ship crews. By 1870, foreign traders began to take up residence on the islands as the copra trade flourished and new trade goods were made available to the people. Islanders cut dried coconut that would be pressed for its oil, which was used for a number of purposes in Europe and America.

Meanwhile, the American Board of Commissioners for Foreign Missions (ABCFM) extended its missionary work from the eastern Caroline Islands to the Marshalls when, in 1857, they put two American missionaries and a Hawaiian aide aboard one of the islands in the group. Thus began the evangelization of the Marshall Islands. Within a few years, the two Americans departed, leaving the mission in the hands of Hawaiian teachers and their new Marshallese converts. The pastors established small schools everywhere to teach the members of their growing communities how to read the Bible, which was then being translated into the local Marshallese language. In the reports that the missionaries sent back to Hawai'i, they counted not just their converts but also the number of "readers" among their membership.

Shortly after the death of Kaibuke, the paramount chief who had protected the missionaries during their first five years, resentment surfaced and chiefs began to retaliate against those Marshallese who had defected to the new religion. For a time they began terrorizing new converts, in some cases even burning down their houses and threatening their lives. But this proved to be the final flailing of a traditional belief system that was quickly being replaced by Christianity. By the end of the 19th century, the Congregational Church was solidly established in the Marshalls, just as it was in the adjacent island groups in Micronesia.

In 1899, Catholics, too, established a foothold in the Marshalls when the German-speaking Missionaries of the Sacred Heart established a mission on Likiep and shortly afterwards on two other islands. The mission school they established on Jaluit a few years later won the reputation of being the best school in the Pacific at that time.

The Germans, who claimed the Marshall Islands as a protectorate, ruled the islands until the outbreak of World War I in 1914. As soon as war had been declared, Japan swept in and took possession of the islands for the duration of the war. At the end of the war, Japan was entrusted with formal authority to govern the islands on behalf of the newly established League of Nations. During the 30-year period of Japanese rule, the Congregational Church continued to increase the size of its membership, which eventually reached 95 percent of the population. Meanwhile, Catholic mission work passed from the Missionaries of the Sacred Heart to the Spanish Jesuits, who soon afterwards withdrew their resident priests and were content to make a single pastoral visit each year.

With the defeat of Japan at the end of World War II, the United States became the administering authority in the Marshalls on behalf of the United Nations Trusteeship Council. The U.S. quickly commandeered two of the northernmost atolls in the Marshalls as test sites for its newly developed nuclear weapons, while Kwajalein became a military base and later a test range for the missiles that were being developed during the cold war era.

During the latter part of U.S. administration, several small denominations were established in the Marshalls. The most successful of these was Assemblies of God, which soon claimed a significant share of the Protestant congregation, but Mormons, Seventh-day Adventists, and Baptists also opened churches. Meanwhile, the Catholic congregation expanded and its influence grew as a result of its special efforts in primary and secondary education on several of the islands.

When the Marshall Islands became independent in 1986, there were no fewer than seven different churches established in the island group. The conversion to Christianity had been completed nearly a century before, and evidence of the social and religious importance of the church could be found everywhere. Yet, for those who knew where to look, remnants of the traditional religion were also easy to find.

Beliefs and Practices

Like peoples in other parts of the Pacific, the Marshallese lived in a world that was teeming with spirits. There were a few spirits who made their home in the heavens, including one deity (Lowa) who created the islands and a group of sister deities who founded the chiefly clans. Generally, however, sky gods were remote from the affairs of humans and almost never consulted by the Marshallese.

Most of the spirits honored by Marshallese resided at a much lower level. They included the spirits of dead relatives who might return at times to possess someone in the family so as to provide valuable information or other assistance. Even today an individual might go into a trance state and take on the voice and mannerisms of a dead relative while speaking to the entire family on behalf of the ancestral spirit. The death of a family member was a critical moment in traditional Marshallese culture, for the spirit had to be placated and sent on its way to the afterlife in a good mood so that it would protect the interests of its family thereafter.

Nature spirits were another category. Usually these spirits were associated with certain plants or bushes or places. A particular reef, for instance, might be regarded as dangerous because of the harmful spirits living there who preyed on women and children. The world of the Marshallese people, like that of other Micronesians, was filled with dangers, many of them caused by superhuman forces. Although most of these nature spirits were fixed to a certain location, some malicious spirits roamed widely. The *mejenkwad*, for example, were a type of cruel female spirit that could fly from place to place bringing death and destruction to different islands.

Marshallese also recognized a variety of other gods, including the god of the ocean, to whom they prayed when fishing and sailing to another atoll. Islanders would call on their guardian spirits when they prepared to cut down a tree to be used in the construction of a sailing canoe. The rituals that were conducted at the start of the breadfruit and pandanus harvest seasons called on a variety of patron gods through prayer and offerings to give abundant food to the people of the atolls. Other rituals were used to invoke the spirits when people made preserved breadfruit or pandanus flour.

Sickness was believed to be caused by the power of the spirits, and so the most effective remedies for sickness also had to be sought from the spirits. To determine who had caused the sickness and how it could be treated, people had recourse to the spirit world. People often had to use different kinds of divination to find answers to these and other questions in their lives. Sometimes they threw a handful of pebbles on the ground and from their pattern tried to discern the answer to their question. Another type of divination was tying knots randomly in strands of coconut or pandanus leaves and counting the number of knots afterwards to find what they needed to know. Helpless in the face of the mysteries that surrounded them, Marshallese turned to the spirits for the knowledge that they were unable to attain on their own.

As Christianity spread rapidly throughout the islands in the late 19th century, the new faith supplanted the traditional religious beliefs and practices. No longer would Marshallese call on their patron gods to assist them, and the offerings and prayers once offered to these gods soon became a thing of the past. Marshallese read the Bible, practiced their new faith, and surrendered the rituals they once practiced so assiduously.

Even so, the spirit world that the Marshallese had once believed in did not disappear entirely. Some spirits continue to roam, Marshallese practice today seems to suggest. People are still said to be possessed by the spirits of the dead today, even if this is not as common as it once was. Many Marshallese still fear venturing onto certain reefs or other places where the nature spirits of old were believed to reside. Some Marshallese still practice divination as their ancestors did, but instead of tying knots in leaf strands, they may open the Bible and let their finger fall upon a verse at random in the hope that the words will shed light on what they are expected to do. Even as they formally practice Christianity, Marshallese today retain a residual belief in much of their old spirit world and in the forces that operated within that world. One could say that for many Marshallese the ancient spirits that their ancestors honored still roam today.

Francis X. Hezel

See also: Entries: Pacific Islander Religious Cultures

Further Reading

Dobbin, Jay, and Francis X. Hezel. *Summoning the Powers Beyond: Traditional Religions in Micronesia*. Honolulu: University of Hawai'i Press, 2011.

Frazer, James. *The Belief in Immortality and the Worship of the Dead*. Vol 3: *The Belief among the Micronesians*. London: Dawson's, 1924.

Swain, Tony, and Garry Trompf. *The Religions of Oceania*. The Library of Religious Beliefs and Practices Series. London: Routledge, 1995.

Tobin, Jack A. *Stories from the Marshall Islands*. Honolulu: University of Hawai'i Press, 2002.

Maryknoll Catholic Missionaries

Maryknoll is a religious missionary organization of secular priests and brothers, sisters, and lay missioners. The priests and brothers form the Catholic Foreign Mission Society of America, popularly known as Maryknoll. The sisters are formally the

Maryknoll Sisters of St. Dominic and are an independent organization closely affiliated with the society.

The Catholic Foreign Mission Society of America (the priests and brothers) was founded for the purpose of preaching the Gospel outside the United States to non-Christians. The society's emphasis is on fostering a local clergy, providing a seminary formation, and preparing candidates for overseas missionary service. In the United States, it engages mostly in education and in the publishing of materials related to missions. Since its founding, however, Maryknoll missioners have kept a presence in the United States, working primarily in Asian American communities.

In early 1911, the Bostonian Fr. James A. Walsh (1867–1936), director of the Society for the Propagation of the Faith, and Fr. Thomas Price (1860–1919), a home (U.S.) missioner in North Carolina, received permission from the archbishops of the United States to establish the American Seminary for Foreign Missions, with instructions to secure the necessary authorization from the Sacred Congregation for the Propagation of the Faith in Rome. That authorization was granted on June 29, 1911. The archbishops then placed the new foundation under the oversight of the bishops, clergy, and laity of the United States.

Mary Josephine Rogers (1882–1955), founder of the Maryknoll Sisters of St. Dominic, was a graduate of Smith College who originally volunteered her services to help Father Walsh with the publication of *The Field Afar*. When the founders of Maryknoll settled in New York, several young women, eager to serve the cause of the mission, came to help with the publica-

tion. Walsh appointed Rogers, who arrived on September 9, 1912, director of the small group of seven "secretaries." As their numbers increased, they became known as "The Teresians of Maryknoll." Eight years later the Teresians, who had petitioned the Vatican to form as a religious community, received a directive establishing them as the Foreign Mission Sisters of St. Dominic; today, they are popularly known as Maryknoll Sisters.

In 1912, after temporary housing in Thornwood and Hawthorne, New York, Maryknoll acquired, with the help of Rogers, 93 acres of farmland on a hill overlooking the Hudson River in Ossining, New York. This location, which has since served as the society's headquarters, was referred to as "Mary's Hill on the Hudson" or as "Mary's Knoll" because of the group's deep devotion to Mary. Its name soon became Maryknoll.

Maryknoll established its first mission in China. On September 7, 1918, Frs. Thomas Price, James E. Walsh, Bernard F. Meyer, and Francis X. Ford left Maryknoll for Guangdong in south China (Father Price died one year later in Hong Kong). The Maryknoll Society soon extended its presence throughout south China and north to Manchuria (Francis Ford later died in a Communist prison in Guangdong and James E. Walsh spent 12 years in a Chinese prison; in 1970, he was the last foreign missionary to leave China during the Communist regime). After China, the Maryknoll priests quickly established missions in 1927 in Korea, the Philippines, and Hawai'i.

The sisters followed very much the same pattern: China (1921), Korea (1924), the Philippines (1926), and Hawai'i (1927),

On September 21, 1921, six Maryknoll Sisters left for China and some six weeks later arrived in Hong Kong and in Yeung-kong (now Yangjiang, Guangdong Province), China. Since then, the Maryknoll Sisters have consistently maintained a presence in all the places, outside of China, noted above, where they founded a number of highly regarded schools, clinics, and hospitals. In all those places, after learning the local language, they also engaged in pastoral, catechetical, and social work.

The Maryknoll Sisters' first mission, however, was in the United States among the Japanese American communities in Los Angeles and Seattle, where they were assisted by the Maryknoll Brothers (members of the society who do not aspire to the priesthood but who live a life of community, celibacy, prayer, and ministry).

The Catholic mission to the Japanese in Los Angeles began in 1920 at the invitation of Bishop Cantwell. The mission to the Japanese in Seattle also began in 1920 at the invitation of Bishop O'Dea. The Maryknoll Sisters opened elementary schools and orphanages and provided social services for the Japanese communities. Less than a decade later, Maryknollers also opened schools in Honolulu (primarily for Japanese students) and a tuberculosis sanatorium in Monrovia, California, where Japanese Americans were among their patients (it is now a retirement home for the Maryknoll Sisters).

After Japan attacked Pearl Harbor on December 7, 1941, President Franklin D. Roosevelt signed, the following February, Executive Order 9066 that allowed military officers to designate the West Coast of the United States and parts of other states, including Hawai'i, military zones from which Japanese and American citizens of Japanese descent were to be excluded and moved to War Relocation Centers. The Japanese were interned in substandard buildings (including horse stalls) in remote "relocation centers," including Manzanar in California and Minidoka in Idaho. Maryknoll Sisters and fathers who had been working with the Japanese in Los Angeles followed them. Two Japanese American Maryknoll Sisters, Bernadette Yoshimochi and Anna Hiyashi, were permitted in 1943 to return to Maryknoll headquarters in New York but opted to live with the Japanese internees in the camps throughout the remainder of their four years of internment. There, the sisters ministered to the spiritual, physical, and educational needs of the internees. Maryknoll Fathers Leo Steinbach and Hugh Lavery, from Maryknoll's St. Xavier Chapel in the Little Tokyo area of Los Angeles, went as well but lived outside the camp and visited daily.

After the end of World War II, many of the Japanese returned to Los Angeles to rebuild their lives as Americans. Their success saw many of them moving out of the community and into the suburbs to guide their children up the American social-economic ladder. Dwindling enrollment in the Maryknoll School led to the closing of the school. It was replaced by the Maryknoll Japanese Catholic Center in 1995. The Maryknollers themselves departed the next year.

Maryknoll School in Honolulu, founded in 1927 and staffed by Maryknoll Sisters who had arrived from their headquarters in New York only days earlier, was initially made up predominantly of Japanese students. Before long, the school was opened to all who desired a Christian education. The school continues today to operate very successfully, albeit without any Maryknollers actively involved in it.

In Chinatowns in San Francisco, New York, Boston, and Chicago, Maryknoll established, or were assigned by local bishops, churches and schools. The priests and sisters provided not only pastoral leadership and education, but also functioned as points of contact between the Asian American communities and the larger society, helping residents, particularly new immigrants, obtain medical and translation services, Social Security insurance, jobs, and education, and otherwise assisted the people in integrating into American life. A number of the Maryknoll priests and sisters who worked in these Chinatown communities had served for many years in Hong Kong and China, where they had learned the Chinese language, so it was logical that they also opened after-hours Chinese-language schools that functioned not only to preserve the home language of the children of immigrants but also served as after-school care for the children of working parents. The Maryknollers have been able to interact with and assist the Chinese in Chinatowns in their own language. Chinatown, New York, is still under the pastoral care of a Maryknoll priest, Fr. Raymond Nobiletti, who had spent many years in Hong Kong.

Boston's Church of St. James the Greater had been founded in 1854 to serve the immigrant Irish community. Just over a century later, the local population was predominantly composed of Cantonese immigrants from China and Hong Kong. Boston's archbishop invited the Maryknoll Sisters, many of whom knew the Cantonese language from their years of work in south China and Hong Kong, to assume responsibility for servicing the needs of a growing non-English-speaking populace. The Maryknoll Sisters' mission on Boston's Tyler Street operated until 1992.

In the 1920s and 1930s, Franciscan priests from nearby St. Peter's Church and the School Sisters of Notre Dame had taught catechism to the Chinese, but the priests and sisters did not know the local Chinese language. St. Therese Chinese Catholic Mission was founded formally in Chicago's Chinatown in 1940 when the archbishop (later Cardinal Samuel Stritch) appointed the Rev. John Mao to start a Catholic church for the Chinese community. After initially holding services at another church, Fr. Mao rented a storefront in Chinatown. Fr. Mao soon after returned to his native Nanjing, China, and the archbishop invited the Maryknoll Fathers to continue the operation of the church. The opening of a school in Chinatown soon followed, staffed by the same School Sisters of Notre Dame. But the sisters soon realized that more than a school was needed to assist the residents, mostly new immigrants, who lacked the skills to succeed in American society. Because the rules of the Notre Dame Sisters did not allow for engagement in social services, the archbishop of Chicago invited the Maryknoll Sisters to take over the fledgling school. The school occupied two large rooms in the On Leong Chinese Merchants Association building (popularly known as "Chinatown City Hall") on Wentworth Ave. The two rooms, divided by huge folding doors, were further divided by bookcases and blackboards to create three rooms for eight grades.

The church and the school provided not only education but also social services. It was echoed by the Chinese Christian Union Church, which occupied a building immediately next door to the original St. Therese church. Christian Union (as it is popularly known) did not have a school, so the children of its members attended the public Haines School nearby.

Both St. Therese and Christian Union held after-school classes in Cantonese, and both served not only educational needs but social ones as well. The after-school Chinese classes provided a safe haven for children of working parents and also helped preserve Chinese traditional values. Christian Union's staff were more permanent, as the St. Therese staff were usually reassigned after several years. Christian Union's Miss Helen Case and Olga Huncke at Haines School were devoted to the education and welfare of Chinatown's children and both made lasting contributions to the community, as did the Maryknollers.

The schools and pastoral work in other Asian American communities have been passed on to non-Maryknoll administrations, but they continue to build on the solid foundations established by Maryknoll and the values the Maryknoll missionaries inculcated.

Although today Maryknoll is no longer a physical presence in Asian American communities outside of New York's Chinatown, the Maryknoll legacy is still very much present in the lifestyles, memories, and values of Asian Americans who inter-

acted with them. As much of their early work has been taken over by both private and public endeavors, Maryknoll has redirected most of its efforts back to its original focus: foreign missions. Maryknoll today is multicultural with members from some 30 countries and continues to serve in some 25 countries in Asia, Latin America, Africa, and some Pacific islands.

Maryknoll describes itself as more than an organization but as a movement whose focus is "making God's love visible in the world." Today, Maryknoll is aided by a third group, the Maryknoll Lay Missioners, men and women who commit themselves for periods of three or more years to serve in foreign missions with the Maryknoll Fathers, brothers, and sisters. Maryknoll also has associates and affiliates who carry on the Maryknoll spirit and ideal in America and throughout the world.

It is a tribute to the early Maryknoll missions among Asian American communities that their work evolved to a level that the Maryknollers have been able to turn over administration to the local community while they direct their efforts to where the need is greater. When missions become local, missionaries have succeeded in their goals.

Raymond Lum, with contributions by
Betty Ann Maheu

See also: Essays: Catholics

Further Reading

Chu, Cindy Yik-yi, ed. *The Diaries of the Maryknoll Sisters in Hong Kong, 1921–1966.* New York: Palgrave Macmillan, 2007.

Kroeger, James H., ed. *The Gift of Mission: Yesterday, Today, Tomorrow: The Mary-*

knoll *Centennial Symposium*. Maryknoll, NY: Orbis Books, 2013.

Lernoux, Penny, with Arthur Jones and Robert Ellsberg. *Hearts on Fire: The Story of the Maryknoll Sisters*. Foreword by Desmond Tutu. Maryknoll, NY: Orbis Books, 2012.

Maryknoll Magazine Online. http://www.mary knollmagazine.org/. Accessed July 15, 2014.

Maryknoll Mission Archives. http://maryknoll missionarchives.org/. Accessed July 15, 2014.

The Maryknoll Story. www.youtube.com /watch?v=mGFYtPw_IIM. Accessed July 15, 2014.

"Vatican Dismisses Maryknoll Priest." http:// www.catholicnewsagency.com/news/vati can-dismisses-maryknoll-priest-from-ord er/. Accessed July 15, 2014.

Matsuri

Matsuri is a Japanese expression that refers to religious and seasonal festivals. Related to the verb *matsuru*, meaning to supplicate, enshrine, or worship, originally *matsuri* were rituals that honored various deities (*kami*) and the spirits of deceased ancestors; rituals also were performed to placate angry *kami* and spirits. In the early history of Japan, these rituals were performed by the head of the community. As such, *matsuri* predates the introduction of Buddhism to Japan.

Matsuri come in various types and sizes, ranging from small ad-hoc rituals to pacify land deities (*jichin-sai*), to family-oriented events such as Hina-matsuri (the Doll Festival, for the healthy growth of girls, celebrated on March 3), to much bigger communal seasonal festivals. Major large-scale festivals include Kamo-mat-suri, popularly known as Aoi-matsuri, and Gion-matsuri, held in May and July respectively in Kyoto, and Tanabata-mat-suri, which takes place in Sendai in August. These *matsuri* attract a large number of tourists from across the country and abroad. Many such traditional *matsuri* are related to agricultural cycles and involve Shintō rituals performed by Shintō priests (*shinshoku*) and shrine maidens (*miko*) to supplicate and give thanks to the *kami*. Deities are often carried around in the *mikoshi*, a portable shrine, which normally marks the climax of the *matsuri*. This is followed by communal feasting with Japanese liquor (*sake*, or *omiki* in this specific context), which has been first offered to the *kami*, and dancing.

Major Buddhist *matsuri* include Hana-matsuri, celebrated on April 8, that commemorates the birth of the historical Buddha (Śākyamuni) in the Mahāyāna tradition. Originally an agricultural ritual, Natsu-matsuri, the "summer festival," is now associated with the Buddhist Obon (or simply *bon*) period. During the Obon season, the spirits of the ancestors return to visit the homes where they formerly lived to be with their progeny. Obon is an occasion to prepare the ancestral altar with special delicacies and flowers to welcome the spirits. Often a priest will be invited for a memorial service. At the end of their three-day visit, the ancestral spirits are given a special send-off. The residents of Kyoto commemorate their return with *Go-zan-no-okuri-bi*, a set of five large "send-off" fires made on the mountainsides on August 16.

In the United States the Japanese community celebrates Hana-matsuri and

Obon-matsuri as major Buddhist events. In addition to these traditional services, the *matsuri* is an occasion to highlight Japanese culture within the larger U.S. community. Thus, the San Francisco Sakura-matsuri held in April is a festive occasion for the various arts and performing organizations to showcase their respective expertise. It is an occasion for enthusiasts of *ikebana* (flower arrangements), *shodō* (calligraphy), and *sumi-e* (ink painting) to exhibit their work. *Buyō* (traditional dance), *koto*, *samisen*, and *shakuhachi* performances are also featured. Other Japanese community–sponsored events take on such names as Nikkei-matsuri, Daruma-matsuri, Aki-matsuri, and Haru-matsuri. These *matsuri* are no longer reminders of their agricultural origins, but are occasions for community solidarity and festivity.

Kieko Obuse

See also: Entries: Obon (Urabon)

Further Reading

Joya, Mock. *Things Japanese*. Tokyo: Tokyo News Service, 1963.

Sugimoto, Etsuko Inagaki. *A Daughter of the Samurai*. Rutland, VT: Tuttle, 1966.

Varley, Paul. *Japanese Culture*. Honolulu: University of Hawai'i Press, 2000.

Matsushita, Eiichi (1930–1984)

Eiichi Matsushita, a native of Japan, was a sociologist. He was an articulate man with an aesthetic sensitivity that few people possess. He also had a complex personality as well as a keen mind. A loyal subject of Japan, he refused to become a citizen of the United States even though he spent most of his life there. His loyalty to Japan, however, was not uncritical. In fact, he often voiced criticism against his beloved homeland.

Born into a samurai-turned-merchant family in Tokyo, Matsushita appeared to have retained many characteristics of the warrior class, such as his sense of loyalty. After receiving his AB degree in sociology from Keio University in Tokyo in 1954, he entered Gettysburg College in Gettysburg, Pennsylvania, in the fall of the same year and obtained yet another AB degree in sociology two years later. In the fall of 1956 he entered Lutheran Theological Seminary in Gettysburg where he obtained his BD degree in 1960. His BD thesis, a sociological study, was on St. Mark's Lutheran Church, Los Angeles, California, where Paul T. Nakamura served as pastor.

After graduation Matsushita briefly served as an assistant pastor at Bethany Lutheran Church in Bronx, New York, before moving to California, where he stayed at St. Mark's Lutheran Church in Los Angeles for a few months. From 1961 to 1962 he was an assistant pastor at Faith Lutheran Church, Long Beach, California, where S. Samuel Ujiie was the pastor. His ministry at Faith was difficult due to racism coming from the Golden Stars across the street, which was an organization for mothers whose sons were killed in the Pacific or in Europe during World War II.

From 1962 to 1963, he was the director of the Philadelphia Planning Study under the auspices of the Board of American Mission (BAM). This sociological study focused on preventing churches from further decline and enabling them to become self-sufficient and service-oriented in their communities. Within a year, Matsushita published his influential study in four volumes with detailed recommendations. The result of his study was the formation of the Center City Parish, a coalition consisting of more than 30 congregations.

The Philadelphia Planning Study was one of the most significant contributions that Matsushita made to the Lutheran Church in America (LCA). It was also a step that Matsushita needed to make his knowledge known and available to the church. In fact, this study earned him a place in the church bureaucracy. Headquartered in Chicago, BAM appointed him in 1963 as assistant secretary for church planning. He held this position until 1968. In that year he became secretary for strategy planning, a position he held until 1972.

Meanwhile the LCA restructured itself in 1972, grouping smaller units into divisions. The BAM came under the umbrella of the Division for Mission in North America (DMNA), which included a department for research and study. Matsushita felt that he was the best qualified person to head the department. But he was passed over for the directorship, which caused him to become bitter about the institution. Instead he was given a position as assistant director for research and planning. In 1976 he felt vindicated when he became the director of the Office for Church and Community Planning, a position he held until his death in 1984.

In his professional life, Matsushita pioneered a study of Lutheran membership and population trends in the 1960s. In 1964 he published "A Theoretical Explanation on Church and Community," followed by numerous studies of LCA congregations and an article on "Population Growth Zero Point" in 1973. He was a founding member of Census Access for Planning in the Church.

Matsushita shared his knowledge and new findings not only with the central LCA staff but also with pastor-developers of new congregations. At their training sessions, he would teach them how to understand the communities in which they would serve and what to look for that would help them in their ministries. He would also describe the characteristics of different types of congregations, including his "point-of-breaks" and "balloon" theories.

Matsushita was among 37 individuals honored by the Evangelical Lutheran Church in America (ELCA) with his portrait on a banner at the Heritage and Hope Village of the ELCA 1997 churchwide assembly in Philadelphia. It was most fitting that the church would honor him in the city where Matsushita made his first significant contribution to the institution as a pastor and churchwide staff leader.

Edmond Yee

See also: Entries: Nakamura, Paul T.

Further Reading

Yee, Edmond. *The Soaring Crane: Stories of Asian Lutherans in North America*. Minneapolis: Augsburg Fortress, 2002.

Yee, Edmond, and J. Paul Rajashekar, eds. *Abundant Harvest: Stories of Asian Lutherans*. Minneapolis: Lutheran University Press, 2012.

Micronesian and Polynesian Traditional Religions

American Indians and Alaskan Eskimos are not the only indigenous peoples in the United States; the continuance of traditional cultures among the atoll-dwelling Micronesians and the Polynesians in both Hawai'i and American Samoa also require recognition. Mostly belonging within the great Pacific Austronesian culturo-linguistic complex, and with the exception of the central Marianas, the traditional religions of these U.S.-held islands share many of the characteristics of the wider Micro- and Polynesian regions. Admittedly the old religions have massively changed under the impact of Christian mission activity and modernization, but many crucial elements remain.

Precontact life was intensely tribal. Even on small atolls, blood revenge warfare was common and warrior bravery extolled; and tribal solidarity and avoidance of misdeeds within one's own tribe or clan was the norm. The early Christian missionaries worked to secure long-lasting intergroup peace in the Northern Mariana Islands, eastern Samoa, and Hawai'i. Their work dissipated intertribal fighting, but aspects of the old religions remained. What were accepted by outsiders as "positive" expressions of reciprocity (ceremonial exchange, trade, intergroup alliances, group transactions, and special rituals at birth, marriage, and death) have survived. Christianity prohibited human sacrifice and cult prostitution, and curbed prolonged feasting, *kava* drinking, and sexually suggestive dancing.

In the Austronesian or Malaya-Polynesian complex, leadership by hereditary chiefs generally prevailed, and in the Polynesian confederacies paramount chiefdoms became kingships, as in the case of Hawai'i. But because Samoa had been subject to the long-inured Tongan empire, the Samoan experience is more ambiguous. In any case, chiefs and the noble families were the recipients of the heaviest flow of goods exchanged, and for receiving sumptuary rights (more gifts at births, marriages, and deaths), the sponsoring of the largest festivities and other entertainments (such as Hawaiian hula dancing) issued from chiefs, noble families, and rulers at the apex of the social hierarchy and was meant to show their generosity. Seniority and paramountcy of chiefs or monarchs were usually based on the ramage system, that is, the ability to trace one's ancestral line to the leader of the first canoe arriving on a given island.

The vertical hierarchy of high or sky gods, down to patron or departmental deities and then to ancestral and minor spirits, and from heaven to earth and down to underworlds, is a feature of Micronesian and Polynesian religions that is reflected in their social structure. This is a key point of distinction with most Melanesian religions, where spiritual beings are visualized as operating more horizontally, and there is a more egalitarian competition for leadership. Thus on the western Micronesian island of Yap, for instance, once the center of an "island empire," there are two great sky gods, Enuunap and Nuuk, who are invoked for tribal security, although the islanders relied on Resiim, the war god, for victory and prosperity, and the heroic culture hero Wonofaat, who achieves such feats that he upstages all the gods.

Wonofaat, the name of a trickster god throughout Micronesia, becomes associated with Jesus for the Yapese; in a legend documented for Ifaluk Atoll, he was the son of "the Middle of Heaven" and a human woman. His painful birth in a fully mature form is made possible by people placing stones from the underwater world on their heads; he becomes accessible as a powerful help to males in improving socioeconomic and sexual relations. Stones, rare in Micronesia, were typically thought to be deposits of the divine. In Yap the habitable world originates from a rock being thrown from the sky, and hollowed limestone disks were used as sacred associated currency and status symbols.

On the Hawaiian Islands, where royal families on each of the main islands were ruled by a monarchy, the vertical image of the universe was pronounced. The highest deity was Kane, the creator of the sky and life on earth. The other primary deities are Ku (lord over war and harvesting), Lono (over storms, water, fertility, peace), and Kanaloa (god of wind and sea, operated on terrestrial and underworld). The fire goddess Pele ruled the volcanoes and various divine family members and demigods. The earth was peopled, not only by humans, but sprites, malevolent spirits in eerie and dangerous places, and spirits of the dead.

Concomitant to this imaging, all royal or chiefly personages (*alii*), who were thought to derive from the skies, were slowly cremated at death and their bones carefully housed. They were believed to be conducted back to the skies by the deity Lo-lupe and revealed as stars. Commoners were buried in shallow graves in selected sand dunes or in caves, but their souls

(*'uhane*) survived and could make their presence felt among the living. Priests (especially those dedicated to Lono) looked carefully to the heavens, especially to the movement of the constellation Pleiades, to schedule the sacrificial rites to perpetuate the worship system. In (American) Samoa, comparable views of the cosmos applied.

Religious functionaries, particularly priests, ritual and technical specialists, and also sorcerers, usually belonged to a middle social stratum. They were responsible for the upkeep of the ritual system, mediating between castes, and meting sanctions against taboo-breakage, even against the disobedience of subject peoples. The Yapese priesthood, for instance, would sometimes threaten to destroy the cosmic fishhook that drew up from the ocean bottom their atoll of Fais, if tribute (*sawei*) was not paid. On Guam, the powerful priesthood (*manmakahana*) held the crucial power balance between the Chamorro "conquerors" on the coast and the subservient inlanders or Manachang. Priests could rise into the ruling nobility, and unproductive nobles could lose their positions. Evidence for such mobility exists for Samoa and Hawai'i, made easier for Samoan priestesses, usually healers (*taulasea*), who married a noble (*taupou*).

In the Hawaiian Islands priests were not only performers of ritual, they were custodians of buildings (including of course the open-air temples), of key artifacts (statues, canoes, etc.), of important family genealogies, mythic texts, chants, taboos, and sorcery power (which royals could deploy against malefactors or enemies). The precontact religion in Micronesia and Polynesia revolved around the fulfillment of socially required obligations. This meant an ongoing commitment to collective warrior activity, with war dances, magic against enemies, careful preparation of weaponry, omen-taking, and sharing of dreams and proverbs. Gift-giving and exchange has persisted. In Samoa woven pandanus mats, symbol of respect toward the nobility, are given on such special occasions as funerals to honor the dead, presented to gods, or wrapped around an effigy in hopes for a miracle, as well as escape from harm.

Generosity in social transactions and offerings to the gods and ancestors generate support within one's community (lineage, clan, tribe), hope for material blessings (reciprocity, common enjoyment in the blessings of the earth), and reinforcement of a shared belief in the cosmic order. People honored leaders for their generosity. The lack of generosity or the neglect of social obligations led to official punishment, illness (typically through ancestral interference, or ghost sickness—*mai autu* as the Samoans called it—because of negligence in honoring relationships), and even death (often through priestly *kahuna* sorcery—in the Hawaiian case—or because they did not attend to the gods). These beliefs still persist.

Traditional Micronesian and Polynesian spirituality has displayed something of a resurgence with the recent spread of postcolonial attitudes and growing respect for environmentally friendly indigenous traditions. While rarely traditional, nostalgia for the old ways seeks to adapt Christian insights into solutions for the future. Many features of the past still lie in "enculturated" church events in the form of celebratory dancing and singing, competitive

gift-giving by congregations, and *kava*-drinking gatherings. But the advocacy of cultural pride has resulted in strident political positions. In Micronesia, for example, the Guamese scholar Vicente Diaz has taken on both American imperialists and Catholic hierarchs with a blend of Marxist ideology, liberation theology, and pride in Chamorro resistance going back to the long wars against the Spanish (1669–1697). In Polynesia, Hawaiian "nativist" urges link with the sovereignty movement (*Ke ea Hawai'i*) that seeks self-governance and redress for the 1893 overthrow of the monarchy. This nativist movement prompted the republication of long-forgotten texts, such as King Kalakau's *The Legends and Myths of Hawai'i* (1888) and Queen Liliuokalani's *Hawai'i's Story* (1898). In *Hawai'i's Story* Liliuokalani, the last reigning queen, issues a plea to "consolidate a united people to advance in the way of civilization." In this attempt to retrieve what is lost, there is a concession that those bad aspects of the precontact religion be transformed, and the complaint that so much good has been dismissed by the pioneer missionaries and later by business exploiters.

Garry W. Trompf

See also: Entries: Pacific Islander Religious Cultures

Further Reading

Dobbin, Jay, and Francis X. Hezel. *Summoning the Powers Beyond: Traditional Religions in Micronesia.* Honolulu: University of Hawai'i Press, 2011.

Friesen, Steven, ed. *Ancestors in Post-Contact Religion: Roots, Ruptures and Modernity's Memory.* Religions of the World. Cambridge,

MA: Harvard University Press, 2001, chapters 3, 10.

Handy, Craighill. *Polynesian Religion*. Millwood, NY: Kraus Reprint, 1985 (1927).

Spiro, Melford E. "Some Ifaluk Myths and Folk Tales." *Journal of American Folklore* 64 (1955): 289–301.

Swain, Tony, and Garry Trompf. *The Religions of Oceania*. Library of Religious Beliefs and Practices. London: Routledge, 1995.

Valeri, Valerio. *Kingship and Sacrifice: Ritual and Society in Ancient Hawai'i*. Translated by Paula Wissing. Chicago: University of Chicago Press, 1985.

Williamson, Robert W. *Religious and Cosmic Beliefs in Central Polynesia*. 2 vols. Cambridge: Cambridge University Press, 1933.

Mid-Autumn Festival

The Mid-Autumn or Moon Festival is the last of the three major festivals (the other two are the Lunar New Year and the Duanwu Jie or Dragon Boat Festival) on the annual Chinese calendar. According to the lunar calendar, the seventh, eighth, and ninth moons constitute the autumn season. The festival falls on the 15th day of the eighth moon, which is the midpoint of the season, hence the name Mid-Autumn Festival. And on that day the moon is always full. According to the *yinyang* system of Chinese philosophy, the moon is classified as yin, a female principle; thus the Mid-Autumn or Moon Festival is a women's festival, celebrated at night.

This festival, interwoven with myths and legends, is associated with poetry, romantic wishes, reminiscing, and, of course, mooncakes and other goodies. While myths and legends gave birth to the festival, poets in traditional China would sing of the beauty of the Moon Goddess or bemoan her loneliness on the moon or gently reprimand her for having swallowed the elixir of life and wonder whether she has any regrets. Young maidens would make their wishes known to the "old man" in the moon, hoping that he would arrange suitable marriages. And the old and young would reminisce about the myths and legends associated with the moon. By doing so they have kept the memory and the tradition alive to this day even in America.

Designations of Mid-Autumn Festival

The Chinese expression for mid-autumn is *zhongqiu*, which first appeared in the *Zhou Li* (*The Rites of Zhou*), an ancient ritual book. The Mid-Autumn Festival is also popularly known as the Yuejie (Moon Festival) and Yuexi (Moon Evening). During the Tang dynasty (618–906 CE) it was also known as Duanzheng Yue (Proper Moon), Zongyue Jie (Second Month of Autumn Festival), and Tuanyuan Jie (Festival of Reunion).

The Chinese character *tuan* means round and so does the character *yuan*, reflecting the round surface of the full moon. As a compound word, *tuanyuan* means reunion, an important concept in Chinese culture. And the notion of reunion on the mid-autumn day goes back as far as the Han Dynasty (206 BCE–220 CE).

Myths and Legends

The ancient Chinese worshiped natural objects, including the sun and the moon. In fact the city of Beijing today still preserves an altar dedicated to the sun and one to the moon, in addition to the ones dedicated to heaven and Eerth. The worship of the moon ceased only after the fall of the Qing Dynasty (1644–1911 CE).

The Goddess. Variant versions of the moon goddess Chang'e date back to antiquity. The earliest record is in the *Shanhai Jing* (*Classic of Mountains and Seas*), an ancient anthology consisting of writings on history, geography, myths, animals, minerals, plants, medicine, religions, nationalities, and so forth. In this work Chang'e appears as Changxi, the wife of Tijun.

The *Guizang*, a work of the Warring States (475–221 BCE), states that Chang'e flies to the moon after ingesting a dose of an elixir of life from Xiwangmu (Queen Mother of the West). She appears in the *Huinan Zi*, a work of 21 essays on a variety of topics that was compiled and presented in 139 BCE to Emperor Wudi (r. 140–87 BCE) of the Han Dynasty by a group of scholars in the court of Prince Liu An (180–122 BCE).

In this version of the tale, Yi (her husband) asks Xiwangmu for the elixir of life. Heng'e (Chang'e) steals and swallows the elixir and flies to the moon. Zhang Heng (78–139 CE) in his book *Lingxian* expanded the story; in this version Chang'e now is the wife of Yi, an archer who shoots down nine of the 10 suns to save the earth from being scorched. In this tale Chang'e steals the elixir of life, flies to the moon, and becomes a toad. The author of this version attempted to make the goddess ugly because of her deed.

By the time of the Yuan Dynasty (1271–1368 CE), a longer version appeared in

Langhui Ji, written by the Daoist priest Yi Shizhen (dates unknown), who based his version on a Song Dynasty (960–1279 CE) work, *Sanyu Tie*. In the Yi version Chang'e is the wife of Yi, the archer with immense strength. The earth is being scorched by 10 suns, but Yi is able to shoot down nine of them, saving the earth and giving people a normal life. To thank Yi for his work, a transcendental immortal gives Yi a pack of elixir of life so that he may become an immortal and ascend to the heavens where he can live forever. But Yi's love for Chang'e runs deep; he does not want to abandon his wife and become an immortal. He entrusts the elixir to Chang'e for safekeeping.

Yi's crafty and mean sycophant disciple Feng Meng also knows about the elixir. So on the 15th day of the eighth moon when Yi is out hunting, Feng attempts to force Chang'e to give up the elixir. To avoid the elixir from falling into his hands, Chang'e swallows the medicine. She immediately feels her body become as light as a swallow; she is unable to stop flying to the moon palace, where she finally settles. Realizing what happened, Yi misses his wife very much. Thereupon he sets up a table in the courtyard with a variety of fruits and other goodies on it and offers them to Chang'e. In memory of his devotion, the people reenact Yi's act of placing sweets out on the 15th day of the eighth moon; thus the origin of the Mid-Autumn Festival. This tale, though based on the much older versions, has a number of variants that are most likely derived from the already established customs.

During the Six Dynasties period (222–589 CE), people began to express sympathy toward the Moon Goddess, pounding medicine in a mortar day in and day out on the lonely moon, and attempted to beautify and humanize her, as reflected in the poems of the subsequent dynasties. However, in the moon palace she also has companions.

The Rabbit. There is no consensus about the legend of the rabbit. Chinese scholars attempted to explain it linguistically. In the poem "Ask Heaven" in the *Chu Ci* (*The Songs of Chu* or *The Songs of the South*), a work composed between the third century BCE and the second century CE, there is a line that literally reads, "Look for the dodder in the stomach." The Chinese character for "dodder" is *tu* while the character for rabbit, written slightly differently, is also read *tu*.

Therefore, some Chinese scholars concluded that the character for dodder (*tu*) actually referred to *tu* (rabbit). This homophonic theory, articulated by Wang Yi (dates unknown) of the Jin Dynasty (265–420 CE), has not been substantiated. In another work, published in 1067 CE, it is stated that the character *tu* (dodder) is read *tu* (as a noun, *tu*, written with a different character, means disciple, apprentice, follower, or believer). And in the local dialect of the former state of Chu (one of the states during the Warring States period), this character referred to "tigers." This homonymic theory leads a modern scholar to conclude that the image of the moon hare is derived from the tiger myth.

There are different versions of this moon hare tale, one found, for example, in *The Takata*. And there is yet another theory, derived from a Buddhist tale in the *Pāli Canon*. It relates that once upon a time there was a beautiful garden with all sorts of flowers, fruits, tender grasses, and water as well as a rabbit, where the holy men often came to meditate.

One evening Buddha also came, transformed himself into a Brahman, and called out sorrowfully that he was hungry and thirsty. When the small animals of the forest heard his cry, they brought him what they themselves normally would eat and begged him to accept their hospitality. The rabbit, however, said that he ate only grass and had nothing worth while to offer but his body. At that moment the rabbit caught sight of a burning coal and threw himself into the fire. But before jumping in the rabbit stopped, picked out the tiny insects in his body, and put them on the ground, saying that he had no right to take their lives even though he was offering his body to the saint.

Buddha, after resuming his own form, praised the rabbit's sacrifice and gave instructions to place the rabbit image on the moon so that it would become a shining example of self-sacrifice. The Daoists subsequently adopted this story and called the rabbit a "Jade Rabbit."

Wu Gang. Besides the Jade Rabbit and the Moon Goddess, there is another character on the moon. His name is Wu Gang. Wu, wishing to become an immortal, practiced the ways of the transcendental immortals. But he made a mistake and was banished to the moon where, to redeem himself, he had to cut down the cassia tree. But as soon as he made a cut, the tree would heal itself.

Whereas the Moon Goddess and the Jade Rabbit are legendary characters, Wu Gang was a historical personality of the Han Dynasty. He was born in Hexi (west of the river, i.e., west of the Yellow River) in the present Shanxi Province. The story of his being banished to the moon to cut down the cassia tree is most likely derived from the Sui (581–618 CE) and Tang Dynasties fiction.

The Cassia Tree. The moon's cassia tree (*guishu*), which is said to be 500 *zhang* (one *zhang* = 3.31 meters) tall, was first mentioned in the *Huainan Zi*. But this tree was also called *suoluo* (*Shorea robusta*) when it was mentioned in the *Yongzhai Suibi* by Hong Mai (dates unknown) of the Song Dynasty. The author simply stated that it was commonly known that there was a *suoluo* tree in the moon, but no one knew of its origin.

However, mention of the *suoluo* tree first appeared in the "Tianchi" chapter in the *Youyang Zazu* by Duan Chengshi (dates unknown) of the Tang Dynasty. It is said that there was suddenly a tree growing from under the bed of a monk in a monastery in Baling. It continued to grow as the monk tried to cut it down. When the foreign monks saw it, they identified it as a *Shorea Robusta* or *suoluo* tree. It was also this author who first introduced the myth of Wu Gang cutting the cassia tree on the moon.

The cassia tree in the Tang dynasty was also known as the *qian* tree. This tale is found in the *Yunji Qiqian*, a work of the Tang dynasty. It further stated that whoever would eat the leaves of the *qian* tree would become a "jade transcendental immortal."

Mooncakes

The origin of the mooncake is obscure, but mention of it is made as early as the Tang dynasty, when cakes were baked into round shapes to look like full moons. It is also said that during the reign of the first Tang emperor Gaozong (r. 618–626), China was under constant attack by the Xiongnü (a Turkish tribe under the Han dynasty). The Tang general Li Jing, however, was able to put a stop to such attacks and returned triumphantly to the capital on Mid-Autumn Day with great pomp and circumstance. A certain Tibetan gave the emperor a box of round cakes. Thereupon the emperor said that perhaps he should invite the moon to share the cakes with him. But in reality he shared the cakes with his ministers. Such sharing became known as a *yuehua fan* (moonlight meal).

Another tale relates how Zhang Shicheng (1321–1367 CE), a leader of the peasant revolt toward the end of the Yuan dynasty (1271–1368 CE), used the occasion of giving mooncakes to summon his followers to rise up against the dynasty on the mid-autumn day by putting a message of revolt in the cakes.

Furthermore, there is yet another tale of the origins of the mooncake. The Qing Dynasty emperor Qianlong (r. 1736–1795 CE) visited the region south of the Changjiang River (Long River) six times during his reign in search of his birth mother. The emperor located his mother in Hangzhou. Overjoyed, she made sweet cakes for him. The emperor thought they were delicious. Hence sweet cakes became mooncakes. This story gives further credibility to the notion that the Mid-Autumn Festival is a Festival of Reunion.

The first written record about mooncakes appeared in the *Mengliang Lu* (Record of Mengliang) by Wu Zimu of the Song dynasty. By the Ming Dynasty

(1368–1644 CE), the records about mooncakes had become quite numerous.

Moon Viewing and the Mid-Autumn Festival

The customs of viewing the moon and making offerings to the moon date back to the Zhou Dynasty (11th century to 771 BCE) and reached their pinnacle during the Tang Dynasty. It is said that the emperor Xunzong (r. 713–756 CE) of Tang built a moon-viewing terrace in the imperial palace so that he and his favorite consort, Lady Yang, could view the moon on the mid-autumn evening. There is also a popular story that the emperor and Lady Yang, under the guidance of Daoists, toured the moon palace and obtained the famous musical piece, *The Rainbow Skirt and the Feathered Coat*. While the story of His Majesty and her ladyship touring the moon palace is fictional, *The Rainbow Skirt and the Feathered Coat* is a historical piece that is still played today. The composition has always been attributed to the emperor, who was far more talented as a musician and composer than as a politician.

The common people, of course, did not have the means to build moon-viewing terraces nor would they have Daoists to guide them to the moon palace. But their moon-viewing activities were equally as enthusiastic and joyous.

As to when the moon viewing became a regularized Mid-Autumn Festival, there is also no general agreement. Some have maintained that it plausibly became a fixed festival during the Sui and Tang periods. Written records of the Song dynasty indicates that it was during the Song period

that the Mid-Autumn Festival was established.

Mid-Autumn Festival in America

Like other immigrants who carried their own culture and festivals when they moved to a new home, the Chinese were no exception. The Mid-Autumn Festival is one festival that has continued today in America. The festival continues to be celebrated with the gifts of mooncakes, imported or locally produced, fruits, and other treats. The children continue to enjoy the rabbit-shaped lanterns. Most of the families, whether living in Chinese enclaves or in the suburbs, continue the tradition of viewing the moon on that night. They set up tables and place on them mooncakes, fruits, and other foods as well as lighted incense. Mooncakes are no longer exclusively round; there are square ones as well. More and more varieties appear in the marketplace each year. While viewing the moon, they also retell the legends of old.

Young maidens today no longer make their marital wishes known to the "old man" in the moon, but they may go out on dates and enjoy an evening of romance. Romantic sentimentalists may bemoan the fact that the advancement of science and technology has dampened, if not totally ruined, the modern-day imagination of the Moon Goddess and her companions. Still, the picture of her flight to the moon continues to adorn the page of the eighth moon in some of the calendars being sold in bookstores and other marketplaces.

The Mid-Autumn Festival carries deep meaning for Chinese persons young and old. Whether young or old, long-settled or newly immigrated, they may feel a sense of sadness to be separated from their loved ones and friends. And yet they may also be comforted by the knowledge, which the Song Dynasty poet Su Shi (1036–1101 CE) also shared, that they are together in spirit when they are viewing the same moon this night.

Edmond Yee

See also: Entries: Chinese New Year; Duanwu Festival

Further Reading

Eberhard, Wolfram. *Chinese Festivals, with Illustrations from the Collection of Werner Banck*. Taipei: Oriental Cultural Service, 1972, chapter 6.

Latsch, Marie-Luise. *Chinese Traditional Festivals*. Beijing: New World Press, 1984, pp. 69–81.

Mongolian American Religions

As practitioners of Tibetan-style Buddhism, many Mongolians have kept their faith alive after arriving in the United States. Mongolians regularly attend Buddhist services and meditation programs where these are available. Because Buddhist temples are limited in the United States, many Mongolians practice Buddhism at home. Christianity is also widespread among Mongolian American communities, and Mongolian

The Dalai Lama (R) greets an audience of Mongolian Americans at the Beacon Theater, October 19, 2013, in New York City. The Dalai Lama was in New York for three days of Buddhist teachings supported by the Richard Gere Foundation. (Robert Nickelsberg/Getty Images)

churches have recently opened in several major American cities.

Kalmyks arriving in the United States in the 1950s became the first significant population to bring Tibetan-style Buddhism to America. Their pioneering efforts included the construction of Tashi Lhumpo Temple in Howell (Freewood Acres), New Jersey. Two more Buddhist temples, Nitsan and Rashi Gempil Ling, have since been constructed in Howell. In August 2008, a special ceremony was held at Tashi Lhumpo to honor two senior monks, Baksha Jampel Dorj and Gen Yonten Gyamtso. The pair have led temple services since the early 1970s, while as of 2010, the 90-year-old Gyamtso still distributed holistic remedies to members of the community.

The Kalmyk high lama Geshe Ngawang Wangyal has also been instrumental in developing the Tibetan Buddhist community in the United States. Geshe Wangyal taught Tibetan studies at Columbia University during the 1960s and 1970s, and he was a mentor to the Tibetologist Robert Thurman. Another important figure in the development of Tibetan Buddhism in America was the Mongol monk Dilowa Gegeen Khutukhtu, a living Buddha who first arrived in the United States in 1949. From his base in Baltimore, Dilowa Gegeen served the Kalmyk-Mongol Buddhist community and was considered its senior authority. He made frequent trips to Howell and paid visits to the Kalmyk Mongols residing in Philadelphia.

On the U.S. West Coast, the main center for Mongolians to practice Buddhism is the Tibetan Center for Compassion and Wisdom (TCCW), located in Mill Valley, California. Arjia Rinpoche, the former abbot of Kumbum Monstery in Amdo and the only Tibetan high lama of Mongol descent, is the leading monk at the center. The center provides occasional services in Oakland, closer to the Mongolian base.

The home of a Mongolian Buddhist will typically contain an altar with Buddhist objects and images. These might include small Buddhist statues, a rosary, a prayer wheel, and at least one photo of the Dalai Lama. Mongolians personalize their altar and may include the picture of a deceased family member. While at home or during their daily routine, Mongolians chant basic prayers, such as "*Om, Mani Padme Hum*" ("Hail! Jewel in the lotus") in private moments of prayer and meditation. Mongolians also perform *ariulukh* (spiritual cleansing), particularly after visiting a lama or going to the temple. To perform this ritual, the adherent will burn crushed juniper leaves in a cup and pass it around his or her body three times while chanting a prayer.

Although Buddhism is the dominant religion in Mongolia, a solid percentage of Mongolians living in the United States are Christians. Missionary groups, including Mormons, Catholics, Protestants, and Seventh-day Adventists, actively seek converts in Mongolia and send them to the United States for religious education and missionary training. Mongolian Christian churches have growing congregations in cities such as Los Angeles, Oakland, Denver, and Washington, D.C.

Michael Kohn

Further Reading

Olna Gazur website: http://www.olnagazur .org/. Accessed July 16, 2014.

Prebish, Charles, and Tanaka, Kenneth, eds. *The Faces of Buddhism in America.* Berkeley: University of California Press, 1998.

Tibetan Center for Compassion and Wisdom website: http://www.tccwonline.org/. Accessed July 16, 2014.

Morikawa, Jitsuo (1912–1987)

Jitsuo Morikawa, a native of Canada, was a leader who exercised tremendous influence on the American Baptist Churches USA (ABCUSA)—its predecessor bodies were known as the Northern Baptist Convention (NBC) from 1907 to 1950 and the American Baptist Convention (ABC) from 1950 to 1972, but in 1972 the convention changed its name to ABCUSA—to reflect the depth of its faith, the breadth of its witness, and its theological integrity. Morikawa was also a gigantic figure among the Asian American Baptists. He enabled them to discover their identity and their impact on the ABCUSA. He also helped the denomination to develop respect for and recognition of the dignity of the Asian American Baptists within the institution. And by enabling the Asian American Baptist churches to grow and to share their cultural, racial, and theological perspectives within the ABCUSA, he expanded the growth of the denomination.

Morikawa began his Christian life as an enthusiastic fundamentalist or evangelical Christian after he was converted by the "hound of heaven" pastor of Maple Ridge Baptist Church in British Columbia, Canada. This marked the beginning of the drastic changes in his life and his theology.

He attended Biola Bible Institute (BBI) in Los Angeles, California, and then the University of California, Los Angeles (UCLA) for further study. His zeal for the Christian faith led him to speak on "Why I believe the Bible to be a supernatural book" in his public speaking class at UCLA. While in Los Angeles he became connected with the American Baptists first through James Fox and later Ralph L. Mayberry of the Los Angeles Baptist City Mission Society. Because of his Baptist connection in Canada, he was ordained at the Immanuel Baptist Church in Pasadena, California, as a Baptist on February 14, 1937, after his graduation from BBI and UCLA. Shortly thereafter many persuaded him to attend seminary. He chose the Southern Baptist Seminary in Louisville, Kentucky. At the seminary Morikawa experienced something totally new—this seminary did not allow African Americans to attend. Due to the American racism then, Morikawa himself was only able to work at the Fifth Street Baptist Church, an African American church led by Augustus Jones, who became one of Morikawa's dearest friends. Another dear friend of his was Mayberry, who spent 37 months working with the immigration office to make possible Morikawa's entry into the United States. Morikawa became a U.S. citizen in June 1954 as the result of the McCarran-Walter Act of 1952.

After his ordination Morikawa became a circuit minister among Boyle Heights, Gardena, and Terminal Island churches in the greater Los Angeles area. During this time he met Hazel Takaii of the Terminal Island church and they were married in 1941.

In the same year Japan attacked Pearl Harbor in Hawai'i, resulting in the U.S.

government's decision in the following year to put more than 100,000 U.S. citizens and legal aliens of Japanese descent into 10 concentration camps across the country. Morikawa was interned at the camp in Poston, Arizona.

During the internment years, some religious institutions decided to provide ministry to the internees. Among them was the American Baptists whose ministry in the internment camps was headed by Mayberry, and later John W. Thomas, another American Baptist, also joined the ministry to the interned Japanese American citizens and the legal aliens. With the help of Thomas, Morikawa was able to leave the camp for three months. He visited Denver, Minnesota, Chicago, and Cleveland where he gave talks in churches. When he was in Minnesota, Morikawa was a house guest of Reuben Nelson, a former general secretary of the ABC. The Nelsons were harassed by telephone calls from neighbors accusing them of disloyalty for entertaining a "Jap."

Morikawa and his family eventually left the concentration camp to settle in Chicago in 1944. The Japanese Protestant ministers then came together and met in Chicago to study and plan ministries with the newcomers from the camps. Morikawa was among them and they formed the United Ministry to Resettlers of Chicago Church Federation (UMRCCF).

In February 1944, First Baptist Church of Chicago voted to install Morikawa as assistant minister. Both Thomas and the then NBC played an important role in this appointment. The internment of Japanese Americans also marked the beginning of consideration of establishing an Asian American Baptist division within the National Ministries of the NBC. But it was Morikawa's appointment to First Baptist Church of Chicago that led to the development of the Asian Baptist Caucus and the securing of a voice in the General Board of the NBC. When the senior pastor Bob Steiger left the church, Morikawa was appointed to take his place. The church became a popular meeting place for Japanese American resettlers out of the camps. Morikawa's wife Hazel commented that "Many romances blossomed. Weddings were quite frequent and Jitsuo tied many good knots." Because of Morikawa's experience at the African American Fifth Street Baptist Church in Louisville, Kentucky, he helped to break the racial barrier at the First Church not only with regard to the Asian Americans but the African Americans as well.

Morikawa's ministry and activities went beyond the UMRCCF and the parish. For example, shortly after World War II and the unjust internment of Japanese Americans in concentration camps, Morikawa along with Paul Nagano and other Japanese Canadian and American leaders established the Japanese Evangelical Missionary Society at the Mount Herman Christian Conference to evangelize the Japanese Americans and Japanese nationals, including those in Japan and South America.

In early 1956, the American Baptist Home Mission Society invited Morikawa to be the secretary of the Division of Evangelism. Morikawa subsequently spent 24 years serving on the national staff—20 of those years as national director of evangelism and the last four years as an associate executive of American Baptist National

Ministries. He was the executive director of American Baptists of the Baptist Jubilee Advance, a five-year national cooperative effort on evangelism among Baptist bodies in the United States and Canada. He founded the Metropolitan Associates of Philadelphia, a five-year ecumenical research study project of lay ministry.

He likewise served on the evangelism committees of the National and World Council of Churches (WCC) and was the chairperson of the North American Working Group of the Missionary Structure of the Congregation, a WCC study project. He was an American Baptist delegate to the WCC Assembly in Evanston, Illinois, in 1954 and in New Delhi, India, in 1961, and also attended its Sixth Assembly in Vancouver, B.C., Canada, in 1983.

A year before his 65th birthday and 12 months from his scheduled retirement, he received an interim invitation from Riverside Church, New York, in 1976 to be the pastor for one year. After that he served the Emmanuel Baptist Church in Ridgewood, New Jersey. In 1978 he received an invitation to serve from the First Baptist Church of Ann Arbor, Michigan, located near the University of Michigan. And there he took steps to begin a lecture series at the university by bringing well-known Christian speakers to the community. Subsequently, after obtaining approval from the university administration, Morikawa also introduced conferences for the faculty and community dealing with ethics and values. He likewise helped the university to establish the Professor of Religious Thought Program to bring well-known theologians, scholars and noted Christians to the university for a semester. The list of individu-

als that this program brought to the campus included Hans Kung, Gustavo Gutierrez, Harvey Cox, Martin Marty, the late Sen. Mark Hatfield, William Sloane Coffin, John B. Cobb, Jr., Joseph Hough, Robert Bellah, and Robert McAfee Brown.

After his retirement from the Ann Arbor church at the end of 1982, Morikawa was elected vice president of the ABCUSA for a two-year term (1984–1985). During this period he was instrumental in the development of racial caucuses, especially the Asian American Baptist Caucus. It was also his conviction that an appropriate theology must be developed that would take individual and personal life with utmost seriousness. He further felt that since public policy and actions of corporate structures exercise significant influence on the welfare of every life, a theology that would hold the institutional and corporate accountabilities was a must for the church. Furthermore he wanted to develop a theology that would address the critical issues of economics, ecology, religions, science, and technology as well. His desire to develop such an appropriate theology seems to coincide with his concern for the Pacific Basin, for he stated that "the future of the Pacific Basin appears to be contingent on . . . how these issues are dealt with [theologically]." By developing and disseminating a unifying, pluralistic theology that seeks reconciliation of all creatures and creation, Morikawa believed that the will and kingdom of God were sought. This was the primary challenge for Asian Americans who would affect the course of history in the Pacific Basin.

Inspired by his life and theology, upon his death, the Morikawa Pacific Rim

Ecumenical Conference was initiated (the name was later changed to the Morikawa Pacific Rim Theology). John B. Cobb, Jr., a theologian and a member of the organization, was convinced that if there were 20 more people like Morikawa around, "American Protestantism could move into creative leadership instead of struggling with issues of church maintenance." To him Morikawa was not only a friend but a hero as well.

Morikawa died peacefully on July 26, 1987. Two days before his death he raised his hand and displayed two fingers, predicting his passing in two days. This gesture prompted Coffin, Morikawa's successor at Riverside Church, to reflect at his funeral service, "He was the only one I know who took the prerogative of God in his own hand and predicted his own demise."

Paul M. Nagano

Further Reading

Chicago Tribune Obituary. http://articles.chi cagotribune.com/1987-07-23/news /8702230844_1_baptist-leader-american -baptist-churches-usa-southern-baptist-the ological-seminary. Accessed July 15, 2014.

Mormons

The Church of Jesus of Latter-day Saints (LDS), widely known as the Mormon church, had missionaries in the Pacific Islands even before the foundation of the Mormon capital, Salt Lake City, Utah, in 1847. Founder and first president of the LDS church, Joseph Smith (1805–1844) sent Addison Pratt (1802–1872) with three other appointees to create a Pacific Island mission in 1843. Pratt, who had worked as a whaler and lived for some months in a Hawaiian village during the 1820s, persuaded Smith that the islanders would be receptive to the Mormon message. Pratt preached in the Hawaiian language through the Tubuai Islands (south of Tahiti and a French Protectorate) until his proselytizing (1844–1847, 1850–1852) was curtailed by orders of the French government, and he could only carry on his work by training missionaries in Salt Lake City. Although Mormons often had difficulty making headway where other missionaries had had an effect, a key point of attraction in LDS preaching was that everyone has a "pre-earth" existence in the sky and that the faithful return to the starry heavens at death, a right Polynesians usually reserved to their royal, chiefly, and noble rulers and which was now proclaimed to be universal. Since the indigenous conception of both cosmos and society was hierarchical and vertical (heaven, earth, underworld), the LDS hierarchical church structure (president, apostles, patriarchs, priestly orders, etc.) also appealed, as did the teaching that Polynesians were lost Israelites. Later LDS teaching in the Pacific had Polynesians sharing origins with the American Indians as the Israel-originated Lamanites referred to in *The Book of Mormon* (the work said to be revealed to Smith by the angel Moroni and revered by Mormons along with the Bible). LDS missions to Lamanites (reaching as far as California by 1831) were meant to reconnect them to the sacred destiny of America, fulfilling the prediction that they would "blossom as the rose" before the Kingdom of God was realized on American soil.

Mongolians line up in a waiting room at the Church of the Latter Day Saints, to get an eye examination and free treatment and glasses next to a picture of the life of Jesus Christ in the Mongolian capital of Ulaan Baator, July 7, 2005. Mongolia is flush with foreign missionaries these days—young Mormons going door-to-door, Korean Christians working with homeless children, and new Catholic churches sprouting up on the grassy steppe. The collapse of communism in 1990 brought religious freedom as well as democracy, opening the doors to proselytizers from around the world. They have flocked to this sparsely populated country wedged between Russia and China, eager for fresh converts. (AP Photo/Elizabeth Dalziel)

In what are now the U.S.-controlled Pacific islands, Mormons are strongest in Polynesia—on the Hawaiian Islands and American Samoa. After preliminary contacts (that involved Pratt), 10 LDS missionaries led by Hiram Clark arrived at Honolulu in 1850, after a royal Edict of Toleration was issued for what were then the Sandwich Islands. By August of the next year five congregations were established with a total of 220 members, rising exponentially to 4,000 by 1854. Among the missionaries was George Cannon (1827–1901), who was popularly received by indigenous Hawaiians for preaching about references to Polynesians in the Mormon scriptures, and who was taken to prophesying the building of a temple on O'ahu. Following his efforts, the second LDS president, Brigham Young (1801–1877), sent a formal letter to Hawai'i's last king, Kamekameha V, announcing that Polynesians were the migrant Israelite group of Hagoth in *The Book of Mormon* text called Alma (63: 5–8); and after Cannon's death, the sixth president,

Joseph F. Smith, initiated plans to build a temple at Laie, Hawai'i's most popular gathering place (on O'ahu's northern tip). During the 1860s increasing numbers of indigenous Mormon converts manifested on the islands of Maui, Kaua'i, and the Palawi basin of Lanai, but special successes in Laie led to the establishment of a sugar cane plantation (1864) that sustained the Mormon community and attracted Polynesian workers from beyond Hawai'i itself. After Hawai'i became a U.S. territory in 1900, immigrant Japanese and mainland Americans added to the following. By 1949, following the founding of the Japanese (later Central Pacific) Mission in 1935, there were 671 Japanese American Mormons.

Mormonism's beginnings on Samoa seemed less auspicious. Of the two indigenous elders starting the mission (1863), Kimo Pelio died and Samuele Manoa was left rather stranded. They had been sent by Walter Gibson, who was declared an LDS "apostate" for embezzling money from Mormons in a colony he formed on Lanai (off Maui) in 1861. The first conversions were never recorded, and officially recognized LDS work had to wait until 1888 with the arrival of Joseph Dean and his wife Florence at Aunu'u (off Tutuila, the main island of U.S. Samoa), sent by LDS political aspirant William King. The Samoan woman named Malaea is famous as the first convert, there being 11,886 in all by 1875, with traditional members of the priesthood attracted and schools founded. Three further missionaries arrived in 1893, concentrating on Tutuila, especially Pago Pago. By 1903, the most important of a number of LDS schools was started at

nearby Mapusaga. In the same year *The Book of Mormon* was translated into Samoan. Interestingly, Mormon followers were stronger on the western side of the island complex (German, 1900–1914, under New Zealand, 1914–1962) than the islands becoming U.S. territory (1899–).

As for U.S.-controlled Micronesia, Mormon beginnings there belong to the postwar period, and indeed, this period saw the greatest growth of LDS numbers in the Pacific in general. Even the Philippines, which was a territory and then commonwealth of the United States from 1900 to 1934 and from 1934 to independence in 1946, did not experience any noteworthy Mormon presence until a decade after the war.

Today, by far the biggest Mormon presence in the U.S. Pacific Island region is Hawai'i, currently showing a membership of 69,872 adherents (just over 5 percent of the total population), with 134 congregations, two temples, and one continuing mission. The largest temple anywhere in the world outside mainland America is at Laie, completed in 1915 and rededicated in 2010 after remodeling. The design combines a suggestion of Mesoamerican architecture and the biblical description of Solomon's Temple and is a world-famous Mormon icon, with over 100,000 visitors a year. In 1955, 35 miles away, the LDS church founded the Church College of Hawai'i (initially a junior college, along with 15 other schools) that in 1974 became Brigham Young University (BYU)–Hawai'i Campus (now with over 2,000 students, mainly from around the Pacific). The year 1963 had already seen the founding of the Polynesian Cultural Center, receiving nearly a million (paying) visitors per year and dedicated by Mormons to the preservation of all Polynesian cultures. The BYU Institute for Polynesian Studies and its journal *Pacific Studies* are important scholarly offshoots of these Mormon concerns.

As for the Samoan Islands, by 1940 U.S. Samoa had only about 640 adherents, yet by now LDS members constitute over 22 percent of the population (even higher in Western Samoa). A key to the church's increasing success lay in the well-serviced Mapusaga High School, which was replaced by one run by the U.S. government in 1974 after having lured many students from the whole central Polynesian region (because boarders were accepted together with day students). The Samoan Eric Faleomavaega became American Samoa's lieutenant governor and the first Mormon non-voting member of the U.S. Congress.

In U.S.-held Micronesia, mission work began in earnest on Guam in 1951, and by 2005 there were 1,669 adherents and four branches (just under 1 percent of the population), more or less the same percentage applying the same year in the Northern Marianas, which received missionaries on Saipan, Rota, and Tinian in 1975 and reached a membership figure of 811. Formerly U.S.-protected, the Marshall Islands and Ponape experienced the first LDS missions as late as 1984 and 1987 respectively, well after the Philippines gained independence from the United States in 1949 after a missionary (Elder George Hinckley) was sent there, in 1961, there now being over 441,000 in the country today.

One also needs reminding that U.S. citizens are heavily engaged in LDS mission work throughout the Pacific Islands, including Papua New Guinea and other Melanesian island complexes. Young American Mormons have been expected to volunteer for a two-year mission period for their church, and they have arrived in the islands by rotation as builders, teachers, and apprentices. Proportionately the biggest Mormon impact has been on Tonga, official data recording near to 15 percent of the permanent resident population in the traditional Wesleyan Methodist stronghold; U.S. citizens work at the temple built there and in well-furbished schools and other service organizations, and their presence has encouraged Tongan migration to Utah, so that paradoxically the largest of all Tongan Free Wesleyan congregations is found in Salt Lake City.

In missionary situations, LDS church members are required to organize themselves into districts and branches (basically well-established and more newly founded congregations). When sufficient numbers have settled, "stakes" (comparable to dioceses) and "wards" (as long-term congregations) come into play (as on Hawai'i). The directives for missions come from the General Authorities at the top of the hierarchy (with the president, his two counselors, and high councils of the church), but the authority is carried out from the bottom up. Each Mormon adherent is encouraged to "advance" (as if deliberately outdoing the Masonic orders) from youthful deacon, teacher, member of the Aaronic, and finally on to the office of elder (where appointed "missionary") and member of the highest priestly order of Melchizedek. The males have the supportive organization of a Mutual Improvement Association and the females a Women's Relief Society; and Mormon families are nurtured by a system of weekly visitations.

The Mormon worldview chimes with the traditional Pacific Island understanding of rewards and punishments, only it is God who is seen as the fundamental bearer of punishment to transgressors of family and church obligations, through ill health, deformities, bad luck, and so on, and God brings blessings of material prosperity, fecundity, and community solidarity to a Mormon congregation abiding by divine commands. On the other hand, stress on the freedom to choose the Mormon way means expressing the right to go against prevailing norms, setting aside overrestraining customs (such as kinship taboos, pressures to adopt out children, traditional dress, etc.) or involving abstinence not only from *kava* but such newly acceptable stimulants as tobacco smoking, alcohol, tea, coffee, and so on. Then again, Mormon belief fits into the typical indigenous islander view that takes the community to comprise both the living and the dead. Ancestors are allowed the opportunity to join the church and enjoy salvation in the next world even though they had never heard of Christ, and this acceptance allows infinite networks of kin to be reconstituted and "sealed" as Latter-day Saints. In the process an alternative class structure is created; it is one that can subsist alongside existing sociopolitical authorities without pretending to overthrow them, while Mormonism, as a very American religion and funded by extensive sources of wealth that bring obvious benefits in terms of housing, education and health care, inevitably "sells" one "American way" across the huge expanse of Oceania.

Garry W. Trompf

See also: Entries: Cambodian Americans and Mormonism

Further Reading

Barker, John, ed. *Christianity in Oceania: Ethnographic Perspectives.* ASAO Monographs, 12. Lanham, MD: University Press of America, 1990.

Britsch, R. Lanier. *Unto the Islands of the Sea: A History of Latter-day Saints in the Pacific.* Salt Lake City: Deseret Books, 1886.

Britsch, R. Lanier. *Moramona: The Mormons in Hawai'i.* Mormons in the Pacific Series. Laie, HI: Institute of Polynesian Studies, 1989.

Finau, Makisi, Ieuti Teeruro, and Jione Langi. *Island Churches: Challenge and Change.* Edited by Charles W. Forman. Fiji: Institute of Pacific Studies, 1992.

Jensen, Andrew. *Latter-day Saint Biographical Encyclopedia.* 4 vols. Salt Lake City: Andrew Jensen History, 1901–1941.

Loveland, Jerery K. "Hagoth and the Polynesian Tradition." *Brigham University Studies* 17 (1976): 1–17.

Ludlow, Daniel H. *Encyclopedia of Mormonism.* 4 vols. New York: Macmillan, 1992.

Pratt, Addison. *The Journals of Addison Pratt: Being a Narrative of Yankee Whaling in the Eighteen Twenties, a Mormon Mission to the Society Islands, and of Early California in the Eighteen Forties and Fifties.* Edited by S. George Ellsworth. Publications in Mormon Studies, 6. Salt Lake City: University of Utah Press, 1990.

Ramstad, Mette. *Conversion in the Pacific: Eastern Polynesian Latter-day Saints' Accounts and Their Development of an LDS Identity.* Studia Humanitatis Bergensia, 19. Kristiansand: Høyslkoleforlaget, 2003.

Swain, Tony, and Garry Trompf. *The Religions of Oceania.* Library of Religious Beliefs and Practices. London: Routledge, 1995.

Muslim *Mosques,* Indian Americans

Indian Americans who are followers of Islam are often referred to as Muslims. Muslims pray at a place of worship known as a *mosque.* The Arabic term for a place of Muslim worship is *masjid,* literally a "place of prostration." *Mosques* are found all over the world, and there is a distinction between a small, privately owned *mosque* and a larger, collective one that offers a place for community and social amenities. Even though the praying can be done in private at home, many Muslims attend *mosques* for prayer or *salat.* The *mosque* offers a place for individuals to collect information, become more educated about the Muslim religion, as well as receive counseling services. The leader of the prayer is known as the *imam.* There are five formal prayers each day, spaced for a constant reminder of God's gifts.

Mosques around the world are varied in design and materials, depending on each Muslim community. However, most *mosques* have the following characteristics: minaret, prayer hall, prayer rugs, *mihrab, minbar,* dome, and shoe shelf. A minaret is a decorative tower that rises above the *mosque* and often varies in style and height. Minarets were originally used as a high point from which to make the call to prayer.

It is not uncommon today for *mosques* to have computerized prayer calls. The prayer hall is a bare room in which the participants can pray by kneeling directly on the floor. There are often a couple of chairs or benches for elderly and disabled worshippers. Copies of the *Qur'an* and other religious reading materials are held in this room. Prayer rugs are kept in the prayer hall and help keep the prayer space clean. Though the prayer hall may be carpeted, individual rugs are often available for use. The *mihrab* is a doorway-shaped indention in the wall of the *mosque.* They are often decorated and ornate. In the *mosque,* near the front of the prayer room, there is a platform known as the *minbar.* This is where religious speeches or sermons are given. The *minbar* is sometimes covered by a small dome. Many *mosques* are decorated with a dome rooftop. The dome is an aesthetic design of the *mosque* and is often decorated with floral or geometric patterns. There is no spiritual or symbolic connotation to the dome. Muslims remove their shoes before entering a *mosque* to maintain cleanliness. A shoe shelf offers a practical space for these shoes to be organized.

Shereen Bhalla

See also: Essays: Muslims

Further Reading

Barker, Chris. *Cultural Studies: Theory and Practice.* London: Sage, 2003.

Renard, John. *The Handy Religion Answer Book.* Canton, MI: Visible Ink Press, 2002.

Rippin, Andrew. *Muslims: Their Religious Beliefs and Practices.* New York: Routledge, 2005.

N

Nāga

When visiting a Thai Buddhist *wat* (temple), even in the United States, one is greeted by an image of the *nāga* (*Phaya Nak* or *Nak*), a mythical serpent that is a ubiquitous motif in the traditional arts of Thailand, especially architecture and sculpture, and in Thai Buddhist culture. *Nāga* is the term used variously to designate the king cobra, the elephant, mountains, and water. While the term may have originated in India, the worship of the serpent as a symbol of fertility and water arose independently in many parts of the world and is especially prominent among the many indigenous communities living along the Mekong River, from its upper reaches in Yunnan Province, China, to its lower sections and delta region in Southeast Asia.

The serpent is believed to be the creator of nature and life. In Thai legends the *nāga* is the protector of devout kings; it assists people to channel rivers for irrigation and construct cities. A Thai folk legend tells of *nāgas* drawing earth from river bottoms to lay the foundation for temples. The *nāga* is the guardian of water. By the same token, it punishes evil rulers and people by releasing an oversupply of water, causing destructive floods. Further, the *nāga* is the mythological support for many of the matriarchic societies in Thailand, Burma, Laos, Cambodia, and Vietnam. *Nāga* as a type of totem appears to have originated in South India.

The *nāga* figures prominently in Thai Theravāda Buddhist lore and culture. In contrast to Brahmanic legends, Buddhism embraced the indigenous *nāga* cult, rather than attacking it. Such accommodation is evident in *wat* or temple architecture and its motifs. *Nāgas* placed on the tiers of *wat* or temple roofs represent the cosmic river of life streaming down to the human world from Phra Sumen. The *wat* is a representation of Phra Sumen or Mount Meru, the mythical mountain at the center of the Hindu-Buddhist cosmology and the Tāvatiṃsa (Skt. Trāyastriṃśa) heaven where Queen Siri Mahāmāyā (Buddha's mother) and other deities reside. *Nāgas* appear on the finial, gable board, balustrade, and along the sides of the stairs leading up to the *viharn* or main temple building. These slithering *nāgas* represent the three ladders that link the heavens with this world. These ladders ascend to *Nirvāṇa*; the gods also use them to descend to earth. In the middle of November, the Buddha uses these ladders to descend from the Tāvatiṃsa heaven after preaching to his mother and the other deities.

The *nāga* is present throughout the Buddha's life. A multiheaded *nāga* caused warm waters to gently bathe the infant Siddhārtha shortly after his birth. The multiheaded *nāga* is especially prominent at the sixth week after the enlightenment. While the Buddha was seated under the mucalinda tree, home of the *nāga* king Mucalinda, a great storm suddenly arose. Thereupon Mucalinda crept out of its lair and coiled its body into seven circles and lifted the meditating Buddha above the rising water. Its seven heads formed a canopy that shielded the Buddha from the storm. Between the 7th and 13th centuries the Mon and Khmer people sculpted the event in stone, a tradition the Thai continued, as well as in other media. *Nāgas* are protectors of the Triple Gems—the Buddha, Dharma, and *saṇgha* (spiritual community).

A final story serves to underscore Buddhism's accommodation of the indigenous *Nāga* cult. A *nāga* desirous of becoming a monk assumed human form. One night shortly after falling asleep, it reverted back to its original shape. The monk who shared the hut was understandably alarmed to find a great snake asleep next to him. After being informed of the deception, the Buddha informed the *nāga* that he could not remain a monk. The *nāga* wept inconsolably. To ease its disappointment, the Buddha administered the Five Precepts (abstaining from killing, stealing, sexual misconduct, false speech, and consuming intoxicants), which if faithfully observed would assure that the *nāga* would attain a human existence in his next life, and thus allowing for entry into the Buddhist order. Further, out of compassion for the *nāga*, the Buddha decreed that henceforth all candidates for the monkhood would be called *nāgas*. Candidates for ordination in Thailand and in the United States are still referred to as *nāgas*.

Boonmee Poungpet

See also: Entries: Dragons; Lotus Flower; Swastika

Further Reading

Aasen, Charence. *Architecture of Siam, a Cultural History Interpretation.* Oxford: Oxford University Press, 1998.

Gosling, Betty. *The Origins of Thai Art.* Bangkok: River Books, 2004.

Jumsai, Sumet. *Naga, Cultural Origins in Siam and Western Pacific.* Bangkok: Chalernit Press and DD Books, 1997.

Nakamura, Paul T. (1926–)

Paul T. Nakamura, a native of Hawai'i, is the first Asian clergy to provide ministry to Asians in North America and an advocate for multicultural ministries. He was born into a large Buddhist family in Hawai'i, where he had a carefree childhood, roaming the natural surroundings of the island. His Christian spiritual journey began when he was in elementary school. His Chinese friend took him to the Episcopal Sunday school and his brother later brought him to the Japanese Congregational Church where he was baptized.

He felt the call to ministry after high school, but his family was not able to support him through college and seminary. So in 1946 he joined the U.S. Army to get government benefits for his schooling after he was discharged. In 1948 he became a student at Gustavus Adolphus College, a Lutheran school in Minnesota. Three years later he was a first-year student at Andover Newton Theological Seminary in Massachusetts. In the intervening years he was either a student there or at Augustana Lutheran Seminary in Illinois. The year 1953 was decisive for him—he became a Lutheran.

In the following year he interned under Lewis and Martha Miller, who were trying to organize a Japanese ministry in Los Angeles. During his internship he met Kikuno Miyagi, his future wife and lifelong partner in ministry, who was attending the Holiness Church there. They were married in 1955 after Nakamura's graduation from Augustana Lutheran Seminary. Together they have two adopted children: a boy, David, and a girl, Joy.

His first taste of Asian American ministry was when he was assigned to work with Lewis and Martha Miller in Los Angeles as an intern. He was ordained in 1955 at St. Mark's Lutheran Church in Los Angeles where he continued to work with Miller until he retired in 1956. In 1957 Nakamura became the pastor of St. Mark's, a multicultural congregation of people from the African American, Japanese American, and Euro-American communities. For the next 16 years, he served the congregation faithfully in spite of two heart attacks in 1969 and 1971.

Another decisive moment in Nakamura's life took place in 1973. He decided to spend the academic year of 1973–1974 in clinical pastoral education. During that year, he did some deep soul-searching and finally concluded that his future ministry was with Japanese Americans. Armed with a promise of support from his friend Yoshimitsu Hokama and a $5,000 gift from the synod, Nakamura began his labor of love in 1975 with the Japanese American community in Torrance/Gardena, a suburb of Los Angeles. In 1998, he formally retired, but he continues to serve the congregation as an interim to this day.

In his long years of ministry, Nakamura has served the community and churchwide ministries in various capacities. He was instrumental in the formation of the Asian Caucus in the Lutheran Church in America and served as its president and secretary. He was a convocator of California Lutheran University, a member of synodical committees, as well as a consultant and then interim director for Asian ministries of the then Commission of Multicultural Ministries, a unit of the Evangelical Lutheran Church in America. He also has been active in the Japanese American community and played a significant role in the Redress Movement in the church and in the sociopolitical arena. In recognition of his services to the church and the community, Nakamura was honored with many awards and commendations by various institutions and agencies.

Nakamura is a gentle giant with a pastoral heart that few persons can match. But he also has his own joys and sorrows. It delights him to see harmony among the congregants in worship and work, but it pains him a great deal "to have a member lapse and join a non-Christian group" and when there were synodical and churchwide staff who "did not involve the concerned parties in the decision-making process."

He values friendship and always expresses his faith in a gentle way. But what has kept him in ministry for more than half a century? The answer is twofold, he maintains, with distinctive humility: "One is [my] loving, patient and supportive family. The other is an understanding congregation that puts up with me, my mistakes and foibles."

Edmond Yee

See also: Entries: Lutherans; Matsushita, Eiichi

Further Reading

Yee, Edmond. "Living Ministry as a Gift: A Profile of Paul Takechi Nakamura." In Lily R. Wu and Edmond Yee, eds. *Church and Discipleship: Asian Lutheran Reflections.* Chicago: Asian Lutheran International Conference, 2005.

Yee, Edmond. *The Soaring Crane: Stories of Asian Lutherans in North America.* Minneapolis: Augsburg Fortress, 2002.

Nepali American Religions

Until the 1990s, when Nepal was still a monarchy, the country was considered the only Hindu kingdom in the world. But after the overthrow of the monarchy, the country was declared a secular state. Almost 90 percent of the population are Hindus, approximately 5 percent are Buddhists, and the remaining 5 percent are Muslims, Christians, Jains, and others. Almost every individual identifies with a religion. Hinduism and Buddhism, which to some extent are inseparable, are widely practiced in the land. One example of the merging of the two religions is seen in the worship of the virgin goddess Kumari, who is selected from the Buddhist family but worshiped essentially by Hindus and Buddhists alike. Having a worship room or a *pūjā* room in every home in Nepal is very common. Going regularly to the temples, monasteries, and *mosques* and churches is also a common phenomenon.

This very religious tradition, which is a part of life of almost every Nepali and a marker of their identity, is carried over to Nepali American homes in the United States. Almost every Nepali American home has a little room or a little space set aside where little stone or metal deities or holy books are placed. The religious rituals naturally are transformed or modified in the new locale, and the daily ritual worship may not be as intense and long as in Nepal, but it is practiced daily when at least an incense stick is lighted in the name of the gods. Nearly all the women of the Nepali American families, if not all men, practice this.

Nepal shares its religious diversity with its South Asian neighbors. The many temples, monasteries, *mosques*, and churches in various cities of the United States are frequented by all the Nepali American families as well as the other Asian American communities on special auspicious days. Programs on certain days of religious festivals are celebrated in temples with worship and feasting. Weddings, the rice-feeding ceremony (*annaprasana*), and the rite of passage (*bratabandha*) are also often carried out in these temples in the United States. Nepali American children grow up learning and embodying the values and norms of their religion. They may grow up as part of the popular culture of the United States, and their language and mannerisms may be similar to those of other Americans, but their religion is always something to which they hold steadfast.

Sangita Rayamajhi

Further Reading

Allen, Michael. *The Cult of Kumari.* Kathmandu: Mandala Book Point, 1996.

Levine, Sarah, and David Gellner, eds. *Rebuilding Buddhism: The Therabada Movement in the 20th Century.* Nepal, Delhi: Orient Blackswan, 2008.

"Nepal." http://countrystudies.us/nepal/33. htm. Accessed July 16, 2014.

Tuladhar-Douglas, William. *Remaking Buddhism for Medieval Nepal*. Delhi: Routledge, 2006.

Nichiren Shōshū

Nichiren Shōshū is a sect of Nichiren Buddhism that experienced great success in the United States from the 1960s to the 1980s. This success was due in large part to its close connection with the lay organization Soka Gakkai, known as Nichiren Shōshū of America (NSA) until the two split in 1991. Since the division, Nichiren Shōshū has maintained a modest presence in the United States. There are currently six temples in the greater metropolitan areas of San Francisco, Los Angeles, Hawai'i, Chicago, New York, and Washington, D.C.

Beliefs and Practices

One of the distinguishing features of Nichiren Shōshū is that it traces its origin to Nikkō (1246–1333), one of Nichiren Daishōnin's (1222–1282) disciples. Nikkō is credited with building the temple at Taiseki-ji at the foot of Mount Fuji. The temple houses the primary object of reverence, the Dai-Gohonzon, a wooden

Nichiren was a Buddhist monk who lived during the Kamakura period (1185–1333) in Japan. Nichiren Buddhism is a form of Mahāyāna Buddhism named after the priest Nichiren, who devoted his life to the enlightenment and happiness of the entire universe. Many legends about Nichiren claimed that he possessed supernatural powers. This is depicted in the noted illustration by Utagawa Kuniyoshi, titled, "Nichiren Calming the Storm." (Historical Picture Archive/Corbis)

maṇḍala inscribed by Nichiren with the name of the *Lotus Sūtra* in Chinese characters and Nichiren's signature. Nichiren Shōshū places emphasis on the importance of the priesthood and highlights its ability to trace a direct line back to Nikkō. This continual priestly lineage, passed down from one high priest to the next, is known as *kechimyaku sojo*, or "Heritage of the Law." Nichiren Shōshū documents describe this as follows: "The Heritage of the Law refers to the master (the Buddha) selecting a single disciple whom he considers to be most suited for his successor and entrusting him with the essence of Buddhism in its entirety. The transmission of the Heritage of the Law is of utmost importance, since the Law would be lost no matter how outstanding the teacher if he had no successor to follow him. . . . Nichiren Shōshū is the only orthodox sect which has handed down the Daishonin's teaching correctly in such an unbroken line" (Nichiren Shōshū, 63). This emphasis on the priesthood also supports a sharp delineation between the priesthood and the laity (*hokkeko*) within Nichiren Shōshū, a fact that becomes particularly relevant for the conflict with Soka Gakkai.

Also unique to Nichiren Shōshū is the belief that Nichiren Daishōnin was the "Original (True) Buddha, the fundamental master of all Buddhas" (Nichiren, 1). This is based on the conviction that Śākyamuni Buddha taught the idea of *Mappō*, a coming time when belief in Buddhism would decline and a more perfect Buddha would appear. Nichiren Shōshū identifies this Buddha as Nichiren and as a consequence renders all previous versions of Buddhism moot.

A final unique feature of Nichiren Shōshū is its belief that the Dai-Gohonzon is what makes enlightenment possible and that it is the sole object of reverence for all people. It identifies other Nichiren-based groups as having either confused objects of worship, such as statues of Shakyamuni Buddha or "counterfeit" Gohonzons. These groups include the Nichiren shū sect based at Mt. Minobu, which the Buddhist Church of America is based on, Risshō Kōsei-kai, Reiyūkai, and Soka Gakkai. Again, from Nichiren Shōshū's perspective it is the unbroken priestly lineage that can guarantee the authenticity and efficaciousness of the Dai-Gohonzon. As a result of this commitment to the Dai-Gohonzon, *tozan* (pilgrimage) to Taiseki-ji is an essential practice.

History

When considering the history of Nichiren Shōshū in the United States it is difficult to separate it from the history of Soka Gakkai. This is because until 1991 Nichiren Shōshū entrusted Soka Gakkai—at the time Nichiren Shōshū of America (NSA)—with guiding Nichiren Shōshū adherents outside of Japan.

In conjunction with NSA efforts, Nichiren Shōshū's early appearance in the United States was via immigrant communities, especially Japanese women who had married American servicemen. This was followed by explosive growth in the 1960s and 1970s through intensive proselytization efforts known as *shakubuku* as well as cultural changes that made Nichiren Shōshū more accessible to non-Japanese, such as using English at meetings. However, at the same time, within NSA there was progressively a less militant commitment to the absolute uniqueness of Nichiren Shōshū in contrast to other traditions.

The tremendous expansion of Soka Gakkai globally and its changing methods and activities distanced it from the Nichiren Shōshū priesthood. Ultimately this led to Nichiren Shōshū cutting off all relations with Soka Gakkai and its members on November 28, 1991. After this formal separation NSA changed its name to Soka Gakkai International while those who left SGI and stayed loyal to the Nichiren priesthood adopted the name Nichiren Shōshū Temple. While there were numerous variables involved in the split, Nichiren Shōshū's distinct emphasis on the importance of the priesthood played a major role. As Daniel Métraux summarizes, "The key questions concerning the Soka Gakkai and Taiseki-ji involve spiritual leadership and responsibility, the correct role of the clergy and laity, the organizational problem of a small provincial priestly order suddenly growing into a mammoth national and international community of believers, and a power struggle between two strong leaders" (Métraux, 326). While Soka Gakkai has gone in a much more progressive direction focused on environmental and social issues, Nichiren Shōshū has consolidated and focused on its core beliefs and traditions, believing that these will ensure true success in the future.

Peter L. Doebler

See also: Entries: Nichiren Shū

Further Reading

Hurst, Jane. "Nichiren Shōshū and Soka Gakkai in America: The Pioneer Spirit." In Charles S. Prebish and Kenneth K. Tanaka, eds. *The Faces of Buddhism in America*. Berkeley: University of California Press, 1998, pp. 79–98.

Hurst, Jane. *Nichiren Shoshu Buddhism and the Soka Gakkai in America: The Ethos of a New Religious Movement*. New York: Garland, 1992.

Inoue, Nobutaka. "NSA and Non-Japanese Members in California." In Kei'ichi Yanagawa, ed. *Japanese Religions in California*. Tokyo: Department of Religious Studies, University of Tokyo, 1983, pp. 99–162.

Métraux, Daniel A. "The Dispute Between the Sōka Gakkai and the Nichiren Shōshū Priesthood: A Lay Revolution against a Conservative Clergy." *Japanese Journal of Religious Studies* 9, no. 4 (1992): 325–30.

Nichiren Shōshū Temple. *Nichiren Shōshū: Basics of Practice*. Rev. ed. West Hollywood, CA: Nichiren Shōshū Temple, 2003.

Snow, David A. *Shakubuku: A Study of the Nichiren Shōshū Buddhist Movement in America, 1960–1975*. New York: Garland, 1993.

Nichiren Shū

Nichiren Shū was founded by Nichiren (1222–1282), a Japanese monk active during the Kamakura period (1185–1333); he was born in present-day Kominato City, Chiba Prefecture, to a fisher family. Nichiren began his lessons on Buddhism under the Tendai monk Dōzenbō (–1276) of Seichōji Temple at the age of 12 and was ordained at 16. He continued his studies at Mt. Hiei, the center of Tendai Shū, at Kōyasan, the major center for Shingon studies, and at other important learning centers. As a result of his wide exposure to Buddhist thought and practice, he concluded that the message of the *Saddharmapuṇḍarika* or *Lotus Sūtra* was the ultimate teaching; and that all sentient beings could attain Buddhahood by chanting the Odaimoku or "sacred title": *Namu-myōhō-renge-kyō*. "*Namu*" means "to praise" and "*myōhō-renge-kyō*" is the Chinese rendering of *Saddharmapuṇḍarika Sūtra*. Nichiren proclaimed his new faith on April 28, 1253.

History

Nichiren did not intend to establish a new school; nor did he give his movement a name. However, his movement came to be known as the Hokke Shū or Lotus School, Nichiren Hokke Shū or Nichiren Lotus School; more simply it is referred to as Nichiren Shū. On October 8, a few days after delivering his final message, Nichiren appointed six of his direct disciples: Nisshō (1221–1323), Nichirō (1245–1320), Nikkō (1246–1333), Nikō (1253–1314), Nicchō (1252–1317), and Nichiji (1250–?) as major disciples without seniority and asked them to care for the other disciples and devotees. They in turn resolved to spread their master's teaching in their own regions. As a result, five major lineages emerged and competed with one another. On the 13th-year memorial service, Nichiji made a pilgrimage to Nichiren's grave and stated his determination to heed his master's words and "convert all the people in the whole world to the Wonderful Dharma [*Lotus Sūtra*]." On New Year's Day of the following year, at the age of 46, Nichiji departed from Shizuoka for the northeastern regions of Honshū and Hokkaidō; and it is believed that he continued on to continental Asia.

After the collapse of the Tokugawa Shogunate (1603–1868), the Meiji government promoted Shintō as the national faith and ordered the many Buddhist traditions to coalesce into seven schools. At present, Nichiren Shū has about 5,200 temples, 8,300 clergy, and 3.8 million members worldwide.

Inspired by Nichiji's example, commemorating the 650th anniversary of its founding, Nichiren Shū launched its modern overseas mission by sending representatives to Korea, Taiwan, Sakhalin, continental China, including Manchuria, and Southeast Asia. Overseas missions in Western countries actually began in 1899, when Takagi Gyōun (1870–1946) was dispatched to attend to the spiritual needs of Nichiren devotees in Hawai'i. Takagi searched on O'ahu and other islands for a suitable site for a temple; he settled on Kapapala Plantation on the island of Hawai'i, where many Nichiren followers had settled. He tirelessly shuttled between the many Japanese plantation communities raising funds for a temple building. He was accompanied by Noguchi Yūkichi, who strapped a statue of Nichiren on his back. The construction of the Kapapala Nichiren Mission started on March 15, 1902, and was completed on May 18 in time for the 650th anniversary of the founding of the Nichiren Shū. Two hundred devotees were present at the dedication ceremony that marked the beginning of Nichiren Shū in Hawai'i.

Takagi also wanted to establish a Nichiren presence in the capital of Hawai'i, Honolulu. The opportunity arose in 1912, when a Shintō priest, Takeshita (first name unknown), representing Katō Jinja, sent a letter inquiring whether Takagi would consider establishing a Buddhist-Shintō worship space. Anticipating problems with such an arrangement and after consulting with his followers, Takagi concluded that it would be best to establish an independent temple. This decision initiated the beginnings of the present Nichiren Mission of Hawai'i in Nu'uanu Valley. There are four other Nichiren temples in the state.

Asahi Nichimyō (1833–1916) sent his disciple Asahi Kanjō (1880–1963) to North America in 1914. After arriving in San Francisco, he traveled to Los Angeles, the home of many devotees. Within a few days after his arrival, the devotees located a hall at a hotel, where he conducted a memorial service for Empress Dowager Shōken (1849–1914). Shortly thereafter, Asahi launched a membership drive and converted a rented house into a temple. On July 12, 1914, Asahi officiated at the opening service for the Los Angeles Nichiren Buddhist Temple. On October 14, Asahi left for Salt Lake City and Seattle to meet with Nichiren Shū devotees, before returning to Japan on December 1. Two years later, in 1916, Oka Ryūchō established the Seattle Nichiren Buddhist Church. Today, the Nichiren Buddhist order of North America consists of 15 temples.

Beliefs and Doctrines

Nichiren lived during the age of *Mappō* or Degenerate Dharma, which the Japanese believed to have begun in 1052. Indeed, natural and man-made events served to only confirm that they were living in a most degenerate age. Corruption was widespread among the aristocracy and Buddhist clerics knowingly violated their precepts. As with other reformist clerics of his day, Nichiren sought a means that would enable Buddhist devotees to transcend suffering and realize enlightenment and Buddhahood. During the course of his studies Nichiren became convinced that the message of *Saddharmapuṇḍarika Sūtra* held the answer. The *Lotus Sūtra* expounds the notion of *busshū* or Buddha-seed. Nichiren stated that the *busshū* is spontaneously given by the Buddha, when we believe and chant the *Daimoku*. The *busshū* is simultaneously planted, matured, and liberated in the mind. In contrast with the idea of *hongaku* or original enlightenment advanced by the *Daijō kishinron* (*Awakening of Faith*), *busshū* is not passive, but is ready to be quickened by the belief in and by chanting the *Daimoku*. This formula is most appropriate during the age of *Mappō*.

Nichiren accepted the Zhiyi's assertion that the *Saddharmapuṇḍarika Sūtra* represents the final and highest truth revealed by the Buddha. Implicit in this statement is the belief that even the most depraved have the potential for and can realize enlightenment with the *Sūtra*. But more crucial, Nichiren concluded that more than simply relating edifying examples of Śākyamuni Buddha's compassion, the *Sūtra* reveals the timeless and absolute Buddha.

The *Lotus Sūtra* has two distinct sections. The first 14 chapters of the *Sūtra's* 28 chapters, especially the chapter on "Expedients," relate how the Buddha skillfully leads unenlightened beings to enlightenment. Zhiyi maintained that Śākyamuni's work among the people was the fundamental reality and truth of his teaching. In contrast, in the second half, especially in the chapter on "The Duration of the Life of the Tathāgata," the *Sūtra* reveals the timeless Buddha. The efficacy of the eternal Buddha compassion is ontologically prior to the historical Śākyamuni's Enlightenment and his compassionate work. The efficacy of the timeless Buddha continues from the beginningless past to the endless future. The second half of the *Sūtra* that reveals the underlying reality of the Eternal Buddha, not the historical Śākyamuni, is the *Sūtra's* core revelation. Nichiren's followers debated the importance of the Absolute Buddha vis-à-vis its compassionate manifestation.

The task of the Nichiren devotee is to realize the Eternal Buddha and to participate in its work. Realization of Enlightenment is possible through the *Daimoku*. Nichiren's belief in the efficacy of the *Daimoku* is grounded in "one thought possesses the 3,000 realms" (*ichinen sanzen*) formulated by Zhiyi. As noted in the entry on Tendai, the notion of "one thought possesses the 3,000 realms" and "one mind [engages] three discernments (meditations)" constitute the content of the twofold meditational method of *zhi* and *guan* or "stillness and insight" (*samatha-vipaśyanā*). Zhiyi maintained that through the exercise of "stillness and insight," the practitioner is able with "one mind" to penetrate the three phases (true, provisional, and middle) of dharmic reality. Implicit in the "one mind [engages] three discernments (meditations)" is the idea of "one thought possesses the 3,000 realms." "Three thousand realms" is a metaphor for "all Dharmas," the building blocks or "psycho-mental markers" through which

the mind apprehends and constructs the phenomenal world. "One thought possesses the 3,000 realms" is, for Tendai, metaphysical. But, it is, for Nichiren, a practical reason for chanting the five syllables: "*myō*," "*hō*," "*ren*," "*ge*" "*kyō*." These five sounds in effect embrace the 3,000 worlds that symbolize the absolute eternal Buddha. And by chanting this phrase the devotee becomes aware of this truth. Nichiren believed that this truth was revealed to him; and because of his awareness of this truth he had a responsibility to propagate the message of the *Lotus Sūtra*.

Additionally, in keeping with the notion of "one thought possesses the 3,000 realms," Nichiren writes in *Risshō Ankoku ron* (*Treatise on Spreading Peace throughout the Country by Establishing the True Dharma*) that when an individual realizes the Eternal Buddha and becomes, in effect, part of the timeless enlightenment, he or she benefits all beings. Thus through the self-realization of an increasing number of individuals, an ideal society comes into being. The method for achieving an ideal world is for devotees to chant the *Daimoku*: "*Namu-myōhō-renge-kyō*." Nichiren writes in *Kanjin honzon shō* (*Treatise Revealing the Spiritual Contemplation and the Most Venerable One*):

His (Śākyamuni's) attainment of Buddhahood is fully contained in the five words: *Myō*," "*Hō*," "*Ren*," "*Ge*," "*Kyō* (*Lotus Sūtra of the Wonderful Dharma*); thus when we uphold the five words, the merits which He accumulated before and after His attainment of Buddhahood are naturally transferred to us.

During his lifetime, Nichiren criticized Pure Land, Zen, and Shingon teachings. In doing so, he provoked the ire of their monks and their powerful supporters. As a result he was persecuted and twice exiled. In 1273 while in exile on Sado Island, in addition to writing a number of major doctrinal treatises, Nichiren created the Daimadara (Great Mandala) that consisted of the names of the *Lotus Sūtra*, Buddhas, Bodhisattvas, and protector deities. He placed the vertically written *Daimoku*, *Namu-myōhō-renge-kyō* in the center of the Daimandara; immediately to the *Daimoku*'s right (the viewer's left) is the name of Śākyamuni Buddha and to its left (the viewer's right) is the name of Prabhūtaratna Buddha. The Daimandara, also known as "*Gohonzon*," is a distillation of Nichiren's understanding of the message revealed in the *Lotus Sūtra*; it is also one of the primary symbols of the Nichiren altar. Other symbols include the seven-jeweled *stūpa* that represents the *stūpa* that rises from the earth in the chapter "Beholding the Stupa of Treasures." When Śākyamuni Buddha was about to expound the *Lotus Sūtra*, a magnificent multijeweled *stūpa* welled up from the earth and suspended itself in midair. Seated within were the Buddhas Prabhūtaratna and Śākyamuni. This spectacle is recreated in the Nichiren altar.

Also making an appearance are four bodhisattvas, Viśiṣṭacāritra (Superior Practices), Anantacārita (Unlimited Practices), Viśuddhacārita (Pure Practices), Supratiṣṭhitacāritra (Firm Practices), and others. The real protectors of the *Lotus Sūtra* are the diligent observance of the tenets of the faith that these bodhisattvas represent. Nichiren believed that he was the incarnation of the bodhisattva Viśiṣṭacāritra, and thus the practioner of the *Lotus Sūtra* and its teachings.

Practices

Chanting of the *Daimoku* and becoming part of the Absolute Buddha's eternal enlightenment and thus participating in creating a better world during the age of *Mappō* appealed to people who inhabited the margins of society. After establishing the notion that the Buddha plants *busshū* or buddha-seed in the mind by the belief in and by chanting the *Daimoku*, Nichiren lobbied against the idea in the *Larger Sukhāvatī Sūtra* that women must be reborn as males before Buddhahood is possible. His stand for spiritual equality attracted many female devotees. These ideas also allowed him to embrace lords of manors, estate stewards, and others.

After being pardoned and released from exile, Nichiren retired in 1274 to Mt. Minobu in today's Yamanashi Prefecture. After becoming ill, he sought therapy at a hot spring in the present Ibaraki. On his way, too weak to continue, he stopped at a follower's estate. He asked his disciple to write a last letter to Hakiri Sanenaga (1222–1297), an important supporter, asking to be buried on Mt. Minobu. Nichiren passed away on October 13, 1282, at 8:00 a.m.

Contributions

Like other faith institutions, Nichiren temples served as a place for spiritual sustenance and a venue for community gatherings during the early period of Japanese immigration to Hawai'i and the continental United States. Nichiren temples and priests link the descendants of their pioneering immigrant forefathers and mothers to their ancestral homeland though a variety of cultural programs and activities. At present, it serves as a spiritual refugee for those seeking the lessons of Nichiren Buddhism. Looking to the future, Nichiren Shū established the Nichiren Buddhist International Center in 1991 and built its facilities in Hayward, California, in 2002 to further the vision of its founder. The purpose of the center is to help overseas missions. For instance, the center promotes awareness of Nichiren Buddhism, translates books and brochures into English from Japanese, and supports workshops and retreats all over the world.

Chishin Hirai

See also: Entries: Nichiren Shōshū; Reiyūkai; Risshō Kōsei-kai (RKK); Soka Gakkai; Tendai Shū

Further Reading

Headquarters of Hawai'i Nichiren Missions. *A Century of Nichiren Buddhism in Hawai'i.* Honolulu: Obun Hawai'i Group, 2003.

Hori, Kyōtsū, and Jay Sakashita, eds. *Writings of Nichiren Shōnin Doctrine 1.* Honolulu: University of Hawai'i Press, 2003.

Hori, Kyōtsū, and George Tanabe, eds. *Writings of Nichiren Shōnin Doctrine 2.* Honolulu: University of Hawai'i Press, 2002.

Nichiren Shū Website. http://nichiren-shu.org/. Accessed July 11, 2014.

Nichiren Shū, ed. *Nichiren Shū Jiten (Dictionary of Nichiren Shū).* Tokyo, 1981.

Nofumi Annaka. "America Nikkeijin no Nichiren Shū Shinkō (An American's faith in Nichiren Shū)." *Nichiren Kyōgaku*

Kenkyūsho Kiyō (Journal of Nichiren Buddhism) 37. Tokyo: Rissho University, 2009.

Risshō Daigaku Nichiren Kyōgaku Kenkyūsho. *Nichiren Kyōdan Zenshi Jō (Complete History of Nichiren Shū, Part I).* Tokyo: Heirakuji shoten, 1964.

Senchu Murano, trans. *The Lotus Sūtra.* 3rd ed. Hayward, CA: Nichiren Buddhist International Center, 2012.

North American Pacific/Asian Disciples (NAPAD)

The North American Pacific/Asian Disciples (NAPAD) are part of the Stone-Campbell movement, which originated in the United States at the turn of the 19th century. It started out as a Protestant reform effort led by figures such as Barton Stone, Thomas Campbell, Alexander Campbell, and Walter Scott. The movement, named after the first three of the founders, rejected creedalism and denominationalism, and espoused Christian unity based on a return to the primitive church, whose blueprint, the founders believed, could be discerned in the New Testament. For this reason, it is sometimes referred to as the Restoration movement. Ironically, however, the movement itself split into three parts—splitting first in the aftermath of the American Civil War, and then again in the second half of the 20th century. In the 21st century, these splits are reflected in the three streams of the movement: the Churches of Christ, sometimes known as A Capella for its disavowal of musical instruments in worship; Christian Churches/Churches of Christ, the most evangelical of the three, sometimes referred to as Independents for their aversion to supra-congregational entities; and the Christian Church (Disciples of Christ), the most progressive of the three, often found at the forefront of ecumenical movements both inside and outside the United States. According to the *2010 U.S. Religious Census: Religious Congregations and Membership Study*, edited by Clifford Grammich et al. (2012), the three streams together comprised about 3.82 million members in the United States in 2010: 786,000 for the Disciples of Christ; 1.45 million for the Christian Churches/Churches of Christ; and 1.58 million for the Churches of Christ. NAPAD's story, which begins in the last decade of the 19th century, has occurred within the context of the Christian Church (Disciples of Christ).

The year 1891 marks the founding of the first Asian Disciple community, and 2010 the year when the Executive Office of NAPAD became a general ministry of the denomination—general in the sense of being responsible to all Disciples within the United States and Canada, as opposed to regional (limited to one cluster of states and provinces) or congregational (limited to a specific congregation). The nearly 120 years of history that has spanned these milestones provokes questions: How did the Asian and Pacific Islander communities evolve during these years? What were the challenges? Who were the key actors? What events proved significant?

North American Pacific/Asian Disciples' history has been one of a confluence of two distinct streams, each arising from a different source in a different period, the first one never gaining momentum, thinning into a weak eddy, rescued from oblivion only by merging with the second stream. Put differently, from 1891 to 1978, Asian Disciples' history was one of marginalization, owing to restrictions imposed on Asians by the dominant society, and sometimes the majority of the church, whereas the history from 1978 to 2010 was one of dynamism and hope, owing partly to the removal of the above-mentioned restrictions but also to a group of determined Disciples who strived to ensure that Asian and Pacific Islander Disciples would find their rightful place in the mainstream of the church.

To understand Asian American Disciples history, we must keep in mind the social atmosphere of the United States in these periods. The aspects of the larger society that particularly affected Asian Disciples were a series of laws that coerced Asians into a marginalized state. One of them was the Naturalization Act of 1790, which disqualified Asians from becoming naturalized citizens. Others were the Chinese Exclusion Act of 1882, which prohibited an entire nation of people from immigrating to the country, and the Immigration Act of 1924, which barred all Asian immigration. In 1952, the racist naturalization law of 1790 was finally repealed, but the number of Asians that could immigrate remained extremely limited. Then in 1965 Congress passed a new immigration law—the Hart-Celler Act—which finally did away with race and national origins as factors in immigration.

Eddying in the Margins, 1891–1977

Sentiments embedded in racialized immigration laws coerced Asians into the margins of American society. Moreover, the racist sentiments were more often than not condoned, if not shared, by U.S. Christians. Even so, it cannot be denied that churches, such as the Disciples of Christ, were among the few institutions that expressed genuine concern for Asian Americans, affording them a context in which to gain dignity and succor. Before 1945 there were nine Asian Disciples communities, seven as independent congregations, two as components of European American Disciple churches. But each of them was on its own, regarded as a mission of one or more local white churches or a missionary agency such as Christian Woman's Board of Missions (CWBM) or the United Christian Missionary Society (UCMS).

It was on January 27, 1891, that the first Asian Disciple community was founded. It was founded as a mission among the Chinese in Portland, Oregon, by the First Christian Church of Portland, in collaboration with CWBM. At the time, Portland had 1,668 Chinese, 9 percent of the city's population; they were subjected to virulent racial prejudices. The church readily attracted Chinese. In 1892 the growth of the community led CWBM to hire a full-time Chinese pastor, Jeu Hawk, who had just graduated from Drake College. In 1900 he resigned from his position and returned to China. That year Hawk's place was taken by Louie Hugh, a convert of Hawk's who also graduated from Drake. During Hugh's pastorate, the Chinese community transformed into a church with its own elders and deacons. Hugh resigned in 1909 to return to China. Thereafter, the church was cared for by two other Chinese ministers, till it was closed in 1924. During its

service of 33 years, the church baptized 77 people. In 1907, encouraged by the work in Portland, CWBM worked with other Disciples to found the Chinese Christian Institute in San Francisco. This mission also grew apace, providing valuable services, baptizing 225 people before it too closed in 1924.

Meanwhile on the East Coast, Chinese were most numerous in New York City. Here the Disciple entity that ministered to the Chinese was Central Church of the Disciples, which later became Park Avenue Christian Church. The community formed around the church's Sunday school, particularly its English and Bible study classes. By 1929, the Sunday school had more than 100 boys, young men, and teachers involved in it, and it was deemed the largest school of its kind in the city. This ministry persisted till 1948, when it ceased because the Sunday school no longer attracted Chinese youth as they were now able to enroll in public schools.

None of the Chinese congregations having survived into the second half of the 20th century, Asian-American Disciples churches that lasted longest were those of Japanese and Filipinos. The work among Japanese began as early as 1901, when Broadway Christian Church in Los Angeles began a night school for a group of Japanese bachelors, teaching English and the Bible. Soon CWBM became involved and in 1908 the ministry developed into the Japanese Christian Church with 10 members, who gathered in a rented building. In the following year, Teizo Kawai, another Drake graduate, was called from Japan to serve as its minister.

The church grew rapidly. By 1914, the Japanese Disciples community moved to a new building, called the Japanese Christian Institute, built and dedicated by CWBM, and the congregation flourished, with its membership rising to nearly 200, becoming a significant presence in the Japanese American community. In 1929, the Japanese Disciples moved to another location to be closer to the heart of the Japanese population in the city. By then, Rev. Kawai had retired and the church was under the leadership of Kojiro Unoura, who pastored the church till 1971. Under Rev. Unoura's pastorate, the church continued to prosper—until 1942, when it closed owing to Executive Order 9066. Four other Japanese Disciples churches were established before 1945. Three of them were in other parts of California: Berkeley; San Bernardino; and Calexico, Imperial Valley. Outside California, a loose Japanese Disciple community was founded in the Arkansas River Valley, Colorado. The third Asian Disciple community that came into being in Southern California before 1945 was that of the Filipinos. It began in 1928 as the Filipino Christian Fellowship, founded by Silvestre Morales, a Disciples of Christ minister from the Philippines, and his younger colleague Felix Pascua, with the support of Dr. Royal J. Dye and his wife Eva Nichols Dye, influential Disciples in Los Angeles. In 1929 the fellowship was adopted as a commission of the State Board of the Disciples in California; and in 1933, the fellowship officially became the Filipino Christian Church (FCC).

Since 1928 the Filipino community gathered at various places—in rented spaces of other churches and commercial establishments. In 1950, it finally acquired its own building, a former Methodist church located at 301 North Union Avenue in Los Angeles. The FCC provided much needed ministry to the Filipinos in the city, most of whom were bachelors relegated to jobs such as dishwashing and crop-picking and often subjected to cruel discrimination. The church was the most successful Protestant ministry in the city for the Filipinos, with its membership reaching 450 at its peak.

The Filipino, Japanese, and Chinese churches served as centers of their respective marginalized communities. None of them could have been established had it not been for the concern the European American Disciples had shown them. That said, it cannot be denied that Asian American Disciples were in a marginalized situation vis-à-vis their white counterparts. This became painfully clear when the dominant church experienced financial distress or when societal forces scapegoated the marginalized. Given this reality, perhaps it is not surprising that six of the nine Asian Disciples communities could not escape closing before 1945. The first Asian Disciples churches to close were those of the Chinese, in Portland and San Francisco, closed in 1924 owing partly to anti-Chinese sentiments. The closure of Japanese churches came in the aftermath of Pearl Harbor with the issuance of Executive Order 9066, which led to the incarceration of around 120,000 Japanese residents, entailing the dissolution of all the Japanese Disciples churches on the West Coast.

Early in 1945, internees of the camps were finally allowed to return to their homes, if they still existed. Many Japanese Disciples returned to California, to Los Angeles. They hoped to reconstitute the Japanese Christian Church at its former site, but they could not do so. The site had been converted into another kind of ministry: All Peoples Christian Church and Center, a multiracial ministry. All Peoples was an innovative and worthwhile ministry, yet it occupied the facilities that had belonged to the Japanese Disciples; and the UCMS, which owned the facilities, decided the facilities would not revert to the Japanese Disciples, partly out of a desire to integrate the Japanese members into the established ministry. The Japanese returnees were invited to join All Peoples. Many, largely Nisei, did, but others, mainly Issei, the first generation, declined. They declined to assimilate into the dominant culture at the expense of their distinct Japanese Christian identity. For a while, this group of Japanese Disciples worshipped separately at All Peoples. Then in 1948, the UCMS finally agreed to their forming into a distinct Japanese Disciples congregation, thus giving birth to West Adams Christian Church.

The post–World War II era brought positive changes to Asian Americans. The Immigration Act of 1952 ruled out race as a factor in the naturalization process—the Chinese Exclusion Law had already been repealed in 1943—and the Immigration Act of 1965 finally eliminated racial and national origins quotas as factors in immigration, enabling Asians to immigrate to the United States on the same footing as Europeans.

After 1945, the Disciples had only three distinctly Asian communities that traced their roots to the prewar period: FCC, West Adams Church (WAC), and the Japanese Disciples community in Colorado. The last of these, given its loose makeup, eventually dissipated. The Japanese congregation in Los Angeles thrived for much of the period between 1945 and 2010. Already by 1952, a two-story educational building had to be built to accommodate increasing Sunday school attendance, which on a given Sunday reached upwards of 250. In the 1960s, however, the church experienced difficulties, buffeted by a variety of societal forces such as the construction of the Santa Monica Freeway, which forced many church members to move away. By the turn of the 21st century, only a handful of elderly Nisei remained. And finally, in 2010, WAC closed as a church for Japanese Americans.

The Filipino Christian Church also thrived between 1945 and 2010. Like WAC, it continued to serve not only its members but also the larger Filipino community in Los Angeles. The church's contributions to Filipino American life were recognized by the city of Los Angeles: in 1998 the city designated the FCC as a historical cultural monument. Compared to WAC, FCC adapted better to the changing times, largely because, unlike Japanese, Filipinos continue to immigrate in large numbers to America. By the end of 2010, FCC remained as the only NAPAD church from the pre-1945 era.

Striving toward the Mainstream, 1978–2010

Filipino Christian Church and West Adams Christian Church have been the

Disciples' link to the earliest years of NAPAD history, but they were not the fount of a new stream of Asian Disciples churches that arose beginning in the 1970s. These congregations have quite different origins. Their origins lay in a vision and the hard work of a group of Disciples—a vision to establish a cohesive Asian and Pacific Islander community that would not be relegated to the margins but integrated into the mainstream of the church. In implementing their vision, the leaders were aided by the progressive atmosphere that prevailed in the country, engendered by the civil rights movement and especially the 1965 Immigration Act.

Most of the Disciples who worked toward the vision were of Asian descent, but the first person to embrace it and act on it was not. That person was Harold R. Johnson (1921–), who served in the general church from 1961 till his retirement in 1990. In 1972, upon his return from a mission trip to Thailand, Johnson developed a deep affinity for Asians and envisioned a denomination-wide structure for Asian Disciples. Asian Disciple were then too few and scattered throughout the country, worshiping mostly in white churches. So the first step Johnson took was to gather like-minded Disciples to form a community of Asian Disciples, and then to persuade the Division of Homeland Ministries (DHM) to support such efforts. Thanks to his persuasiveness, on July 27–28, 1978, an informal consultation of Asian Disciples was held in Indianapolis, Indiana. Aside from Johnson, conferees included Jane Pouw Felty, Luz Bacerra, Grace Kim, and Janet Casey-Allen. This consultation resulted in the creation of the Fellowship of Asian American Disciples (FAAD).

In April 1979, again under the auspices of DHM, a more formal consultation took place at Spencer, Indiana. It attracted additional Asian Disciples, for example, Itoko Maeda, David T. Kagiwada (1929–1985), and James and Maureen Osuga. The consultation designated Johnson as the staff liaison between Asian Disciples and DHM, decided to publish a newsletter for the community, and discussed needs that had to be met to establish a viable Asian Disciples community, needs such as appointing a DHM staff member dedicated to Asian Disciples. At the consultation, the group adopted a new name, the American Asian Disciples (AAD), with "American" understood to refer to Asians in both North and South America.

In 1980, October 6–8, a convocation of AAD was held in Indianapolis, Indiana. This proved to be another crucial gathering. There the Executive Council of AAD was formed, with David T. Kagiwada elected as convener (later called moderator), Janet Casey-Allen as secretary/treasurer, and newcomer Soongook Choi (1933-2002) as newsletter editor. Choi would eventually emerge as an outspoken leader of NAPAD, forming along with Johnson and Kagiwada the triumvirate of NAPAD founders. At this meeting, it was decided that AAD would hold a convocation every other year, alternating with the General Assembly, while the Executive Council would meet every year.

In 1982, July 28–August 2, AAD held its second convocation on the campus of the University of California at Berkeley. At this gathering, AAD agreed to seek official recognition and budget and staff support from the denomination. It also agreed to search for ways to increase the number of Asian Disciples, individually and congregationally; and enhance Asian Disciples' representation on the boards of the church. AAD's efforts paid off: in June 1984 the General Board of the denomination formally recognized AAD as a constituency of the Christian Church (Disciples of Christ), opening a way for it to negotiate with DDH for staff and program support.

On July 10, 1985, David T. Kagiwada died. To honor the memory of this articulate and passionate Disciple, a scholarship was established to support seminarians of Asian/Pacific Islander background. In October 1989, an Asian Ministries Consultation was held in Chicago, participated in by the AAD Executive Council and select leaders from DHM and other parts of the denomination. The consultation resulted in a proposal to embed AAD in the general structure of the denomination.

The proposal of the 1989 consultation was followed up by the Executive Council. As a result, in 1991 the General Assembly approved the creation of a DHM staff position dedicated to ministering to and developing the Asian and Pacific Islander Disciples community. Subsequently, in February 1992, Geunhee Yu was appointed as associate for American Asian Ministries in DHM's Center for Congregational Growth and Vitality (later renamed as the executive pastor for American Asian Disciples Ministries). Yu was officially installed at the 1992 AAD Convocation, held on the campus of the University of Southern California in Los Angeles. At the time, there were about

17 Disciples churches whose members were primarily Asian.

Asian American Disciples continued to grow. In 1993, Disciples of Christ Korean Fellowship was organized; in 2000, it changed its name to the Korean Disciples Convocation. In July 1994, at Woodstock, Illinois, the AAD held its eighth convocation. It turned out to be the largest AAD convocation held to date, with over 100 people participating. At the convocation, Geunhee Yu explained challenges he faced in his position. He noted that apart from his salary and travel allowance, there was hardly a budget for Asian ministries in DHM, limiting his ability to develop Asian congregations. Yu's report caused members to be more attentive to raising funds for AAD programs. The 1996 convocation was held in conjunction with Pacific Islanders Asian American Ministry (PAAM) of the United Church of Christ, July 26–28, 1996, at Chapman University, in Orange, California. There, the community adopted a new name for itself, North American Pacific/Asian Disciples, to better signal its openness to diversity.

At the next NAPAD Convocation, held July 30–August 1, 1998, at Mills College in Oakland, California, Jeri Sias was elected new moderator for the next two years. In her tenure, Sias worked hard to place NAPAD more squarely in the general structure of the church. To this end, a NAPAD Structure Task Force was formed and a visioning conference was held in Indianapolis in March 2000 to plot NAPAD's course for the next 10 years. The conference attracted about 50 leaders from NAPAD, general units, regions, and theological institutions; and the conferees crafted a document that urged, among others, NAPAD and the general church to better relate to each other.

The conference's document was endorsed by the 2000 NAPAD convocation, held July 27–29 in Indianapolis. To implement its goal of becoming embedded in the general church, NAPAD obtained the support of the Standing Committee on Renewal and Structural Reform, which made preliminary recommendations on matters related to structural issues of the denomination. And in 2002 the Standing Committee, on behalf of NAPAD, submitted a restructure proposal to the General Board of the denomination. This proposal sought to move the office of the executive pastor of NAPAD from DHM to the office of the general minister and president. In the end, the proposal failed, as it was rejected by the General Board. The General Board offered an alternative proposal, which would remove the executive pastor's office from DHM but make it an independent NAPAD commission, instead of placing it in the office of the general minister and president. But this proposal was rejected as it would overburden NAPAD with financial obligations.

The work of restructuring was not taken up until 2008. That year, August 6–9, NAPAD held its 15th convocation in Stony Point, New York. The community appointed a Restructure and Constitution Renewal Task Force (RCRT). The formation of the task force was motivated by a new development in the denomination. That year the General Board approved the formation of a Mission Alignment Coordinating Council (MACC), entrusted with streamlining and better integrating general units of the church. Given NAPAD's

desire for restructure shown at the 2000 Vision Conference, it was assumed that the new alignment would bring significant changes to NAPAD, and RCRT was charged to prepare for the change, particularly by amending the constitution and bylaws of the community.

After deliberating for a year, in April 2009, MACC submitted a nine-point proposal to the General Board. One of them was GB-09-066: "The NAPAD Executive Pastor will be accountable to a NAPAD executive board and the ministry as a whole will have a covenantal relationship to the General Board." The General Board adopted the proposal, making the new arrangement effective January 1, 2010. Consequently, the office of the executive minister of NAPAD was allowed to move out of the DHM and become a distinct unit of the general church and have access to services and equipment shared by the general units, which considerably lessened NAPAD's overhead.

At its 16th convocation, held in Seattle, Washington, August 4–7, 2010, NAPAD adopted a new set of bylaws and affirmed the work of MACC. On November 22, 2011, Geunhee Yu retired from the office of the executive pastor of NAPAD after nearly 20 years of service in the post, having ably shepherded NAPAD's full integration into the general structure of the denomination. Under his leadership, NAPAD churches increased in numbers from less than 20 to over 90, with over a dozen ethnic groups represented. Nominated to be Yu's successor was Jinsuk (John) Chun, a former deployed staff of the Pacific Southwest Region in charge of Asian and Pacific Islander ministries. A new day was dawning in the community and NAPAD was no longer eddying in the margins but striving in the mainstream of the Christian Church (Disciples of Christ).

Timothy S. Lee

See also: Entries: Kagiwada, David

Further Reading

Lee, Timothy S. "From Coerced Liminality to In-Beyond the Margin: A Theological Reflection on the History of Asian-American Disciples." *Call to Unity* 9 (September 2008).

Yu, Geunhee. "Asian American Disciples." In Douglas A. Foster, Paul M. Blowers, Anthony L. Dunnavant, and D. Newell Williams, eds. *The Encyclopedia of the Stone-Campbell Movement*. Grand Rapids, MI: Eerdmans, 2004, pp. 40–41.

Obon (Urabon)

Urabon or simply Obon, the Japanese variant of the Sanskrit *Ullambana*, is a Buddhist service of gratitude offered to the ancestors. Its origins are obscure, but many scholars trace it to the tale of Jaratkāru, who appears in the Indian epic *Mahābharata* (I, 13–14; 45–48). According to this account, Jaratkāru chances upon a large pit over which a number of persons are suspended upside down by a single root of grass that was being gnawed at by a rat. He learns that they are the ancestral spirits of his deceased father and ancestors. They find themselves in their predicament, not by their doing, but because Jaratkāru, who chose to become an ascetic and celibate, would leave no heirs and thus end the family linage. Moved, Jaratkāru promises to marry and produce an heir. Buddhists reworked the story by featuring Maudglyāna, one of Buddha's 10 great disciples, who rescues his mother from *preta*, the realm of hungry ghosts. *Preta* is the second lowest of six *gatis* or realms through which beings transmigrate. The lowest is hell, the others in ascending order are: (3) the animal realm, (4) the *asuras* (constantly fighting demigods) realm, (5) the human realm, and (6) the *deva* or heavenly realm.

The *Nihon Shoki* (Chronicles of Japan) reports that Obon was first observed during the reign of Emperor Saimei on the 15th day of the seventh lunar month in 656. The court sponsored a service in 733 and annually thereafter. The Japanese evolved Obon into a three-day festival of great joy, because they believed and still believe that their ancestors return from their spiritual abode to be with their progeny. Prior to the introduction of Buddhism, the Japanese celebrated *tama matsuri* or the "welcoming of the spirits festival." Observed twice annually, at the end of the year and at the end of summer, this indigenous celebration welcomed the ancestral spirits of the fields, water, and other nature deities to solicit their assistance for good planting conditions and abundant harvests. The Obon celebration was eventually absorbed into the summer *tama matsuri* festival, and the end of year festival was abandoned.

Reminiscing about her childhood during the early 20th century in *A Daughter of the Samurai*, Etsuko Inagaki Sugimoto describes the preparations her grandmother and mother took to welcome the ancestral spirits at Obon. They made special offerings and placed them on the *butsudan* (family altar), where the ancestral tablets were placed. She writes of her anticipation as follows:

> Like all children I always looked forward with pleasure to [the] visit of the ancestors, but after Father's death, I felt a deep personal interest, and my heart was beating with ex-

Clarine Shimada, 79, dances in the Obon festival at a Buddhist church in San Jose, California, July 13, 2003. The traditional Japanese Obon folk dance is a Buddhist festival to honor ancestors as an expression of gratitude for life. The Obon honors the spirits of the deceased and has taken place annually for centuries at Japanese Buddhist temples. (AP Photo/The News Tribune, Jensen Walker)

citement, as the family met at the shrine.

When it was time for the ancestral spirits to return at dawn on the fourth day of their three-day visit, the family placed offerings and a lantern in a miniature canoe fashioned from a pampas mat. The offerings would sustain their visitors and the lantern would light the way. They hurried to the river, floated the offering-filled canoe, and watched it drift downstream. This ritual is still observed in a number of locatations in Japan. In Hawai'i *toro nagashi* or floating of the lantern has become a community event that coincides with Memorial Day.

Obon is a major service; and *hatsu obon* or first obon refers to the first service for those families who lost loved ones during the past year. For these families, the service is especially poignant. The return of the ancestral spirits is an occasion for great joy that is expressed through the *bon odori* or *bon* dance. Typically the *yukata*-clad dancers circle around a *yagura*, a wooden scaffold on which the musicians and singers provide the music. The late summer "Bon season" is an important part of the present-day culture and life of Hawai'i and

North America. Buddhist temples use the occasion to highlight Japanese cultural arts with exhibits and a food bazaar. The Ghost Festival (see entry on the Ullambana Assembly) is the Chinese counterpart of the Bon Festival.

Ronald Y. Nakasone

See also: Entries: Ghost Festival/Zhongyuan Festival; Qingming Festival

Further Reading

Aston, W. G., trans. *Nihongi: Chronicles of Japan from the Earliest Times to A.D. 697.* Tokyo: Japan Society, 1896.

Joya, Mock. *Things Japanese.* Tokyo: Tokyo News Service, 1958.

Matsunaga, Daigan, and Alicia Matsunaga. *Foundations of Japanese Buddhism.* 2 vols. Los Angeles: Buddhist Books International, 1974.

Menon, Ramesh, trans. *The Mahābhārata: A Modern Rendering.* New Delhi: Rupa, 2004.

Sugimoto, Etsuko Inagaki. *A Daughter of the Samurai.* Rutland, VT: Charles E. Tuttle, 1966.

Okinawan (Ryūkyūan) Spiritual Culture

The spiritual culture of the Okinawan (Ryūkyūan) people (or *Uchinaanchu* as they refer to themselves in their native tongue) residing in Hawai'i and the continental United States is a complex blend of archaic indigenous shamanic and animistic beliefs and ancestral veneration that has been reinforced and honed by centuries of interaction with Chinese faith traditions, especially Confucianism, and with Japanese Buddhism. The belief that they share the world with innumerable disembodied spirits and that their identity is linked to their genealogy are formalized in family, kin group, and community rituals.

Okinawans in Hawai'i and Continental United States

The exodus of Okinawans from their homeland was prompted in large part by the demand for cheap labor after the end of the African slave diaspora, Japanese imperial designs after World War I, and post–World War II U.S. military strategy. Statistics published by the Okinawan Prefectural Government reveal that between 1899 and 1911, 13,335 Okinawans sought work overseas, mostly as agricultural laborers. Of this number 10,250 settled in Hawai'i and 863 migrated directly to the continental United States. At the end of World War I Japanese entrepreneurs recruited Okinawan laborers to populate and to work in the newly acquired League of Nations–mandate territories once held by Germany in the Southeast and Northeast Pacific. Further, the 1920 collapse of world sugar prices and the subsequent loss of employment forced many Okinawans to seek work abroad. Okinawans migrated to South and East Asia (21,047) and to South America (31,243) between 1927 and 1940. By 1940, 75,318 persons, approximately 15 percent of the population, had migrated overseas (Tamamori and James, 2000: 75).

In the aftermath of vanquishing the Japanese defending the island of Okinawa, the U.S. military requisitioned prime farmland, much of which it still holds. Additionally, after 1946 more than 180,000 out of an estimated 332,000 Okinawans and their descendants living abroad were repatriated back to war-shattered Okinawa and its outlying islands. This large influx of people resulted in a lack of employment opportunities that prompted a second wave of migration. Between 1948 and 1993 most of the 17,714 Okinawan immigrants ventured to South America. Many Okinawan women also left as brides of U.S. servicemen stationed on Okinawa. Interest in emigration waned after the late 1960s with the growing prosperity of Japan and as overseas immigrants began returning to Japan and Okinawa.

At the present, the two largest concentrations of Okinawans in the United States reside in Hawai'i and greater Los Angeles, where approximately 50,000 and 15,000 persons, respectively, claim to be Okinawan. These communities include first-, second-, third-, fourth-, and even fifth-generation persons of Okinawan descent, each with varying degrees of affiliation with their ancestral homeland.

Beliefs and Practices

The basis for Okinawan spiritual culture can be extrapolated from the *Omorosōshi*, an anthology of 1,553 shamanic poems that preserves the earliest aspirations and memories of the Okinawan people. From these poems we learn that the ancient Okinawans believed that they shared the world with innumerable animate and inanimate spirits, and that they had, and still have, great reverence for their elders and ancestors and for the wisdom they acquired from their life experiences. This reverence, evident in the ritual expression of their spiritual culture, is reinforced by Confucian notions of filiality.

First and foremost is the prominent presence of the *ubutidan* (Jpn. *obutsudan*), the ancestral altar that enshrines the *tōtōmē* or *ifee* (Jpn. *ihai*), memorial tablets of successive generations of ancestors in the main room of a traditional home. The *futuki* (Jpn. *hotoke*) or ancestral spirits are believed to reside in memorial tablets and thus are able to observe the daily comings and goings of their progeny. The living attend to their ancestors through regular offerings and by reporting births, marriages, and other significant events. The 1st and 15th days of each lunar month are set aside for formal rituals. Before merry-making, relatives visiting from abroad will approach the ancestral altar.

In addition, the numerous tombs that can be seen on hillsides and beachfronts also speak of the Okinawan respect for their ancestors. Families make periodic pilgrimages to the family tomb, in which the remains of successive generations are interred. Special effort is made to visit the site on *usīmīsai* or "spring equinox festival" that is observed during the third lunar month, a custom adopted from the Chinese observance of *Qingming*. On this occasion, the family will clean the grave site and repair the tomb, before conducting a service and sharing a meal at the site. Another important rite is *ubun*, which is observed on the 13th, 14th, and 15th of the seventh lunar month that corresponds to the Japanese Buddhist Obon. On this occasion the family prepares the ancestral altar with a festive array of offerings to welcome the ancestral spirits on the 13th day. On the 15th day, the family sends off their ancestors to their spiritual abode, *nirai-kanai*. Memorials that mark the anniversary of death are also occasions for family rituals. These rituals reinforce family solidarity and an individual's awareness of his or her place among the generations. The oldest person of the family, usually a female, is the lead celebrant; a professional ritual specialist is not required. These family-oriented rituals contrast with Japanese custom that normally requires the services of a Buddhist cleric.

In addition to offering incense and *uchikabi*, the burning of ritual money, in traditional Okinawa the women would prepare special dishes that typically include *rafuté* (glazed pork); deep-fried tofu and sweet potatoes, stewed *gobo* (burdock), turnip, and *konbu* (pork wrapped in kelp); *kamaboku* (fish cake), and *mochi* (rice cakes). These dishes are arranged in neat rows in an *ujū*, multitiered lacquered boxes or arranged on a plate. Confectionery, fruits, stalks of sugar cane, and *awamori* (Okinawan *sake*) are also offered. Recently, these traditional offerings have been replaced by other celebratory dishes and liquors. At the end of the service, these offerings are consumed. Families in Hawai'i and the continental United States have simplified the food offerings and rarely share meals at the grave site. They often return home or retreat to a restaurant to share a meal.

Diasporic Okinawan families and communities continue the reverence for their ancestors by observing many of these traditional rituals, albeit in different guises. Children are constantly reminded of the sacrifices of their immigrant forebears by regular private and community memorial services. I have not come across nor have I made any formal survey of Okinawan households, but personal observation and anecdotal evidence suggest that most Okinawan families have an ancestral altar, make regular offerings, but do not mark the traditional fortnightly rituals with any particular observance. Offerings to the ancestors are observed on New Year's Day, memorial rites that mark the anniversary of death, and other days of family significance. Families also make an effort to visit the grave sites on Memorial Day, Mother's Day, and Father's Day, which are American observances. The anniversaries of deaths, birthdays, and the Buddhist Obon are also occasions to visit grave sites.

Most recently, many Okinawa prefectural organizations sponsor Irei no hi or Day to Honor the Departed Spirits for those who perished during the Battle of Okinawa. Irei no hi, June 23, marks the formal end of the Battle of Okinawa.

Additionally, Okinawan families honor their elders with a series of late life celebrations. *Kajimaya* or the 97th birthday is especially celebratory. *Kajimaya* is based on the Chinese 12-year zodiac cycle. The first birthday is celebrated with great fanfare; thereafter the 13th, 25th, 37th, 49th, 61st, 73rd, and 85th birthdays are especially auspicious. Some Okinawan communities sponsor a special party to celebrate the longevity of their elders in conjunction with Keirō no hi or Respect for the Aged Day, a recently established Japanese national holiday on the third Monday of September. These late life celebrations together with the mortuary rites and memorial observances underscore the belief that the corporeal and spiritual constitute a continuum. With the end of corporeal life, the individual continues his or her spiritual life.

"Sister-Protector," Ritual Sites

Okinawans carried many portable aspects of their traditional spiritual culture to their new homes, but not the formal structure and rituals of the national faith that was headed by the office of the *chifijin* (Jpn. *kikoeogimi*), or national priestess. The office was established by Shō Shin (1465–1527; r. 1477–1526), the third monarch of the second Shō Dynasty. The *chifijin* appointed the regional and local priestesses, *nuru* (Jpn. *noro*), who in turn supervised the village *nīgami* (Jpn. *ne-gami* or root-deity) and other subordinate functionaries.

Okinawans believe females to be spiritually gifted, an idea that can be traced to ancient Ryūkyū, when the islands consisted of consanguineous settlements centering on a founding family. At this time the expression *kami* or deity was synonymous with *fu* or "mother," whom the ancients associated with *kan'unna* or "female-deity." These designations—*kami, fu,* and *kan'unna* (Jpn. *kami onna*) are rooted in the belief that women were more in tune with the unseen spiritual world, and thus better able to tap its resources and to communicate with beings dwelling in that realm. The spiritual power of the female is personified in the personality of the *unarigami* or "sister-protector," who shields the male members of her family from harm. For their part, the men labor to provide the material needs of the family and attend to matters outside the family. This sister-brother partnership provided the rationale for Ryūkyūan polity

and the establishment of the office of the *chifijin ganashii mee* who together with the king shared the responsibility for ensuring the well-being and prosperity of the nation. This dual sovereignty system—a partnership of the highest spiritual and secular authorities—is celebrated in Ryūkyūan creation myths and folklore, and is still operative in all levels of present-day Okinawan society and its overseas communities.

During the Ryūkyū Kingdom the *chifijin* conducted rituals of thanksgiving, offered prayers for peace, and observed memorials for the royal ancestors to ensure the well-being of the king and the nation. However, the 1879 Japanese annexation and the forcible exile of King Shō Tai (r. 1848–1879) and his court to Tokyo essentially dismantled the office. The chief-priestess, a daughter of Shō Iku (r. 1835–1847), chose to remain behind; her sacerdotal responsibilities were too important to abandon. Although the last *chifijin* died in 1944 (Lebra, 1966:121) memories of nationhood continue through the *munchū*, the family clan. Most significant is the *Agari umāi* or Eastern Pilgrimage. Once led by the *chifijin*, it recalls the mythical origins of the Ryūkyūan people. Two of the most revered sites are Haiinju and Ukinju, artesian springs that watered the first rice field. Indeed, even today, families and individuals observe *kā umāi* or "well pilgrimage" in and around their village to honor and give thanks to the water *kami* (spirit) from which their ancestors drew life-giving water. Revered well sites are referred to as *uganju* and are essential aspects of the indigenous animistic tradition.

Another important site is the *utaki* or sacred grove. The *utaki* is associated with the burial site of the founding family—*nīya* (Jpn. *neya*) or root house of the traditional village. Located in the hills or nearby woods, the focal point of an *utaki* is the *ibi*, a stone representing common ancestral spirits. On the *utaki's* grassy clearing the *nuru* (Jpn. *noro*) or local priestess or priestess leads the rites of *umatī* (Jpn. *matsuri*) that coincide with planting and harvesting. One of the more significant rites is *gung-watī umatī* that celebrates the rice harvest. The temperate climate in the southern islands allows for this festival to be celebrated on the 15th day of the fifth lunar month.

Interestingly, the office of the *chifijin* did not include the *yuta* or shaman in the state sacerdotal hierarchy system. The *yuta* is recognized at an early age by the community and by other *yutas* to be endowed with shamanic (*saadakaumari*) and paranormal powers (*kamidari*). It appears that the *yuta's* nonrational powers of clairvoyance and prognostication, and her ability to traverse the spiritual realms and communicate with the unseen could not be quantified, and thus was beyond state control. Perhaps it is for these reasons that Shō Shōken (1617–1675) and Saion (1682–1761), chief councilors during the kingdom, deemed the *yuta's* powers to be irrational and superstition. They issued decrees to ban their activities. The Japanese also attempted to exterminate the *yuta* in the early 20th century. But these attempts failed. The *yuta* still enjoys great popularity, probably because she can divine the needs of the ancestral spirits, remind the living of those ritual responsibilities they may have forgotten, and identify auspicious days for marriage, travel, starting a new venture, and other important undertakings. The *yuta* is the only spiritual personality that has been active in the overseas Okinawan community.

Ronald Y. Nakasone

See also: Entries: Ijun

Further Reading

Hijirida, Kyoko, and Tomoko Oshiro. *Introduction to Okinawan Culture.* n.p., 2011.

Lebra, William P. *Okinawan Religion, Belief, Ritual, and Social Structure.* Honolulu: University of Hawai'i Press, 1966.

Nakasone, Ronald Y., and Susan Sered (2005). "Ritual Transformation in Okinawan Immigrant Communities." In Karen I. Leonard et al., eds. *Immigrant Faiths: Transforming Religious Life in America.* Walnut Creek, CA: AltaMira Press, 2005, pp. 79–98.

Nakasone, Ronald Y., ed. *Okinawan Diaspora.* Honolulu: University of Hawai'i Press, 2002.

Sakihara, Gary K. "Okinawan Household Survey." In *Uchinanchu: A History of Okinawans in Hawai'i.* Honolulu: University of Hawai'i/United Okinawan Association of Hawai'i, 1981.

Sakihara, Mitsugu, ed. *Uchinanchu: A History of Okinawans in Hawai'i.* Honolulu: University of Hawai'i/United Okinawan Association of Hawai'i, 1981.

Sakihara, Mitsugu. *A Brief History of Early Okinawa Based on the* Omoro sōshi. Tokyo: Honpo shoseki, 1987.

Tamamori, Terunobu, and John C. James. *Okinawa: Society and Culture.* Naha: Bank of Ryūkyūs International Foundation, 2000.

Wacker, Monika. "*Onarigami,* Holy Women in the Twentieth Century." *Japanese Journal of Religious Studies* 30, nos. 3–4 (2003): 339–59.

P

Pacific and Asian American Center for Theologies and Strategies (PACTS)

Pacific and Asian American Center for Theologies and Strategies (PACTS) emerged from the quickening of "ethnic consciousness in the late 1960s" that inspired and challenged the Asian American and Pacific Islander clerics and laity from mainline Christian denominations to reexamine their Christian faith and its theological underpinnings. To this end PACTS worked to address the needs of Pacific and Asian Americans, with special attention to the local ethnic congregations, and to promote the training of leaders through seminaries and other institutions of higher education. PACTS fulfilled these objectives through numerous programs that assisted the local churches, collected and distributed resources, developed study guides, and produced publications. This entry reviews the history of PACTS and its contributions.

History

In his *Director's Report*, Roy I. Sano, the first director, traces the inspiration for the idea of and the establishment of PACTS. He recalls the Rev. Dr. Woodie White, the general secretary of the Commission on Religion and Race, urging Asian Americans "to dream of a center for reflection, strategizing, and leadership training of both clergy and laity" at the United Methodist Church Asian Caucus held at Santa Monica, California, in March 1970. He remembers also that at the June 21, 1971, National Conference of Christian Work among the Chinese in America, the Rev. Wilbur Choy outlined the need for a training center; Rev. Frank Mar echoed the same sentiment.

The following February, Choy convened a meeting of like-minded clerics to explore the establishment of a center dedicated to highlighting the religious needs of Asia Americans. Choy together with the Revs. James Chuck, Paul Wu, Dennis Loo, George Nishikawa, Sano, and Canon James Pun met regularly for a year. Nishikawa assumed the chair after Choy was elected to the United Methodist episcopacy. At the conclusion of the March 1973 planning retreat at Mills College in Oakland, California, the participants issued "Statement of Priorities and Programs" to establish the Asian Center for Theology and Strategies (ACTS).

The Statement called for ACTS to (1) develop programs of higher education, specifically in the seminaries, to address the concerns of religious challenges of Asia Americans and their faith institutions; and (2) relate to the Asian American communities beyond the churches. ACTS would give voice to the spiritual concerns of Asian Americans, develop new structures to understand and address these concerns, and foster a new spirit of faith. The center would conduct workshops to train and foster theological reflection, negotiate with seminaries to introduce programs to nurture Asian American religious denominational leaders, and produce publications to disseminate news and developments, and share concerns.

ACTS was initially based at Mills College, where Sano, the first director (1972 to 1980), was chaplain and assistant professor of religion. When Sano was appointed professor of theology and director of PACTS at the Pacific School of Religion in 1977, ACTS moved its office to its campus in Berkeley, California. On March 26, 1974, ACTS was incorporated as a 501(c)(3) nonprofit entity with the state of California as the Asian American Center for Theologies and Strategies. The growing numbers of Pacific Islanders, especially in Hawai'i and California, prompted ACTS to rename itself Pacific and Asian Center for Theologies and Strategies (PACTS) in 1977.

Rev. Lloyd Wake served as director from 1980 to 1985. Subsequent directors were Fumitaka Matsuoka (1985–1987); Julia (Matsui) Estrella (1987–1995); and Debbie Lee (1995–2000). The active and long-serving staff members included Kathleen Thomas-Sano and Clifford Alika, Ruby Okazaki, and Miya Okawara.

PACTS continued its original program mission in the 1980s, but expanded to include women in ministry; ministry with immigrants, refugees, and native peoples; racial and ethnic concerns; and human rights. During this period PACTS partnered with Pacific, Asian, and North American Asian Women in Theology and Ministry to draw attention to the theological and ministerial concerns of Asian women. PANAAWTM's interest in racism, identity, and sexism within the Asian American community, as well as tokenism and marginalization within U.S. society, meshed with PACTS' vision. In 1991 PACTS described itself as "an ecumenical center for research, resourcing, recruiting, training, and consciousness-raising, with foci on the Pacific and Asian American constituencies, to promote the fulfillment of God's mission through the ministries of the churches and the service of community groups." PACTS' activities expanded to include ministry with gays and lesbians.

Contributions

The Asian American leaders who met in the early 1970s to found PACTS acknowledged the gains made through the theological acculturation of Euro-American Christianity. Many mainline Protestant denominations established Asian American "desks" in response to rising ethnic awareness in the late 1960s. In addition to sensitizing the denominations to their Asian membership and reaching out to new constituencies, PACTS sponsored seminars, workshops, and travel intensives, and collected resources to address institutional racism in religious institutions and the concerns of women laity and clerics, gay and transgender, and other minority communities. Evidence of PACTS' activities is documented in the 20 file boxes in the GTU archives.

PACTS collected and compiled considerable resources and developed study guides related to the Asian American and Pacific Islander religious and spiritual experience. In 1976 Sano compiled "The Theologies of Asian Americans and Pacific Peoples," a seminal collection of reflective essays and studies that articulated the long-suppressed voices of minority communities of faith. This unpublished work is a treasure trove of early reflections by future Asian and Pacific Islander scholars and theologians articulating the need for an Asian American theology, and discussing racial identity, racial discrimination in religious institutions, and the practical concerns of Asian and Pacific Islander peoples living and worshiping in and with mainline religious institutions. Similar concerns were highlighted in the quarterly *Branches: A Pacific and Asian American Journal of Faith and Ministry*. PACTS also disseminated information and news through *Pacific People: Occasional Newsletter of Pacific and Asian Americans*. In 1999 PACTS published *Unfaithing U.S. Colonialism* (Dharma Cloud Publishers), which memorialized the 1898 U.S. takeover of Cuba, Guam, Hawai'i, Philippines, and Puerto Rico.

PACTS established the Pacific Asian American Center for Christian Education (PAACE) to disseminate materials produced by the departments of various denominations for their Pacific and Asian American constituencies. It also collected academic papers and reflections on the Pacific Islander and Asian American experience. PACTS further developed study guides on history projects and teaching courses for local congregations. These courses offered guidelines on how to study, understand, and interpret the Pacific and Asian American experience and contributions within its historical and sociological context.

Significantly, PACTS' programs moved beyond "exclusively" mainline Christian denominational concerns to give voice to persons victimized by war and poverty, who otherwise have no venue to voice their suffering. This entry highlights two of its more memorable projects.

PACTS partnered with the U.S. Japan Committee for Racial Justice, an organization committed to giving space to "survivors" of racism in the Pacific-Asia region to tell their stories, and convened a series of *Tochi wa Inochi* (Land Is Life) events. The first convened in Okinawa; subsequent events were held in Guam, Vieques, Marshall Islands, and Hawai'i in approximately five-year intervals. The June 19–23, 1996 *Tochi wa Inochi* event coincided with the 51st anniversary of the Battle of Okinawa, the last major battle of World War II. As the title of the conference series suggests, the organizers linked people with their homeland. Land provides sustenance and identity. War, in turn, not only defiles the land, but uproots people from their homes. Survivors related their struggles to reclaim their homelands from nuclear and chemical pollution, the result of weapons development. Perhaps the most riveting testimony emerged from the voices of Korean and Filipino women who were forced by the Japanese Imperial Army to be sex slaves (200,000 women during World War II).

PACTS also focused on "experiential" learning. One such exposure trip was led by Ruth Cortez of the Philippines, a student at the Pacific School of Religion. Cortez arranged for the participants to experience homelessness in the Philippines and its link to the militarization by arranging stays in homeless camps, visits to Catholic Faith-Based Organizations, conversations with political prisoners opposed to the Marcos regime, and visits to the former U.S. naval base at Subic Bay (closed in 1992) and other military sites. To understand worker poverty, the participants stayed with farmers in the countryside and fishermen and their families. Experiences such as these provided antidotes to academician reports.

Throughout its history, PACTS was in continual transition, grappling with its mission, programming, funding support, and staffing. At the end of the last century, these issues became overwhelming. Kyle Miura assumed the directorship in 2000. On November 16, 2001, the PACTS board formally voted to disband and ended its ties with the Graduate Theological Union (GTU) on May 31, 2002. Its files and extensive resource library, including the Jitsuo Morikawa (1987–1975) Memorial Library, are housed in the GTU where the collection can be accessed under Pacific and Asian American Center for Theology and Strategies Collection, 1972–2002. PACTS remained dormant until 2011, when it registered its nonprofit status with the state of Hawai'i, where it continues its work.

Julia Keiko Higa Matsui Estrella

See also: Essays: Bible and Asian Americans; LGBT Asian Americans and Christianity; *Entries:* Estrella, Julia Keiko Higa Matsui; Sano, Roy I.; Wake, Lloyd K.

Further Reading

Pacific and Asian American Center for Theology and Strategies Collection. 1972–2002.

Flora Lamson Hewitt Library, Graduate Theological Union. The collection consists of 20 boxes of files that includes 11 series. They are (1) board minutes, (2) program files, (3) PACTS newsletters and journals, (4) funding, (5) subject files, (6) resource library, (7) photographs, (8) audio cassettes, (9) videotapes, (10) videotapes, and (11) computer disks.

Pacific Islander Religious Cultures

According to the 2010 U.S. census, there were 1.2 million people who identified themselves as Native Hawaiians and other Pacific Islanders. "Native Hawaiian or Other Pacific Islander" refers to a person who has origins in any of the indigenous peoples of Hawai'i, Guam, Samoa, or other Pacific Islands. They include people who also marked the checkboxes "Native Hawaiian," "Guamanian or Chamorro," "Samoan," "Polynesians such as Tahitian," "Tongan," and "Tokelauan, Marshallese, Palauan, and Chukese." People of Melanesian origins such as Fijian, Guinean, and Solomon Islander are also included. The Native Hawaiian and Other Pacific Islander population was the race group most likely to report multiple races in the 2010 census. They were one of the fastest-growing race groups between 2000 and 2010.

The religious beliefs of Pacific Islanders—those people who inhabit the islands of Micronesia, Melanesia, and Polynesia—reflect centuries-long efforts of missionaries to Christianize the area. Spanish priests brought Roman Catholicism to the islands in the mid-1600s. Catholic and Protestant missionaries from Europe began visiting

Mormons from the Polynesian Culture Centre (Brigham Young University) liven up the birthday celebration of King Kamehameha the Great. (Rico Leffanta/Dreamstime.com)

the area in the early part of the 19th century. In the mid-1800s North American missionaries representing the Church of Jesus Christ of Latter-day Saints established churches there. Despite Christian influence, some Pacific Islanders continue to practice animistic religions, and many Christian Pacific Islanders mix indigenous beliefs with modern doctrine. The Pacific Islands have also become home to several non-Christian religions.

The voyages of James Cook (1728–1779) sparked British and European interest in the Pacific. Known to the British and Europeans as "noble savages," the Hawaiians and other Pacific Islanders were considered to possess pre-Adamic innocence. In 1796 the London Missionary Society

sent a ship called *Duff* with 29 missionaries to the Pacific, and early work began in the "Society Islands" of Tahiti. European missionaries were dependent on local Christians for translation, and Pacific Islanders were the missionaries themselves of the Pacific. Denominational rivalry and international political developments influenced the missionary efforts of the Western churches.

Christianity is the predominant faith of Hawai'i and the other Polynesian societies. In the Marquesas and Society Islands, Protestant traditions are followed by slightly more than half the population, while another 30 percent are Roman Catholic. On the Cook Islands, the Cook Island Christian Church is the largest Protestant denomination and includes more than 60 percent of the population. The only established non-Christian religion is the Baha'i faith. Samoa is 98 percent Christian and primarily Protestant Methodist. Catholics, Seventh-day Adventists, and Mormons also maintain churches on the island. In Hawai'i, the predominant religion is Roman Catholic, followed by the Church of Jesus Christ of Latter-day Saints and other Protestant faiths. A minority of Hawaiians belong to non-Christian faiths, including Judaism, Buddhism, Islam, and Hindu.

More than 400,000 people populate the islands of Micronesia. Catholicism is the dominant religion on Guam and Kiribati, while Protestant religions claim a larger majority on the other Micronesian islands. Established faiths include the United Church of Christ, Mormon, Baptist, Seventh-day Adventist, Salvation Army, and Jehovah's Witness. The influence of early animistic religions is evidenced by Christian Micronesians' veneration of ancestors, references to spirits, and worship of icons. Traditional magic is often mixed with modern Christian beliefs. Non-Christians are a minority in Micronesia and include followers of the Baha'i faith. A small community of Buddhists has been established on the island of Pohnpei.

Unlike Asian Americans on the U.S. continent, Pacific Islander Americans have had opportunities to make a place for themselves more readily. They have lived in a society where racial divisions have not been drawn sharply. Such a landscape created greater opportunities for them to weave their religions and cultures into their life fabric to seek to change their societies of rich diversity. The collective wisdom of their ancestors offered them the foresight to know that their world was changing and that they would have to adjust. That their cultures have survived and continue to thrive is a testament to their foresight and alternative worldviews of other possibilities.

Fumitaka Matsuoka

See also: Entries: Aloha Spirit; *Kava;* Marshall Islands, Religion in; Micronesian and Polynesian Traditional Religions; Samoan Spirituality; Sovereignty; Tongan Spirituality

Further Reading

Fadiman, Anne. *The Spirit Catches You and You Fall Down: A Hmong Child, her American Doctors, and the Collision of Two Cultures.* New York: Farrar, Straus and Genoux, 1998.

Garrett, John. *Footsteps in the Sea: Christianity in Oceania to World War II.* Geneva, Switzerland: World Council of Churches, 1992.

Iwamura, Jane Naomi, and Paul Spickard, eds. *Revealing the Sacred in Asian and Pacific America.* New York: Routledge, 2003.

Takaki, Ronald. *Raising Cane: World of Plantation Hawai'i.* New York: Chelsea House Publishers, 1994.

Pakistani American Religions

Religion plays an integral role in shaping Pakistani and Pakistani American identity, cultural etiquette, and social norms. The majority of Pakistanis practice Islam and are of the Sunni sect, although there is a significant representation of Pakistani Shiites. Islam is an especially potent aspect of Pakistani national ideology and sense of

Pakistani and other Muslims attend Friday prayers at the Makki Masjid Community Center of Brooklyn. The large Pakistani community, that has made its home along Coney Island avenue, joined Muslims around the world in mourning the loss of former Pakistani Prime Minister Benazir Bhutto. The opposition leader was assassinated in Pakistan during a Political rally on December 27, 2007. (Richard H. Cohen/Corbis)

self because Pakistan was founded specifically as a nation for the majority Muslim populations in the eastern and western regions of British India (eastern Pakistan was later to become the independent nation of Bangladesh). The particular form that Islam takes in the context of Pakistan is deeply intertwined with elements of non-Muslim South Asian culture and rituals as well as feudalism and patriarchy. Hinduism, Christianity, and Zoroastrianism are also practiced by a small minority of the Pakistani population.

Most Pakistani immigrants who came to the United States in the 1970s and 1980s brought with them a strong sense of culture and religion, establishing makeshift *mosques* when they first settled in the country. Over time, as Pakistanis climbed up the socioeconomic ladder, large Islamic centers and *mosques* were built to cater to this fast-growing community. While in wealthy suburbs and larger cities *mosques* tend to be ethnically specific, in smaller towns across the nation Pakistani Americans attend *mosques* that are more multicultural, mixing with other South Asian, Arab, East Asian, and African American Muslims. *Mosques* as institutions have served as a space for religious edification as well as socialization and community building. Most Pakistani parents deem it important to send their children to the Islamic equivalent of Sunday school, where youth are taught to read the *Qur'an*, learn the five pillars of Islam, and follow the teachings of Muhammad as ethical and moral guidelines. Like the other Abrahamic faiths, Islam's emphasis on monotheism, prayer, and charity are considered central to religious edict. In terms of religiously informed cultural etiquette, many Pakistani families encourage modesty in dress for women and limited gender interaction, although most Pakistani women do not wear the *hijab* or Muslim veil, which is more culturally enforced in the Middle East. Other important aspects of Islamic observance include celebrating the Eid holidays, observing Ramadan as the month of fasting, eating *halal* meat (which is butchered in a particular manner decreed by Islamic law), and avoiding pork and alcohol.

Although most first-generation Pakistani immigrants held on to a deeply culturalized form of Islam that mixed South Asian rituals with more orthodox religious practice, they also focused on assimilating to secular American norms in the public sphere and kept religion strictly confined to the home or the *mosque*. However, as second- and third-generation Pakistani Americans come of age, they have generally tended to ascribe to one of two diverging paths in terms of their religious identity. Many young Pakistani Americans have tended toward complete secularization whereby the label "Muslim" is similar to that of "Jewish" in its connotation of being less a religious marker and more of an ethnic identity. Such Pakistani Americans generally consider themselves

"nonpracticing" Muslims who will celebrate religious holidays and obey some religio-cultural norms in terms of marriage, but generally do not observe Islamic practices. On the other hand, there is a growing number of young Pakistani Americans who identify strongly with Islam and have in fact started a trend toward establishing a specifically *American* form of Islam. This population has made it a point to disassociate religion from the South Asian cultural influences of their parents' generation, forming Muslim Student Associations on university campuses, proudly donning outward symbols of religion such as the *hijab* and growing a beard, attending national Islamic conferences, and finding new role models in the form of African American and other convert scholars and sheikhs. Particularly after the events of 9/11, many young observant Pakistani Americans have been adamant in defending the fact that their Islamic and American identities are in congruence with each other and that Islam, like Christianity and Judaism, can become part of the American fabric. This generation of Pakistani Muslims has engaged in activism and cultural production as a way of establishing themselves in the American context, all the while furthering their knowledge of Islam. Many young Pakistani American women will mix wearing jeans and fashionable Western tops with the *hijab*, and there has been a rise in Muslim American comedians, artists, filmmakers, and musicians of Pakistani descent. This transformation in young Pakistani American Muslim identity has not only increased interaction between American Muslims across ethnic and racial boundaries, but has also fostered interfaith collaboration and dialogue.

Another interesting stream in Pakistani America is the rise of Islamic Sufi practices. A reaction to the worldliness and materialism that infected mainstream Islam, Sufism is a distinct sect known for the exploration and development of the inner, mystical self. Sufis believe it is possible to draw close to God in his Divine Presence in this life through meditation, self-discipline, and pilgrimage. This form of "mystical" Islam has slowly spread to the West and is practiced by some Pakistani Americans who find it less political and more spiritual than orthodox Islam.

Rabia Kamal

See also: Essays: Islamophobia; Muslims

Further Reading

Cohen, Stephen C. *The Idea of Pakistan.* Washington, DC: The Brookings Institution, 2004.

Haddad, Yvonne Y. *Muslims in America: From Sojourners to Citizens.* New York: Oxford University Press, 2002.

Mohammad-Arif, Aminah. *Salaam America: South Asian Muslims in New York.* London: Anthem Press, 2002.

Williams, Raymond B. *Religion of Immigrants from India and Pakistan.* New York: Cambridge University Press, 1988.

PANA Institute. *See* Institute for Leadership Development and Study of Pacific and Asian North American Religion (PANA Institute)

Polynesian Traditional Religion. *See* Micronesian and Polynesian Traditional Religions

Presbyterian Churches of Japanese Heritage

In the Presbyterian tradition of American Protestant Christianity there are currently 18 churches of Japanese heritage. They are primarily in California but they also are in Philadelphia, Pennsylvania; Chicago, Illinois; Seattle, Washington; and Ogden and Salt Lake City, Utah. A majority began as outreach missions from the "mother church" in San Francisco. The Japanese Presbyterian Conference (JPC) was founded in 1905 to maintain an ethnic relationship. They have continued to maintain an ethnic relationship as the JPC, which meets annually providing a national forum for lay and clergy leadership to make decisions that affect the ongoing changes in their encounter with the wider society. In California the JPC churches are divided into north and south regional groupings of lay and clergy leaders who meet periodically during the year to discuss local and regional matters, which may then be brought to the annual National Conference. The clergy meet annually in retreat to identify issues and to seek resources that may address both clergy and lay issues facing the JPC locally, regionally, and nationally. However, over the last decade the value of meeting as the original JPC dwindled until it was disbanded. They now acknowledge their Japanese heritage, but no longer feel the need to be organized based on that former identity.

Historical Context

The first Asians to come to North America in any substantive numbers were the

Chinese who participated in the Gold Rush of 1849, and who built the Pacific or western portion of what was to become the Transcontinental Railroad between 1863 and 1869. Developers turned to cheap and expendable Chinese labor to perform the dangerous work of blasting mountains, digging tunnels, building bridges, and laying rail beds. Despite their contribution, the Chinese faced considerable discrimination. The U.S. Congress passed the Chinese Exclusion Act in 1882. Subsequently it passed the Geary Act in 1892 that extended the Exclusion Act with additional onerous new restrictions. In need of labor, developers recruited Japanese laborers, who because of their numbers soon began to establish their own businesses, communities, and *nihonmachis* (Japantowns) that became centers of their social, cultural, and religious activities.

By 1900 the largest numbers of Japanese were in northern California: San Francisco had 1,781, Sacramento County 1,209, and Alameda County 1,149. In addition, Monterey County had 710, Fresno County 598, San Joaquin County 313, Santa Clara County 284, Contra Costa County 276, and Santa Cruz County 235. Southern California, primarily Los Angeles County, had about 500. With the exception of San Francisco most Japanese settled in rural areas of these counties. By 1920, however, the number had boomed to nearly 72,000; and by 1930, the Japanese American population had grown to nearly 97,500. The 1930 U.S. Census Bureau counted 35,390 Japanese immigrants in the Los Angeles area. The population increase is attributed to births and migration from other areas on the West Coast such as

Seattle, Washington, and especially from the U.S. territory of Hawai'i. The Gentlemen's Agreement of 1907 between the United States and Japan restricted Japanese immigration; but the agreement was never ratified by the U.S. Congress and expired in 1924.

Early Asian American Converts

The oldest Asian American Christian congregation to be established in North America was the Chinese Presbyterian Church, now called the Presbyterian Church in Chinatown, San Francisco. Like other Protestant denominations at the time, the Presbyterian Church designated its outreach to temporary and permanent immigrant populations from Asia as "foreign missions" and thus under the denomination's Board of Foreign Missions. The congregation of four members was formally established on November 6, 1853, with the leadership of the Rev. Dr. William Speer, who served in Canton, China. He arrived in San Francisco on November 6, 1852 with a working knowledge of Cantonese and a call from the Presbyterian Board of Foreign Missions to evangelize to the city's Chinese population. He opened a dispensary and a school at the church; he published *The Oriental*, the first English/Chinese bilingual newspaper in the United States; and he fought for the repeal of an anti-Chinese mining tax. Since its beginnings, the church has continued a tradition of supporting social services, including education, low-income housing, health services, and youth programs. It had a century-old partnership with Presbyterian House (now named

Donaldina Cameron House) that first provided safety and rehabilitation to Chinese women who had been trapped in the sex slave trade. Its mission gradually expanded to a full range of Christian social services and youth programs, dovetailing well with the congregation's vision. In 1925 the Presbyterian denomination transferred Chinatown Church's jurisdiction from its Board of Foreign Missions to the Board of National Missions.

Records of Howard Presbyterian Church in San Francisco reveal that in 1869 a number of Japanese were attending the church's Sunday school and studying a Chinese-language translation of the Bible. It is not clear whether or not this group had any influence on what was to have a significant impact on the development of Christianity among Japanese in San Francisco and subsequently throughout California, namely, the Fukuinkai (Gospel Society). In the early 1870s several men working at the boardinghouse of the Boys High School on Sutter Street had begun studying English with the school's vice principal and his wife, Mr. and Mrs. Wilson, both of whom resided at the boardinghouse. They were Nishimaki Toyosaku, Tachibana Naruhiko, and Yoshida Masaru, who subsequently began attending the First Congregational Church located at Post and Mason Streets, where in 1874 they became acquainted with Kaji Tamenari, Koyano Keizō, and Ninomiya Anji.

The six men met on Sundays to learn English and for Bible study. Through the assistance of the church's women's association, the men rented a room in the Chinese Mission building of the Methodist Episcopal Church. The manager of the mission building and head of the Chinese Mission for the Methodist Church, Otis Gibson (1826–1889), taught the Bible and invited them to worship. Other young men joined the group. In 1877 Gibson baptized two of them and later three more. On this basis they organized the Fukuinkai in October of that same year with a formalized order of regulations and leadership.

At this point the Fukuinkai was a nondenominational and independent Japanese organization guided by Christian principles that stressed the importance of "eradicat(ing) the evil way of life." The Fukuinkai's two prongs for upright living included (1) moral reform and (2) charitable work such as a night school for teaching English and assisting the newly arrived to find jobs and housing. Another powerful motivating factor for the Fukuinkai was to express not only their perceived "Christian" values, but also their values as Japanese within a hostile dominant cultural environment. Like the Chinese the Japanese experienced racial discrimination and fear of the larger community that was due in part to the growing Japanese military and technical advances.

During the initial period of the Fukuinkai, Gibson assumed more and more of the Fukuinkai's leadership. By 1881 the men such as Koyano and Nishimura who had come from the Congregational Church became increasingly uncomfortable with Gibson's and the Chinese Mission's influence. This disaffection led to the Congregationalist members splitting off and forming the Tyler Fukuinkai, named for its location on Tyler Street (now Golden Gate Avenue).

Formalized on June 4, 1881, the Tyler Fukuinkai received support from such luminaries as the Japanese consul general Yanagitani Kentarō and Mr. (first name unknown) Fletcher, owner of the Ichiban Company. Having left the influence of the Methodists, the Tyler Fukuinkai turned to the Presbyterians. Rev. Robert McKenzie, who subsequently went on to become president of the San Francisco Theological Seminary (Presbyterian), was especially helpful during this organizational period.

Another split in the original Fukuinkai occurred in 1883 after some members expressed a desire to disassociate themselves from the Chinese Mission of the Methodist Episcopal Church. They wanted to return to the original nondenominational character of the Fukuinkai. Some 30 members left in August to establish themselves on Stevenson near Second Street. However, this group was not able to maintain itself as an independent organization, and after only one month a majority merged with the Tyler Fukuinkai.

The California Methodist Episcopal Conference recognized the remnant Fukuinkai as a mission in September 1885. The following year the new Japanese Methodist mission moved out of the Chinese Mission into the building next door. In the meantime the group continued to help Japanese newcomers adjust to life in America and gradually rebuilt itself after its previous loss of membership. At its annual gathering in September 1886 the Conference of the California Methodist Episcopal Church formally received the Fukuinkai as one of its congregations.

As in the case of the Methodist Fukuinkai, the Tyler Fukuinkai continued its outreach to Japanese newcomers, immigrants, or short-termers such as students or businessmen. Although Bible studies and worship services continued, many of the activities focused on the practicalities of adjusting to a new living environment, jobs, housing, language, and other things. The increase of nonreligious membership prompted a number of influential Presbyterian leaders, including Rev. McKenzie, to encourage the establishment of a Japanese church. A conference was called during which a resolution passed to establish a church. This was presented in petition form to the Presbytery of San Francisco, which was meeting at St John's Presbyterian Church on April 28, 1885. On May 9 a committee of the Presbytery received 17 members from other churches and 16 more by profession of faith at the Tyler Fukuinkai on Golden Gate Avenue. These latter were baptized at a subsequent meeting of the committee on May 16, and at that point the First Japanese Presbyterian Church of San Francisco was officially established under the care of San Francisco Presbytery.

The San Francisco Presbytery only provided Sunday preachers until the Presbyterian Board of Foreign Missions assigned a permanent representative and superintendent for the Japanese Mission on the Pacific Coast. Since many of the young men were students who planned to return to Japan, the Presbyterian Church considered this effort to be missionary work. The students would be sent back to Japan as missionaries among their own people.

From the example of the Presbyterian Church's response to the early Chinese and Japanese presence in the United States, it can be seen that the Protestant denominations understood their relationship to the Asians in North America in the context of "foreign missions." Protestant denominations saw themselves as bringing the "civilizing message" of Jesus Christ to the world and saw the immigrant in America as alien and in need of being "civilized/Christianized."

Growth and Development

The Presbyterian Board of Foreign Missions acted quickly in providing supporting leadership by assigning Earnest Adolphus Sturge, MD, PhD (1865–1934) to this first church. As a result of health problems, Dr. Sturge returned as a medical missionary to Thailand. He had hoped to work with the Board of Foreign Missions' Chinese Mission in San Francisco, but there was no position available. In the summer of 1885 he turned his attention to the burgeoning possibilities among the Japanese. He worked closely with the newly formed church by preaching, leading Bible study classes, and supporting efforts to establish a Japanese YMCA, which became the focus for the education emphasis of the Presbyterian Board's mission.

Without lessening its educational emphasis, the board and the church with Sturge's guidance began to reach out to the growing Japanese agricultural laborers in rural California. These efforts took the form of day and night schools, educational classes, and the establishment of libraries, women's societies, and kindergartens.

From 1913 the focus centered on the family and Sunday school. More and more women had been allowed to immigrate to be with their husbands or to meet their husbands for the first time ("picture brides"). By this time there were between 7,000 and 8,000 children (Nisei—second-generation Japanese Americans born in the United States with U.S. citizenship). Baptisms among these Nisei children and their participation in Sunday school increased dramatically. The growing presence of the Japanese/Japanese American population was accompanied by an increase in anti-Japanese sentiment. The California Legislature passed the Henry-Webb Land Act in 1913 that denied aliens who were ineligible for citizenship the right to own land or to lease agricultural land for more than three years. Japanese aliens acquired property in the name of their American-born children.

Under these trying times Dr. Sturge felt that Japanese churches should become better to meet the needs of their people. In July 1914 the First Japanese Presbyterian Church began to worship together with the Japanese Congregational Church. Later that year on October 4 the churches formed the Federated Japanese Church of Christ of San Francisco, an arrangement that continued through the war years, the period of incarceration in the "relocation camps," until the return of the Japanese Americans to San Francisco and the rebuilding of their lives, at which point the federation dissolved.

During the 1918 Spanish flu pandemic Dr. Sturge set up an emergency clinic at the Japanese Reformed Church. His wife Eugenia worked alongside him. Sadly, she contracted the flu and passed away. Some years prior the Federated Japanese Church of Christ had moved to 1500 Post Street. The Sturges had their home right next door at 1516 Post Street. With his wife's passing Dr. Sturge gave their residence and all of its contents to the church to be used for the Japanese community in his wife's memory. Representing the church, Mr. Kiyoshi Tomizawa accepted the deed from Dr. Sturge. The church has remembered Mrs. Eugenia Sturge by building the Sturge Memorial Building.

In 1921 Dr. Sturge resigned as superintendent of the Japanese Presbyterian Mission on the Pacific Coast, though he continued to serve on its session, which is the governing board of the local Presbyterian congregation; he resigned in 1923. Coincidentally, the oversight of the Japanese Presbyterian Mission was transferred from the Board of Foreign Missions to the Board of Home Missions.

Dr. Sturge moved to San Mateo just south of San Francisco in 1927. His residence again became the foundation of a Japanese American congregation growing through its Sunday school. It was subsequently named Sturge Presbyterian Church. In 1932 Rev. Hata, pastor of the Federated Japanese Church of Christ of San Francisco, resigned and Dr. Sturge was called back to the San Francisco church. Though Dr. Sturge passed away a short two years later, his work with the Sunday school had a powerful impact on children, youth, and young adults alike. Already he had had a profound influence on a generation of young men who entered into the ministry and with lay leaders, who were the "missionaries" from the San Francisco church to other areas where Japanese had settled.

Transition

Before Dr. Sturge's passing, the first English-language worship service for Nisei and by Nisei was held in the Sturge Memorial Building on May 14, 1933. Until this the Japanese Presbyterian church had been an Issei (first-generation) Japanese-language church. The Japanese language and the first-generation Issei continued to dominate and maintain primary leadership until the 1950s when the Nisei finally came into their own. During this period from 1933 until 1957 the Rev. Dr. Eiji Kawamorita led the San Francisco church through this generational transition.

After Kawamorita's retirement, Rev. Howard Toriumi served the English- and Japanese-speaking members of the congregation. The issue of language ministry had faced the congregation for many decades. Although most Nisei spoke Japanese to one degree or another, their primary language tended to be English. Thus, there had been a need to provide Sunday school instruction in English, then worship services. By the time Rev. Toriumi assumed the pastorate of the Japanese Church of Christ, English was dominant; however, a considerable minority was Japanese-speaking. Until this point there had been two people to share the language ministries. The Japanese-speaking ministry began to languish and participation began to dwindle.

After a decade of tremendous change and challenge Toriumi resigned in 1960 to take a JPC pastorate in Los Angeles. He was replaced by the bilingual Rev. Nicholas Iyoya in 1962. He was also suited for the societal changes that would be sweeping America. Trained at the University of Chicago Graduate School and Union Theological Seminary in New York, he had the skills and social consciousness to address discrimination, civil rights, justice, community organizing, fair housing, and other pressing issues.

War and Postwar Years

The Second World War/Pacific War had a powerful effect on the Japanese American community, already viewed as unwanted immigrants and discriminated against. The rise of Japan as a dominant military power in Asia stirred up racial fears in the American public well before the outbreak of war. With the attack on Pearl Harbor Japanese Americans, especially those on the West Coast, were viewed as enemy aliens who were subject to Executive Order No. 9066, which authorized the military to issue "civilian exclusion orders," moving both aliens and "non-aliens" (American-born citizens) to designated "evacuation" (detention) sites in various parts of the country. Ninety-two percent of the Japanese American population living in the continental United States, men, women, and children, were placed behind barbed wire fences with guard towers housed with armed soldiers.

The faith community continued its activities. Buddhists and Protestants held interdenominational services. Roman Catholics and Seventh-day Adventists held separate services. Members of the Federated Japanese Church of Christ continued to be served by their ministers. Rev. Dr. Eiji Kawamorita and the newly ordained Howard Toriumi, a Nisei pastor, assisted. Toriumi's was an unusual story. At the time of the evacuation order he was a second-year student at San Francisco Theological Seminary (SFTS). Sensing the seriousness of this situation for the ministry among Japanese

Americans, the Presbytery of San Francisco (district governing body) took the extraordinary measure on April 28, 1942, of receiving Toriumi into the care of the San Francisco Presbytery from the Sacramento Presbytery, approving him for licensure (preaching in the Presbyterian pulpit) and ordaining him to the full "ministry of word and sacrament" as a minister in the Presbyterian Church all on the same day.

The majority of the members of the San Francisco church were sent to the relocation center in Topaz, Utah. Some of the hardships were documented by David Tatsuno of the San Francisco church, who smuggled a small handheld motion picture camera into Topaz.

Following the end of World War II, Japanese Americans gradually returned home. Some were able to regain their homes and farms, but the majority could not. The Federated Japanese Church of Christ was able to receive its buildings. Rev. Kawamorita and a succession of students from SFTS helped to settle the returnees by putting their lives back together and rebuilding the congregation. In 1949 Rev. Howard Toriumi became Dr. Kawamori's permanent assistant ministering to the English-speaking Nisei.

While an influx of postwar *Shin-Issei* (new Issei) immigrants helped to reinforce the Japanese-speaking Issei membership, the demographics of postwar Japanese Americans favored the eventual rise in numbers and to leadership of the Nisei. The federation with the Congregation Church ended in 1953. And with the closure of the Japanese American Evangelical and Reformed Church, a number of Nisei families joined the Japanese Church of Christ.

A significant development began in 1948 when concerned leaders from the various faith congregations in San Francisco founded the Shyūkyōka Konwa-kai (Gathering of Religious Persons) to foster understanding and better communication among leaders of Buddhist, Christian, and independent Japanese religious congregations that had been providing temporary housing and assistance to returnees and those who were dispossessed of their homes. As a result, the community was better able to leverage its resources and extend much needed assistance. In addition, the formation of the Shyūkyōka Konwa-kai would lead to other cooperative housing projects.

A study group formed within Christ United Presbyterian Church, formerly the Japanese Church of Christ (Presbyterian), began to dream about the possibility of providing housing for low-income elderly in the Japantown area. The idea soon interested other congregations seeking to meet the needs of the Japanese American community. Fortuitously in January 1968 the San Francisco Redevelopment Agency awarded the Post, Laguna, Sutter, and Octavia streets' sought-after 16 parcel site in the Japantown area to the informal Shyūkyōka Konwa-kai to develop. As a result, Shyūkyōka Konwa-kai incorporated as a nonprofit organization and renamed itself the Japanese American Religious Federation (JARF) (Nichibei Shūkyō Renmei) on June 1, 1968. Membership in JARF was by institution from the religious groups in the Japanese American community and two additional groups, the San Francisco Ministry to Nursing Homes and the Society of St. Francis, an Episcopal monastic community to which two Japanese monastics belonged.

Because of the religious nature of the JARF association, a new nonprofit with 501(c)(3) status was incorporated as JARF Housing, Inc. on April 11, 1972, to develop, own, and operate Nihonmachi Terrace, FHA Project No. 121-44284-NP-R, Section 236 of the National Housing Act, a facility of 245 units of low-income and affordable housing, the majority for seniors. The project broke ground on February 23, 1974, and opened its doors in January 1975.

Transformation

Rev. Nicholas Iyoya, who actively participated in the Nihonmachi Terrace Project, resigned in 1971. The following year Rev. David Nakagawa took on the task of not only representing Christ United in the low-income senior housing project, but also guiding the congregation in the relocation and building of its new structures on the northwest corner of Sutter and Laguna (1500 Sutter St.). During Rev. Nakagawa's pastorate the church celebrated its 100th anniversary in 1985.

Throughout its history this San Francisco Japanese Presbyterian church saw continuity and change. A racial-ethnic church, it continually strived to establish its place within the wider cultural society in a manner true to its changing identity and by its contributions to that society. With a fine musical sense, Rev. Nakagawa reaffirmed worship as an expression of joy and wonder while continuing to encourage the importance of racial and economic justice. He championed the role of education in a unique way. He was a "younger" Nisei, closer to the experience of Sansei (third-generation) Japanese Americans than to those of his own generation. He saw the Sansei growing up, going to school, and experiencing the same issues as their counterparts among Chinese and other Asian Americans. They had generational similarities that bound them together in a way that superseded their ethnic and cultural roots. Chinese American, Korean American, and biracial families were joining the life of the congregation.

Toward the end of his ministry Rev. Nakagawa masterfully approached a young elementary school teacher who had been raised in the Cameron House program of the Presbyterian Church of Chinatown to come and lead a summer camp program, similar to that at Cameron House. For 14 years Steve Woo headed Christ United Presbyterian Church's summer program. At its peak it drew between 250 and 300 elementary school–age children, providing an educationally stimulating nine weeks' summer program that also was the equivalent of a full day's child care for busy working parents, known as CUPC's (pronounced "cup-see") Summer Camp program. Youngsters of predominantly Asian American background came from all over the city. It was the largest such program of any church-related program of any denomination, white or racial ethnic, in San Francisco. Also at its core the program trained high school and college–age youth in leadership skills, mentoring them to be camp leaders and counselors.

After Rev. Nakagawa's resignation in 1987 the congregation continued to gradually take on a more and more Asian American cast. During the author's 12-year tenure

the congregation saw the final passing of its original Japanese-speaking Issei generation. As a bilingual-bicultural individual, he assiduously stressed the value of Japanese-language ministry, while at the same time he welcomed the changing character of the congregation. Also as a board member and officer of both JARF and JARF Housing, Inc., he helped to create a new housing nonprofit that sought to meet the increasing need for intermediate health care housing in the form of an assisted-living facility for the Nisei generation. It was named Kokoro (heart/mind). Intentionally constructed to provide a culturally and spiritually expressive environment reflecting the continuity and ever-changing face of the Japanese American experience, it addressed a vital need in that community.

From 2002 to the present the Rev. Grace Suzuki has continued to oversee the changes incarnated among its members and provide new directions for the church while honoring its Japanese heritage. The church has provide a focus on family and youth of the present-day Asian American experience with its bicultural, biracial, indeed multiethnic backgrounds, and maintained a Japanese-language ministry for *Shin* and *Shin-shin* [New (1950s) and New-new (post-1970s)] Issei: a church for 21st-century America.

Other East Asian Communities

One of the fastest growing segments of Asian American communities in the Presbyterian Church is the Korean heritage. Suffice it to say, the connection to the Presbyterian tradition in Korea is due to the highly successful proselytizing efforts of American Presbyterian missionaries from the latter half of the 19th century. So successful were they that by far the majority of Christians in Korea from that time to the present have some relationship to the Presbyterian tradition. When coming to the United States, Koreans have been quickly drawn to expressing their ties to this form of Christian tradition.

Filipinos and Vietnamese are also postwar immigrant communities like that of the Koreans who reflect their home country's cultural experience with the Christian religion. Both Filipinos and Vietnamese had been colonized by European countries that were primarily Roman Catholic in their cultural/religious stance. In the case of Filipinos it was Spanish Catholicism and in the case of Vietnamese it was French Catholicism. Thus, the contact with the Presbyterian tradition was for most primarily upon coming to the United States, initially through social service outreach by local congregations or by the regional jurisdictions (presbyteries) that saw a need to reach out to the growing immigrant population in their areas.

Filipino and Vietnamese Presbyterian churches tend to be small "new church developments" within their ethnic enclaves. Interestingly, the first Filipino Presbyterian congregation was organized by the Rev. Venus Manguiat, Jr., a graduate of Union Theological Seminary of Manila. He and a small number of like-minded Filipinos gathered together in August 1980 to form an ecumenical fellowship. The following year an organizing membership of 78 petitioned the Presbytery of San Gabriel to be the Filipino Community Presbyterian Church of Southern California. It was formally estab-

lished on November 8, 1981. At present it is a "nesting" congregation with the First Presbyterian Church of Azusa, California. With the exception of two non-Filipino ministers who assisted "between" pastors, pastoral leadership has come from Filipino ministers who had had ministerial training or led congregations in the Philippines.

Following the end of the Vietnam War in 1975, U.S. churches were encouraged to "adopt" Vietnamese families to assist them in adjusting to American life and the English language. It also included acquainting them with American holidays and significant church observances. For many Vietnamese immigrants this became their introduction to Protestant and, particularly in this case, Presbyterian Christianity. National and regional agencies of the denomination provided resources in identifying the needs of various racial-ethnic communities and implementing ways of assisting them. If the Filipino Presbyterian communities began to coalesce in the early 1980s, Vietnamese Presbyterian communities have done so in the latter half of the first decade of the 21st century.

Compared to the Korean American Presbyterian churches, the numbers of Filipino and Vietnamese congregations are few and scattered throughout the country. The majority of Vietnamese congregations are located in concentrations of Vietnamese communities on the West Coast in southern and northern California and Washington state, on the Gulf Coast of southeastern Texas and western Florida, and a few on the East Coast.

Two examples are the Pittsburgh Vietnamese Presbyterian Fellowship that nests in the Pleasant Hill Presbyterian Church of Pittsburgh, Pennsylvania, and the Vietnamese Grace Community Presbyterian Church nesting in Bethany Presbyterian Church of Sacramento, California. The Pittsburgh Fellowship began in February 2008 with 12 members under the leadership of Rev. Thang Toan Chu, who had previously been a pastor in Detroit, Michigan. However, because of a medical emergency, Rev. Chu and family moved to California to care for his brother. In the transitional period Rev. Dan Van Nguyen, who had come from Vietnam, assisted the fledgling fellowship during its search for permanent pastoral leadership. This was fortuitous for them in that with the support of the New Church Development office of the Pittsburgh Presbytery, Rev. Nyugen became the permanent replacement in the following year. Membership has risen to 25.

Led by Pastor Philip Khanh Trinh, the Vietnamese Grace Community Presbyterian Church is very active within the Vietnamese community of the wider Sacramento area of northern California. Rev. Trinh also provides leadership to the national Presbyterian Church's National Vietnamese Presbyterian Council as its stated clerk. This position provides both clerical support and ecclesiastical guidance to this national body within the wider denomination. Like the Pittsburgh Fellowship, Grace Community is in a nesting relationship with another established congregation and in 2008 began reaching out to the Vietnamese immigrant community in the wider Sacramento area of northern California. Its membership is primarily a Vietnamese-speaking congregation; however, it does have an active youth contingent, which is being educated in an English-language environment, and a few non-Vietnamese members.

In addition to the Filipino and Vietnamese communities, the Presbyterian Church (USA), largest of the Presbyterian denominations in the United States, has denominational organizations of Asian background for Cambodian, Laotian, Indonesian, Thai, and Taiwanese communities as well.

Donald C. Drummond

See also: Entries: Japanese American Christianity

Further Reading

Blain, Doug. "The 1920 Anti-Japanese Crusade and Congressional Hearings." *Seattle Civil Rights and Labor History Project*, a website of faculty and students of the University of Washington. 2005. http://depts.washington.edu/civilr/Japanese_restriction.htm. Accessed 27 December 2013.

Cooper, Bruce C. *Riding the Transcontinental Rails: Overland Travel on the Pacific Railroad 1865–1881*. Philadelphia: Polyglot Press, 2005.

Drummond, Donald C. "The Creation of JALFI: A Senior Assisted Living Project in the Japanese American Community." Organizational Project, University of San Francisco, San Francisco, CA. 1998.

Holland, Clift L., comp. *The Japanese Community*. http://www.prolades.com/glama/la5co07/japanese_community.htm. Accessed July 11, 2014.

One Hundredth Anniversary History Committee. *The Church's One Hundred Years in the Japanese Community*. pp.1–8.

Presbyterian Mission Agency. *The National Vietnamese Presbyterian Council*. 2013. http://www.presbyterianmission.org/ministries/asian/national-vietnamese-presbyterian-council-nvpc/. Accessed July 11, 2014.

Suzuki, Lester E. *Ministry in the Assembly and Relocation Centers of World War II.* Berkeley, CA: Yardbird, 1979.

Tatsuno, David. 2006. "Topaz Memories." Washington, DC: Library of Congress, National Film Registry, 2006. Also available in DVD format produced in 2006 by KTEH, PBS, San Jose.

Teaching with Documents: Using Primary Sources from the National Archives. Washington, DC: National Archives and Records Administration 1989.

Yoshida, Ryo. "A Socio-historical Study of Racial/Ethnic Identity in the Inculturated Religious Expression of Japanese Christianity in San Francisco 1877–1924." PhD dissertation, Graduate Theological Union, Berkeley, CA, 1989.

Project Dana

Sponsored by Moʻiliʻili Hongwanji Mission, one of the 35 temples of the Honpa Hongwanji Mission of Hawaiʻi of the Jōdo Shinshū Hongwanji Denomination of Buddhism, Project Dana was established in 1989 by co-founders Mrs. Shimeji Kanazawa and Mrs. Rose Nakamura. Project Dana is an interfaith volunteer caregivers program meeting the needs of the frail elderly, disabled persons, and family caregivers in Hawaiʻi. *Dāna* or generosity refers to the first of the six *pāramitās*, or perfections that Mahāyāna Buddhist devotees are encouraged to cultivate; the other five are *sīla*, morality; *kṣānti*, patience; *vīrya*, perseverance; *dhyāna*, meditation; and *prajñā*, wisdom. *Dāna* is defined as selfless giving from a compassionate heart without desire for recognition or reward. This expression of compassion, the giving of joy and happiness, helps to relieve sentient beings from suffering. The form of compassion in the act of *dāna* is the dynamic manifestation of wisdom.

Project Dana provides a variety of support services through a corps of trained volunteers and is located throughout the state of Hawaiʻi on the islands of Oʻahu, Hawaiʻi, Maui, and Kauaʻi. In addition, there are three Project Dana sites in California and two in Japan. In California the Dana Project is supported by volunteers of the Fresno Betsuin Buddhist Temple in the city of Fresno, Venice Hongwanji Buddhist Temple in the city of Venice, and San Mateo Buddhist Temple in the city of San Mateo. In Japan, the Shinshuji Temple in Sapporo City, Hokkaido, and Tsukiji Betsuin Temple in Tokyo have also established a Dana Project.

As a member of the National Volunteer Caregiving Network with headquarters in West Virginia, Project Dana's volunteers are guided by the universal principle of *dāna* and contribute toward the well-being of the frail elderly, disabled persons, and family caregivers. At its initial developmental stages of interfaith volunteer caregiving across the nation, Mrs. Kanazawa served as trustee representing the Buddhist community. Project Dana was given its name by the late Rev. Ruth Tabrah (1921–2004).

The projected increased growth among the elderly necessitates compassionate options to help elders maintain the independence and dignity they deserve, and at the same time, contribute toward their well-being by providing caring assistance and support services.

Project Dana is particularly mindful of elders who desire to live at home—many who are isolated and lonely. With the ever-increasing number of older adults and greater demands on existing services, the program fills important social service gaps by providing much needed assistance for friendly visits and respite services; transportation to medical appointments, grocery shopping, and religious services; and telephone visits, minor home repairs, and light housekeeping. Home safety assessment and education are also offered as part of Project Dana's services. A trained staff coordinates and facilitates a caregivers' support group for caregivers to help alleviate the stress that may come with continuous caregiving. Each service has the same goal in mind—that of allowing elders to live at home among family and friends and share in the life of their community.

Project Dana serves as a referral and linkage agency working closely with over 200 community agencies, both public and private, to ensure a continuum of services to the elderly. The program is firmly dedicated to supporting Hawai'i's older adults and family caregivers through a holistic and best practice approach.

Project Dana's headquarters is located at Mo'ili'il Hongwanji Mission in Honolulu, Hawai'i, and its small and capable staff works closely with its coalition of 32 church and community organizations to provide services to Hawai'i's elders. Volunteers are the heart of Project Dana, and without them, the program would not be able to provide its much needed services. They are members of the various faith-based organizations, the community, and educational institutions, or individuals who are interested in serving the growing population of the elder community. The majority of Project Dana's volunteers are devoted seniors, and in some instances, families volunteer together and provide an all-important intergenerational service of compassion and love spanning across the generations. Each volunteer receives an orientation and training, and volunteers are sensitive to diverse cultures and traditions. Project Dana provides continued education and training in many areas of interest and concern regarding elders for its volunteers and the community at large. The process of matching an elder and volunteer is done carefully to meet the needs of the recipients through the gifts, talents, and abilities of the volunteers.

Through the support of government and private foundation grants as well as donations from organizations and individuals, Project Dana has been able to maintain its services since its inception. Services have been provided to over 1,000 persons by over 850 volunteers totaling in excess of 50,000 hours annually.

Throughout the years, aging in place has become a global, national, state, and local concern. Hawai'i leads the nation in longevity. Hence, the Buddhist responsibility in caring for the elderly plays a key role in volunteer caregiving through churches and temples.

Rose S. Nakamura and Myra Ikeda

See also: Entries: Honpa Hongwanji Mission of Hawai'i

Further Reading

http://www.projectdana.org/. Accessed May 28, 2013.

Roof, Wade Clark, and Mark Silk, eds. 2005. *Religion and Public Life in the Pacific Region: Fluid Identities.* Walnut Creek, CA: Altamira Press.

Q

Qingming Festival

The origin of the Qingming (Pure and Bright) Festival observed by Chinese in the United States dates back to antiquity, but today it is an amalgamation of the Cold Food Festival, the old Qingming Festival, and the tradition of sweeping the graves. This entry gives an overview of these three traditions.

The Cold Food Festival

There is no consensus on the origin of the Cold Food Festival, which occurs 105 days after the winter solstice. It was traditionally associated with the Jie Zitui story that dates back to the early Spring and Autumn period (770–476 BCE) and/or an astronomical phenomenon.

The Jie Zitui Tale. In brief, Zhonger, a noble scion of the Jin principality, was in self-exile to avoid being murdered by a treacherous minister. He was accompanied by a small group of loyal followers, among them Jie Zitui.

After wandering about for a long while, the group ran out of food. Zhonger was on the verge of starvation. Jie Zitui quietly cut off a piece from his leg and roasted it for Zhonger. After 19 years of exile, Zhonger regained power and rewarded his followers, but he neglected Jie Zitui. Thereupon

Ching Lee holds a stick of incense as she bows in front of the Chi Sin Buddhist & Taoist Association tent during the Chinese Qingming, or Tomb Sweeping Day, at Skylawn Funeral Home and Memorial Park in San Mateo, Calif., April 5, 2014. Qingming which literally translates to Clear and Bright, is a time of year when Chinese families visit the graves of their ancestors to clean the gravesite and pay their respects. (Jeff Chiu/AP/Corbis)

Jie and his mother went to live high on a mountain.

The following year, reminded that he had failed to reward Jie, Zhonger sent out

Maple Han kneels in front of his sister's grave during the Chinese Qingming, or Tomb Sweeping Day, at Skylawn Funeral Home and Memorial Park in San Mateo, California, April 5, 2014. (Jeff Chiu/AP/Corbis)

a search party that found Jie living on the mountain. Jie Zitui refused to return to serve his prince again. Zhonger personally went to invite him back to court, but Jie would not budge. Hoping to smoke him out, Zhonger ordered the mountain burned. After the fire subsided, Jie and his mother were found burned to death while holding onto a willow tree. To memorialize his faithful servant, Zhonger ordered that there should be no fire on the day Jie and his mother died. Hence the day became a Cold Food Day.

Both Zhonger and Jie Zitui were historical personalities whose tale of woe was recorded in the *Zuo Zhuan* (*The Zuo Commentary*), a work of the Warring States period (475–221 BCE); the tale also appears in the *Lü Shi Chunqiu* (*The Spring and Autumn of the House of Lü*), a Qin (221–207 BCE) and Former Han (206 BCE–208 CE) period work; and the *Shi Ji* (*Records of the Historian*) by Sima Qian (145–ca. 86 BCE). But these historical records make no mention of Zhonger ordering the mountain to be burned to smoke out his friend.

The first reference that mentions Jie being burned to death is found in the 29th chapter of the *Zhuang Zi* by Zhang Zhou (dates unknown). But now it is generally agreed that Zhuang Zhou really did not write this part of the book; the chapter is a much later addition. The following Han dynasty books also mention Jie being burned to death: the *Han Shi Waizhuan* by Han Ying (dates unknown) and the *Xin Xu* by Liu Xiang (dates unknown).

The Astronomic Phenomenon. The *Zhou Li* (*The Rites of Zhou*—see entry on Confucian Rituals for details) states, "In the second moon of spring the bell with wooden clappers sounded, signifying the prohibition of fire in the realm." This led Du Gongzhan (dates unknown), who annotated the *Jing Chu Suishi Ji* (*Records of Years and Seasons of Jing and Chu*) of the Sui dynasty (581–618 CE), to note, "This means the third moon of spring is the time for the fire to come out." In other words, if the prohibition of fire takes place in the second moon, then the third moon is the time for rekindling the fire. Thus, the Cold Food Festival in ancient times took place toward the end of the second or at the very beginning of the third moon in the spring.

Consequently, some scholars speculate that the prohibition of fire is linked with the relationship between the ancient custom of supplication for rain and the Chinese zodiacal constellation of the Dragon, one of the 28 constellations. They further point out that rain and fire just do not mix. Hence, the prohibition of fire occurred.

Taking this thought a step further, Chen Jiujin, a modern scholar, argues that the prohibition and the rekindling of fire is associated with the positions of Orion and Mercury, which are hidden from each other. Thus Chen concludes that the prohibition and the rekindling of fire refer to the appearance and disappearance of these two stars. The rekindling of fire in the third moon points to the reappearance of Mercury in the east. This notion of the astronomic phenomenon being associated with the Cold Food Festival may also have something to do with the star worship of the Chinese.

The Sweeping of the Graves. Prior to the Zhou Dynasty (11th century–771 BCE), sacrifices to the ancestors took place at the ancestral temples, not at their graves. With the establishment of the Zhou Dynasty, graves along with sacrifices at the burial sites became more and more popular. By the time of Confucius (551–479 BCE), the practice had become an established norm. Meng Zi (372–289 BCE), in the *Mencius*, Book IV:B:33, tells of a man from the state of Qi who deceived his wife and concubine about his association with men of wealth and consequence, but he actually begged for food from people who made sacrifices at the graves.

While this story does not give a fixed date, by no later than the mid-Tang Dynasty (618–907 CE), the practice of making sacrifices at the grave site in the spring had become fixed for Qingming.

Cold Food Festival: A Historical Note

The *Hou Han Shu* (*History of the Later Han*) relates an incident concerning the Cold Food Festival with Jie Zitui in the biography of Zhou Ju, who became a provincial governor of the Ping Zhou (which included part of the present Shanxi and part of Shaanxi, Hebei Province, and Inner Mongolia). When Zhou learned that the people commemorated Jie by eating cold food for one month to the detriment of their health, he reduced the observance to three days. For the same reason, Cao Cao (115–220 CE) ordered a prohibition on eating cold food altogether, but to no avail. In the *Yezhong Ji* by Lu Hui of the Jin Dynasty (265–420 CE), there is also information associating the Cold Food Festival with the Jie Zitui story.

From these sources it is probably safe to state that Jie Zitui historically had nothing to do with the Cold Food Festival, but people commemorated him on the occasion of this festival.

The Qingming Festival

The term Qingming is one of the 24 solar terms on the lunar calendar. According to the lunar calculation, Qingming marks 107 days after the winter solstice or 15 days after the vernal equinox. This custom was established during the Southern-Northern dynasties (420–589 CE). Initially Qingming was not an established independent festival, but more likely a simple acknowledgment. In ancient China the year was divided into two parts, the *yin* and the *yang*. The *yang* was from the third to the eighth moon, while the *yin* was from the ninth to the second. During the *yin* part of the year, the sky was drab and the air heavy and cold. Thus people generally stayed indoors, with men repairing old agricultural tools and making new tools while the women performed their domestic chores, such as mending and weaving.

But in the third moon, the air is pure (*qing*) and the sky bright (*ming*)—hence *qingming* became the name of the festival or activity. People would come out to celebrate spring's return to the earth. The

activity was called *taqing*, or "treading the green grass." People would go up to high places, which were associated with spirituality, to breathe the fresh air and to enjoy the spring scenery. On the way, they would gently tug at one another's sleeves to become reacquainted after the long winter.

Qingming was also a time of romance. Boys and girls would walk along the opposite sides of the riverbank, singing love songs and throwing willow twigs at the one whom each had selected to become their lifelong partner. Should the chosen one be receptive, one party would cross the river and together they would disappear into the bushes for a romantic tryst; a wedding would be scheduled after the fall when food was abundant.

This activity is described in some poems in the *Shi Jing* (*The Book of Poetry*), a book in the Confucian canon. However, this custom was discontinued probably at the beginning or shortly after the Spring and Autumn period, which coincided with the rise of urbanization.

The Emergence of the New Tradition

Qingming became a formally established festival through a long evolution. The process merged the activities of the Cold Food Festival being extended beyond its designated period into the day of Qingming, and the sweeping of the grave custom being associated with the Cold Food Festival. The date of the Cold Food Festival was only two days before Qingming, which marked the beginning of spring. It is difficult to tell exactly when the sweeping of the graves or the making of sacrifices to the ancestors began to be associated with the Cold Food Festival. But the general consensus is that it most likely took place after the Qin dynasty.

Here we have three separate activities—treading the green grass, that is, Qingming, the Cold Food Festival, and sweeping the graves—converging together within a short period of time. It is not hard to see how the activities can be mixed or extended to the realms of others. It is most likely by the time of the Tang dynasty that the Cold Food Festival and the Qingming activities had been rather thoroughly merged. Thus by the time of the Northern Song dynasty (960–1127 CE), Qingming had taken over the function of the Cold Food Festival and had become an established independent festival. Hence making sacrifices to the ancestors at their graves also became an activity of Qingming. And by the time of the Ming (1368–1644 CE) and Qing (1644–1911 CE) dynasties, the Cold Food Festival no longer existed.

The Activities. Even though the Cold Food Festival disappeared during the Ming-Qing period, many of its activities were incorporated in the Qingming Festival, such as cockfighting, egg coloring, egg fights, ball-playing, swinging on swings, and hook throwing. But Qingming had its own unique activities as well. As previously mentioned, originally Qingming was a time to celebrate the spring's return and to get reacquainted with neighbors and friends on the way to the high places as well as a time of romance for the young.

There was also the custom of "sticking willow twigs into the ground" and "the wearing of the willow wreath [on the head]." The ancient Chinese believed in the existence of the soul after a person died. And the willow is a very hardy plant, growing anywhere under any conditions. If a twig is stuck into the ground, it will in time take root and become a tree. Perhaps it is due to this belief that people around the time of Qingming began to engage in the activities of sticking willow twigs into the ground and wearing willow wreaths on their heads. Sometimes they also hung willow wreaths on their front doors.

As time went by other activities such as storytelling by blind men, instrumental music concerts, wrestling, and so forth became part of the observance. So even though the Qingming Festival was also called the Ghost Festival, it was not an occasion for sadness or fear, but a time of joy, hope, and merriment.

Modern-Day Qingming Festival

Since the fall of the Qing dynasty in 1911, the Qingming Festival continues to be observed, especially in rural China. The people keep up with the tradition of cleaning the weeds from and putting new soil on graves. However, many activities associated with this festival are no longer practiced. The offering of sacrifices also differs from locale to locale and from urban areas to rural locations. In addition, some locales have also introduced tree planting activities into the festival.

Qingming Festival in the United States

As previously stated, this festival is observed across the United States by Chinese

Americans at cemeteries where their ancestors were buried. The date of observance spans from the weekend before to the one after the festival, as well as on the day of Qingming. The character of the festival, however, has been modified. First of all, there is no need to remove weeds and to put new soil on graves anymore; this is done by the ground staff.

Second, from the *Mencius* we learn that the ancient people offered cooked meats and wine at the ancestral graves. This practice is still observed by some traditional families. The ancient customs of the "hanging of paper" and the "burning of paper money" (i.e., paper money for the dead) continues to be observed by some families. Today ancestors are offered candles, incense, fruit, cakes, flowers, and houses and cars made of paper. After the sacrifice, all the edible items are taken home to be consumed by the families. But some families, perhaps being members of other faiths or less traditional, simply bring flowers to the graves.

Third, most of the traditional activities associated with this festival are largely nonexistent. In their stead cemeteries with a large Chinese population have in recent years initiated Buddhist or Daoist ceremonies for the dead and serve a buffet lunch for the living. The festival continues to be observed with joy and hope (minus the merriment, of course) as it always has been.

Edmond Yee

See also: Entries: Confucian Canon; Confucian Rituals; Confucianiam; Duanwu Festival; Ghost Festival/Zhongyuan Festival; Obon (Urabon); Ullambana Assembly

Further Reading

Eberhard, Wolfram. *Chinese Festivals, with Illustrations from the Collection of Werner Banck*. Taipei: Oriental Cultural Service, 1972, chapter 2.

Latsch, Marie-Luise. *Chinese Traditional Festivals*. Beijing: New World Press, 1984, pp. 46–54.

Mengzi. *Mencius*. Vol. 1. Translated by D. C. Lau. Hong Kong: The Chinese University Press, 1979.

R

Rajan, Frederick E. N. (1949–)

Frederick E. N. Rajan, a native of India, was the highest Asian Lutheran church official in North America, holding the position of executive director for the Commission for Multicultural Ministries (CMM) in the Evangelical Lutheran Church in America (ELCA) from 1992 to 2006. Born into a devout Christian family in the southernmost part of India, he grew up in the Arcot Lutheran Church, founded by the Danish Missionary Society.

After high school he entered the Annamalai University where he obtained a BA degree in economics in 1971, and two years later an MA degree in economics from Madras University. During his university days, he was active in the Student Christian Movement. After marrying his wife Sheila, they immigrated to the United States in 1976. He became a student at Faith Evangelical Lutheran Seminary (FELS), Tacoma, Washington.

After completing his MDiv and MTh degrees at FELS, Rajan went on to spend three years in Clinical Pastoral Education (CPE) at Hermann Hospital, Houston, Texas, where he received basic, advanced, and supervisory-level training.

While he was in CPE training, he simultaneously completed a two-year congregational internship at House of Prayer Lutheran Church, Clear Lake City, Texas. In 1985 Rajan was ordained in the Lutheran Church in America after accepting a call to Holy Trinity Lutheran Church, Irving, Texas.

During the formation of the Evangelical Lutheran Church in America in the 1980s, a small group of persons vigorously encouraged the church officials to recognize the necessity of multicultural ministries in North America—including the importance of having a unit in the new church to be responsible for such ministries and to serve as a watchdog for justice within the institution. Thus with the birth of the ELCA in 1988, the CMM was established.

In 1988, Rajan joined the staff of CMM as the associate director for advocacy. In response to the dearth of people of color as writers for church publications, he organized the first-ever people of color writers workshop and trained a cadre of writers for the church from the communities of color. Many of these participants not only became regular writers for church publications, but also institutional leaders. He developed a comprehensive antiracism training program, which continues to be used in the ELCA and in other denominations. He actively worked with the U.S. federal government through the Office for Governmental Affairs, ELCA, in addressing the Japanese Redress Bill, the American Indian Self-Determination Act, and the increase of minimum wage for workers.

In 1989, he was appointed director for Multicultural Mission Strategy. This involved leading the development of a national strategy, which ultimately transformed the ELCA, a nearly 100 percent Anglo-American–dominated institution, into making a commitment to be a multicultural church. To help the ELCA to fulfill its commitment, Rajan initiated an annual Multicultural Mission Institute, offering practical ways for all participants to learn cross-culturally and for the institution to become more aware of the reality and gifts of multicultural America. To extend the reach of these institutes, a series of books and booklets were also published and educational videos produced to promote multicultural ministry.

In 1991, Rajan was elected to a four-year term as the executive director for CMM. With this election he became the first Asian to hold such a high office among all Lutheran denominations in North America. He was subsequently reelected to two more terms. During his tenure as executive director, he forged partnerships with other mainline Protestant denominations such as the United Church of Christ, Presbyterian Church USA, Reformed Church in America, and the Episcopal Church in addressing and developing programs to strengthen multicultural ministry. He worked tirelessly with the Lutheran Church–Missouri Synod in publishing an African American Lutheran hymnal, *This Far by Faith*, the first-ever joint effort between these two churches. Rajan also established strong ties with Asian Lutheran churches in Asia.

Recognizing that the Arabs and Middle Easterners were not yet included at the multicultural table, he enabled the ELCA to recognize the Arab and Middle Eastern ministry as the fifth distinct ethnic ministry. Upon his conclusion of service, Mark Hanson, presiding bishop of the ELCA, said, "As executive director of the Commission for Multicultural Ministries, Fred Rajan has been a strong voice calling the Evangelical Lutheran Church in America to be an increasingly multicultural and intentional anti-racist church. Pastor Rajan has called this church to accountability, not only for our broad commitments, but also in our policies and practices . . . and has played a key role in the development of the ELCA's five ethnic-specific ministry strategies. While carrying out his work on behalf of the ELCA, he has always deepened connections with our ecumenical partners."

In addition to his responsibilities in the ELCA, Rajan organized with global church leaders an International Multicultural Ministries Forum in 2000 under the auspices of the World Council of Churches and served as its chair for seven years (1999–2006). This forum coordinated global conferences and produced numerous publications. For five years (200–2005), he also served as chair of the Inclusiveness and Justice Commission of the National Council of the Churches.

In recognition of his contributions to the church, Pacific Lutheran Theological Seminary, Berkeley, California, in 2002 honored Rajan with an honorary Alumni Award. The Academy of Ecumenical Indian Theology and Church Administration of the Gurukul Lutheran Theological College and Research Institute in Chennai, India, awarded him a doctor of divinity degree.

After leaving the ELCA in 2006, he joined Advocate Health Care—a ministry of the ELCA and the United Church of Christ—as its vice president for mission and spiritual care at Advocate Good Shepherd Hospital. In 2009 he assumed additional responsibility as the vice president for mission and spiritual care at Advocate Condell Medical Center. Both of these organizations are located in the suburbs of Chicago.

Rajan "is a man for others in both private and public life." Privately he provides support to his family in India as well as for theological education there. He established a Frederick and Sheila Rajan Scholarship Fund at Gurukul Lutheran Theological College and Research Institute, Chennai, India, to provide scholarships to Dalit women students pursuing theological studies. He meets his friends' needs, material and spiritual, with equal magnanimity.

Since 1985, Rajan has served the Asian American community faithfully in many capacities, such as by being a member of multicultural writing teams, an officer of the association, and currently, the president of the Asian Lutheran International Conference and a member of its editorial board.

Edmond Yee

See also: Entries: Lutherans; Matsushita, Eiichi; Nakamura, Paul T.

Further Reading

Yee, Edmond. *The Soaring Crane: Stories of Asian Lutherans in North America*. Minneapolis: Augsburg Fortress, 2002.

Yee, Edmond. "Speaker of Truth, Life, and Vision: Frederick E. N. Rajan." In Lily R. Wu and Edmond Yee, eds. *Asian Spirit Journey: An Anthology of Devotions and Prayers*. Chicago: Association of Asians and Pacific Islanders, 2003.

Ramadan

The name Ramadan refers to the ninth month of the Islamic lunar calendar, which has become synonymous with the daily fasting observed during this period. Among Islam's various religious obligations, Ramadan is perhaps the most widely observed by Muslims (the adherents of Islam) and most familiar to non-Muslims, particularly in the more culturally diverse metropolitan regions of the United States and other countries.

The practice of fasting in Ramadan is commonly known as one of the "five pillars" that form the basis of Muslim religious life, next to the basic testimony of faith, *shahāda* ("I attest that there is no god but the One God, and that Muhammad is His messenger"); the regular performance of the ritual prayer, *salāt*; the giving of alms, *zakāt*; and the pilgrimage (*hajj*) to the holy city of Mecca. Islam's holy scripture, the *Qur'an*, explains Ramadan's importance thus: it was in this month (in the year 610 CE) that the first verbal revelations of this same *Qur'an* descended upon an Arab merchant named Muhammad in the language of his people, thus initiating him as the prophet of his age and cultural milieu, indeed of all mankind. The *Qur'an* enjoins the believers (that is, monotheists who accept the authenticity of Muhammad's prophethood) to honor this pivotal event by abstaining from all food and drink from the first light of dawn until sunset, after which time the fast may be broken. Thus, the cycle of fasting and fast-breaking is repeated every day of the 29 to 30 days of Ramadan, whose beginning and end are

A Muslim American family has their picture taken during the traditional outdoor Eid al-Fitr celebrations, July 28, 2014, in the Brooklyn borough of New York. The Eid holiday marks the end of the Islamic holy month of fasting. (Robert Nickelsberg/Getty Images)

determined by the appearance of the new sickle moon.

The revelatory event described in the *Qur'an* can be seen as the beginning of the religion of Islam, for it is in the *Qur'an* that the basic metaphysical principles and behavioral standards of the Muslim community are expressed explicitly. In a broader sense, Islam understands itself not as a newly invented religion but simply as the ultimate expression and confirmation of the age-old monotheistic doctrine represented by innumerable earlier prophets, including Abraham, Moses, and Jesus; nonetheless, it is the *Qur'an*'s particular language and the person of Muhammad that define the flavor of Islam as it is commonly understood: as a monotheistic religion separate from other traditions. In remembering Islam's origins, Ramadan thus celebrates the tradition's uniqueness while at the same time always remembering its universality.

Ramadan can represent a strenuous adjustment for many Muslims, because of the fasting itself as well as because of the altered sleep patterns that usually accompany the restricted eating schedule—particularly when the month (which shifts backward in time yearly about 11 days, relative to the solar year) falls in the longer days of summer. In many Muslim countries workdays are therefore shortened to accommodate the associated difficulties. On the other side of this daytime asceticism, however, is an intensified enjoyment of the evening and night, owing to both the heightened pleasure of eating and drinking (often in a festive familial or communal atmosphere) and an increased focus on devotional practices, including special Ramadan prayers and recitations of the *Qur'an*.

Ultimately, the spiritual practice of fasting serves to strengthen and rejuvenate one's inner connection to and understanding of the Islamic spiritual path, but at the same time it provides a unique opportunity to awaken compassion for those compelled by need to go hungry. In this latter spirit, Ramadan has the status of a particularly auspicious time for the giving of alms (obligatory in Islam) and the performing of acts of charity in general.

The important holiday known as Eid al-Fitr (Arabic, festival of the breaking of the fast) or Şeker Bayramı (Turkish, festival of sweets) marks the end of the fasting period and thus falls on the first day of the month of Shawwāl following Ramadan. On this day, fasting is expressly prohibited and special prayers are held in *mosques*. Most Muslims celebrate Eid al-Fitr for about three days, taking time to dress in their most festive clothes, prepare generous feasts, and visit family and friends with holiday greetings. Regarding the details of these celebrations, as of Ramadan in general, one would be mistaken in speaking of a typical "American" Ramadan tradition; the United States is home to Muslims from the most diverse cultural backgrounds (Afghan, Chinese, Uzbek, Indonesian, Indian, and so forth), each with its own individual traditions, which differ in the details—just as surely as one culture's cuisine differs from that of all others—despite the common ground of shared religious principles.

Neal Kenji Koga

See also: Entries: Eid al-Adha, Festival of Sacrifice

Further Reading

Esposito, John. *The Oxford Dictionary of Islam*. New York: Oxford University Press, 2003.

Muhammad Asad, trans. and editor. *The Message of the Qur'ān*. Rev. ed. London: The Book Foundation, 2008.

Schimmel, Annemarie. *Islam: An Introduction*. Albany: State University of New York Press, 1992.

Ratanasara, Havanpola (1920–2000)

Havanpola Ratanasara was born in the Sri Lankan village of Havanpola. With his parent's permission, he became a novice monk at the age of 11, taking full ordination nine years later at the age of 20. He went on to obtain his first university degree from the University of Sri Lanka, then a postgraduate degree and diploma for educational research from Columbia University in New York, and finally a PhD in education from the University of London in 1965.

In his early years, he participated in numerous international seminars and conferences, presenting papers on various topics. In 1957 at the personal request of the prime minister of Sri Lanka, Ratanasara was asked to represent Sri Lanka as a delegate to the United Nations, the first Buddhist monk awarded this honor. He is reported to have said during an interview in 1958 on being a United Nations delegate, "You Americans believe in atomic bombs, hydrogen bombs and all those things. Well, we don't. We are a peace-loving people and want no association with any power bloc." He founded the Post Graduate Institute of Pali and Buddhist Studies at the University of Kelaniya in Sri Lanka in 1978.

In 1980, Dr. Ratanasara immigrated to the United States, settled in Los Angeles, and devoted himself to the promulgation of inter-Buddhist, interreligious understanding and education. He initiated the establishment of the Buddhist *Saṇgha* Council of Southern California, an organization of Buddhist clergy of all traditions, and served as its president. He also served as executive president emeritus of the American Buddhist Congress, a national organization of Buddhist temples and organizations, of which he was a founding member. In 1983, he founded the College of Buddhist Studies, Los Angeles, and was the president and a member of the academic staff.

Ratanasara played an active role in interreligious understanding for 20 years. He served as a board director for numerous international conferences on religion and peace. He was a member of the Executive Council of the Interreligious Council of Southern California and served as a vice president. He also served as co-chair for the Buddhist–Roman Catholic dialogue in Los Angeles. In 1992 Ratanasara was named the chief *saṇgha* nayake (judicial patriarch) for the Western Hemisphere for his lineage, formalizing his role as chief advisor of his tradition. In 1995 he founded the Buddhist Studies International Center in Iriyaweteya, Sri Lanka, which has become a center for those who want to study Buddhism and meditate in a true Buddhist cultural setting. To celebrate its opening,

Ratanasara's 1969 *Buddhist Philosophy of Education* was reprinted.

Ratanasara was firmly committed to interfaith dialogue based on what he understood to be commonalities among various religions. He reaffirmed this commitment in a paper titled "The Importance of Interfaith Dialogue" presented in July 1996 at the Intermonastic Dialogue at Gethsemani Monastery, Louisville, Kentucky. At the time of his death on May 26, 2000, he was working on *The Path to Perfection: A Buddhist Psychological View of Personality*.

Kusala Bhikshu

See also: Entries: Sri Lankan American Religions

Further Reading

Mitchell, Donald W., and James A. Wiseman, eds. *The Gethsemani Encounter: A Dialogue on the Spiritual Life by Buddhist and Christian Monastics*. London: Continuum International Publication Group, 1997.

Ratanasara, Havanpola. *Buddhist Philosophy of Education*. Los Angles: Havanpola Ratanasara, 1995.

Woo, Elaine. "U.S. Buddhism Leader Havanpola Ratanasara Dies." *Los Angeles Times*, 2000. http://articles.latimes.com/2000/jun/02/local/me-36637. Accessed 30 June 2014.

Reincarnation in Dharmic Religions

Reincarnation is one of the popular concepts discussed in various spiritual and religious teachings, such as Hinduism, Buddhism, and Kabbalah. Various cultural groups such as Chinese, Hindus, Tibetans, Indonesians, Egyptians, Celtics, Greeks, and Australian aborigines believe that one's soul travels and transmigrates into different forms when one dies. Souls can be reincarnated into different bodily shapes, celestial beings, humans, animals, insects, or plants.

While the concept of reincarnation is known cross-culturally, it is probably most frequently referred to within Asian and Asian American communities that practice dharmic religions such as Hinduism and Buddhism. The transmigration and reincarnation of one's soul, or atman, based on Hindu and Buddhist teachings, is determined by one's karmic deeds and connections—the "law of *karma*." Hindus and Buddhists believe that human interactions are interdependent and that one's actions have ethical consequences. One's fate, development, and deterioration are not random acts but based on one's causal and karmic connection. For example, it is believed that within the Tibetan community, the reincarnations of the Dali Lama—Panchen Lama, Karmapa, Rinpoche, and other spiritual teachers—are connected to their past life and deeds. Some believe that certain spiritual *gurus*—who are teaching Buddhism in the United States or in Europe—are reborn in the "Western world" so they can teach Dharma (i.e., Buddhist teachings) to Westerners and Asians and Asian Americans in the Western Hemisphere. In the Tibetan community, there is a verification process to recognize that a *Tulku*—which literally means "living Buddha" or enlightened Tibetan lama—Rinpoche, or a lama, is a reincarnation of a previous celestial being. For example, the Dali Lama is believed to be the reincarnation of the Compassion Buddha (Avalokitesvara).

It is also believed within the Asian and Asian American communities that certain celestial beings reincarnate into a lower level of being to perform certain duties, as addressed in the Hindu notion of "avatar." For example, it is believed that Vishnu, one of the Hindu Trinity (*trimurti*) who preserves and maintains cosmic order, has 10 different incarnations, who appear among humanity as avatars. Each incarnation descends with the specific purpose of rescuing humankind from great danger. For example, some believe that the seventh avatar of Vishnu is Lord Rama, whose heroic story is depicted in one of the most important mythological Hindu epics, The *Rāmāyaṇa*; his eighth avatar is Lord Krishna, whose teachings are revealed in the Hindu sacred scripture *Bhagavad-Gītā*; and his ninth avatar is Buddha, who relieves human sufferings and helps spread spiritual teachings to China, East Asia, and the rest of the world. There have been discussions regarding how many incarnations Vishnu or Krishna have: some believe that Vishnu has more than 10 incarnations, and some believe that Krishna has infinite reincarnations (as discussed in another sacred Puranic Hindu text, Bhagavata Purana). In fact, it is possible that every human being is a reincarnation of Krishna. The notion that Krishna has innumerable reincarnations is in accordance with the Buddhist belief that everybody possesses the Buddha nature and Buddha is within everybody ("You are the Buddha, and Buddha is you"). The dharmic implications of reincarnation for Asian and Asian American Buddhists (or any Buddhist regardless of ethnicity) is to reach enlightenment (Hindu *moksha* or Buddhist *Nirvāṇa*) so that one's soul does not linger in the cycle of birth and rebirth called *saṃsāra*.

Rueyling Chuang

Further Reading

Algeo, John. *Reincarnation Explored*. Wheaton, IL: Theosophical Publishing House, 1987.

Fishbane, Eitan. "A Chariot for the Shekhinah: Identity and the Ideal Life in the Sixteenth-Century Kabbalah." *Journal of Religious Ethics* 37(3) (2009): 385–418.

Head, Joseph, ed. *Reincarnation: A East-West Anthology*. Wheaton, IL: Theosophical Press, 1967.

Reiyūkai

Founded in 1930 by Kubo Kakutarō (1892–1944) and Kotani Kimi (1901–1971) with the purpose of creating a better society by incorporating into daily life the philosophy of Shakyamuni Buddha as found in the *Lotus Sūtra*, Reiyūkai promotes a variety of different activities advocating the importance of self-transformation through honoring one's parents and ancestors. The U.S. headquarters are in Pasadena, California, and the U.S. branch currently has 1,150 registered members.

History

While working at the Ministry of the Imperial Household after being acknowledged for his outstanding work as a construction engineer, Kubo Kakutarō became worried about the social chaos and the deteriorating ethical behavior exhibited in Japan during the Taisho era (1912–1926). Searching for a method that would guide people properly, preserve the best traditions of Japan, and establish a peaceful world, Kubo came upon the *Lotus Sūtra*. Through his study and practice, Kubo became convinced that honoring one's own ancestors and simultaneously seeking internal transformation and improvement would result in the significant realization of family unity, advancement of social welfare, and peace in society. Deciding to dedicate his life to propagating this philosophy, Kubo resigned his position at the Ministry of the Imperial Household and founded Reiyūkai with his sister-in-law Kotani Kimi on July 13, 1930.

Responding to the traditional idea that honoring and remembering one's ancestors needed to be performed by a Buddhist temple, Kubo, inspired by the increase in literacy through compulsory education, promoted the idea that individuals could read and recite the *Sūtra* on their own and thereby honor and remember their ancestors without depending on Buddhist monks. In support of this, Kubo edited the "Blue Sūtra" as an excerpt of the *Lotus Sūtra* for use by members. This idea of individual empowerment struck a chord in the hearts of many Japanese people living during these turbulent years in Japan, and the organization experienced tremendous growth before, during, and after World War II, up to 1950. Reiyūkai has continued to increase its membership worldwide.

Reiyūkai also faced many challenges. Risshō Kōsei-kai split off from Reiyūkai in 1938 and many splinter groups separated from Reiyūkai during the 1940s and 1950s. After Kubo passed away in 1944, the organization endured such tests and worked to adapt to changing circumstances while holding to its original values. Remaining true to Kubo's fundamental principle of Reiyūkai being a leader in social welfare activities, Kotani, as president, led members in promoting a wide variety of service activities such as assisting war orphans, supporting the methamphetamine elimination campaign, visiting and volunteering at sanatoriums, supporting centers for people with handicaps, and conducting charity fund drives. After visiting the United States and Europe as a goodwill ambassador at the request of the Japanese Red Cross Society, Kotani concentrated her efforts on cultivating youth, founding the Reiyūkai Youth Group Society in 1954 and constructing a leadership-training center for young people, Mirokusan, in 1964. The organization continues to cultivate new leaders for society in the present day.

Currently, Reiyūkai is active in more than 25 countries and regions and the "Blue Sūtra" has been translated into numerous Asian and European languages. The organization has various programs that focus on social welfare, particularly among youth (Reiyūkai Youth Group Society) and those with special needs (Reiyūkai Social Welfare Center). The organization also maintains education centers that aim at fostering individual and social change, including the Azabudai School Education Institute, the Lifelong Learning Volunteer Exchange Center, and the Inner Trip Foundation, which supports international student exchange.

The history of Reiyūkai in the United States can be traced to the 1950s and 1960s as its teachings arrived via Japanese immigrant families. Reiyūkai's fundamental idea—honoring and remembering one's ancestors without depending on a Buddhist priest or adhering to traditional Japanese Buddhist customs—was attractive to many Japanese American families who led the organization during its early years in serving the Japanese American community. It was registered as a nonprofit organization in 1972 and officially became the first overseas branch office of Reiyūkai in 1973. Today, the U.S. headquarters is recognized as Reiyukai America.

While the organization primarily served Japanese American families early on, there is a greater variety of ethnicities and backgrounds among members today. Recent activities such as a Family Day Festival, a "Letter to My Parents" contest, and a Remembering National Heroes Day, along with other environmental and humanitarian activities, support Reiyūkai's current efforts to go beyond ethnic or religious boundaries and support individual and communal flourishing. Reiyūkai operates permanent activity centers in Pasadena and National City, California, with activity groups present in Honolulu, Chicago, and East Coast locations.

Belief and Practice

Reiyūkai advocates incorporating Śākyamuni Buddha's teachings into daily life to increase one's awareness of self and others and their interdependence, thereby alleviating suffering in its many forms and promoting social solidarity. This includes becoming aware of the different causes and effects of karmic relations that individuals have inherited from their ancestors and resolving the negative aspects while enhancing the positive aspects. Reiyūkai focuses on the realization of world peace by starting with individual harmony. Some of the many practices promoted by Reiyūkai are described below.

Reverence for One's Ancestors. First, in support of Reiyūkai's emphasis on filial piety, both toward one's living family as well as one's ancestors, Kubo instituted the Family Posthumous Name (*sōkaimyō*), a symbolic plaque of one's past ancestors representing both paternal and maternal sides of the family, as well as Reiyūkai's Posthumous Name (*hōmyō*) to be inscribed in a registry, which may include all one's ancestors and family members, including children and the unborn, and distant relatives. These are installed in each household in a place of honor (*hōza*) where the "Blue Sūtra" may be recited.

Get-Togethers. Next, as a means to self-development and social solidarity, Reiyūkai encourages members to invite others to the organization (*michibiki*) and to have communal gatherings (*tsudoi*). Both activities aid self-reflection by placing the individual in a social setting where he or she sees oneself in relation to others. The gatherings, beginning with *Kotai Hōza* in 1928, are opportunities for members to share both positive and negative life experiences, including how involvement in the activities of Reiyūkai has positively affected their lives. Besides supporting member growth, the gatherings also serve as a key means to communicate the principles and efficacy of Reiyūkai membership.

The *Lotus Sūtra*. Since its main principles are based on the *Lotus Sūtra* and the *Sūtra* itself is recited as part of the practice, Reiyūkai recites the *daimoku*, the phrase "*Namu-myōhō-renge-kyō*," which Reiyūkai translates as: "I devote myself to the Sūtra of the Lotus Flower of the Marvelous Dharma." This activity impacts the other practices of Reiyūkai, distinguishing it from other groups based on Nichiren Buddhism that also recite the *daimoku*.

Through these practices, one can realize the roots of one's life, both where one comes from and where one is going, through the action of honoring and remembering one's ancestors and creating wide and deep life-connections right now though significant get-togethers. In these ways, Reiyūkai presents an opportunity to make changes in oneself that lead to the cultivation of human qualities that, in turn, can improve society.

Peter L. Doebler

Further Reading

Clarke, Peter B. "'Success' and 'Failure': Japanese New Religions Abroad." In Peter B. Clarke, ed. *Japanese New Religions in Global Perspective*. Richmond, UK: Curzon, 2000, pp. 272–311.

Ellwood, Robert S., and Shimazono Susumu. "New Religious Movements: New Religious Movements in Japan." In Lindsay Jones, ed. *Encyclopedia of Religion*. 2nd ed. Vol. 10. Detroit: Macmillan Reference USA, 2005, pp. 6572–75.

Hardacre, Helen. "Sex-Role Norms and Values in Reiyukai." *Japanese Journal of Religious Studies* 6, no. 3 (1979): 445–60.

Hardacre, Helen. *Lay Buddhism in Contemporary Japan*. Princeton, NJ: Reiyūkai Kyōdan, 1984.

McFarland, H. Neill. *The Rush Hour of the Gods: A Study of New Religious Movements in Japan*. New York: Macmillan, 1967.

Ogata, Ichitaro. (2008). *Thus Have I Heard—Encountering, Learning from, and Living by the Influence of Mrs. Kimi Kotani.* Tokyo: Reiyukai, 2008.

Reader, Ian, Esben Andreasen, and Finn Stefánsson, eds. *Japanese Religions: Past and Present.* Honolulu: University of Hawai'i Press, 1993.

Reiyukai America Website. http://www.reiyukai-usa.org/. Accessed July 15, 2014.

Reiyukai Website (English). http://reiyukaiglobal.org/. Accessed July 15, 2014.

Thomsen, Harry. *The New Religions of Japan.* Rutland, VT: Tuttle, 1963.

Rinzai Zen

Rinzai Zen-shū is the Japanese lineage of the Chinese Linji Chan (Zen) School, which was founded during the Tang Dynasty (607–918) by Linji Yixuan (Jpn. Rinzai Gigen, d. 867). Zen was introduced to Japan as early as the Nara period (647–794), but it did not take root until Myōan Eisai (1141–1215) returned from his second trip to China, where he received his *inka* (seal of Dharma succession) from Xuan Huichang (n.d.), a Linji master. He returned in 1191. After overcoming resistance to establishing a new Buddhist tradition, in 1202 he founded Kenninji Temple in Kyoto. Originally trained as a Tendai (Ch. Tianti) monk, Eisai combined Zen meditation with Tendai rituals. His successors, Shūhō Myōchō (Daitō Kokushi, 1283–1337) and Musō Soseki (1275–1351), evolved Rinzai Zen into a distinctively Japanese institution. During the Muromachi period (1336–1573) the purveyors of Rinzai melded Zen ideas (such as emptiness, transiency, and selflessness)

Reverend Raitei Arima, Superintendent Priest, Rinzai Zen-shū, Shokokuji-ha, Shokokuji Monastery in Japan addresses an audience, March 26, 2012, at the National Gallery of Art in Washington, DC. On the occasion of the Cherry Blossom Centennial Celebration, which was one year after a tragic earthquake in Japan, the Imperial Household Agency of Japan loaned one of its most important national treasures, the entire Colorful Realm of Living Beings, for the first time. (Karen Bleier/AFP/Getty Images)

with Japanese aesthetic sensibilities (asymmetry, simplicity, spontaneity, "agedness," and tranquility) to give rise to the Higashiyama culture. Much of what is commonly understood to be traditional Japan—*chadō*, *ikebana*, *Noh* drama, *sumi-e* painting, architecture with its distinctive *washitsu* (Japanese-style room) with its distinctive *fusuma* (sliding panels), *tatami* (straw mats), *shoji* (paper screens), *tokonoma* (decorative alcove), and *karesansui* (dry landscaping)—emerged at this time. After this burst of creative activity, Rinzai entered a period of stagnation until Hakuin Ekaku (1681–1769) revived the tradition through his *kōan* training methods that serve as the framework for modern Rinzai Zen practice.

Today Rinzai is not a single organized body. Rather, it is divided into 14 branches identified by their head temples, of which half are based in Kyoto. The largest and most influential is the Myōshinji branch, founded in 1342 by Kanzan Egen Zenji (1277–1360). The other 13 branches are Nanzenji and Tenryūji, both founded by Musō Soseki; Daitokuji, founded by Shūhō Myōchō; Tōfukuji, founded by Enni Ben'en (1202–1280); Kenninji, Kenchōji, Engakuji, Kokutaiji, Kōgakuji, Eigenji, Hōkōji, Shōkokuji, and Buttsūji.

These 14 temples are organizational divisions that arose from temple history and teacher-student lineage, and do not represent sectarian divide or difference in fundamental practice. These head temples preside over approximately 6,000 temples, 40 monasteries, and one nunnery. The Myōshinji, with approximately 3,500 temples and 19 monasteries, has one temple in Hawai'i.

At the time of its founding in 1932 by Rev. Okamoto Nanshin, the Paia Myōshinji Rinzai Zen Temple on Maui was the only Rinzai temple in the United States and its territories. A native of Okinawa, Okamoto was educated and trained in Kyoto. Before immigrating to Hawai'i, he was the abbot of Torinji Temple on Ishigaki Island. Rev. Oshiro Kiyoshi, a native of Tomigusuku, Okinawa, who succeeded Okamoto, was instrumental in rebuilding the temple after the 1946 tsunami. With a membership of approximately 130 families, the temple serves the spiritual needs of the Okinawan community. The temple is also a venue for Okinawan (Ryūkyūan) culture.

The first Rinzai master to address an American audience was Shaku Soyen (1869–1919), who spoke at the 1893 Chicago World Parliament of Religions. Before returning to Japan, he spent nine months in the San Francisco area, where he established a small *zendō* at the home of Alexander and Ida Russell, where he led *zazen* meditation sessions and lectured. Shaku was followed by Rev. Senzaki Nyozen (1876–1958), who taught at various sites in California until his death in 1958. Senzaki's friend and colleague Okamoto of the Paia temple translated and published his *On Zen Meditation* in 1938. Another Rinzai pioneer was Rev. Sasaki Shigetsu, better known by his clerical name, Sokei-an (1882–1945), who was active in New York. In 1931, his small group was incorporated as the Buddhist Society of American, later renamed First Zen Institute of America. One of his most active supporters was Ruth Fuller Everett, an American socialite and the mother-in-law of Alan Watts (1915–1973). Shortly before his death in 1945, Sokei-an and Everett wed and she took the name Ruth Fuller Sasaki (1892–1967). Some of the more prominent recent Rinzai Zen teachers include Rev. Sasaki Kyosan Jōshū (1907–2014), who founded the Mt. Baldy Zen Center in California, and Rev. Shimano Eidō Tai (1932–), who established the Dai Bosatsu Zendō Kongōji in New York State. Rev. Ōmori Sōgen (1904–1994) founded Daihonzan Chōzen-ji, the first

Rinzai headquarters temple established outside of Japan, in Honolulu.

Beliefs and Practices

Zen emphasizes that the truth and reality of Buddhism resides in the enlightenment of Śākyamuni Buddha and that all beings have the potential for attaining a similar experience. The realization of this potential is not to be found in the written documents, no matter how sacred, but through *zazen* or sitting meditation, *koan* practice, and *samu* (physical labor). The goal of Zen is *kenshō*, "seeing one's true nature"; it is an expression that is often used interchangeably with satori, "comprehension" or "understanding." *Kenshō* is the initial insight or awakening, not full enlightenment; it is the portal to a lifetime of post-*kenshō* training aimed at deepening this insight through the activities of daily life.

In contrast to Dōgen's Sōtō Zen tradition that emphasized *zazen*, Hakuin employed *koan* (Ch. *kongan*) practice. The *koan* is a pedagogical device designed to prod, heighten, and test a student's understanding of the Zen experience. *Koans* are often framed in the form of a "riddle" that forces a student to confront the limits of rationality and ordinary logic. Consider the following *koan* by Hakuin. Clapping his hands, he queries, "This is the sound of two hands clapping. What is the sound of one hand clapping?" The *koan* is an examination that does not call for a doctrinal or rational response. It does not ask the student for his or her opinion or judgment. If the student had attained an understanding of the basis of the *koan*, he or she would respond appropriately, either verbally and/or

with some action. The encounter between teacher and student is direct and immediate. When the student's mind (understanding) meets the teacher's mind, the Dharma is transmitted. Case Six of the *Mumonkan* recalls the moment at Mt. Gṛdhrakuta (Vulture Peak) when Śākyamuni Buddha lifted a flower to those who had gathered to receive his teachings. Everyone was silent. Mahākāśyapa broke into a broad smile. Whereupon Śākyamuni said,

I possess the true Dharma eye, the marvelous mind of Nirvana, the true form of the formless, the subtle Dharma Gate, independent of words and transmitted beyond doctrine. This I entrust to Mahākāśyapa.

A thousand years later Bodhidharma (ca. fifth–sixth century), the transmitter of Zen from India to China, explained the meaning of Zen:

A special transmission outside the scriptures,
[that is] not to be founded upon words and letters;
By pointing directly to [one's] mind It lets one see into [one's own true] nature [Buddhahood].

In *koan* practice, should the student's response be unsatisfactory, the teacher will ask the student to wrestle with it during *zazen* meditation and in the course of daily life. By forcing the student to realize the limits of language and rationality, the exercise prods the student to tap and release the Buddha-mind to transform his or her basis for life. After the initial *kenshō* experience, the student must continue to deepen the realization and make it visible in every thought, word, and act. Every event is an opportunity and every object replete with the lesson of the Buddhadharma. The Zen life is one of increasing authentic spontaneity with maturity. Such spontaneity can be seen in the drawings and calligraphy of Hakuin, who revealed his deepening stations of spiritual maturity.

The idea of *samu* or engaging in spiritual exercises beyond the meditation hall can be traced to Baizhang Huaihai (720–814), who coined the famous maxim: "No work, no food." Baizhang expected Zen monks to approach agricultural and all manner of manual labor with the same attitude as sitting meditation. Work is much more than simply working in the fields: it is a spiritual exercise. Through work, a practioner takes charge of his or her spiritual exercises and contributes to the welfare of the community.

Contributions

As noted above, the impact of Rinzai Zen on the early immigrant experience has been largely confined to the Okinawan American community on Maui. However, it has had a broad and deep impact on the arts. D. T. Suzuki's (1870–1966) lectures at Columbia University in the early 1950s and his writings influenced many artists, poets, writers, and composers. In the mid-1950s, writers associated with the Beat Generation took a serious interest in Zen, including Joyce Johnson (1935–), Jack Kerouac (1922–1969), Allen Ginsberg (1926–1997), Kenneth Rexroth (1905–

1982), and Ruth Weiss (1935–). In 2009, "The Third Mind: American Artists Contemplate Asia, 1860–1989" at the New York City Guggenheim Museum showcased the impact of Zen influences on such abstract expressionists as Franz Kline (1910–1962), Sam Francis (1923–1994), Phillip Guston (1913–1980), Robert Motherwell (1915–1991), Jackson Pollack (1912–1956), David Smith (1906–1965), and Mark Toby (1890–1976). These artists drew inspiration from the expressive spontaneity of *Zenga* (Zen paintings) and Zen-inspired calligraphers such as Morita Shiryū (1912–1998) and Inoue Yu'ichi (1916–1985). Composer John Cage (1912–1992), who also attended Suzuki's lectures, came away with the idea that the purpose of art is "to wake people up." To this end he composed *4'33"*, a piece in which the performer sits in front of a piano without playing a note for 4 minutes and 33 seconds. The performance is bracketed by the performer lifting and closing the piano lid. The ambient sounds from the audience provide the "sounds" of the piece. The "unusual" performance forced the audience to appreciate silence or "no-sound." The Zen idea of immediacy provided a rationale for minimalism, an art and design movement that set out to expose the essence of an object by eliminating all nonessential features and concepts.

Ronald Y. Nakasone

Further Reading

Dumoulin, Heinrich. *Zen Buddhism: A History*. Vol. 2: *Japan*. New York: Macmillan, 1990.

Hisamatsu, Shin'ichi. *Zen and the Fine Arts*. Tokyo: Kodansha International, 1971.

Matsunaga, Alicia, and Daigan Matsunaga. *Foundation of Japanese Buddhism.* Vol. II: *The Mass Movement.* Los Angeles: Nembutsu Press, 1973.

Miura, Isshū, and Ruth Fuller Sasaki. *Zen Dust, the History of the Kōan and Kōan Study in Rinzai (Lin-chi) Zen.* New York: Harcourt, Brace & World, 1966.

Paia Zen Mission. http://rinzai-maui.org/. Accessed July 15, 2014.

Sekida, Katsuki, trans. *Two Zen Classics: Mumonkan and Hekiganroku.* Edited and introduced by A. V. Grimstone. New York: Weatherhill, 1977.

Suzuki, Daisetz T. *Zen and Japanese Culture.* New York: Pantheon Books, 1959.

Tanabe, George J., and Willa Jane Tanabe. *Japanese Buddhist Temples in Hawai'i.* Honolulu: University of Hawai'i Press, 2013.

Westgeest, Helen. *Zen in the Fifties: Interaction in Art between East and West.* Zwolle Amstelveen: Waanders; Cobra Museum Voor Moderne Kunst, 1996.

Risshō Kōsei-kai (RKK)

Established in 1938 by Nikkyō Niwano (1906–1999) and Naganuma Myōkō (1889–1957), Risshō Kōsei-kai (RKK) is a lay Buddhist organization in the Nichiren Buddhist tradition and is an offshoot of Reiyūkai. The North American headquarters are in Irvine, California; designated churches are in Los Angeles and Pearl City, Hawai'i; and Dharma Centers are in many major U.S. cities. RKK teaches the relief of suffering and establishment of peace based on the teachings of the *Lotus Sūtra*, practices a particular type of group counseling called *hōza*, and is highly active in interfaith relations and peace and human rights activism.

History

Nikkyō Niwano (originally Shikazo Niwano) and Naganuma Myōkō (originally Naganuma Masa) founded Risshō Kōsei-kai in 1938. The name may roughly be translated as a group meeting to support each other in rightly following the Buddha's teaching. Both Niwano and Myōkō were from the working class and were former members of Reiyūkai. RKK sources suggest the departure was based on differences in understanding regarding the contemporary relevance of the *Lotus Sūtra*. An alternative explanation is put forth by Harry Thomsen: "The reason for the secession was not a profound doctrinal difference, but rather Niwano had become conscious of his abilities as a leader and wanted to become independent." Regardless of the reason, RKK carried over many of the practices of Reiyūkai, and its basis in the *Lotus Sūtra* links the organization to other new Japanese religions based on Nichiren Buddhism such as Soka Gakkai or Nipponzan Myōhōji.

After the Second World War RKK experienced phenomenal, continual growth. This rapid growth was challenged in the mid-1950s through a series of events that tarnished RKK's public image. These included the so-called "Zōshiki incident" in 1951 in which a mother reportedly committed double-suicide with her son after an RKK fortuneteller foretold the son's death. In 1954 a former convert, Shigeru Shiraishi, brought legal action against RKK, claiming that RKK's teachings and activities put it in violation of the Religious Corporation Act. This was followed by a property dispute in 1955 with allegations of improper dealings. Then, from 1955, the *Yomiuri Shinbun* newspaper carried out an offensive attack in numerous articles against RKK, ranging from its real estate dealings to its methods of proselytization. Throughout this period there were also investigations by governmental bodies that led to sharp criticism of RKK. The combination of these factors contributed to a decline in membership in 1956. The organization also faced internal conflict at this time as supporters of Myōkō challenged Niwano's leadership. Indeed, as Kiyomi Morioka shows, the organization was moving toward having Myōkō as the single leader; however, her death in 1957 brought this to an abrupt end.

With Niwano in sole control and the organization's structure and teaching refined as a result of the 1950s controversies, RKK resumed its pattern of growth and focused attention on interfaith relations and peace and human rights activism. Niwano helped organize the first World Conference for Religion and Peace in 1970 and was the first president of the Asian Conference for Religion and Peace. Other associations include support for UNICEF and the International Association for Religious Freedom.

The presence of RKK in the United States can be traced to December 1951 when Tomoko Ozaki, a coffee farmer in Kona, Hawai'i, joined the organization. It spread throughout the Hawaiian Islands through grassroots communication, especially among women. In September 1958 Niwano officially recognized Hawai'i as the first overseas congregation of RKK. After this *hōza* counseling centers were progressively established. In 1969, Ozaki was ordained as the first American-born minister of RKK. However, subsequent head ministers have primarily been sent from Japan. RKK has maintained a presence in the continental United States since at least the 1970s and currently has centers in many major U.S. cities.

Nichiko Niwano (1938–), son of Nikkyō Niwano, has been president since 1991, and the designated next president is Kosho Niwano, Nichiko Niwano's daughter. Recent activism includes programs addressing disarmament, hunger, and nuclear energy, including a statement calling for the curbing of the use of such energy in the wake of the Fukushima Dai'ichi Nuclear Power Station disaster caused by the 2011 earthquake in Japan.

Belief and Practice

With its primary doctrinal beliefs based on the *Lotus Sūtra*, RKK embraces many basic Buddhist beliefs such as the centrality of the Three Treasures, the Four Noble Truths, the Law of Twelve Causes, and the Eightfold Path. However, while similar to other Nichiren groups, RKK sees itself as the true lineage of Nichiren. It advocates breaking the cycle of *karma* and transmigration though repentance (*zange*), which is recognizing one's ignorance and aiming to live a perfect life. Through such individual action RKK aims for "the revival of true Buddhism as the means to bring full enlightenment to every individual and make perfect Japanese society and the world at large." In keeping with this eschatological vision, RKK divides modern history into three phases: 1938–1957 (Age of Tactful Teaching); 1958–1977

(Age of Manifestation of Truth); 1978–present (Age of Unlimited Manifestation of Compassion).

The core practice is daily recitation of portions of the *Lotus Sūtra* in the morning and evening before a home or temple altar, including the *daimoku*, the phrase, "*Nam-myōhō-renge-kyō*," an expression of devotion to the *Lotus Sūtra*. The primary object of devotion, or *gohonzon*, is a particular statue of the Buddha purported to have been revealed to Nikkyō Niwano through his study of the *Lotus Sūtra*. The statue is made up of a standing figure on a lotus flower. The figure's hands are held in the *abhaya mudra*, the right hand raised and the left hand hanging by the hips, both palms facing outward. The gesture indicates peace, protection, and benevolence. Behind the figure is a cloud-shaped halo on which smaller images of four bodhisattvas sit. While meant to represent Śākyamuni, since he is believed to have been one with the Eternal Buddha that sustains the universe, revering the image of Śākyamuni is seen as a means of paying homage to the Eternal Buddha. The most important version of the statue is housed in RKK's Great Buddha Hall in Tokyo.

The second main activity is a kind of small group counseling with a leader called *hōza* or, according to RKK, Circle of Compassion. The activity involves sitting (*za*) in a circle and "attempt[ing] to find solutions to problems in the light of Buddhist principles (*hō*)." During the session, members share problems or questions and in turn give advice. Shamanistic practices also played a significant role in the early years of RKK, including onomancy, reading one's future based on the Chinese characters of one's name, but it is unclear how significant such practices may be today.

Also significant are the 1st and 15th days of each month, designated as days of *Uposatha*, modeled on early meetings of Śākyamuni and his followers. These are days set aside for testimony sharing, *hōza* counseling, and creating an overall sense of community. In addition, members observe memorial days throughout the year, in particular remembering significant events from the life of Śākyamuni Buddha, Nichiren, and Nikkyō Niwano. There are also memorial days observed monthly dedicated to Nikkyō Niwano (4th of each month), Myōkō Naganuma (10th), and Śākyamuni Buddha (15th).

Finally, RKK also maintains active publications, including a quarterly magazine, *Dharma World: For Living Buddhism and Interfaith Dialogue* in English; *Saṇgha in Motion*, a bimonthly newsletter for the United States; as well as a monthly newsletter, *Shan Zai*, in multiple languages.

Peter L. Doebler

Further Reading

Anderson, Richard W. "Risshō Kōseikai and the Bodhisattva Way: Religious Ideals, Conflict, Gender, and Status." *Japanese Journal of Religious Studies* 21, nos. 2–3 (1994): 311–37.

Clarke, Peter B. "'Success' and 'Failure': Japanese New Religions Abroad." In Peter B. Clarke, ed. *Japanese New Religions: In Global Perspective*. Richmond, UK: Curzon, 2000, pp. 272–311.

Ellwood, Robert S., and Shimazono Susumu. "New Religious Movements: New Religious Movements in Japan." In Lindsay Jones, ed. *Encyclopedia of Religion*. 2nd ed. Vol. 10. Detroit: Macmillan Reference USA, 2005, pp. 6572–75.

Guthrie, Stewart. *A Japanese New Religion: Risshō Kōsei-kai in a Mountain Hamlet.* Ann Arbor: Center for Japanese Studies, University of Michigan, 1988.

McFarland, H. Neill. *The Rush Hour of the Gods: A Study of New Religious Movements in Japan.* New York: Macmillan, 1967.

Morioka, Kiyomi. "Attacks on the New Religions: Risshō Kōseikai and the 'Yomiuri Affair.'" *Japanese Journal of Religious Studies* 21, nos. 2–3 (1994): 281–310.

Niwano Nikkyō. *Lifetime Beginner: An Autobiography.* Translated by Richard L. Gage. Tokyo: Kosei, 1978.

Reader, Ian, Esben Andreasen, and Finn Stefánsson, eds. *Japanese Religions: Past and Present.* Honolulu: University of Hawai'i Press, 1993.

Thomsen, Harry. *The New Religions of Japan.* Rutland, VT: Tuttle, 1963.

S

Samoan Spirituality

Anthropologists and linguists trace the origins of the Samoans to Austronesian-speaking people of present-day south China, who made their way to Taiwan. Between 5000 and 2500 BCE and for the next 1,000 years, the Austronesian migration continued southeast to the Philippines, Borneo, Indonesia, and as far west as Madagascar; in 1200 BCE, migrants journeyed east to Melanesia and in 500 CE, to Micronesia. Venturing further, they made landfall in Fiji about 1100 BCE. Three hundred years later they set sail for the islands of Tonga and later northeast to Samoa. The Fiji-Tonga-Samoa Crescent evolved the distinctive Polynesian culture, which includes Hawai'i, Rapa Nui (Easter Island), and Tahiti. A cultural and linguistic divide later developed between Fiji to the west and Tonga and Samoa to the east.

History

The Dutch explorer Jacob Roggeveen (1559–1729) in 1722 became the first known European to have sighted the Samoan Islands. He was followed by the French explorer Louis-Antoine de Bougainville (1729–1811), who named the islands the Navigator Islands in 1768 because of the extraordinary seafaring skills of the inhabitants. Thereafter, French, British, German, and American ships routinely anchored in Pago Pago Harbor for refueling and provisions during the 19th-century whaling era. International rivalries resulted in the Tripartite Convention of 1899 that partitioned the 1,170-square-mile archipelago. The eastern islands of Tutuila in 1900 and Manu'a in 1904 became American Samoa (formerly Western Samoa), an unincorporated territory of the United States, with the Ratification Act of 1929. All civil, judicial, and military powers rest in the president of the United States. Persons born in American Samoa are American nationals, but not U.S. citizens, and they are not allowed to vote in U.S. presidential elections. They are free to live and work anywhere in the United States.

The 2010 U.S. Census Bureau reported 55,519 Samoans living in American Samoa. Of this number approximately 92 percent are native Samoans, who constitute the second most numerous Pacific Islanders under U.S. hegemony, after the native Hawaiians. It is estimated that more than 180,000 Samoans and their progeny live in Hawai'i and the continental United States. Honolulu, Hawai'i, has the largest Samoan population, while there are large numbers in the states of California, Washington, Utah, and Alaska.

The western islands became German Samoa after Britain vacated all claims in exchange for Germany's termination of rights in Tonga. During World War I, New

Zealand troops landed in 'Upolu unopposed on August 29, 1914. New Zealand controlled Samoa under the League of Nations mandate until 1962 when the Independent State of Samoa became the first small-island country in the Pacific to become independent; it joined the Commonwealth of Nations in 1970 and the United Nations in 1976. The Bureau of Statistics of the Independent State of Samoa reported a population of 187,820 in 2011.

Beliefs

Unlike the Hawaiians and their other Polynesian cousins, the Samoans did not create outward signs—temples or altars—of their spiritual underpinnings. Their Polynesian cousins referred to them as "godless." Except for a few totems, the absence of any material manifestation of a spiritual culture confounded the Christian missionaries. Traditional Samoans inhabited a sacred world and every aspect of their lives was sacred. What need was there for sacred spaces and symbols? Sacredness was crystallized in *fa'a Sāmoa* or the Samoan Way and was played out through *vā tapuia*, the covenantal relationships between and among people and with the natural world. *Vā tapuia* is the unseen protagonist in the film *The Orator.*

The 106-minute film focuses on Saili, a dwarf and poor taro farmer; his wife, Va'aiga; his teenage stepdaughter, Litia; and Poto, their antagonist. The family is an outcast; it has no social standing in the community and is under constant threat by other villagers and Va'aiga's family. Saili summons the courage to become a *tulāfale,*

an orator, to protect his family, ancestors, and his land. At the climax of the film, Saili travels with Litia to reclaim Va'aiga's body so they can give her a proper burial, and so she can be at home with her family. Earlier, unannounced and uninvited, Poto entered Saili's home, and stole the body of his sister, Va'aiga, while Litia was mourning her mother. Deep into digging her grave, Saili was unaware.

This simple narrative reveals the spiritual power of *vā tapuia.* Poto seriously breached *vā tapuia* at least three times. First, he stole into Saili's house; second, by removing Va'aiga's body, he forcibly disconnected her from her family and her preferred resting place. Third, as a *matai* or chief, Poto failed to uphold the dignity of his office by failing to recognize covenantal bonds between Va'aiga and her family. It is because of *vā tapuia* that Saili finds courage and self-worth, and reclaims Va'aiga's body. For an appreciation of *vā tapuia* we turn to Samoan mythology.

Traditional Samoa shares with its Polynesian cohorts the notion of an uncreated creator. Tagaloa (Hawaiian, Kanaloa) is the progenitor of the sun, moon, and heavenly bodies, Earth and all its inhabitants—animate and inanimate, corporeal and disembodied. Samoans inhabit a sacred world wherein all things and all beings are kin. Additionally, as descendants of Tagaloa, all existences and their relationship to each other are *tapu* or sacred and forbidden. *Tapu* means that the individual and the space of every being and thing is to be honored and not violated. Additionally, each thing and person possesses mana or power/prestige. Each person or thing has a role and a responsibility to ensure the well-being of every other person and thing.

Vā tapuia or the sacred covenant between and among individuals is played out through *vā-feāloaloa'i*, a set of protocols or etiquette that govern social relationships. A child must be respectful of his or her parents and teachers; a commoner must respect the judgment and authority of the *matai* or chief and honor the knowledge and orator skills of the *tulāfale*. The chiefs in turn must respect the right of every person to speak. Properly observed, *vā-feāloaloa'i* mediates conflicts and misunderstandings.

Samoan society centered on the *āiga* or extended family that is headed by a *matai* and the office of the *tulāfale* or "talking chief." A village normally consists of several *āigas*, each headed by its respective *matai* who is responsible for the well-being of all persons under his charge and is custodian of its assets. The *matai* also represents the family at the *fono* or village council that meets at *malae*, the village square, to enforce and adjudicate breaches of *tapu* and to determine matters of community concern, such as war. The *matai* also assumes responsibility for the conduct of his *āiga* who breaches a *tapu*, such as rape, against a member of another family. Among the many *matai* is the *ali'i sili* or high chief.

The *tulāfale* is especially adept in oratory, a most respected skill in an oral tradition. A repository of history, genealogy, tradition, and protocol, the *tulāfale*'s knowledge is essential for ceremonial protocol, for the exchange of property, marriage proposals, and negotiating between *āigas*. Skilled in language, the *tulāfale* is also a poet. In contemporary Samoa, the *tulāfale* functions as an advisor and debater on matters of public policy and is expected to be thoroughly informed on traditional lore and custom. This is the guise Saili assumes.

Saili and Litia arrive at the funderal for Va'aiga that her biological family is sponsoring. Standing with the symbols of the orator—*to'oto'o* (staff) in his right hand and a *fue* (whisk) over the right shoulder—Saili's very presence reprimands Poto for his breaches of *tapu*. As a *matai*, Poto is responsible for the well-being of his *āiga*, a role at which he is adept. Earlier he persuaded the village elders to lift their 17-year banishment of Va'aiga and allow her to be buried in the village; the lifting of the ban in effect justifies his kidnapping of Va'aiga's body. But his actions are totally dismissive of her wish to remain with Saili and Litia, not to return to the family and village that banished her. Poto also disregards the fact that Saili is from a different *aiga*. His contempt not only breaches the *tapu* between different *aigas*, but diminishes the mana or prestige that should be central to the character of a *matai*. A *matai* is elected. Poto violated the trust of his *āiga*.

Saili, for his part, states that Va'aiga is his wife and the mother of Litia; and that her rightful place is with them, but more poignantly, he states that she belongs between his heart and lungs, where her being cannot be desecrated by the worms and birds, should she be buried in her natal village. The final scenes are of Saili and Litia returning home with Va'aiga's body and Saili sitting on her grave, cradling a child.

The filmmaker chooses not to include a scene of Poto submitting himself to *ifoga*, a ritual gesture of apology to right the violations of *vā tapuia*. But the implication is clear. Normally a person submitting to *ifoga* arrives at dawn and sits wrapped in a finely handwoven mat in front of the victim's home. The victim or his or her family can either accept the supplicant's gesture of *ifoga* or ask for his life. Should the family accept the *ifoga*, the *tapu* is remedied by an exchange of valuables. The film does include a series of scenes relating to the ritual of *ifoga*. Three men who earlier bullied and injured Saili sat for days in front of Saili's family home in the hope that their apology would be accepted.

The film is filled with other metaphors that highlight the authority of *vā tapuia*. It is not the intent of this entry to critique the cultural lessons and aesthetic merits of *The Orator*, but it is worthwhile mentioning the pervasive authority of *vā tapuia*. Saili's diminutive stature contrasts with Poto's imposing frame, which in turn is dwarfed by the authority of the sacred covenant. Though he was counseled to ignore Saili's presence, custom required Poto to change into his ceremonial *tapa* garments to engage in an oratory exchange. Ironically, throughout the film the outcast Va'aiga is seen patiently weaving an *'ie tōga* that Litia finishes after her mother dies. The *'ie tōga* or "treasured mat" is never used to sit or sleep on, rather it is a valuable cultural artifact produced by women for such ceremonial exchanges as the bestowal of the title of *matai*, weddings, and funerals. The value of an *'ie tōga* resides in the craftsmanship, and the woman's skill determines her place and identity in the community. Litia unfurls the *'ie tōga* that Saili offers to Poto. The outcast family upholds the sacred covenant of *vā tapuia*, the very heart of *fa'a Sāmoa*.

Vā tapuia also extends to the natural world. The reverence for the sacredness of nature is demonstrated by harvesting a tree to build a house or to hew a canoe. Before a tree is cut, the woodcutter performs a *faalanu* or chant that seeks a pardon from the forest god *Manuvao* (forest bird) and to thank the tree for availing itself to satisfy a need. During times of regrowth, certain trees and plants were *tapu* from being cut. Similar rituals are performed by fishermen and farmers.

Samoan Christianity

In 1830 John Williams of the London Missionary Society (Congregationalist) arrived at Sapapalii, a village on the northeast coast of Savari'i Island, on the *Messenger of Peace* with eight Tahitian and Rarotongan (Cook Islander) teachers. The London missionary experienced great success. Within 12 years, in 1848, the first Samoan version of the New Testament was published and the Old Testament in 1855. But Christianity was not accepted without considerable thought. The chiefs convened the entire community to consider the advantages of accepting a new god. The material wealth and technological superiority of the Europeans convinced the people that the Christian God was superior to their own gods. They were also cognizant of the goddess Nafanua's prophecy: a new god would supersede the rule of the old gods.

The Samoans readily took to Christian ideology for a number of reasons. First, the notion of a creator God was also present in Tagaloa, mentioned above. Second, Christian moral sanctions outlined by the Ten Commandments were present in the notion of *tapu* that was supported by *vā tapuia*. Third, the *ifoga* ritual that obligates the *matai* to take responsibility for the actions of his family parallels Christ's death that atones for the sins of others. Fourth, the Samoans understood the Christian Church service to be *tapuaiga* or "worship," a notion that referred to sacred undertaking. Fishing, for example, is a sacred undertaking that involves the entire community. The community would invoke the gods to ensure the fishermen's safety and for an abundant catch. The sacredness of *tapuaiga* is reflected in the proverbial expression, "*E le sili le ta'i i lo tapuai*" (Of the two roles, the tapuaiga is more important than the fishing expedition). The *tapuaiga* ends when the fishermen utter the phrase "*Malo le tapuai*" (Gratitude for the *tapuaiga*).

As of February 2013, the World Christian Database showed the religious affiliations of American Samoa to be 98.3 percent Christian. Of this figure the CIA Factbook estimates that 50 percent are Christian Congregationalist, 20 percent Roman Catholic, and 30 percent Protestant and other faiths that include a small number of Chinese Universalists, Buddhists, and Baha'i, as of February 2013. The Church of Jesus Christ of Latter-day Saints website reports a membership of 15,411 with 37 congregations in American Samoa.

Finally, as in other immigrant communities, the churches serve as community centers, reminders of tradition, and the homeland. Samoans living stateside rely on their *āiga* for support. Families shelter anyone who needs a place to stay and pool their resources to assist their kin. *Fa'a Samoa* is still operative.

Ronald Y. Nakasone

See also: Entries: Pacific Islander Religious Cultures

Further Reading

Church of Jesus Christ of Latter-day Saints. http://www.mormonnewsroom.org/facts-and-statistics/country/american-Sāmoa. Accessed October 1, 2013.

Fischer, Steven Roger. *A History of the Pacific Islands*. New York: Palgrave, 2002.

Holmes, Lowell D., and Ellen Rhoads Holmes. *Sāmoan Village, Then and Now*. 2nd ed. Fort Worth, TX: Harcourt Brace Jovanovich, 1992.

Lan, Iakapo Yan. Personal correspondence. September 25, 2013.

Mead, Margaret. *Coming of Age in Sāmoa, a Psychological Study of Primitive Youth for Western Civilization*. New York: Morrow Quill Paperbacks, 1928.

The Orator (*O le tulāfale*). Produced by Catherine Fitzgerald; written and directed by Tusi Tamasese. New Zealand Film Commission and Sāmoan Government, 2011. 106 min.

Peteru, Maiava Carmel. n.d. "O le tōfā manao, A Sāmoan Conceptual Framework for Addressing Family Violence." http://www.familyservices.govt.nz/documents/working-with-us/programmes-services/pacific-framework-Sāmoan-fa2.pdf. Accessed October 6, 2013.

Purcell-Sjölund, Anita L. "Exploring 'Sāmoaness' in the Sāmoan Language Film, *The Orator* (O le Tulāfale). http://du.diva-portal.org/smash/get/diva2:536569/FULLTEXT01. Accessed October 1, 2013.

Sāmoa Bureau of Statistics. http://www.sbs.gov.ws/. Accessed September 25, 2013.

Tui Atua Tupua Tamasese. "Clutter in Indigenous Knowledge, Research and History: A Sāmoan Perspective." 2004. http://www.msd.govt.nz/about-msd-and-our-work/publications-resources/journals-and-magazines/social-policy-journal/spj25/clutter-in-indigenous-knowledge-25-pages61-69.html. Accessed September 30, 2013.

Sano, Roy I. (1931–)

Roy I. Sano, a native of Berkeley, California, born into a Japanese immigrant family, was a bishop of the United Methodist Church. Bishop Sano's parents converted to Christianity upon the death of their third child. The Sanos were sent to Poston War Relocation Center in 1942; Sano was then 11 years old. Sponsored by a Quaker family, the Sano family left Poston for Pennsylvania, where they worked as agricultural laborers. It was during this time that Sano felt a call to the ministry. After World War II, the Sanos returned to California. Sano is married to Kathleen Thomas-Sano and is the father of three children.

Sano majored in American history at the University of California at Los Angeles. During college he served student pastorates at Oxnard, California (1950–1954) and as associate pastor at Christ Church in Santa Maria, California. He was ordained deacon in 1954 by Bishop Donald H. Tippett. He earned a minister of divinity degree at Union Theological Seminary, New York City, in 1957. While in seminary he served as minister of education for the Japanese American congregation of the United Church of Christ in New York City. After graduating from seminary, he became a

Bishop Roy I. Sano is a retired Japanese American Bishop of the United Methodist Church. Bishop Sano was elected to the Episcopacy in 1984, and served the Denver and Los Angeles areas. Retired since 2000, he lives in Oakland, California. (Glen Martin/The Denver Post via Getty Images)

member of the California-Nevada Annual Conference of the United Methodist Church. Sano earned a master of theology degree from the GTU in 1968 and completed his doctoral studies in philosophy at Claremont Graduate School in 1972.

Sano was instrumental in establishing and guiding Pacific Asian Center for Theologies and Strategies (PACTS) through its initial years. In one of its first initiatives, Sano as the director of ACTS (later PACTS) inquired: Why over its long history has the Pacific School of Religion (PSR) never appointed an Asian American faculty person? After two years of meetings with faculty and administration with little progress, he rallied the Asian American community to lobby and educate the larger community about the need for racial and ethnic tenure-track professors. These efforts led to his appointment as professor of theology and director of Pacific and Asian American Ministries.

At the same time he was also director of PACTS. Sano, in this capacity, worked to involve the local Pacific Islander and Asian American churches and communities to explore and reimagine a Christian theology that addressed their ethnic and cultural experience. He also worked to ensure that racial ethnic professors were considered for tenure-track appointments at the seminaries.

Sano served as director of PACTS and PSR professor until he was elected to the United Methodist Episcopacy in 1984 by the Western Jurisdictional Conference. He was assigned to the Denver Episcopal Area and served for eight years on the United Methodist General Board of Global Ministries. He was the first Japanese American

to become a bishop of the United Methodist Church. He retired in 2000.

Julia Keiko Higa Matsui Estrella

See also: Entries: Pacific and Asian American Center for Theologies and Strategies (PACTS); United Methodism

Further Reading

Russell, Jesse, and Ronald Cohen, eds. *Roy I. Sano.* New York: Books on Demand, 2012.

Santo Niño

The Santo Niño or the Holy Child is one of the most popular Catholic religious devotions in the Philippines and among the Filipino diaspora scattered all over the world. The devotion is represented by a revered statue—the 12-inch wooden figure of Jesus Christ as a little boy, formally dressed in a resplendent red robe filigreed with golden floral-and-leaf patterns. Despite its diminutive size, the statue exudes opulence. It is adorned with jewelry, consisting of a chain of old Spanish coins; a fleece garnished with emeralds, rubies, and diamonds, as well as a golden ram pendant said to have been a gift from the Spanish monarch Charles III. More diamonds, 44 in all, complete the image's 22-carat gold crown, which was given by then Philippine first lady Imelda Marcos in honor of the country's quadricentennial year of Catholicism. The Santo Niño's right hand is raised in imitation of a pontiff's blessing, and slightly below the extended middle and index fingers stands a golden scepter, also encrusted with jewelry. The image's left hand holds a golden globe on top of which is a cross overlaid with pearls.

The luster of the image's vestments is in contrast to its dark facial features. Its black, curly hair frames a puce face with ebony eyes and long, jet-black eyelashes and eyebrows. The face is definitely that of a boy before the age of five, impish-looking, with chubby cheeks, a narrow, high nose, and a mischievous grin. It does not at all resemble the facial characteristics of its millions of Filipino devotees.

Its dissimilarity can be explained by its origins. The image was brought to the island of Cebu in the central Philippines by Portuguese explorer Ferdinand Magellan, who led a Spanish-funded expedition to find a new commercial route to the Spice Islands in 1519. It is typical of Baroque art, carved in Flanders, Belgium, which was a Spanish territory at that time. When Magellan's expedition anchored in Cebu in 1521, they encountered the indigenes, led by their chieftain Humabon and his wife Humamay. Historians do not give a reason for the surprising turn of events a week after the encounter, but subsequent to the initial hostility from both sides Humabon and Humamay agreed to be baptized, together with about 800 of their followers. Magellan, through the Italian explorer and scholar Pigafetta, gave Humamay the image of the Santo Niño at her baptism. It is believed that Humamay treated the image as a local deity.

Historical traces of the Santo Niño image disappeared after the death of Magellan at the hands of Lapu-Lapu, Humabon's rival chieftain, and the return to Spain of the few remaining expeditionary forces that included Pigafetta. However, the image would reappear 44 years later in 1565 when a new Spanish expedition headed by Miguel Lopez de Legazpi returned to Cebu and set fire to a village to disperse the natives. A Spanish sailor found the Santo Niño statue in one of the huts, inside a pine box and covered by a white cloth, similar to the way in which the indigenes protected their own animist figures.

Historians have surmised that after Magellan's death, the Cebuanos reverted back to their animist practices and incorporated the image into their belief system. As proof, they point to the actions of the villagers upon their return to their settlement. Having discovered the loss of the image, the indigenes formed a representation to the Spanish officials to offer gold and provisions in exchange for the icon. The natives feared that the image's disappearance from their midst would mean a poor harvest and other calamities. They also asserted that the figure did not come from Magellan but had been in their possession since time immemorial.

The Spanish, for their part, regarded the finding as a miracle, prompting Legazpi to decree an annual celebration honoring the Santo Niño. A church made of wood and cane was built to house the image. A fluvial parade involving the Spanish fleet and a procession with the participation of the natives installed the image in its new home, beginning the yearly ritual when the figure is paraded from its sanctuary to the place where it was found.

The festivities first took place on April 28 when the statue resurfaced. However, the date was moved to January when the Catholic Church declared the second Sunday after Epiphany the feast of the Holy Name of Jesus. Although the celebration still happens in January, it has been moved to the third Sunday of the month. The Santo Niño is now encased in glass and housed at the Basilica Minore del Santo Niño de Cebu, which was built on the original sanctuary site. Administered by the Augustinian order, the basilica is now a place of pilgrimage where hundreds of thousands of devotees converge to take part in the Sinulog, the annual observance of the feast of the Santo Niño, which is unrivaled in the Philippines in religious and secular pomp and pageantry.

During the Sinulog, the image is taken out of its glass case for a fluvial parade, where it is joined by a flotilla of boats and yachts that are lavishly decorated with flowers and bunting as helicopters shower it with petals, leaves, and confetti. From the wharf, the image is processed through the streets of Cebu, which are lined with pilgrims tossing flowers in its path amidst the beating of drums and the clapping of hands. After a high mass at the Pilgrim Center, an open-air, theater-like structure within the basilica compound, the baptism of the first native converts is reenacted. The event is followed by a winding afternoon procession through the narrow streets of Cebu until the image is returned to its case inside the basilica.

Continuously punctuating the festivities during the Sinulog are shouts of "*Pit Señor*" from the ocean of humanity that follows the regal image. The expression is short for "*Sangpit sa Señor*," a Cebuano phrase meaning "to call, ask, or plead to the king." Pilgrims believe that the Santo Niño figure is miraculous, and they call to it for healing and the granting of their petitions.

After a day of religious devotion, the celebration turns secular the next day when a grand parade takes over the streets, featuring dancing and revelry, accompanied by a trade and food fair, complete with rock bands and contests.

The Santo Niño's popularity can be attributed to its antiquity and longevity, a sign of its resilience and ability to withstand adversity, reflecting the lives of most Filipinos. However, believers point to the image's miraculous power as its main attraction. Stories of the Santo Niño saving the lives of fishermen caught in storms out at sea are passed on from one generation to the next. Students, job hunters, and the sick give testimonials on how the image has transformed their lives by granting their prayers. The Sinulog, from the Cebuano word *sulog* ("water current"), originally referred to a prayer dance of supplication.

Although Cebu is the unquestioned capital of the Santo Niño devotion, the religious practice has spread throughout Catholic Philippines. Churches all over the archipelago possess their own local version of the Santo Niño image, mostly replicas of the Cebu icon. However, the image in Tacloban, Leyte province, is said to be older than the one in Cebu, and the Santo Niño celebration in Aklan province called the Ati-Atihan rivals the Sinulog in popularity. During the Ati-Atihan, the people paint their faces black and dance in the streets to the hypnotic beat of drums and shouts of "*Hala bira*," loosely translated as "to perform something with gusto or force."

The Santo Niño devotion has circled the globe in the wake of Filipino migration. In the United States, the image can be found in Catholic churches with many Filipino American worshippers. These churches have also become the focus of festivities honoring the Santo Niño, such as picnics, dances, and parades sponsored by Cebuano associations on the third Sunday of January. Novenas to the Santo Niño are regularly scheduled, following the pattern set by the devotion in Cebu.

The city of San Francisco in California used to hold an annual Santo Niño festival and parade until the early 1980s. But the citywide event ceased after a series of lawsuits between competing Cebuano associations over the use of the name "Santo Niño de Cebu."

Other U.S. cities with notable Santo Niño devotions are Philadelphia and Tampa. The Augustinian order from Cebu gave the Old St. Augustine Church in Philadelphia an exact replica of the image of Santo Niño from the Basilica Minore. The replica has been permanently enshrined in the Philadelphia church, and a mass is held every Sunday for the devotees. The Filipino American community in Philadelphia holds their version of the Sinulog every third Sunday of January, but a much more elaborate celebration, called a "Summer Sinulog," is held every third Sunday of August, close to the feast of St. Augustine.

The Filipino American community built a shrine to the Santo Niño at St. Paul's Catholic Church in Tampa, Florida, in 2010. One of its biggest funders claims to have been physically healed by the Santo Niño after having suffered a stroke. The shrine was a culmination of 10 years of sustained devotion and fundraising by the community. As a display of the devotion's popularity and the importance of the shrine, every third Sunday in January Filipino Americans from all over the United States gather for a Sinulog celebration at St. Paul's. Participants bring their own Santo Niño images, holding them high over their heads during the procession, and shout "*Pit Señor*." Scholars of transnationalism and migration have commented that the sustained display of devotion and Filipino cultural forms surrounding the image of the Santo Niño de Cebu expresses more than just religiosity, but a diasporic consciousness connecting the homeland with transnational settlement.

Ofelia O. Villero

See also: Essays: Catholics; *Entries:* Aglipay, Gregorio; El Shaddai; Filipino Protestants

Further Reading

Bautista, Julius J. *Figuring Catholicism: An Ethnohistory of the Santo Niño de Cebu.* Quezon City, Philippines: Ateneo de Manila University Press, 2010.

Florendo, Abe, ed. *The Holy Child Devotion in the Philippines.* Manila, Philippines: Congregacion del Santisimo Nombre del Niño Jesus, 2001.

Tondo, Josefina Socorro Flores. "Popular Religiosity and the Transnational Journey: Inscribing Filipino Identity in the Santo Niño Fiesta in New Zealand." *Asia Pacific Journal of Anthropology* 11, nos. 3/4 (September–December 2010): 219–44.

Satsang

Satsang, which literally means "being in association with truth," is a modern philosophical concept derived essentially from ancient Hindu philosophy. This philosophy can be broadly divided into two categories: Advaita philosophy (nondualism)

Priest Gurdeep Singh of Nanaksar Gurdwara temple in Brampton, Ontario. The Nanaksar Satsang Sabha of Ontario has been fighting immigration for three years to keep Priest Gurdeep in their Brampton congregation. (Carlos Osorio/Toronto Star/Getty Images)

and Dvaita philosophy (dualism). The former claims that there is only one Truth /Reality that is absolute, known as Brahman, and the multiple factors that seem to exist are just illusion or mere reflection, or perceptions of the Brahman, the absolute source of all beings. In other words, the Creator is absolute and real, and creation is only illusion, as it is only the reflection of the Creator that is limited and prone to one's perception, and thus unreal.

Adi Sancaracharya (780–820 CE) developed a systematic Advaita philosophy gleaning thoughts and interpretations from preceding Hindu philosophers. Advaita philosophy upholds a view that there is essential oneness between the source of creation (Brahman) and the creation

(self) itself, because there is only one absolute existence as Brahman (the source of all).

Largely inspired by Advaita philosophy, Ramana Maharshi (1879–1950 CE) reinterpreted Advaita philosophy as *satsang* philosophy, which is also described as neo-Advaita. Ramana Maharshi claimed that he had experienced Enlightenment or awakening through *satsang* (being in association with truth), a state in which there is absolute lack of self-awareness. According to *satsang* teachings, enlightenment can be experienced and attained by anyone through spiritual seeking and discipline. The students/disciples/followers of *satsang* philosophy help educate and bring awareness to people and encourage them to experience *satsang*, which is a way to achieve absolute liberation.

Eastern religion began to slowly achieve prominence in the West when the scriptures and religious literature were translated into English at the end of the 18th century. By the 19th century Eastern philosophy had become influential in the West, and in 1893, Swami Vivekananda (1863–1902) founded the first Hindu organization.

There are several branches/denominations of *satsangs* in the United States: Ramana satsangs, Shiv Yog satsangs, Satsang with Mooji, Radha Soami Satsang Beas, and multiple independent *satsang* centers containing members of both Eastern and Western origin. Brat Lal, a Radha Soami *guru*, first visited the United States, followed by Ram of Peepal Mandi. In 1911, Data Dayal went on an international tour and visited the United States. Bhagat Singh Thind, an offshoot *guru* of Radha Soami Satsang Beas, settled in America and preached a mixture of Sant Mat, Radha Soami, Sikh, and Occult doctrines. He was modestly successful in his venture and gathered several hundred disciples. Bhagat Singh Thind also wrote a number of books with Radha Soami-related themes, including his most famous treatise, *Radiant Road to Reality*. Kirpal Singh (1894–1974), founder of Ruhani Satsang, Sawan Singh of Radha Soami Satsang Beas, and Paul Twitchell in Washington, D.C. also have established several *satsang* centers and gathered multiple disciples who continue to carry on the mission of *satsang*.

Understanding *Satsang*

Satsang, like any new philosophical concept, not only carries its original conceptual meaning, but also misconceptions. Being aware of this fact, teachers of *satsang* continue to offer clarifications of what *satsang* means, and what it is not. *Satsang* means something different in diverse contexts when it is used in the postmodern era. It is used to mean a concept, a state of mind, a sanctuary, a meeting place, and a religious institution or association. However, *satsang* originally described a spiritual experience rather than a concept or philosophy, or an association.

Satsang believers claim that there is only one truth, and the rest of what we see and perceive is mere illusion. According to *satsang* philosophy, a perceiver is often influenced by several factors that obstruct him or her from being able to perceive "the truth." However, self-denial and disassociation with other factors of life help a person to attain *satsang*, which brings enlightenment and awakening. *Satsang* teachings emphasize that *satsang* is an experience rather than knowledge.

Satsang is mostly explained in conceptual or other dimensional terms. It is a state of mind in complete connection with truth, where external factors and distractions are shunned through the practice of meditation. *Satsang* is connected to and in communication with one's soul, where one completely loses association with anything but the soul. It is believed that during *satsang* one goes into a state of nonexistence and complete annihilation of self, which is a quintessential characteristic of *satsang* experience. However, *satsang* is a temporary state of being, which could last depending on one's spiritual discipline and seeking. It is normal that the awakened person comes back to a normal state of being where she or he will begin to feel herself or himself or the surroundings. It is also believed that those who experience *satsang* will be in an elevated state spiritually, emotionally, and morally, and they will be the seekers of higher objectives than worldly and material things. People who experience *satsang* will strive to recapture it repeatedly so that they may become more and more spiritually awakened. People seeking *satsang* are supposedly those who have no interest in or regard for the self as they are on the verge of denying it. Therefore *satsang* philosophy advocates that *satsang* is a true solution to the world's problems, which are largely the result of selfishness and materialism. *Satsang* is not necessarily a temporary state if the seekers wish to spend all their time in it.

Misconceptions

Satsang teachers clarify that *satsang* sanctuaries are only the venues that create the atmosphere to experience *satsang*. They define that *satsang* is not a social institution or a spiritual association or a religious group or a social club within Hinduism; rather it is a state of mind that each individual can experience on her or his own, with intentional spiritual seeking to attain *satsang*, or to be in communion with truth or one's soul irrespective of place and time. However, a place that is commonly called *satsang* is where mood and attitude are created through spiritual guidance to help an individual to attain the *satsang* state of being.

Satsang is essentially being, not learning. It is neither not taught nor learned. It is not a skill or a talent, but an inward aspiration for associating with truth. According to *satsang* this association happens when a person enters into complete blankness without any influence or memory or distraction from external factors or internal data. It is a state where one goes into complete amnesia of what the world has offered and enters into a new state where nothing exists but the truth and the soul. This is the ideal state of *satsang* or enlightenment. *Satsang* is giving up everything, such as beliefs, notions, intentions, desires, and illusions, which is the secret of freedom. *Satsang* is complete detachment to self as in body and other and associating with soul, which is real and absolute, untouched and unpolluted by any external factors such as emotions or knowledge. This absolute truth is also known as soul, conscience, and the Truth as in "*Sat*."

Satsang as a Movement

The *satsang* philosophy adopted by many disciples has become a movement and gained popularity mostly in the West through the students and followers of Ramana Maharshi. Although *satsang* is essentially not an institution or organization, it represents an institution because of the organized structure and institutional elements that are associated with it. *Satsang* keeps a general structure that is common among many individual centers that carry the title *Satsang* even though they are not necessarily connected institutionally. However, there is a connection through the disciples and followers and their *gurus* as they all carry the same mission of *satsang* philosophy. Therefore in popular culture *satsang* not only comes across in philosophical or conceptual terms but also in structural terms such as building or organization. *Satsang* is a meeting place where questions and answers and time spent with a *satguru*—a teacher of truth—can occur. *Satsang* is deemed a place for learning about Truth from a *satguru* (a teacher of Truth who has often experienced *satsang*, a teacher who helps people to attain *satsang*). *Satsang* is also perceived as a movement, especially in the West, that leads people to be enlightened and awakened.

Satgurus, who advance it as a mission, believe *satsang* is the path to peace. Thus there are *satgurus* such as Vasant (male, Norway), Vartmann (male, Australia), Susanna (female, Sweden), Shantimayi (female, United States), Rahasya (male, Germany), Arjuna (male, United States), Anamika (female, Israel), and Gopalji (male, Holland). Rajaneesh (the founder of the Osho movement who died in 1990), Poonjaji (1910–1997), a disciple of Ramana Maharshi (1879–1950), Paul Brunton, Andrew Cohen, Russell Williams, and Karl Renz have given prominence to the enlightenment movement both in the East and the West. Today the Shivyog *satsangs* are established across North America in approximately 41 locations. Similarly Radhasoami Satsang Beas are established in all other Western countries.

Satsang is a movement because its followers intentionally and conscientiously use media and other commercial means to reach the people with the message. Although *satsang* is supposed to be an independent and individualistic experience, there are instances when the disciples claim that they have experienced spiritual transmission of enlightenment from their *guru*. In other words, a *satguru* can induce enlightenment in a disciple.

General Structure of Satsang: A Meeting Place

Satsang is a definite meeting place and a time when a group of people gather to engage in spiritual conversation with a *satguru*, who usually gives a short speech and then opens for questions. *Satsangs* are popular in the West mainly because of the affirmation and structured teaching that it offers to the people in diaspora who experience displacement and therefore seek identity. *Satsang*, which was originally introduced as a concept alone, has become an institution or structural organization, or a *satsang* network in the West. Now *satsang* also typically involves certain spiritually motivating activities such as meditation, chanting, a short discourse, reading and reflecting on scriptures and their interpretations. *Satsang* does not dwell much on religion per se, but emphasizes a way to enlightenment. Thus *satsang* is a spiritual concept that has taken the shape of a movement spreading across India and in other parts of the world, East and West. *Satsangs* are conducted in different forms as informative *satsangs*, guidance *satsangs*, *bhav satsangs* to increase spiritual emotion. *Satsangs* follow a certain order; however, much of what is discussed are matters of soul rather than religious or institutional matters. The topics that are discussed in each *satsang* vary based on the *satguru* who teaches in a particular *satsang*. Some of the topics that *satsangs* discuss could include "Embody your intelligence, voice, love, power, and gender"; "Embody the radiance, warmth and stillness of your authentic self"; "Cultivate compassion; realize radical aliveness; experience your wholeness," which are not necessarily philosophical but spiritual in content. Thus the enlightenment that *satsang* advocates is not only a one-time phenomenon but a process of spiritual growth that leads to ultimate enlightenment.

Surekha Nelavala

See also: Entries: Han; Hindu Canon; *Kava*

Further Reading

Brunton, Paul. *A Search in Secret India.* London: Rider, 1972.

Cohen, Andrew. *Autobiography of an Awakening.* Corte Madera, CA: Moksha Press, 1992.

Godman, David, ed. *The Fire of Freedom: Satsang with Papaji.* Lucknow, India: Avadhuta Foundation, 2007.

Jaxon-Bear, Eli, ed. *Wake Up and Roar: Satsang with H. W. L. Poonja.* Vol I. Novato, CA: The Gangagi Foundation, 1992.

Jaxon-Bear, Eli, ed. *Wake Up and Roar: Satsang with H. W. L. Poonja.* Vol II. Novato, CA: The Gangagi Foundation, 1993.

Juergensmeyer, Mark. *Radhasoami Reality: The Logic of a Modern Faith.* Princeton, NJ: Princeton University Press, 1991.

Lane, David C. *The Radhasoami Tradition.* New York: Garland, 1992.

Sadguru. *Don't Polish Your Ignorance . . . It May Shine.* Mumbai: Jaico, 2011.

Seichō no Ie (SNI)

Established by Taniguchi Masaharu in 1930, Seichō no Ie (SNI) is a movement unaffiliated with any traditional faith tradition. While it maintains offices around the globe, outside of Japan its most significant presence is in Brazil. The organization's U.S. headquarters are in Gardena, California. SNI teaches that the present world of suffering as perceived by the five senses is an illusion. However, humans, as children of the divine, may learn to perceive the true reality, or *jissō*, a world of harmony and peace that eternally exists. The primary text of SNI is *Seimei no Jissō*, written by Taniguchi, and the central practice is a particular kind of mediation, *shinsokan*.

History

Seichō no Ie (lit. "house of growth," glossed on one of the organization's websites as "the home of infinite life, wisdom and abundance") was founded in 1930 by Masaharu Taniguchi (1893–1985). At first it functioned as a publishing company for the monthly magazine *Seicho-no-Ie* as well as Taniguchi's voluminous writings, a blend of Buddhist, Christian, and Shintō elements that also drew on Western philosophical thought. Before the establishment of the organization, Taniguchi had been active in publication work and intellectual leadership in the Omotokyō, a faith tradition founded by Deguchi Nao (1836–1918). Taniguchi claimed to have received a divine revelation on December 3, 1928, through which he learned that the present world of suffering as perceived by the five senses is an illusion. However, humans, as children of the divine, may learn to perceive the true reality behind this illusion, a world of harmony and peace that eternally exists. According to Taniguchi, rather than being a new religion, SNI was beyond religion, the essence that other religions pointed to. At first followers were allowed to continue in the faith tradition that they had been part of, but eventually a ritual system unique to SNI developed.

During the war Taniguchi was a strong advocate for emperor worship and SNI was active in supporting the wartime effort. While he was censored for a time after the war, Taniguchi was active again from the 1950s. (For more on Taniguchi and SNI during the prewar and wartime periods see Reichl, 2011, 74–77). After the death of Taniguchi in 1985, his son-in-law Seichō Taniguchi assumed leadership and attempted to distance SNI from its wartime associations and emphasize pro-peace activities. Recently there has also been an increased focus on environmental issues, such as the "Zero Carbon" movement, which aims to neutralize the carbon footprint of SNI activities. This concern with the environment has continued under Taniguchi Masanobu, the son of Taniguchi Seichō, the current leader since 2008.

It was during the interwar years that SNI came to America, arriving in Hawai'i in the 1930s. The group was given a special dispensation from 1943 to the end of the war, allowing it not only to remain active but to grow as it provided support to the families of the members of the Japanese American battalion who looked to it to provide memorial services and prayers for their relatives killed in battle. After the war, growth in the United States slowed and the organization has always been made up of largely Japanese Americans. Current membership numbers are unavailable but as of 1997 membership was about 2,500

with women constituting 60 percent. The organization is aware that its close ties to Japanese culture may inhibit growth in the United States. Such an awareness is evident in a May 2008 mailing from Reverend Abe Tetsuya, acting chief of SNI Hawai'i Missionary Area, to members in Hilo, Hawai'i, that encourages changing ritual activities that have too strong an association with Japanese culture, such as bowing. At the same time, SNI faces resistance to such changes among members who prefer the traditional practices, requiring careful negotiation as the organization moves forward.

Beliefs and Practices

SNI asserts three basic teachings. First is that the "True Image" (terminology used on the organization's English website) or *jissō* is the real world, a world created by an absolute deity and that exists in harmony with this deity. The phenomenal world that we perceive through our senses may distort this True Image. Second, all phenomena are manifestations of the mind, including words and actions. Mind is flexible and may either perceive a negative, distorted world, or be a conduit for aligning the perceived world with the True Image. Third, all faith and religious systems are manifestations of the True Image.

Drawing especially on Buddhist and Christian notions (although not necessarily representing these accurately), SNI teaches that since the absolute deity is only good, it could not create sin and therefore sin is an illusion. The sin of humans is to even conceive of sin. This principle is extended to deny any negative thing in practice, such as sickness, enemies, or death, recognizing that these do not exist. Indeed, part of SNI's attraction may be found in its attempt to respond to a myriad of practical, daily issues relevant for all people, ranging from physical and emotional problems to financial and social ones. Salvation from such illusory problems is recognizing one's connection to the divine and the recovery of one's innate freedom and true nature in the immediate world. SNI does not deny an afterlife, but the emphasis is on the possibility of a perfect world in the here and now through the unlimited potential each human contains. SNI also suggests that overcoming differences in faith traditions is only possible by recognizing the absolute divinity that is only partially represented by other faiths.

The primary text of SNI is *Seimei no Jissō* (*The Truth of Life*), written by Taniguchi Masaharu and made up of 40 volumes. Also of importance are four holy *Sūtras* based on purported revelations to Taniguchi, *Prayerful Song to Praise and Bless the Holy Missioners, Nectarean Shower of Holy Doctrines, Song of the Angel*, and *For Spiritual Healing*. In addition to the sacred texts, SNI also publishes periodicals including the monthly *Truth of Life* in English.

The central practice of SNI is a particular kind of mediation, *shinsokan*. Also allegedly revealed directly to Taniguchi, the practice aims to instill an intuitive knowledge that one is a true child of the absolute deity and therefore perfect. It entails five elements: (1) a formal posture or *seiza*, which aligns one with cosmic forces; (2) breathing done through *gasshō*, a unique hand position held in front of the face; (3) invocation, acknowledging oneself as a child of absolute deity, leaving the world of senses, and entering the realm of *jissō*; (4) words of meditation made up of repeating the divine attributes such as infinite wisdom, love, life, abundance, joy, and harmony; and (5) a final affirmation. Besides *shinsokan* there are also communal services, which include reciting a part of the sacred writings, a message based on the *Seimei no Jissō*, and testimonies by adherents regarding the personal efficacy of SNI. Finally, symbolic imagery is largely absent from SNI since various figures and imagery in different faith traditions are understood to exhibit only a partial truth of *jissō*. However, SNI does employ a principal image made up of Chinese characters representing a variant writing of *jissō*, which is meant to point to the one True Image behind every other sacred image.

Peter L. Doebler

Further Reading

Asai, Yumiko, and Christopher A. Reichl. "Generational Patterns in Code-Switching and Mixing among the Members of a Japanese New Religion in Hawai'i." *The Journal of Intercultural Studies* 29 (2002): 1–14.

Chapel, Gage W. "Synthesizing Eastern and Western Religious Traditions: The Rhetoric of Japan's Seicho-No-Ie." *Journal of Communication and Religion* 12, no. 1 (1989): 14–21.

Ellwood, Robert S., Jr. *The Eagle and the Rising Sun: Americans and the New Religions of Japan.* Philadelphia: Westminster Press, 1974.

Reader, Ian, Esben Andreasen, and Finn Stefánsson, eds. *Japanese Religions: Past and Present.* Honolulu: University of Hawai'i Press, 1993.

Reichl, Christopher Albert. "The Globalization of a Japanese New Religion: Ethnohistory of Seichō no Ie." *Japanese Religions* 36, nos. 1–2 (2011): 67–82.

Reichl, Christopher Albert. "Ethnic Okinawan Interpretation of Seichō no Ie: The Lineal Descendant of Ijun at Home and Overseas." *Japanese Society* 3 (1998/99): 120–138.

Stalker, Nancy K. *Prophet Motive: Deguchi Onisaburō, Oomoto, and the Rise of New Religions in Imperial Japan.* Hononlulu: University of Hawai'i Press, 2008.

Yanagawa, Kei'ichi, ed. *Japanese Religions in California: A Report on Research Within and Without the Japanese-American Community.* Tokyo: Department of Religious Studies, University of Tokyo, 1983.

Sekai Kyūsei-kyō Izunome (Church of World Messianity)

Sekai Kyūsei-kyō Izunome (hereafter Izunome), also known as the Church of World Messianity, is one of the so-called New Japanese Religions that emerged in the first half of the 20th century. Izunome aims to create a paradise on earth by resolving spiritual, physical, psychological, and social problems through different purification practices. The organization came to the United States in the 1950s and continues to maintain a modest presence with approximately 2,700 members in North America. This entry will briefly survey the beliefs and practices of Izunome followed by a sketch of its general history.

Beliefs and Practices

Izunome believes that humans have departed from a natural law that underlies all things. Departing from this law, or God's will, has led to all sorts of physical, psychological, social, and environmental problems, problems that threaten humans with destruction. The goal of Izunome is to reverse these problems and create an ideal world of peace and prosperity; in short, to make paradise on earth. This fundamental worldview is based on the belief that the founder of Izunome, Okada Mokichi (1882–1955), received a special revelation showing him how to create this change, a revelation he then passed on by establishing Izunome. Mokichi is referred to as *Meishu-sama* (enlightened spiritual leader) and even after his death he is seen as a "supreme heavenly intercessor."

The primary object of worship in Izunome is Sōzō Sushin, the God of Creation, who wills that paradise be built on this earth so that mankind can follow the will of God. Izunome is thus primarily an eschatological belief system, heavily emphasizing a chronological view of history that is going through drastic change from a bad past to a better future.

In order to accomplish this goal of creating a true, good, and beautiful paradise for humans in harmony with God's will, what is required is purification (*jōka*). The different practices of Izunome serve this goal of purification. The main practice is *jōrei* ("purification of soul"), a ritual of channeling light for spiritual and physical healing. The Izunome website describes *jōrei* as a "divine light or love light from God that purifies the spiritual body by dispelling the clouds within," thereby restoring the receiver to "their original state, that of a true child of God." Izunome also claims that *jōrei* creates physical, psychological, and social well-being. An essential part of making *jōrei* effective is wearing an *ohikari*, "a golden medal contained in a small bag worn by the member around the neck like a pendant" that serves to transmit the divine light. So while physical health is one of the benefits claimed by Izunome, it is important to recognize that such a benefit is based on spiritual purification.

Another essential purification practice is installing an ancestral altar in one's house, a *mitamaya* ("Sacred Spirit House"). The purpose of this is to appease or purify evil ancestral spirits who are seen as causes of misfortune.

Other important purification practices include nutrition and art, and these are supported by established organizations associated with Izunome. Nature farming—a kind of organic farming practice that does not use fertilizers—emphasizes the close connection between physical and spiritual well-being and the need to follow Natural Law. Izunome also sees both natural and artistic beauty as important ways humans may attune themselves to Natural Law. Specific activities include a unique school of Japanese flower arrangement called *Sangetsu*, two art museums—the Hakone Museum of Art in Hakone, Japan, and the MOA Museum of Art in Atami, Japan—and several sacred gardens, which serve as "models of the paradise of earth." These practices serve as a means to cultivate physical, psychological, social, and spiritual well-being for an individual and this in turn aids the larger goal of universal transformation.

Finally, it is important to note that Izunome is egalitarian. Anyone who receives *jōrei* may pass it on to others; the activity is not restricted to a hierarchical elite.

Likewise, Izunome takes a broad ecumenical perspective, generally accepting the truth of all religions.

History

Okada Mokichi started Izunome on January 1, 1935. In his youth he suffered from ill health, endured the deaths of his wife and children, and experienced financial ruin from the global economic depression and the great Kanto earthquake. Such hardships constitute the background of his religious experience and are significant for understanding Izunome's emphasis on health and prosperity. Before founding Izunome, Okada was a member of the spiritual organization Ōmoto-kyō, which also practices a form of healing by transmitting light through the hand. In 1926, Okada claimed to have received a divine revelation through which he learned both about the true nature of things as well as his unique role in bringing paradise to earth.

Okada strongly believed in the efficacy of beauty in purifying the individual and creating change. He collected art and established the Hakone Museum of Art in 1952. As a result of his legacy, the MOA Museum of Art was established in 1982. Also, the *Sangetsu* school of flower arrangement was established in 1972 based on his practice.

Izunome came to the United States in February 1953 when two missionaries came to Hawai'i and then to Los Angeles in 1954. The Los Angeles location has been the most successful. Within the United States, the group has attracted both Japanese Americans and Caucasians, particularly females over the age of 40. Yutaka

Tisdall-Yamada suggests that Messianity has functioned for Japanese-descendent members "primarily as a social center for an ethnic community" while Caucasian members often come for its specific religious content. The current headquarters are in Hackensack, New Jersey, and Izunome claims the current North American membership is around 2,700. Thus Izunome has not found the same kind of success in the United States as it has in Brazil or Thailand where it claims 410,000 and 660,000 members, respectively.

Peter L. Doebler

Further Reading

Clarke, Peter B. "Modern Japanese Millenarian Movements: Their Changing Perception of Japan's Global Mission with Special Reference to the Church of World Messianity in Brazil." In Peter B. Clarke, ed. *Japanese New Religions in Global Perspective.* London: Routledge, 2000, pp. 129–181.

Matsuoka, Hideaki. *Japanese Prayer Below the Equator: How Brazilians Believe in the Church of World Messianity.* Lanham, MD: Lexington Books, 2007.

Sekai Kyūsei-kyō Izunome. "Asia, Oceania." http://www.izunome.jp/en/border/asia/. Accessed February 25, 2014.

Tisdall-Yamada, Yutaka. "The Symbolic Image of Ancestors in the Church of World Messianity." *Japanese Journal of Religious Studies* 18/2–3 (1991): 151–64.

Selma (California) Japanese Mission Church

Selma Japanese Mission Church (1917–2011) was a unique 94-year experiment in Buddhist-Christian interfaith cooperation and sharing among the farming community of Selma, California. Much of the initial motivation and detail for this experiment has been lost and must be extrapolated from the recollections of interviewees who recalled the memories of their predecessors, as well as from oblique references found in scattered documents. The following narrative sketches the shared experiences and vision of one interfaith community.

A Shared Past

Japanese immigrants began settling in California's San Joaquin (Central) Valley during the early 1900s, in response to the need for agricultural laborers. These hardworking immigrants quickly established their own farms and businesses, including a *Nihonmachi* (Japanese business district) on the south side of the town of Selma. As the Japanese community grew, so did their need to share community resources. Selma Issei (first-generation Japanese) were deeply committed to a single group serving the Japanese community. Upon arriving in town, new Japanese immigrants, regardless of religion, would be visited by representatives of the settled Japanese community, Buddhist and Christian, and asked to lend financial support. After a decade of fundraising, sufficient donations were assembled to purchase a Japanese community center in Selma.

In 1916, the Selma Japanese community established a committee of Buddhist and Christian Japanese residents to locate and secure a suitable venue for a community center that could be used for religious and cultural events. They selected the former Christian Church of Selma on Whitson

Street between Second and Third Streets. The building and property were purchased for $400. Full conveyance of the property was transferred on February 5, 1917, to six U.S.-born Nisei (second generation) minors, whose Japanese-born parents were prohibited from owning land. The original owners were children from both Buddhist and Christian families.

In 1938 the community group incorporated with the state of California as the not-for-profit Selma Japanese Mission Church. Due to discrimination and to appear as innocuous as possible, Japanese Buddhists in the United States regularly adopted names and practices that conformed to mainstream religious practices and perceptions. The use of the expression "church" (from the Greek *kuriakos* meaning "belonging to the Lord," which designated a Christian place of worship) was one such adjustment. "Church" is not synonymous with *bukkyōkai* (literally, Buddhist association), which is the proper expression for a Buddhist temple. The Selma Japanese Mission "Church" was neither a Christian nor a Buddhist organization, rather, it was a nonreligious community group founded by Japanese immigrants. Within the organization, however, were two religious fellowships: one for local Japanese Buddhists and one for local Japanese Christians.

The Selma Japanese Mission Church's building remained unused and vacant for the duration of World War II while persons of Japanese ancestry, Buddhist and Christians alike, were forcibly sent to relocation camps. The Selma Japanese Mission Church reopened in 1946 when members from both the Christian and Buddhist fellowships returned home. The first religious programs each fellowship held were religious classes for their children.

In 1954, the church sold the property to Friis Hansen and Company. Proceeds from the sale, along with donations from the membership, were used to purchase a two-and-a-half-acre parcel at 2415 Floral Avenue and to erect a new facility. Construction began on a new, larger facility in April 1955 across from the cemetery. The new building was dedicated on February 11, 1956. During the ensuing years, membership declined as founders of the Selma Japanese Mission Church passed away and their descendants left local farms and settled elsewhere—often moving out of agricultural work. In 2011 the building and land were sold to the Thomas-Robinson Funeral Home. The proceeds were divided by the number of surviving members, to be distributed directly to religious nonprofits. Among the Buddhist fellowship members, most funds were given to the Fresno Betsuin Buddhist Temple and their membership was transferred to the temple in Fresno upon closure of the Selma Japanese Mission Church. Within the Selma Christian fellowship, many members chose to donate their portion of the proceeds to the United Japanese Christian Church of Clovis in gratitude for years of providing clergy support, while a few donated to local Protestant Christian churches where they now held membership.

Sharing Spaces

Members of the Selma Japanese Mission Church shared resources, space, and experiences in unique ways. First and foremost the fellowships shared worship and religious education space. Members of the church were welcome to attend either or both Buddhist and Christian worship services and religious instruction classes for children, which were held independently on different days of the week.

Evening worship services were conducted by Fresno clergy from the Buddhist temple and the Japanese-member Christ United Methodist Church (which merged with the Japanese Congregational Church in 1990 to become the United Japanese Christian Church of Clovis). After both worship services, held on different nights of the week, family and friends remained for fellowship and a potluck meal.

Memorial services for members of the Selma Japanese Mission Church, whether a member of the Buddhist or Christian fellowship, featured a special arrangement. Both fellowships would offer a traditional memorial service led by their clergy, one after another. At Buddhist memorial services members from the Selma Christian Fellowship would represent the Christian community during the Buddhist incense offering ritual. Between services the altars were changed. Following the last service everyone enjoyed a shared communal meal.

The Selma Japanese Mission Church on Whitson Street was the venue for the local chapter of the Young Buddhists of America, the Selma Buddhist Club, and the Selma Women's Association, which began in 1924 as the Bisaka Club, to meet and to host events. Clergy from the Fresno temple provided worship leadership and support for Buddhist fellowship members.

In 1929, Japanese youth from Selma First Methodist Church, supported by Edith Tsuruda of the national Methodist Church's Board of Missions and Lola Brown of the Selma Methodist Church, organized a Japanese Christian fellowship in Selma for Protestant Christian Japanese living in the area who had been attending churches further away. Clergy from Fresno's Christ United Methodist church provided worship leadership, Bible study, and pastoral care; the Selma Methodist Church and Selma Baptist Church assisted with Sunday School teachers and support for youth groups. The Selma Fellowship participated in regional Methodist events such as the Fresno Japanese Methodist Epworth League. In January 1941, Christ Methodist Church started the Fresno Nisei Church held on Sunday evenings. Youth would gather in different locations in the greater Fresno area. On the third Sundays they met in Selma.

After the attack on Pearl Harbor both fellowships ceased meeting. Programming at the church for both the Buddhist and Christian communities was reactivated in the summer of 1946. After World War II, a joint Buddhist-Christian Memorial Day Service was held annually in Selma, a still common practice among Japanese-Americans nationwide. The interfaith ritual eulogized the local Christian and Buddhist Japanese American servicemen who died during the Second World War. In later years the annual service honored veterans, deceased members of the military and their relatives, and all ancestors. Memorial plaques honoring deceased servicemen were placed on the walls of the church.

The facility on Floral Avenue was fully shared by members of the Selma Japanese Mission Church, Buddhist and Christian alike. The rectangular building included an entryway, a main hall with a stage, meeting rooms used for classes, a kitchen, and bathrooms. A Buddhist altar was permanently placed in the main hall; it was enclosed behind sliding doors when not in use. A portable altar with its attendant cross and candles would be carried in for Christian services. In 1956, a few months after moving into the new property, the Christian fellowship asked the board of the interfaith Selma Japanese Mission Church to purchase a cross, candleholders, offering plates, and a purple cloth to be used in their worship services, as well as during the annual interfaith Memorial Day Services. The request was approved by the multifaith board. Since its inception, the Selma Japanese Mission Church was a Japanese community group that pulled leadership from both the Christian and Buddhist fellowships.

Sharing Experiences

As was true in many Japanese immigrant communities, Christian and Buddhist children learned their ancestral language together. The Whitson Street facility hosted a *Nihongakko* (Japanese-language school) that drew students from Selma and beyond. The first students were transported to and from class in Yoshinhei Torii's horse-drawn buggy. The first graduating class in 1918 included 11 students. The school operated through 1941.

Nisei (second-generation Japanese) recall attending both Buddhist and Christian Sunday school classes, which were held weekly on Sundays. Childhood exposure to both religions created strong bonds between neighbors and led to interfaith marriages.

The church's annual springtime picnic, a highlight of the year for the local Japanese community, included fun and games for persons of all ages. The Selma Japanese Mission Church also sponsored a Tencho Setsu (Japanese Culture Festival) in November. And there were movie nights featuring Japanese films projected onto sheets in lieu of a projection screen. At these events and other cooperative events Christians and Buddhists worked side by side to plan and implement events. All funds raised were used for the church, the broad organization that hosted both the Buddhist and Christian fellowships. They understood themselves to be a Japanese community first, and Buddhist or Christian second.

Shared Vision

With declining membership in both the Buddhist and Christian fellowships, members questioned the future of the Selma Japanese Mission Church. In 2011 it was decided to sell the property and close the church. Members of the Buddhist fellowship moved their memberships to the Fresno Betsuin Buddhist Temple. Their Japanese altar was given to the temple. Members of the Christian fellowship chose to move their memberships to area congregations, most opting to join the United Japanese Christian Church in Clovis.

On March 16, 2014, during the United Japanese Christian Church's "Year of Heritage," an 81-inch-tall granite Japanese pagoda lantern located in the church's Japanese Garden and a shorter lantern located at the entrance to the church were dedicated to honor Selma's Japanese interfaith community. During the dedication service all attendees pledged their commitment to keep the story of this interfaith community alive as the youth presented surviving members with symbols of appreciation. One of the members recalled that this was a community "that got along just fine" and all hoped their multifaith experiment would be tried again.

Kathryn M. Schreiber

See also: Entries: Japanese American Christianity; Japanese American Religions; Japanese American Religious Federation (JARF); Japanese Evangelical Missionary Society (JEMS); Jikei Kai: Japanese Benevolent Society

Further Reading

Buddhist Churches of America, ed. *Buddhist Churches of America, 75 Year History, 1899–1974.* Vol. 1. Chicago: Nobart, 1974.

Fresno Buddhist Temple. "About Us." www .fresnobuddhisttemple.org. Accessed September 30, 2013.

Nakasone, Ronald Y. *School Prayer: A Buddhist Response.* San Francisco: Buddhist Churches of America, 1985.

United Japanese Christian Church. "History of the Selma Mission Church." In *The Focal Point.* Clovis, CA: United Japanese Christian Church, August 2012. Reprinted from *Fresno Betsuin Buddhist Temple (1901– 1986).* Fresno: Fresno Betsuin Buddhist Temple, 1986, pp. 94–95.

United Japanese Christian Church. "History of the UJCC: How We Got Here." www.ujcc life.com. Accessed September 30, 2013.

United Japanese Christian Church. "Selma Christian Fellowship: 1929–Present." In *This Is My Story, This Is "Our Song"; United Japanese Christian Church. 100th Anniversary of Christ United Methodist Church and 85th Anniversary of Japanese Congregational Church.* Clovis, CA: United Japanese Christian Church, 1993.

Waugh, Isami Anfuku, and Alex Yamato. "A History of Japanese Americans in California." In *Five Views: An Ethnic Historic Site Survey for California.* Sacramento: State of California, Resources Agency, Department of Parks and Recreation, Office of Historic Preservation, 1988, pp. 158–202.

Seventh-day Adventist Church

The Seventh-day Adventist (SDA) Church is a Protestant Christian denomination known for its emphasis on the Sabbath, Saturday worship, and the return of Christ. Whereas orthodox Christianity traditionally recognizes Sunday as the divinely ordered day of rest, this sect defines itself in part on restoration of Sabbath observance on the last—or "seventh day"—of the week, as defined in the Pentateuch (cf. Gn 2:2-3; Ex 20:8ff; Rv 1:10; Acts 20:7). Adventism arose from the Second Great Awakening, and more particularly the Millerite movement started by William Miller; Seventh-day Adventism was formally distinguished from other Adventist groups in 1863. This sect is the largest and most well known of several such Adventist communities that developed in New York State in the early to mid-19th century.

Miller in 1933 prophesied that Christ was to return on October 22, 1844, and when that did not happen (the "Great Disappointment"), the tenor of proclamation shifted away from date predictions to that of the date as being rather the beginning of a spiritual judgment that would later culminate in the Second Coming. Following that shift, Joseph Bates ("apostle of the Sabbath") then advocated Saturday worship, and the idea comprised the first issue of *The Present Truth* (now *The Adventist Review*) in 1849. Two other figures, James S. and wife Ellen G. White, were central to the group's formulation, as well as to Adventism today, since White was not only an early example of feminine leadership in a Protestant church, but her many prophecies and writings are still hotly debated. One impacting vision she claimed to have had was that of three angels evangelizing throughout the globe, which aided a change in the church's attention toward international missionary activity. In the 1860s, the church moved to Battle Creek, Michigan, and then in the late 20th century to Maryland (Silver Spring and later Takoma Park), where it is governed presently by the General Conference.

The "28 Fundamental Beliefs" form the doctrine for the church, adopted in 1980 (revised in 2005), though extending from an earlier genesis. The Holy Scriptures as the "infallible revelation of [God's] will" is the first of these ordinal tenets, and there are several others that are distinctive or defining:

- Six: "In six days the Lord 'made the heaven [sic] and the earth' and all living things upon the earth, and rested on that seventh day of that week."

- Eight describes the "Great Controversy" between Christ and Satan, which informs current reality and its strife, though the ultimate victory has been won by Jesus.

- Thirteen reveals the church's self-identification as "remnant" in an age of "widespread apostasy," driving the sense of mission.

Baptism is the formal entry into the church, conducted by immersion, and along with communion it comprises a common Reformational formulation of two sacraments. Adventists are Trinitarian (publically professed in the 1931 SDA *Yearbook* "Statement of Beliefs"), and many of the theological notions extend from Arminianism. They follow Protestant ideas about the Bible and justification by faith; however, while they are considered Evangelicals, they reject the notion of "once saved, always saved" (predestination). The Sabbath as Saturday is greatly emphasized, such that even Friday evenings may be used to prepare for it (e.g., Vespers), wherein most activities, save family events and nature outings, are to cease. Sunday worship is very much frowned upon, to the point of being viewed as "idolatry," and sometimes apocalyptic concerns are associated with such deviation—that is, that the state will at some point mandate Sunday worship. In the early years Adventists were "premillennial" in expecting Christ to come before a thousand-year reign, but the "Great Disappointment" restrained such belief in later years. Nevertheless, the understanding today is one of a millennium in which the righteous will be renewed in heaven for the first 1,000 years after Christ's return, after which they will return with the New Jerusalem. Health and conscious living also are a significant part of the religion's focus: a "holistic relationship with God, self, and others" is outlined in the Commandments—and often it extends to specific practices, like vegetarianism and kosher observance.

Saturday observances typically start with Sabbath school and are followed by a worship service along the lines of modern Evangelicalism, though perhaps more subdued in many aspects. The Lord's Supper, communion, is practiced four times each year, and included in each of these liturgies is a foot-washing ceremony (whereas Catholic churches perform such washings once a year on Holy Thursday).

Adventists tend to follow conservative religious values, where abortion is discouraged and only heterosexual marriages are conducted and recognized. They are active throughout the world in evangelization and missionization, including disaster relief efforts. Loma Linda University and Medical Center (California) is their largest and most well-known institution in North America. The international scope of the organization must help to foster a sense of appreciation for ethnic diversity where "people from all backgrounds or ethnicities are equal in Jesus." The structure of church governance follows a presbyterian polity, where each church is directed by elders, in addition to the overseeing General Conference. Pastors are usually male, though this standard has seen some change, however measured, in recent years.

The relationship to interfaith and ecumenical movements has often been tenuous at best, and even to this day the SDA Church does not readily embrace ecumenism. It is not part of the World Council of Churches, though it has participated as an observer. Since the gradual dogmatic integration of belief in the Trinity in the first part of the 20th century, relationships with other churches have significantly improved—a process that has garnered greater respect in Protestant circles.

During the 1950s, there was significant dialogue with other Evangelicals, fostering a greater sense of parity. These meetings were prompted especially by Donald Grey Barnhouse and Walter Martin's comprehensive study of Adventism, which formally saw the group not as against Christianity but rather "heterodox" in doctrine. In certain instances Catholicism and other Protestant churches have been associated with "Babylon" (cf. Rev 17). Founding member Ellen White has come under scrutiny for various reasons internally and externally, one of these being the accusation of plagiarism. Some of the church's conservative positions have resulted in countermovements, such as SDA Kinship International, a social network formed in 1976 for LGBT Adventists. In popular culture the most well-known splinter from SDA has been the infamous "Branch Davidian" group that operated out of a compound near Waco, Texas, where David Koresh (1959–1993) and scores of others died in the 1993 Waco siege when they were suspected of holding weapons illegally. Another group, the Seventh-Day Adventist Reform Movement, formed in Europe over controversies in World War I, but since 1949 has been headquartered in the United States (currently Roanoke, Virginia).

The North American Division of the church is the greatest sender of missionaries to foreign lands. In this division there are just over one million members, amidst a total population of about 345 million. Some churches combine worship and specific Asian American populations, especially in

Hawai'i and the San Francisco Bay Area, where there are individual Chinese, Japanese, and Filipino SDA churches. A quick review of the Adventist website reveals that Pacific Islanders and Asian Americans have embraced the faith. In the early 20th century, the children of Japanese immigrants in Hawai'i became Adventists and were thus able to attend medical school. The participation of Asian and Pacific Islander Americans in the tradition merits a more systematic study.

Adventism in general is recognized for its emphasis on health, and this facet is especially true of American Adventism, which boasts of introducing commercial cereal breakfasts to the U.S. diet through John Harvey Kellogg (1852–1943), a medical doctor who was an Adventist until his disfellowship in 1907. John Harvey's brother, William—also a Seventh-day Adventist—founded the Kellogg Company, known for its brand of cornflakes. More recently, Adventism has been featured in studies conducted by the U.S. National Institutes of Health—particularly in its successes in increasing longevity. Dan Buettner's series of books have also featured Adventist contributions to preventive medicine.

Larry M. Taylor

Further Reading

Aamodt, Terrie Dopp, et al. *Ellen Harmon White: American Prophet.* New York: Oxford University Press, 2014.

Bull, Malcom, and Keith Lockhart. *Seeking a Sanctuary: Seventh-Day Adventism and the American Dream.* Bloomington: Indiana University Press, 2007.

Carnes, Tony, and Fenggang Yang, eds. *Asian American Religions: The Making and Re-making of Borders and Boundaries.* New York University Press, 2004.

Fernandez, Gil G., and Far Eastern Division of Seventh-Day Adventists. *Light Dawns over Asia: Adventism's Story in the Far Eastern Division 1888–1988.* Silang, Cavite, Republic of the Philippines: Adventist International Institute of Advanced Studies, 1990.

Fraser, Gary E. *Diet, Life Expectancy, and Chronic Disease Studies of Seventh-Day Adventists and Other Vegetarians.* New York; Oxford: Oxford University Press, 2003.

Land, Gary. *Historical Dictionary of Seventh-Day Adventists.* Landham, MD: Scarecrow Press, 2005.

Shamanism, Modern

The terms "shamanism" and "shaman" trace their origin to the Evenki (Tungusic) *šamán*, an expression that was introduced to the West at various times in the 17th century by European travelers returning from Siberia. Some scholars have traced the expression to the Vedic *śram*, meaning "to heat oneself," which gave rise to *śramana* or ascetic (one who practices austerities), who consumes (purifies) mental and spiritual impurities through heat (fire). The expression filtered into Central Asia about 300 CE, and East Asia where it appears as *shamen* in China and *shamon* in Japan. Today, "shamanism" refers to a variety of practices found throughout the world in which the shaman enters into altered states of consciousness to interact with spirits or disembodied beings. This characterization can be traced to such scholars as Mircea Eliade (1907–1986), who defined shamanism to be a "technique of religious ecstasy"; and to Hori Ichirō (1910–1974), who offers the following

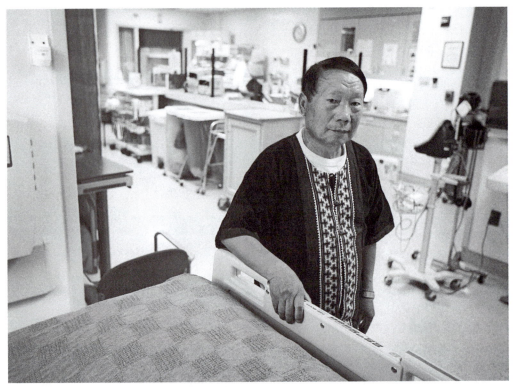

Fai Pha Chang, a Hmong shaman from Merced, stands in a hospital room at Merced's Mercy Medical Center, September 28, 2009. He is authorized to perform some minimal ceremonies at the hospital after going through classes on hospital policies. (Craig Kohlruss/Fresno Bee/MCT/Getty Images)

expanded definition. Shamanism is a "magical, mystical, often esoteric phenomenon that has taken shape around the shaman, a person of unusual personality who has mastered archaic techniques of ecstasy (trance, rapture, separation of the soul from the body, etc.)."

Beyond this focus on the personality and powers of the shaman, shamanism is a very complex spiritual culture with innumerable and continually evolving strands. Scholars have not arrived at a definitive definition. At the moment "shamanism" is a heuristic expression that guides researchers to identify an outlier tradition without a

standard canon and institution structure. This entry can only introduce some conceptual paradigms through which the shamanic tradition and experience may be understood by those outside its various traditions. We begin with a note on some of the presuppositions that support the shamanic worldview and proceed to sketch the personality of the shaman, its calling, training, and powers; we illustrate these points with select examples. We conclude with some thoughts of its persistence, place, and prospects in Asian and Pacific Islander communities in the United States. This entry relies heavily on the popular media and should be read in conjunction with the entry on the Hezhen (Nānai), which introduces a living Tungusic shamanic tradition.

Shamanic Worldview

Descriptions of the shamanic experience and its practices presuppose the presence of multiple worlds that are inhabited by innumerable ancestral and other disembodied beings. These worlds are not mutually exclusive, but interactive, and their boundaries are porous, making it possible for the shaman to communicate with and travel to different realms, and for denizens of these realms to intrude into our corporeal world. The existence of multiple worlds and the reality of disembodied beings are essential to the 86-minute 1988 anime fantasy film *My Neighbor Totoro* by Miyazaki Hayao. The narrative revolves around Satsuki and Mei, the two young daughters of Professor Kusakabe Tatsuo, and their adventures with friendly wood spirits in postwar rural Japan.

The film opens with the three moving into a long-abandoned house in the countryside to be near their mother, who is recuperating at a nearby hospital. Shortly after settling in, the younger Mei sees rabbit-like ears peeking through the overgrown weeds in the garden. Following the two small magical creatures though a tunnel-like passageway to the hollow of a great camphor tree (*kusunoki*) in the sacred precincts of a Shintō shrine, she meets and befriends their larger cohort, whom she identifies as Totoro. She drifts into sleep on top of her newfound friend. Shortly thereafter, Satsuki finds her sister fast asleep in a clearing; there is no Totoro. Mei is unable to convince Satsuki and her father that Totoro is indeed real. Later the three visit and pay homage to the spirit of the *kusonoki* tree, a gesture that tacitly affirms the presence of spirits in all existence—animate and inanimate, a fundamental reality of the Shintō tradition. Not to belittle Mei, her father tells the girls that Totoro is the "keeper of the forest," who appears when it wants to.

The film portrays the more magical and beneficent qualities of spirits, not their dark and malevolent aspects, which will be taken up later. The title of the film, *My Neighbor Totoro*, underscores the neighborly intimacy with beings of another world. Like good neighbors visiting each other's homes, Mei, Satsuki, and Totoro travel freely between each other's worlds. Mei moves from her world through a "tunnel-like passageway" to Totoro's world; Totoro for its part seems to just appear, not needing a passageway. The passageway, a common metaphor in the shamanic experience, takes the form of a bridge in *Aoi no Ue* and other *Noh* plays. The bridge also features prominently in Daoist funeral rituals, wherein by crossing the bridge, the spirit of the deceased is gently led to the world of the ancestors. Similarly, the ladder and raft are metaphors that crystallize the idea of a conduit between worlds that make possible "astral" travel and the feasibility of communication between worlds, exploited by the shaman.

The sacred forest is the magical dwelling place of tree and other spirits. The towering *kusunoki*, which the family honors, represents the three realms of reality and their continuum. Its roots dig deeply into the underworld, the trunk represents this world, and the branches reach the heavenly realms. (Chamorro culture associates the underworld with paradise; Ryūkyūan culture posits *nirai kanai* or "paradise" and the home of the ancestors that lies beyond the horizon beneath the sea.) The tree, a symbol of the shamanic universe, is a motif that appears in Buddhist iconography in the form of the *chattavali* or parasols that arises above the *aṇḍa* or hemispheric dome of the early *stūpa*; in East Asia the *stūpa* evolves into the pagoda that is topped by the *chattavali*. The sacred mountain, another shamanic symbol, continues in Buddhist art and architecture.

Halfway through the film, the girls learn that their mother will not be able to return home. A disappointed and worried Mei sets off for the hospital with a fresh ear of corn. Her disappearance prompts a futile search by Satsuki and the neighbors. With night approaching and out of desperation, Satsuki returns to the camphor tree and pleads for Totoro's help. Earlier in the film, Satsuki offers an umbrella to Totoro while they were waiting in the rain at the bus stop. Reciprocating her thoughtfulness, Totoro appears and summons the Catbus that effortlessly carries Satsuki to the lost Mei. Having rescued Mei, the Catbus then whisks the sisters over the countryside to a tree branch overlooking their mother's hospital room. They learn that their mother caught a minor cold and is otherwise doing well. Relieved, the Catbus transports the sisters back home and disappears. Alerted by the outside commotion, the father, who is visiting, goes to and lifts the window to find Mei's gift, an ear of corn on the outside sill.

Mei's gift is a tangible gesture of warmth and reciprocity toward her mother. This mutually affirming and beneficial relationship is a common theme in the shamanic experience between the ancestral spirits and their living progeny. The spirits of deceased ancestors take a special interest in the well-being of their descendants, who in turn honor them by remembering them through rituals and sacrifices. In Korea, the Marianas, Myanmar, the Ryūkyūs, and elsewhere, living descendants turn to their ancestral spirits for guidance and help. These practices also evolved into communal practices. Farmers made offerings to ensure abundant rain and good harvests. Fisherfolk and hunters turned to their ancestral spirits for good catches and for a safe return. The many local planting and harvest festivals observed in Japan are reminders of these collective observances.

Shamanic practice also turns to other spirits for help. Thus, for example, Thai merchants often enshrine and make daily offering to Nang Kwak, who invites good fortune, especially in the form of money. Taxi drivers in Thailand enshrine any number of deities on their dashboard to ward off accidents. The Japanese secure sacralized amulets from shrines and temples for protection against fires, automobile accidents, and misfortune, and to invite good fortune, safe childbirth, and passing university entrance examinations.

Spirits

We can only speculate on the origins and motivation for positing the reality of ghosts and spirits; but they no doubt recall a time when our early ancestors, acutely sensitive to the life-energy that pervaded the world and its denizens, did not distinguish between spiritual and corporeal realities and between animate and inanimate beings. Pascal Khoo Thwe, who grew up in a remote village in the Shan States of Myanmar, provides a window to such primal sentiments in his memoir, *From the Land of Green Ghosts, a Burmese Odyssey*. He writes,

> I was brought up not only among my ancestors, but among ghosts and fairies as well. Ours is a ghost and spirit culture, and for us the presence of ghosts is as natural as reincarnation is to the Buddhists. . . . Ghosts and spirits of the past were introduced into our daily lives with prayers and mantras, and they lived and ate with us like members of our families. We knew they were there; we felt their presence, we heard their voices in ourselves and in the forests and farms around us. . . . We took their existence for granted. Someone who saw a ghost would not expect to shock anyone whom he told of his experience—it would be a plain matter of fact. They were part of us, and we part of them. (Thwe, 17–18)

Thwe recounts such a reality when he overheard his grandmother speaking to the spirit of her recently deceased spouse, who had told her that he would be returning seven days after his death. Thwe records his grandmother's words.

> "Is it you, La Pen? I did everything you ordered for your funeral. I hope I have been a dutiful and faithful wife to you. But this house belongs to the living, not the dead. You know that. Please go back to the grave; to your new home. Go back to where you belong. I will meet you again when I am dead." (Thwe, 93–94)

Note the ease between the spirit of La Pen and his wife. She gently reminds him that he no longer belongs to the realm of the living, and that she fully expects to join him. La Pen's death was not unexpected; in addition to preparing himself for his transition, he was actively involved in his funeral arrangements. Still his spirit yearned nostalgically for the familiar; he returned only to be reminded that he now has a new home and that he has entered a new phase of his continuing being. The yearly visit of ancestral spirits at Obon is an occasion for great joy and celebration in the Japanese Buddhist community.

In addition to reiterating the existence of multiple worlds, the permeability of their boundaries, and the reality of spirits that were evident in *My Neighbor Totoro*, La Pen's return reveals two other features of Thwe's shamanic world. First, the end of corporeal existence is not the end of the life of an individual, and second, however intimate the relationship may have been in the corporeal world, the dead belong to the world of the spirits.

Thwe does not write about the transition from corporeal to spiritual being, but in traditional Ryūkyūs and Japan the transformation from corporal and spiritual being traditionally occurred over 33 years. The spirit of the deceased accomplishes this change with the aid of the proper mortuary and memorial rituals that are sponsored by his or her progeny. At the conclusion of the 33rd-year memorial service, the *tootoome* (Jpn. *ihai*) or memorial plaque that is inscribed with the deceased's name is ritually burned and placed on the ancestral altar; henceforth, shorn of individuality, the person is honored as a *kami* or deified ancestral spirit. While these memorial rituals have been seamlessly incorporated by Buddhist practices, their shamanic origins are clear. Buddhist mortuary and memorial rituals practiced in Hawai'i and the continental United States observe this pattern.

Second, while the relationship between spiritual ancestors and their living descendants may have once been intimate, now, belonging to different worlds, they are not to live together. Belonging to different realms or orders of existence, they are ontologically different beings. The danger for the living of such cohabitation, especially among husband and wife, is a popular cinematic genre. Such an example is dramatized in the 1999 Thai film *Nang Nak*, directed by Nonzee Nimibutr. The film recounts the love between Maak and Nak. Local lore recalls that in the 19th century, Mae Nak Phrakhanong had a difficult delivery and both she and her child died in childbirth. Her husband Maak was away at war. On his return Maak finds Nak and their baby at home. He happily resumes his life with Nak and their child; but warned and badgered by neighbors, he discovers that they are indeed specters. Frightened, he immediately flees. Angered at the neighbors for exposing the blissful spell she has cast, and angry that Maak has abandoned her and the child, Nak's vengeful spirit pursues him and the village men who set fire to her home. Only the shamanic prowess of an accomplished ascetic is able to persuade Nak's spirit to return to her grave. The unnatural cohabitation with spirits is also one of the themes of *Ugetsu*, a 1953 black-and-white Japanese film directed by Mizoguchi Kenji (1898–1956). Such close association with the deceased is unnatural and portends sure death for the living. In *Nang Nak* and *Ugetsu* the power of the Buddhist Dharma or truth offers protection. The capacity to see that they are under the spell of specters liberates, albeit painfully, Maak and Genjurō in *Ugetsu*. We shall return to these two personalities later.

Nak and Miyagi in *Ugetsu* die unexpectedly. Unprepared for death and thus confused, their spirits were not able to successfully adjust to their new status. Such disorientation is common for spirits who have separated from their corporeal bodies from sudden and unnatural deaths such as accidents and violent deaths. In Myanmar such spirits return to this world as "green ghosts." Some return to avenge wrongs that were committed against their persons or families. The practice of appeasing vengeful spirits persists in Hawai'i. In 1913, Yamaguchi Susumu carved an image of Jizō Bosatsu (*Kṣitigarbha Bodhisattva*) to pacify vengeful spirits that lurked in and around Kawaihapai Bay, Mokuleia, O'ahu. The vengeful spirits that once lurked in the bay have since been pacified; the drownings have since ceased.

As mentioned, when Mei, Satsuki, and their father paid homage to the camphor tree, they acknowledged the intrinsic sacredness of its indwelling spirit. The Thai refer to this indwelling spirit or soul with the expression *winjaan*, the psychobiological force that remains with an individual though cycles of birth and death. This belief meshes well with the Buddhist notion of the sacredness of all existence. Thus Buddhist monks have been able to successfully prevent deforestation by ordaining trees into the priesthood and wrapping their trunks with sacred robes. The Thai writer Angkarn Kalayaanaphong even goes so far as to attribute a voice to plants, and most of all compassion. Surprised to learn that plants can talk and grateful for their generosity, Grandma says, "Your compassion lies secreted deeply with you. You are able to bring forth your generosity and your magnanimous mercy so that I can feel the delight of the divine power that has revived my strength and vigor." The plants respond in unison, "In fact, the deities have bestowed souls on all living things." "Soul" is a translation of *winjaan.* Thai Buddhist ontology presumes that beings possessing *winjaan* have a voice (Kalayaanaphong, 1987, 85).

The Shaman

The shaman, an intermediary or messenger between the human world and the spirit world, is often consulted by individuals and the community to explain unusual events or phenomena, including dreams. The shaman also possesses the ability to travel to and through different worlds to locate and communicate with wayward spirits who have left their bodies. These paranormal powers that are beyond ordinary perception and knowing are not easy to come by. Carmen Blacker in *The Catalpa Bow* describes the rigorous and prolonged exercises of the various categories of Japanese shamans. The special diet, austerities, and training in concentration and ritual lead to a transformation of the psyche that can access and tap the shamanic powers. While these paranormal powers are to serve others, they have also been misused in the form of hexes and curses.

The pattern of initiation and training that prepares the shaman to access, channel, and accumulate spiritual powers to serve the community is present in the Buddhist ascetic experience. The model for the Buddhist ascetic is Buddha, who experimented with austerities and meditation. Buddhist documents recount the different psychospiritual stages Siddhārtha Gautama ascends during the night before the enlightenment. Settling into meditation, Siddhārtha recollects his past lives early into the night. At the second watch (late night into early morning), he becomes cognizant of the laws that govern the birth and death of all beings. These initial phases of insights are attributable to his experience with shamanic exercises. A contemporary understanding of the shamanic view of multiple worlds and lives appear in *Uncle Bunmee, Who Can Recall His Past Lives*, a 2010 Thai film written, produced, and directed by Apichatpong Weerasethakul, which received the Palme d'Or at the 2010 Cannes Film Festival. In the film, Uncle Bunmee is visited by his deceased wife and others; in a series of surrealistic scenes he recalls his previous births. During the final watch (early morning to dawn), Siddhārtha comes to understand that reality is the fortuitous coming together of countless "observable particulars," including events, and that spiritual health is the result of individual volition. This third insight represents a shift from shamanic "magic" to a philosophical and ethical basis for understanding physical and spiritual illness.

If in fact Buddhist documents correctly describe Siddhārtha's spiritual ascent, the descriptions of the initial two stages summarize his mastery of shamanic method and powers. Siddhārtha's experience also explains the presence of many of the shamanic elements in Buddhist thought and practice. This presence recognizes the many forces that course through the universe and animate the human experience; instead of repudiating or suppressing them, the Buddhist tradition embraces and directly confronts them. In the *Kṣitigarbhapaṇidhāna Sūtra* (*Vows of Bodhisattva Kṣitigarbha*), beings from throughout the 10 quarters, including innumerable spirits and disembodied beings, assemble to hear the Buddha recount Bodhisattva Kṣitigarbha's great compassion. Kṣitigarbha traverses the six *gatis* or realms. He is especially concerned with those malevolent spirits who have fallen to the lower realms; they are in need of the most help. Ghosts and malevolent spirits are often understood to be incarnation of Buddhas and bodhisattvas, who invoke fear of wayward ways.

Shamanic elements have long been present in Buddhist ritual practice. Buddha allowed spells and magic for protection against snakebites. Magic spells in the form of mantras appear in the early Mahāyāna *Sūtras*, notably the *Prajñāpāramitā Hṛdaya* or *Heart Sūtra*. Avalokiteśvara says that *prajñāpāramitā* or the perfection of wisdom is the great spell (*mantra*), the spell of great knowledge, the utmost spell, the unequaled spell, the allayer of all suffering. This *Sūtra* is part of the daily ritual of the Korean and Japanese Zen traditions. These and other shamanic elements began to be systematized from about the beginning of the sixth century in the form of Mantrayāna, and later in Tantrayāna. In sum this development produced rituals, spiritual algorithms that acknowledge the innumerable benign and malevolent forces coursing through the universe, and harnessed them in the service of attaining enlightenment. Tantrayāna in the form of Shingon is a vital part of the American Buddhist experience.

Additionally, the paranormal powers of the shaman are commonly understood to be "gifts" that need to be accepted and cultivated. In present-day Ryūkyū (Okinawa) a young girl is recognized by the community at an early age to have *saadakaumari* or "gifted with a capacity for spirituality." At some point, she is "seized" by the *kami* or spirit(s); but should she resist her "calling," she experiences physical and health problems, an existential crisis on which standard medical diagnoses and therapies have no effect. However, once she decides to assume the responsibility of the office, the maladies subside and disappear. At this point, the shaman or *yuta*-to-be (*yuta* are always women) visits other established *yuta* for confirmation and training, and makes pilgrimages to sacred sites in preparation for her responsibilities. Mitake Shina, founder of the Ishizuchi Shrine in the Moʻiliʻili district of Honolulu, was possessed by Takayama no Takagami. The pattern of "seizure," acceptance, and training is also present in the Hmong *txiv neeb* shamanic experience in the United States. Thus possessed, the shaman acquires the ability to communicate and negotiate with the spirits to help the physically and emotionally sick.

Whether one is called to or chooses the profession, shamanic initiation and training sensitizes the shaman to heretofore unknown psychic and spiritual rhythms that are present through the universe. Indeed, ancient Buddhist documents recount psychic changes, including expanded powers of the mind, that occur after prolonged meditative exercises. Reports of these experiences lend credence to the idea that there is more to the human experience than what can be empirically verified.

Shamanic Healing

Possessed with the powers of clairvoyance, clairaudience, and divination, much like a Western-trained physician, the shaman offers a diagnosis, identifies the cause or causes, and suggest ways, including rituals, to pacify and/or exorcise spirits that may have seized an individual. An individual's spiritual equilibrium is thrown out of kilter when the spirit leaves the individual by fright or the person is possessed or seized by a marauding spirit(s). The goal of shamanic healing is to alleviate traumas affecting an individual's spirit and restore well-being or balance and wholeness that includes the physical body.

Spirit- or soul-loss, reported by Anne Fadiman in *The Spirit Catches You and You Fall Down*, is perhaps best known. The narrative revolves around Lia Lee (1982–2012), who was born in Merced, California; she was the first child to be born in the United States to Nao Kao Lee, her father, and Foua Yang, her mother. Lia experienced her first seizure at three months of age and was diagnosed with epilepsy by a resident at Merced Community Medical Center. However, in Hmong culture such seizures, referred to as *qaug dab peg* ("the spirit catches you and you fall down"), are evidence of the ability to enter and journey into the spirit realm. It is a most honorable condition to have been chosen to host a healing spirit.

Lia slipped into a coma after a grand mal seizure in 1986 at the age of 4 years and lived in a persistent vegetative state for 26 years. While her American physicians attributed her condition to brain damage, the Lees attributed her condition to soul-loss. Lia's soul left her body when her sister Yer slammed the door and frightened it out of the body. They employed shamans to perform spirit-calling rituals to invite her spirit back, in the belief that once her spirit returned, she would be revived. The shamans were unsuccessful in locating and communicating with her spirit/soul to return to her body. The Burmese, Chinese, and Chamorros also have soul-calling rituals; these rituals are performed immediately after death, inviting the spirit of the deceased to return to his or her body, and thus to continue their corporeal life. Soul-calling is integral to the Chinese ritual; it is performed to determine death; if the soul fails to return, the person is pronounced dead.

In addition to exorcising malevolent spirits that have seized or possessed the spirit of an individual, shamanic rituals are performed to strengthen the spirit of an individual. The Thai observe *suebchata*, a ceremony intended to reinforce the spirit on the occasion of a person's 60th birthday and other auspicious birthday milestones. In the northeast Isaan region, families sponsor *sookwan*, a ritual to reenergize a person's spirit-essence by inviting all ancestors to assist in this task. This ceremony is not limited to frail elders, but anyone who needs to have his or her life-spirit reenergized. Any person who had a significant role in an individual's life is invited to participate. The ritual can be performed by either a cleric or by an elder. Such spirit revitalization rituals are performed by the present-day Hawaiian community at age 50, then every 10 years until age 70, then at 75 and every 5 years or so with a *luau* (celebratory feast).

The shaman is consulted to explain unusual phenomena and dreams. Living on a farm in rural Hawai'i, I distinctly recall my mother being extremely agitated by the crowing of a pet hen. When I asked why, she replied, "Hens never crow." The next day, accompanied by my father, they consulted a shaman and learned that they had neglected a long-forgotten ancestor. My mother spent the next day busily preparing special sacrificial dishes for the service, which we were all required to attend. I do not recall whose spirit we neglected to make offerings to, but immediately after the service, the hen stopped crowing. Stories of neglected ancestral spirits still abound in the Okinawan (Ryūkyūan) and Japanese communities. Unappreciated spirits can cause all manner of trouble. The need to memorialize the dead is part of the Japanese Buddhist ritual calendar. In addition to the private memorial rituals, rituals such as the summer Obon and *Eitaikyō* services publicly honor the deceased. The *Eitaikyō* (perpetual memorial service) is especially important, because it honors those ancestral spirits who have no living descendants to remember them.

In the film *Nang Nak*, the local priest attempted to thwart Nak's spirit's attempts to claim Maak's life; his attempt included secluding Maak in a sacred space cordoned by candles and sacred string, and monks chanting sacred Buddhist texts. But it took the knowledge and power of a powerful Buddhist ascetic to coax Nak's wandering spirit back into the grave, where he was able to capture it. A Buddhist priest plays a similar role in *Ugetsu*. The priest writes sacred Buddhist incantations on the body of Genjirō, Miyagi's wayward husband, to exorcise the vengeful spirit of Lady Wakasa with whom he is involved. At least within Thai and Japanese shamanic cultures, the paranormal powers of the shaman can be superseded by the properly trained Buddhist ascetic.

The shaman exercises his or her powers by first donning the shamanic costume and other symbols of the office before entering into ecstatic trance or séance. Shamanic rituals are often accompanied by ritual dance and drumming. I refer the reader to the entry on Hezhen (Nānai) shamanism for further clarification of their function and symbolism, for comments on the shaman as healer and the rogue shaman.

Conclusion

Shamanism and its practices persist in the Asian and Pacific Islander American communities in a number of guises. Anecdotal evidence filtered through community informants suggest that the shamanic experience still animates the respective Asian communities and individuals in the guise of rituals and attitudes that have been appropriated by Buddhism and other institutional traditions. With the exception of the Hmong community, shamanic practices operate outside of formal institutions and below the "radar"; the efficacy of a shaman is shared by word of mouth and normally closed to persons outside the community. That such "secret practices" exist is supported by creative literature. In addition to *From the Land of Green Ghosts: A Burmese Odyssey* by Pascal Khoo Thwe, the shamanic experience figures prominently in Maxine Hong Kingston's *The Woman Warrior, Memoirs of a Girlhood among Ghosts*, Nora Okja Keller's *Comfort Woman*, Quang Van Nguyen and Marjorie Pivar's *Fourth Uncle in the Mountain*, George Crane's *Bones of the Master*, and the poems and essays of many other Asian American writers.

Pacific Islander communities continue to be animated by their ancestral spirituality. The entries on Samoan, Tongan, and Chamorro spirituality reveal that these and other island peoples have adjusted and adopted their respective shamanic cultures of respect for their ancestral spirits through the family and their respect and responsibility for the natural world. In the face of Westernization and modernization, the Hawaiians have evolved strategies to preserve their ancient culture and teachers through the *halau* (schools) such as the *hula* and to honor their ancestors through the *'ohana* or family. The shamanic tradition is especially rich in Hawai'i. Glen Grant has collected a number of stories in *Obake, Ghost Stories in Hawai'i* that touch on aspects of the shamanic experience.

The shamanic tradition has been systematically suppressed, for example by the Japanese in the Ryūkyūs after its annexation in 1879 and by the Soviets in Siberia, and denigrated by established faith institutions. More subversive, however, have been the rationality of science and the practical impact of modern medicine that cast suspicion on the shaman's paranormal powers to harness the ancestral and other spirits, and more fundamentally the shamanic worldview. Yet, the *New York Times* reported on September 19, 2009, that Mercy Medical Center in Merced, California, formally recognized the legitimacy of the cultural and therapeutic function of traditional healers, the first ever such program in the United States. The hospital approved nine shamanic rituals, including "soul calling" and chanting, that can be performed in the clinical setting. These rituals, in conjunction with Western biomedicine, recognize the need to heal the whole—spiritual and physical—person. This is a stunning breakthrough, since rationality and logic, including modern medical practices, have long questioned the efficacy of shamanic methods and techniques. This development in Merced tacitly recognizes, at least, some of the presumptions of the shamanic worldview and the role of the shaman. But inexplicable dreams, the appearance of spirits from other worlds, and the possibility of "astral travel" continue to excite the imagination. We communicate with our ancestral spirits by resonating with the rhythms of the spiritual worlds. Totoro will appear only when we abandon ourselves to the magical world of spirits.

Ronald Y. Nakasone

See also: Essays: Spirituality; *Entries:* Chamorro Spirituality; Hawaiian Religion; Hmong Shamanism; Korean Shamanism; Okinawan (Ryūkyūan) Spiritual Culture; Samoan Spirituality; Tongan Spirituality

Further Reading

Alpers, Antony. *The Legends of the South Seas: The World of the Polynesians Seen through Their Myths and Legends, Poetry, and Art.* Oxford: Oxford University Press, 1970.

Balzer, Marjorie Mandelstam, ed. *Shamanic Worlds, Rituals and Lore of Siberia and Central Asia.* Armonk, NY: North Castle Books, 1997.

Blacker, Carmen. *The Catalpa Bow, a Study of Shamanistic Practices in Japan.* London: Unwin Paperbacks, 1982.

Brown, Patricia Leigh. "A Doctor for Disease, a Shaman for the Soul." *The New York Times.* September 19, 2009.

Crane, George. *Bones of the Master: A Buddhist Monk's Search for the Lost Heart of China.* New York: Bantam Books, 2000.

Conze, Edward. *Buddhist Wisdom Books, Containing the Diamond Sūtra and the Heart Sūtra.* London: George Allen & Unwin, 1958.

Conze, Edward. *Buddhism: Its Essence and Development.* New York: Harper and Row, 1959.

DuBois, Thomas A. *An Introduction to Shamanism.* Cambridge: Cambridge University Press, 2009.

Eliade, Mircea. *Shamanism, Archaic Techniques of Ecstasy.* Princeton, NJ: Princeton University Press, 1984.

Fadiman, Anne. *The Spirit Catches You and You Fall Down.* New York: Noonday Press, 1997.

Grant, Glen. *Obake: Ghost Stories in Hawai'i.* Honolulu: Mutual, 1994.

Hori, Ichirō. 1975. "Shamanism in Japan." *Japanese Journal of Religious Studies* 2, no. 4 (December 1975): 231–88. David Reed, translator.

Kalayaanaphong, Angkarn. "Grandma." In Herbert P. Phillips, et al., eds. *Modern Thai Literature.* Honolulu: University of Hawai'i Press, 1987.

Kingston, Maxine Hong. *The Woman Warrior, Memoirs of a Girlhood among Ghosts.* New York: Vintage Books, 1975.

Mizoguchi, Kenji. *Ugetsu.* 1953. 94 mins. Tokyo: Daiei.

Nakasone, Ronald Y. "Late Life, Mortuary, and Memorial Rituals in the Japanese Community." *Journal of Religious Gerontology* 15, no. 4 (2003): 3–14.

Nimibutr, Nonzee. *Nang Nak.* 1999. 100 min. Bangkok: Tai Entertainment.

Nyuyen, Quang Van, and Marjorie Pivar. *Fourth Uncle in the Mountain, the Remarkable Legacy of a Buddhist Itinerant Doctor in Vietnam.* New York: St. Martin's Press, 2004.

Robinson, Richard H., and Willard L. Johnson. *The Buddhist Religion, a Historical Introduction.* 3rd ed. Belmont, CA: Wadsworth, 1970.

Thwe, Pascal Khoo. *From the Land of Green Ghosts: A Burmese Odyssey.* New York: HarperCollins, 2002.

Walter, Mariko Namba, and Eva Jane Neumann Fridman, eds. *Shamanism: An Encyclopedia of World Beliefs, Practices, and Culture.* Santa Barbara, CA: ABC-CLIO, 2004.

Shin Buddhist Music

Jōdo Shinshū, one of the largest Pure Land denominations of Buddhism in Japan, is represented in the United States by several different communities, the largest of which is the Buddhist Churches of America (BCA), a national umbrella organization with more than 60 affiliated communities across the country. The BCA traces its history back to the late 1800s when a number of Shin priests were sent by their parent organization, the Nishi Hongwanji in Kyoto, to minister to the needs of Japanese migrant workers who had been immigrating to both Hawai'i and the mainland United States for some decades. They quickly established the Buddhist Mission of North America, which was renamed the Buddhist Churches of America during the internment of Japanese Americans during World War II. The organization continues to serve the needs of the Japanese American community while reaching out, as it has for most of its history, to the larger American Buddhist population. Thus, American Shin Buddhism can be seen as negotiating a space between their historical Japanese roots and attempts to acculturate to normative American religious customs. This dual nature of American Shin Buddhism is perhaps clearest in its music.

Shin Buddhist music in the United States can be roughly divided into four broad categories:

1. *Shōmyō* or chanting *Sūtras* and other sacred texts
2. *Gāthā* or hymns
3. *Taiko* ensembles
4. *Gagaku* or classical Japanese court music

The last two categories, *taiko* and *gagaku*, are not, strictly speaking, Shin Buddhist music. That is to say, they are not limited to a Shin Buddhist context but are instead part of the larger world of classical Japanese music. In the case of *taiko*, for example, the term itself merely refers to Japanese drums, and the style of *taiko* music most commonly found in the United States traces its roots to the post–World War II *taiko* revival in Japan, which was imported to the United States via Saiichi Tanaka in the late 1960s. It was during this time that Sansei (third generation) Japanese Americans were beginning to formulate a specifically Asian American identity against the backdrop of the civil rights era, and *taiko* served as a way to challenge the stereotype of the "passive Asian" while claiming a connection to their Japanese roots. It was not long, however, before *taiko* became popular outside of the Japanese American community, and today most *taiko* ensembles are pan–Asian American in character.

Gagaku, classical Japanese court music played with traditional instruments such as the *biwa, koto*, and *shō* (mouth organ), is also not limited to the Shin Buddhist context where it is sometimes referred to as *hōraku* (lit. Dharma music). Like *taiko*, *gagaku* has become increasingly popular in the Japanese American context more recently, perhaps reflecting a desire to reconnect with individuals' Japanese roots. Both *taiko* and *gagaku* are performed at special occasions or festivals, most notably during Obon festivals where large *taiko* ensembles accompany the Obon dance to celebrate and memorialize the dead. Moreover, to the extent that both *taiko* and *gagaku* are not limited to the Shin Buddhist context, nor indeed to a strictly Japanese American context, the remainder of this entry will focus instead specifically on Shin Buddhist music.

Ritual Context for Shin Buddhist Music

The vast majority of BCA-affiliated and other American Shin Buddhist communities hold a weekly worship service at a local temple. This is a clear departure from normative Shin Buddhist temple practice in Japan where Shin Buddhists generally only attend temple services during large holidays or festivals and the resident priest or minister will instead visit members' homes to perform specific rituals, memorials, and rites. In the United States, owing to a tendency to adapt to normative Protestant Christian standards, Shin Buddhists attend weekly Sunday services, a service that provides the ritual context for the communal chanting of texts and singing of songs.

Whereas the Sunday service varies from temple to temple across the United States, its most basic form is as follows. The service begins with the ringing of a large *kansho* bell located somewhere outside the main worship hall or *hondo*. The ringing of the bell calls the *sangha* community members to gather in the *hondo* where they will presently be joined by the minister and his or her assistant minister. A lay member of the community will serve as officiant, directing the congregation to the texts that will be chanted or sung. Generally, the community will begin by chanting a shorter *Sutra*, followed by taking refuge in the Three Treasures (the Buddha, the Dharma, and the *sangha*), singing a *gāthā*, and listening to the minister deliver a Dharma talk, or sermon. There may be a second chant or song sung following this sermon, and at some point before, during, or after the service, members are expected to *ōshoko* (offer incense) at the main altar. On most Sundays, there is a small social gathering following the service.

Shōmyō Sūtra Chanting

At least once during the service, *sangha* members will collectively chant a *Sūtra* text. There are a limited number of texts specific to the Jōdo Shinshū tradition: selections from the so-called Three Pure Land *Sūtras*; commentarial literature by Jōdo Shinshū patriarchs such as Shandao and Nāgārjuna; and devotional poems (*wasan*) written by the tradition's founder, Shinran Shonin. Some texts, such as the *San Butsu Ge*, are chanted more frequently or on specific occasions such as a memorial service or holiday. And, of course, throughout the service, members will recite the *nembustu*, a short, *mantra*-like phrase in praise of the Buddha Amida, "*namu-amida-butsu*." Reciting the *nembutsu* often precedes the *Dharma* talk, for example, and is a part of most of the *Sūtra* chants as well. Historically, Shin Buddhists were known for spontaneously chanting the *nembutsu* during ritual observances, a phenomenon that is not as common in contemporary practice.

Shōmyō, or the chanting of Buddhist sacred texts, has a long history in Japan that borrows heavily from Chinese styles of musical chanting, which in turn may be based on ancient Indian traditions. The Japanese style that American Shin Buddhists have inherited is based on a pentatonic scale of five basic notes. *Sūtras* are generally chanted in their classical Japanese readings at a steady rhythmic pace with one syllable per beat in sets of five or seven. A minister will lead the *saṇgha* through the chant, and most texts have a specific section for the cantor to chant solo with response from the congregation. Generally, time is marked by the striking of bells, gongs, or an *ōdaiko* drum. As mentioned, reciting the *nembutsu* during or immediately after a chant is common.

Whereas Shin Buddhist ministers are given extensive training in the proper way to chant their tradition's sacred texts, lay members rarely receive such guidance apart from their relationships with local ministers. As a result, participation in the communal chanting of texts varies across different local communities, reflecting individuals' comfort with the classical chanting style. Moreover, as Shin Buddhism developed in North America over the course of the 20th century, attempts were made to render the classical Japanese style of chanting into contemporary English, often through direct translations of the *Sūtras*. Hence, it is common to see in service books traditional Japanese musical notations with English translations beneath them. This in some sense can be read as the community making explicit attempts to relearn its tradition in response to the process of Americanization that may have distanced it from its Japanese roots. However, some Buddhist leaders have questioned the utility of direct translation, noting that this, too, is based on the Protestant Christian assumption that textual exegesis is more important than psychological or spiritual development; that is, it may be more important to *perform* the chant than to intellectually understand its content.

American *Gāthā*

In addition to chanting sacred texts, services are marked with the singing of hymns or *gāthā*. In the American Shin context, these hymns most closely resemble Protestant Christian hymns in genre and style. However, their complex and nuanced history is worth deeper exploration than the simple assumption of linear acculturation from Japan to the West. Many *gāthā* were written at the turn of the 20th century; others are centuries-old Japanese folk songs or modern adaptations of Shinran Shonin's *wasan* set to Western-style music. Still others are more contemporary works composed over the last few decades. And *gāthā* have been composed by Japanese, Japanese American, and Euro-American Buddhists alike.

The most widely used collection of Shin Buddhist *gāthā* today is the *Shin Buddhist Service Book* compiled in 1994 by the BCA Department of Education. (The book also contains the *Sūtras* regularly chanted as well as notes on temple services and etiquette.) The *Service Book* contains 68 *gāthā*, as well as instrumental and choral music compositions, roughly evenly divided between English and Japanese. Whereas several songs were composed specifically for the creation of the *Service Book*, the book also includes a substantial number of *gāthā* from previous volumes, songs written, composed, or set to modern Western music as early as the 1890s. Like the chanting of sacred texts, some songs are more popular than others, and some are sung only on special occasions. For example, "In Lumbini's Garden," a song composed by Paul Carus in the early 1900s, is regularly sung on Hanamatsuri to celebrate the birth of the historical Buddha. The song "White Ashes," based on an epistle written by 15th-century Shin Buddhist reformer Rennyo Shonin with music by American composer Lou Harrison, is often sung during memorial services.

It should also be noted that the *Service Book* by no means represents the extent of contemporary American Shin Buddhist *gāthā* or musical repertoire. Most temples, in addition to standard BCA service books, have their own local collections of songs culled from other Shin Buddhist collections or compositions by local musicians. Moreover, many temples have talented musical members who compose original songs in a variety of genres for Sunday services, which may never be written down or recorded. In sum, *gāthā* creates a space within the service for individuals to creatively express their own Buddhist identities and share these expressions with the community as a whole.

Conclusion

The Shin Buddhist experience in the United States is closely linked to the Japanese American experience, an experience that has been marked by World War II internment. Internment and racial prejudice has forced the community to carefully negotiate a specifically Japanese as well as American identity, and one can see tension within the community to hold fast to its Japanese roots while creatively engaging and adapting to normative white American cultural customs. Ritualized music is one space where this tension is sharply on display.

Attempts to translate Japanese *Sūtras* and other sacred texts into modern English for the purpose of ritual chanting have generally failed. The pentatonic scale of these chants does not lend itself naturally to English, and as mentioned above there is a sense that the value in such chanting is not intellectual understanding but spiritual practice. Furthermore, ritual practices can be slow to change; generally, rituals are performed because they have always been performed, in this way, and ritualists are resistant to adapt them too far from their assumed "right" method. Thus, the chanting of Shin Buddhist sacred texts can be read as an attempt by the community to retain its specifically Shin Buddhist and Japanese identity.

The history of American Shin, however, does not end with its Japaneseness. The community has consistently engaged with non–Japanese Americans, engagement that has had significant influence on the ritual life of the community. This is self-evident in the singing of Shin Buddhist songs and *gāthā*. Not only is the music itself performed in a style imported to Japan and Jōdo Shinshū from Western European sources, but many of the songs sung were themselves written or composed by non-Japanese converts to the tradition. When the most recent service book was compiled, an attempt was made to exclude *gāthā* that were "too Christian" or whose popularity had waned. It is interesting to note that the attempt was not to create a more "Japanese" collection but rather a more "Buddhist" collection, suggesting then that the community embraced songs and compositions that fulfilled this objective regardless of their source. Contemporary music makers similarly eschew rigid ethnic categorizations, and thus *gāthā* and other Shin Buddhist songs can be seen as the antithesis to *Sūtra* chanting: a space for creative and innovative expressions of Shin Buddhist practice and faith.

Scott A. Mitchell

See also: *Essays:* Arts and Cultural Production; *Entries:* Honpa Hongwanji Mission of Hawai'i; Imamura, Yemyō

Further Reading

Ama, Michiro. *Immigrants to the Pure Land: The Modernization, Acculturation, and Globalization of Shin Buddhism.* Honolulu: University of Hawai'i Press, 2011.

Goa, David J, and Harold G. Coward. "Sacred Ritual, Sacred Language: Jōdo Shinshū Religious Forms in Transition." *Studies in Religion* 12, no. 4 (1983): 363–80.

Malm, William P. *Traditional Japanese Music and Musical Instruments.* Tokyo: Kodansha International, 2001.

Masatsugu, Michael K. "'Beyond This World of Transiency and Impermanence': Japanese Americans, Dharma Bums, and the Making of American Buddhism during the Early Cold War Years." *Pacific Historical Review* 77, no. 3 (2008): 423–51.

Mitchell, Scott A. "Sunday Morning Songs." *The Pure Land* 22 (2006): 127–38.

Terada, Yoshitaka. "Shifting Identities of Taiko Music in North America." *Senri Ethnological Reports* 22 (2001): 37–59.

Wells, Keiko. "Shin Buddhist Song Lyrics Sung in the United States: Their History and Expressed Buddhist Images (2), 1936–2001." *Tokyo daigaku taiheiyō* 3 (2003): 41–64.

Williams, Duncan Ryûken, and Tomoe Moriya, eds. *Issei Buddhism in the Americas.* Urbana: University of Illinois Press, 2010.

Wong, Deborah. *Speak It Louder: Asian Americans Making Music.* New York: Routledge, 2004.

Shingon

The Kōyasan Shingon Missions of North America and Hawai'i are not-for-profit corporations affiliated with the Kōyasan Shingon Shū headquartered in Wakayama, Japan. Shingon Buddhism was founded on the teachings of Kūkai, also known as Kōbō Daishi or Odaishisama (774–835), a Japanese priest active during the Heian period (794–1185). "Kōyasan" refers to the site where Kūkai established a monastery and the Sect's administrative center; it is also the site where he rests in "perpetual meditation." "Shingon" is the Japanese reading of the Chinese *zhenyan*, literally, "true word," which is in turn a rendering of the Sanskrit "*mantra.*"

Beliefs and Doctrines

According to Shingon lore, Vajrasattva, after having been initiated by Mahāvairocana Buddha into the deepest mysteries of the Buddhadharma, retreated into an iron tower in southern India for centuries, until Nāgārjuna entered it, according to one version of this legend, to receive the *Vajraśekhara Sūtra* (*Kongōchō-kyō*), one of the tradition's two major canonical sources. The other is the *Mahāvairocana Sūtra* (*Dainichi-kyō*), which articulates the theoretical foundation of the sect. The *Vajraśekhara Sūtra* describes the process for becoming a Buddha. Both *Sūtras* advance the idea that all beings possess the virtues of the Mahāvairocana Buddha and are able to realize Enlightenment and instantly become a Buddha with their very own bodies. The tradition relies also on the *Susiddhikara Sūtra* (*Sōshitsuji-kyō*), the

Prajñāpāramitānaya Sūtra (*Risshu-kyō*), and the *Yogi Sūtra* (*Yugikyō-kyō*) for canonical support. As evidenced in his writings, the tradition maintains that Kūkai properly understood these canonical sources. His most important treatises are *Benkenmitsunikyōron* (*On the Differences between the Exoteric and Esoteric Teachings*), *Sokushinjōbutsugi* (*Meaning of Becoming a Buddha in This Very Body*), *Shōjijissōgi* (*Meanings of Sound, Sign, and Reality*), *Unjigi* (*Meanings of "Hūm"*), and *Hizōhōyaku* (*Precious Key to the Secret Treasury*).

Kūkai categorized the Buddhist tradition into Mikkyō (esoteric teaching) and Kengyō (exoteric teaching). This distinction is based on a rationalization that there are two classes of Buddhas—*Dharmakāya* and *Nirmāṇakāya*—each with its respective method of transmitting the Dharma or teaching. *Dharmakāya* refers to the absolute body/being of the Mahāvairocana Buddha, who through the experience of enlightenment embodies perfect understanding of all aspects of reality. The *Mahāvairocana Sūtra* and other canonical documents articulate directly and immediately the form and content of Mahāvairocana's Enlightenment. In contrast, the Nirmāṇakāya or "transformed-body/being" is a manifestation or expression of Mahāvairocana Buddha. The historical Śākyamuni is a Nirmāṇakāya Buddha; he is a pale imitation of the absolute Mahāvairocana. Moreover, Śākyamuni employed *upāya*, pedagogical devices such as parables, illustrative stories, and aphorisms that might heighten a devotee's spiritual awareness, but did not illuminate the real and true experience of true reality and Buddhahood. Additionally, the exoteric method is long and laborious toward the realization of enlightenment.

Accordingly, Kūkai advanced the notion of *sokushin jōbutsu*, realizing Buddhahood with one's body. Buddhahood is not simply an intuitive realization, nor is it to be realized after death. Buddhahood or Enlightenment and its attendant virtues are to be realized through one's present physical body and lived in this present life. Buddhahood is possible because all beings share and are thus identical to the Mahāvairocana Buddha (*rigu no jōbutsu*). Most are unaware that they are originally endowed with enlightenment. Realizing Buddhahood or enlightenment involves both the compassion emanating from Mahāvairocana Buddha and the practitioner's acceptance of and receiving it (*kaji no jōbutsu*). This idea is crystallized in the expression *kaji*. *Ka* means "to add" or "to increase." *Ka* is thus a gift that Mahāvairocana gives or bestows; and *ji* is acknowledging this gift and cherishing it. This "giving" and "accepting" is consistent with the fundamental Buddhist insight of *pratītyasamutpāda*, namely, that the universe is an interconnected web of things, beings, and events.

The practitioner quickens an appreciation of *kaji* when he or she becomes aware that his or her activities are expressions of the "mysterious" activities of the Mahāvairocana. Kūkai refers to these activities as *sanmitsu* or Three Mysteries. *Sanmitsu* catalogues the dynamism of Mahāvairocana's deeds (*mudra*), voice (*mantra*), and thoughts in graphic form (*maṇḍala*) that constitute the movement, sounds, and landscape of the cosmos, the Mahāvairocana. All movements give expression to Mahāvairocana's body, all sounds are rhythms of his voice, and the comprehension of these realities are crystallized in the *maṇḍala* that visualizes his mind. All objects of the six senses constitute the form, resonance, and pattern of the cosmic mind-body of Mahāvairocana. Every phenomenon thus is *hosshin seppō*, an expression of Mahāvairocana's preaching. This appreciation is deepened through the ritual practice of *sanmitsu*.

In addition, identity with the mind-being of Mahāvairocana Buddha results in a heightened awareness, which is initially short lived, but can be sustained beyond ritual. This synchronicity also has healing qualities. The priest can perform *kaji* healing rituals to restore the well-being of the sick. Countless testimonials affirm the efficacy of *kaji* healing rituals.

While Mahāvairocana Buddha may be formless and thus rationally incomprehensible and inexpressible, on the basis of *kaji* the Three Mysteries interpenetrate and are one with the activities of sentient beings. The practitioner can realize this formless reality through the meditative ritual practice of *sanmitsu* that integrates *mudras* (symbolic hand gestures), *mantras* (voiced sounds), and *kansō, kannen* (visualization focusing on *mandalas* or Sanskrit *siddham* letters). With the increasing mastery of *mudras*, *mantras*, and visualization, the practitioner's actions, speech, and thoughts come to resonate with the Three Mysteries (action, speech, and thoughts), the language through which the Mahāvairocana Buddha (Dharmakāya or absolute reality) communicates and manifests itself. By participating in the *samādhi* (mindful stillness) of the Mahāvairocana, the practitioner realizes his or her original enlightenment. The intent of ritual practice is to mirror the Mahāvairocana's being and activity in oneself, and thus confirm for oneself the reality and dynamism of Dharmakāya. When Mahāvairocana suddenly surfaces, the once innate but unrealized enlightenment becomes manifest (*kentoku no jōbutsu*). This experience confirms the practioner's perfection of the Three Mysteries, and he or she is now a fully awakened Buddha. Śākyamuni Buddha and Kōbō Daishi actualized their original Enlightenment in their own lives. By penetrating the cosmic language of Mahāvairocana, the practioner also gives credence to *hosshin seppō* and *sokushin jōbutsu*.

History and Administrative Structure

In 2002, more than 1,000 followers from Japan and more than 800 followers from throughout the United States gathered to celebrate the centennial of Rev. Hōgen Yujiri's efforts to establish the Lāhainā Daishidō on Mau'i in 1902. However, even as early as 1885, Shingon followers had been holding services at various *daishidō* (shortened from Kōbō Daishidō) in private homes and temporary meeting halls throughout the islands. In 1915, the Kōyasan Shingon Mission of Hawai'i was established to administer the 12 Kōyasan Shingon temples present on the islands. In 2013 Bishop Sohko Kuki and 13 other priests served the needs of their followers in eight temples. All priests have been trained and certified by the parent organization, Kōyasan Kongōbuji Headquarters in Japan. Kōyasan Shingon Mission of

Hawai'i is an active member of the Hawai'i Buddhist Council that is comprised of the major Japanese Buddhist denominations in the islands.

There are several Shingon temples and numerous *daishidōs* (organized Kōbō Daishi meeting places) on the U.S. mainland. Three temples are located in Los Angeles, one in Fresno and Sacramento, and two in Seattle. There are also long-standing *daishidōs* in San Jose, Berkeley, and Santa Rosa. Shingon temples are independent institutions, but are granted temple status by Kōyasan Headquarters. The stringent rules for becoming a temple account for numerous *daishidōs*. Ministers are assigned by Kōyasan Headquarters. The head ministers for the Los Angeles, Sacramento, and Seattle temples are Issei (first-generation immigrants) from Japan. The *sōkan* (bishop) of North American Shingon Mission administers and directs its propagation and ministerial activities within the continental United States. The *sōkan* is elected from among the North American priests. Likewise the *sōkan* for the Shingon Mission of Hawai'i is elected from among its priests. The temple of the elected *sōkan* becomes the headquarters in Hawai'i.

Practices

Shingon temples serve the spiritual, existential, and social needs of their lay membership and their priests. Of the many needs, mortuary and memorial services that mark important milestones in an individual's and family's life cycle are probably the most significant. Each of the 13 Buddhas and bodhisattvas who appear on the Taizōkai and Kongokai *mandalas* highlight the 13 milestones of the 33-year-long memorial cycle. After the funeral rites, the tradition observes the 7th, 14th, 21st, 28th, 35th, 42nd, 49th, and 100th days, and the 1st year, 3rd year, 7th year, 13th year, and 33rd year after death. Thus Fūdō Myō'ō (Acala) is the patron of the first 7th-day memorial service; Shaka Nyorai (Śākyamuni) is the patron of the second or 14th-day memorial service. The other Buddhas and bodhisattvas in sequence are Monju Bosatsu (Mañjuśri), Fugen Bosatsu (Samantabhadra), Jizō Bosatsu (Kṣitigarbha), Miroku Bosatsu (Maitreya), Yakushi Nyorai (Bhaiṣajyaguru), Kannon Bosatsu (Avalokiteśvara), Seishi Bosatsu (Mahāsthāma), Amida Nyorai (Amitābha), Ashuku Nyorai (Akṣobhya), and Dainichi Nyorai (Mahāvairocana). Kokuzō Bosatsu (Ākāśagarbha) is the patron for the 33rd-year memorial service. In addition, most temples observe Obon and its accompanying Bon *odori* (dance), the annual summer observance that welcomes the spirits of the deceased ancestors back home.

In addition, the temple is the venue for regular congregate and special services, including the *homa* or fire ritual throughout the year. The *homa* ritual offers followers the opportunity to renew their commitment to self-cultivation by inscribing their yearnings to expunge undesirable negative energy generated by detrimental thoughts and desires on pieces of wood. During the ritual, the priest feeds the ritual fire, symbolically expunging detrimental thoughts and desires that inhibit the realization of Buddhahood. Followers also inscribe their aspirations and requests for blessings, which when consumed will be transported to the Buddhas and bodhisattvas dwelling in spiritual realms.

The temples are venues for spiritual education and practice. To this end many temples have *daishikōs* (classes and seminars) that offer instruction on Buddhist thought and practice, especially the teachings of Kūkai. Temples also offer instruction on meditation, particularly *aji kan*, meditation on the visualization of the Sanskrit letter अ, "A," and breathing techniques. The letter "A" represents the moment immediately before Mahāvairocana (highest reality) manifests itself. When the practioner identifies with the letter "A," he or she enters the reaches of highest reality and experiences a transformation of thoughts, speech, and action. This transformation can also be accomplished by breathing techniques. In addition to Sunday Dharma schools, temples are venues for *goeika*, a form of Japanese Buddhist music that includes singing praises and the use of small hand-held bells and gongs. From time to time temples will organize a Shikoku Pilgrimage to visit the 88 temples and sites associated with Kūkai.

The local temples are important centers for community activities. During and after World War II local temples assisted with the reintegration of the Japanese returning from the internment camps. Temples regularly sponsor *taiko* drumming classes and Japanese-language schools. The Boy Scout troop sponsored by the Los Angeles Koyasan Buddhist Temple is one of the oldest in America and was personally commended by President Roosevelt before World War II at a White House ceremony. Temples offer *omamoris* (talismans) that are imbued with the protective spirit of the Buddha or bodhisattva who was activated during the ritual. In Hawai'i some of the priests handwrite as many as 10,000 individual talismans for large events. In Los Angeles this can be as many as 2,000. Some temples have been active in the development of senior living facilities in their locales.

Select temples are authorized to take on *deshi* (disciples), who receive instruction on the Shido Kegyo (the Fourfold Practices) to become a licensed priest and on meditation techniques. Normally an aspiring priest attends precepts ceremonies lectures, and ordination in Japan. However, materials for the basic 108 days of training are now in English. Kōyasan has certified Rev. Eijun Eidson, who has been given the title *Denju Ajari* (transmission master), to conduct and provide instruction on the complete collection of 259 rituals at the Kōyasan Shingon at Tenchiji Temple in Fresno, California. The training is identical to that in Japan, except that it is conducted in English and Sanskrit. Twelve persons from Japan, mainland United States, and Hawai'i have received instruction on the 1,000-page collection and its 3,000 pages of commentary.

Tenchiji Temple has a library of approximately 45,000 books, 15,000 journals, and 10,000 periodicals in religious studies. It includes many Japanese and Chinese texts. It is also the repository for Dr. David Chappell's library collection (9,000 volumes). The library materials are open to the clergy and scholarly public by appointment.

Eijun Bill Eidson

See also: Entries: Buddhist Meditation

Further Reading

Abe, Ryuchi. *The Weaving of Mantra.* New York: Columbia University Press, 2000.

Arai, Yusei. *Shingon: Japanese Esoteric Buddhism: A Handbook for Followers.* Edited by Eijun Bill Eidson and Harada Shoken (Atsuyo). Fresno, CA: Shingon Buddhist International Institute, 1997.

Hakeda, Yoshito S. *Kūkai: Major Works.* New York: Columbia University Press, 1972.

Hashimoto, Shinnin. *A History of Shingon Buddhism in Hawai'i.* Wakayama: The Headquarters of Kōyasan Kongōbuji Temple, Department of Foreign Mission, 2006.

Iwatsubo, Shinko. *Tenchi: Heaven Earth.* Edited by Eijun Bill Eidson and Harada Shoken (Atsuyo). Fresno, CA: Shingon Buddhist International Institute Kōyasan Buddhist Temple, 1962.

Kūkai. *Shingon Texts.* Berkeley, CA: Numata Center for Buddhist Translation, 2004.

Murakami, Yasutoshi. *Language of the Japanese Heart: Kūkai.* Edited by Eijun Bill Eidson and Harada Shoken (Atsuyo). Fresno, CA: Shingon Buddhist International Institute, 2013.

Payne, Richard. *Tantric Ritual of Japan: Feeding the Gods—The Shingon Fire Ritual.* New Delhi: Aditya Prakashan, 2001.

Shiba, Ryotarō. *Kūkai the Universal: Scenes from His Life.* Torrance, CA: Heian International, 2003.

Snodgrass, Adrian. *The Matrix and Diamond World Mandalas in Shingon.* Buddhism Satapitaka Series, nos. 354–55 (1997).

Yamasaki, Taiko. *Shingon: Japanese Esoteric Buddhism.* Edited by Morimoto Yasuyoshi. Fresno, CA: Shingon Buddhist International Institute, 1993.

Shinnyo-en

Shinnyo-en is a lay Japanese Buddhist order based on the *Mahāparinirvāṇa Sūtra*; *shinnyo* is Japanese for *tathatā*, a Buddhist expression that refers to the "real and true nature of all existent things and beings." *En* means "garden." The English translation of the order's name is Order (borderless garden) of Truth.

History

Shinnyo-en was founded by Itō Shinjō (Itō Fumiaki, 1906–1989) and his wife Tomoji (Uchida Tomoji, 1912–1967). After completing his studies at Daigōji in Kyoto, Japan, in 1943, Itō realized that he was indeed privileged to have been able to spend six years formally studying and practicing in a monastery; most people do not have the means to receive such formal training. As a result of this epiphany, Itō resolved to find a way for all people to have a similar opportunity. Thus in 1946, he founded the independent Shinnyo order that was recognized by the Japanese government to be a bona fide faith-based organization in 1953. Itō Shinjō is known by his followers through his priestly name of Kyōshu-sama (*kyōshu*, literally head or founder of a sect; *sama* is an honorific).

In 1970, Itō journeyed to the United States and discovered that Shinnyo-en had already taken root through the efforts of its devotees in their respective communities. Practitioners in Hawai'i established the first Shinnyo-en temple outside of Japan in 1971. Shinnyo-en dedicated a temple in San Francisco in 1982, the first temple on the continental United States. At present there are over 100 temples and training centers in or around major cities such as New York, Chicago, Seattle, San Francisco, Los Angeles, São Paulo, London,

Paris, Milan, Munich, Singapore, Sydney, Taipei, and Tokyo. Currently the order claims more than one million Shinnyo-en practitioners worldwide. Shinnyo-en at present is led by Itō Shinsō (Itō Masako, b. 1942), Itō's daughter. Shinnyo-en is based in Tachikawa, a suburb of Tokyo.

Beliefs

The beliefs and practices of Shinnyo-en are primarily based on the *Mahāparinirvāṇa Sūtra*, a Mahāyāna Buddhist document, commonly referred to as the *Nirvāṇa Sūtra*. According to Shinnyo-en thinking the major thrust of the *Sūtra* can be summed in three propositions that correspond to propositions common to Mahāyāna Buddhism: (1) the Buddha is eternal and unchanging; (2) all beings possess the Buddha-nature; and (3) there are "four perfections": permanence, bliss, self, and purity (*jō raku ga jō*). These three propositions correspond to the metaphysical, ontological, and existential foundations of Shinnyo-en thought. The first and second propositions state the metaphysical and ontological basis for Shinnyo-en, respectively, and guarantee the third. With regard to the eternality of the Buddha and truth, Itō essentially maintains the life and death of Siddhārtha Gautama to be incidents. The truth of the impermanence and interdependent quality of all existences is eternal. Further eternality is extended to the innate presence of the Buddha-nature in each person. Thus the potential for Buddhahood is a real possibility in this present life. The "four perfections" are realized through the practice of *sesshin* (meditation practice). Shinnyo-en practice must be un-

derstood through *bakku daiju* and *reinōsha* (spiritual medium).

Bakku daiju is rendered by the order as "to lift away and shoulder the suffering of followers." It is one of the more distinctive notions in Shinnyo-en doctrine. In traditional Buddhism, *bakku daiju* refers to the bodhisattva's compassion to take on the suffering of all sentient beings. In Shinnyo-en the altruistic function associated with *bakku daiju* is performed by Ito's deceased children for the sake of the devotees. This reality was established by Itō's first son, Chibun (Motofumi, 1934–1936, posthumously known as Kyōdōin among the followers; "in" is a posthumous title, usually reserved for persons of prominent social standing), who contacted his mother 100 days after he passed away on June 9. When Tomoji received a spiritual message (*reigen*), she entered into a trance and communed directly with the spiritual world. His death was later interpreted to be a sacrificial act for the sake of his parent's spiritual mission.

A second tragedy struck when Itō's second son, Yūichi (posthumously known as Shindōin among the followers), died on July 2, 1952, at the age of 15. Itō interpreted Yuichi's death to be sacrificial, to sustain the order. The two brothers, Kyōdōin (one who guides people to [true faith in] the teaching) and Shindōin (one who guides people to truth), are collectively referred to as Ryōdōji-sama (Two virtuous boys), who were sent to the spirit world by their parents to relieve the suffering of the Shinnyo-en devotees. Their deaths established and opened a path to the Shinnyo spiritual world to assist Shinnyo-en devotees to follow the Buddha and to do good for others. Shinnyo-en teaches that Shindōin lifted our suffering (*bakku*) and Kyōdōin shoulders our suffering (*daiju*). *Baku* or "expunging suffering" is an alternative expression of *in'nen giri* or the cutting off of suffering. In traditional Buddhism *daiju* is used to articulate the magnanimous receiving of acceptance of the suffering of others. The Shinnyo-en devotee understands *bakku daiju* simply means worldly blessing and protection.

The lifting (*bakku*) and shouldering (*daiju*) of suffering by the two sons is directly related to the role played by Tomoji, who is posthumously known as Shōjuinsama (one who embraces or accepts all; mother of embracement). Shinnyo-en teaches that after the elimination of karmic obstacles through the agency of the two sons, their mother opened the path to enlightenment for all beings. The expression *shōju* is related to the bodhisattva's passion to embrace and receive all beings and lead them to enlightenment. Whereas the passing of the first son was of a particular importance to the order's early years, the death of Shōjuin-sama on August 6, 1967, at the age of 55 is understood to extend compassion to all beings. The deaths of their two sons and the death of the founder also have soteriological functions.

Practices

The basic practice of Shinnyo-en to enlightenment is *sesshin* meditation. The traditional meaning of *sesshin* refers to a prolonged or intense meditation session; but for Shinnyo-en it means "touching one's heart, one's buddha nature, the heart of others, and the heart of buddha" (Shinnyo-en, 40) with the aid of a *reinōsha*, a spiritual medium. There are two forms of *sesshin* training, structured and unstructured. Structured *sesshin* refers to training that is offered at the conclusion of a service with the assistance of a *reinōsha* or spiritual guide who communicates messages from the spiritual world (*reigen*) to each practitioner to uncover his or her Buddha nature by reflecting on the root causes of one's spiritual challenges, to realize the interdependent nature of all existence, and to understand how one's thoughts and actions affect oneself and others. It should be noted that the members of the Itō family residing in the spiritual realm send messages to guide and counsel their devotees. The source of the spiritual power (*reinō*) that the spiritual guide (*reinōsha*) taps into is the same as Shōjuin-sama (Tomoji) had access to. Prior to meeting and marrying Kyōshu-sama (Itō Fumiaki), Tomoji had perfected her shamanic powers that she inherited from her grandmother and aunt. It was through her influence that Shinnyo-en owes its *sesshin* and *reinōsha*.

Shinnyo-en is cognizant of the criticism of the need for the *reinōsha* and beliefs in the efficacy of disembodied spirits. To distinguish itself from popular magic, fortune telling, and shamanic miracles, Shinnyo-en simply states that the power of enlightenment releases all manner of powers that are inherent in Dharmakāya.

The *reinōsha* also urges the practioner to practice harmony, gratitude, kindness, and acceptance. The resulting insights are to be applied in unstructured *sesshin* that are practiced in daily life through the Three Practices: (1) *otasuke*, sharing the Dharma (teaching) to equip others with the means to overcome spiritual challenges and fulfillment; (2) *kangi*, sincere offerings that support activities within the *saṇgha* (community), as well as to nonaffiliated charitable and philanthropic organizations and activities; (3) *gohōshi*, serving others by giving time and physical support. To this end, Shinnyo-en counsels its practioners to recognize that each moment is an opportunity to gain new insight and that the activities of daily life are occasions for cultivating wisdom, loving-kindness, and the compassion of a Buddha. This realization results in the "four perfections": permanence, joy, self, and purity (*jō raku ga jō*). The Shinnyo-en devotee is aided by Kyōshu-sama, Shōjuin-sama, and Ryōdōji-sama.

Cultivating the Three Practices counteracts greed and craving, the causes of human suffering. The order thus encourages its practitioners to serve their communities by engaging in volunteer and philanthropic efforts. For example, since 1970, practioners have engaged in weekly cleaning of public spaces such as streets, parks, and train stations at over 6,000 locations around the world. Established in response to the 1995 Great Hanshin earthquake, the Shinnyo-en Relief Volunteers (SeRV) provides its practitioners with an avenue for volunteer service. Since its inception, SeRV volunteer aid workers have responded to the Russian tanker *Nakhodka* oil spill in the Sea of Japan in 2004, massive typhoons in Taiwan in 2001, the Indian Ocean earthquake and tsunami of 2004 in Sri Lanka and Thailand, and the great eastern Japan earthquake and tsunami of March 2011. Examples of philanthropic organizations based in the United States are the Shinnyo-en Foundation, Izumi Foundation, and Nā Lei Aloha Foundation.

Through these philanthropic activities, Shinnyo-en practitioners strive to create a Buddha-world. This effort is possible through *tōkō*, the collective efforts that quickens the good-roots (qualities) of all beings and Buddha's compassion. To enter this world the practitioner must experience *bakku-daiju*, salvation through interaction with the spiritual world.

Ronald Y. Nakasone

Further Reading

Clarke, Peter Bernard. *Japanese New Religions in Global Perspective.* London: Routledge, 2000.

Clarke, Peter Bernard, and John Nelson, eds. *Handbook of Contemporary Japanese Religions.* Leiden: Brill, 2012.

Cornille, Catherine. "New Japanese Religions, between Nationalism and Universalism." In Peter B. Clarke, ed. *Japanese New Religions.* Richmond, UK: Curzon Press, 2000.

Hubbard, Jaime. "Embarrassing Superstition, Doctrine, and the Study of New Religious Movements." *Journal of the American Academy of Religion* 66, no. 1 (1998): 59–92.

Pantzikas, Anton, ed. *Shinjo: Reflections.* Boston: Somerset Hall Press, 2009.

Sakashita, Jay. "Shinnyoen and the Transmission of Japanese New Religion Abroad." PhD dissertation, University of Stirling, 1998.

Shinnyo-en Website. http://www.shinnyoen.org/. Accessed July 15, 2014.

Shinnyo-en. "The Vision and Art of Shinjo Ito: USA Tour, Buddhist Ripples." Tokyo: International Affairs Department of Shinnyo-en, 2009.

Shinnyo-en. *Aiming for Nirvana.* Tachikawa: Shinnyo-en, 1993.

Shinrankai

Shinrankai, also known as Jōdo Shinshū Shinrankai, is an offshoot of the mainline school Jōdo Shinshū Honganji, known in the United States as the Buddhist Church of America. The group was established in 1958 when its founder, Takamori Kentetsu, a Honganji priest, separated from the mainline school.

Shinrankai distinguishes itself by claiming that Jōdo Shinshū Honganji misinterprets Shinran Shonin's basic teachings about Buddhism. "Shinrankai claims that the doctrines of Honganji are very vague and that they fail to help people actually attain salvation; Shinrankai demands more emphasis on teaching people that they can attain final salvation in the Pure Land (Jōdo)" (Kenshin, 2011, 44). For general information on the beliefs and practices of Jōdo Shinshū, see the separate entry.

Shinrankai has a small presence in the United States. The headquarters and main temple are in Gardena, California, and there is also a center in Honolulu, Hawai'i. The organization has a publishing arm, *Ichimannendo*, which offers translations of Takamori's writings including the introductory text *You Were Born for a Reason: The Real Purpose of Life*. Extensive information on Shinrankai in English, apart from the group's own publications, is not readily available.

Peter L. Doebler

See also: Entries: Buddhist Churches of America; Higashi Honganji; Honpa Hongwanji Mission of Hawai'i

Further Reading

Kenshin, Fukamizu. "The Situation of Japanese Traditional Buddhism in the Web 2.0 Era: Who Attacks and Who Guards the Religion?" In Erica Baffelli, Ian Reader, and Birgit Staemmler, eds. *Japanese Religions on the Internet: Innovation, Representation, and Authority.* London: Routledge, 2011, pp. 39–61.

Shintō

Shintō, the indigenous spirituality of the Japanese, refers to an outlook and lifestyle grounded in a sentiment of the innate sacred nobility of the natural world and every animate and inanimate denizen who is part of it. The sacredness that animates all existences is referred to as *kami*, who are present everywhere, especially in auspicious objects and beings. This belief is so deeply interwoven into the fabric of society and culture that even those Japanese who profess not to hold such sentiments readily participate in its domestic and communal rituals. Domestic or family rituals include such milestones as births, coming-of-age celebrations, weddings, and other felicitous occasions. Yearnings for safe childbirth, success in examinations and business, luck in finding a soulmate merit a visit to the shrine or other sacred sites. The origins of *matsuri* or festivals are linked to a community's collective experience that includes planting and harvesting, and mitigating the causes of disease and natural calamities. *Matsuri* also emerged from guilds. Fisherfolk not only celebrate good catches, but also conduct rituals for safe passage while at sea. The overriding sentiment underlying these rituals is a sincere gratitude for the gifts that nature provides to nourish life and well-being; and for the assistance of mythical and personal ancestors for safe passage through this world.

This entry is an overview of the above introduced Shintō sentiments that played out primarily in Hawai'i. Information on the Shintō experience in Hawai'i is sparse. This entry is constructed from tidbits of information from a variety of sources, including oral histories and personal recollections. It begins with the origins of Shintō and touches on its practices and beliefs.

History

The expression "Shintō" or the "way of *kami*" first appears in the eighth century *Nihon Shoki* (720) as an effort to highlight the indigenous spiritual tradition vis-à-vis Buddhism, a foreign faith. However, rather than an ideological confrontation, the Japanese opted for *shinbutsu shūgō*, a syncretism of Buddhism and Shintō that was formally articulated a century later in *honji suijaku*, a notion that advanced the idea that *kamis* are emanations of buddhas and/or bodhisattvas. Thus, for example, Amaterasu Ōmikami, the sun goddess, was identified with Dainichi Nyorai (Mahāvairocana), the sun Buddha. As a result, with the exception of a few shrines, most notably Ise Jingū, the more politically astute Buddhists took control of the shrines and erected temples within the compounds; Shintō functionaries wore Buddhist robes and chanted Buddhist *Sūtras*. Toward the end of the Edo period (1615–1868) *kokugaku* (native studies) intellectuals, particularly Moto'ori Norinaga (1730–1801), tried to recover the "true Japanese spirit" embedded in the *Nihon Shoki*, the earlier *Kojiki* (712), the lyrical poetry of the *Man'yoshū* (759?), and other ancient documents. In addition to recounting the origins of the universe and Japanese people, these early documents assumed, for example, that the corporeal and disembodied worlds are inhabited by countless *kami*. First and foremost is the benevolent Amaterasu Ōmikami, the original ancestor of the imperial family and by extension the Japanese nation. The emperor is the corporeal representative of the life-giving Amaterasu Ōmikami. Norinaga and other "native studies" intellectuals set the stage for *shinbutsu bunri*, the separation of Shintō from Buddhism. Following the 1868 overthrow of the Tokugawa Bakufu, the Meiji era (1868–1912) restored the emperor as the head of state. During the same period the country saw the emergence of *kokka* or State Shintō and *kyōha* or Sect Shintō.

State Shintō

The Meiji government derived much of its justification for State Shintō from Ōkuni Takamatsu (1792–1871), who advocated a return to *hongaku* or "original teachings," an expression that indentifies the Japanese spirit before the introduction of Chinese and other nonindigenous cultures. Such a spirit, Ōkuni argued, would quicken the "Japanese Way" in the citizenry and would in turn resist Western colonization and secure Japan as a modern nation. Ōkuni and other nationalists did not consider State Shintō to be a spiritual tradition, but an ideology that would remind the Japanese of their emperor's divinity, their divine ancestry, and the divinity of the land of Japan—rallying cries for nationalism.

In 1868 the government revived the long-defunct Department of Shintō that was first promulgated in 701. The department and its many subsequent incarnations began the process of separating Shintō from Buddhism and its role in the government. During the Tokugawa era (1615–1867), much like the office of the county clerk, temples were keepers of vital statistics. In 1871, the department established a 12-tiered administrative structure to consolidate the estimated 200,000 shrines scattered throughout the country under the aegis of Ise Jingu, the ancestral shrine of the imperial family dedicated to Amaterasu Ōmikami, Toyouke no Ōmikami, the *kami* of food, clothing, and shelter, and other *kami* prominent in Japanese mythology. This act justified the emperor's position as the head of state. The government also charged priests with the task of *shūshin* or moral culture that is inherent in the Japanese by virtue of their divine ancestry and the sacredness of their homeland. The government codified this moral posture in the 1890 *Kyōiku chukogo* or Imperial Rescript on Education; it became in effect a sacred document, which students were required to recite regularly. The rescript exhorted students to be loyal and filial to the emperor, the divine descendant of the Amaterau Ōmikami, to courageously support the state, and to protect the imperial family. It was an effort to counter excessive Western influences, provide a basis for public morality, and unify the people.

State Shintō also played a key role in Japan's empire-building project. The Japanese government established shrines in territories it occupied—Formosa (present-day Taiwan), the Ryūkyūs (present-day Okinawa Prefecture), Korea, and Nan'yo (South Pacific islands acquired through the League of Nations mandate)—so the people would become loyal subjects. Reminders of Japanese colonialism, most of these shrines were dismantled after the war. Although the government sponsorship of shrines ended with the nation's defeat in 1945, Japanese identity still remains closely linked to Amaterasu Ōmikami, the imperial family, and Japanese identity.

Sect Shintō

The government's initiative to consolidate the shrines met with resistance from a number of *kōs* or "spiritual confraternities" that believed their respective faith traditions did not fall under the directives of State Shintō. The primary contention of these *kōs* hinged on the *kami* to be honored. The government agency mandated that the four *kamis* that appear in the *Kojiki* be enshrined and worshipped. The four are Ame no Minakanushi no Kami, Takamimusubi no Kami, Kammusubi no Kami, and Amaterasu Ōmikami. Izumo Taisha and other *kōs*, which enshrined and worshiped other *kamis*, objected. The government recognized 13 independent *kōs*. They are Fusokyō, Izumo Oyashirokyō, Jikkokyō, Konkōkyō, Kurozumikyō, Misagikyō, Ontakekyō, Shinrikyō, Shinshukyō, Shintō Shuseiha, Shintō Taikyō, Shintō Taiseikyō, and Tenrikyō. Konkōkyō, which enshrined Konkodaijin, and Tenrikyō, which believed in Tenri-Ō-no-miko, successfully petitioned to be reclassified after the war's end.

Shrines are no longer supported by the government, but by in-kind and monetary donations by their devotees.

Today Jinja Honchō, the Association of Shintō Shrines, administers approximately 80,000 shrines. The association sets certain standards for shrines and priests; it publishes books and other literature and deliberates on important appointments. Membership is voluntary and it is estimated that more than 90 percent of shrines are part of the association. Other than this loose association, the tradition does not have a centralized bureau that issues directives about what to believe or how to interpret its "doctrines." The Shintō faith is not centered on beliefs, but the tradition does expect a devotee to follow a lifestyle that includes developing purity of heart, gratitude, and reverence toward all manner of *kami*. A fuller discussion of some of its beliefs and practices follows.

Shintō in Hawai'i

Japanese immigrants to Hawai'i carried with them their Shintō culture, where it became an essential component in the spiritual and cultural life of the community. However, because its rituals and symbols supported the ideology of imperial Japan, shrines and devotees experienced U.S. government and societal pressure during and immediately after World War II. These and other factors led to the closure of many shrines and the dismantling of their organization, which resulted in the loss of their records and memories. Maeda Takakazu estimates that Japanese immigrants established at least 59 shrines, a number culled from newspapers, magazines, newsletters, diaries and other unpublished sources, and oral history. This number does not include shrines erected in the cane fields that asked for abundant harvest, or shrines at harbors from which fishermen set out to sea, or shrines erected in private homes and gardens. These once numerous shrines have long vanished.

Today only a handful of the larger shrines with institutional links to Japan are active. Of the five shrines—Konpira Jinsha, Lāhainā Daijingu, and the Wailuku Izumo Taisha—Maui once hosted, only the 1915 Mau'i Jinsha and the Ebisu Kotohira Jinsha in Ma'alaea Harbor remain. Mau'i Jinsha was established by Rev. Matsumura Masaho, who arrived from the Big Island a year earlier. Matsumura returned to Japan in 1936; he was succeeded by Rev. Koakutsu Hatsuhiko. Six years later, he was replaced by Rev. Masao Arine Masao, a Maui boy who went to Japan in 1941 to receive formal training. While studying he met his future wife, Yamaguchi Torako, a Waipahu girl who had returned to Hiroshima with her mother and sister when she was seven. Less than six months after their return to Hawai'i, Pearl Harbor was attacked. As U.S. citizens, they at first avoided internment. However, Rev. Arine was later interned at the military camp in Haiku, Maui. After Arine's death in 1972, his wife assumed the responsibilities of Mau'i Jinsha and the Ebisu Kotohira Jinsha. As of 2013, at the age of 99, she continues to offer services one Sunday each month. In 1978 the shrine was placed on the National Register of Historical Places. The architect Takata Ichirō designed a traditional *nagare*-style shrine; it was constructed without the use of nails by

Tomokiyo Sei'ichi and Takada Ichisaburō, first-generation immigrants.

Of the five shrines that once served Kaua'i, only markers remain. One such marker is on the grounds of the Kapa'a Sands resort. The four active shrines on O'ahu are Daijingu Temple, Hawai'i Kotohira Jinsha–Hawai'i Dazifu Tenmangu, Hawai'i Izumo Taishakyō, and Ishizuchi Jinja. Many of the shrines in Hawai'i are associated with shrines of the homeland of the immigrants. The recently established Tsubaki America and Tsubaki Kannagara Jinja are not part of the early Japanese immigrant experience.

Daijingu Temple. Rev. Goshi Mino'o established the first Daijingu shrines in Hilo and Kaua'i in 1898; these shrines were dedicated to Amaterasu Ōmikami; a shrine to the goddess was established in Honolulu in 1905. Rev. Kawasaki Masato founded the Honolulu Daijingu Temple in 1916 in the Liliha district of Honolulu. The U.S. government closed and confiscated the shrine at the outbreak of World War II, and the resident priest, Kawasaki Kazoe, and his family were detained and eventually repatriated to Japan. At the conclusion of the war the Kawasakis returned to reestablish the shrine in Nu'uanu district in a renovated residence.

Hawai'i Kotohira Jinsha–Hawai'i Dazifu Tenmangu. In 1920, Rev. Hirota Hitoshi established Hawai'i Kotohira Jinsha, when he carried a *Gobunrei* (a part of the *kami*) enshrined at the Kotohira-gu in Kagawa Prefecture to his residence at 1256 North King Street. He served as *gūji* (head priest) until his death in 1925. He was succeeded

by Rev. Donkai Okazaki, who moved to the Nawili'wili Daijingu on Kaua'i in 1927. He in turn was replaced by Rev. Misao Isobe, who was dispatched by Shirasaki Hachimangu in Japan. The U.S. government closed the shrine at the onset of the war and in 1943 interned and deported the Isobe family to Japan. The shrine did not resume its activities until 1947. The following year, the federal government seized the property under the Trading with the Enemy Act and in 1949 announced its intent to sell the property. The shrine association immediately retained the services of a law firm to challenge the government (*Kotohira Jinsha v. McGrath*) and won. It was the first lawsuit ever initiated by a Japanese organization against the federal government, paving the way for similar suits. To mark the start of a new beginning, Kotohira Jinsha officially changed its name to Hawai'i Kotohira Jinsha and was incorporated as Hawai'i Kotohira Jinsha Kyōdan in 1951.

Kotohira Jinsha is dedicated to Konpirasan (Omononuchi-no-mikami), the patron of seafarers; it is the largest and most active shrine on the islands. In 1952 the shrine received the *Gobunrei* of Sugawara no Michizane (845–903), the patron of learning, enshrined at the Dazaifu Tenmangu of Saifu City, Fukuoka Prefecture. Hence the present name, Hawai'i Kotohira Jinsha–Hawai'i Dazifu Tenmangu. In addition, the grounds host Shirasaki Hachimangu of Yamaguchi Prefecture, Suitengu of Kurume City, Fukuoka Prefecture, Inari Jinja of Kyoto, Otaki Jinja of Otake City, Hiroshima, and Watatsumi Jinja of Tokushima Prefecture. Most of these shrines and the *kamis* they enshrined are from locales where many immigrants are from. Ōtaki Jinja was established by Sugimoto Tei'ichi and more than 120 other immigrant families from Ōtake City; the shrine is dedicated to the guardian *kami* of the city. There are approximately 25,000 Hachiman shrines throughout Japan; Hachiman is the deified name of Emperor Ōjin (r. 270–310), who is revered as the protector of the country and a god of war. Inari is the *kami* of agriculture; the fox serves as its messenger. Suitengu shrine is dedicated to safe childbirth. Watatsumi Jinja enshrines the tutelalry *kami* of the sea.

Mentioned also in the Kotohira Jinsha history is the Katō Jinsha, formally located in the Kukui district of Honolulu; it was closed at the outbreak of the war. The Kukui Redevelopment Project Agency offered the shrine building to the community, but there were no takers; it was demolished in September 1962. The original Katō Jinsha is dedicated to the deified spirit of the warlord Katō Kiyomasa (1561–1611) of Higo Province (present-day Kumamoto Prefecture).

Izumo Taishakyō Mission of Hawai'i. Rev. Miyao Katsuyoshi founded the Hawai'i Izumo Taishakyō in 1906 in Honolulu; but a shrine was not erected until 1923. The City and County of Honolulu requisitioned the shrine's property during the war. The city returned the shrine building in 1962 in very poor condition. It was moved to its present location on Kukui Street and restored. Interestingly, the U.S. government did not dissolve the shrine during the war, probably because it was one of the 13 *kōs* that were classified as Sect Shintō and not associated with State Shintō. The shrine enshrines the spirit of Ōkuninushi, who is believed to be the original leader of Izumo (present-day Shimane Prefecture). In Shintō mythology he is the ruler of the unseen world of spirits and magic, and the patron of nation-building, farming, business, and medicine.

Ishizuchi Jinja. The Ishizuchi Shrine in the Mo'ili'ili district of Honolulu had its origins when Takayama no Takagami appeared before Mitake Shina (1877–?) on January 17, 1913. Earlier that morning, Mitake announced, "Today an honored *kami* is coming." That evening Miyake was completely possessed by Takayama no Takagami, who announced, "I am Takayama no Takagami; I will borrow Shina's body and save everyone." Mitake did not know the identity of the *kami*. Only later did she learn that Takayama-no-Takagami is enshrined in Ishizuchi Jinjas that are scattered throughout the Inland Sea region. Having no spiritual training, Shina returned to Japan between 1914 and 1915 to be trained and certified by Ishizuki headquarters. Differing from the *kami* of other shrines, whose spirits were brought from Japan, the *kami* enshrined at the Ishizuchi Shrine appeared on its own. It did have a *chigi*, the X-shaped forms on both sides of the ridge beam, and the *katsuōgi*, cylindrical forms that sit perpendicular on the roof ridge. The Uesugi Gi'ichi family, who lived just below the shrine, maintained the shrine. Joe and Margie Pang and other old-timers remember the *tengu* image prominently placed on the altar; a similar image hangs at the Mo'ili'ili Ishizuchi shrine. Tengu is associated with Sarutahiko Ōmikami, the principal Shintō deity of the physical world. After the war, the shrine paraphernalia were packed and sent back to Japan

Wakamiya Inari Shrine. Formerly located in Kaka'ako and built in 1914, the shrine has survived three moves. From Kaka'ako it was moved in 1918 to a South King Street location that is currently occupied by the McCully Bicycle Shop. Saved through community effort, it was moved in 1979 to the Waipahu Cultural Gardens Park for restoration, to become a part of Hawai'i's Plantation Village. A small group of devotees still tend to it, but it is in poor condition. There was no formal blessing to rededicate it, so it is essentially just a shell. In the 1980s, the *temizuya* or ritual water purification basin was part of a neighbor's landscaping. The characteristic *kitsune* or fox and *koma inu* or lion-dog, guardian mascots associated with the shrine, have long disappeared. It was painted in bright red, typical of Inari shrines in Japan. An architect known only by the name Haschun designed the shrine.

In addition to their spiritual functions, Shintō shrines and priests served as purveyors of Japanese culture and identity. Much like the Buddhist temples, shrines built Japanese-language schools and offered a venue for festivals and other community activities. Kotohira Jinsha sponsored a Japan-Hawai'i Goodwill Sumo Tournament in 1956 between the All Japan High School Champions and Hawai'i Sumo Champions.

Tsubaki America and Tsubaki Kannagara Jinja. In 1986 Rev. Yukitaka Yamamoto, the 96th high priest of Tsubaki Grand Shrine in Mie, Japan, established the Tsubaki America Shrine in Stockton, California. The shrine venerates Sarutahiko no Ōmikami and his consort Amenouzume no Mikoto. The former is the principal *kami* of the earth; the latter is the *kami* of the arts, marriage, and joy. Amaterasu Ōmikami is also enshrined there. Tsubaki America relocated in 2001 to Granite Falls, Washington, to join with Tsubaki Kannagara Jinja, founded in 1992 by Rev. Koichi Barrish.

Beliefs and Practices

The *Kojiki*, *Nihongi*, and other ancient documents reveal that all manner of animate beings and inanimate things owe their existence to *kami*, a noble and sacred spirit that infuses life and vitality. While *kami* may be everywhere and in all objects such as rocks and trees, and all beings, including humans, the Japanese normally identify *kami* with awe-inspiring natural phenomena and personalities who have demonstrated exceptional accomplishments. Perhaps the most famous natural *kami* is Mt. Fuji. Jimmu (ca. 660–585 BCE), the first emperor, and Emperor Meiji (1866–1912) have been deified as *kami*. Ancestral spirits are also referred to as *kami*. The above mentioned Kato Jinsha deified the spirit of Kato Kiyomasa, a warlord of Higo during the Azuchi-Momoyama era (1568–1615).

Consistent with the belief that humanity shares and interacts with the world and its denizens are sacred, the Shintō "lifestyle" is one of gratitude for the blessings bestowed by *kami* and to their ancestral spirits. Such a lifestyle is demonstrated through a sincere relationship with *kami* and through affection toward and cooperation with others that share the world. The devotee is expected to observe the proper ritual offerings and prayers, to make pilgrimages to sacred sites, and to remember to make sacrifices to their deceased ancestors. Neglect of any or all rituals can and often will invite *wazawai* (misfortune, calamity, curse). The *kami* in turn responds in a manner that is appropriate to the devotee's reverence or neglect thereof. A visit to the family grave or sponsoring a simple service is often enough to mollify a neglected ancestral *kami*. Traditionally *wazawai* was thought to be a form of *tsumi* (pollution, misfortune) that needed to be exorcised by *harae*, physical and/or spiritual purification, before the individual was allowed to reenter the community.

Shrines are also established to appease angry spirits. Daizifu Tenmangu, for example, was built to pacify the *goryō* (angry and vengeful spirit) of Sugawara no Michizane (845–903), who was ousted from his position as the minister of the right, the second highest political post at the court. After his exile and subsequent death, the capital, Kyoto, was ravaged by a series of natural calamities and those who engineered his ouster suddenly died. In an effort to pacify his spirit, Michizane was posthumously pardoned, promoted in rank, and enshrined as Tenman, Kitano Daimyōjin, the highest rank of a *tenjin* or heavenly personality. These actions mollified Michizane's spirit; he is now honored as a *kami* of learning and literature. His shrine at the Kotohira Jinsha-Daizifu Tenmangu is frequented by students wishing for success in their educational pursuits. The practice of appeasing vengeful spirits

continued during the early immigrant experience. Alarmed at the number of drownings of children and fishermen in 1913, Yamaguchi Susumu carved an image of Jizō to pacify vengeful spirits that lurked in and around Kawaihapai Bay, Mokuleia, O'ahu. Jizō (*Kṣitigarbha*) is a Buddhist spiritual hero, not a Shintō *kami*, but in the popular Japanese mind, he is identified with Sae no Kami, who is often seen in thoroughfares that lead into villages. In the *Kojiki*, Sae no kami stands watch on the boundary that divides the world of the living and the dead. Jizō is certainly the most appropriate *kami* for safeguarding from drowning. In his Buddhist guise, Jizō promised Śākyamuni Buddha that he would traverse the six hells and assist those in suffering until the future Maitreya appears. Jizō continues to fulfill his promise; the vengeful spirits that once lurked in the bay have since been pacified; drownings have ceased. The image was moved to the Wahiawa Ryūsenji temple in 2004.

It is not possible to build a shrine to mollify every vengeful spirit, but it is possible to control them through *harae*, a general expression for purification ceremonies designed to counter misfortune and pollution and restore ritual purity. Washing hands before approaching the *kami* is a form of *harae*. Before a bout, sumo wrestlers sprinkle salt to purify the ring of spirits that may be lurking nearby. New homes and new undertakings are blessed to avoid misfortune. Salt is sprinkled at the entryway after returning home from a funeral. This ritual prevents the spirit of the deceased, who may have followed the mourner home, from entering the house. Death is a form of *kegare* or pollution or defilement. *Kegare* from death still has considerable force in the Japanese community. If a death in the family has occurred, the traditional New Year pilgrimage to the shrine is forgone and New Year greeting cards are not sent.

In addition to appealing for protection, Japanese appeal to *kami* for protection from misfortune. *Yakudoshi* or "age of bad luck" is widely observed by Japanese in Hawai'i. The 42nd year for men and the 33rd for women are especially dangerous. In Japanese the numeral 4 is pronounced *shi* and 2 is voiced *ni*. Forty-two or *shini* in a different context means "to die." The number 33 is pronounced *sanzan*, which in a different situation can mean "disaster." Men and women who come of age can mitigate or even avoid the misfortunes of *yakudoshi* by visiting a shrine and/or sponsoring a large party. The present usage of the expression possesses little of its former meaning. The *kanji* or ideogram pronounced *yaku* means "misfortune" or "bad luck"; but the *kanji* for "duty" or "responsibility" is also pronounced *yaku*. Originally, *yakudoshi* marked an auspicious milestone that called for a celebration of longevity (*toshi iwai*). A person reaching a *yakudoshi* age underwent rituals of purification by abstinence and confinement and engaged in some sacred activity.

The *matsuri* or festivals that punctuate the calendar year are expressions of joy and gratitude, and celebrate the agricultural cycle, mark coming of age milestones, and other events specific to the community. These celebrations, especially the planting and harvest *matsuri*, are shared by the entire community, regardless of faith affiliation. Some of the more important obser-

vances are *hatsumode, momo no sekku, tango no sekku, tanabata*, and *shichi-go-san. Hatsumōde* is the first visit to the shrine in the New Year. The devotee recommits him/herself to a life of gratitude and asks *kami* for health and prosperity for him or herself and for the family. Celebrated in early February, *setsubun* marks the first day of spring according to the lunar calendar. *Momo no sekku* marks the blooming of the peach blossoms; the third day of the third month is Girl's Day. *Tango no sekku* is the season of the iris; the fifth day of the fifth month is Boy's Day. *Tanabata* or star festival celebrates the meeting of the deities Orihime and Hikoboshi (represented by the stars Vega and Altair respectively) who meet only once a year on the seventh day of the seventh lunar month. On this occasion wishes are written on color strips of paper and hung on bamboo sprays. *Shichi-go-san* (Seven-Five-Three) marks the rite of passage for girls seven and five years of age, and boys five or three years of age. On the 15th of November children wearing traditional kimonos visit the shrines to pray for health and for protection against misfortune.

Miyamairi is the custom of bringing a newborn to a shrine a month after birth. On this visit the priest blesses the child and wards off any pollutants. Shrines also provide, for a fee, *omamori*, amulets to hang on the car's rear view mirror for protection from accidents. There are amulets imbued with the spirit of a protector *kami* to ensure protection of the home from fire and other calamities, safe childbirth, success in business, and luck in finding love. Priests often perform purification rituals at the construction of a new home. They are called to exorcise homes from the pollution of death or bless a new venture.

While the shrine is a sacred site where the *kami* can be invited and where the people can experience its presence, traditional Japanese families maintain a *kamidana* or home shrine where daily offerings are made. Families often place images of *shichifukujin*, the seven *kamis* of good fortune, and other symbols on the *kamidana* to ensure longevity, happiness, and luck. But perhaps the most ubiquitous presence of the Shintō lifestyle is the Japanese obsession with cleaning, especially during the waning days of December. The home must be spotless to welcome the New Year.

Michael Maricio

See also: Essays: Spirituality; *Entries:* Hezhen (Nānai) Shamanism; Japanese American Religions; Shamanism, Modern

Further Reading

Cali, Joseph, and John Dougill. *Shintō Shrines, A Guide to the Sacred Sites of Japan's Ancient Religion.* Honolulu: University of Hawai'i Press, 2013.

Herbert, Jean. *Shintō: At the Fountain-head of Japan.* London: George Allen & Unwin, 1967.

Maeda, Takakazu. *Hawai no jinsha shi [History of Shintō shines in Hawai'i].* Tokyo: Daimeido, 1999.

Hawai'i Daijingu. http://www.hawaiidaijingu .com/history/. Accessed May 1, 2013.

Hawai'i Kotohira Jinsha–Hawai'i Dazaifu Tenmangu. http://www.e-shrine.org/. Accessed May 1, 2013.

Sho, Calligraphy

Sho (as it is referred to in Japan; Ch. *shu*) or calligraphy is the simple exercise of writing *kanji* (Ch. *hanzi*) and phonetic script to communicate thoughts, feelings, and information. Its origins can be traced to pictographs inscribed on bone, turtle shells, and other surfaces that expressed yearnings for good harvest, aspirations for health and safe passage through life; many of the inscriptions asked for prognostications for war. While *kanji* may have originally been inspired from images of the natural world (and some graphs still hint at their physical inspirations), they became increasingly abstract. Their numbers proliferated, resulting in regional variations and often multiple versions of a single *kanji*. Thus, among the many reforms Shi Huangdi (r. 221–210 BCE), the first Qin emperor, initiated after unifying China was the standardization of the script for ease of communication and to expedite trade and taxation. Today there are five script styles: (1) *tensho* (Ch. *zhuànshū*) or seal script, (2) *reisho* (Ch. *lìshū*) or clerical script, (3) *kaisho* (Ch. *kǎishū*) or regular script, (4) *gyōsho* (Ch. *xíngshū*) or semicursive script, and (5) *sōsho* (Ch. *cǎoshū*) or cursive or running script. The seal and clerical script are rarely used today, except for seals and the occasional inscription. Typographical variants of *kaisho* or regular script are used for newspapers, books, and other printed media. The semicursive *gyōsho* and cursive or running *sōsho* styles are used to take notes, write letters and poetry, and employed for other informal occasions.

Sho culture spread to Korea, Japan, Vietnam, Manchuria, and other regions impacted by Chinese civilization, where the mastery of the brush and the visual qualities of the written word were one of the four measures of scholarly accomplishment.

(The other three are *qin* [Jpn. *koto*] or zither, *qi* [Jpn. *go*] or bead board game, and *hua* [Jpn. *ga*] or painting.) This entry introduces the traditional method of the study of *sho*, the aesthetics of line and space, and concludes with some remarks on the modern *sho* and its practice in the United States.

Aesthetic and creative interests quicken the *sho* artist to explore ideographic styles and developments, to give expressive shape to their meanings, to play with their constructions (form and stroke order), to explore the potential and limitations of the soft brush and the textures of ink and paper, and to give form to feelings and thoughts through line, space, and time. Since *kanji* are abstractions signifying objects, sounds, feelings, and ideas, the art of *sho* is nonfigurative, nonobjective, and nonrepresentational; it can be properly called abstract art. The art of *sho*, like abstract expressionism, is interested in giving spontaneous form to the inner life. Centuries of exploration have generated an aesthetic vocabulary that mirrors the subtleness of the soft brush together with the range of the texture of inks and the texture of different writing surfaces.

Aesthetics of Line (Form)

Lines are all around us. Seen from afar my arm is a line; similarly, a brush, a plastic pipe, and the edge of the stage are lines. Some lines are harsh and cold; others are soft and fluid; others are dynamic and bold. The visual qualities of strength, warmth, steadfastness, rhythm, volume, and playfulness are some aesthetic values of line that are prized in the art of *sho*.

Writing *sho* is, in many ways, a performance. The ink marks that appear on the paper are traces of the more expansive hand and body movements, and more fundamentally the intent and personality of the artist. Rhythm mirrors the breath and concentration; it is the "thread" that holds a single or a series of *kanji* together with varying degrees, the aesthetic qualities of strength, warmth, steadfastness, and playfulness mentioned above. Spontaneity issues forth after years of practice.

Aesthetics of Space

The aesthetic sensibilities of East Asia place a prime value on space, an essential element in the art of *sho*. Space is most difficult to appreciate and understand, because one is accustomed to seeing form and color, not space or emptiness. The art of *sho* identifies physical, temporal, and aesthetic space.

Space and form, the interplay of black form and white space, are reciprocal and inseparable. Space, the white unmarked surface, has a physical presence that enriches line; and line in turn gives life to space. Space is not a passive medium in which forms are located or where events occur, rather it defines form and is the source from which it emerges. Form creates space, but it is space that gives meaning and efficacy to form.

In addition to its physicality, "space" also possesses the meaning of *ma*, "pause" or "point in time"; it is an aesthetic element that gives life to space. In dance *ma* is referred to as *omoi-ire* (lit. to put one's thoughts into; i.e., to ponder, reflect on, or meditate on), or pause, often imperceptibly, and is intended to transport the observer out of time. Like form and space, movement and rest are complementary. Likewise, timelessness is meaningful only in time. For composer Takemitsu Toru (1930–1996) *ma* is silence that "gives life to sound and removes it from its position of primacy." Silence isolates sound, thereby accentuating it. Space, the counterpoint of form, enriches line.

Ma is often responsible for the "accidental" splattering of ink that appears on the writing surface when the brush lingers over the paper or pauses while writing. What is seen to be "accidental" is *futo*, or "natural process." During medieval Japan (13th–17th centuries) the adverbial form of *shizen*, "by chance," described the unintentional "happenings" that occurred during the creative process. These "happenings" were understood to be integral to the creative process, not obstacles or mistakes. Likewise in *sho* unexpected ink drips and bleeding into the paper are integral aspects of the art, not mistakes.

In addition to the momentary "pause" wherein the *sho* artist gathers his thoughts and strength before committing ink to paper, the construction of the ideogram together with the rhythm of the breath and body necessitates *ma* moments. The complex movements required to write the ideographs for *okushi*, "memory and imagination," illustrate the technical use of *ma*. The brush enters the paper to create the *risshinben*, "left-side standing 'heart'" radical with the first "dot" on the far left. The bleeding indicates that the brush lingered momentarily, allowing a bit of extra ink to flow on to the paper, before soaring upward and to the right to form the second

"dot." After another momentary pause the brush jumps upward and slightly to the left to begin the long downward vertical stroke. The downward momentum powers the brush upward to the upper reaches of the writing surface, where it enters the paper and begins to compose the *tsukuri*, right-side component of *oku*, "memory." The cursive form of *tsukuri* or left-side component requires the brush to execute a series of brisk zigzag horizontal strokes as it progresses downward. The moments of "rest" are located at those transition points where the brush changes direction. The final "rest" occurs on the far right at the end of the *shitagokoro*, "bottom heart" radical that forms the *ashi* or foot section of the ideogram. The pause signals another gathering of the breath and strength, before the brush leaps to execute the first downward stroke of the second ideogram *shi*, "imagination" or "thought." The rhythm of breath and movement propels the brush to complete the upper half of the *kanji*. The thin sword-like slashing downward diagonal stroke that begins at the middle of the ideogram forms the first stroke of *kokoro*, "heart" or "mind." The brush leaps up and to the left to begin the heavy diagonal line that comes to a point, before executing the final two "dots" that complete the character. One of the joys of "reading" ideograms is to follow the movement of the brush. In addition to rhythm, lines of these two *kanji* exhibit a number of aesthetic qualities—strength, warmth, steadfastness, rhythm, and playfulness—that add visual interest.

Lastly, *ma* refers to "space" that links the art and the viewer. Art has the power to reach beyond the physical confines to embrace and flow through the viewer, drawing him or her into an uncommon world. A great work of *sho* draws the viewer to the spaceless abode of the writer's *kyōgai* or "spiritual dwelling place." Ordinarily *kyōgai* refers to one's socioeconomic station, but in Japanese Buddhist culture the expression refers to a "capacity for life," nurtured through a long and vital involvement in life. The artless rhythm of the very late works of the Rinzai Zen master Hakuin Ekaku (1685–1768) exhibits a formless landscape of equanimity and uncommon ease; it is a topography that draws the viewer to commune with a rarefied formless reality. Such a landscape is revealed by the brush of Furukawa Taiko (1871–1968), who at the age of 91 wrote *sho rō ju ta* ("pine-tree," "old or elder," "longevity," and "many") or "The pine tree [reminds this] elder of [his] longevity." Furukawa's lines become progressively more animated as the brush moves toward the bottom of the poem. Furukawa's strength is demonstrated by an abandoned freedom of movement and almost total disregard of form, especially in the final two ideographs: *ju* and *ta*. His rendering for *ju*, "longevity" is unprecedented in that such a rendering is not found in *kanji*-sample dictionaries; but more significantly, both *kanjis* were executed with total abandon.

Modern *Sho*

Modern *sho* has its origins in the early 20th century, when after nearly 300 years of isolation, *sho* artists rediscovered the ideographic forms from the fringes of Chinese culture. Differing from the staid official style, these "outliner" scripts revealed the creative potential of the brush. In the early 1950s, Franz Kline (1910–1962), Robert Motherwell (1915–1991), and other abstract artists were drawn to the expressiveness of *sho*. Action painting by Jackson Pollock (1912–1956) highlighted spontaneity in the creative process, a major element in the art of *sho*. In response to the large canvases on which abstract expressionists created their work, Inoue Yu'ichi (1916–1985), Morita Shiryū (1912–1998), and other Japanese *sho* artists, who exhibited in Europe and South America, also used large brushes and sheets of paper that highlighted the forceful spontaneity of the soft brush. Later contemporary Korean and Chinese calligraphers would soon follow.

Please note that the calligraphy images mentioned in this entry can be viewed in "Formless Form: The Aesthetics of *Sho* (Calligraphy)," cited in the bibliography.

Ronald Y. Nakasone

See also: Essays: Arts and Cultural Production; *Entries:* Arabic (Islamic) Calligraphy

Further Reading

Harrist, Robert E., Jr., and Wen C. Fong. *The Embodied Image, Chinese Calligraphy from the John B. Elliott Collection.* Princeton, NJ: The Art Museum, 1999.

Hisamatsu Shin'ichi. *Zen and the Fine Arts.* Translated by Gishin Tokiwa. Tokyo: Kodansha International, 1971.

Morita, Shiryū. *Sho—ikikata no katachi* [*Sho—the Form of Life*]. Tokyo: NHK, 1968.

Munroe, Alexandra. "*Circle*—Modernism and Tradition." In *Japanese Art after 1945: Scream Against the Sky.* New York: Abrams, 1994, pp. 83–124.

Nakasone, Ronald Y. 2005. "A Buddhist View of Teaching and Learning in the Later Years." *Aging and Spirituality* 17, no. 2 (Summer 2005).

Nakasone, Ronald Y. "Formless Form: The Aesthetics of *Sho* (Calligraphy)." *Arts in Religion and Theological Studies* 21, no. 2 (2011): 4–11.

Nakata, Yūjirō, ed. *Chinese Calligraphy*. Translated by Jeffery Hunter. New York: Weatherhill/Tankosha, 1982.

Westgeest, Helen. *Zen in the Fifties, Interaction in Art between East and West*. Amsterdam: Waanders, 1996.

Winther-Tamaki, Bert. *Art in the Encounter of Nations: Japanese and American Artists in the Early Postwar Years*. Honolulu: University of Hawai'i Press, 2001.

Shunryū Suzuki (1904–1971)

Shunryū Suzuki, founder of the San Francisco Zen Center, the first Zen Buddhist monastery established in the West, is arguably the single most important figure in the spread of Sōtō Zen throughout North America.

Suzuki was born into a small Sōtō temple just south of Tokyo. At the age of 12, he decided to train with Rev. Sōon Suzuki (1877–1934), one of his father's disciples. Sōon took to calling him "crooked cucumber," a nickname for his absent-minded, idealistic, quirky disciple. From a young age, he excelled in the classroom. At Komazawa University, he majored in Zen and Buddhist studies, and minored in English. After graduating, he expressed an interest to teach Zen Buddhism in America, but Sōon Suzuki fiercely opposed the idea and encouraged him instead to train at Eiheiji, one of the Two Head Temples of Sōtōshū in Japan. He was assigned to be the attendant of Ian Kishizawa (1865–1955), a well-known Sōtō Zen teacher and scholar. Suzuki also trained for some time at Sōjiji, the other Head Temple of Sōtōshū. Even after returning to Sōon Suzuki's temple in 1932, he continued studying with Kishizawa.

Suzuki landed in San Francisco on May 19, 1959, to become the resident priest of Sōkōji. He arrived at a most opportune moment. Partly through the efforts of Alan Watts (1915–1971), a pivotal figure who popularized Eastern philosophy in the West, beatniks of the 1950s and hippies of the 60s were exploring alternatives to war, racial discrimination, pollution, poverty, and other concerns. They were attracted to the peaceful reputation of Buddhism, especially the Zen emphasis on living a simple life in tune with nature and its aesthetics.

Suzuki opened Sōkōji's doors to these "counterculture" Americans and taught them to cultivate the wisdom of nonduality through the practice of single-minded sitting meditation (*shikantaza*). In 1962, he founded the San Francisco Zen Center, which quickly grew; so much so that in 1966, it purchased Tassajara Hot Springs in the Los Padres National Forest. This became Tassajara Zen Mountain Center, the first Sōtō Zen monastery in the West. In 1969, Sōkōji's board of directors asked Suzuki to resign as their resident priest because he was spending more time with his Western students than with the Japanese American members of the temple. In 1969, the San Francisco Zen Center purchased a large building at 300 Page Street in San Francisco, which is now known as City Center.

The San Francisco Zen Center has fostered a large network of affiliated Zen centers, mainly in the Bay Area, with connections to like-minded groups throughout the United States. Its main locations are Tassajara—the monastic arm of the organization;

City Center—a facility that sponsors meditation retreats, study groups, and recovery groups; and Green Gulch Farm—a farm located 30 miles north of San Francisco that produces and sells large amounts of organic vegetables to support the Zen Center.

Suzuki died of cancer in late 1971. Although he had lived for only 12 years in the United States, he rode the crest of a swelling interest in Zen and made a major contribution toward establishing Sōtō Zen in North America. Shortly before his death, *Zen Mind, Beginner's Mind* was published. A collection of his talks, this book remains a bestseller of contemporary Zen literature.

Daigaku Rummé

See also: Entries: Buddhist Meditation; Rinzai Zen

Further Reading

Chadwick, David. *Crooked Cucumber: The Life and Teaching of Shunryū Suzuki.* New York: Three Rivers Press, 2000.

Suzuki, Shunryū. *Not Always So: Practicing the True Spirit of Zen.* Edited by Edward Espe Brown. San Francisco: HarperCollins, 2002.

Suzuki, Shunryū. *Zen Mind, Beginner's Mind.* Edited by Trudy Dixon. New York: Weatherhill Press, 1970.

Sikh American Legal Defense and Education Fund (SALDEF)

Founded in 1996, the Sikh American Legal Defense and Education Fund (SALDEF) is the nation's oldest Sikh American civil rights and education organization. SALDEF seeks to empower Sikh Americans by building dialogue, deepening understanding, promoting civic and political participation, and upholding social justice and religious freedom for all Americans. SALDEF envisions a nation in which Sikh Americans are recognized and respected as a vibrant and integral part of the United States, and appreciated for their shared values of service, social justice, and an unshakeable belief in freedom and equality for all.

SALDEF was founded as a virtual, volunteer organization, with a handful of volunteers from various professional backgrounds scattered throughout the nation. The group initially focused on educating the public about Sikh Americans and their faith, as well as monitoring media misrepresentations of Sikhs. The volunteer nature of the organization sought to embody in action a central tenet of the Sikh faith, *seva*, selfless service of others. The service was targeted to fill a very specific, relatively ignored area of great need for Sikh Americans, a community comprised primarily of immigrants that were still finding their place in U.S. society. Sikh Americans needed advocates to monitor their representation in the Western media, which so often mischaracterized Sikhs as members of the Hindu religious tradition, or as terrorists.

Early on, the members of the organization realized that Sikh American civil rights were often circumscribed by the lack of knowledge most members of the community had about U.S. law and their rights under it. To help address this, the organization produced and distributed a "Know Your Rights" card that community members could carry in their wallet. The idea has since expanded to "Know Your

Yuvkaran Gahley serves guests during a Sikh tradition called a Langar, which is a group dinner of vegetarian fare, July 30, 2014. The event, held in the Rayburn foyer, was hosted by the Sikh American Legal Defense and Education Fund's SikhLEAD Internship program and was the first time in the Sikh Americans' 125-year-old history that a Langar has been held on Capitol Hill. (Tom Williams/CQ Roll Call/Getty Images)

Rights" forums, which SALDEF has held throughout the country since 2002.

Understanding the need for accurate, easily digestible information about Sikh Americans, their history, and their faith tradition, the organization produced various publications to educate media, law enforcement, politicians, as well as interested fellow citizens. The first of these was a pamphlet entitled *Who Are the Sikhs?*, which offers a brief introduction to Sikh Americans and the Sikh faith. This was soon followed by a short brochure called "Welcome to the Gurdwara," which details the culturally appropriate etiquette and attire for visitors to a Sikh sacred site,

easing any apprehensions they might have. The brochure was designed to help members of the media and local officials more easily access Sikh American communities that they served, as well as to encourage Sikh communities to hold open houses for their neighbors to learn about them and their beliefs. To further this end, the organization annually distributes a business card–sized document containing images of, and basic facts about, Sikh Americans, which it encourages community members to hand out to friends with whom they would like to share something about their community and religious beliefs.

SALDEF has produced a number of publications, some of which are also available in Punjabi, on such topics as school bullying, hate crimes, employment discrimination, and recommendations for law enforcement when interacting with Sikh Americans. These resources represent an important contribution to those interested in learning and/or teaching about the Sikh American community, offering information that is clear, concise, accurate, verifiable, and accessible to a wide variety of audiences.

SALDEF was the first Sikh American organization to provide free legal support to those whose civil rights had been violated by connecting community members with pro-bono attorneys. In 1997, the organization made a singular contribution to Sikh American civil rights by assembling a legal database of federal and state court opinions relating to Sikh Americans. It achieved its first major legal victory representing a *granthi*—the caretaker of the *gurdwara* and reader of the scriptures during religious ceremonies—who faced charges of carrying a concealed weapon in September 1999. Gurbachan Singh Bhatia, 69, was arrested by local police after a minor traffic accident, while returning from a religious ceremony blessing the new home of a local Sikh American family. Local police detained him for carrying a *kirpan*, a small, religious sword that is a religiously mandated article of faith for Sikhs who have taken a vow to live according to the ideals of the Sikh way of life. Thanks to the organization's intervention through a letter-writing campaign, raising funds, and finding legal assistance, the case was dismissed and an important legal precedent

established. SALDEF continues to regularly receive requests for assistance with *kirpan* cases throughout the country.

Through this and other cases, the organization learned the importance of educating local law enforcement officials, who are the ones most likely to encounter Sikh Americans while on the job. This has become a signature aspect of SALDEF's work. Central to the group's efforts in this area has been the production, in partnership with the U.S. Department of Justice, of a groundbreaking training video for law enforcement entitled *On Common Ground*. Similarly, SALDEF created a training program for first responders in July 1999. Its Law Enforcement Partnership Program (LEPP) has now trained well over 100,000 local, state, and federal law enforcement officials in over 150 agencies, including the Federal Bureau of Investigation (FBI), the U.S. Department of Justice (DOJ), and the police forces of New York City; Boston; Washington, DC; Las Vegas; Columbia, Missouri; Des Moines, Iowa; Jamestown, North Carolina; Charlestown, West Virginia; Pittsburgh, Pennsylvania; Eugene, Portland, and Salem, Oregon; and numerous other cities and towns. As a result of the relationship SALDEF has fostered with the Washington, DC Metropolitan Police Department, its chief has issued a call welcoming turban-wearing Sikhs into the force. This basic right to employment while maintaining their religious requirements is something Sikh Americans in many areas of the country have had to fight for, or are still denied.

SALDEF has partnered with the DOJ, the Transportation Security Administration (TSA), and the Department of Homeland

Security (DHS) to produce and distribute posters to increase awareness about Sikh Americans. In August 2004, the DOJ released a poster titled "Common Sikh American Head Coverings." The TSA published a similar poster the following year. In 2006, DHS released a poster providing information about Sikh Americans and the *kirpan*.

Initially named the Sikh Mediawatch and Resource Task Force (SMART), the organization changed its name and focus to meet the needs of the nation's Sikh community in the aftermath of the terrorist attacks of September 11, 2001. In the wake of the terrorist attacks, the racially and religiously identifiable Sikh American community disproportionately suffered from a massive, national hate crime epidemic against those perceived as Muslim. SALDEF worked to explain to the media, politicians, and law enforcement officials who Sikh Americans were, what they believed, and that they were among those suffering from hate crimes and racial profiling by law enforcement and at airport security.

SALDEF representatives worked with high-level federal government officials to address the problems Sikh Americans and others were experiencing in the midst of the national trauma. As the only established Sikh American civil rights entity at the time, SALDEF met with Transportation Secretary Norman Mineta, forming an important and efficacious working relationship for the organization and the community. In response to reports of racial and religious profiling at airports after 9/11, SALDEF offered critical background information to the FAA to enable the "appropriate and sensitive" handling of Sikh

American passengers. In response to the first reported incident of illegal turban removal by airport security screeners after 9/11, the organization conducted an awareness and protocol training about Sikh Americans at Albany International Airport. Ongoing discussions with the TSA continue to address the profiling Sikh Americans still encounter as de facto policy in many airports throughout the nation.

In the years since 2001, SALDEF has continued to engage in conversation with such seminal political figures as the director of the FBI, U.S. attorney general, secretary for the Department of Homeland Security, and the assistant attorney general for civil rights, addressing many other issues of interest to Sikh Americans. A hallmark of the organization's success has been its ability to open channels of communication to the highest levels of government, from which Sikh Americans had previously been excluded. SALDEF was recognized on the floor of the U.S. House of Representatives for its contributions in conducting multiple congressional briefings on civil rights issues including hate crimes, workplace discrimination, and racial profiling.

As the needs of the community evolved after 9/11, SALDEF was inundated by civil rights, legislative, employment, and accommodation issues on a much greater scale than ever before, necessitating a broad expansion of its work on behalf of Sikh Americans. A brief synopsis of some prominent recent cases provides a perspective on the diversity of cases the organization, and the Sikh American community, continue to confront in the United States.

In 2007, SALDEF worked on behalf of Satnam Singh, a Sikh American incarcerated in Vermont, regarding a potential policy change that would have restricted Mr. Singh's right to maintain his turban. In response to SALDEF's inquiry, Robert Hofmann, commissioner of the Vermont Department of Corrections, formally accepted changes in policy to respect a prisoner's religious rights. Among others, changes included recognizing the *Khanda* as a religious symbol, allowing prisoners to maintain their turbans in all areas of the institution, and an implementation of a redress process.

Since mid-2007, SALDEF has made dozens of official complaints in response to naturalization delay concerns from community members, some waiting over four years. This led to a meeting with U.S. Immigration and Customs' enforcement director, Emilio Gonzalez, who offered assurances that steps were being taken by the DHS and the FBI to address the thousands of applicants waiting for their naturalization applications to be processed due to name checks, and that "significant results" would be seen within six months.

SALDEF continues its early work in the area of media monitoring. A New Jersey affiliate of *ABC News* apologized to SALDEF and the Sikh American community in early 2008 for misrepresenting Sikhs as Muslims. In a news report, a correspondent showed video footage of a Sikh American while discussing a Muslim neighborhood and concerns over affairs in Pakistan. Within 24 hours of receiving SALDEF's letter, correspondent Jeff Rossen and ABC apologized to SALDEF and the Sikh American community and promptly removed and edited the video depicting the misrepresentation.

Throughout its history, but especially since 9/11, SALDEF has received a steady stream of complaints of discrimination in the workplace, by private businesses, and in dealings with local government officials. In the summer of 2009, SALDEF initiated a campaign to overturn an Oregon law prohibiting public school teachers from wearing religious clothing or articles of faith in the classroom—effectively banning observant Sikhs from the entire profession. SALDEF's work led the Oregon Speaker of the House to remark that "the commitment and effort of the Sikh American Legal Defense and Education Fund played a key role in ensuring that every Oregon citizen has the right to teach in our classrooms while maintaining religious free exercise." SALDEF has also helped numerous individuals deal with instances of employment discrimination, and contacted the Department of Motor Vehicles in a number of states because of difficulties encountered by Sikh Americans attempting to obtain a driver's license without being forced to remove their turbans.

In April 2011, Arizona's legislature attempted to push through a bill that would have removed Balbir Singh Sodhi's name from the state's 9/11 memorial, to sell it for scrap metal. Mr. Sodhi, a Sikh American business owner, was the first American to die in the hate crime epidemic that followed 9/11. A protest led by SALDEF flooded Arizona governor Jan Brewer's office with 7,500 letters in less than three days, forcing her to meet with the Sodhi family and veto the bill.

SALDEF also engages in policymaking discussions, offering explicit recommendations on issues of relevance to Sikh

Americans. In the wake of the August 2012 massacre in the Oak Creek *Gurdwara* in Wisconsin, SALDEF worked with the community and other Sikh organizations to serve the needs of the local and national Sikh American communities. In subsequent congressional hearings, SALDEF joined a coalition of community service nonprofit organizations that urged policymakers to pass strong legislation to prevent, document, investigate, and combat hate crimes, an ongoing and growing problem for racialized non-Christian communities in the United States.

SALDEF also regularly organizes presentations to schools, conferences, and special groups around issues such as how to deal with hate crimes and school bullying. SALDEF also reaches Sikh American youth by presenting at youth camps, where children are taught about the types of bullying, methods for preventing such harassment, and the need for students to document and report the incidents to their parents and teachers.

SALDEF has endeavored to serve the educational, occupational, and networking needs of the community's young adults through its SikhLEAD program. One part of this program, designed to facilitate an increase in the number of Sikh Americans committing themselves to public service, places college students in congressional internships. This not only provides these young adults with exposure to the legislative and policymaking process but with invaluable networking opportunities. By providing an entree into national politics, this program will help expand the pool of eligible candidates for political positions from the Sikh American community in the coming years.

An even more significant aspect of SikhLEAD is the remarkably successful Leadership Development Program. This initiative seeks to inspire, train, and support talented and highly motivated Sikh Americans as they develop skills and contacts that will be indispensable when they assume their place as community leaders. In training cadres of future leaders and activists, SALDEF offers leadership training, personal development, and networking/bonding opportunities for the participants. The program also introduces participants to a host of successful community mentors from throughout the nation, with whom the program participants can network and develop long-term relationships. Several graduates of the program have already achieved remarkable success in terrain as diverse as university-level student elections, the television show *American Idol*, and collecting, shaping, and performing the stories of Sikh Americans interviewed throughout the country.

Ultimately, the gains SALDEF has been able to help foster in its relatively brief existence have broadened civil and human rights, ensuring greater religious freedom and making the nation more free and democratic for all Americans. SALDEF's multifaceted action plan to institute change on behalf of the Sikh American community continues to evolve to best suit the changing needs of the community.

Jaideep Singh

See also: Essays: Islamophobia; Religion, Race, and Orientalism; *Entries:* Indian American Sikhs; South Asian Americans Leading Together (SAALT); Sikh Foundation, The

Further Reading

SALDEF Annual Reports, 2010–2013.

SALDEF Website. www.saldef.org. Accessed July 11, 2014.

Sikh Canon

Compiled between 1469 and 1675, the 1,430-page *Gurū Granth Sahib* is the sacred canon of the Sikh tradition. It is a collection of *rags* or hymns that describe the wonders of Wahegurū (the Divine) and the oneness of humanity. A secondary, noncanonical literature is the *Janam Sakhis* that relates the life stories of the *gurus*. This entry provides a brief overview of the content, development, and role of the *Gurū Granth Sahib* in Sikh worship, ritual, and life.

The fifth Sikh *guru*, *Guru* Arjun (1563–1606), together with the scribe Bhai Gurdas (1551–1636), gathered poetic expressions from the first five *guru* teachers, including his, and 15 great Hindu *bhagats* ("devotees") and Muslim saints that resonated with the insight of *Guru* Nānak into the *Ādi Granth* (*ādi* means "primal"; *granth* means "book"). The editorial basis for their selection was verses that penetrated into and revealed Wahegurū. Rather than metaphysical treatises or theological injunctions, insights into Wahegurū were to be consumed and savored through poetry set to music. The 10th *guru*, *Guru* Gobind Singh (1666–1807), appended 115 hymns composed by the ninth *gurū*, *Guru* Tegh Bahadur (1621–1675), to the *Ādi Granth*. He also added the *Dasam Granth* (*Tenth Book*), his own composition. While some scholars believe the *Dasam Granth* to be separate from the *Gurū Granth Sahib*

(McLeod, 1990, 6–7), the Sikh community accepts the expanded text as part of their canon. *Guru* Gobind Singh announced that the *Guru Granth Sahib* (*sahib* is an honorific) was his successor, ending the historical lineage of *gurus*. In the Sikh tradition, a *guru* is a teacher who intuits and reveals the divine and transcendental Wahegurū. The *Gurū Granth Sahib* is the ahistorical ever-present *guru*.

The *Ādi Granth* consists of three distinct parts, opening with the "*Japji*," the prayer for the morning. The opening section includes three daily prayers. The "*Japji*" (meditation) has 38 stanzas and two couplets by *Guru* Nānak; it is recited at sunrise. It begins with the *Mūl Mantar* (*Mantra*):

OM
One Universal creator God,

The Supreme Unchangeable Truth—*Ikk Ōnkār* [*Ik* means "one" or "united"; *on*, "supreme"; *kār*, "formless"]

The Creator of the Universe,
   Beyond Fear,
Beyond Hatred, Beyond Death,
   Beyond Birth, Self-Existent,
by the Guru's Grace

The "*Rahiras*" (supplication) consists of nine hymns, four of which were composed by *Guru* Nānak, three by the fourth *guru*, *Guru* Ramdas (1538–1581), and two by *Guru* Arjan; it is chanted at sunset. The "*Sohila*" (praise) has five hymns; three by *Guru* Nānak and one each by *Guru* Ramdas and *Guru* Arjan; it is recited before retiring for the night. The five stanzas of the "*Sohila*" remind the

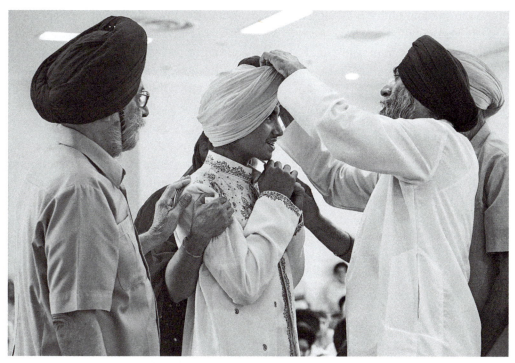

Guransh Singh, 14 (center), participating in his Dastar Bandi, a ceremony unique in the Sikh community where a young male decides to start wearing a turban, in Washington, D.C., July 19, 2010. (Marvin Joseph /The Washington Post/Getty Images)

devotee of his or her relationship with Wahegurū. The first stanza asks the devotee to imagine being united with Wahegurū. The second reminds the devotee that Wahegurū is the singular and only reality. The third emphasizes the underlying harmony of the entire created world as it worships Wahegurū. The fourth stanza focuses on the importance of the name(s) of Wahegurū in relation to human suffering. The final stanza reminds the devotee to serve others.

The hymns in the main body of the *Ādi Granth* consist of 31 subsections that are derived from the 31 classical Indian *rags*, musical modes. In addition, some of the hymns are set in folk musical patterns. The 31 *rags* are divided into 14 *rags* and 17 *raginis* (nonclassical *rags*). The *rags* are arranged chronologically, beginning with the *Guru* Nanak, the first *guru*, and proceeding to the fifth. The hymns of the *bhagats* form a later and distinct section. The final section of the *Adi Granth* contains miscellaneous hymns, including those associated with the seasons, not set in musical mode. The final section is the *Rāgmālā* (garland of musical modes), a hymn of 12 stanzas. Singing is usually accompanied by a *tablua*, a set of hand drums.

At sunrise, the *Gurū Granth Sahib* is brought in from the *sachkhand* (the room in a *gurdwara* where the *Gurū Granth Sahib* rests at night) and placed on the *takht* and opened. This opening ritual is the *prakash*, "making light manifest." It is opened at random and the hymn that appears is read in full. This ritual, *hukam*, is to understand the "command" of the *guru's* message that appears in the hymn and apply it to their lives. The *Gurū Granth Sahib* remains open throughout the day. At the end of the day it is closed in a ritual called *sukhasan* and returned to the *sachkhand*. When being transported, the *Gurū Granth Sahib* is carried on the head; it is not to be touched with unwashed hands or placed on the floor.

The *Gurū Granth Sahib* is recited at rituals of transitions such as births, weddings, and funerals, and at times of crisis. Each of these is marked by an important ritual linked to the text. At the birth of a child, the *Gurū Granth Sahib* is opened and the first letter from the first full verse on that page decides what the first letter of the child's first name will be. At death, Sikhs prefer bodies to be cremated and the scripture is integral to the ritual. The "Soliha," for instance, is recited after the body is bathed and readied for cremation. During a 10-day mourning period the entire *Gurū Granth Sahib* is read. It is also read in its entirety for *Akhand Path*, a ceremony performed at felicitous events, such as the birth of child, or during times of crisis.

In the *gurdwara* ("doorway to the guru"), site of communal worship, the *Gurū Granth Sahib* is accorded great honor and attended to with all the trappings of royalty, like the former living *gurus*. The *Gurū Granth Sahib* is placed on a raised platform known as *takht*, a throne-like dais at the front of the devotional space. It is covered with *rumalas*, silken cloths, to honor it and protect it from heat, dust, and pollution. Above the *takht* is a *palaki*, an honorific canopy. An attendant constantly waves a *chaur*, a flywhisk-like fan. The arrangement is reminiscent of a royal court. If at all possible, Sikhs will devote a separate room to enshrine the *Gurū Granth Sahib* in their homes.

Before entering the sacred space, the Sikh devotee engages in ritual purification that includes removing the shoes and covering the head. The devotee bows before entering and sits on the floor. The pattern of congregational worship can be divided into two categories: *Katha*, the reading of the holy hymns followed by their explanation, and *Kirtan*, the singing of the hymns. A *granthi* (narrator), male or female, is the ceremonial reader for the *Gurū Granth Sahib*. The *granthi* is the principal religious functionary of the tradition and the caretaker of the *Gurū Granth Sahib* and trustee of the donations.

Reading, listening, singing, or sitting in the presence of *Gurū Granth Sahib* constitute the core of Sikh ritual and devotion. The passages in the *Gurū Granth Sahib* are sacred and are not to be altered in any way. It is written in Gurmukhī, a script derived from and a systemization of *lande/mahajani*, a business shorthand that *Guru* Nānak must have used as a young business professional (Singh, 1995, 17). But *Guru* Nānak believed that Waheguru is accessible through any language.

Maura Helen Schmitz

See also: Entries: Indian American Sikhs

Further Reading

Ādi Granth, The, or the Holy Scriptires of the Sikhs. Translated by Ernest Trumpp. New Delhi: Munshiram Manoharlal, 1970.

Gill, Rahuldeep Singh. "Scriptures." http://www.patheos.com/Library/Sikhism/Origins/Scriptures.html. Accessed May 1, 2014.

Mann, Gurinder Singh. *The Making of Sikh Scripture*. New York: Oxford University Press, 2001.

McLeod, W. H. *Textual Sources for the Study of Sikhism*. Chicago: University of Chicago Press, 1990.

Shackle, Christopher, and Arvind Mandair, eds. *Teachings of the Sikh Gurus: Selections from the Sikh Scriptures*. New York: Routledge, 2005.

Singh, Nikky-Guninder Kaur, trans. *The Name of My Beloved: Verses of the Sikh Gurus*. San Francisco: Harper San Francisco, 1995.

The Sikh Foundation

The Sikh Foundation is a nonprofit and nonpolitical organization that was started in 1967 by Dr. Narinder Singh Kapany with multiple objectives—to pass on the Sikh heritage to the growing Sikh diaspora in the West, particularly the youth; introduce the world to the ethics, mysticism, arts, literature, and heroism of the Sikhs; contribute Sikh perspectives to issues of common human concern; advance Sikh culture by advancing the tradition of critical and creative thinking that gave birth to the faith; and generate the highest quality resources for the study of Sikhism. It is in the pursuit of these aims that the Sikh Foundation has been able to deeply impact the areas of Sikh studies, Sikh art, publications, and heritage conservation.

The Sikh Foundation pioneered the establishment of chairs of Sikh studies in universities with the Kundan Kaur Kapany Chair of Sikh & Punjabi Studies at the University of California–Santa Barbara in 1998. Subsequently, it has set up three more chairs of Sikh studies at the University of California–Riverside, University of California–Santa Cruz, and California State University–East Bay. The foundation has also organized many conferences and supported the teaching of the Punjabi language at the University of California–Berkeley, Stanford, and Columbia.

The foundation has also played a leading role in the promotion of Sikh art through major art exhibits at leading museums, including the Victoria & Albert Museum, London; the Royal Ontario Museum, Toronto; the Asian Art Museum, San Francisco; the Rubin Museum, New York; the Smithsonian, Washington, D.C.; the Santa Barbara Museum of Natural History; and the Fresno Art Museum. To commemorate the 35th anniversary of the Sikh Foundation, the Satinder Kaur Kapany Gallery of Sikh Art was established at the Asian Art Museum in San Francisco in 2003.

In collaboration with UNESCO, the Sikh Foundation undertook the renovation and conservation of *Guru* ki Maseet, a 17th-century *mosque* at Sri Hargobindpur in Punjab, India. This *mosque*, built by the sixth Sikh *guru* Hargobind Rai for his Muslim subjects, is a unique symbol of communal harmony.

Along with these projects the Sikh Foundation also provides the community with high-quality educational products on Sikhism such as books on all aspects of Sikh art and culture, journals, calendars, posters, displays, greeting cards, videos, CDs, tapes, DVDs, and other Sikh pride-building products. A selection of books published by the Sikh Foundation includes

Warrior Saints by Amandeep Madra and Paramjit Singh (1999), *Boy with Long Hair* by Pushpinder Kaur (1999), *Sikh Art and Literature* edited by Kerry Brown (1999), *Bindhu's Wedding* by the Singh Twins (1999), *Sacred Writing of the Sikhs* published by UNESCO and the Sikh Foundation, *The Name of My Beloved* by Nikky G. K. Singh (1995), and *Games We Play* by Puspinder Kaur (2013).

A journal, *The Sikh Sansar*, was published from 1972 to 1977. This journal was widely circulated in the United States and Canada. A directory of Sikhs living in the United States and Canada was also prepared. Following the assault in 1984 by the Indian government on the Golden Temple and other Sikh temples in India, the Sikh Foundation published full-page advertisements in leading newspapers in New York, Chicago, Washington, D.C., Los Angeles, and San Francisco. This was followed by the publication of a newspaper, *The Sikh Times*, in 1984–1985.

The website of the Sikh Foundation offers its readers a selection of Sikh-related articles and writings for all age groups including games, puzzles, and other educational material for children. The online store makes available a plethora of products including books, magazines, posters, CDs, DVDs, calendars, and so on.

The Sikh Foundation offers its perspective on various topics of human interest through participating in TV talk shows, publishing books on religion and culture, engaging with law enforcement agencies, and giving books to public libraries and other institutions.

Sonia Dhami

See also: Entries: Indian American Sikhs

Further Reading

Bigelow, Anna. "Tying Bonds of Unity at *Guru ki Maseet.*" *The Tribune—Chandigarh*, February 24, 2001.

The Sikh Directory. http://fateh.sikhnet.com /Directory. Accessed October 1, 2013.

The Sikh Foundation Webpage. www.sikh foundation.org. Accessed July 11, 2014.

Sikh Gurus

The term *guru* is used in South Asian languages to denote a (usually spiritual) teacher, but there are four specific ways in which the term is used in Sikhism. Throughout the most sacred Sikh scripture, the *Gurū Granth Sahib*, God is frequently referred to as "*Guru*," and modern-day Sikhs refer to God as *Waheguru*, which may be translated as "The Great Teacher." Both of these instances point to the Sikh understanding of God as the greatest of teachers, in the sense that all wisdom and liberating knowledge are from God. *Guru* is also the title given to each of the 10 spiritual masters, or divinely inspired teachers of the Sikh tradition (see below). The third usage of the term refers to the *Gurū Granth Sahib* (which can be translated as *Venerable Book That Is Guru*). Finally, the term is used to refer to *Guru panth*, the worldwide Sikh community as *guru*. Since there is no pope, priesthood, or official hierarchy in Sikhism, theological decisions are to be made democratically or by individual Sikhs through consulting the Sikh scriptures.

The 10 Human Gurus of Sikhism

Guru Nanak Dev (1469–1539) was the first of the 10 human *gurus* of Sikhism and lived during a time of religious interaction—and sometimes overt conflict—between the Muslim Mughal Empire (descendants of the Mongols who ruled much of South Asia from the mid-15th to the mid-19th centuries) and the majority Hindu population under their rule. At about age 30, he went to pray and bathe in a river, but disappeared for three days. Upon his miraculous return, he declared:

> There is neither Hindu nor Muslim, so whose path shall I choose? I shall follow God's path. God is neither Hindu nor Muslim and the path which I follow is God's. (*Janam Sakhi* tradition)

After this revelation, *Guru* Nanak traveled and preached for the rest of his life. His teachings, which emphasize devotion to one universal God, were revealed in the form of poetic hymns set to musical accompaniment, 974 of which appear in the *Gurū Granth Sahib*.

The second *guru*, *Guru* Angad Dev (1504–1552), formalized the *gurmukhi* (from the mouth of the *gurus*) script that the *Gurū Granth Sahib* would come to be written in, and composed 62 poetic couplets, which are included in the *Gurū Granth Sahib*. The third *guru*, *Guru* Amar Das (1479–1574), composed 907 of the hymns in the *Gurū Granth Sahib* and institutionalized the *langar* meal, the community-sponsored meal that is still served today to all people who visit a *gurdwara* (Sikh place of worship), without respect to race, caste, or social status. *Guru* Ram Das (1534–1581), the fourth *guru*, composed 679 hymns in the *Gurū Granth Sahib*, including the *Laava* (the Sikh wedding hymn), and established the town that is today known as Amritsar, the most sacred city for Sikhs.

The fifth *guru*, *Guru* Arjan Dev (1563–1606), composed 2,218 hymns in the *Gurū Granth Sahib* and compiled these and the hymns of the first four *gurus* into a written canon. He also constructed the *Harimandir Sahib* (known as the Golden Temple), the most sacred site for Sikhs, in the city of Amritsar. In 1606, *Guru* Arjan Dev was martyred by the Mughal emperor Jahangir (becoming the first martyr of Sikhism), an event that would have an indelible impact on Sikh history.

Guru Hargobind (1595–1644), the sixth *guru* and the son of *Guru* Arjan, introduced the concepts of *miri* (worldly authority) and *piri* (spiritual authority) to the guruship. At this point in history, the guruship assumed more political authority as subsequent *gurus* oversaw the Sikhs defending themselves against the Mughal Empire. The seventh *guru*, *Guru* Har Rai (1630–1661), was *guru* during a time of relative stability and oversaw a period in which the number of Sikhs was rapidly expanding. *Guru* Har Krishan (1656–1664), the son of *Guru* Har Rai, became the eighth *guru* at five years old. He is popularly revered for his great compassion: while caring for victims of smallpox, he succumbed himself at only seven years of age.

The ninth *guru*, *Guru* Tegh Bahadur (1621–1675), contributed 115 hymns to the *Gurū Granth Sahib*. He was martyred by the Mughal emperor Aurangzeb (who sought to convert his entire empire to Islam) while defending the religious rights of Hindus. The 10th *guru*, *Guru* Gobind

Singh (1666–1708), was the son of *Guru* Teg Bahadur and became *guru* during a time in which Sikhs were particularly under attack by the Mughal empire. *Guru* Gobind Singh instituted the Khalsa (the pure), an initiated group of Sikhs who would wear the "Five Ks," or five symbols of their faith. Although he did not add hymns to the *Gurū Granth Sahib*, *Guru* Gobind Singh composed the 1,428-page *Dasam Granth* (*Book of the Tenth Guru*), the second most revered Sikh scripture. Finally, *Guru* Gobind Singh ended the succession of human *gurus*, transferring the guruship to *Gurū Granth* and *Gurū Panth*.

Sikh Gurus Today

Among Sikh Americans, as among Sikhs worldwide, the *gurus* are revered as divinely inspired moral exemplars. Stories from the lives of the *gurus* are used to teach ideal moral behavior to both children and adults. Patterns of venerating the Sikh *gurus* in the United States also mirror those found worldwide. Images of the *gurus* are commonly hung in Sikh homes and businesses, but are not used for devotional purposes in *gurdwaras*. The *Gurū Granth Sahib* is revered as the eternal living *guru* of Sikhs and is treated as the embodiment of the 10 human *gurus* and the continuing presence of the divine inspiration carried by each of them. Sikhs view visiting a *gurdwara* as coming into the presence of the living *guru* and bow deeply in front of the scripture as a sign of respect. Throughout services, the *Gurū Granth Sahib* is placed on a *manji sahib*, a bedded throne-like platform covered by a canopy, thus signaling the respectful treatment of the scripture as the living *guru*.

Charles M. Townsend

See also: Entries: Indian American Sikhs

Further Reading

Cole, W. Owen. *Understanding Sikhism*. Edinburgh: Dunedin Academic Press, 2004.

McLeod, Hew. *Sikhism*. London and New York: Penguin Books, 1997.

Singh, Pashaura. *Life and Work of Guru Arjan*. Oxford, New York, and New Delhi: Oxford University Press, 2006.

Sri Granth (searchable online *Guru Granth Sahib*). http://www.srigranth.org. Accessed July 16, 2014.

Soka Gakkai

Soka Gakkai International (SGI) is a lay Buddhist organization with roots in Nichiren Buddhism, particularly Nichiren Shōshū. Established in the United States in the early 1960s, it existed under the name Nichiren Shōshū of America (NSA) until 1991, after which it changed its name to Soka Gakkai International–USA (SGI-USA). Of the so-called New Japanese Religions Soka Gakkai has become the largest and most ethnically diverse. According to the organization's own estimates there are currently 126,806 members in the United States. According to information obtained from SGI-USA headquarters, California had the largest membership in 2013, claiming 37,655 members.

Beliefs and Practices

Soka Gakkai was a lay association of the Nichiren Shōshū sect until 1991 and its beliefs and practices generally adhere to the main teachings of Nichiren Buddhism. Nichiren Buddhism was founded by the former Tendai priest Nichiren Daishōnin (1222–1282). Nichiren viewed the *Saddharma Puṇḍarīka* or *Lotus Sūtra* as the most important of Buddhist teachings, particularly the idea that the Buddha-nature is already within all sentient beings and that enlightenment can be attained through the wisdom of the *Lotus Sūtra*. Individual enlightenment in turn engenders social peace. Nichiren taught that three great secret laws of Buddhism would appear in a period when the Buddha Dharma was in decline, known as *mappō*. The three laws were the importance of the *Dai-Gohonzon*, the *daimoku*, and the *kaidan*.

Daimoku is both the phrase "*Nam-myōhō-renge-kyō*," variously translated as "I devote myself to the Mystic Law of the *Lotus Sūtra*" or "hail to the wonderful Dharma *Lotus Sūtra*," and the activity of invoking the phrase through chant.

The *Dai-Gohonzon* is a wooden *maṇḍala* inscribed late in life by Nichiren with the name of the *Lotus Sūtra* in Chinese characters and Nichiren's signature surrounded by the names of individuals representing various life conditions, ranging from demons, teachers, and heavenly kings to bodhisattvas and Buddhas. The object of highest veneration in Nichiren Shōshū Buddhism, it is housed at the head temple, Taisekiji, at the foot of Mt. Fuji. It is thought to embody the Dharma and also to embody Nichiren, who, as an incarnation of the eternal Buddha, infused his enlightenment into his original *gohonzons*. A copy of the *Dai-Gohonzon*, a *gohonzon*, is given to the adherent in a formal ceremony, *gojukai*, and is placed on the home altar. Saying the *daimoku* in front of the *gohonzon* is known as *shodai* and is considered to be highly efficacious for the realization of one's own true nature and for the attainment of supreme enlightenment. Practitioners may also engage in *gangyo*, the exercise of reading sections of the *Lotus Sūtra*, especially the 2nd chapter and the 16th chapter, emphasizing the teachings of the inherent Buddha-nature of all sentient beings and that Buddhahood is attained from within rather than externally. Chanting the *daimoku* before the *gohonzon* thus constitutes the core practice of Soka Gakkai and is the means to bring about spiritual transformation in the individual or, as the second president Josei Toda called it, "human revolution." Practice brings one into harmony with the basic rhythm of the Dharma that underlies the universe, enabling individuals to face the challenges of their own lives and to realize, according to the organization's website, "one's unique life purpose." Then through individual change social and global change can begin.

Finally, Nichiren taught that the *kaidan*, the most important Buddhist sanctuary, would appear in the age of *mappō*. Nichiren Shōshū has identified Taisekiji temple as the *kaidan*, and as a result pilgrimage to Taisekiji has always been essential. Since the occlusion of the group by Nichiren Shōshū in 1991, Soka Gakkai members have been prohibited from entering Taisekiji.

While chanting the *daimoku* continues to be the core practice of Soka Gakkai, the break with Nichiren Shōshū has led the organization into more progressive directions, prioritizing lay leadership, especially among women and minorities. While Nichiren Shōshū, and Nichiren Buddhism in general, claim exclusivity, Soka Gakkai has shown a greater tolerance for other faith positions. The overall emphasis now is on personal, social, and global peace and prosperity, starting with the individual, and a firm belief in the possibilities for happiness and peace in this world, rather than one to come. SGI-USA currently engages in numerous cultural, educational, and social initiatives including advocating for peace and disarmament, ecological sustainability, human rights, and intercultural and interfaith dialogue.

History

The history of Soka Gakkai can be easily organized according to its three presidents: Tsunesaburo Makiguchi (1871–1944), Josei Toda (1900–1958), and Daisaku Ikeda (1928–). Founded by Makiguchi in 1937, Soka Gakkai originally started as Sōka Kyōiku Gakkai (Value Creation Education Society). Focused on Makiguchi's ideas of progressive education that stressed individual initiative, benefit, and critical thought, at first the organization had no connection to Nichiren Shōshū. After his own conversion to Nichiren Shōshū, Makiguchi practiced chanting with others in his education club. While there was no formal association between the two, Makiguchi's education advocacy and his faith commitments became more connected to the point that he and other Sōka Kyōiku Gakkai leaders were imprisoned in 1943 for treason due to their opposition to State Shintoism. Makiguchi died in

prison in 1944. His close disciple Josei Toda was released in 1945 and would become Sōka Kyōiku Gakkai's second president in 1951.

It was Toda who, after the war, shifted the organization's focus from education to spiritual practice, supported by his religious vision informed by Nichiren's idea of *kosen-rufu*, a term that connotes both the conversion of the world to true Buddhism and a utopian vision of a world peace and harmony. In 1951 he changed the name to Soka Gakkai and formally made the organization a lay association of Nichiren Shōshū, placing members under the authority of the Nichiren priesthood and giving them access to priest services such as weddings and funerals. The association between Soka Gakkai and Nichiren Shōshū would provide mutual benefits for many years, giving Soka Gakkai institutional legitimacy and providing Nichiren Shōsū with new members, financial resources, and contemporary relevance. At the time of Toda's death in 1958 the movement had experienced phenomenal growth in Japan thanks to its aggressive form of proselytization known as *shakubuku*.

Daisaku Ikeda became president of Soka Gakkai in 1960. Under his leadership the organization would grow considerably in its membership, geographical coverage, and variety of activities. While *shakubuku*-style proselytization continued, Soka Gakkai also extended its reach through cultural and political institutions. Ikeda established the Soka Gakkai Culture Bureau in 1961, which produced public-image friendly projects such as the Tokyo Fuji Art Museum, the Min-On Concert Association, and Soka Schools. Politically,

Soka Gakkai became active in 1955, sponsoring candidates and eventually forming its own party, Komeito, in 1964. The close association of a "religious" group with a political party caused controversy and eventually Soka Gakkai formally separated itself from Komeito. Such a direct involvement in politics has never been a priority of SGI-USA. Perhaps most significantly, Ikeda shifted the focus of Soka Gakkai to global outreach. During the 1960s the organization expanded globally, including its establishment in the United States.

Soka Gakkai's first American members were primarily Japanese immigrants, especially Japanese women who had married American servicemen. Through their efforts families and friends were brought into contact with the group. In 1960 the first formal organization was founded, Soka Gakkai of America. The name was changed to Nichiren Shōshū of America. An American headquarters was established in Santa Monica, California, in the early 1960s under the informal leadership of Masayasu Sadanaga who would later change his name to George Williams. Intensive *shakubuku* grew the organization's numbers through street solicitation, home meetings, college activities, and large cultural festivals. Through these efforts Soka Gakkai in America experienced explosive growth in the 1960s and 1970s.

Among the new religious movements that emerged from Japan in the mid-20th century, Soka Gakkai has had the most success in attracting new members, and it is also the movement that has become the least tied to Japanese ethnicity. In early stages diversification could result in tension, such as using chairs when reciting the *Sūtra* instead of sitting on the floor, or translating key teachings into English, questioning how essential the Japanese language was for practice. Rather than being an insular means to protect one's Japanese identity, Soka Gakkai was seen as something that transcended ethnicity. Indeed, the early decision to use English at meetings is one key reason Soka Gakkai was able to reach out to non-Japanese individuals.

According to SGI-USA, they do not keep track of ethnic data anymore, but a study by Phillip Hammond and David Machacek in 1997 found that Caucasian Americans were the largest ethnic group, constituting about 42 percent of membership, while Asian Americans constituted 23 percent. There were also a significant number of African Americans and Latinos. As an international movement that encourages members to think of themselves as "global citizens," the cultural link between Soka Gakkai and Japan has been more or less severed. Indeed, sociological studies in the United States, Britain, and Australia have suggested that it is Soka Gakkai's global perspective that attracts many adherents in postindustrial societies, individuals who value a cosmopolitan outlook and self-expression. Inasmuch as SGI-USA aims to cultivate world peace and intercultural exchange, its ability to transcend association with any particular ethnic group may be viewed as a success.

The separation from Nichiren Shōshū reinforced the weakening of Soka Gakkai America's connection to its Japanese roots. As growth leveled by the end of the 1970s, outreach shifted from aggressive proselytization to a focus on social, cultural, and educational activities. At the same time there was less militant commitment to the uniqueness of Nichiren Shōshū, a position strongly advocated by Toda. In this way Ikeda recast the idea of *kosen-rufu* to mean the broad dissemination of, rather than the conversion of the world to, Nichiren Buddhism. The tremendous expansion of Soka Gakkai globally and its changing methods and activities distanced it from the Nichiren Shōshū priesthood. After this formal separation from Nichiren Shōshū the organization as a whole changed its name to Soka Gakkai International. Those who left SGI and stayed loyal to the Nichiren priesthood adopted the name Nichiren Shōshū Temple. One of the greatest obstacles posed by the break was obtaining copies of the *gohonzon* for new adherents since only the priests were authorized to consecrate additional *gohonzons* based on the original. However, SGI obtained a version transcribed by Nichikan Shonin in 1720, which serves as the basis for *gohonzons* issued today.

Overall, the break with Nichiren Shōshū has proved of little consequence, even enabling SGI-USA to pursue its progressive agenda further. While the core practice of *daimoku* is still a central part of its identity, SGI-USA currently engages in a wide variety of cultural, educational, and social initiatives. Supporting this work are Soka Gakkai's extensive publications, particularly the weekly newspaper *World Tribune*, published since 1964, and *Living Buddhism*, a journal published since 1981 (titled *Seikyo Times* until 1997). Awareness of changing demographics is seen in the fact that subscribers to the *World Tribune* in the United States can receive language supplements in Japanese, Chinese, Korean, Thai/Cambodian, French, and Portuguese. Completely Spanish versions of both are also published, *La Tribuen del Mundo* and *Esperanza*. Finally, SGI-USA's activities extend beyond the bounds of SGI-USA proper through para-institutions founded by Ikeda such as the Ikeda Center for Peace, Learning, and Dialogue in Cambridge, Massachusetts and Soka University of America in Aliso Viejo, California, drawing the organization full circle back to the Nichiren Buddhist–inspired value education of Makiguchi.

Peter L. Doebler

Further Reading

Clarke, Peter B. "'Success' and 'Failure': Japanese New Religions Abroad." In Peter B. Clarke, ed. *Japanese New Religions in Global Perspective*. Richmond, UK: Curzon, 2000, pp. 272–311.

Coleman, James William. "Soka Gakkai: Engaged Buddhism in North America." In Paul David Numrich, ed. *North American Buddhists in Social Context*. Leiden: Brill, 2008.

Inoue, Nobutaka. "NSA and Non-Japanese Members in California." In Kei'ichi Yanagawa, ed. *Japanese Religions in California*. Tokyo: Department of Religious Studies, University of Tokyo, 1983.

Kisala, Robert. "Soka Gakkai: Searching for the Mainstream." In James R. Lewis and Jesper Aagaard Petersen, eds. *Controversial New Religions*. Oxford: Oxford University Press, 2005, pp. 139–52.

Machacek, David, and Phillip E. Hammond. *Soka Gakkai in America: Accommodation and Conversion*. Oxford: Oxford University Press, 1999.

Machacek, David, and Bryan Wilson, eds. *Global Citizens: The Soka Gakkai Buddhist Movement in the World.* Oxford: Oxford University Press, 2001.

Prebish, Charles S. *Luminous Passage: The Practice and Study of Buddhism in America.* Berkeley: University of California Press, 1999.

Seager, Richard Hughes. *Buddhism in America.* New York: Columbia University Press, 1999.

Seager, Richard Hughes. *Encountering the Dharma: Daisaku Ikeda, Soka Gakkai, and the Globalization of Buddhist Humanism.* Berkeley: University of California Press, 2006.

Waterhouse, Helen. "Soka Gakkai Buddhism as a Global Religious Movement." In John Wolffe, ed. *Global Religious Movements in Regional Context.* Burlington, VT: Ashgate, 2002.

Songkran

Celebrated for three days between April 13 and 15, Songkran marks the beginning of the New Year for the Thai and many other South and Southeast Asian cultures. A national holiday in Thailand, for Buddhists the festival is a time for remembering their ancestors, for visiting the *wat* or temple, family and friends, and more recently for water-splashing and carousing. The term *Songkran*, derived from Sanskrit astronomy, originally referred to the annual passage of the sun through the zodiac. Today Songkran is associated with the sun leaving the constellation of Aries and entering Taurus in April, when there are an equal number of hours during the day and night, a celestial event known as *maha-songkran* (the supreme cycle). Songkran was originally a lunar holiday, but is now celebrated on fixed days.

On the first day, devotees normally visit a temple to offer flowers, candles, and incense to the Buddha. While an image of the Buddha is carried around the temple grounds, devotees sprinkle sacralized water on it as a gesture of respect. The sprinkling of the Buddha recalls the sweet rain that fell on the infant Siddhārtha shortly after his birth. Subsequently, devotees also sprinkle water on monks; after the drenching, the abbot dons a new robe that he has received and proceeds to share his reflections on the *Dhamma* and bless the congregants.

For Buddhists, another important event is Bangsukun Atthi, a ritual that transfers merits to deceased family members and relatives to assist and ease the transition toward a better rebirth. For this event, families will bring the corporeal remains of their ancestors to the temple. In the past, the remains were buried under the bodhi tree on the temple grounds, and there was no need to bring the corporeal remains to the *wat*. For some communities Songkran is an occasion to honor the guardian spirits of the village and town, a vestige of an ancient and pre-Buddhist practice. In an effort to begin the New Year afresh, homes are cleaned so that they are spotless. In the past in Central Thailand, household chores such as gathering firewood and fetching water were prohibited during Songkran.

Devotees often build *chedis* on the grounds of temples with sand from a nearby river. The sand-*chedi* symbolizes the site of the Buddha's remains, a holy undertaking. This activity is also an oppor-

A woman pours water over a Buddha statue at the Songkran and Thai Food Festival held at Wat Buddharangs in Homestead, Florida, April 15, 2012. The Songkran Festival is the traditional Thai New Year, and is celebrated with a religious ceremony and public festivities. People enjoy splashing water on each other as they believe that water will wash away bad luck, and splashing water over friends or anyone will give them a New Year blessing. When the young pour scented water on their elders' hands, the elders, in return, wish them good health, happiness and prosperity. (J. Pat Carter /Corbis)

tunity to return to the temple grounds all of the sand that had been removed by footwear during the previous year. New clothes and personal items along with other ritual objects, such as banana, sugarcane, and jackfruit leaves are brought to be sprinkled with sacralized water. These items are used for auspicious occasions during the year. The final highlight of Songkran is the sprinkling of scented water on the hands of elders. The elders are presented with flowers, candles, incense, new clothes, betel nuts, acacia water, and perfume. Betel nut is a symbol of respect and hospitality. In the past acacia water was used as soap. Once the elders receive the gifts, they will sprinkle the acacia water and the perfume on top of the heads of the young and offer their blessings. After the formalities are completed, people douse water on each other and celebrate the advent of the New Year, often with great gusto. Songkran is accompanied with overabundance of food and spirits.

The Songkran festival is very much related to water. It is believed that the sprinkling and splashing of water invokes the monsoon rains. Water is also a symbol of fertility and purification, and used simply for cooling. April is the hottest time of year. Water is used widely in different ceremonies and rites of passage.

Thai Buddhist communities in the United States continue many of these traditional Songkran rituals, albeit modified to accommodate the American workweek. Thus the major elements of Songkran are held over two weekend days. Songkran is an occasion to visit the *wat* to reaffirm Buddhist and cultural roots, for children to perform the traditional dances and music they practiced throughout the year, to consume traditional cuisine and meet friends. It is also an occasion to highlight Thai culture to the larger community.

Boonmee Poungpet

See also: Entries: Thai American Religions

Further Reading

Gerson, Ruth. *Traditional Festivals in Thailand.* Oxford: Oxford University Press, 1996.

Ishii, Yoneo. *Saṇgha, State, and Society: Thai Buddhism in History.* Translated by Peter Hawkes. Honolulu: University of Hawai'i Press, 1986.

Watt, David K. *Thailand: A Short History.* New Haven, CT: Yale University Press, 1984.

Sōtō Zen

Sōtōshū, a major Japanese Zen Buddhist tradition in Hawai'i and the continental United States, traces its ideological underpinnings to the insights Eihei Dōgen Zenji (1200–1253) received from Tiandong Rujing Chanshi (Jpn. Tendō Nyojō Zenji, 1163–1228), the 13th patriarch of the Chinese Caodong or Sōtō Zen linage. Dōgen returned to Japan in 1227 or 1228 and later founded Eiheiji Temple. The Japanese Sōtō tradition recognizes Dōgen, together with Keizan Jōkin Zenji (1268–1325), who es-

tablished Sōjiji Temple, to be its "Two Founders." Keizan Jōkin and his disciples popularized the Sōtōshū tradition among the common people by moving away from the strict monastic discipline set forth by Dōgen. At present, there are approximately 15,000 Sōtō Zen temples throughout Japan and 30 training monasteries, including the two most important, Eiheiji and Sōjiji.

History—Hawai'i

Sōtōshū formally established itself in Hawai'i in 1903 when the Rev. Sen'ei Kawahara (?–1908) founded Taiyōji in Waipahu, O'ahu, and Rev. Ryōun Kan (1854–1917) established Zenshūji in Wahiawa, Kaua'i (the temple relocated to Hanapepe in 1977). There are currently seven other active temples. Sōtō Mission of Hawai'i, Shōbōji Betsuin, in the heart of Honolulu, was founded in 1913. In 1921 Shōbōji became the head temple of the denomination's Hawai'i district, and its chief priest or *sōkan* became its administrative head. Ryūsenji, located in Wahiawa in central O'ahu, was established in 1904. Mantokuji Sōtō Mission of Paia, Maui, was founded in 1906. In 1914, Daifukuji Sōtō Mission was established in Kona, Hawai'i. In 1915, Taishōji was founded in Hilo, also on the island of Hawai'i. Founded in 1918, Taiheiji is located in Aiea on O'ahu. Founded in 1927, Guzeiji Sōtō Mission is the only Buddhist temple on the island of Molokai. As of 2013 these nine temples provide the spiritual needs for approximately 1,700 families who offer regular financial support.

Sōtōshū temples were originally established to serve the Japanese immigrant communities that were attached to the sugar plantations. The communities welcomed the priests, who embodied the customs and traditions of their homeland. In addition to their clerical responsibilities, the priests established Japanese-language schools and assisted the Japanese community in innumerable ways to living in a foreign country. The temples also served as community centers and venues for long-established festivals. Present-day temples and clerics continue to serve the spiritual needs of the descendants of the first immigrants with weekly Sunday services, annual rituals to celebrate important milestones in the life of the Buddha and the temples' founders. Priests lead the weekly *zazen* or sitting meditation and study sessions, and perform marriage ceremonies, funerals, and memorial services. The temples carry on as community and cultural centers, offering lessons in martial arts, flower arranging, tea ceremony, folk dancing and singing, and Japanese drums. Sōtō Mission of Hawai'i Shōbōji founded Sōtō Academy, a K–6 elementary school, where in addition to its regular curriculum, Japanese language and Kumon math are offered. The state of Hawai'i accredited the academy in 1990.

History—Continental United States

Like the Sōtō Zen temples in Hawai'i, the temples on the continental United States primarily serve the spiritual and social needs of the Japanese American community. At present, there are five Sōtō Zen temples, all in California. Founded in 1922, Zenshūji in Los Angeles has the largest membership. Sōkōji in San Francisco, the second oldest, was established in 1934. The other three are Long Beach Buddhist Church (1957), Sōzenji in Montebello (1972), and Monterey Zenshūji Soto Zen Temple in Monterey (1955). These five temples serve approximately 360 families and 43 individual members.

Sōtōshū devotees residing in and around Little Tokyo in Los Angeles invited Rev. Hōsen Isobe (1877–1953), who was at the time in Hawai'i, to establish Zenshūji Sōtō Mission. Isobe and his community faced strong anti-Japanese sentiments. Like other Japanese Buddhist temples, Zenshūji Sōtō Mission provided a refuge where the immigrant community could continue to nurture their spiritual identity and stay connected with the homeland. The community collected and sent relief aid to the victims of the 1923 Great Tokyo Earthquake. In 1924 the U.S. government passed the Immigration Act of 1924 or Johnson–Reed Act, including the National Origins Act and Asian Exclusion Act.

Responding to the Japanese attack on Pearl Harbor in 1941, President Franklin Delano Roosevelt (1882–1945) signed Executive Order 9066 incarcerating Japanese nationals and Japanese American citizens, who were believed to be threats to the national security. Zenshūji, like other Japanese Buddhist temples, warehoused the belongings of its members, who were allowed to take only two suitcases of their personal effects with them. Likewise the temples served as hostels for the returning internees while they rebuilt their lives. As a result of this dislocation, many members of the community moved away from the Little Tokyo area of Los Angeles, eroding the Zenshūji's membership and its financial base. Zenshūji celebrated the 90th anniversary of its founding in 2012.

In 1937, Zenshūji was designated as Ryōdai Honzan Betsuin Zenshūji, head temple of the North American District. With this designation its *sōkan* or head priest became the director of the Sōtō Zen Buddhism North America Office, a jurisdiction that extends from Canada to Panama. Rev. Banjō Sagumo (?–1956) served as the first director. Initially the director exerted most of his energies on the needs of the Japanese American community. However, as a result of the great interest in Zen Buddhism that emerged in the late 1950s, the director's responsibilities now include supervising more than 50 Sōtō Zen centers and more than 360 American Sōtō Zen priests scattered throughout North America.

Rev. Shunryū Suzuki (1904–1971), who served as the resident priest at Sōkōji from 1959 to 1969, played a large role in the spread of Sōtō Zen beyond the Japanese American community. Suzuki arrived in San Francisco at a most opportune moment; it was the end of the Beat movement and just before the social movements of the 1960s. Persons associated with these movements were searching for alternative visions and approaches to the Vietnam War, racial discrimination, pollution, and poverty. In the meantime, D. T. Suzuki's (1870–1966) lectures and writings on Buddhism and Zen, in particular, appealed to many intellectuals and artists, who were drawn to the Zen emphasis on simple living, being in tune with nature, the nonviolent nature of Buddhism, and its art and aesthetics. While the teaching and practice of Sōtō Zen was available at Zenshūji, Sōkōji, and other temples, they were not accessible to those who did not speak Japanese.

Shunryū Suzuki, who spoke English, attracted many beatnik and hippie types to the morning *zazen* sessions at Sōkōji; they soon outnumbered the Japanese American membership. This led to the establishment of the San Francisco Zen Center in 1962, which together with other subsequent centers provided an opportunity for persons who wanted to engage in *zazen* meditation and to learn about different aspects of Buddhist thought and culture. Today these centers offer meditation retreats, instruction for sewing robes, and meditation paraphernalia, as well as outreach opportunities in prisons, hospices, and with homeless people, based on Buddhist ideals of wisdom and compassionate practice.

These interests stand in contrast with the Japanese American devotees who grew up in the temple and for whom temple membership is a family and cultural tradition. While Obon, the festival honoring their ancestors, and the spring and autumn Ohigan are traditional Buddhist services, the Japanese American membership associate them as rituals that connect them with their ancestors and events that foster community solidarity. They associate the temple with funeral and memorial rites, and weddings and births that mark important personal and community milestones. *Shōtsuki hōyō* is a monthly service in memory of those members who passed away during the month; their names are read as part of the service.

Rev. Dainin Katagiri (1928–1990) and Rev. Hakuyū Maezumi (1931–1995) were also instrumental in spreading Sōtō Zen's teaching and practice beyond the Japanese American community. Katagiri assisted Suzuki with the establishment of the San Francisco Zen Center. In 1972 he relocated to Minneapolis, Minnesota, to establish the Minnesota Zen Meditation Center and later Hōkyōji Zen Practice Community. He returned briefly to the San Francisco Zen Center to guide it through an especially difficult period. He returned to Minnesota in 1984 where he died in 1990. He left 12 Dharma heirs (disciples who were given formal permission to be full-fledged priests). Hakuyū Maezumi is another influential figure. He founded Busshinji, also known as the Zen Center of Los Angeles, in 1968 and certified 12 Dharma heirs, ordained 68 priests, and administered the Buddhist precepts to more than 500 practitioners. Maezumi died unexpectedly while visiting Japan.

Beliefs and Practices

Dōgen Zenji was ordained at a young age; but during the course of his study, he was troubled by what seemed to be a contradiction. It appears that his question emerged from the following passage that appears in the *Mahāparinirvāṇa Sūtra* (*Nirvāṇa Sūtra*): "All living beings in their entirety have the Buddha-nature: the Tathāgata abides [in them] constantly, without changing at all." If all sentient beings possess the Buddha-nature and the Tathāgata or Buddha is present in all beings, why, then, did Śākyamuni Buddha and all previous Dharma masters need to undergo such rigorous spiritual training?

Dōgen visited many Japanese Buddhist teachers and inquired about his question,

but did not receive a satisfactory answer. Finally, he was advised to go to China. After three years of intense study under Rujing Chanshi, Dōgen had a spiritual awakening. He explains in the "Busshō" (Buddha-nature) chapter in the *Shōbōgenzō* (*Treasury of the True Dharma Eye*) that the Zen student must verify for him or herself the reality and truth that indeed he or she possesses the Buddha-nature and that the Tathāgata (Buddha) resides in him or her. To this end the student must first bring forth the aspiration to awaken to his or her Buddha-nature and practice the form of meditation known as *shikantaza*.

While often translated as "just sitting" and usually associated with sitting in meditation, *shikantaza* is properly not a practice. "Practice" implies a goal or end to be achieved. Since Buddha-nature is intrinsic, that is, it resides in each person, there is no need to engage in *zazen* meditation to realize Buddhahood or enlightenment. This is the way it is from the viewpoint of the Dharma and for one who has verified this reality for him or herself. However, from the viewpoint of the ego-self, there is always a separation between the self and other things. According to the Sōtō Zen teaching, it is necessary to verify for oneself the nature of this reality. For this reason, it inevitably becomes necessary to start with the practice of *shikantaza*, the objective of which is to eliminate the sense of separation between the ego-self and other things. Rather than only sitting in *zazen*, this practice must be carried out in every activity that in and of itself affirms the reality of the Buddha-nature and is thus an expression of enlightenment. In the end, *shikantaza* is a description of the awakened state of someone who has let go of dualistic consciousness as well as the name of one form of *zazen*.

To be sure, sitting in *zazen* is the central practice in Sōtō Zen, but practice is not restricted to *zazen* meditation. In 1227 or 1228, the year he returned from China, Dōgen clearly states in *Fukanzazengi* (*A Universal Recommendation for Zazen*) that *zazen* is not restricted "to sitting." The goal of practice is to eliminate the illusion that one's self is separate from one's actions and that the self is separate from all things and beings. The spiritual end for Sōtō Zen is to awaken to the essential oneness of all things, beings, and events. It is to realize that every existent thing has always been, is, and will be within the causal connections of interdependence. To be aware of and live with this awareness in one's daily life is Zen realization. Dōgen summarized the essentials of this reality in "Genjōkōan" (Manifesting Suchness): "To study the Way of Buddha is to study the Self; to study the Self is to forget the ego-self; to forget the ego-self is to be enlightened by all things."

In Japan, *zazen* practice is traditionally associated with monks and nuns. While there have always been lay persons who have practiced meditation, it is not possible for most people to engage in extended and intense *zazen* meditation. For such devotees Dōgen prescribed the *shishōbō* or four true teachings of generosity, loving speech, actions that benefit others, and mutual identification. By observing these virtues in daily life, the lay person can let go of the belief in the self and realize the self in all things. These four practices figure prominently in the *Shushōgi* (*The Meaning of Practice and Realization*), a document that was created from quotations from Dōgen Zenji's *Shōbōgenzō* at the end of the 19th century to encourage and outline the doctrine that would lead to proper living as a means to awaken to one's Buddha-nature and to affirm the Buddha in him- or herself.

Conclusion

Zenshūji and other Sōtōshū temples that serve the Japanese American community are experiencing declining membership. This is due in part to the passing of those elders who founded the temples. Those issues that prompted the founding of the temples—cultural and ethnic nostalgia, a refuge from the pressures of discrimination, and a venue for traditional events—are no longer pressing concerns. Their children and grandchildren have many other spiritual options and do not have the strong ties to Japanese culture and society that their elders once did. Whether the present membership can reconnect with the spiritual resources of Sōtōshū or rekindle its ancestral ties or remake itself to adjust to modernization to support the existence of its temples are open questions. The membership and its priests are experimenting with ways to continue to serve the needs of their Japanese American constituencies and to attract those who may wish to practice and study Zen Buddhism in such a context.

Daigaku Rummé

See also: Entries: Rinzai Zen

Further Reading

Asai, Senryō, and Duncan Williams. "Japanese-American Zen Temples: Cultural Identity and Economics." In Duncan Williams and Christopher Queen, eds. *American Buddhism*. London: Curzon Press, 1998, pp. 20–35.

Hori, G. Victor Sōgen. "Japanese Zen in America: Americanizing the Face in the Mirror." In Kenneth Tanaka and Charles Prebish, eds. *The Faces of American Buddhism*. Berkeley: University of California Press, 1998, pp. 49–78.

Oyama, Kōryū. *History of Hawai'i Sōtōshū 1903–1978*. Honolulu: Shōbōji Sōtō Temple, 1978.

Preston, David. *The Social Organization of Zen Practice: Constructing Transcultural Reality*. New York: Cambridge University Press, 1988.

Sekkei Harada. *The Essence of Zen*. Boston: Wisdom, 2008.

South Asian Americans Leading Together (SAALT)

South Asian Americans Leading Together (SAALT) is a national nonprofit organization that endeavors to ensure that the voices and perspectives of South Asian Americans are included in policy discussions of social justice, immigration, and diversity in the United States. A nonpartisan group, SAALT's strategic initiatives to accomplish these goals include public policy analysis and prescriptions, partnering with South Asian American organizations and other allies, mobilizing community members to act, and leadership development training.

SAALT's guiding principles reflect its dedication to social justice and reform. In particular, the organization attempts to give voice to the most disempowered segments of the South Asian American community in an effort to improve their lives

and facilitate access to their rights. To accomplish this, the group regularly partners with regional and national South Asian American community groups and organizations, in addition to other groups focused on civil rights and immigrant advocacy. Analysis from such ground-level coalition and community building informs SAALT's public policy positions, through which it seeks to influence local, state, and national politics. The group also strives to encourage the development of a pan–South Asian American identity— one not limited by the divisive characteristics of ethnicity, religion, generation, and class, while still respectful of national, religious, and cultural identities. Transparency is an important core value of the organization, which promises wide information sharing, open communication, and decision making based on group consensus.

SAALT originated in 2000 as a board of concerned individuals focused on leadership development within the politically underrepresented South Asian American community. The group decided to develop a video addressing the rapidly growing problem of hate crimes against South Asian Americans at the close of the 20th century. In the midst of that project, the terror attacks of 9/11 transformed the work they were doing on the video project and the organization itself. In the coming months, the organization transformed into one with a much greater emphasis on policy advocacy and community education.

During this critical time for South Asian American communities, SAALT offered direction and information to government agencies and politicians regarding the ground-level effects of special registration, detention of suspected immigrants, interrogation of detainees, and racial and religious profiling. In addition to producing the video examining the ongoing impact of hate crimes against South Asian Americans, SAALT's first report detailed incidents of bias against the numerous non-Christian communities of color targeted in the wake of 9/11. In conjunction with numerous civil and immigration rights groups, the organization helped represent the South Asian American community at a national press conference at the Japanese American memorial in Washington, D.C. The groups and communities joined together to call for an end to what became the greatest hate crime epidemic in modern U.S. history.

In 2004, the organization received a grant that enabled it to open an office in New York City and hire paid staff. A subsequent organizational three-year plan added capacity and coalition building to the group's strategic initiatives. Over the next three years, community dialogues were initiated in Chicago, Philadelphia, Edison (New Jersey), New York City, San Francisco, and Houston.

Moving to the Washington, D.C. area in 2005, SAALT rapidly expanded its community services in 2006, beginning with a drive to expand the membership base. The group's 2006 activities included election monitoring, release of a report about South Asian American electoral participation, initiation of a community empowerment project in New Jersey, and membership in the National Coalition of Asian Pacific Americans and Detention Watch Network.

This coalition-building exemplifies SAALT's efforts to reach out to non–South Asian American organizations, particularly pan–Asian/Pacific American service organizations that have historically failed to appreciate and address issues specific to South Asian American communities. As a sign of the group's immense progress in highlighting the issues confronting South Asian Americans, Deepa Iyer—SAALT's first executive director who guided the group's direction on policy advocacy, programs, and partnerships from 2004 until 2013—was appointed chair of the National Council of Asian Pacific Americans. Similarly, SAALT has also partnered with the National Network for Immigrant and Refugee Rights and the Leadership Conference on Civil and Human Rights.

Among the community-level initiatives organized by SAALT is a national day of community service, begun in 2003, to inspire and foster civic engagement among South Asian Americans. Each year, thousands of people throughout the country contribute volunteer service, guided by the theme "Stand together, serve together." In 2007, the group initiated SAALT Circles, quarterly informational conference calls to discuss issues affecting community members. These community forums offer a safe space to share experiences, build community, and strategize to effect positive change. Also in 2007, the group joined a racial justice campaign to end the unfair targeting of South Asian American merchants in Georgia by law enforcement, arrested for unknowingly selling customers the ingredients to make methamphetamines.

With the majority of South Asian Americans being immigrants, SAALT prioritizes the rights and welfare of immigrants. The issues the group seeks to address include the difficulties in attaining permanent legal status and citizenship, the implementation of harsh enforcement initiatives targeting the community, like the National Security Entry-Exit Registration System, discriminatory profiling, and immigration policies that can result in their deportation for low-level offenses. In this capacity, in 2007 SAALT testified before the U.S. House of Representatives' Immigration Subcommittee about immigration reform, and the United Nations' Special Rapporteur about civil and immigrant rights issues. SAALT favors "a just and humane approach to immigration reform that includes a path to legalization for undocumented immigrants; elimination of the visa backlog; robust worker protections; and enforcement provisions that respect civil rights and due process."

Also in 2007, SAALT coordinated the first National South Asian Summit, bringing over 150 individuals together for a congressional briefing and advocacy workshops. By 2013, the National South Asian Summit had grown to include over 375 advocates, activists, and allies, including representatives from over 30 South Asian community groups from throughout the nation. The summit offered more than 40 issue-based workshops, panels, plenaries, and caucuses, and a congressional briefing with community leaders about data on immigration reform. In addition, a briefing about immigration reform, health care access, and hate crimes included panelists from the White House, U.S. Department of Justice, U.S. Department of Health and Human Services, and the White House Initiative on Asian Americans and Pacific Islanders.

In 2008, the organization expanded, adding a policy director and program assistant, while continuing its growth in providing community services. SAALT released an "issue brief" regarding problems affecting South Asian American communities in New Jersey, joined the campaign seeking justice for Indian migrant workers exploited by employers on the Gulf Coast, held a roundtable discussion in Michigan, conducted a briefing in the New Jersey state house, released a brochure about changes in the naturalization process in three South Asian languages, and coordinated the formation of a National Coalition of South Asian Organizations (NCSO) with 34 members.

NCSO is a network of community-based organizations with common beliefs regarding how to precipitate social change, which serve, organize, and advocate for South Asian American communities. The coalition offers a forum through which the member organizations can enhance the effectiveness of their work, while nurturing productive relationships with groups and individuals with similar goals and principles. NCSO has released a policy platform directed at stakeholders, community members, and policy makers. This "National Action Agenda" was designed to rectify the long absence of South Asian American concerns from policy debates and political decision making at the local and national level.

The coalition's action agenda includes nine items, each with detailed recommendations: civic and political participation, civil rights and civil liberties, data collection, economic justice, gender equity, health care, immigrant rights, LGBTIQ rights, and youth empowerment. A by-product of this initiative is the 2011 campaign, "An America for Us All," which attempted to mobilize community members around the 10th anniversary of the terror attacks of 9/11. The campaign asked community members to reflect on the events of 9/11 and what has since transpired within South Asian America. In particular, focus was placed upon the impact of unfair policies implemented by the government and the xenophobic rhetoric so prevalent in public discourse. Ultimately, the campaign called upon participants to work together to help the United States live up to its founding ideals of fairness and equality, while respecting and appreciating our society's increasing diversity.

SAALT has engaged in a census awareness campaign focusing on the South Asian American community to ensure its accurate representation. This was followed in 2011 and 2012 by the implementation of the "South Asian Vote!" campaign, which sought to expand South Asian American electoral participation through voter education. To ensure South Asian Americans have equal access to the nation's electoral process, SAALT monitors elections, conducts exit polling of South Asian American voters, conducts voter registration, and works to ensure the provision of language access for South Asian American voters.

Among the most crucial aspects of the group's work is leadership development. SAALT seeks to enhance the leadership skills of individuals within non-profit organizations through the NCSO, working to build a pipeline of leaders. Programs focusing on youth and college students seek to nurture and train future community

leaders. For example, SAALT's RISE UP! Young Leaders Institute (YLI) offers college students an opportunity and avenue through which to develop leadership skills, connect with fellow activists and mentors, and explore social change strategies around issues that affect South Asian American communities. The institute is designed to cultivate skills to deepen knowledge and awareness, strengthen and nurture relationships with diverse communities, and empower young leaders to be agents of change. The 2013 YLI paid particular attention to the increasingly documented bullying and bias confronting South Asian American youth. Participants explored South Asian American history, social change movements, the intersections of identity and power, the effects of xenophobia upon targeted minorities and society, and resources for addressing racial and religious harassment.

In addition, the Advocates for Community Empowerment (ACE) Project guides community-based organizations through intensive trainings designed to enhance the efficacy of their advocacy work. The program endeavors to teach practical organizing skills and strategies, offer opportunities for cross fertilization of ideas from peers and trainers, and provide individual technical assistance to participating organizations.

In addition to the reports it issued about hate crimes after 9/11 and South Asian American electoral participation, SAALT has released several reports to help guide their policy recommendations. A 2007 report, "Building Community Strength," focused on the needs and opportunities of South Asian American organizations.

Integrating a needs assessment with interviews with members of 31 community-based groups, the report highlights best practices within South Asian American community organizations. It also offers recommendations for better serving South Asian American communities, further research, and focused efforts.

In 2009, SAALT released "Washington DeSi: South Asians in the Nation's Capital" to help alleviate the lack of information available about the South Asian American community in the Washington, D.C. metropolitan area, home of the fifth largest South Asian American population in the country. In conjunction with the Asian Pacific American Legal Resources Center (APALRC), SAALT launched the South Asian Community Empowerment (SACE) project, which included a multi-language needs assessment, focus groups, interviews, and relationship-building with community organizations. The report analyzes surveys from nearly 200 respondents, in addition to information gathered from focus groups.

Also in 2009, SAALT's Deepa Iyer and Priya Murthy published a piece in the *St. John's Journal of Legal Commentary* entitled "Courting the South Asian Vote: One Step Forward, Two Steps Back," which studies the pattern of how South Asian Americans have been "othered" through interrogating racist and xenophobic political discourse. The article details how such practices can restrict South Asian American participation in the U.S. political process. This was followed in 2010 by "From Macacas to Turban Toppers: The Rise in the Xenophobic and Racist Rhetoric in American Political Discourse,"

which further demonstrated the impact of such bigotry-laden discourse on South Asian American political participation and civic engagement. Additional reports have offered stories of success, resistance, and resilience in the South Asian American in the decade after the watershed events of 9/11 ("Community Resilience"), and narratives of racial and religious profiling ("In Our Own Words").

Jaideep Singh

See also: Essays: Islamophobia; *Entries:* Sikh American Legal Defense and Education Fund (SALDEF)

Further Reading

SAALT Website. www.saalt.org. Accessed July 11, 2014.

Sovereignty

Sovereignty is the idea that a geographical location, an ethnic or racial group, a state, or a nation is entitled to self-rule. Sovereignty among Pacific Islanders operates in a historical and complex space, since many of the islands are either current colonial territories or are dealing with social issues brought about during colonialism. Sovereignty is significant because it motivates Pacific Islanders to argue for and actively seek increased sovereignty for themselves.

Oceania is divided into three geographical and ethnic groups: Melanesia, Micronesia, and Polynesia. These groupings, while simplifying discussions of specific Pacific Islanders, is a label arbitrarily placed upon these groups of people by Dumont d'Urville in the 1820s. Melanesia, meaning Black group, is the islands of Solomon, Vanuatu, Fiji, New Caledonia, and

Papua New Guinea. Micronesia is the islands of Guam, Mariana, Micronesia, Marshall, Palau, and Kiribati. Polynesia is the islands of Samoa, Tonga, Aotearoa, Tahiti, Cook, Marquesas, Rapa Nui, and Hawai'i. Tonga, Samoa, and Fiji are estimated to have been populated around 1500 BCE, Aotearoa around 800 CE, Rapa Nui and Hawai'i around 400 CE, and the Marquesas around 300 CE.

By 1900, most of the Pacific Islands were a possession of Britain, France, Germany, or the United States. In 1643, Fiji was spotted by Abel Tasman and in 1774 by Captain Cook. The HMS *Bounty* with Captain William Bligh made contact in 1789 and again in 1792. Captain James Wilson stopped in Fiji in 1797. Fiji became a member of the British Empire in 1874. Laborers from India were brought to work in Fiji in 1879. In 1916, Indian immigration to Fiji ended. Most of the laborers chose to stay in Fiji, since they had been assured of permanent residence status. In 1929, Indian Fijians gained a representative in the Legislative Council. Fiji began moving toward independence in 1961 with full independence in 1970.

Magellan spotted Guam in 1521. In 1565, Spain colonized Guam. Guam became a U.S. territory in 1898 with the end of the Spanish-American War. During World War II, the United States evacuated their personnel from Guam, and from 1941 to 1944 Japan controlled Guam. After World War II, the U.S. Navy returned to Guam and began to govern Guam. In 1950, the Organic Act of Guam made the inhabitants of Guam U.S. citizens. Chamorros are indigenous to Guam, but are now a minority among the population.

Missionaries arrived in 1828 and translated Samoan into a written language. Germany gained possession of Samoa in 1879, with annexation of Western Samoa in 1899. At the same time, the United States annexed Eastern Samoa. Western Samoa has been independent from Aotearoa since 1962, and American Samoa has been an unincorporated territory of the United States since 1900.

In 1643, Abel Tasman spotted Tonga. A civil war erupted in 1799 and ended in 1852 with Taufa'ahau as king. Tonga made a treaty with Germany in 1876 and became a German protectorate. In 1879, Tonga made a treaty with Britain and became a British protectorate. The British government had government control until 1905. Tonga became independent and a member of the Commonwealth in 1970. Papua New Guinea became a German protectorate in the late 1870s, and became self-governing in 1973, with full independence in 1975.

Currently, Pacific Islander sovereignty is a complicated and highly politically charged topic. It is further complicated by environmental issues, that is, global warming and rising sea levels that will overtake many of the Pacific Islands. What are Pacific Islanders without Pacific Islands? What becomes of their sovereignty when there is no land over which sovereignty can be achieved?

Niccole Leilanionapae'āina Coggins

See also: Entries: Pacific Islander Religious Cultures

Further Reading

Campbell, I. C. *A History of the Pacific Islands*. Berkeley, CA: University of Hawai'i Press, 1989.

Coffman, Tom. *Nation Within: The Story of America's Annexation of the Natives of Hawai'i.* Kihei, HI: Koa Books, 2009.

Kame'eleihiwa, Lilikalā. *Native Land and Foreign Desires: A History of Land Tenure Change in Hawai'i.* Honolulu, HI: Bishop Museum Press, 1992.

Kauanui, J. Kēhaulani. *Hawaiian Blood: Colonialism and the Politics of Sovereignty and Indigeneity.* Durham, NC: Duke University Press, 2008.

Merry, Sally. *Colonizing Hawai'i: The Cultural Power of Law.* Princeton, NJ: Princeton University Press, 2000.

Silva, Noenoe K. *Aloha Betrayed: Native Hawaiian Resistance to American Colonialism.* Durham, NC: Duke University Press, 2004.

Sri Lankan American Religions

Sri Lanka is a multiethnic and multireligious country. The numerical majority of the country, the Sinhala people, are predominantly Buddhist. Of the country's minority groups, Tamils are largely Hindus. But in both Sinhala and Tamil communities, there are small enclaves of Christians and Catholics. Sri Lanka is also home to adherents of Islam. While all the groups are covered here, the primary focus is on Sri Lankan American Buddhists and Hindus because they are the largest groups in the United States, and because they brought to America thinking and traditions that are not part of the Judeo-Christian belief system that generally defined the American religious landscape, particularly before the passage of the 1965 Immigration Act.

There are two main Buddhist sects, Theravāda and Mahāyāna. Theravāda is the older sect of the two, where the teachings of the Buddha in the original form are better preserved. Sri Lanka is a Theravāda Buddhist country. In American cities with significant numbers of Sri Lankan Buddhist immigrants, there is at least one Sri Lankan Buddhist temple sustained by voluntary community donations. The resident monks are usually Sri Lankan and are sponsored by the communities they serve. But non–Sri Lankan monks ordained in the Theravāda tradition reside in some temples such as the Bhavana (Meditation) Center in West Virginia. Buddhist temples are built according to traditional architectural design, but in the United States, some are located in homes or former churches. Still, they all attempt to organize the use of space to reflect those temples back in the homeland. Most Buddhist immigrants also have small shrines in their homes—a traditional practice.

Among the most important features of every Buddhist temple are one or more statues of the Lord Buddha, and when establishing temples in the United States, the communities usually bring the major statue from Sri Lanka. The statues are installed above a surface on which devotees can place their *pūjā* items—offerings of flowers, incense, and other items. The offerings symbolize the "noble qualities" of the Buddha such as kindness, compassion, wisdom, and generosity that devotees should try to cultivate.

The focus of Buddhist teachings is mental development by getting rid of "defiling thoughts" such as anger, hatred, and jealousy, and cultivating "wholesome thoughts" mentioned above. Buddhism is based on a theory of *saṃsāra*, or rebirth, and proper

Sri Lankan monks demonstrate outside the White House in Washington, October 4, 2006. Dozens gathered to condemn attacks by Tamil Tiger rebels in their homeland and to express appreciation of the U.S. authorities following the arrest by the FBI of people in the United States who sought to purchase weapons for use by the Tamil Tigers. (Jason Reed/Reuters/Corbis)

mental cultivation will ensure that both the present and future existences are positive ones because Buddhism does not subscribe to a creationist theory. The Buddha (who was a human being) taught that that the existence, sustenance, and destruction of the universe result from natural processes and that individuals are their own "refuge." They shape their future lives, based on the consequences of their volitional actions.

The most important religious event for Sri Lankan Buddhists is Vesak, the full-moon day in May. It was on Vesak days that the Buddha's birth, enlightenment, and passing away occurred. On this and other important Buddhist holy days, monks or-

ganize religious activities for adults and children. Most temples in America also offer regular meditation classes as well as Buddhism and Sinhala-language classes, and organize other community events such as the traditional New Year celebrations in April.

Sri Lankan Buddhist temples do not charge for *pūjā* or other events, and all services offered by the monks are free of charge. The relationship between monks and the lay community is reciprocal: the community provides the monks with food and other necessities, and monks teach them the Dhamma (Buddha's teachings), fulfill people's religious needs, and perform other social services. People also invite monks to their homes for the giving of alms, or at times of illness or other need to chant *pirith* (blessings). Therefore in America, people often give monetary donations to monks for incidental expenses such as travel.

Hindus believe in a supreme god who is formless and unknowable and who created, sustains, and will ultimately destroy the universe in a cyclical process. But most people seek to know him and someday to find liberation from the cycle of rebirth by reunifying with him. So ancient sages gave the formless god hundreds of forms, and from early times, Hindu beliefs and concepts were communicated through iconographic symbols. The most powerful in the Hindu pantheon of deities are the male gods Shiva and Vishnu, and the goddess who, like the gods, is known by multiple names. Each deity represents aspects of the supreme God in the form of *shakti* or energy. Most Hindus worship both Shiva and Vishnu, but are more strongly allied to one or the other. The majority of Sri Lankan Tamils are Shivites.

In Hindu philosophy, two important components are family life and spiritual life, and to instill family values in people, Shiva, for instance, is represented as a family unit. He and his wife, Parvati, have two sons, Ganesh and Muruga. Among Sri Lankan Tamils, Muruga is the most beloved among all the gods, and the Murugan Temple in Maryland maintained by Sri Lankan American Hindus is dedicated to him. The temple celebrates religious and cultural festivals, conducts religion and language classes, and offers both religious and life-cycle rituals.

In Hinduism, *pūjā* means the ritual worship of images of the deities. Devotees express their love and devotion, and draw near to the Divine through *pūjā*. The various deities represent various powers, and people do *pūjā* before important undertakings and to commemorate different life-cycle events. Lord Ganesh, for example, is the remover of obstacles, and Hindus generally start the New Year with a Ganesh *pūjā*.

Some rituals, such as *Abhisheka* and *Navaratri*, are quite elaborate and sponsorships vary accordingly. In the *Abhisekha* ritual, the image of the deity is honored by bathing with various ingredients, including rosewater, milk, yogurt, honey, and sandalwood water. During the *Navaratri* festivities, three goddesses—Parvathi for strength, Lakshmi for wealth, and Saraswathi for knowledge—are worshipped for three nights each, on nine consecutive nights. Both men and women can sponsor *pūjā* in the temples, and they may be done by individuals at domestic shrines.

Virtually all Sri Lankan Muslims adhere to the Islamic faith, though the majority follow the Sunni tradition. But whether they belong to the Sunni or the Shia sects, like all other Muslims, their cultural identities are strongly tied to their religion. So Sri Lankan American Muslims attend neighborhood *mosques* operated by Muslim peoples of other ethnicities.

The Christian and Catholic Sri Lankan Americans also attend neighborhood churches of other American communities and participate in social service acts such as feeding the homeless. They share the same biblical teachings and celebrate

Easter, Christmas, and other important religious events in the Christian calendars.

Usha Welaratna

See also: Entries: Ratanasara, Havanpola

Further Reading

Fuller, C. J. *The Camphor Flame: Popular Hinduism and Society in India*. Princeton, NJ: Princeton University Press, 1992.

Leonard, Karen Isalksen. *The South Asian Americans*. Westport, CT: Greenwood Press, 1997.

Walpola, Rahula. *What the Buddha Taught*. London: The Gordon Fraser Gallery, 1978.

Swami Prabhavananda (1893–1976)

Swami Prabhavananda, a philosopher, writer, and spiritual leader, was sent to the United States by the Ramakrishna order to continue the work begun by Swami Vivekananda (1863–1902) to spread the teachings of Sri Ramakrishna (1836–1886). After graduating from Calcutta University, he joined the Ramakrishna Order of India. After arriving in 1923 and serving as an assistant minister of the Vedanta Society of San Francisco, he moved to Portland and established the Vedanta Society of Portland. In 1929 he relocated to Los Angeles and the following year founded the Vedanta Society of Southern California.

In addition to establishing a number of branches in Southern California, Prabhavananda wrote and translated a number of books to make accessible the spiritual traditions of India to the West. His 1962 *Spiritual Heritage of India* is an intimate exposition of the many strands of Indian

spiritual traditions. In the foreword to the 1979 reissue, Huston Smith comments on Prabhavananda's rich and holistic grasp of his Indian tradition. Prabhavananda's translations include *Shankara's Crest-jewel of Discrimination, The Song of God: Bhagavad Gita*, and *How to know God: The Yoga Aphorisms of Patanjali*; these were written with Christopher Isherwood.

Prabhavananda's comprehensive knowledge of Indian thought attracted Aldous Huxley (1894–1963) and Gerald Heard (1879–1971), among other notables. In *My Guru and his Disciple*, Christopher Isherwood described his more than three decades (1939–1976) as a student of Prabhavananda. Cyriac Muppathyil's *Meditation as a Path to God-realization* published by the Pontifical Gregorian University in Rome examines how Hindu and Christian meditation are a meeting point for Hindu-Christian dialogue.

Ronald Y. Nakasone

See also: Entries: Hindu Canon; Indian American Christians

Further Reading

Isherwood, Christopher. *My Guru and His Disciple*. Minneapolis: University of Minnesota Press, 2001.

Swami Prabhavananda. *Spiritual Heritage of India*. Hollywood, CA: Vedanta Press, 1979.

Swami Vivekananda (1863–1902)

On May 31, 1893, an ochre-robed sadhu (monk), boarded a ship at Mumbai, India, to attend the Parliament of the World's Religions in Chicago. He had not been

Temple volunteers Ronald Harris, top and Reginald Matthews, both of Chicago, cover up a statue of Swami Vivekananda at the Hindu Temple of Greater Chicago, July 11, 1998, in Lemont, Illinois. The statue honors Vivekananda as the first man to bring Hindu religion and the practice of *yoga* to America. (AP Photo /Frank Polich)

him to speak. Thus on September 11, 1893, the 30-year-old swami opened his address with, "Sisters and Brothers of America . . ." to which the 7,000 attendees inexplicably offered applause lasting for more than three minutes. Continuing, he said, "I thank you in the name of the most ancient order of monks in the world; I thank you in the name of the mother of religions; I thank you in the name of millions and millions of Hindu people of all classes and sects." He ended with a plea for the end of sectarianism, bigotry, and fanaticism. He reiterated with a more expansive plea at the final session on September 27:

> If the Parliament of Religions has shown anything to the world it is this: It has proved to the world that holiness, purity, and charity are not the exclusive possessions of any church in the world, and that every system has produced men and women of the most exalted character. In the face of this evidence, if anybody dreams of the exclusive survival of his own religion and the destruction of others, I pity him from the bottom of my heart, and point out to him that upon the banner of every religion will soon be written, in spite of resistance: "Help and not Fight," "Assimilation and not Destruction," "Harmony and Peace and not Dissension."

invited to attend, and most certainly, not to address the parliament. However, after a chance meeting with John Henry Wright (1852–1908) of Harvard University, who was impressed by the monk's knowledge and charisma, the professor arranged for

Named Narendranath, Swami Vivekananda was born on January 12, 1863, to Vishwanath Datta, a successful attorney, and Bhuvaneshwari Devi. Narendra excelled in school. At Calcutta University he studied Western philosophy and history. He exhibited a deep interest in the spiritual life; even as a child he practiced meditation and pondered the existence of God. In 1881, when he first met Sri Ramakrishna Paramahansa (1836–1886) at the Kali Temple in Dakshineshwar, he asked without hesitation,

"Sir, have you seen God?"

"Yes, I have. I see Him as clearly as I see you, only in a much more intense way."

Narendranath had found his master.

Shortly thereafter Ramakrishna asked his disciples to wear ochre robes and sent them out to beg food, thus initiating the Ramakrishna order. After Ramakrishna discarded his mortal body in the early hours of August 16, 1886, Narendra assumed the leadership and established the first *math* or monastery of the Ramakrishna order in Baranagar (north Kolkata). In 1887 Narendranath took the vows of *sannyasa* (renunciant) and the name Vivekananda.

Vivekananda learned from Ramakrishna that all living beings were embodiments of Brahma, the source, the all-pervading and eternal reality; and that service to humanity is to render service to Brahma. Ramakrishna's message was a departure from traditional Vedanta thought that maintained activity is a means for preparing the mind for meditation and knowledge of Brahma. Vivekananda thus left the monastery to discover India. During his travels, he was appalled by the poverty and backwardness of the people. He concluded that the most pressing need was food, other daily necessities, and education. The poor needed training in improved methods of agriculture and other village industries. But more importantly, the poor needed faith that they belonged to and possessed *Atman*, the divine soul of Brahma. While the poor participated in the rituals and festivals, they failed to understand and apply the ennobling principles of Vedanta teachings in their lives.

While wrestling with the ideals of Vedanta and the practical realities of India, Vivekananda learned of the Parliament of the World's Religions. His friends and supporters encouraged him to attend the parliament. For his part, he believed that the parliament would provide the forum to present Ramakrishna's Vedanta teaching and a platform to appeal for help to uplift the poor.

After the parliament, Vivekananda remained in the United States for nearly two years. In addition to lecturing in Chicago, Detroit, Boston, New York, and other cities, in 1894 he founded the Vedanta Society of New York. In June and July 1895, he lectured to a dozen of his disciples at Thousand Island Park in New York. He delivered a series of lectures in England in 1895 and again in 1896, sharing his insights of India's spiritual heritage. In November 1895 he met Margaret Elizabeth Noble (1867–1911), who as Sister Nivedita worked to educate poor girls. In May 1896 Vivekananda met Max Müller (1823–1900), who would write a biography of Ramakrishna. He also visited other European countries; in Germany he met the Indologist Paul Deussen (1845–1919).

Vivekananda left for India on December 16, 1896, from England, stopping in France and Italy before arriving in Colombo, Sri Lanka, on January 15, 1897. In Colombo he gave the lecture "India, the Holy Land." In this and other lectures he repeatedly highlighted the applications of Vedanta principles to uplifting the people, eliminating the caste system, promoting science and industrialization, addressing widespread poverty, and ending colonial rule. These lectures were collected in *Lectures from Colombo to Almora.*

Despite declining health, Vivekananda left for the West for a second time in June 1899. He was accompanied by Sister Nivedita and Swami Turiyananda (1863–1922). Following a brief stay in England, he continued on to the United States, where he established the Vedanta Society of San Francisco in 1900. That same year he traveled to Paris to participate in the Congress of Religions. He visited Brittany, Vienna, Istanbul, Athens, and Egypt before returning to Kolkata on December 9, 1900. Due to his deteriorating health, Vivekananda was unable to attend the Congress of Religions in 1901 in Japan; instead he made pilgrimages to Bodhgaya and Varanasi.

On July 4, 1902, Vivekananda awoke early, went to the chapel at Belur Math, and meditated for three hours, after which he lectured to his students and discussed the plans for a Vedic college in the Ramakrishna Math with colleagues. At 7:00 p.m., he went to his room, asking not to be disturbed; he died at 9:10 p.m. while meditating. He was cremated on a sandalwood funeral pyre on the bank of the Ganges in Belur, opposite to where Ramakrishna was cremated 16 years earlier.

Ramakrishna Mission

Soon after his return to Kolkata, on May 1, 1897, Vivekananda founded the Ramakrishna Mission that emphasized "renunciation and service." In early 1898 he acquired a sizable plot of land at Belur on the west bank of the Ganges River to build a monastery. The Ramakrishna Mission and Ramakrishna Math established a pattern of monastic life that fuses ancient monastic ideals to the conditions of modern life. The curriculum gives equal importance to personal illumination and social service; the math is open to all. The mission has established and maintains hospitals and charitable clinics, training centers for nurses, orphanages, and homes for the elderly. It has also been involved in disaster relief operations during famine, epidemic, fire, flood, earthquake, cyclone, and communal disturbances. The mission is also active with rural and tribal welfare. Education is another focus. It has established universities, colleges, vocational training centers, high schools and primary schools, teacher-training institutes, as well as schools for the visually handicapped.

The worldwide branches of the Ramakrishna order outside of India are generally known as Vedanta Societies. These branches are primarily involved in spiritual, pastoral activities, and social service. In the United States the society is dedicated to raising awareness of the Vedanta spirituality through offering instruction in meditation and public lectures. Since Vivekananda emphasized "doing," with the exception of the state of West Bengal, the Vedanta Society does not formally memorialize its founder or any special milestone. The citizens of West Bengal celebrate their compatriot's birthday on January 12.

Jayanta Bhowmik

See also: Entries: Hindu Canon; International Society of Krishna Consciousness (ISKCON)

Further Reading

Houghton, Walter R. *The Parliament of Religions and Religious Congress at the World's Columbian Exposition.* Chicago: F. T. Neely, 1893.

Vivekananda, Swami. *Complete Works of Swami Vivekananda.* 9 Vols. India: Advaita Ashrama, 2001.

Swastika

The swastika is a symbol formed by two perpendicular intersecting lines, with four arms bent at right angles, giving the appearance of rotation. The word "swastika" is taken from the Sanskrit root *su-asti*, meaning "well-being," "good fortune," or "prosperity." However, usage of the symbol itself appears much earlier in archaeological records than this name for it. This symbol has seen very wide usage throughout human history, being found in ancient archaeological remains from India, China, Egypt, Persia, Rome, and Greece, and also within more recent archaeological evidence from Native American, Celtic, Germanic, and Nordic peoples. It has been used by these cultures variously as a symbol for the sun, the four cardinal directions, the continuing cyclical rotation of the four seasons and other natural cycles, and, nearly universally, as a symbol of good fortune. The swastika's appearance in the folklore of different Asian American cultures has primarily come through its associations in multiple religious traditions from Asia.

South Asian Americans can point to the particularly long history of the swastika in the Indian subcontinent. Its earliest known appearances in archaeological materials are dated around 2500 BCE from the Indus Valley Civilization in modern-day India. Hindus have associated the swastika with *samsāra*, the cycle or "wheel" of birth, death, and rebirth. They have also associated it with the sun and used it as a symbol of the Hindu god Vishnu. These usages of the swastika have been continued in South Asian American folklore.

For Jains in India and in the United States, the swastika continues to have great importance as a central image. For Jains, the swastika itself represents *samsāra*, with the four arms representing the four levels of existence; that of the gods, of humans, of animals, and of the underworld.

For Buddhists also, the swastika has long been seen as a symbol for *samsāra*. For Theravāda ("School of the Elders") Buddhists—who have come to the United States primarily from Thailand, Burma, Cambodia, Laos, and Sri Lanka—the swastika has also been seen as one of the traditional auspicious markings of the Buddha's footprints, which are popular images in Theravāda Buddhist iconography and material culture. For Chinese Buddhists, the swastika has been considered a symbol of the "seal" of the Buddha's infinitely compassionate heart. For this reason, Chinese icons of the Buddha—such as the Hsi Lai Temple in Hacienda Heights, California—often depict a swastika on the Buddha's chest. Within Daoism and broader Chinese and Chinese American culture, the swastika is a symbol of luck or prosperity and is used to represent 10,000, this number itself being symbolic of infinity. Thus, for Daoists, the swastika is a symbol of infinite luck.

Due to its 20th-century appropriation by Nazi Germany and accompanying associations with Nazi aggression and anti-Semitism, usage of the swastika in the United States after World War II has been controversial. There have been several instances of the swastika appearing on consumer products imported from Asia, with companies having to recall or issue apologies for the offense these products have caused to consumers in the United States who are unaware of the swastika's meanings outside of Nazi Germany. However, with the swastika being such a central symbol in several major Asian religions, there have been calls by many Asian Americans for a movement toward reclaiming the swastika from its relatively recent negative associations with Nazi Germany and anti-Semitism.

Charles M. Townsend

See also: Entries: Dragons; Lotus Flower; *Nāga*

Further Reading

MacArthur, Meher. *Reading Buddhist Art: An Illustrated Guide to Buddhist Signs and Symbols*. New York: Thames & Hudson, 2002.

Quinn, Malcolm. *The Swastika: Constructing the Symbol*. London and New York: Routledge, 1994.

"Reclaiming the Swastika": http://www .reclaimtheswastika.com/. Accessed July 16, 2014.

T

Tai Chi. *See Taiji Quan*

Taiji Quan

Taiji quan, or, in the Wade-Giles system of Romanization, *tai-chi ch'uan* (often referred to simply as *taiji*), is a Chinese internal martial art that literally translates as "supreme ultimate fist or boxing." *Taiji* is a series of slow movements with poetic names such as "grasp bird's tail" and "strum the lute." Often misidentified as fundamentally Daoist or religious in nature, *taiji* is actually a secular physical practice whose stated goals originally included both national and personal health. However, *taiji* has become part of the repertoire of American Daoism (see Daoism) and thus should be considered part of Asian American religious culture.

This entry will discuss the term *taiji* as a philosophical concept, the applications of this concept in medicine and healing, cultivation practices, and popular martial art forms such as *taiji quan* (also known as *tai-chi chuan*) in the North American culture.

Historical Developments

Variously translated as "the Great Ultimate" or "the Supreme Ultimate," *taiji* is an ancient Chinese philosophical concept that describes the primordial state of the cosmos immediately before any type of differentiation. In this state of predifferentiation, all things are included and balanced, but as an undivided whole.

The Daoist classic *Daode Jing* (written approximately in the fourth century BCE) famously states that the cosmos was derived from the *taiji*, which birthed the two complementary bipolarities (*yinyang*), which in turn begot the four phenomena (*sixiang*) and from which the eight trigrams (*bagua*) were born.

The two complementary bipolarities refer to yin and yang, while the four phenomena refer to the cosmological directions that are identified by four constellations. The eight trigrams are major patterns that can be used to explain and predict all things that happen in the cosmos. However, all these levels of differentiations are derived from a balanced whole, which is the Great Ultimate, or the *taiji*. The reversal of this process of differentiation is an important goal of the Daoist cultivation practices. The human world consists of a web of endless differentiations, whereupon the Daoists try to return to the state before differentiations, and preferably to the state of *wuji* (the limitless ultimate, or the state of nondifferentiation), understood as the original Dao or the ideal state of being.

A popular visual representation of the *taiji* is what is known as the *yinyang* fish diagram. The diagram consists of a circle with two complementary halves that also

853

include a dot of the opposite within each other; the circle that includes both yin and yang in their endless cycle of becoming each other is the *taiji*. All movements in the cosmos are initiated from this basic principle of constant transformations between yin and yang to maintain a balanced whole.

Although the *yinyang* fish diagram (and the concept of *taiji* as well) is mostly associated with the Daoist tradition, *taiji* as a concept first appeared in divination literature that predated religious Daoism. The *Yi jing* (or *I Ching*, Book of Changes), one of the popular divination manuals, was selected by Confucius as a classic for his curriculum for scholarly training. In other words, Confucians have historically used *taiji* as a basic concept for understanding the structure and working of the cosmos.

Neo-Confucians of the 12th century explained and reinterpreted *taiji* extensively to differentiate the Confucian usage of the term from their Daoist contemporaries. One of the most drastic interpretations was introduced by neo-Confucian philosopher and educator Zhu Xi (1130–1230), who equated *taiji* (predifferentiation) to *wuji* (nondifferentiation), essentially arguing that there is no state of being with higher meaning than that of *taiji*, and in turn denying the legitimacy of the Daoist path of cultivation with the goal of attaining the original Dao.

In more recent centuries, the concept of *taiji* has been applied to medicine and healing, cultivation practices, and most notably martial arts. Many contemporary *taiji quan* (also known as *taichi chuan*) masters attribute the founding of this mar-

tial art form to the Daoist immortal Zhang Sanfeng (whose dates range between the 13th and 17th centuries), after observing a bird fighting with a snake on the holy Daoist mountain of Wudang Shan. Instead, *taiji* was developed in the early 17th century (though some scholars date its first public appearance as late as the 19th century) by the Chen family patriarch, a retired military man, in the now-famous Chen family ancestral village, located in present-day Henan Province.

Yet the roots of *taiji* go much deeper. Longevity and meditative practices have always been among the most important concerns of Chinese culture in general. An unearthed tomb from 168 BCE contained an illustration of various people engaged in stretching, self-massage, and gymnastics. Known as the *Daoyin tu*, this chart shows that cultivation techniques were part of everyday Chinese culture 2,000 years ago. Beyond these, longevity techniques may include breathing exercises, sexual hygiene, gymnastics, and diet and herbs, but their aim is always to guide the *qi*. The ideal of the body functioning in harmony was a moral as well as a physical ideal, and it formed the first stage in the quest for immortality.

Beliefs and Practices

***Taiji* and the Human Body.** To understand how the concept of *taiji* is applied in actual practices, we must look at how Chinese conceptualize the human body in relation to the cosmos. Essentially, the cosmos as a comprehensive system operates with its inherent principles, and we can observe the manifestation of these same principles by seeing the same patterns on all levels of the cosmos. From constellations in the sky, landscapes in nature, to human societies, and to the smallest organisms, the same principles apply. Likewise, the human body, as part of the cosmos, also shares the same general principles. Furthermore, different levels of the cosmos, regardless of scale, correspond and interrelate through these shared principles. This is known as the correspondence theory. *Taiji* as a philosophical concept is widely applied to the daily lives of the Chinese people precisely because it is believed that universal principles such as *taiji are* consistently manifested in all levels of human experiences. Therefore, *taiji* as the ideal state of being, where yin and yang are balanced and continually co-creating, is equally as important for understanding the cosmos as it is important for understanding the human body.

As traditional Chinese medicine and healing methods (most notably acupuncture) become increasingly popular in mainstream America, the theories behind the medical practices are also disseminated outside of the Chinese American circle. One important goal in traditional Chinese healing is to attain and maintain the optimal balance within the human body. Although the Chinese healers may or may not employ the term *taiji* in their description and explanations of the optimal balance, the therapeutic practices they employ on the patients, and the cultivation methods that they practice themselves and often teach to their patients, all aim for a state of co-existence and balance of yin and yang in the human body.

Taiji Quan. Today, there are five main styles of *taiji*, each named after the family most associated with it. The Chen style is the oldest, but the best known and most widely practiced is the Yang style. Although there is no record of the first *taiji* class taught in America, it is doubtful that the first wave of Chinese immigrants in the mid-19th century practiced what we know today as *taiji* at all. They were mostly from South China, and *taiji* practice was centered in the north. Moreover, this first generation arrived between the 1850s and the 1880s, yet *taiji* gained public popularity in China only in the late 19th and early 20th centuries, thanks to Yang Chengfu (ca. 1886–1935), to whom most of the original Yang-style *taiji* instructors in the United States trace their lineages. (Indeed, Yang remains the most popular style of *taiji* in the United States.) The first visual representation of *taiji* in America may be a newsreel from the 1930s depicting Chinese immigrants in California practicing it en masse.

The first American *taiji* books published in English were by European American authors Edward Maisel (1937–2008) and Sophia Delza (1903–1996). A modern dancer from New York City, Delza wrote *Body and Mind in Harmony* (1961) as a straightforward guide to the practice, a book still in print today. Maisel's *Tai Chi for Health* was published the following year. Maisel, who founded the Tai Chi Institute of America in New York City in 1961, attempts to excise anything overtly Chinese from *taiji*. While Delza uses simple line drawings to illustrate positions, Maisel's photographs show white men in loafers, slacks, shirt, and tie—everything but a sports jacket. His language recalls cheerful 1950s physical fitness boosterism. Chapter subheadings include "A Way to Remain Youthful," "Never a Feeling of Strain," and "Tai Chi Prevents Freak Injuries."

Indeed, Maisel's conception of spiritual achievement owes more to Norman Vincent Peale's "power of positive thinking" than to Chinese thought. Maisel writes that *taiji* can give you "greater mental powers," can act as a "safe tranquilizer," and "furnishes strong motivation." Expert testimony comes not from Chinese sources, but from physicians working in New York City hospitals. For Maisel, *taiji* is compatible with the American values of optimism and activism.

One of the first Chinese to teach *taiji* to non-Chinese in North America was Da Liu (1904–2000) who taught at the United Nations in New York beginning in 1956. He wrote several books that conflated *taiji* with Taoism, now all out of print, including *The Taoist Health Exercise Book* (1973), *The Tao of Health and Longevity* (1978), and *The Tao of Chinese Culture* (1979). Cheng Man-ch'ing (Zheng Manqing, 1901–1975) had a wider impact on *taiji* in America, thanks to his numerous students who have continued to teach. Born in eastern China, a former bodyguard for the Nationalists, Cheng taught *taiji* at the Military Academy in Shanghai. He moved to New York City in 1964 and shortly thereafter founded the Shr Jung T'ai Chi School. He was also a painter, a doctor of Chinese medicine, and, according to those who knew him, a legendary colorful character. Although he wrote his first *taiji* book in Chinese in 1950, his first successful book in English was *T'ai Chi:*

The Supreme Ultimate Exercise (1967), in collaboration with his American student Robert K. Smith.

Two important popularizers of *taiji* in America were both connected with Esalen, the retreat center in Central California best known for giving birth to the human potential movement. Although *yoga* and other movement arts were taught at Esalen, according to historian Eugene Taylor, *taiji* "was the movement therapy that became most popular . . . chiefly through Gia-Fu Feng" (1999, 245). Feng (1919–1985), a friend of Esalen founder Richard Price, was the only Chinese American on the full-time staff. The second figure, Al Chungliang Huang (1937–), was a regular visitor to Esalen who often conducted seminars with his friend Alan Watts (1915–1973). Like Cheng and Feng, Huang was born into a privileged family in China. Huang's family left for Taiwan in 1949, where he had an Americanized upbringing, and in 1955, Huang moved to Los Angeles to pursue a degree in architecture. He met Alan Watts in 1961 and they began co-teaching classes at Esalen in 1965. Huang founded the Living Tao Institute, a loosely organized nonprofit where Huang, as of 2012, continues to teach free-form *taiji*, combined with Chinese philosophy and calligraphy.

Huang's most famous book, *Embrace Tiger, Return to Mountain: The Essence of T'ai Chi*, first published in 1973 (and featuring a somewhat patronizing introduction by Alan Watts), is a transcription of a week-long Esalen workshop held in 1971. The book's appeal may be due to the way Huang undercuts the Orientalist discourse now creeping into discourse about *taiji*.

Huang insists *taiji* should not be made into just an "Oriental thing." He equates *taiji* with *yoga* and Zen.

Beginning with Da Liu, we see a pattern emerging—Chinese immigrants from elite Confucian literati backgrounds who teach *taiji* in America as part of their heritage, while also expounding on health and longevity practices, and teaching cultural practices such as calligraphy, meditation, and Chinese philosophical classics such as the *Yi Jing, Daode Jing* that all educated Chinese would be familiar with. The combination of these activities, in the American popular imagination, added up to something called "Daoism."

Taiji spread quickly during the late 1960s; it was taught in YMCAs, community centers, and nursing homes, particularly in California and New York but throughout the country as well. *Taiji* instructors came to include non-Chinese teachers, as well as a new generation of post-1965 immigrants from China and Taiwan, many of whom came to North America to attend graduate school and who taught *taiji* at their universities. These immigrants were necessarily not from elite literati backgrounds and thus did not conflate *taiji* with Daoism. Today, *taiji* is part of American popular culture, depicted in television commercials and in "for dummies" paperbacks.

In Canada, one also finds the more recent "Taoist Tai Chi" created by Moy Lin-shin (1931–1998), a Cantonese immigrant to Canada. In Toronto, he founded the Taoist Tai Chi Society (TTCS) in 1970 and a Daoist temple called Fung Loy Kok Temple a decade later. There are centers in most Canadian cities and several in the United States, notably in Tallahassee, Florida, and Boulder, Colorado. The society has a growing presence in Europe and the Caribbean as well. Master Moy, the founder and spiritual leader, was born in Guangdong in Southern China. He moved to Hong Kong in 1948 to escape the revolution. There, he trained at the Yuen Yuen Institute, which was established by Longmen monks from Canton. Moy immigrated to Canada in 1970, both to teach martial arts but also as a Daoist missionary. He modified standard Yang-style tai chi and coined the term "Taoist tai chi." As Moy's original students left Toronto, Taoist *taiji* clubs sprung up around Canada and later in the United States.

The TTCS raises awareness by emphasizing the health benefits of practicing *taiji* and the service aspect of belonging to the society. In fact, the TTCS bases its identity around the practice of this trademarked style of *taiji*. Moy modified the commonly taught Yang style of *taiji* by adding a bend in the waist so that the torso is at a 45-degree angle and fully extending the arms, which are rounded in Yang style.

Emily S. Wu and Elijah Siegler

See also: Entries: Daoism; Daoist Rituals

Further Reading

Cheng, Man-ching, and Robert K. Smith. *T'ai Chi: The Supreme Ultimate Exercise for Health, Sport, and Self-Defense*. Rutland, VT: Tuttle, 1967.

Delza, Sophia. *T'ai Chi Ch'uan: Body and Mind in Harmony*. North Canton, OH: The Good News, 1961.

Huang, Al. *Embrace Tiger, Return to Mountain: The Essence of Tai Chi*. Moab, UT: Real People Press, 1973.

Jou, Tsung Hwa. *The Dao of Taijiquan: Way to Rejuvination.* Rutland, VT: C. E. Tuttle, 1989.

Liao, Waysun. *The Essence of T'ai Chi: Selections from the T'ai Chi Classics on the Great Power and Inner Meaning of the Ancient Martial Art.* Boston: Shambhala, 2007.

Maisel, Edward. *Tai Chi for Health.* New York: Holt Rinehart & Winston, 1963.

Robinet, Isabelle. "*Wuji* and *Taiji*: Ultimateless and Great Ultimate." In Fabrizio Pregadio, ed. *The Encyclopedia of Taoism.* London: Routledge, 2008, pp. 1057–59.

Taylor, Eugene. *Shadow Culture.* Washington, DC: Counterpoint, 1999.

Wong, Kiew Kit. *The Complete Book of Tai Chi Chuan: A Comprehensive Guide to the Principles and Practice.* Rutland, VT: Tuttle, 2002.

Taiwanese American Religions

Historical Background

Taiwanese Americans are a post-1965 Asian American group that is largely middle class and educated. While religious survey data on Taiwanese American religion is imprecise because Taiwanese are rarely disaggregated from data collected on Chinese Americans, the closest estimations number Taiwanese Americans to be about 20–25 percent Protestant Christian, 20–25 percent Buddhist, and 50 percent nonreligiously affiliated. These numbers are strikingly different from the religious demography of Taiwan, where Christians comprise a mere 3.9 percent, Buddhists 35.1 percent, and the vast majority practice a popular religion that is a mixture of Buddhism, Daoism, and folk religion. These numbers suggest that at least for the first generation, Taiwanese American religion is often a story of religious change after coming to the United States.

To fully understand Taiwanese American religion, one must situate Taiwanese Americans and their faith practices in their historical and contemporary lived experiences as immigrants in the United States. The Taiwanese American population is largely composed of immigrants who migrated to the United States after the 1965 passage of the Hart-Celler Act and their offspring. Due to a combination of both U.S. immigration policies that have preferred highly educated immigrants and economic push factors from Taiwan, Taiwanese American immigrants are predominantly college-educated and professional. Their second-generation offspring have followed in their parents' educational footsteps. For example, in Los Angeles County, 71 percent of Taiwanese adults have a college degree, according to the 2000 Census. It is important to note that Taiwanese Americans represent a particular demographic subset of all Taiwanese—educated, upper middle class, and, particularly among men, scientifically trained. These factors have influenced the shape of Taiwanese American religion and have made it distinctive from religion in Taiwan. Most Taiwanese who come to the United States are not very religious. This is because the population of immigrants draws from the subset of the *least* religious among the Taiwanese—the educated, the majority of whom are educated in the sciences. Many Taiwanese Americans claim that they were not religious but observed some religious rituals for sake of family tradition of ancestral veneration. Because so much of Taiwanese religion revolves around the extended family, distance from the family in Taiwan makes most Taiwanese Americans even less inclined to maintain traditional Taiwanese religions. Both the initial lack of religiosity and distance from the family makes some Taiwanese immigrants more open to conversion to other religious traditions in the United States.

Among Taiwanese immigrants who are religious, they are more inclined to belong to institutionalized religions such as Buddhism or Christianity—religions that have "modernized," so to speak, and are more compatible with a Western, scientific worldview. Again, class and education are factors. Folk religious traditions that are associated with the working class and less educated in Taiwan are hardly visible in the United States, where the Taiwanese population is largely educated and middle class.

Finally, as a predominantly immigrant population, the immigration experience, and themes of dislocation and settlement figure prominently in the religions of Taiwanese Americans. Like other immigrant groups, religious institutions serve both spiritual and social functions for the larger Taiwanese American community. Religion is an invaluable social network for newly arrived Taiwanese. Taiwanese Americans use religion to expand their social circles, grow their businesses, learn English, and so on. Taiwanese American religious institutions are *ethnic* institutions and are spaces for them to congregate among their own, to celebrate and preserve Taiwanese traditions, and to pass these on to the second generation. In short, religious institutions help Taiwanese immigrants gain a

foothold in a new land. For this reason, religious institutions are the most popular and important source of community gathering among Taiwanese Americans, even for those who are not religiously affiliated. Indeed, the dramatic growth in the number of converts to Christianity in the United States among Taiwanese Americans is largely due to the success of Christian churches in meeting the social needs of Taiwanese immigrants. So too, some Buddhist and other non-Christian Taiwanese religious institutions have adopted social activities and services in the United States to both attract and meet the needs of Taiwanese American devotees.

Beliefs and Practices

Christianity. Taiwanese American Christianity is a largely Protestant phenomenon. The early cohort of Taiwanese immigrants were disproportionately Protestant Christians, and they established Christian churches and fellowships as important centers in the Taiwanese community in the late 1960s and early 1970s. Canadian and American Protestant missionaries to Taiwan had converted Taiwanese to Protestant Christianity as early as 1860. The Presbyterian Church played an important role in the early Taiwanese American community, particularly among the *Benshengren*, or the Han Chinese who migrated to Taiwan before 1949. The Presbyterian Church has historically been, and continues to be, a strong proponent of Taiwanese independence and a critic of the Kuomintang government in Taiwan. While the Presbyterian Church continues to play an important role in Taiwanese American

Christianity, its membership has diminished as independent, evangelical Taiwanese American and Chinese American churches have increased in popularity. Most notable among these are the Evangelical Formosan Church (EFC) and Ling Liang Tang or Bread of Life Christian Church. Both of these organizations have planted churches all over the world. For example, the Evangelical Formosan Church (EFC) was established in the early 1970s and has now planted over 100 churches, mostly in the United States, but also in Taiwan, New Zealand, Australia, Canada, and Costa Rica. Taiwanese American Christianity is influenced considerably by both the larger American evangelical and larger global Chinese Christian movements.

Some Taiwanese immigrants attend exclusively Taiwanese churches. But many attend Chinese churches that draw Han Chinese from China, Southeast Asia, and Taiwan. Ethnic factors such as if one is a *Bengshenren* or a *Waishengren*, linguistic factors such as if one is more comfortable with Taiwanese or Mandarin, and political factors, such as whether one is pro–Taiwan independence, may influence the church that Taiwanese Americans attend.

Conversion and Social Factors. The Taiwanese American church, and Christianity in general, plays a far more pronounced role in the lives of Taiwanese in the United States than in Taiwan. For this reason, a significant number of Taiwanese convert to Christianity after migrating to the United States. As mentioned earlier, part of this is due to a predisposed openness to conversion among Taiwanese immigrants. And

part is due to the role of Christian churches in easing the settlement and migration process of Taiwanese immigrants in the United States. Church leaders are quite aware of the challenges that Taiwanese immigrants face in the United States. Taiwanese American churches have taken the leadership in providing social spaces for ethnic fellowship, often sponsoring events that serve the larger Taiwanese American community. Churches are intensely social places where service and social activities can occupy most of church members' free time. For example, church members may spend a large part of their Sundays attending services in the morning, eating lunch, and then attending choir practice or fellowship meetings. Weekends often involve Friday night meetings and social events. Families with children are particularly attracted to Taiwanese American churches because they provide programs that promote traditional Taiwanese values and culture. Taiwanese immigrants are attracted to the Taiwanese American church because it reconstructs the extended kinship network that they have lost in the process of migration.

The Second Generation. Most Taiwanese churches have an English-language service for the second generation, in addition to a Taiwanese-language and/or Mandarin-language service for the first generation. Indeed, the programs for the second generation are a large draw for the first generation, who are eager for their children to be among Taiwanese and away from the perceived corrupting influences of American culture. Church programs for youth include Sunday school, choir, orchestra, Friday night fellowship meetings, summer camps, vacation Bible school, retreats, and more. Taiwanese American churches may have abundant programming for school-aged children; however, these are often lacking once the second generation reaches college age and beyond. Some churches may successfully incorporate a second-generation Taiwanese American adult congregation. But the second generation frequently complains that they lack autonomy in decision making and are still treated as children in the church. For this reason, many second-generation Taiwanese American adults do not remain in the Taiwanese American church, and it is questionable whether there will be an identifiable Taiwanese American Christianity beyond the first generation. The second generation is not necessarily abandoning the faith, but is increasingly attracted to pan–Asian American churches that are composed of the second generation and beyond. Here they are able to congregate with other East Asian Americans who have similar cultural values and racial experiences as themselves. The Christianity of the second generation is also notably different from that of the first generation. These pan–Asian American churches function less as assimilatory vehicles, and incorporate more of, and are arguably indistinguishable from, American evangelical Christianity.

Buddhism

Buddhism in Taiwan underwent radical transformation and revival just as immigration to the United States began in the 1960s and 1970s. The emphasis in what is often called "modern Chinese Buddhism" shifted in two ways: from religious practice and education solely among monastics to laypeople, and from the afterlife to this life. Once perceived by the educated as quaint, traditional, and superstitious, Chinese Buddhism underwent a modern transformation and acquired a popular following starting in the mid-1970s, particularly among women in the rising Taiwanese middle class. Taiwanese Buddhists who immigrated before the 1980s had few religious options in the United States. Unlike Christianity, where laypersons could easily establish Bible studies and Christian fellowships, Buddhists did not develop similar lay organizational counterparts until much later. Some Taiwanese Buddhists maintained personal practices at home, others drifted from religious practice, while still others even converted to Christianity for the ethnic community.

Taiwanese Buddhist organizations established Dharma centers and temples in the United States beginning in the mid-late 1970s, 10 years after the initial founding of Taiwanese American Christian organizations. Several well-known Taiwanese Buddhist organizations such as Tzu Chi, Fo Guan Shan, and Dharma Drum have established centers and temples in the United States that enjoy considerable popularity. Most well known among these is Fo Guan Shan's Hsi Lai Temple in Southern California that attracts over 700 people every weekend. Many of Hsi Lai's visitors and devotees are not Taiwanese, but Chinese American, Vietnamese American, and white Buddhists.

For the most part, Taiwanese American Buddhists practice Mahāyāna Buddhism, with an emphasis on Chan and Pure Land practices. Devout Taiwanese American Buddhists maintain altars in their homes where they pray, meditate, and chant. Many Taiwanese and Taiwanese Americans have a special devotion to Guanyin, or the Avalokitesvara Bodhisattva. And many of the devout chant the *Heart Sūtra* as part of their regular practice. Some of the devout, particularly housewives, are active volunteers at the temple.

While maintaining many features of Buddhism in Taiwan, these temples have had to adapt considerably to the American religious environment. For example, some temples meet weekly on Sundays with Dharma and chanting services, and with laypersons playing substantial leadership roles in teaching, charity work, and social activities. Like Taiwanese American churches, Buddhist temples have played an important role in assimilating new immigrants to the United States and have expanded from mere spaces of religious ritual to community centers that organize social gatherings, sporting events, children's camps, and so on. Others have maintained a more traditional approach, with monastics concentrating on religious ritual and education and with limited involvement of laity. Unlike Taiwanese American Christian organizations, many Taiwanese American Buddhist organizations have also actively incorporated whites into their communities, some of whom have even taken vows and become monastics under a Taiwanese Dharma master.

There is considerable variation in how Taiwanese Americans practice Buddhism in the United States. In contrast to Christianity, where Christians are expected to attend Sunday services and the church plays a central role in one's devotional life, the temple is far more peripheral to Buddhist practice. Some of the most pious Buddhists do not attend the temple at all. Many Buddhists will attend multiple temples, but not one on a regular basis. Despite temples' best efforts to propagate the Dharma and introduce a new kind of everyday lay Buddhism, a significant number of temple visitors use the temple as they did in Taiwan, visiting on special holidays and as a place to pray in times of special need. As such, the temple can be regarded as what one Taiwanese Dharma master fondly calls a "spiritual gas station," where devotees can load up on spiritual fuel when they need it.

Second Generation. Children's religious education is relatively new to Taiwanese Buddhism. As such, not all temples offer programming for the second generation. Part of the difficulty lies in the linguistic and cultural divide between the monastics, many of whom are recent immigrants, and the Americanized second generation. Temples struggle to maintain the second generation. There has been some success, particularly in areas such as Southern California where there is a large Taiwanese American population, to draw the college-age second generation to Buddhism. But in general, temples offer few programs for youth beyond elementary school. Many temples have English Dharma classes, but these are often geared toward the white converts and have limited appeal to Taiwanese American youth. Taiwanese American parents similarly express difficulty in passing on and explaining their Buddhist faith to their children. Once adults, most second-generation Taiwanese Americans do not maintain Buddhist practices. They are alienated from an American Buddhism that is largely composed of white converts, but also do not feel comfortable with the Taiwanese Buddhism of their immigrant parents.

The Nonreligious and Other Religions

About half of Taiwanese immigrants claim no religious affiliation in the United States. American religious surveys, however, do not capture the fullness of Taiwanese American religiosity. Even though the nonreligious do not consider themselves religiously observant, they do participate in "religious" practices that are inextricably connected with Taiwanese cultural practices. For example, it is not uncommon for the nonreligious to display icons of the Maitreya Buddha, or Laughing Buddha, in their homes and businesses as he is a popular Taiwanese cultural figure. Many continue to participate in rituals of ancestral veneration when at home in Taiwan. Some visit the temple on special holidays such as the Lunar New Year or will visit for good luck. And some will even seek divination services that are normally associated with Taoist temples in Taiwan.

Some Taiwanese immigrants will visit popular religious temples, in particular, Daoist temples and temples devoted to the special devotion of certain deities such as Matsu, the goddess of the sea. However, these are usually temples established by earlier and contemporary working-class Chinese immigrants from Hong Kong, China, and Southeast Asia. As mentioned

earlier, Taiwanese American religious institutions have largely been Protestant and Buddhist. This reflects the class-specific nature of Taiwanese American immigration.

Although not in large numbers, Taiwanese Americans are also Catholics, Mormons, Jehovah's Witnesses, Seventh-day Adventists, and Jews. Because there are so few Taiwanese Americans within these faith traditions, they rarely have their own ethnic congregations but belong to American or Chinese American congregations. Finally, some Taiwanese Americans are members of Yiguandao, the Way of Unity, a new religious movement from Taiwan.

Carolyn E. Chen

See also: Entries: Chinese American Religions; Hsi Lai Temple; Tzu Chi Foundation U.S.A.

Further Reading

Chandler, Christopher Stuart. *Establishing a Pureland on Earth: The Foguang Buddhist Perspective in Modernization and Globalization.* Honolulu: University of Hawai'i Press, 2004.

Chen, Carolyn. *Getting Saved in America: Taiwanese Immigration and Religious Experience.* Princeton, NJ: Princeton University Press, 2008.

Lee, Jonathan H. X. "Creating a Transnational Religious Community: The Empress of Heaven and Goddess of the Sea, Tianhou /Mazu, from Beigang to San Francisco." In L. A. Lorentzen, J. J. Gonzalez, K. M. Chun, and H. D. Do, eds. *Religion at the Corner of Bliss and Nirvana: Politics, Identity, and Faith in New Migrant Communities.* Durham, NC: Duke University Press, 2009, pp. 166–83.

Lin, Irene. "Journey to the Far West: Chinese Buddhism in America." *Amerasia Journal* 22 (1996): 106–32.

Tarthang Tulku (1935–)

Tarthang Tulku (1935–) was born in the mountains of Golok in the far northeast of Tibet, a region located in the present southeastern corner of Qinghai Province, China. His father, Sogpo Tulku, Pema Gawey Dorje (b. 1894), was a respected physician and holder of the Nyingma Vidyadhara lineage. Before he was two years old, he was recognized as an incarnate tulku and given the name Kunga Gellek by Tragyelung Tsultrim Dargye (b. 1866). At the age of nine, he entered the Tarthang Monastery. He left his homeland for Sikkim in 1958 via Bhutan and made his way to the University of Varanasi, India, where he taught for six years. During this time he established Dharma Publishing in 1963. He entered the United States in 1968 and settled in Berkeley in 1969 with his wife, the poet Nazli Nour. He is perhaps the earliest and most important teacher of the Nyingma, oldest of the four Tibetan Buddhist lineages in the United States. The Nyingma lineage is comprised of the mo-

The Copper dome of the first Tibetan Buddhist Temple constructed in the U.S. shines in the coastal sun 30 miles north of Jenner, California. A quadrangle of 50 rooms encloses the temple, which can be seen in clear weather from 40 miles out at sea. The complex, known as Odiyan, was built over eight years by volunteers who are devotees of Tibetan Lama Tarthang Tulku. (Bettmann/Corbis)

nastic and celibate Red Saṇgha (community, order) and noncelibate White Saṇgha. Individuals would move between these two *saṇghas* in response to changing circumstances and proclivities.

Shortly after settling in Berkeley, Tarthang Tulku established the Tibetan Aid Project to support the Tibetan refugee community and to preserve their Tibetan heritage. In 1971 in a further effort to preserve Tibetan culture and introduce Tibetan Buddhism and culture to the West, he relocated Dharma Publishing to Berkeley, California, and in 1972 he founded the Nyingma Institute. Further, in 1983, Tarthang Tulku established the Yeshe De for the purpose of preserving and distributing sacred Tibetan texts. More than 20 million texts have been distributed. He established the Copper Mountain Mandala, Odiyan Retreat Center in Sonoma, California, in 1975; it is a monastic community that fosters meaningful work, and that is dedicated to the cultivation of the life and culture of Tibetan Buddhism. Among Tarthang Tulku's more recent projects is the Mangalam Research Center of Buddhist Languages, dedicated to teaching Buddhist languages. It began in 2009 and is located in downtown Berkeley.

Tarthang Tulku has written over 40 books on a variety of topics. Some of the more popular ones are *The Sacred Art of Tibet* (1972), *Gesture of Balance—a Guide to Awareness, Self Healing and Meditation* (1977), *Time, Space, and Knowledge: A New Vision of Reality* (1977), and *Teachings from the Heart* (1989).

Ronald Y. Nakasone

See also: Entries: Tibetan American Religions

Further Reading

Fields, Rick. *How the Swans Came to the Lake: A Narrative History of Buddhism in America.* Boston: Shambhala, 1992.

Lopez, Donald. *Tibetan Buddhism and the West.* Chicago: University of Chicago Press, 1999.

Prebish, Charles S. *Luminous Passage: The Practice and Study of Buddhism in America.* Berkeley: University of California Press, 1999.

Tendai Shū

Established in 1973, the Tendai Mission of Hawai'i is not part of the early Japanese immigrant spiritual experience. However, Tendai Shū merits an entry, because its monastery on Mt. Hiei, Enryakuji Temple, not only guards the northwest sector of the former capital of Kyoto from malevolent spirits, but more importantly, incubated the founders of Japanese Buddhist movements that emerged during the Kamakura era (1185–1333). Hōnen, the patriarch of Jōdo-shū; Shinran, the founder of Jōdoshin-shū; Nichiren, the originator of Nichiren Shū; Eisai, who established Rinzai-shū; and Dōgen, the originator of Sōtō-shū, at one time or another studied at Enryakuji Temple. Kūkai, the founder of Shingon-shū, is the exception.

History

"Tendai" is the Japanese rendering of "Tiantai," the name of a mountain in Taizhou in South China, where Zhiyi (531–597) lived and taught. Building on Huiwen (515–577), Huisi (ca. 550), and others, the Tiantai patriarch Zhiyi consolidated and systematized the many strands of Buddhist thought to establish a tradition with a distinctive Chinese flavor. Three of his most important works are *Miaofa wenju* (*Profound Meaning of the* Sadharmapuṇḍarika [Sūtra]), *Miaofa lianhua jing xuanyi* (*Commentary on the* Lotus Sūtra), and *Mohe zhiguan* (*Great stillness and contemplation*). These texts are transcriptions of his lectures by his disciple Guanding (561–632). As the titles of the first two documents indicate, Zhiyi appealed to the *Sadharmapuṇḍarika* or *Lotus Sūtra* for his interpretation of Buddhist thought and practice. The first extols the import of the *Lotus Sūtra*; and the second is a line-by-line commentary. Delivered late in his life the *Mohe zhiguan* (Jpn. *Mahā shikan*) represents Zhiyi's most mature and systematic thinking; it details different meditation types and their respective requirements that led to the development of Chan (Zen) and Pure Land Buddhism. These and other writings provided the basis for Japanese Tendai and the subsequent development of Japanese Buddhist movements.

Saichō was familiar with Zhiyi's thoughts through the texts that the Vinaya (Precept) master Ganjin (Jianzhen, 688–763) introduced to Japan. However, since the texts contained errors, Saichō traveled to China to secure accurate copies and to acquire other texts not yet known in Japan. During his eight-and-a-half-month sojourn, Saichō collected 450 volumes and 230 sections of Buddhist documents. Another purpose was to receive official sanctions from Tiantai and other traditions. He received the seal of transmission—approval to teach—from Xiuran (n.d.) of the Zhanlin Temple of the Ox Head school of Chan (Zen). He also received the seal of trans-

mission from the Esoteric master Weixiang of Guoqing Temple. Both temples are located on Mt. Tiantai. Daosui (559–?) and Xingman (n.d.) passed on the seal of the Tiantai school. Finally, Daosui initiated Saichō into the Bodhisattva Precepts.

Upon his return in 805, Saichō began to fuse these four traditions into Tendai-hokke-shū (Tendai-Lotus school). The following year he received permission to annually accept two *nenbundosha*, aspirants who chose to be ordained into his newly formed sect. The first ordinations did not take place until 810. In 818 Saichō petitioned the court for permission to establish an independent Mahāyāna *kaidan*, ordination platform, based on the *Brahmajāla Sūtra* (Jpn. *Bonmōkyō*). Prior to this, monastic ordinations took place at Tōdaiji Temple in Nara under the ancient Vinaya Precepts. The older and established Nara schools fiercely opposed such a move; they maintained that the Mahāyāna ordinations were meant for the laity, and not for clerics. Nonetheless in 822, seven days after Saichō's death at 56, Emperor Saga (785–842) approved his petition. Those ordained in Tendai-hokke-shū were required to train for 12 years in either *shanagō*, a course of study devoted to the Tantric teachings, or *shikangō*, a curriculum devoted to *hokke enryō*, the Perfect Teaching of Buddha based on the *Lotus Sūtra*. Enryakuji became a center of Buddhist learning. At one time Mt. Hiei hosted 3,000 monasteries that housed students from all Buddhist persuasions.

With close ties to the aristocracy and the imperial family, Japanese Tendai did not have close ties with farmers, tradespeople, and other commoners who immigrated to

Hawai'i. Tendai Shū did have a presence in prewar Hawai'i with the 1918 establishment of the Tendai Fudō-son Temple located at 834 South Hotel Street in Honolulu. Unable to recover after its closure soon after the December 7, 1941, attack on the U.S. Naval base at Pearl Harbor, the temple dissolved in 1950. Reverends Matsumoto Kokan and Matsumoto Myosei, immigrants from Kumamoto Prefecture, established the Palolo Kwannon Temple, a Tendai affiliate, in Palolo Valley on O'ahu in 1935. The Tendai Mission of Hawai'i was established as a project of the Overseas Missionary Society of the sect. An accomplished artist, Bishop Ara Ryōkan, quickly established the Hawai'i Institute of the Arts that offered instruction in Japanese painting, dying, and calligraphy. In 1982 the Tendai Mission established the Hawai'i Institute to provide young people an opportunity to learn ancient Japanese martial arts and the Japanese language. Rev. Jikyu Rose established Koganji Jizo-in, a Tendai affiliate temple, in 1975. Rev. Ryosei Akase first enshrined the Fureai Kannon in a small worship space in the Leeward Nursing Home she founded. In 1997 she established the Makaha Kannon-in Temple within sight of the nursing home. In 1995 Rev. Monshin Paul Naamon established Tendai New York Betsuin in New York State.

Beliefs and Doctrines

Zhiyi grounded his understanding of Buddhist thought and practice on the ideas and spirit of *Sadharmapuṇḍarika Sūtra*; but he relied on Mādhyamika and Yogācāra doctrinal developments to systematize his belief on the inseparability of doctrine and practice. Simply, doctrine and its underlying theoretical support guide the goals of practice and its methods; practice reaffirms the validity of the theory. To this end he arrived at three distinctive doctrinal positions and two signature meditation principles. The three doctrinal positions are *wushi bajiao* (Jpn. *goji hakkyō*) or "five periods and eight teachings," *sanqian yuanju* (Jpn. *sanzen engu*) or "perfect containment of the 3,000 realms," and *sandai yuanyong* (Jpn. *santai enyu*) or "identity of the three (phases of reality) truths." The two meditation principles are *yinian sanqian* (Jpn. *ichinen sanzen*) or "one thought possesses the 3,000 realms," and *yixin sanguan* (Jpn. *isshin sankan*) or "one mind [engages] three discernments (meditations)."

The "five periods and eight teachings" is a *jiaoxiang panshi* (Jpn. *kyōsōhanjaku*) or classification system that attempts to reconcile the massive amount of Buddhist documents that entered China. Whereas Indian observers witnessed the gradual evolution of Buddhism culture, the earliest discourses and the most abstract documents arrived almost simultaneously. The sheer number of documents and their seemingly contradictory ideas bedeviled the Chinese. How could one man, however brilliant, deliver so many discourses over a single lifetime?

The "five periods" is a chronological division; and the eight teachings refer to the method and nature of Buddhist teachings. In the *Lotus Sūtra* the Buddha offers Zhiyi justification for dividing Buddha's 50-year teaching career into five periods. Since most people were not fully ready to appreciate the rarefied import of his enlightenment, the Buddha devised any number of expedient means to lead people to the *Lotus Sūtra*. The *Lotus Sūtra* is the final and highest teaching and supersedes all other teachings. Zhiyi divided the teaching career of the Buddha into the time of Avataṃsaka (three weeks); the time of the Deer Park, when he preached the *Āgamas* or earliest *Sūtras* (12 years); the time of Vāipuliya or development (8 years), when he introduced the teachings of Mahāyāna; the time of wisdom (22 years), when he shared the wisdom of mature Mahāyāna; and the time of the Lotus (8 years). Zhiyi explains this fivefold division by using the metaphor of the light from the sun. Just as the angle of the sun's rays illuminates the mountain peak at the break of day, Buddha preached the *Avatamsaka Sūtra* that describes the profound experience of Enlightenment. However, since his description left listeners dumbfounded, Buddha modified his pedagogy to gradually introduce the Dharma (teachings) through parables, stories, and more readily understood teachings; this is the time of inducement. The third and fourth periods refer to the time of development and deepening understanding of the Dharma, just as the rising sun gradually illuminates more and more of the mountainside. At noon the sun shines on the highest peak and deepest valleys equally. This is the time of the Lotus. All beings—the most spiritually gifted and the most depraved—equally receive the fruit of the Buddha's teaching and experience that leads to enlightenment. This can be accomplished through the *Ekayāna* or one vehicle articulated in the *Sadharmapuṇḍarika Sūtra*. Zhiyi included the *Mahāparinirvāṇa Sūtra* during this final period, because it reaffirmed the idea that all sentient beings are to become Buddhas.

Zhiyi divides the "eight teachings" into methods and the nature of the teaching. The four methods are abrupt, gradual, secret, and indeterminate. The abrupt or sudden is for those with the highest capacity, who can understand the Dharma without any preliminary instruction; this is the time of Avataṃsaka. The gradual teaching refers to graded instruction. The secret or special method is designed to match the needs and capacity of each individual. The indeterminate refers to those occasions when Buddha preaches to a gathering of many people and each understands and receives the Dharma according to his or her needs and capacity. The nature of teaching includes analytical, synthetic, special, and round or perfect. The analytical method is for those who benefit from a rational explanation of the core principles of the Dharma. Others may be more receptive to understanding the Dharma synthetically or intuitively. The special teaching is reserved for the most adept bodhisattvas. The perfect or round teaching refers to lived experience of the Dharma, wherein all things interpenetrate; it is the middle path.

Zhiyi identified two distinct divisions among the 28 chapters of the *Sadharmapuṇḍarika Sūtra*. The first 14 chapters detail the eternal Buddha living among the people and devising all manner of means to teach them. The message is one of the universality of liberation from suffering and that every being possesses the potential to realize Buddhahood. The second half of the *Sūtra* describes the underlying reality of the universe. Zhiyi maintained that the work of Śākyamuni among the people is the most important, namely that everyday reality is the truth of the universe. The basis for such assertion is found in the opening section of the second chapter on "Expedient Means." The passage reads,

Buddha and only the Buddha can exhaust [know] the real nature of all *Dharmas* [phenomena]; [every *Dharma* has ten characteristics; they are] form (external appearance), nature (internal characteristics), essence (both external and innate characteristics), potential (innate ability or power), function, (direct-) cause, conditions (indirect cause, context), result (of direct cause and conditions), effect (emergence of a tangible fact), and essential integrity (of the above nine aspects).

For Zhiyi, each and every Dharma possesses and thus reveals the totality of reality. There is no underlying reality that supports the appearance of a Dharma or object. What is apprehended by the senses is a Dharma's true and real reality. The 10 characteristics are explained below.

Doctrine—Meditation

The opening line of Guanding's preface to the *Mohe zhiguan* reads, "Stillness and insight (*śamatha* and *vipaśyanā*) [possess a] clarity and tranquility beyond anything known by earlier generations." This passage crystallizes the essence of Zhiyi's confidence in the meditation exercises and their fruit of "clarity and tranquility" to intuit and dwell in true reality. "*Zhi*" (Skt. *śamatha*; Jpn. *shi*) or "stillness" is the quiescent original nature of mind, free of distractions. From this dwelling place, the mind slides into *guan* (Skt. *vipaśyanā*; Jpn. *kan*) or "insight" that contemplates the reality of all Dharmas. *Zhi* and *guan* are like the wings of a bird; they are to be practiced simultaneously.

The mechanics and content of *zhi* and *guan* are crystallized by the two meditational principles of "one mind [engages] three discernments (meditations)" and "one thought possesses the 3,000 realms" that correspond to the doctrines of the "identity of the three (phases of reality) truths" and the "perfect containment of the 3,000 realms."

The basis for "one mind [engages] three discernments (meditations)" is the counterpart of the Tiantai assertion that every Dharma possesses the three phases of reality: empty, provisional, and the middle. This claim is a reinterpretation of the 18th verse of the 24th chapter of the *Mūlamadhyamakakārikā* (*Middle Stanzas*), where Nāgārjuna (ca. 150–250) equates *pratītyasamutpāda* with *śūnyatā* and the middle path. *Pratītyasamutpāda* or dependent co-arising refers to the phenomenal world of change; all existent Dharmas or existent objects or events is the temporary coming together of separate component parts. Created Dharmas do not have substantial reality or being and are described to be *śūnyatā* or empty of an enduring identity. *Pratītyasamutpāda* and *śūnyatā* are two aspects of the same reality; the former refers to its provisional nature and the latter is its true reality. Zhiyi highlights the third phase, the middle way;

it is the living reality of the enlightenment. Through the exercise of "stillness and insight," the practioner is able with "one mind" to discern the three phases of dharmic reality. The identity of the three phases of reality explains the capacity of the Buddha to live in the world of change while dwelling in mindful equanimity. Just as water beads off the lotus flower, the enlightened person lives untainted in the world of passions.

Implicit in the "one mind [engages] three discernments (meditations)" is "one thought possesses the 3,000 realms" that mirrors the "perfect containment of the 3,000 realms." "Three thousand realms" is a metaphor for "all Dharmas," the building blocks or "psycho-mental markers" through which the mind apprehends the phenomenal world. Zhiyi arrives at 3,000 by integrating (1) the 10 spiritual realms or levels that the human mind possesses, (2) the 10 characteristics of Dharma, and (3) the three aspects of reality discussed above.

The spiritual realms are hell, beasts, hungry ghosts, *asuras* or fighting spirits, human, *śrāvaka*, bodhisattva, and Buddha. Before the advent of Buddhism, Brahmanic beliefs held that an individual transmigrates through the first six realms. Note that these are physical realms. Zhiyi appended four Buddhist realms and asserted that an individual transmigrates through psycho-spiritual, not physical, realms during the course of a lifetime or even a day. Even persons who dwell in the deepest hell possess the realm of the Buddha and can thus achieve enlightenment. Likewise, even the best among us can unleash the depravities of a hellish being when conditions are adverse. Each of these 10 realms

contains the other nine, for a total of 100 realms. Moreover, each of these 100 realms contains the 10 Dharma characteristics listed above for a total of 1,000. Finally, each of the three worlds—sentient beings, nonsentient beings, and the five *skhandhas* (matter, perception, mental concepts and ideas, volition, and consciousness) or five aggregates that constitute mental, physical, and all other elements in this phenomenal world—contains the 1,000 attributes of the 100 realms. Each of the three worlds embraces 1,000 realms, for a total of 3,000 realms. These 3,000 realms are embraced in a single thought; hence the phrase "one thought, 3,000 realms." "One mind [engages] three discernments (meditations)" and "one thought possesses the 3,000 realms" constitute the basis and content for the Tiantai meditation.

Meditation Practice

In chapters three and four of the *Mohe zhiguan* Zhiyi discusses the conditions for cultivating *zhi* or *śamatha* and *guan* or *vipaśyanā* and lists four different forms of "stillness" (Skt. *samādhi*). These are: (1) *changzuo sanwei* (Jpn. *jōza zanmai*), sitting in meditation for 90 days without engaging in any other practices; (2) *changxing sanwei* (Jpn. *jōgyō zanmai*), circumambulating an image of Amida Buddha while reciting the *nembutsu* for 90 days; (3) *banxing sanwei* (Jpn. *hangyō zanmai*), the practice of focusing on the truth of the *Lotus Sūtra* while walking and sitting; and (4) *feixing feizuo sanwei* (Jpn. *higyō hiza zanmai*), neither walking nor sitting. Zhiyi lists under this last method miscellaneous types and methods of "stillness." While the 10 spiritual realms constitute the primary content of meditation, Zhiyi mentions the contemplation on evil. Such meditation is consistent with the idea of the three aspects of reality and the 3,000 realms that embrace all of reality. Evil as well as good thoughts surface during meditation practice. When evil thoughts arise, Zhiyi advised not to suppress them, but to dispassionately observe them.

The above categories of meditation became the core of Japanese Tendai practice after Ryōgen (912–984) became abbot in 966. In addition to rebuilding the many structures that had been ravaged by fire, Ryōgen restored discipline among the monks. He also reassessed the mission of Buddhist monastic education and focused the curriculum on the *Lotus Sūtra* and *hangyō zanmai*, also known as the *hokke sanmai*, and the *nembutsu* recitation that Ennin (794–864) integrated into *jōgyō zanmai*, a technique he learned during his nine years at Mt. Wutai. With this new orientation, the monks thus customarily recited the *Lotus Sūtra* in the morning and practiced *nembutsu* recitation in the evening. Nichiren Shū emerged from devotion to the Lotus. Through the efforts of Genshin (942–1017), the practices focusing on Amida Buddha and recitation of the *nembutsu* inspired Ryōnin (1071–1132) to found the Yūzū nembutsushū, Hōnen to establish Jōdo Shū, and Shinran, Jōdo Shinshū.

Mappō

Convinced that Japan had entered *Mappō* or Age of the Degenerate Dharma, Gen-

shin argued in the *Ōjōyōshū* (Essentials of Birth in the Pure Land) that *jiriki* or "self-power" traditions such as Zen, Shingon, and even Tendai were of no avail. The only hope for enlightenment and Buddhahood was to rely on *Tariki* or "Other-power" of Amida Buddha's compassionate vow to welcome all beings, no matter how depraved, to the Pure Land. To this end, he recommended visualization of Amida Buddha. In contrast, Honen and later Shinran would favor the *nembutsu*, the recitation of Amida Buddha's name.

The idea of *mappō* entered Japan during the Nara period (646–794). It was the last of three historical phases that projected the gradual corruption of the Dharma as it moved further from its source. This degeneration is marked by the yardsticks of teaching, practice, and realization. During the first phase, the Age of the True Dharma, which extends for 500 years after Buddha's death, the Dharma is a living reality; it is properly understood, sincerely practiced, and realization or enlightenment is attained by many. At the end of the first age, humanity enters the Age of the Counterfeit Dharma, 1,000 years during which the Dharma and practice are present, but realization is rare. Indeed, after the master's passing, great thinkers emerged who produced learned treatises on the meaning of the Dharma, great universities were established to preserve and transmit the tradition, and great monasteries trained eager aspirants. During the last age, 1,500 years after the passing of the Buddha, the Dharma is preserved in the treatises that were written in the previous age, but understanding is shallow. Devotees no longer engage in practice and attainment is not possible.

The Japanese believed that the age of *mappō* began in 1052. Indeed, natural and man-made events served only to confirm that they were living in the age of *mappō*. The war between the Taira and Minamoto clans at the close of the Heian period (866–1085) devastated the country; the capital of Kyoto was ravaged by *sōhei* (priest-warriors) from Mt. Hiei; the 1177 fire and the 1180 whirlwind destroyed large portions of the capital. Corruption in high places was rampant, especially among the clerics. Among the 32 hells described in the *Ōjōyōshū*, Genshin reserved the most horrific to those clerics who professed loyalty to the Dharma, but knowingly violated it in the most obscene manner.

Hongaku, Original Enlightenment

Not only did the established Nara Buddhist schools dispute the institutional credentials of Saichō to establish an ordination platform, but Tokuitsu (ca. 781–842), a Hossō monk, challenged key doctrinal points. The principal issue revolved around their respective assessment of human nature. Saichō maintained that all beings possess the Buddha-nature and therefore Buddhahood was assured. This position is supported by *Sadharmapuṇḍarika*, *Mahāprajñāpāramitā*, *Avataṃsaka*, and other Mahāyāna documents. The Hossō tradition and its Indian Yogācāra predecessor maintained that Buddhahood or enlightenment is possible for most beings, except for the *icchantika*, a class of beings who do not have the seeds or potential for Buddhahood. The school arrived at its position by observing human nature and its

analysis of the persistence of irredeemable karmic energy that persists in the human psyche of evildoers. This issue is more fundamental. Will there ever be a time when the Buddha will not be needed? This may be a spurious question, but if sometime in a distant eon when all beings have attained Buddhahood and there are no beings to be liberated from suffering, what will become of the Buddha? The eternal Amida and Vairocana Buddhas will not be needed. Will they cease to exist? By positing the *icchantika*, the Yogācārins assured the eternality of the Buddha and the Dharma.

The idea that all beings possess the Buddha-nature posed conceptual problems regarding women attaining enlightenment. Saichō and Kūkai revealed the misogyny of their era when they prohibited women from entering their respective monasteries for fear of their polluting presence, especially during their menstrual cycle. In *Muryōjūkyō shaku* [*Notes on the Sukhāvatīvyūha-sūtra*] Hōnen acknowledged the contradiction between the ideals of universal Buddhahood and the diminished possibilities of women articulated in the *Larger Sukhāvatīvyūha-sūtra*. While the 18th vow assures birth in the Pure Land for all beings, the 35th vow was established especially for women, who are especially burdened by the strength and depth of their *karma*. Women who sincerely and reverently recite Amida Buddha's name will be transformed into men and be led personally by Amida of the Pure Land. Like Hōnen, Shinran concluded that the object of Amida's vows is evil persons, including women who by virtue of their gender are especially burdened by deep-rooted passions. In the 60th hymn in *Jōdo wasan* (*Hymns on the Pure Land*) Shinran writes:

Profound is Amida's compassion!
He demonstrates his wondrous
  wisdom
By establishing the Vow to making
  men of women
And leads them to Buddhahood.

Shinran and Hōnen reiterate the view of the Chinese Pure Land master Shandao (613–681) concerning the necessity of women taking on the male gender to ensure the possibility of Buddhahood. Interestingly, Shinran's Pure Land tradition still chants the 35th vow as part of the funeral liturgy for women.

The slightly younger contemporaries, Dōgen (1200–1260) and Nichiren (1222–1282), were highly critical of the traditional Buddhist centers for discriminating against women. Dōgen affirms the presence of Buddha-nature in all beings in "*Busshō* (Buddha-nature)" in chapter 22 of *Shōbōgenzō*. In "*Raihai Tokuzui* (Prostrating to the essence of attainment)," the eighth chapter, he vents his anger against those who do not offer the same opportunity of Buddhahood to women. "To discriminate against women and attempt to keep them from attaining Buddhahood is the conduct of utter fools, who seek to mislead humankind." He goes on to say, "To destroy the evil sacred places [that deny women to enter, worship, and practice] is the best way to requite the Buddha's benevolence." Like Dōgen, Nichiren (1222–1282) too leveled harsh criticism toward traditional centers that discrimi-

nated against women. In a response to a query by the female priest Sen'nichi, Nichiren writes,

[T]he *Lotus Sūtra* is the greatest, and that greatest doctrine in the *Lotus Sūtra* is the doctrine of salvation for women. Thus, even should all the women of Japan be despised and rejected by all other *sūtras* in the canon, what does it matter as long as salvation is assured by the authority of the *Lotus Sūtra*?

Nichiren's response relies on Zhiyi's classification system of Buddhist teachings; the *Lotus Sūtra* represents the culmination of the Buddha's teaching. Nichiren consistently championed the capacity of women to realize enlightenment.

Esoteric Practices

While waiting for his ship to depart, Saichō met the esoteric master Shunqiao, a disciple of Śubhākarasiṃha (637–735), and was initiated into Tantrayāna or Vajrayāna, the third and final development of Indian Buddhist thought. Although the goal is still Buddhahood, Tantrayāna departs from early Mahāyāna in the methods to this end. While Śākyamuni delivered his teachings openly, the student of Tantra would need to be initiated before receiving instructions directly from a *guru* or teacher. The goal of Tantric rituals— mantra (efficacious phrases), mudra (efficacious gestures), and *maṇḍala* (efficacious visualizations)—is to resonate with the voice, movement, and mind of Vairocana Buddha. It was believed, and still believed by many, that mastery of such rituals can harness the energy that flows through the universe. Once harnessed, the energy can be directed to pacify disease, ward off danger, foster prosperity and merit making, and destroy enemies. These powers correspond to the three classes of Buddhist heroes who enter the *maṇḍala* through the coercion of *mantra*.

The Japanese court was very interested in harnessing these powers and thus sponsored Tendai and Shingon priests to perform rituals to pacify such vengeful spirits as Sugawara no Michizane (see entry on Shintō). In 970 Emperor Seiwa sponsored a *goryō-e* (meeting with the spirits) service at Yasaka jinja in Kyoto in response to an epidemic that swept through the country that spring. This is the beginning of the annual Gion Matsuri festival. While this is a perversion of Tantric rituals, a realistic Saichō promoted the study of tantric doctrine and ritual to cater to the whims of his patrons. These elaborate rituals were also seen as entertainment that relieved the boredom of court life.

Because Saichō was with Shunqiao only briefly, it is doubtful that he was initiated into the more complex Tantric rituals. When he returned to Japan, he was constantly asking his nemesis Kūkai, who had spent considerable years studying in China, to borrow texts and for instructions in esoteric rituals. Relations between the two finally ruptured when Kūkai refused to lend a rare Tantric text unless Saichō became an initiate and studied with him for three years. The development of Tendai esotericism was left to Ennin, Enchin (814–891), and Annen (ca. 841–ca. 901).

Aesthetics

The poet Fujiwara no Shunzei (1114–1204) introduces his *Korai fūtaishō* (*Notes on the poetic style though the ages*) with the opening lines of Zhiyi's *Mohe zhiguan* that was quoted above. It is not possible to know exactly how Fujiwara understood "stillness and insight" (*śamatha* and *vipaśyanā*). But modern commentators place great value in clarity and stillness realized in meditation practice as the basis for aesthetic appreciation and creativity. Poetry opens the *kokoro*, translated as "heart" or "mind," to see, hear, and feel reality. An example of dwelling in "stillness" is a haiku by Bashō (1644–1694), who gives poetic form to the momentary reality of the sound of a frog breaking the surface of the still pond.

An old pond, ah!
A frog jumps in,
The sound of water.

Even in the English translation, we can sense the "stillness" of mind that enabled Bashō to appreciate the immediacy of the water's splash. Subjective clarity enabled the poet to apprehend a sensory event, and "insight" made it possible to penetrate the living reality of transiency. The *haiku* crystallizes a key Tendai position, namely the "identity of the three (phases of reality) truths."

The poet's subject was not the sound of water, but the authenticity of his feelings quickened by the event. Such genuine sensibility is crystallized in the phrase *mono no aware*, coined by Moto'ori Norinaga (1730–1801). This phrase articulated what he believed to be sensitivity to the transiency of things in *Genji Monogatari* [*Tale of Genji*] by Murasaki Shikibu (ca. 973–ca. 1014). *Mono* means "thing" or "things" and *aware*, roughly translated, means "poignancy." Thus *mono no aware* means the "sadness of things." Lady Murasaki identifies with and feels in "things" their fleeting existence. With gentle but sad appreciation for the momentary, she gives aesthetic life to the cardinal Buddhist truth of *anitya* or impermanence. Indeed, *mono no aware* is a pervasive undercurrent in the visual and literary arts. Kawabata Yasunari (1899–1972) expressed such sentiment in the tenor and content of his 1968 Nobel acceptance speech. He quotes wistful joy in the poetry of Myōe (1173–1232) and Dōgen upon seeing the winter moon.

The capacity of the poet (artist) to quiet the mind and intuit the nature of things and delight in color, form, and sound is the "Way" of poetry (art). By giving form to these intense feelings, poetry is the aesthetically crystallization of the "perfect containment of the 3,000 realms." Thus Fujiwara writes, "Enlightenment is nowhere other than in worldly passions."

Conclusion

Zhiyi transformed an Indian spiritual tradition into a Chinese institution, which in turn provided Saichō and others the resources to forge Buddhism with a Japanese flair. While the direct impact of Tendai Shū in the Japanese American community may have been minimal, its twofold curriculum at Enryakuji inspired the development of the major Japanese Buddhist denominations that appeared during the Kamakura era. The idea of *hongaku*, original enlightenment, and the belief that Amida's compassionate vow is meant for the most humble, provided common folk with the confidence to persevere. Most of the immigrants to Hawai'i and the continental United States came from areas where the Lotus and Pure Land based teachings had deep roots.

Ronald Y. Nakasone

See also: Entries: Jōdo Shū (Pure Land Sect); Nichiren Shū; Rinzai Zen; Shingon; Sōtō Zen

Further Reading

Dōgen. *Shōbōgenzō* (*The Dharma-eye and treasury*). Translated by Gudo Wafu Nishijima and Chodo Cross. Berkeley, CA: Numata Center for Buddhist Translation and Research, 1975.

Donner, Neal, and Daniel B. Stevenson. *The Great Calming and Contemplation: A Study and Annotated Translation of the First Chapter of Chih-i's Mo-ho chih-kuan.* Honolulu: University of Hawai'i Press, 1993.

Groner, Paul. *Saichō: The Establishment of the Japanese Tendai School.* Berkeley, CA: Berkeley Buddhist Studies Series, 1964.

Heisig, James W., et al. *Japanese Philosophy: A Sourcebook.* University of Hawai'i Press, 2012.

Kasahara, Kazuo, ed. *A History of Japanese Religion.* Translated by Paul McCarthy and Gaynor Sekimori. Tokyo: Kosei, 2001.

Kawabata, Yasunari. *Japan, the Beautiful, and Myself.* Translated by Edward G. Seidensticker. Tokyo: Kodansha International, 1966.

Kurihara, Toshie. "A History of Women in Japanese Buddhism: Nichiren's Perspective on the Enlightenment of Women." *Journal of Oriental Studies* 13 (October 2003): 94–118.

Lotus Sūtra, The. Translated by Tsugunari Kubo and Akira Yuyama. Tokyo: Bukkyō Dendō Kyōkai, 1991.

Marra, Michael F., ed. *Japanese Hermeneutics: Current Debates on Aesthetics and Interpretation.* Honolulu: University of Hawai'i Press, 2002.

Matsunaga, Alicia, and Daigan Matsunaga. *Foundation of Japanese Buddhism.* Vol. 1. Los Angeles: Buddhist Books International, 1976.

Robinson, Richard H., and Willard L. Johnson. *The Buddhist Religion: A Historical Introduction.* Belmont, CA: Wadsworth, 1997.

Shinran. *The Collected Works of Shinran.* Vol. 1. Translated by Dennis Hirota, et al. Kyoto: Jōdo Shinshū Hongwanji-ha, 1997.

Tenrikyō

Tenrikyō, literally the "Teaching of Heavenly Reason," was founded in Japan in 1838 by Nakayama Miki (1798–1887). For Tenrikyō followers she is not just the founder, but is the parent of humankind; she is therefore called Oyasama or "Our Beloved Parent." Nakayama is believed to have three basis attributes: the Shrine of God, the Parent of the Divine Model, and the "Ever-Livingness."

As the Shrine of God, Nakayama's mind is that of God, but her body is human. This reality was made manifest when God the Parent entered Nakayama on October 26, 1838. For nearly two decades, however, this reality and her message received little attention; she was in fact mocked and ridiculed. It was only after she began performing miracles and healings that people began to believe that she was the incarnation of God the Parent. Step by step she shared the teaching of God the Parent, prepared the service for salvation, and offered the grant of healing. More important, she demonstrated how one can live joyously. Her life models *yokigurashi*, the joyous life, and is thus regarded to be the Parent of the Divine Model. She composed *Mikagura-uta* (*Liturgical songs*) and *Ofudesaki* (*Tip of the writing brush*) in Japanese *waka* poetry format and with Japanese phonetic syllabary, without the use of Chinese ideograms.

Her claim as a living god invited oppression, first from Buddhists and Shintoists, and eventually from government authorities, who claimed that she was causing disorder in society. Police harassment was intense and Oyasama was imprisoned at least 17 times. She passed away on January 26, 1887, at the age of 90, wishing the spiritual growth of her followers.

The Tenrikyō faith maintains that Oyasama did not die, but withdrew from physical life and became "invisible." She lives eternally and continues her work. Devotees can still "visit" her at Kyōsōden, her residence in Tenri where she is attended to in exactly the same manner as she was during her corporeal existence. The belief in her "Ever-Livingness" has been enhanced by the testimonies of those who have been healed of incurable diseases through service and prayer. At present, Tenrikyō has approximately two million adherents. Its spiritual center is the Jiba, the site where humankind was originally conceived by God the Parent. Located in Tenri City (named after Tenrikyō), this "Jiba of Origin" attracts nearly one million pilgrims and visitors each year.

Tenrikyō in the United States

After Oyasama "became invisible" in 1887, Tenrikyō spread quickly and widely throughout Japan. Within 10 years, Tenrikyō followers increased from about 20,000 to approximately 3,130,000 at the end of 1896. In the early 20th century representatives were dispatched to Hawai'i and North America. Typically, these representatives were "solo missionaries"; they received no support from Japan. An example of such a person was Kanzawa Tsunetarō (1873–1944), who in 1927 established the first Tenrikyō church in San Francisco. After arriving in San Francisco in 1903, he "took up various jobs, such as working for the railroads and in coal mines, before starting his own laundry business" to support his missionary work. Later, however, due to the illness of his children, he resolved to fully devote himself to the Tenrikyō mission. Kanzawa passed away at the age of 77 in 1944 while interned at the Department of Justice Detention Camp in Santa Fe, New Mexico. Like other Japanese and Japanese Americans in Hawai'i and the continental United States, Tenrikyō devotees were "under suspicion for their loyalty" to the United States.

In Hawai'i, after establishing the first church in Honolulu in 1929, Tenrikyō launched additional churches at the rate of almost one a year until the war broke out on December 7, 1941. Tenri leaders "were questioned by FBI agents and sent to internment camps on the mainland." The churches were closed, but those who remained continued their faith, performing the services behind closed doors until their ministers returned. After the war, Tenrikyō regained its momentum and furthered its reach into North America. Currently, there are 96 churches in the two dioceses—62 in North America (U.S. mainland and Canada) and 34 in Hawai'i. The precise number of current Tenrikyō devotees is difficult to ascertain, because the tradition does not have a rite through which one officially becomes a believer. The number of devotees can only be approximated by the number of persons who are initiated into leadership positions. The need for leaders is indicative of the membership.

Tenrikyō has two "clerical" positions: *yōboku* and *kyōto*. To receive the title of *yōboku*, an individual must attend and complete *besseki*, nine comprehensive lectures on Tenrikyō at the headquarters in Japan. Those certified as *yōboku* are intermediaries, who interpret and propagate Tenrikyō teachings and administer the grant of the *sazuke* or "healing." Instructions for becoming a *yōboku* appear in *Ofudesaki*. As of 2013 Canada has 161, the U.S. mainland 1,275, and Hawai'i 566 *yōbokus*. Those who have attained the position of *yōboku* and wish to become a *kyōto* must successfully complete a primary three-week training course at the headquarters. As of 2013 Canada has 63, the U.S. mainland 506, and Hawai'i 270 *kyōtos*.

Recognizing the need to adapt to the changing needs of its core membership—second- and third-generation English-speaking Japanese American devotees—Tenrikyō has embarked on "localizing" its spiritual mission. The tradition understands that the faith is evolving cross-culturally and changing with successive generations. The "localization" project requires a strong sense of pride, identity, and connection with others. A young leader of Tenrikyō in America stated, "We need to have pride in our faith. We need to have conviction and confidence in our faith. . . . One means to do that is to understand what other people believe . . . so that we can have a common reference point in engaging in our missionary work."

Beliefs

Composed between 1869 and 1882, the 17-volume *Ofudesaki* is a collection of 1,711 poems that channel the teachings of God the Parent through Oyasama's brush. It is one of Tenrikyō's three most important scriptures; the other two are the *Mikagura-uta* and the *Osahizu*, which is the compiled record of oral revelation through Nakayama's spiritual successor, Iburi Izō (1833–1907). The *Ofudesaki* poems provide instructions for returning the human mind to its "original, pristine condition." When "returning to the origin," the mind becomes like clear water (*Ofudesaki*, 3: 7–21). The poems offer instruction on the necessary step-by-step return to the "original condition" in ways that are appropriate to the time, place, and spiritual maturity of all human beings (*Ofudesaki*, 6: 15).

The basic tenet of the Tenrikyō teaching is that humankind and the world were created by God the Parent who desires humanity to have a joyous life. Accordingly, all conditions for the joyous life are already provided by God, who works in the world and in the human body. In other words, human beings are nurtured by God, and the natural environment is also sustained by God. Humans are allowed to use their bodies created by God the Parent. The body is "borrowed"; it is "a thing lent," or "a thing borrowed."

Another important tenet is that the mind is the true self. Although God desires humans to help one another with a bright and joyous mind, they often harbor self-centered thoughts that are contrary to the intent of God the Parent. Selfish and self-centered thoughts are improper, but they are not indicative of innate evil. "The root of illness lies in our own mind" (*Mikagura-uta*, 10: 10). The improper use of the mind is like "dust" and can be swept away through the service, prayer, proper conduct, and by helping others. God informs the devotee that he or she has gathered "dust" through some bodily disorder. Physical suffering is thus a signal and is a reminder to correct the misuse of the mind. The human mind and body are linked, and God is the mediator.

Death is not eternal departure, but the transition into a new life. When people die, they return their body to God. They shed their "old" bodies, like removing a garment, and returning to this world with a new body. Successive births and deaths are part of the continuum of life, where the joyous life is to be achieved. God as Parent guides human beings along the path of their spiritual growth by urging them to purify the mind. When the mind is purified, the joyous life is experienced.

Practices

In daily life Tenrikyō devotees are guided by *tannō* and *hinokishin* that should be practiced for a lifetime. *Tannō* refers to the understanding that what happens in and around our lives are the workings of God. Since these happenings are guiding messages from God the Parent, the devotee should receive events positively and with joy. *Hinokishin* (literally, contribution of the day) refers to any act performed to help others without any thought of reward; such an act is an expression of the devotee's gratitude for God the Parent's daily blessing and protection. These faith-motivated acts can take any form and be done at any time. *Hinokishin* is instilled as a basic attitude of daily living, such as simply uttering a kind word, or a response to disaster relief activity that engages thousands of people. A unique example of *hinokishin* occurred in 1971. At that time Tenrikyō devotees sent 10,000 coconut seedlings from Hawai'i to assist in a beautification project in Okinawa, a gesture that fostered U.S.-Japan relationships. Tenrikyō churches practice *hinokishin* in their communities. A notable example is the membership of Tenrikyō America West Church in San Francisco in the Japanese American Religious Federation, a consortium of faith congregations that have built low-income senior housing.

Tsutome refers to ritual services that engage the five senses. In addition to speech, services include *teodori*, hand gestures, and musical accompaniment. Services are all inclusive. Those who are visually or physically challenged participate by singing; those who are hearing impaired participate through their hand gestures. In addition to the regular morning and evening congregate services, Tenrikyō followers often engage in special services that petition God the Parent for help and protection and expressing their gratitude. Tenrikyō's most important *tsutome* is performed on the 26th of each month at the sacred Jiba. Symbolically demonstrating God the Parent's working at the time of human creation, this service is performed for universal salvation. It is the foundation of all services and the inspiration for the monthly service performed at churches and mission centers throughout the world.

Sazuke (divine grant) is administered to those suffering physical disorders. It is performed only for the benefit of others. Restoring health through *sazuke* is the first step toward the awakening to the working of God. By healing the mind, the devotee nurtures his or her spiritual growth. For those who administer the healing prayers of *sazuke*, this activity is fundamental for their salvation. "By saving others, we are also saved" (*Ofudesaki*, 3: 47).

Finally, Tenikyo is a tradition of simplicity. Its teaching is grounded in the simple premise that God the Parent created humankind at the Jiba to experience the "joyous life." The ritual and practice of *hinokishin* and *sazuke* remind devotees that the "joyous life" is realized through service to others. By leading others to the "joyous life," the devotee also experiences it. Simplicity is also reflected in the service format. Its liturgy, *tsutome*, does not vary, even when occasion and purpose varies. The sanctuaries standing at the Jiba of Origin are simple unadorned buildings providing a vast space for worship.

Has such simplicity focused on the fundamentals helped Tenrikyō to be localized in cultures outside Japan—in the United States, for example? Or is it itself already culturally bound and has this prevented cultural adaptation? For more than a century since its first missionary arrived from Japan, the Tenrikyō Church in America has broken down the wall of cultural boundaries tenaciously, and its efforts will continue.

Ikuo Higashibaba

Further Reading

Mikagura-uta, the Songs for the Service. Tenri: Tenrikyō Church Headquarters, 1967.

Ofudesaki. Tenri: Tenrikyō Church Headquarters, 1993.

Short History of Tenrikyō in Hawai'i. Honolulu: Tenrikyō Mission Headquarters of Hawai'i, 1987.

Tenri Forum 2006: New Frontiers in the Mission. Tenri: Tenrikyō Overseas Mission Department, 2009.

Tenrikyo Website. http://www.tenrikyo.or.jp /eng/. Accessed July 16, 2014.

Traces of the Founder. Los Angeles: Tenrikyō Women's Association of America, 1994.

Thai American Religions

Beginning from the middle of the 1960s, prompted by the liberalization of U.S. immigration policies and by the American military presence in Thailand during its involvement in the wars of Vietnam, Laos, and Cambodia, the initial flow of Thai immigrants to the United States corresponds with both the advent of Theravāda Buddhism in the United States through mission and diaspora and with a decisive cultural turn toward Eastern spirituality as an alternative to mainstream religion in America. Thais in America come from one of the largest countries in mainland Southeast Asia, which, until 1932, was known to the world as Siam, and where the Theravāda form of Buddhism has been the dominant and vitalizing force throughout the region since at least the 11th century. Prior to 1965, neither Thais nor Theravāda Buddhism had any significant presence in America. By the 1990s, however, both were firmly established in communities throughout North America. These developments have opened a new chapter not only in the religious history of Asians in America, but more broadly in the long history of Buddhism's gradual geographical and cultural diffusion since its emergence in Northern India some 2,500 years ago.

The impetus to formally establish Thai Buddhism in America and build the first Thai *wat* (temple-monastery) in the United States was initially the concern not of Thai immigrants but of royal, ecclesial, and civil authorities in Thailand who, in the mid-1950s and 1960s, sought to expand Thai Buddhism beyond its national borders. It was during this auspicious period, known as the Jayanti celebration commemorating the 2,500th anniversary of the Buddha's *parinibbana* (his passing into *Nirvāṇa* at death), that Thailand began to conceive of itself as a world center of Buddhism and funded the development of the first transnational temples under royal patronage in India with the construction of Wat Thai Buddha-Gaya in 1959 and with the establishment of Wat Buddhapadipa in the United Kingdom in 1965. An obscure museum of Tibetan objets d'art on New York's Staten Island was to be the third outpost in this ambitious global effort, but the plan was aborted in 1966 when complications with the proposed site surfaced. A group of Thai immigrant and American-

Monk Master Chaiya stands by boxes of donated relief supplies for the victims of Cyclone Nargis at the Chaiya Meditation Monastery, May 11, 2008, in Las Vegas, Nevada. Members of the Buddhist monastery shipped the items to Thailand where relief supplies were staged before heading into Myanmar. The cyclone devastated the southwest part of Myanmar on May 3 killing more than 28,000 people and leaving an estimated 1.5 million in need of aid. (Ethan Miller/Getty Images)

born Buddhists did, however, successfully form the Buddhist Study Center in New York as a legal entity in 1965 and, with the assistance of a monk from the London temple, eventually established Wat Vajradhammapadip a decade later. This development, along with the formal establishment of Wat Thai in Los Angeles in 1972— America's first and largest Thai temple— presaged a new bottom-up, lay-centered approach to the institutionalization of Theravāda Buddhism in the United States, one that nevertheless cultivated close links with Thai royalty and high-ranking civil servants but was largely led and financed by a growing, if widely dispersed, immigrant Thai population in America. The new trend continued to gain momentum throughout the 1970s with the establishment of temples serving major metropolitan areas across the continental United States, including Washington, D.C. (1974), Chicago (1976), Denver (1976), and San Francisco (1979), and necessitated the formation of the Council of Thai Bhikkhus in the United States to act as a liaison for missionary monks (*dhammaduta*) coming from Thailand to serve these emerging communities. Today 105 wats can be found scattered throughout North America in 32 states, including six temples in Canada. In addition to these, there are 32 Thai Christian church communities located primarily in California and Texas. The first Thai *mosque*, Masjid Al-Fatiha, was established in 1993 in the town of Azusa, a predominately Hispanic community about 30 miles northeast of Los Angeles.

In contrast to the Thai church or *mosque* where the universal features of the religion tend to be emphasized, the wat in America is often more culturally specific. It functions both as a religious center for preserving and transmitting the Buddhadhamma (the doctrines, laws, and teachings of the Buddha) and as a social space for promoting and performing Thai cultural practices and values. Religious activities commonly associated with the daily life of a temple involve chanting in Pāli (the liturgical language of Theravāda Buddhism), going for refuge to the Buddha, *Dhamma*, and *Sangha* (teacher, teaching, and community of monks); taking the Five Precepts (*pancasīla*) or vows to abstain from (1) the taking of life, (2) stealing, (3) sexual misconduct, (4) lying, and (5) intoxicants; obtaining "blessings" (*anisamsa*); engaging in "merit-making" (*tham bun*) activities such as offering alms to the *sangha*; performing ceremonies for ritually transferring merit by decanting sacralized water (*krùadnáam*); and participating in rituals (*tham yan*) such as those involving the recitation of protective chants (*paritta*), the dispersal of holy water, tying a sacred string around one's wrist, and holding a sacred cord that

ritually links participants to each other, the monks, and the central Buddha image. Participation in such activities effectively binds monks and laity, the living and the dead, men and women, children and parents, teacher and student, younger people and older people together into moral relationships of mutual reciprocity governed by social hierarchy and gender. They also publicly affirm the Buddhist worldview based on the natural law of cause and effect and its consequentialist ethic of *karma* (action) and rebirth, and they articulate core Thai values such as generosity and hospitality and the Buddhist ideals of equanimity and compassion.

These principles and values are often enacted in social relationships mediated by the temple. The practice of ordaining young men as novice monks, even for a brief period during summer vacation rather than the traditional three-month rains retreat in Thailand, helps ensure they become responsible adults after disrobing. Ordaining also generates merit for one's parents, especially one's mother who is owed a "milk debt" for the sacrifices she made during pregnancy and as one's primary caregiver. Daughters, too, are expected to repay this debt. However, ordination for them has never been a possibility since the nun's order was never established in Thailand. Instead, they are expected to financially support and care for their parents. It is the fulfillment of this obligation that may, in fact, be one of the key factors driving women's decision to migrate. Nearly two-thirds of all Thais in the United States today are women. Recent research finds many of these women not only send remittances back home to support their families, but over the last four decades they have emerged as a catalyzing force in the propagation of Theravāda Buddhism in the United States (Perreira, 2008).

Significantly, the eclecticism endemic to the religious milieu of Thailand, including "pre-Buddhist" or animistic "folk Buddhist" practices such as the cult of charismatic monks and relics, the worship of Brahmanic deities, elaborate spirit-calling ceremonies (*pithi riak khwan*), yantric tattoos, the distribution of magical amulets, fortune telling, dashboard shrines, and spirit cults have not, thus far, figured prominently in the religious life of the *wat* in America. What is striking, however, is the demographic diversity associated with the temple and the implications this holds for the future. The "parallel congregations" identified in early research (Numrich, 1996) have given way to communities that are increasingly interracial, multiethnic, and integrated. Though still predominately Thai, the community is also constituted by non-Thai husbands, children of mixed families, people of other religious faiths, and Laotian, Cambodian, Vietnamese, and Indian immigrants. Even local neighbors who live within the vicinity of a *wat* can be found participating at all levels of the temple's social and devotional life. Such rich diversity among first-generation immigrants is unprecedented in the history of Asian religions in America and underscores the broad appeal of both Thai Buddhism and Thai culture.

Todd LeRoy Perreira

See also: Entries: Thai Buddhist Immigrant Culture; Thai Buddhist Immigrant Spirituality; Thai Religious Foodways

Further Reading

Bankston, Carl L., III, and Danielle Antoinette Hidalgo. "Temple and Society in the New World: Theravāda Buddhism and Social Order in North America." In Paul David Numrich, ed. *North American Buddhists in Social Context*. Leiden, the Netherlands: Brill, 2008, 51–85.

Cadge, Wendy, and Sidhorn Sangdhanoo. "Thai Buddhism in America: A Historical and Contemporary Overview." *Contemporary Buddhism* 6(1) (2005): 8–35.

Numrich, Paul David. *Old Wisdom in the New World: Americanization in Two Immigrant Theravāda Buddhist Temples*. Knoxville: University of Tennessee Press, 1996.

Padgett, Douglas M. "The Translating Temple: Diasporic Buddhism in Florida." In Charles S. Prebish and Martin Baumann, eds. *Westward Dharma: Buddhism beyond Asia*. Berkeley: University of California Press, 2002, 191–217.

Perreira, Todd LeRoy. "The Gender of Practice: Some Findings among Thai Buddhist Women in Northern California." In Huping Ling, ed. *Emerging Voices: Experiences of Underrepresented Asian Americans*. New Brunswick, NJ: Rutgers University Press, 2008, 160–182.

Perreira, Todd LeRoy. "*Sasana Sakon* and the New Asian American: Intermarriage and Identity at a Thai Buddhist Temple in Silicon Valley." In Tony Carnes and Fenggang Yang, eds. *Asian American Religions: The Making and Remaking of Borders and Boundaries*. New York and London: New York University Press, 2004, 313–337.

Thai Buddhist Immigrant Culture

Thailand is a strongly Buddhist country. Approximately 95 percent of its 67 million citizens are followers of Theravāda

Buddhism; most of the remaining 5 percent are Muslims; but Christians and other faith traditions are also present. Theravāda Buddhism was introduced in the 13th century from Sri Lanka to Sukhothai, the first Tai kingdom. ("Tai" refers to the population of descendants of speakers of a common Proto-Tai language; in contrast "Thai" refers to the Siamese or Tai Siam people, one branch of this Tai ethnolinguistic group, who settled in the Chao Phraya valley and are the ancestors of modern Thailand and the Thai people.) The doctrines and practices of Theravāda (literally, the teaching of the elders) permeate virtually every aspect—daily life, the arts, and architecture—of Thai culture. It is part of the Thai identity. However, while scholars may revere Theravāda for preserving the original teachings of the Pāli canon, the Buddhism that is currently believed and practiced has incorporated archaic and animist beliefs long present in Tai culture and elements of Hindu-Brahmanism. A pantheon of spirits, magic, spells, charms, and amulets add color to the spiritual landscape. Tai spirituality is motivated by improving one's socioeconomic and spiritual station in this and subsequent lives.

Beliefs and Practices

Archaic Tradition. Long before contact with Indian culture, including Buddhism, the Tai people possessed a spiritual tradition that included a pantheon of spirits, which can be categorized in three types. These are *khwan* or "life essence," *phii* or "spirits," and *thaeaen*, "deities" or "forces of nature." Every sentient being, including

humans, is imbued with a life essence, a vital force that animates that being; it leaves when its host organism dies. *Khwan* implies "ego" and "spirit." The *khwan* may also flee the body it inhabits when it experiences a severe shock, any sudden change, and by being frightened by evil spirits. With the *khwan* absent the body loses its zest for life, weakens, and may eventually die. A *tham khwan* ritual can incite a wayward *khwan* to return; there are also rituals to fortify a lethargic *khwan*. While the *khwan* resides in their bodies, Thais believe that they are blessed with happiness, security, and prosperity. Thus the *khwan* is associated with grace, morale, and prosperity. An individual's life-essence can be ritualistically bound to the body by tying the wrists with holy thread. At death one becomes a *phii*, the spirit of the deceased, who watches over its living relatives; but it can also be menacing if it is ignored or unhappy. It requires regular offerings. *Thaeaen* represent such natural forces as wind, rain, earth, and sky. These spirits are also the embodiments of natural entities, such as trees, rice, or diseases.

Perhaps the most ubiquitous expression of the ancient tradition are the spirit houses that can be seen along roadsides and in the compounds of virtually every house, office, hotel, hospital, public building, and even on the grounds of the most modern skyscrapers in Bangkok. Spirit houses are erected to mollify the original residents of the land and provide them a place to live. The current occupants "lease" the land from these spirits. Different designations of spirit houses indicate the kind of spirits who dwell in them. Thus *San Phra Phūmi* refers to those spirit houses erected for the original inhabitants of the land on which a building is constructed. These spirits prefer Thai-style houses made from wood, and more recently from more durable materials. Their size varies, but normally they are about the size of a rather large birdhouse. The present occupants of the land make daily offerings to honor these guardian spirits and to secure their protection for their household and families. Failure to honor the spirits invites misfortune and bad luck.

The second type of spirit house is the *San Lak Muang*. Built for the guardian spirits of a city, these houses are erected near the City Pillar that marks the site of the city's founding. The *San Lak Muang* for the city of Bangkok is located near the Grand Palace and the Temple of the Emerald Buddha. A third kind of spirit house is the *San Chao*; these are built for the deities and spirits of charismatic personalities who are revered for their moral integrity and supernormal powers. These last two kinds of spirit houses, often quite large and beautifully decorated, are normally situated on a large parcel of land. Dedicated to the *Phra Phrom* (Brahma), the Erawan Shrine is prominently located on the precinct of the Erawan Hyatt Hotel in central Bangkok. Many Thais make pilgrimages to these shrines to ask for favors and for wise guidance. Spirit worship is also a source of solace.

In addition to honoring the spirits with homes, the archaic tradition requires long and complex mortuary and memorial rituals. Mortuary rituals symbolically separate the world of the living from the dead. At funerals, the neck, arms, and feet of the deceased are bound, symbolizing severance from his or her ties with the family and possessions. Clothes are put on backwards for those who died from an accident or unnatural causes, reminding the deceased that he or she is no longer a denizen of this world. An unnatural death is especially troublesome, since the individual's karmic destiny has not been fulfilled, and his or her *phii* or spirit, confused with this abrupt change, believes that it still belongs to the world of the living. It may even steal the body of another person.

While the ancient tradition honored the deceased, the veneration of ancestors is particularly important to Thais of Chinese origin. Confucian filiality requires honoring deceased parents and elders in the same manner as when they were alive. Three annual occasions are of particular importance: Qingming, Sart Chin, and the Chinese New Year.

On Qingming, which falls on the third day of the third lunar month (early April), the family visits the ancestral tomb. After cleaning the tomb and offering sacrifices, the family shares a meal at the grave site. This ritual reinforces family ties. Sart Chin (Ch. *yulan pen* or Festival of Hungry Ghosts) is observed on the 15th day of the seventh lunar month (August). On this occasion, the ancestral spirits return to visit their progeny. In anticipation, families prepare offerings of food and ritually burn money, effigies of clothing, and other articles necessary in the afterlife, for the comfort of the ancestral spirits. The ancestors are also honored at New Year's. These rituals demonstrate gratitude to the ancestors and reinforce family solidarity; they are also consistent with the Buddhist emphasis on gratitude as an essential virtue, which when observed, results in beneficial *Karma* in this life and subsequent lives.

In their search for supernatural assistance people turn to amulets and charms, collectively called *khrüangrang-khongkhang*, whose power lies in the material from which they are fashioned, but mostly from the psychic power transferred to them. Thus transformed, amulets and charms ward off evil spirits and invite luck and prosperity. Amulets take many forms. The most popular amulets are that of the Buddha in meditation, especially ones that were made and sacralized by monks famed for their paranormal powers. Other popular amulets are of famous monks (*kechi-ajarn*) and such Hindu deities as the elephant-head god Ganesh (*Phra Pik Kaned*) and Jetukam Ramathep, an amulet named for two princes of the Srivijaya kingdom of southern Thailand. Charms or *yantra* (*mantra*) or "magic spells" inscribed on strips of paper or cloth and *sak yan* (tattoos) are also sought after. Respected monks offer amulets and charms in exchange for a promise by the recipient to observe the five Buddhist precepts and for using their supernatural power only for good and without thought of momentary gain or fame. The recipient is reminded that their potency depends on his or her moral conduct. These monks have in short appropriated the archaic spiritual tradition to serve the *ratanatrai* (Skt. *triratna*) or the Triple Gems—the Buddha, the *Dhamma* (teachings), and the *Saṇgha* (the community of his disciples, particularly monks). Likewise, erecting shelters for the spirits and offering them food are understood to be expressions of *metta*, loving kindness. And

the merit generated from such deeds can be transferred to all beings, even to disembodied spirits themselves.

Confidence in the potency of amulets and charms can be traced to the ancient Tai and Āyurvedic medical theory that assumes illness occurs when an individual's makeup is out of balance and to notions of the power of indwelling spirits. As noted earlier, in addition to an individual's indwelling *phii*, countless other *phiis* abound in nature. *Phiis*, who have a reciprocal relationship with the individual and the community, can be called upon to intervene in a beneficial manner. Through chants of holy texts and/or "magic spells," *phiis* can be quickened to aid in healing the body or rebalancing the mind and body. Alternatively, spiritual merits can be transferred to an individual via an amulet or charm to restore balance.

The popularity of amulets and charms in postmodern Thailand is evidence of the persistence of archaic beliefs. The Tai, like other Southeast Asian people, have long believed that they share the world with innumerable disembodied spirits. Properly honored, these spirits will aid individuals and their families to pass through their time in this world. To ignore these spirits, or worse still, to treat them with contempt, will surely invite disaster. For many Tais the traditional spiritual belief and practice is a convenient way to deal with the threats and dangers of daily life. These beliefs and their associated practices contrast with the rationality of the Buddhist notion of *kamma* and the arduous observance of Buddhist morality and meditation practice.

Buddhist Contribution. Radically different from the ancient Tai beliefs in spirits, Buddhism is based on the theory of *kamma* (Skt. *karma*), a rational law of cause and effect, and successive lives. Simply, meritorious deeds generate good results; evil deeds result in bad outcomes in this and successive lives. A spiritual tradition based on the logic of *kamma* and individual responsibility need not fear spirits intent on intruding on spiritual cultivation, nor does it need to appeal to *phiis* and *thaeaens* for assistance. The idea that the realization of *paññā* (Skt. *prajñā*) or spiritual insight and *nibbāna* (Skt. *Nirvāṇa*) are achieved through individual effort does not depend on outside assistance. Still, the idea of *kamma* reinforces present-day Thai Buddhists' interest in merit making for a better future through the observance of the Buddhist precepts and through the cultivation of the meditation practice of *samatha-vipassanā.*

Based on the efficacy of generating good deeds, the Buddha prescribes in the *Dīgha Nikāya* and *Anguttana Nikāya* the *puññakiriyā-vatthu* or 10 meritorious activities for gaining happiness in this present life and in the next life. They are *dāna-maya* or generosity, *sīla-maya* or observing the precepts, *bhāvana-maya* or mental development, *apacāyana-maya* or humility, *veyyāvace-maya* or service to others, *pattidāna-maya* or sharing merits with others, *pattāna-modanā-maya* or rejoicing in the merits of others, *dhamma-desanā-maya* or teaching the *dhamma* (Dharma or teaching of Buddha), *dhammassavana-maya* or listening to the *dhamma*, and *ditthujukamma* or right views. These 10 deeds serve as the basis for a devotee's moral and spiritual development, which when observed also benefits others. Special emphasis is placed on *cāga* or generosity, *sīla* or morality, and *bhāvanā* or meditation.

Generosity involves the giving of monetary and material necessities to monks and *wats* (temples). It also includes donating expertise, time, and caring for the poor and the needy. Generosity directed toward supporting the monks and their institutions is the most meritorious. Such donations enable monks to dedicate their lives to spiritual development and to carry out their clerical responsibilities. The more monks deepen their understanding, the more spiritual guidance they can offer in relieving the stresses of modern life. This symbiotic relationship between the clergy and laity accounts for the persistence of Buddhism in Thailand across the centuries. It is customary to dedicate the merits one has acquired through these gifts to friends or foes, living or deceased. One major merit-sharing occasion is the late September Sārd Festival (giving merit to the departed), dedicated to deceased ancestors and relatives.

The practice of *sīla* is another means for accumulating merit and for spiritual development. This practice involves observing the precepts to discipline the mind, sense organs, and conduct. Lay devotees observe *panca-sīla* or five precepts; those who aspire to gain more merit may choose to observe three additional precepts. *Samanera* or novices observe 10 precepts. The *bhikkhu* (Skt. *bhikṣu*) or monk observes 227 precepts, and the *bhikkhuni* (Skt.

bhikṣuni) or nun observes 311 precepts. The five precepts are moral observances, whereas the eight and 10 precepts include spiritual practices.

Panca-sīla has both negative and positive aspects. The negative aspects are taking life, taking what is not given, adultery and sexual misconduct, lying, and using intoxicants. Their respective positive counterparts or *Panca-dhamma* are the cultivation of *metta* (Skt. *maitrī*) or love as in the reverence for life; *cāga* or generosity; *dāna* or sharing and giving; *santos* or contentment with one's situation; *sacca* or truthfulness as in honesty and sincerity; and *sati* or mindfulness as in awareness and alertness.

A teacher and not a lawgiver, Buddha advised that the virtue in the precepts lay in the cultivation of good *kamma* for oneself and others. The individual cultivates the precepts in accordance with his or her capacity and situation. Observing the precepts is a self-imposed obligation. Those who are unable or unwilling to follow the precepts are regarded as being ignorant and in need of instruction and guidance. Such persons are not sinners to be punished and condemned. Understanding, rather than fear of punishment, is the motivating rationale for following the precepts. Similarly, any violation of a precept is an opportunity to remake one's life. Thus instead of brooding over the past and clinging to guilt, individuals should resolve to avoid repeating a transgression. Such a resolution generates good *kamma* that is conducive for spiritual development. Thai Buddhists find consolation in this sympathetic attitude toward human weakness.

The Thai laity devotees do what they can to observe the spirit of the precepts. Some become vegetarian, although vegetarianism was not advocated by Buddha, to demonstrate *metta*. Others observe the eight precepts on the days of the full moon and new moon and during Vesak celebrations that honor Buddha's birth, enlightenment, and death. On these occasions, the devout will don white robes and spend 24 hours at the temple, free from family commitments and away from worldly pleasures for spiritual cultivation. They meditate, chant, study, and observe the eight precepts *(attha-sīla)*. The three additional precepts are to abstain from sex, refrain from eating after noon, and refrain from wearing bodily ornaments, using perfumes, dancing, singing, playing music, or seeing shows, and from using large and high beds or seats.

Morality and meditation are the two aspects of spiritual practice necessary to attain insight and final emancipation. The two are intertwined, like fire and flame. They crystallize the fundamental teaching of Buddhism that is to avoid evil, to do good, and to purify the mind. The mind is purified by cultivating *samatha* and *vipassanā*. *Samatha* refers to the calming of the mind, one-pointedness that leads to *vipassanā* wherein the mind intuits reality as it really and truly is. The practice of *samatha* and *vipassanā* is both practical and spiritual. Mindful concentration and insight is an effective stress management tool; its practice also accrues spiritual merit by reducing desires. Many Thais will practice *samatha* for 5–10 minutes each day to still the mind by mindfully inhaling and exhaling in the presence of the image of the Buddha. A few cultivate *vipassanā* under the guidance of a meditation master. The practice involves the entire being and mind and leads to an understanding of *paṭiccasamuppāda* (Skt. *pratītyasamutpāda*), the 12 links of dependent-arising, the *tilakkhaṇa* (three marks of existence): *anicca* or impermanence, *dukkha* or suffering, and *anatta* or no-self. This insight leads to an attitude of nonattachment toward the self, material possessions, and worldly pleasures, and the ultimate release from suffering. Only a few practice *vipassanā* to prepare for a good or peaceful death that leads to rebirth in the higher realms in *saṃsāra* or no rebirth at all.

Indian Hindu Contribution. The impact of Indian culture is evident in traditional festivals. The mid-April Songkran, the most important observance of the year, marks the seasonal shift from arid heat to humid rains and a new year. Songkran is associated with the Indian festival of Holi that celebrates the coming of spring, good harvest, and fertility. On this occasion people visit their local *wat* to pray for a good year. Lo Ching Cha, the Giant Swing Ceremony, which originated in southern India, appeals for plentiful rain to ensure a bountiful harvest; the ceremony is conducted by Brahmin priests. Loy Krathong festivities honor all sources of water and ask for forgiveness for polluting them. According to lore, Loy Krathong originated during the Sukhothai period by Nang Nopanas, who wanted to honor the water spirits at the end of the rainy season.

Conclusion

Like their cohorts in the homeland, the Thais living in the United States enlist the help of their archaic, Buddhist, and Hindu traditions to improve their socioeconomic and spiritual station. How these beliefs and practices play out in the immigrant Thai community are discussed in the entry on Thai Buddhist Immigrant Spirituality.

Sudthaporn Ratanakul

See also: Entries: Thai American Religions; Thai Buddhist Immigrant Spirituality; Thai Religious Foodways

Further Reading

Gerson, Ruth. *Traditional Festivals in Thailand.* Oxford: Oxford University Press, 1996.

Kitissa, Pattana. *Mediums, Monks, and Amulets: Thai Popular Buddhism Today.* Chiengmai: Silkworm Books, 2012.

Law, Bimals Chun. *The Buddhist Conception of Spirits.* Delhi: Bhartiya, 1974.

MacDoniel, Justin Thomas. *The Lovelorn Ghost and Magic Monk.* New York: Columbia University Press, 2011.

Reichart, Peter A., and Pathawee Khongkhunthian. *The Spirit Houses of Thailand.* Chiengmai: White Lotus Press, 2007.

Sparkes, Stephen. *Spirit and Souls, Gender and Cosmology in an Isan Village in Northeast Thailand.* Bangkok: White Lotus Press, 2005.

Tambiah, Starley Leyaroja. *The Buddhist Saints of the Forest and the Cult of Amulets.* Cambridge: Cambridge University Press, 1984.

Tambiah, Starley Leyaroja. *The Cults of Spirits in North-East Thailand.* Cambridge: Cambridge University Press, 1970.

Terwiel, Barend Jam. *Monks and Magic: An Analysis of Religious Ceremonies in Central Thailand.* Copenhagen: NIA Press, 2012.

Yoshinori, Takeuchi, ed. *Buddhist Spirituality: Indian, Southeast Asian, Tibetan, and Early Chinese.* Delhi: Motilal Banarsidass, 1995.

Thai Buddhist Immigrant Spirituality

Most Thais living and working in the United States identify with the adage: "To be Thai is to be Buddhist." But a closer examination quickly reveals that traditional Thai Buddhism is a blend of indigenous animism and Indian Brahmanism. This entry will briefly describe how these beliefs and practices play out in the immigrant Thai community in the United States. It also includes a section on the role of the *wat* or temple. It begins with an overview of Thai immigration. Much of the writer's observations are based on interviews with the clerics and devotees from Wat Mongkolratanaram and Wat Buddhunsorn located in the San Francisco Bay Area. Other monks with long experience in the United States living in other parts of the country also offered their insights.

History

Chang and Eng, the Siamese Twins, a circus sideshow attraction, were the first Thai immigrants, arriving in the United States about 1830. Thai immigration to the United States was virtually nonexistent until the immigration laws in 1965 lifted the stringent quotas for non-Europeans as a result of the civil rights movement. The first Thai immigrants were a small number of nurses and physicians who were recruited to fill shortages in U.S. medical facilities. Immigration began in earnest during and after the Vietnam War, in which Thailand was a U.S. ally. The approximately 5,000 Thais who entered the United States by 1970 were primarily doctors, nurses, engineers, businessmen, and wives of U.S. Air Force personnel; women outnumbered men three to one. Subsequent immigration inflow of skilled and unskilled workers is the result of globalization. According to the 2010 U.S. Census, there were 237,583 people who identified themselves as Thai or part-Thai.

The large number of Thais living in the United States prompted the Saṅgha Council of Thailand, on the recommendation of Ven. Art Arsabha Mahathera (1903–1989), one of the nine heads of the Mahasangha, the highest administrative council of monks, to dispatch Thai monks to attend to the spiritual and social needs of Thai living in the United States in 1969. This action marks the official establishment of Thai Theravāda Buddhism in the United States. In 1972 the local devotees in partnership with the Saṅgha Council of Thailand established the first Thai Buddhist *wat* or temple, Wat Phuttapratheep, in Los Angeles. A second Thai *wat* was founded in Washington, D.C. in 1974. The first Thai American Buddhist Association was established in Los Angeles in 1970 to support Thai immigrants and promote Thai culture; these associations are found in areas with sizable émigré populations. By 2011, 95 Thai *wats* were established across the country. Monks are hand-picked by the Saṅgha Council of Thailand. Before being sent, these Phra Thammathut or missionary monks are given training in world politics, international economics, Thai culture and customs, counseling, public relations, and methods of teaching and propagation.

Beliefs and Practices

Since entering the United States in the 1970s, the Thai immigrant experience has exhibited three forms of Buddhist spirituality: traditional, popular, and modern. Traditional and popular Buddhism continue the beliefs and practices of the homeland; in contrast, modern Buddhist spirituality, still very amorphous, can be characterized as more rational and existential.

Traditional Buddhism. Traditional Buddhism is shaped by the notions of transmigration, rebirth, and *kamma* (Skt. *karma*), whose ultimate goal is rebirth in *Nibbhana* (*Nirvāṇa*) that is realizable through the cultivation of *boon* or merit-making. The rituals and devotional practices for acquiring merit are designed to reap better circumstances in this life and a better life in the next incarnation. The ordained monk is most favorably situated to realize *nibbāna*, because his life is devoted to the study of sacred texts, observing the precepts, meditation, and sharing the merits he has acquired with the laity. In contrast, the lay devotee cannot fully commit his or her energies as would a cleric; he or she needs to earn a living to care for the family. The lay devotee for his or her part earns merit by offering alms to the ordained clergy and serving the *wat*, by participating in the rituals, including chanting the sacred Pāli texts, by listening to *Dhamma* (Skt. Dharma) lessons, by meditating, and by receiving sacred water (*nam mon*) and other blessings administered by the monks.

The offering of alms and service to the *wat* are especially important avenues of earning merit for women. Most engage in one or another form of lay practice, which includes *Sanghika-dana* (community offering). They are always busy preparing food that sustains the monks, cleaning, gardening, and volunteering for all manner of tasks. The exercise of merit-making eliminates selfishness and nurtures generosity, virtues that ultimately lead to *Nibbhana*. Merit is earned by participating in *Thet Mahachat* (The Great Birth) and other rituals.

In addition to the communal ritual cycle, a devotee earns merit by observing important personal milestones with rituals performed by a monk at the *wat*. A boy having his first haircut by the abbot earns merit. Visits to the temple on birthdays and other important personal milestones also garner merit. Devotees earn merit by offering gifts and food to the monks who perform funerals. Parents often have their sons ordained as novices, who then live at the temple for brief periods. Because full-fledged female ordination is not allowed in the Theravāda tradition, women participate in *Buat Chii Phram*, a temporary ordination in which they observe the eight precepts, don white robes, and need not shave their hair.

Popular Buddhism: Magic Monks and Spirit Worship. Since many Thais are also animists, monks frequently receive requests to perform rituals of prognostication, carry out exorcisms, and sacralize (*pluksek*) amulets and images. These practices are rooted in archaic beliefs that we share the world with disembodied beings, including ancestral spirits, and that shamans have the powers to manipulate these spirits. Requests for these rituals are indicative of a deep yearning for personal well-being, security, success, and for assurance of a safe passage through life.

This yearning is evident in personal household shrines and the ubiquitous shrines that are tended to at Thai-owned restaurants. Such shrines honor an array of deities with a number of sacred images and symbols. It is not uncommon for altars to have Buddhist images, Chinese and Hindu deities. Photos or images of King Chulalongkorn (1853–1910), a popular devotional figure, and famous monks can also be found. The altar above the reception counter at Your Place Thai Cuisine in Berkeley is a prime example. A figure of a Thai-style Buddha commands the center. Sharing the altar are two laughing Chinese Buddhist images, the Daoist Fu, Lu, Shou deities of good fortune, prosperity, and longevity, a replica of the Emerald Buddha of Wat Phra Kaew, the image of the monk Luang Po To, a figurine of Nang Kwak, and an assortment of other images and symbols. Each of the images was sacralized in Thailand and once again in the Bay Area. To the left of the shrine is another large portrait of Luang Po To (1788–1872), the most influential spiritual mentor of King Mongkut (1808–1868) and King Chulalongkorn.

Nang Kwak is honored on two other shrines in the restaurant's dining area. She is an incarnation of Mae Po Sop, the rice goddess, who is the Siamese (Tai) version of the Hindu goddess Sri Lakshmi. A consecrated Nang Kwak figure used by Thai shopkeepers is a benevolent spirit who invites good fortune, especially in the form of money, and is thus the patron of merchants. The position of her right hand resembles the Japanese *maneki neko* (welcoming cat) who beckons customers. The restaurant has a shrine dedicated to the Chinese deity of the land on which the building is erected.

Magic is not encouraged in Buddhism. Nevertheless, monks are often asked to bless a new house or car or exorcise evil spells. The common rationale for their "use of magic" is that such rituals support morale and fortify the spirits of those who experience bad dreams, are depressed by a death in the family, are concerned over bad omens, or are stressed from being unemployed. These "magic" rituals are accompanied by Buddhist messages and counseling. In Thailand "magic" rituals are normally performed by shamans. "Magic" is discreetly practiced in the United States. Non-Buddhist deities are housed and worshiped in periphery areas of the *wat*.

The persistence of folk traditions can be traced to the Thai belief that the natural world, including human beings, possesses physical and immaterial aspects. Further, these spirits reside in such natural objects as trees, mountains, forests, rivers, houses, and even rice grains. Thus, before felling a tree, the traditional woodcutter would seek permission from the spirits of the forest. These beliefs existed well before the introduction of Indic spiritual traditions. Thais worship Indra, a major Indian deity, and the four-faced Brahman as spirits who can bring prosperity and luck. Likewise Thais believe Lord Buddha, the figure of the Emerald Buddha, and Luang Po (revered monks) to be powerful personal protectors who can also lend their powers to secure their homes, villages, cities, and nation. Buddhist monks and shamans may invoke and/or appropriate any spirit to ease the burden of their clients.

Modern Buddhism. Educated professional Thai immigrants and the second-generation Thai Americans are drawn to the rationality of their Buddhist faith. They are interested in the stress-reducing benefits of meditation, studying, and understanding the sacred texts. Their interest is quickened in part by modernization and the secular American society, the reputations of the Dalai Lama and Thich Nhat Hanh, and popular Buddhist culture. They understand that Thai Buddhism, its *wats*, and its clerics will need to adjust to American society for their children and future generations.

A retired nurse and a longtime civil service employee for the city of San Francisco, who settled in the United States over 30 years ago, are examples of "modern" Buddhists. While they routinely participate in the regular and special rituals, they visit their *wat* on other days, which, as they emphasize, are for themselves, to cultivate their spirit. On these special days, they observe the Buddhist precepts, chant, meditate, and engage the abbot on the finer points of the *dhamma*. Both women are community leaders; in addition to helping with the traditional temple activities, they serve on the *wat*'s governing board, fundraise, and offer instruction on Thai culture and language to Thai American youths. In contrast to Thailand, women in the United States have freedom to undertake nontraditional leadership roles. They, too, mentioned that to know Thai culture is to know Buddhism. At home they continue to observe the precepts, chant, meditate, read books, and learn from CD series and YouTube videos. Their favorite contemporary monks are the British Venerable Thanissaro Bhikkhu and the progressive Venerable W. Vajiramedhi, who apply Buddhist teachings to daily life.

The Thai *Wat* (Temple)

The *wat* has multiple functions. Spiritually, the *wat* is the place for monks to live the Buddhist life, to share Buddhist teachings, to perform rituals and ceremonies, and to offer counseling. For the laity, the *wat* is where they can learn about Buddha's *dhamma* and to cultivate *boon* or merit by making offerings to the clerics and serving the temple. The temple serves as a community center, where the devotees can attend lectures on all manner of topics, receive medical care and social services, and participate in cultural and social activities. In addition to these activities, the *wat* in the United States assists newly landed immigrants with material assistance, advice and counseling, temporary housing, and employment referrals. The *wat* also assists the Thai government in issuing and renewing passports and national identification cards. During our conversation Thammarit Jankunti, a retired Thai American who has lived in the United States for 40 years, sums up the role of the *wat* for the émigrés:

Feeling lonely, alienated by a new environment, full of stress, and depression about their work and life,

Thais turn to the *wat* for emotional and spiritual comfort. It is a place of joy, entertainment, and solace for both children and adults. Being at the *wat* for one or two hours is like being in Thailand. Though their life and work in America is full of stress and frustrations, the *wat* helps us to be hopeful and in good spirits.

The *wat* is a place of comfort to Thai women who experience the difficulties of international marriages. The website of a California *wat* encourages such women to introduce their spouses to the *wat* and to practice *dhamma* together. Participating together will improve their relationship and relieve the wife's depression. Others, who are lonely, stressed from child-rearing, and with marital problems, visit the *wat* for solace.

The *wat* is the center and purveyor of Thai tradition and culture that includes Thai food, Thai classical music and dance, Thai language, and Thai etiquette. Parents bring their children to the *wat* to learn what it means to be Thai, which means to be generous and humble, and to be respectful of their parents and the elderly. To this end parents will often send their sons to the *wat* to be ordained as novices or monks for brief periods. This custom tacitly reinforces the perception that Thai identity is intimately linked to their Buddhist faith, rather than ethnicity. The *wat* thus is the locus of group cohesion, identity formation, and the venue for cultural transmission. It is the spiritual, cultural, and educational center that promotes and preserves Thai culture and nationality. In the United States the *wat* serves a similar

function; and in additional it is a venue where Thais can gather for fellowship and to reconnect with their homeland. Thai culture and identity is transmitted through Buddhist Sunday schools that teach Thai language, culture, and customs, as well as the Buddhist faith to Thai youths and interested non-Thais. Like *wats* in the homeland, in addition to Veska Pūjā and other Buddhist celebrations, the U.S. *wat* sponsors such traditional festivals as Songkran, the New Year Water festival, and Loy Krathong, the festival of lights. The *wat* also sponsors Father's and Mother's Days, which mark the birthday of the king and queen. On these occasions, Thais don their national costumes. It should be noted that the Thai *wat* also serves the ethnic Khmer (Cambodian) and Laotian American communities.

The Thai *Wat* as a Civic Movement

The laity, who helped to found their *wats* and related associations, became more seasoned with democratic forms of religious polity and became active in community politics. One example from the mid-1990s involved the Berkeley Thai Buddhist community, when neighbors filed an appeal with the city to shut down the 25-year Sunday food offering that supported Wat Mongkolratanaram and its programs. The food service offered Thai cuisine in exchange for a donation. The neighbors sued, arguing that the temple was operating as a commercial enterprise in a residential zone, and that the activity violated their right to reside in peace. Abbot Phra Manas argued that the activity of food offering and donations was the religious duty of Theravāda Buddhists. Because in the United States monks cannot walk the streets "begging" for food and alms as practiced in Thailand, the Sunday food offering is a religious activity for templegoers, and lets the volunteer food preparers and servers earn merit for this and their next lives.

The suit culminated in 2008 when the complainants petitioned the Berkeley City Council. In response the Thai community garnered support from the University of California at Berkeley's student senate. More than 2,000 signed a petition to save the Sunday food service. The Berkeley City Council unanimously (9–0) rejected the petition. Dionne Jirachaikitti, a community advocate with the Asian Law Caucus, observed, "To a new generation of Thai Americans, this issue marked the first time second-generation Thais in America have come together to organize for a cause." The issue was an "example of religious exclusion aimed at communities of color, in particular immigrant communities, that are less aware of zoning laws and more vulnerable to attack."

Conclusion

The beliefs and practices of Thai immigrants continue the traditions of their homeland, albeit modified for the American context. Devotees, who observe traditional and popular practices, see Buddha and his teachings and the multitude of spirits of their archaic beliefs to be forces that can be manipulated through ritual. In contrast, modern devotees understand the Buddha and his teachings as vehicles for self-cultivation and appreciate the moral rationality of *kamma.* These tendencies are not mutually exclusive. Thai immigrants often appeal to more than one strand of Buddhism. Both strive to acquire merit in this life and the next life. The *wat*, its rituals, and other activities are essential supports for their Thai identity. Missionary monks wear three robes: the traditional, the popular, and the modern.

Thai immigrant Buddhists continue to follow a traditional practice of Theravāda Buddhism, but as ethnic and spiritual minorities, they are conscious and appreciative of their spiritual traditions. At the moment, no new movements have surfaced that might alter the traditional pattern. But change can be seen in the details. Services are now held on the weekend, especially Sundays, the only time when most devotees are free from work. Traditional ritual times and dates are shifted and compressed. Rituals that lasted two or three days are now abbreviated to a day or to half a day. The daily morning alms round has been replaced by the opportunity to offer food to the monks on the temple grounds. One concession Thai Buddhism has made to accommodate its American experience is the invention of the wedding ceremony. In keeping with Buddhist Vinaya, monks in Thailand do not perform weddings. The key question is what beliefs and practices will future generations of Thai preserve? How will they balance their American experience with their cultural and spiritual identity? With globalization, real-time communication, and massive population movements, the immigrant Buddhist experience may become no different from its experience in Thailand.

Prasong Kittinanthachai

See also: Entries: Thai American Religions; Thai Buddhist Immigrant Culture; Thai Religious Foodways

Further Reading

Cadge, Wendy. *Heartwood: The First Generation of Theravāda Buddhism in America.* Chicago: University of Chicago Press, 2005.

Esterik, Penny Van. *Taking Refuge: Lao Buddhists in North America.* Tempe: Arizona State University, 1992.

Gombrich, Richard, and Obeyesekere. *Buddhism Transformed.* Princeton, NJ: Princeton University Press, 1988.

Kitiarsa, Pattana. *Mediums, Monks, and Amulets: Thai Popular Buddhism Today.* Chiang Mai: Silkworm Books, 2012.

McMahan, David L. *The Making of Buddhist Modernism.* Oxford: Oxford University Press, 2008.

Numrich, Paul David. *Old Wisdom in the New World: Americanization in Two Immigrant Theravāda Buddhist Temples.* Knoxville: The University of Tennessee Press, 1996.

Prebish, Charles S., and Martin Baumann, eds. *Westward: Dharma Buddhism beyond Asia.* Berkeley: University of California Press, 2002.

Seager, Richard Hughes. *Buddhism in America.* New York: Columbia University Press, 1999.

Terwiel, Barend Jan. *Monks and Magic: Revisiting a Class Study of Religious Ceremonies in Thailand.* Copenhagen: Nordic Institute of Asia Studies Press, 2012.

Thai Religious Foodways

Food plays an important role in the Thai American family and religion. Sharing meals is a time for bonding. Typically rice, the main staple, is served first to those seated around the table; subsequently, individuals help themselves with their own utensils or a common serving spoon for small portions of side dishes (*kap khaao*) that are placed in the center. Thai American food is eaten with a spoon and fork. The fork is used for pushing food on to the spoon. Chopsticks and a soup spoon are used for noodle dishes.

Families often offer food to monks at the temple or those who visit their homes, not only to provide them with nutritional intake, but as a devotional gesture to the Buddha and his teachings. Giving alms to monks (*tak baat*) by placing food in a monk's alms bowl is a customary practice of merit making (*tam bun*).

Thai American food is a blend of native culinary traditions and ingredients that have been influenced by India, China, neighboring Southeast Asian cultures, and American cuisine. The result is a diverse and multiflavored cuisine of spicy, sweet, sour, salty, and sometimes bitter dishes. Basic ingredients are chili peppers, cane or palm sugar, lime or tamarind juice, fish sauce, and shrimp paste. Some Thai restaurants may cater to the American palate by decreasing the intensity of flavors or substituting with similar Thai ingredients. The best place to experience authentic Thai dishes is probably in Thai American homes or at local Thai American temples.

Preparing dishes is not a rigid process, as cooks rely upon their experience with smell and taste to produce the desired flavor. Preparation of dishes is usually quick and includes boiling, steaming, grilling, stir-frying, or frying. A mortar and pestle are used to pound ingredients together to make salads, pastes, relishes, or sauces.

Ajahn Raywat collects rice during the "tak bat" or donation of rice to the monks, an important part of Buddhist merit making, during the Ok Phansa services to mark the end of Buddhist Lent at Wat Pa, in Chandler, Arizona, October 24, 2010. Buddhist Lent is a time devoted to study and meditation. Buddhist monks remain within the temple grounds and do not venture out for a period of three months starting from the first day of the waning moon of the eighth lunar month (in July) to the fifteenth day of the waxing moon of the eleventh lunar month (in October). Ok Phansa Day marks the end of the Buddhist Lent and falls on the full moon of the eleventh lunar month. (Jack Kurtz/ ZUMA Press/Corbis)

Rice, whether white rice (*khaao suai*) or sticky (*khaao niao*), is essential for meals. Although rice can be a singular dish such as fried rice (*khao pat*), side dishes (*kap khaao*) are the accompaniment. This may consist of curries, soups, stir-fries, salads, and meat or seafood dishes.

There are many types of curries (*kaeng phet*), which contain such basic ingredients as dried or fresh chilies, onions, garlic, galangal, lemon grass, kaffir lime leaves, and shrimp paste, which are all mashed into a paste. Soups include varieties of *kaeng jeut*, a simple broth with few seasonings, and *tom yam*, a soup with a spicy and sour base. Like *kaeng phet*, coconut milk or other ingredients are added to create a variety of soups.

Spicy and sour salads (*yam*) have a sauce typically containing lime juice, fresh chilies, fish sauce, and sugar. *Yam* can be made with green papaya, green mango, glass noodles, winged beans, pomelo, and seafood. Stir-fry dishes are multitudinous and range from stir-fried meats, vegetables, or a mixture. Chili paste (*nam prik*) is a relish made by mashing shrimp paste, chili peppers, and garlic, seasoned with lime juice and palm sugar. There are many variations, which can be eaten with vegetables that are raw, boiled, grilled, fried, or pickled, or accompanied with fried or steamed fish.

Noodles are prepared in a variety of ways such as a single dish of noodles in a soup broth (*kuaitiao nam*), or without a soup broth but briefly dipped into hot water (*kuaitiao haeng*). Noodles may be doused in gravy (*kuaitiao rat naa*), used in a salad, baked, or stir-fried like *pat thai*. Noodle forms include rice noodles, which come in different widths, yellow or wheat-based egg noodles (*ba mii*), glass noodles (*wun sen*), and *khanom jiin*, another form of rice noodles commonly eaten with curries.

Desserts (*khong waan*) are also numerous. The fundamental ingredients of desserts are rice flour, sugar, coconut, and coconut milk. Additions include sticky rice, fruits, tapioca, pumpkin, corn, or egg yolks.

A *samrap*, or set meal with several *kap khaao* dishes, is shared between more than one person. In a *samrap*, there must be a variety of colors for attractiveness and a balance of tastes and textures for the dishes to complement each other. For example, a tangy *tom yam* would go well with an omelet, or a *kaeng jeut* would be paired with a spicy stir-fry dish.

Heather E. Nakasone

Further Reading

Cummings, Joe. *World Food: Thailand*. Sydney: Lonely Planet, 2000.

Phromsao, Kannika, Nantha Benjasilarak, and Prayat Saiwichian, eds. *Samrap Thai* (Thai Cuisine). Chiang Mai: Wannarak, 1999.

Thompson, David. *Thai Food*. London: Pavilion Books, 2002.

Theravāda Buddhism

The 1970s have been described as a decade of stagflation, an unprecedented mixture of double-digit unemployment and inflation rates. These economic conditions impacted how Vietnamese, Cambodian, and Laotian refugees were received in the wake of the fall of Saigon in April 1975. Theravāda Buddhist temple building came with a backlash from xenophobic neighbors who—under the guise of zoning laws and regulations—invoked their privilege supported by the ideology of white supremacy in attempts to stop the building of temples in their neighborhoods, as evidenced by an example in Silver Spring, Maryland, where, in 2008, neighbors counted cars and kept detailed records and photos of people visiting the temple during festival celebrations. The Maryland State Supreme Court denied the group, then known as the Khmer Buddhist Society, a permit to build a temple on Newtown Hilltop. Afterwards, the Newtown Zoning Board presented the Khmer Buddhist Society with an order to "cease all religious services and festivals permanently." In the late 1980s Laotian refugees in Rockford, Illinois, a rural blue-collar town, faced extreme violence in their attempt to build a temple on a small farmstead on the outskirts of town. The Laotian temple was the target of a firebomb and drive-by rifle fire. Although Burmese Buddhist communities have not received that level of opposition with respect to their establishment of religious temples, the Aloh/taw Pyayt Dhamma Yeiktha (APDY) in the city of El Sobrante, California, received complaints from its predominantly white neighbors soon after the home temple was established in November 1998. Joseph Cheah notes that members of the Burmese Buddhist community "received complaints from the city that there were 'weird' gatherings of people there and they were cultish." Here again, neighbors complained about noise, traffic, and parking. Because most residents would deny that they possess any discriminatory sentiment or religious bias against the presence of a non-Christian place of worship in their neighborhood, the words "traffic" and "noise" have, at times, become code words for covert racism.

Unlike their Cambodian and Laotian neighbors, Thai Americans did not come to the United States as refugees. The first settlements of Thai immigrants did not appear until the late 1960s, immigrating to America for many different reasons. Thai migration to the United States was fueled in the 1960s and 1970s by Thailand's social and political upheaval in combination with changes in U.S. immigration policy that lifted the ban on immigration from Asia. The Immigration and Nationality Act of 1965 also established a preference for skilled labor. Therefore, the first wave of Thai immigrants primarily consisted of doctors, nurses, and other white-collar professionals. In particular, a shortage of nurses in the United States drew large numbers of Thai immigrants. In the late 1960s the American government began to give a warm welcome to Thai nurses by offering green cards to them upon their landing on American soil. Additionally, an increased number of Thai students immigrated for educational purposes, although that goal was not achieved as easily as expected. Thai exchange students faced financial hardships, and unexpected scholastic demands were compounded by language problems that made successful completion of a degree impossible. Those who dropped out did not return to Thailand, but instead, found unskilled and semi-skilled jobs. Later, when their student visas expired, many petitioned for a change of status to permanent resident. Since the passage of the Immigration Reform and Control Act of 1984, a change in status became nearly impossible. Further, another group of Thai immigrants came as wives of U.S. service personnel stationed in Thailand during the Vietnam War. Similar to immigrants from other parts of the world, Thai immigrants brought their religion and religious institutions with them. The growing number of Thai temples throughout the United States attests to the growing presence of Thai Americans. According to Todd LeRoy Perreira, there are roughly 105 *wats* scattered throughout North America in 32 states, including six temples in Canada. Nearly 30 percent of the temples are located in California.

The formation of Thai Buddhism in America unfolded in two phases. Initially it was a top-down formation that was spearheaded by royal, ecclesial, and civil authorities in Thailand, who in the mid-1950s and 1960s sought to expand Thai Buddhism beyond its geographical and national borders. During this period,

Thailand envisioned itself as a "world center of Buddhism." As such, it funded the development of the first transnational Thai temples under royal patronage in India in 1959 with the construction of Wat Thai Buddha-Gaya, then in the United Kingdom in 1965 with Wat Buddhapadipa. There were also plans to construct a Thai temple in New York's Staten Island, but the plan was aborted due to complications, while simultaneously a group of Thai immigrants and American-born Buddhists successfully formed the Buddhist Study Center in New York as a legal entity in 1965. This event, followed by the 1972 establishment of the first and largest Thai temple in Los Angeles, foreshadowed a new bottom-up, lay-centered approach in the institutionalization of Thai Buddhism in the United States. "In June 1971 a mission of Thai monks led by Ven. Phra Dhammakosacharn arrived in Los Angeles, and lay people began to raise funds to purchase land. In 1972, land was donated and construction began on a main hall, a two-story Thai-style building that was completed and dedicated in 1979." The bottom-up approach maintained close links with Thai royalty and high-ranking civil servants, but was financed and led by the growing Thai immigrant population in America. Wendy Cadge notes, "Buddha images for the shrine hall and two sets of scriptures were carried to the United States by monks and lay people from Thailand, and in 1979 His Majesty the King and Her Majesty the Queen of Thailand presided over the casting of the principal Buddha image for the temple at Wat Po (officially called Wat Phra Chetuphon, or the Monastery of the Reclining Buddha) in

Thailand." Throughout the 1970s Thai immigrants established Thai temples in several metropolitan areas: Washington, D.C., Chicago, Denver, and San Francisco. This growth in the United States necessitated the formation of the Council of Thai Bhikkhus to act as liaison for the missionary monks that were coming from Thailand to serve the growing community; the council was established in 1977.

Jonathan H. X. Lee

See also: Entries: Berkeley Thai Temple, Wat Mongkolratanaram; Buddhist Churches of America; Chinese Temples in America; Watt Samaki

Further Reading

Cadge, Wendy. *Heartwood: The First Generation of Theravāda Buddhism in America.* Chicago: University of Chicago Press, 2005.

Numrich, Paul David. *Old Wisdom in the New World: Americanization in Two Immigrant Theravāda Buddhist Temples.* Knoxville: University of Tennessee Press, 1996.

Perreira, Todd LeRoy. "Thai Americans: Religion." In Jonathan H. X. Lee and Kathleen Nadeau, eds. *Encyclopedia of Asian American Folklore and Folklife.* Santa Barbara, CA: ABC-CLIO, 2011, p. 1110.

Thich Duc Niem (1937–2003)

Venerable Thich Duc Niem was born into the Ho family in Binh Thuan Province, Vietnam. At age 13, he left home to study under Venerable Thich Minh Dao of Long Quang Temple. Subsequently he studied with the Venerables Thich Tri Thang, abbot of the temple in Phan Rang, Thich Thien Hoa, Thich Tri Quang of An Quang Temple in Saigon, and Thich Tri Thu at

Hai Duc Buddhist Academy in Nha Trang, Vietnam. In 1962, he graduated from South Vietnam Buddhist College at An Quang Temple in Saigon. Besides Buddhism, he also studied traditional academic subjects. After graduating with a bachelor of arts from Van Hanh University in 1966 he became the principal of Bodhi High School in Long Xuyen City and director of Bodhi School in Binh Duong province.

In 1969, he won a scholarship to study at the National Pedagogic University of the Republic of China (Taiwan), where he earned an MA in 1972 and a PhD in Chinese language and literature, and philosophy. In 1978, while he was studying in Taiwan, he was invited to be the chair of the Refugees Boat People Rescue Association (in Taiwan). In this capacity, he helped countless of his country folk.

In 1979, Thich Thien An invited Thich Duc Niem to teach at the University of Oriental Studies in the United States; he later served as its deputy director. He went on to establish Ananda Publishers, which printed Buddhist *Sūtras* in Vietnamese for worldwide distribution. In June 1981, he formally established the International Buddhist Monastic Institute (Phat Hoc Vien Quoc Te) to train aspiring devotees, to propagate the Dharma, and to preserve Vietnamese traditional culture. He served as a certifier for the Transmission of the Complete Precepts at the City of Ten Thousand Buddhas in 1979. For more than 20 years, he led the effort to publish periodicals, translate and compile Buddhist *Sūtras*, and write essays. He published and distributed at least 235 Buddhist-related texts.

Thich Duc Niem's scholarship and his quiet and steady leadership earned him great respect in the Vietnamese Buddhist immigrant community.

Ronald Y. Nakasone

See also: Entries: Vietnamese American Buddhists

Further Reading

Nguyen, Cuong Tu, and A. W. Barber. "Vietnamese Buddhism in North America: Tradition and Acculturation." In Charles S. Prebish and Kenneth K. Tanaka, eds. *The Faces of Buddhism in America*. Berkeley: University of California Press, 1998, pp. 129–46.

Quang Minh, Thich. "Vietnamese Buddhism in America." Electronic Theses, Treatises and Dissertations. Paper 1589. 2007.

Thich Thien An (1926–1980)

Ven. Thich Thien An was born in Hue, Vietnam. He was a Thien (Zen) Buddhist monk, a professor of Asian thought, the founder of the International Buddhist Meditation Center in Los Angeles, and a refugee relief worker.

Born into a Buddhist family, he entered the monastery at the age of 14 and was later sent to Japan to further his studies. He received a doctorate in literature at Waseda University in Japan in 1963. After returning to Vietnam, he helped to establish the Van Hanh Buddhist University in Saigon. In 1966, he arrived as an exchange professor at the University of California, Los Angeles. He had fully intended to return after a year, but was persuaded to remain by his students. He founded the International Buddhist Meditation Center on South New Hampshire Avenue in Los Angeles in 1970; three years later he established the University of Oriental Studies.

The aftermath of the fall of Saigon on April 30, 1975, resulted in a large influx of refugees to the United States. The U.S. government approached Thich Thien An to assist in the resettlement effort. In addition to his clerical responsibilities Thich Thien An and his students raised funds to purchase apartment buildings to house the refugees, organized English classes, and helped in countless other ways to help ease the trauma of those fleeing their homeland to transition into American life. In September 1980 he complained of not feeling well. Physicians discovered a brain tumor that had metastasized from a cancer of the liver. He died on November 23, 1980, at the age of 54.

He encouraged interfaith conversation and cooperation and promoted mutual understanding between religions and Buddhist sects, as well as trained new generations of monks and nuns to propagate the Dharma in the Western world. The many American monks and nuns he ordained continue to propagate the Dharma at his center and other Vietnamese temples. He wrote *Zen Philosophy, Zen Practice* and *Buddhism and Zen in Vietnam*. Many consider Thich Thien An to be the first patriarch of Vietnamese Buddhism in America.

Ronald Y. Nakasone

See also: Entries: Vietnamese American Buddhists

Further Reading

"Ven. Dr. Thich Thien-An." International Buddhist Meditation Center. http://www.urban dharma.org/ibmc/ibmc2/suto.html. Accessed July 16, 2014.

Tianhou, Empress of Heaven

History and Origins

Tianhou is popularly venerated as the Empress of Heaven, but dually venerated as the Goddess of the Sea. The early Chinese pioneers traveled across the Pacific Ocean in little wooden junks, and on those junks there was an altar to Tianhou. If they were lucky and landed on the shores of the California coast, they immediately returned thanks to her for safely guiding their junks to America. Hence, she is commonly enshrined in historic Chinese temples throughout California, in Weaverville, Oroville, and Marysville, to name a few. In addition, new temples are being established in the newer ethnic Chinese communities in Los Angeles and San Francisco. The tale of how a village girl became the Empress of Heaven is also a very popular religious folktale in Chinese American communities, especially among the Taiwanese American communities.

She is the highest-ranking female deity in the vast and patriarchal Chinese folk pantheon. In Taiwan and Fujian, Tianhou is popularly known as Mazu/Mazupo. The goddess Tianhou/Mazu ranks second only to the Buddhist bodhisattva Guanyin as a female object of popular devotion throughout the cities and villages of China's coastal provinces.

The cult of Tianhou is based on the worship of a maiden named Lin Moniang (Miss Lin, the Silent One) who is said to have lived from 960 to 987 CE on the island of Meizhou in the Minnanese Putian district of Fujian Province. There are numerous myths and legends surrounding

The main shrine in the Ma-tsu Temple U.S.A. The shrine is dedicated to Meiguo Mazu, or "American Mazu," who is venerated by Taiwanese Americans in the San Francisco Bay Area. (Courtesy of Jonathan H. X. Lee)

her life, but the most widely held belief largely conforms to the same outline. Miss Lin was born on the 23rd day of the third lunar month in 960 CE into a pious family, variously described as humble fisherfolk or as local gentry. Her father is frequently identified as a virtuous but low-ranking Confucian official. She is described as having one to four brothers, and sometimes even as many as five sisters. The bodhisattva Guanyin, who gave her mother a magic pill, made her conception possible. In another version, Guanyin of the South Sea (Nanhai Guanyin) visited her mother in a dream and gave her an *utpala*, or blue lotus, to swallow, and 14 months later she gave birth to Lin Moniang.

From day one, Miss Lin demonstrated herself to be unique. As a baby she had been mute, not making any sounds or even a little cry during the first few months of her mortal life, which is why her family named her the "Silent One." As a young girl, she was credited with several special qualities, with a wide range of special traits and skills for someone her age. By the age of five, she was said to have been inspired by an image of Guanyin, and to have been able to recite the *Guanyin jing*; by age eight she was credited with being well versed in the Confucian classics. By the age of 10, Miss Lin set her heart on the Buddha and began studying the *Sūtras* and the practice of meditation, which was unusual for someone her age. Hence, by 11 she was renowned for her knowledge of the principal Buddhist *Sūtras*. Her manners were beautifully impeccable; her demeanor graceful; she carried herself with dignity to the extent that no one dared to question her. So by the age of 13, after acquiring a noble and fair reputation as a young virtuous girl, to no one's surprise she found favor among the religious figures of her village.

Then one day, she was accepted as an inspired disciple under the tutelage of a religious master, Xuantong, who frequently visited her family. The master said to Tianhou, "You, being born with a heart full of compassion and good virtue, are destined to be the savior of the mortals." Thereupon, he became her teacher in Daoist inner alchemy and practices, in addition to Buddhist meditation. Many years later, through her perseverance and sacrifice, Tianhou gained incredible spiritual achievement and insight. Casting slight variations in these accounts aside, Miss Lin was endowed with great spiritual powers that she gladly used in the service of others, out of her innate sense of compassion.

Two core events occurred in her legendary life. First, by age 16 while playing with a group of friends by an old water well, she encountered a Daoist fairy or old water spirit. The friends immediately fled upon seeing the fairy, but Miss Lin knelt down and greeted the fairy with sincere respect. Afterwards, the fairy presented her with a bronze talisman/charm and disappeared. Soon after, Miss Lin used the charm to ex-

orcise evil spirits, heal diseases, help others whenever possible, and perform many shamanic tasks. More importantly, from that day on, she had magical powers that enabled her spirit to travel outside her body, a special talent that she would invoke many times as a mortal before her apotheosis as an immortal goddess.

The second core incident occurred later on, wherein Miss Lin seemed to have fallen asleep or become entranced at her weaving loom. While in this state of dream (or trance), her spirit drifted far out to sea, saving her father and brother (or brothers) in a capsized boat amidst a violent storm. In a number of versions, she was unable to save one of her brothers. In other versions, it was her father that she was unable to save, due to her mother calling her back to waking life in the midst of her rescue. As a result, Lin Moniang was inconsolable. When the survivors subsequently returned to port with vivid recollections of having seen or heard her in the storm, her reputation as a miracle worker spread to neighboring villages along the Fujian coast.

The process by which Miss Lin transformed from mortal girl, to goddess, to the Empress of Heaven is a seemingly straightforward one. Miss Lin's dedication in helping her family and others in perilous situations, in addition to the state, especially while at sea, coupled with her many magical powers, earned her the respect, support, and devotion of her early believers and continues to do so.

Temples to the Empress of Heaven

The first temple dedicated to the Empress of Heaven was established during the early

1850s with the first wave of Chinese immigration to the United States in search of gold. Today, the Tien Hau Temple is celebrated as the "oldest" Chinese temple in America and is visited by tourists throughout the year. As immigration policies changed after the passage of the 1965 Immigration Act, Taiwanese immigrants established the second large-scale Empress of Heaven temple to their Mazu in the mid-1980s. The Ma-tsu Temple of U.S.A. was established in San Francisco and is officially registered as a nonprofit religious institution. This temple was established as a branch of the Chaotian Temple in Beigang, Taiwan. Today, the Ma-tsu Temple of U.S.A. has relocated to 30 Beckett Street. The temple's stated mission is to advocate the virtues of Mazu, benevolence, uphold the Buddhist Dharma, teach the principles of human kindness and relations, and promote social morality.

As a result of the Vietnam War and the large wave of Sino-Southeast and East Asian refugees who resettled in America, more Empress of Heaven temples were established on the American religious landscape. Over the past three decades the landscape of Chinese America was significantly reconfigured by Indo-Chinese immigrants who arrived in the U.S. following the legislation of the Indochina Migration and Refugee Assistance Act of 1975, the Refugee Act of 1980, and the Amerasian Homecoming Act of 1987. As the United States pulled out of the disastrous Vietnam War in 1975, about 130,000 Vietnamese who were generally highly skilled and well educated, and who feared retaliation for their close association with Americans, were airlifted by the U.S. government to bases in the Philippines, Guam, and Wake Island in the northern Pacific Ocean. This first wave of refugees was subsequently followed by a major exodus out of Vietnam, Laos, and Cambodia that began in 1978 and lasted into the mid-1980s, totaling virtually five million people. There were also clusters of refugees that flooded into the neighboring South and Southeast Asian countries: Thailand, Malaysia, Indonesia, the Philippines, and Hong Kong—at a rate that ranged from 2,000 to as many as 50,000 refugees per month. Thousands of refugees fleeing Vietnam, Laos, and Cambodia escaped in ramshackle wooden boats or precarious rubber dinghies, hence, they were called boat people. Unable to deal with the massive influx of refugees, the host countries began to expel them. To counter the humanitarian crisis, President Jimmy Carter ordered the Seventh Fleet to seek vessels in distress in the South China Sea. A sizeable percentage of refugees coming from Vietnam, Laos, and Cambodia were of ethnic Chinese backgrounds, speaking either Cantonese or the Chaozhou dialects. Many were also devotees of the representation of Tianhou as the sea goddess. Many boat people recounted having seen a "red light" shielding their boats from wind and rain, from heat and sun, which they associated with Chau Ba Thien Hau (Our Lady Tianhou). In Taiwan the iconographic "red light" is recognized as *Mazu huo* (Mazu fire). The immediate effect of this mass migration is reflected in new temples dedicated to Tianhou founded by Indo-Chinese Americans.

At present, there are two large Tianhou temple complexes in the urban landscape of Los Angeles. One temple is located in the economically challenged Latino community of Lincoln Heights, while the other is a palatial complex in Los Angeles' Chinatown. The latter is the 6,000-square-foot, $2 million Sino-Vietnamese Thien Hau Temple, completed in September 2005. It was first established in 1983, occupying a Christian church. The temple gained increasingly greater public support through the years because the goddess, Thien Hau, was efficacious. Although Vietnamese immigrants from the Camau Association established the Thien Hau Temple, its patronage includes Sino-Vietnamese, Sino-Khmers, and Sino-Thais who speak Chaozhou, as well as other Cantonese immigrant Americans. Additionally, the Elderly Indo-Chinese Association's Tianhou Temple, also founded in the early 1980s, primarily serves Chaozhou- and Cantonese-speaking immigrant Americans from Southeast Asia. These new Tianhou (Thien Hau) temples are markedly distinct from Ma-tsu Temple U.S.A. in that they, much like the Tianhou temples in Hong Kong, are not preoccupied with associating themselves with the Mazu cult in Meizhou, China.

Community Ritual Tradition

Currently, there have been no reported multiple day celebrations at the Ma-tsu Temple U.S.A. during Mazu's birthday. In traditional Chinese settings, Mazu's birthday celebration would feature huge bonfires, firecrackers, big banquets, and continuous religious rituals performed in the temple by Daoist masters, and performances of Chinese operas to entertain the goddess. This type of traditional celebration is still practiced in Hong Kong, Taiwan, and Fujian at major Tianhou/Mazu temples.

The smaller scale celebration of Mazu's birthday at the Ma-tsu Temple U.S.A. does not include the traditional celestial inspection tour in which she views the state of her immediate realm and extends her protection to the community. Instead, the Ma-tsu Temple U.S.A. takes advantage of the Chinese New Year Parade, usually in February or early March, by participating in it to provide the goddess with an opportunity to make her celestial inspection tour. During the American version of Mazu's inspection tour, she views the state of the world and extends her protection to the community, thus mediating between Chinese and non-Chinese culture while expanding the parameters of her religious sovereignty. One of the main functions of Mazu's tour is to unify the community. Mazu is able to accomplish this because as a symbol of Chinese religious culture, she reminds both the Chinese and non-Chinese viewers of something that is Chinese.

In the case of Mazu and her participation in the San Francisco Chinese New Year parade, there are two levels of understanding and symbolism. One, to the immigrant Chinese Americans participating in Mazu's celestial inspection tour, it is an event full of religious meaning. To many viewers, the carriage carrying Mazu and her two attendants walking in front of her with loud firecrackers exploding in the San Francisco Chinese New Year Parade are but a distinctive aspect of Chinese American culture, mingled with dragon dances and young Chinese American children dressed up in traditional Chinese clothes. Symbolically, the firecrackers are used to scare away demons as she inspects her precinct. Mazu's participation in the parade extends far beyond the core expression of secular cultural exchange; instead it is a concession to an inspection later—on her birthday sometime in April. The Ma-tsu Temple U.S.A. views her participation in the parade as her inspection tour, deeply rooted in rich religious symbolism. The by-product is the American version of her inspection tour that serves a religious and secular function. Each year during the parade, she becomes an honored symbol of traditional Chinese religious culture for both the Chinese Americans and non-Chinese viewers.

The Ma-tsu Temple U.S.A. actively invites visitors to participate in their celebrations as a form of cultural exchange. For example, during the Chinese New Year Parade, they warmly accepted non-Taiwanese/Chinese volunteers to be flag carriers, horn blowers, and incense carriers. They even went as far as letting the volunteers wear Mazu's two generals' costumes. After the parade, they invited all the volunteers to participate in the ritual return of Mazu to her throne, followed by a meal where a special soup was served. Lastly, they invited everyone to revisit the temple on any occasion.

Religious Significance

The goddess Tianhou/Mazu ranks second only to the Buddhist bodhisattva Guanyin as a female object of popular devotion throughout the cities and villages of China's coastal provinces: Guangdong, Zhe-jiang, Jiangsu, Shanghai, Shandong, Hebei, Henan, Liaoning, Fujian, Xianggang, and Aomen. Tianhou is also popular in the Chinese diaspora in: Brazil (São Paulo), Burma, France (Paris), India, Indonesia (Java), Japan, Malaysia, Mexico, Penang, the Philippines, Singapore, Thailand, Vietnam, and the United States (Los Angeles, San Francisco, and Honolulu).

The Empress of Heaven, the Goddess of the Sea, Tianhou/Mazu is the second most popular object of devotion in China, Taiwan, and the Chinese diaspora where the bodhisattva Guanyin is venerated. There is a sense among their devotees that Tianhou/Mazu is the daughter, sister, or reincarnation of the compassionate Guanyin. Contemporary veneration of Tianhou/Mazu is heavily politicized. In Taiwan, they view her as a symbol of their independence and sovereignty, while in mainland China she is seen as a potential symbol of unification.

There are contemporary tales of the Goddess of the Sea, Empress of Heaven, safeguarding her devotees from natural disasters, such as seasonal droughts, but her salvation does not end there; instead, modern tales depict her shielding her devotees from American bombs during World War II in Taiwan.

Jonathan H. X. Lee

See also: Entries: Chinese American Religions; Chinese Temples in America; Daoism; Guanyin; Taiwanese American Religions

Further Reading

Bosco, Joseph, and Puay-peng Ho. *Temples of the Empress of Heaven.* Hong Kong: Oxford University Press, 1999.

Lee, Jonathan H. X. "Contemporary Chinese American Religious Life." In James Miller, ed. *Chinese Religions in Contemporary Societies*. Santa Barbara, CA: ABC-CLIO, 2006.

Lee, Jonathan H. X. "Creating a Transnational Religious Community: The Empress of Heaven, Goddess of the Sea Tianhou/Mazu, from Beigang, Taiwan to San Francisco U.S.A." In Lois Ann Lorentzen, Joaquin Jay Gonzalez III, Kevin M. Chun, and Hien Duc Do, eds. *On the Corner of Bliss and Nirvana: Politics, Identity, and Faith in New Migrant Communities*. Durham, NC: Duke University Press, 2009.

Nyitray, Vivian-Lee. "Becoming the Empress of Heaven: The Life and Bureaucratic Career of Tianhou/Mazu." In Elisabeth Bernard and Beverly Moon, eds. *Goddesses Who Rule*. New York: Oxford University Press, 2000.

Tibetan American Religions

Tibetan Americans come from an ancient kingdom nestled in the upper reaches of the Himalayan Mountains, which are some of the tallest and most treacherous mountains in the world. Their country of origin, Tibet, overlooks India to the south and China to the north. In 1949, it was invaded and occupied by Communist China, which resulted in a massive outward flight of Tibetan refugees, many of whom sought political asylum in nearby India, while some made their way to the United States. Since the 1950s, many ethnic Tibetans have been attracted to America, mainly to escape political and religious persecution in their country of origin, where ethnic Chinese immigrants are quickly becoming the new majority and the Chinese-led government is enforcing an assimilation policy. Others have come as a result of chain migration, usually having been sponsored by a family member who came before them. Many Tibetan Americans living in exile, due to the Chinese takeover of Tibet, continue to actively participate in a nationalist independence movement for a Free Tibet. The rallying point of this independence movement is the 14th Dalai Lama, Tenzin Gyatso, who is the contemporary religious leader of Tibetan Buddhism and head of state living in exile. This movement also enjoys popular support from many non-Tibetans living in the United States. Many non-Tibetan Americans are sympathetic to the Dalai Lama's cause. He has been featured in several Hollywood blockbuster films such as *Kundun*, *Red Corner*, and *Seven Years in Tibet*. Meditation books authored by the Dalai Lama are top sellers online and in American bookstores.

The founder of Buddhism is Siddhārtha Gautama (ca. 480–400 BCE), an ancient Hindu prince who broke away from Hinduism, with its rigid hierarchical caste system and complex religious rituals, in search of answers to the perplexing questions of poverty, sickness, old age, and death. In the process, he experimented with austere and extreme yogic practices and meditative techniques, although ultimately he settled on the golden mean of everything in moderation, nothing in excess, in his quest for personal enlightenment (Buddha-hood) and greater societal well-being. Buddha attracted and continues to allure many new followers who, in turn, pass down his teachings to their students, who have carried his religion all over the world. Early on, Buddhism branched out into three primary schools of thought: Theravāda Buddhism, Mahāyāna Buddhism, and Varjayāna Buddhism. Theravāda Buddhism mainly is practiced in Thailand, Sri Lanka, Burma, Cambodia, and Laos. It has sometimes been referred to as the "way of the elders" because every young man apprentices for two years under a master monk to learn the way to enlightenment. Mahāyāna Buddhism is the tradition found in China, Mongolia, Korea, and Japan. It is sometimes compared to Protestantism, wherein people pray to God directly, versus Catholicism, where they often pray through saints, because, under this tradition, people tend to discern the path to enlightenment directly for themselves through their own experiences with nature and the deities, although this is an incomplete definition. Finally, Varjayāna Buddhism is found in Vietnam, Nepal, and Tibet. The term Varjayāna Buddhism is often used interchangeably with Tibetan Buddhism, or Tantrism, to refer to the religion of Tibet, which is a melding of Buddhism and Bon, indigenous beliefs in lake, sky, and mountain spirits.

Varjayāna Buddhism was introduced as a "state" religion in ancient times by rulers over relatively small fiefdoms, who probably viewed it as a handy vehicle through which to garner a broader base of support and organizational structure to further legitimate their claim to power. In Tibet, this religious movement took the form of a theocracy based on Tantric incarnation theology and local spirit beliefs. One way to understand this particular kind of theology is to consider it in terms of metaphysical archetypes or exemplary models of human beings or the stories of creation. Tantric Buddhism shares commonalities with Brahmanism and Hinduism, and other forms of Buddhism, as it also begins from the point of an archetype. For example, it also teaches that the search for enlightenment is like an ancient pearl diver, unadorned by a scuba tank, plunging deep down on the ocean floor for that most precious of pearls, the *atman* of the Brahmans, the absolute and all-transcendent in Buddhism. An unenlightened person believes he or she has an individualized mind and unique self, or ego, but this is an illusion that gives rise to the belief in an individual soul.

Some Tibetan Buddhists, however, interpret this to mean that the one cosmic mind alone is itself unique. Life from this perspective is composed of a myriad of cycles of time and life-bearing emanations. The one cosmic mind appears to be differentiated, but that is an illusion as it is being reflected by subsidiary minds that can only see a tiny bit of the picture. Just as the sun gives off innumerable rays that reach the earth, and a single cloud releases countless raindrops that go into the same ocean, humankind is but a complex of mental illusions. If human beings were not mentally one, according to this teaching, there would be no collective hallucination of the world. If each individual's mind were separate and unique, each person would have his or her own distinctively illusionary world, and no two people would see the world in the same way. Since our consciousnesses are collectively one, we can see the same trees, mountains, sky, and lakes. Therefore, there is one illusionary mind conscious and unconscious to all human beings in which all subsidiary creatures of nature are part. In many ways and to different degrees, there are some commonalities in the variant Buddhist schools of thought. Buddhists, generally, believe that ignorant people are those who lack the ability to "see" the living incarnate in nature, and by extension, fail to follow the five golden precepts (thou shall not kill; thou shall not steal; thou shall not lie; thou shall not drink to excess; and thou shall not engage in sexual misconduct).

Tantric Buddhism incorporates ritualized magic, some of which is found in all branches of Buddhism, and is more deeply rooted in earlier forms of Hinduism. However, when Mahāyāna Buddhism entered Tibet, it intermingled with ancient Tibetan shamanic Bon religious beliefs and practices, which gave rise to a distinctive and separate new branch of Varjayāna Buddhism. Tibetan rituals may include personal and communal magical practices aimed at transforming one's consciousness and entering into a Buddhist state of enlightenment or communion with bodhisattvas (compassionate Buddhas in the ethereal world) or other enlightened beings. Such rituals may include creating *maṇḍalas*, or designs symbolizing the universe, chanting, dancing, playing musical instruments, repeatedly prostrating oneself, and visualizing while meditating. Varjayāna Buddhism grew to become the state religion of Tibet as early as the mid-seventh century, when Tibet was expanding on all sides and engaging in political negotiations with its neighbors. King Songzen Gambo first adopted Buddhism as the state religion because it promised to peacefully unite people of different cultures in a way that was harmonious and respectful of their right to exist. Legend has it that he had two wives, one from Nepal, another from China, who encouraged him to propagate Mahāyāna Buddhism in Tibet.

Tibetan Americans have carried their unique cultural and religious heritage to their new homeland. They continue to modify and adapt many of their religious rituals and traditions to accommodate the changing landscape and social institutions of the United States. Some ritual practices are ongoing, especially those pertaining to individual and communal forms of worship and prayer, or meditation, aimed at transforming one's consciousness so as to better achieve a state of enlightenment. However, it is not yet possible to enact other ritual practices such as sky-burials in the United States. While in Tibet monks and lamas were cremated, ordinary people usually preferred to have a sky-burial. They believed that after the dead person's soul embarked on its journey to reincarnation, the body remained as a carcass. For the first three days after death, the body should not be touched, after which, if the family had enough money, they brought in monks to stay with the dead person, while chanting and performing proper rituals to ensure an auspicious rebirth. During this time, the entire text of the Tibetan Book of the Dead was recited to the departed. The body then would be washed, placed in a fetal position, and wrapped in white cloth. Lamas chanted to guide the soul while leading a ritual to the charnel ground. At the site, the body was cut up into small pieces and placed on a mountaintop as a food offering for birds of prey. This practice is known as *Jhator*, literally, the giving of alms to the birds. It is considered an act of great generosity to allow others to be nourished by one's own remains. As well, it is believed that vultures, or to use the colloquial expression, *Dakini* (sky dancers), are the equivalent of angels for they carry the deceased into heaven, which is believed to be a windy place where souls await reincarnation. This giving of human flesh to vultures is considered honorable because it spares the lives of small animals that the birds might otherwise prey upon. It is said that once upon a time, a Buddha named Sakyamuni fed his flesh to a hawk to spare a pigeon to demonstrate his virtue. While this practice is no longer in place in Tibetan American communities, where cremation ceremonies are more commonly practiced, many associated rituals such as chanting sacred texts to guide the spirit in the ethereal world continue, in modified form, in keeping with ancient Tibetan religion.

Kathleen Nadeau

See also: Entries: Kingdom of Tonga; Trungpa, Chögyam; Wangyal, Ngawang

Further Reading

Evans-Wentz, W. Y. "Introduction." In *The Tibetan Book of the Great Liberation.* London: Oxford University Press, 1973.

Maguire, Jack. *The Essential Buddhism: A Complete Guide to Beliefs and Practices.* New York: Pocket Books, 2001.

Willis, Michael. *Tibet: Life, Myth, and Art.* London: Duncan Baird, 1999.

Tongan Spirituality

The Kingdom of Tonga is an archipelago of approximately 170 islands in the South Pacific, 40 of which are inhabited. The population, in its 2011 census, was 103,036 people. Religiously, the people of Tonga adhere to four main religious affiliations: the Free Wesleyan Church of Tonga (37 percent), Church of Jesus Christ of Latter-day Saints (17 percent), the Free Church of Tonga (16 percent), and Roman Catholic (11 percent). Varied other Christian denominations account for an additional 14 percent of the Tongan population. Members of non-Christian religions make up 4 percent of the national population, while 1 percent of the population reported having no religious affiliation.

Tongan Americans are the third largest Polynesian population in the United States and reflect the religious preferences of the population of their homeland. In the 2010 U.S. Census, there were 57,183 people who reported Tongan ancestry. Seventy-seven percent of the Tongan population in the United States lives in three states, California (40 percent), Utah (23 percent), and Hawai'i (14 percent). The popularity of Utah as a migratory destination of Tongan immigrants is directly related to the rising popularity of the Church of Jesus Christ of Latter-day Saints (Mormons) in the nation of Tonga. This will be further discussed later in this entry.

Beliefs and Practices

According to E. E. V. Collocott (1919), the Tongan creation myths refer to the islands being created through a divine pair, male and female, called Biki and Kele. The offspring of Biki and Kele brought forth the material realm and all of its components that became the nation of Tonga. Early Tongan religious understanding held that the chief of Tonga was in this divine lineage and was the *Tui Tonga*, a supreme chief and lord of the people. Thus, the *Tui Tonga* served as the living connection to the community of spiritual beings that brought forth the Tongan Islands.

This connection to the divine community can be observed in the "Tongan Way" (*Anga' fakatonga*), a concept that permeates the culture and identity. Hansen (2004) reports that the *Anga' fakatonga* is the animating principle of Tongan life, characterized by a generous sense of charity and selflessness that is extended to family, friends, and community. The Tongan Way extends familial relationships and courtesies to those who are not members of the immediate family. It is a point of pride among Tongans, and imparting such generosity to future generations is understood as the task of Tongan parents. To be authentically Tongan is to engage the Tongan Way. The lifestyle is embedded as the first aspect of traditional culture and the challenge to preserve it faced by immigrants to America is defined as the foremost obstacle to be overcome in the retention of the Tongan culture. Nonetheless, the Tongan Way exemplifies the communal nature of the Tongan people, stemming from the original community of deities that brought forth the land and the people.

The communal sense of the Tongan people can also be understood through an observation of the *kava* ritual. *Kava* creates a euphoric response in the body and acts similar to alcohol. *Kava* is a sacred drink derived from a pepper root and is drunk in highly ritualized ceremonies in many Pacific island nations. In Tonga, the ritual begins by seating the participants in an elliptical arc according to a specific hi-erarchical order. When present, the king or, in his absence, the highest ranking individual or an individual to be honored is seated at the center of the ellipse. The *kava* is prepared according to an ancient ritual. Once formal commands have been given by the presiding person of importance, the *kava* is shared in order of rank, highest to lowest, among the participants. As the *kava* drinking progresses, the issues of the day are discussed. This ceremony contains both a sense of sacrifice because the *kava* has some paralyzing properties, and a means of communication with the divine. As the ritual continues into the night, the discussion may clarify the direction of the tribe, community, or nation. Thus, guidance and movement, perhaps even divine instruction, are known through a communal, albeit hierarchical, interaction.

Christianity was introduced in Tonga in the late 18th century, but early efforts to evangelize the archipelago were abandoned by the turn of the 19th century. The Wesleyan denomination (Methodist) sent missionaries to Tonga in 1824. Within seven years, the Tongan king had converted to the Methodist denomination, taking the Christian name of George. King George created a monarchical constitution similar to that of Great Britain. Following the king's conversion, conversions to Methodism were plentiful. Simultaneously, Roman Catholic missionaries were entering the South Pacific region. Due to the size of the region and a lack of focus on one particular island chain, the growth of Roman Catholicism was not as fast as Methodism.

While Christian morality became the new norm, the communal aspect of the Tongan culture, the Tongan Way, presented challenges. It was common that the commandment against stealing was viewed as purely utilitarian by the Tongans, referring only to items needed for use by individuals. An unused saw, for example, would be considered common property should a neighbor have need for it. Such utilitarian attitudes toward private property challenged the common notions of morality held by typical 19th-century European Christians.

The adoption of Christianity by the Tongan people was not without strife. In 1885, the premier of Tonga, also a Methodist minister, Shirley W. Baker, convinced the king to break from the main denomination and to form the Free Wesleyan Church of Tonga. This disruption of coherence in the main Christian church of Tonga allowed for the entrance and expansion of other denominations, particularly the Church of Jesus Christ of Latter-day Saints (Mormons). The growth of both Mormonism and Roman Catholicism was also fostered by church-sponsored schools established to educate children.

Tongan immigration to the United States is a relatively recent phenomenon that hinged on two principal factors: religious and economic. Migrations did not begin on a consistent basis until after 1965, when the United States relaxed immigration laws for non-Europeans. Religiously, initial migrations to the United States were often the result of intense missionary activity in Tonga by the Mormon church and as a result of conversions to the Mormon church. Mormon families would often sponsor Tongan individuals in their migration to the United States. The result is that Utah has the second largest concentration of Tongans in the United States. Economically, as native Tongans began to realize that an individual could make, on average, 10 times the amount of money of their family members at home, the migrations increased. By 1996 the Tongan economy was afloat due to remittance monies sent back to Tonga from working family members overseas.

The increasing Tongan population in the United States has not come without challenges to the sense of Tongan culture. In an effort to re-create Tongan culture in the United States, many families do all they can to pass the Tongan Way to their children through an emphasis on the communal nature of the culture, solidarity with all Tongans in diaspora, and the hope of altruistic sharing. The American culture, however, contradicts such values, and Tongan immigrants are often faced with the challenge of attempting to keep their children within the culture of their homeland while living in a culture that does not share such values. Parents and other extended family members stand in the gap between the culture of home and the culture of the United States.

While religious affiliation is often a place where cultural expressions are embraced, respected, and encouraged, particularly American religious traditions can contradict the Tongan tradition. In many cases, church leadership in the United States has discouraged or banned particular celebrations, dances, or rituals that the American church leadership has deemed inappropriate to the decorum of the faith. *Kava* rituals were frowned upon by the missionaries that brought Methodism to Tonga. A tradition of women dancing and having money physically stuck on them by the participants of the celebration in an effort to raise money for the honoree(s) at a wedding, anniversary, or birthday has been discouraged by the Mormon leaders. This type of dance at a Catholic celebration, however, is allowed. At one church in Arizona, a priest celebrating his anniversary of ordination received the tribute of the parishioners through this type of dance. Inconsistencies between prohibitions and allowances of such celebrations often cause conflict within migrant Tongan Americans who may be seeking a balance between assimilation into the dominant culture and retention of the traditions and celebrations of the culture they have been born into. Children born in the United States, however, are more likely to see the ways of the island culture as a burden, while seeking to integrate more fully within the mainstream American culture.

The Tongan people have an innate sense of solidarity with others. This sense transcends particular religious affiliation, but is often a challenge to those who have migrated to the United States who would seek to retain the cultural values of their homeland. The Tongan Way and the interchange of ideas that take place in a *kava* ceremony stand as a contrast to the American Way of individualism and toeing the "party line" as an employee of a major corporation. Religious belief in those who have come to the United States may serve both the retention of the culture and the loss of it.

Larry Fraher

See also: Entries: Kava; Pacific Islander Religious Cultures

Further Reading

Collocott, E. E. V. "A Tongan Theogony." *Folklore* 30, no. 3 (September 1919): 234–38. Online at http://www.jstor.org /stable/1255664.

Collocott, E. E. V. "The Supernatural in Tonga." *American Anthropologist*, New Series, 23, no. 4 (October–December 1921): 415–44. Online at http://www.jstor.org /stable/481279.

Goodman, Michael A. "Church Growth in Tonga: Historical and Cultural Connections." In Reid L. Neilsen, Stephen C. Harper, Craig K. Manscill, and Mary Jane Woodger, eds. *Regional Studies in Latter-day Saint Church History: The Pacific Isles*. Provo, UT: Religious Studies Center, Brigham Young University, 2008: 37–54. Online at http://rsc.byu.edu/archived /regional-studies-latter-day-saints-history -pacific-isles/3-church-growth-tonga -historical-and-cultural-connections.

Hansen, Moana. "The Loss and Transformation of the Tongan Culture and Its Effect on Tongan American Families in Utah." 2004. http://people.westminstercollege .edu/staff/mjhinsdale/Research_Journal_1 /mo_paper.pdf. Accessed June 2, 2013.

Hirschman, Charles. "Problems and Prospects of Studying Immigrant Adaptation from the 1990 Population Census: From Generational Comparisons to the Process of 'Becoming American.'" *International Migration Review* 28, no. 4 (Winter 1994): 690–713. Online at http://www.jstor.org /stable/2547154.

Turner, James W. "The Water of Life: *Kava* Ritual and the Logic of Sacrifice." *Ethnology* 25, no. 3 (July 1986): 203–14. Online at http://www.jstor.org/stable/3773584.

United States Department of State. "International Religious Freedom Report 2010: Tonga." http://www.state.gov/j/drl/rls /irf/2010/148900.htm. Accessed June 12, 2013.

Urbanowicz, Charles F. "Drinking in the Kingdom of Tonga." *Ethnohistory* 22, no. 1 (Winter 1975): 33–50. Online at http:// www.jstor.org/stable/481279.

Tripiṭaka (Buddhist Canon)

The Tripiṭaka (Pāli, Tipiṭaka) refers to the Buddhist canon. *Tri* means "three" and *piṭaka* is "basket," but here it refers to the three categories of sacred documents. The first, *Sūtra Piṭaka* (Pāli, *Sutta Piṭaka*), refers to the documents attributed to the teaching of the Buddha; the second, *Vinaya Piṭaka*, is the collection of the rules of conduct; the third, *Abhidharma Piṭaka* (Pāli, *Abhidhamma Piṭaka*), is the collection of commentaries. Only a small portion of the tremendous literary output of Buddhist documents remains; and only a fraction of this has been rendered into English. This entry begins with an overview of the history and development of the Buddhist canon. The second section reviews the use of the canon among the Asia American Buddhist traditions.

History

The collection and systemization of the Tripiṭaka began with the First Buddhist Council (*Saṃgīti*, literally, to recite) at the Sattapanni Caves in Rājagṛiha (present-day Ragir), three months after the death of Buddha in ca. 480 BCE. According to Buddhist lore 500 of the leading disciples led by Mahākāśyapa were present when Ānanda, renowned for his great memory, recited over seven months all that he heard in the presence of the Buddha. As a first cousin and later personal attendant for the last 25 years of Buddha's life, Ānanda had been a constant companion and was present at more discourses than any other. He began each of his recitations with the phrase, "Thus have I heard at one time," and continued by recalling the place and naming those in attendance, before relating the words of the Buddha. *Sutras* conclude with the words to the effect, "Upon hearing the Buddha's words, those present rejoiced, accepted, and believed the Teachings." Except for rare exceptions, the Buddhist *sūtra* follows this aforementioned format. Another of the 10 leading disciples, Upāli, recited the *Vinaya*, the monastic rules that were instituted to govern the ordained clerics and the lay community. Those in attendance made oral corrections. At this time the *Sūtra Piṭaka* and *Vinaya Piṭaka* were compiled. The need for clarifications over disagreements led to the composition of commentaries that resulted in a third category, the *Abhidharma Piṭaka*, at a later date.

The First Council met, not to compile or commit to writing, but to recite and confirm what had been committed to memory. In keeping with ancient Brahmanic practice, Buddhists continued to transmit the Dharma (teaching) orally for four centuries. The earliest historical mention of the *sūtras* being recorded comes from Sri Lanka, when Emperor Asoka (ca. 274–36 BCE) sent his son Mahinda (third century BCE) together with scriptures written in Pāli to a people whose language was Singhalese. The difficulties of transmitting the Dharma in another language necessitated recording it on palm leaves and later on paper.

Many unknown authors composed *sūtras* centuries after the Buddha's passing. Critics questioned the value and authenticity of these later compositions that were not recited at the First Council. Followers of Mahāyāna, on the other hand, asserted that while these later compositions might not have been spoken by the Buddha, they nonetheless articulate the import of his teachings. One of the justifications Mahāyānists advanced for the authenticity of these later *sūtras* was that since enlightenment or Buddhahood is open to everyone, the teachings of later disciples who intuited the same truth as the Buddha are equally genuine. The 1901 publication of *Bukkyō tōitsu ron* (*On the unity of Buddhism*) revived the controversy, when the Japanese scholar and cleric Murakami Senshō (1851–1929) asserted that Śākyamuni is the sole historical Buddha and that Amitābha Buddha is an ahistorical abstraction of an ideal personality. This assertion challenged Pure Land orthodoxy. He went on to say that with the exception of the Bodhisattva Maitreya, the other bodhisattvas that appear in Mahāyāna *sūtras* are personifications of the highest ideals of Buddhist wisdom and compassion. Murakami went on to write that faith in the Buddhadharma should not be contingent on the historicity of the Amitābha Buddha.

Historically, of course, it is most likely that the earliest sections of the *Prajñāpāramita*, *Avataṃsaka*, *Saddharmapundarīka* (*Lotus*), and other early Mahāyāna *sūtras* that emerged between a century before and after the Common Era were liturgical chants that gave voice to the spiritual sentiments of different communities of devotees. Their systematic and metaphysical content have led scholars to determine that the *Laṇkāvtāra* and the *Vajracchedikā* (*Diamond*) *Sūtras* appeared later and the *Mahāvairocana Sūtra* and the *Vajraśekhara Sūtra* even

later. Each new ideological development of the Buddha's original teachings has been accompanied by the appearance of new *sūtras*, *śāstras* (commentaries), and other expressions. The canon is continually evolving and being added to.

As noted above, Upāli recited the *vinaya*, the behavioral guidelines conducive to attaining enlightenment. The laity was expected to observe the five cardinal precepts (abstaining from killing, stealing, lying, imbibing intoxicants, and sexual misconduct); clerics were expected to adhere to the *prātimokṣa* (Pāli, *pātimokkha*). *Prāti* means "towards" and *mokṣa* (Pāli, *moksha*) means "liberation." In the Theravāda tradition of Sri Lanka and Southeast Asia, fully ordained monks (*bhikṣu*; Pāli, *bhikkhu*) observe 227 rules; and fully ordained nuns (*bhiksuni*; Pāli *bhikkhunī*), 311. The Chinese monastic tradition also observes similar rules. Even today the *prātimokṣa* is recited by the monastic clergy throughout the world fortnightly to guard against transgressions.

The need to systematize ideas and to "guard" against misinterpretations gave rise to the *śāstras*, treatises or commentaries that offer a more rational account of the content of a *sūtra* or a tradition. Nāgārjuna (ca. 150–250) systematized the ideas of the *Prajñāpāramita Sūtras* with the *Mūla Mādhyamika kārikā* (*Middle Stanzas*). Vasubandhu (ca. 400–500) for his part condensed the tenets of the *Sarvāstivāda* in the 610-verse *Abhidharmakośa śāstra*. Completed in 430, the *Visudhimagga* (*Path of Purity*) by Buddhaghoṣa is a comprehensive manual that condensed and systematized the theory and practice of the Theravādan tradition.

The Tripiṭika

Disputes over the *Vinaya* rules led to the convening of a second council at Vaiśālī about 380 BCE, 100 or so years after the Buddha's *Nirvāṇa* (death). The controversy centered between those who favored a more liberal interpretation of the *Vinaya* and those who favored a more rigid observance of the precepts. Asoka convened the Third Council in Pāṭaliputra (present-day Patna) about 235 BCE to eliminate confusion and establish orthodoxy. Meanwhile the Sri Lankan Theravādins convened a Third Council in the first century BCE at Aloka Lena (present-day Alu Vihara). Kaniśka (first century BCE) convened a Fourth Council in Kashmir to systemize the Sarvāstivāda doctrines. The proliferation of commentaries was no doubt generated by the sectarian differences that can be traced to the Buddha's attitude toward his own insight and teaching. According to Edward Conze, he "stressed that he was a guide, not an authority, and that all propositions must be tested, including his own." As Buddhism settled in different countries, more documents were added to the Tripiṭika. The primary editions of the current Tripiṭika appear in Pāli, Chinese, and Tibetan. A number of Sanskrit documents are extant, but they are not collected in a canon.

The Pāli Tripiṭika is the canon of the present Theravāda tradition. In addition to the *Vinaya Piṭaka* and *Sutta Piṭaka*, the Pāli canon includes seven works in its *Abhidhamma Piṭaka*. The Theravāda's Pāli Tripiṭika is the only extant canon from among the 18 Nikāya (sectarian) schools that were once active. Remnants of other canons exist in Sanskrit and Chinese translations; but most have been lost. In or about 1165 the Sri Lankan King Parākramabāhu (1153–1186) convened the Fourth Council to reform the discipline of the increasingly corrupt Buddhist community and to compile and edit the *sūtras* and commentaries. This effort resulted in the present Theravāda Tripiṭika.

Fearing for the future of their culture and the Buddhadharma under British rule, in 1868 Burmese Buddhist groups convened a council at Mandalay. As a result of this Fifth Buddhist Council, Buddhists engraved in stone the Pāli *sūtras* and built 450 temples in which to house them. In 1954 the Burmese convened the Sixth Council in Rangoon. As a result the Pāli canon was published in Burmese script to commemorate the 2,500th anniversary of Śākyamuni's passing.

While the Chinese and Koreans have published earlier collections, the most definitive edition of the Chinese Tripiṭika is the 100-volume *Taishō Shinshū Daizōkyō* (*Taishō Revised Tripiṭika*). This edition of the Chinese Buddhist canon and its Japanese commentaries was spearheaded by Takakusu Junjirō (1866–1945). In addition to the *Vinaya*, *Sūtra*, and *Abhidhamma Piṭaka*, the *Taishō Revised Tripiṭika* includes works of famous Indian clerics, and histories and catalogues of Buddhist scriptures composed in China and Korea. Its 5,320 titles are bound in 100 volumes. Chinese translations and commentaries are in Volumes 1–55. Japanese works are in volumes 56–85. Volumes 86–97 contain Buddhist-related drawings; and volumes 98–100 are texts of different indexes of Buddhist texts in Japan.

The Tibetans divided texts into two broad categories: the *Kangyur*, "Words of the Buddha" and the *Tengyur*, "Commentaries." The *Kangyur* is divided into the *Vinaya*, *Perfection of Wisdom sūtras*, other *sūtras*, and *tantras*. Currently there are about 12 available versions of the *Kangyur*, including the *Derge, Lhasa, Narthang, Beijing,* and *Stog Palace*, named from the place of publication. In addition to Buddhist texts, the Tibetan texts include works dealing with logic, grammar, medicine, and the arts and crafts.

Doctrinal Uses of the Canon

Buddhists turn to the documents in the Tripiṭika for doctrinal justification and for ritual. This entry mentions only a single example. The following passage from the *Avataṃsaka Sūtra* is one of the primary justifications for the mind-only doctrine advanced by the Yogācāra tradition.

> Like a skillful painter, the mind
> sketches all worlds,
> Creating the whole of reality,
> including the five *skhandhas*
> (elements of existence).
> Mind, Buddha, and sentient beings,
> Amongst these three, there is no
> difference.
> Mind and Buddha are by nature
> without limit.
> One who understands Mind to be
> the creator of every world,
> Intuits the Buddha and his true
> essence.
> (*Avataṃsaka Sūtra. Taishō*, Vol. 9,
> p. 465c)

Another influential document is the *Sadharmapuṇḍarika* or *Lotus Sūtra*. The *Sūtra* provided Zhiyi (531–597) the justification for his interpretation of Buddhist thought and practice, which subsequently provided the basis for Japanese Tendai and the development of many Japanese Buddhist movements. (See entry on Tendai Shū.) Shinran (1173–1263), the founder of Jōdo Shinshū Buddhism, drew inspiration from the Amida Buddha's unconditional compassion articulated in the *Larger Sukhāvatīvyūha Sūtra* and other Pure Land scriptures. (See entry on Buddhist Churches of America.) Korean monks and intellectuals were particularly interested in Tiantai, Huayan, and Chan thought. (See entry on Korean Buddhism.)

More recently the Japanese aesthetician Yanagi Sōetsu (1889–1969) appealed to the *Larger Sukhāvatīvyūha Sūtra* as the canonical basis for his *mingei* (folk art) aesthetics and philosophy. Buddhist scholars look to the ideas of *pratītyasamutpāda*, an extension of the law of *karma*, articulated in the *Avataṃsaka Sūtra, Abhidharmakośaśāstra*, and other texts, to advance Buddhist reflections on bioethics, the environment, and other concerns.

Ritual Use of the Canon

While academics use the Tripiṭika to justify their insights and interpretations, clerics and devotees turn to the documents for didactic and ritual purposes. The *Dhammapada* is one of the most popular collections of Buddha's sayings; the original appears in the *Khuddaka Nikāya* of the Pāli canon. For his part, in the *Dhammapada Atthakatha* (Commentary) Buddhaghoṣa identifies the occasion and context that prompted each of the Buddha's responses. Another popular source for inspiring the Buddhist life is the *Jataka* tales that are also found in *Khuddaka Nikāya*; the more than 500 edifying stories praise the compassion and wisdom the Buddha demonstrated in his previous lives.

In addition to these edifying tales, *sutras* and sections of *sutras* are recited in rituals. Koreans recite the *P'anya simgyŏng* (*Prajñāpāramitā Hṛdaya* or *Heart Sūtra*) and portions of the *Ch'ŏsugygyŏng* (*Dabei Zhoujing*; *Thousand-hand Sūtra*) daily. The *Smaller Sukhāvatīvyūha Sūtra*, commonly chanted at funerals, describes the beauty of the Pure Land and the beings who reside there. The Vietnamese service book complied by the Sagely City of 10,000 Buddhas of Ukiah, California, includes passages from three major Mahāyāna traditions: Zen, Pure Land, and Esoteric. The morning recitation includes the "Shurangama Mantra," the "Great Compassion Mantra," the *Heart Sūtra*, and passages associated with Pure Land and Esoteric Buddhism. The evening recitation includes the *Amitābha Sūtra* and passages from other Pure Land texts. Similarly the Jōdo Shinshū–affiliated Buddhist Churches of America's *Seiten* (literally, *Holy Scriptures*; simply, *Service Book*) contains scripture for daily and special rituals.

The *Chanting Book, Pāli Language with English Translations* contains passages from the Theravāda Pāli canon, meditations, popular prayers, blessings, and petitions that the Thai tradition regularly uses in the United States. The funerals and memorial chants appear in Section 6 and are taken from seven books of the *Abhidhamma*. These chants are reminders that life is transient, suffering is endemic to the human condition, and the self is illusionary. One of the most frequently recited is the "Dhammasanganī" (Enumeration of phenomena) that is chanted at the crematorium or grave site before cremation and/or burial and for memorials.

The introduction of the *Chanting Book* offers four traditional reasons for chanting. First, chanting brings to mind the teaching of the Buddha that reinforces and inspires the Buddhist life; second, chanting purifies the mind and is a means to gain merit toward enlightenment; third, in addition to providing emotional relief from stress, chanting with others quickens a sense of belonging. Finally, chanting is an expression of respect for the Buddha, Dharma, and *Saṇgha*, the community of monks.

Conclusion

The 500 leading disciples who gathered for the First Council assembled to recite (*saṃgīti*) and recollect the words of the Buddha. Like the disciples at the First Council, devotees reciting a *sutra* or sections of a *sutra* are, "ritualistically," in the "presence" of the Buddha and are "hearing" the master speak. The ritual of reciting the words of the Buddha (*sūtra*) links to Buddhism's founder and the original community; the exercise is also an affirmation of the universality and eternality of the Dharma. For many devotees reciting and copying the *sūtras* are devotional exercises that bring great spiritual merit.

Ronald Y. Nakasone

See also: Entries: Buddhist Education; Buddhist Meditation

Further Reading

Beikoku Bukkyōdan kaikyōshi kai, ed. *Seiten* (*Service Book*). San Francisco: Beikoku Bukkyō dan, 1974.

Conze, Edward. *Buddhism: Its Essence and Development.* New York: Harper and Row, 1959.

Conze, Edward. *A Short History of Buddhism.* London: Unwin Paperbacks, 1980.

Council of Thai Bhikkhus in the U.S.A. *Chanting Book.* Houston: Wat Buddhavas of Houston, 2006.

Dharma Realm Buddhist Association. *Van Phat Thanh Thanh Nhat Tung Nghi Quy* (*Daily Recitation Handbook in Sagely City of Ten Thousand Buddhas*). Burlingame, CA, 2008.

Dutt, Sukumar. *Buddhist Monks and Monasteries in India: Their History and Their Contribution to Indian Culture.* London: George Allen and Unwin, 1962.

Fukuura, Seibun. *Bukkyō bungaku gairon* (*An Outline of Buddhist Literature*). Kyoto: Nagata, 1970.

Hirakawa, Akira. *A History of Indian Buddhism, from Śākyamuni to Early Mahāyāna.* Translated by Paul Groner. Honolulu: University of Hawai'i Press, 1990.

Mizuno, Kōgen. *Buddhist Sūtras: Origins, Development, Transmission.* Tokyo: Kosei, 1982.

Murakami Senshō. *Bukkyō tōitsu ron* (*On the Unity of Buddhism*). 3 vols. Tokyo: Shoshi shinsui, 2011.

Trungpa, Chögyam (1939–1987)

Chögyam Trungpa was a charismatic, albeit controversial, Tibetan personality. As the 11th reincarnation of the 14th-century Trungpa Künga-gyaltzen, who was the incarnation of Maitreya Bodhisattva, Chö-

Chögyam Trungpa Rinpoche (1939–1987) was a Tibetan Buddhist meditation master and acclaimed teacher of Tibetan Buddhism. In 1974, he founded the Naropa University (formerly Institute) in Boulder, Colorado. This was the first accredited Buddhist university in North America. (Kenn Bisio/The Denver Post/Getty Images)

gyam Trungpa was the abbot of Surmang Monastery in the rugged Kham mountain region that straddles the present-day Tibet Autonomous Region and Sichuan Province, China. Chögyam Trungpa belonged to the Kagyü lineage, one of the four major Tibetan Buddhist traditions. He also trained in the Nyingma tradition, the oldest of the lineages, and was an advocate of the *ri-me* (nonsectarian) movement that sought to consolidate the teachings and methods of the different Tibetan Buddhist traditions.

With a small number of colleagues, when the Communist Chinese entered Tibet Trungpa fled on horseback and on foot through the Himalayas to India in 1959. The Dalai Lama appointed the 20-year-old monk to be the spiritual advisor to the Young Lamas Home School in Dalhousie, India. In 1963 he entered Oxford University to study comparative religions, philosophy, and the fine arts. For a number of reasons, including a car accident that partially paralyzed the left side of his body in 1970, Trungpa abandoned his monastic vows and married 16-year-old Diana Pybus. The couple moved to the United States where he established Tail of the Tiger (now known as Karmē-Chöling) Meditation Center in Barnet, Vermont. In less than 20 years, he established Varjadhatu, Shambhala Training, and the Naropa Insitute, and authored *The Sacred Path of the Warrior, Cutting Through Spiritual Materialism*, *The Myth of Freedom*, *Crazy Wisdom*, and other books.

Desiring to firmly root the Buddhist Dharma (teaching) in the West, Chögyam Trungpa established Vajradhātu, an umbrella organization for a number of meditation centers. He developed Shambhala Training, an approach to meditation for those who were not interested in Buddhism. Inspired by Shambhala, a mythical realm of peace and purity mentioned in Indo-Tibetan documents, Shambhala Training proposed to cultivate a sacred outlook, gentleness, mindful awareness, and determination to create an enlightened society. Fundamental to Shambhala Training is appreciation for the basic goodness and inherent dignity of oneself, others, and the world.

In 1977 at Trungpa's urging, Naropa Institute applied for regional accreditation from the North Central Association of Colleges and Schools. Naropa Institute received accreditation in 1986 and became Naropa University, a private liberal arts college that incorporates meditation practice in its curriculum. Located in Boulder, Colorado, the university takes its name from Naropa (1016–1100), the rector of Nalanda University.

Chögyam Trungpa's often outrageous, unexpected, and bizarre behavior has been understood to be an expression of *yeshe chölwa* or "crazy wisdom," a characteristic of memorable Buddhist personalities. "Crazy wisdom" refers to an innocent condition of mind or a being who is completely awake, unfettered by social convention. He consumed liberal amounts of alcohol, smoked heavily, and it is rumored that he used cocaine. On more than one occasion, he would appear totally drunk, but deliver brilliant and cohesive lectures on rarefied points of meditation. He was reported to be sexually promiscuous and to have transmitted AIDS to his partners. Chögyam Trungpa died of cardiac arrest on September 28, 1986, in Nova Scotia, Canada, and his body was cremated at Karmē Chöling.

Ronald Y. Nakasone

See also: Entries: Tibetan American Religions

Further Reading

Midal, Fabrice. *Recalling Chögyam Trungpa.* Boston: Shambala, 2005.

Mukpo, Diana. *Dragon Thunder: My Life with Chögyam Trungpa.* Boston: Shambala, 2008.

Trungpa, Chögyam. *Cutting through Spiritual Materialism.* Boston: Shambala, 1987.

Trungpa, Chögyam. *Crazy Wisdom (Dharma Ocean)*. Boston: Shambala, 2001.

Seager, Richard Hughes. *Buddhism in America*. New York: Columbia University Press, 1999.

Tu Weiming (1940–)

Tu Weiming is one of the most renowned Chinese Confucian scholars (scholars in traditional Confucianism assumed the role of the priest in performing rituals) in America, if not in the world, today. Born in Kunming, Yunnan Province, China, Tu moved to Taiwan at an early age, where he obtained his BA degree (1961) at Tunghai University before coming to the United States for his advanced training. He received both his MA (1963) and PhD (1968) degrees from Harvard University. He taught at Tunghai University, Taiwan, Princeton University, and the University of California at Berkeley before returning to Harvard University in 1981 as professor of Chinese history and philosophy.

As of 2014 Tu holds the following positions: director of the Institute for Advanced Humanistic Studies at Peking University,

From left, Peking University President Xu Zhihong, Peking University Council Chairman Min Weifang, Director of Harvard Yenching Institute Tu Weiming, and former U.S. President George H. W. Bush speak to one another at the opening ceremony of the 2005 Beijing Forum on November 16, 2005, in Beijing, China. The Beijing Forum, held from November 16 to 18, is an international academic forum focusing on academic and cultural exchange. Bush was in Beijing for a two-day seminar on China-U.S. relations. U.S. President George W. Bush was scheduled to arrive in Beijing on November 19 for a three-day visit to China. (China Photos/Getty Images)

director of the Harvard-Yenching Institute, Harvard-Yenching professor of Chinese history and philosophy and of Confucian studies, and a professorship in the Department of East Asian Languages and Civilizations, Harvard University. His third position is unique in that he is the first to become a named professor of Confucian studies in America.

He has authored and edited more than 30 books in Chinese and English and published more than 150 articles, essays, and interviews. Some of his books in English have been translated into Chinese. Tu has received six honorary degrees from various universities and holds honorary professorships at Renmin University, Zhejiang University, and Shanghai Academy of Social Sciences, all of which are in the People's Republic of China. He was the recipient of the Second Thomas Barry Prize at the United Nations and the Tenth T'oege Prize in South Korea. He has given endowed lectures in Hong Kong, India, and South Korea. Tu has assumed a wide range of administrative positions in academia. His other services to the academic community are equally impressive.

As a Confucian scholar, Tu is audacious and visionary in his articulation of the future of Confucianism. As early as 1986 he published an article, "Toward a Third Epoch of Confucian Humanism: A Background Understanding," in which he argued that the potentiality of a third Confucian revival was real and forthcoming. Three years later he revised his 1976 monograph *Centrality and Commonality: An Essay on Chung-yung* by adding a chapter titled "On Confucian Religiousness," when the question whether or not Confucianism is a religion was hotly debated. In this chapter he addressed the crucial and timely question, "What is the Confucian way of being religious?" He defined it as "ultimate self-transformation as a communal act and as a faithful dialogical response to the transcendent" (Tu, 1989, p. 94). He further pointed out that "Confucian religiosity is expressed through the infinite potential and the inexhaustible strength of each human being for self-transformation" (Tu, 1989, p. 94). This was followed by two volumes published successively in 2003 and 2004 titled *Confucian Spirituality*, which he co-edited with Mary Evelyn Tucker.

Some of his selected books are *Confucian Thought: Selfhood as Creative Transformation*; *Centrality and Commonality: An Essay on Confucian Religiousness* (a revised and enlarged edition of *Centrality and Commonality: An Essay on Chung-yung*); *Humanity and Self-Cultivation; Way, Learning, and Politics; Essays on the Confucian Intellectual; Confucian Tradition in East Asian Modernity: Exploring Moral Education and Economic Culture in Japan and the Four Mini-Dragons* (editor); *Confucianism and Human Rights* (co-editor with Wm. Theodore de Barry).

Edmond Yee

See also: Entries: Confucianism

Further Reading

Chinese Civilisation Centre. www.cciv.cityu .edu.hk. Accessed July 14, 2014.

Tu, Weiming. *Centrality and Commonality: An Essay on Confucian Religiousness*. Revised and enlarged edition of *Centrality and Commonality: An Essay on Chung-yung*. Albany: State University of New York Press, 1989.

Tu Weiming Website. tuweiming.net. Accessed July 14, 2014.

Tule Lake

The Tule Lake Pilgrimage was inaugurated by students and activists in the late 1960s. Initially, informal groups traveled to the site of many WRA (War Relocation Authority) camps to learn more about the experiences of those who had been interned during World War II. The pilgrimage was a part of the political and social activism of Nisei and Sansei who were seeking political redress and an official apology from the United States government for the internment. The Tule Lake Committee organized their first pilgrimage in 1978; as of 2012, there have been 19 official pilgrimages. (Pilgrimages to other WRA camps, most notably Manzanar, have also taken place on a regular basis since the 1970s and 1980s.) These events have served a variety of purposes; they educate younger generations about the experiences of Issei and Nisei who were imprisoned during the war, and they have provided a platform from which Nisei can share their memories. The pilgrimages have also served to reconcile families, communities, and friends whose lives were thrown into chaos by the events of World War II.

Tule Lake, located in northern California on the Oregon border, was the home of one of the 10 War Relocation Authority detention centers established during World War II. It was the only "segregation center," heavily armed and enclosed by barbed wire, because it housed 18,000 members of the Japanese community who were considered disloyal. When the United States government circulated a questionnaire that asked if they were willing to serve in the military and swear unqualified allegiance to the United States and renounce allegiance to Japan, families were divided. Answering "yes" rendered noncitizen Issei stateless and asked Nisei to fight for a country that imprisoned them. Those who answered "no" to either or both of those questions were branded disloyal and sent to Tule Lake. More than 5,000 Nisei who renounced their citizenship as a protest or to preserve family unity were sent to Tule Lake.

According to Joanne Doi, returning to Tule Lake is a spiritual experience on many levels. In addition to providing a space for communal reconciliation and recognition of the painful events of the past, the pilgrimage is an opportunity to "give voice to a complex silence" of those who were victimized and shamed by their country and their parents' country. This silence, she suggests, can refer to the unwillingness (or inability) of Nisei survivors to talk about their experiences with their children, a silence that instigated their search for answers. Silence is also an integral part of all religious ceremonies and practices; prayer and meditation consecrate silence. The Tule Lake Pilgrimage has used silence to open up a space for Nisei to share their memories. The pilgrimages stimulate dialogue and reconciliation between Nisei who faced shame and ostracism and their children who very often knew nothing about their family history. The pilgrimages are organized as retreats where dialogue is encouraged. Many Nisei who had never spoken about their experiences were moved to speak during the pilgrimage. By using sacred terminology, the organizers reinforced a sense of reverence and respect for the suffering of their community and families.

Although the pilgrimages are deliberately nonsectarian, they elicit comparison to both Western and Asian religious traditions. Pilgrimages to sacred sites—places of miracles and shrines dedicated to teachers and saints—commemorate pain, suffering, and transcendence. Pilgrimages to natural sites—mountaintops or forest groves—validate the idea of sacredness in the beauty of everyday life. The Tule Lake Pilgrimage invites Buddhists and Christians to remember, forgive, and reconcile in a setting that is both beautiful and gives rise to painful memories.

The pilgrimage takes on secular and sacred meaning; it is political and personal, an attempt to forge reconciliation but also an opportunity to remind the larger community to never forget. Because the event typically takes place on or around the Fourth of July, the pilgrimage can also be considered an expression of patriotism, albeit one that is often tinged with bitterness.

In 2006, Tule Lake Camp was designated a National Historic Landmark; in 2008 it was made a part of the World War II Valor in the Pacific National Monument, designations that will ensure the preservation of the camp.

Lori Pierce

See also: Entries: Japanese American Internment, Remembrance, and Redress

Further Reading

Densho. "Sites of Shame: An Overview of the Japanese American Detention Centers." http://www.densho.org/learning/default .asp?path=sitesofshame/SitesOfShame.asp. Accessed July 16, 2014.

Doi, Joanne. "Tule Lake Pilgrimages: Dissonant Memories, Sacred Journey." In Jane Naomi Iwamura and Paul R. Spickard, eds. *Revealing the Sacred in Asian and Pacific America.* New York: Routledge, 2003, pp. 273–89.

National Park Service. "Tule Lake Unit: World War II Valor in the Pacific Monument." http://www.nps.gov/tule/historyculture/in dex.htm. Accessed July 16, 2014.

Tule Lake Committee. "History of Tule Lake Concentration Camp and Pilgrimage." http://www.tulelake.org/. Accessed July 16, 2014.

Tzu Chi Foundation U.S.A.

Tzu Chi (Ciji) Foundation is a large and multifaceted Buddhist organization based in Taiwan, best known for its charitable activities and altruistic ethos. Tzu Chi represents the fastest-growing humanistic or this-worldly lay Buddhist movement in the Chinese cultural sphere in the 21st century, and it is one of the world's largest nonprofit relief and charity organizations. Worldwide this lay Buddhist organization claims more than five million followers, with branches in 39 countries; it has implemented rescue and relief work in over 61 countries, including Afghanistan, Iran, El Salvador, and South Africa.

Its extraordinary growth is among the notable features of the Taiwanese Buddhist revival of the late 20th century. It is also intertwined with the social and political changes that marked Taiwan's transition to democracy and the growth of an urbanized middle class. Although it is still headquartered in Taiwan—where it is one of the

Residents who were displaced by floodings receive blankets, cash, and food supplies from the Chinese Buddhist Tzu Chi Foundation during relief distribution to some 1,000 families at the floodstricken city of Marikina east of Manila, Philippines, November 19, 2009. Hundreds of thousands of residents were affected by the worst flooding in 42 years in the capital following back to back typhoons and tropical storms that also killed more than 800 people. (AP Photo/Bullit Marquez)

largest, richest, and most powerful religious groups—over the years Tzu Chi has grown into a complex organization with vast resources and an impressive global footprint. In terms of its membership, it is primarily a lay organization; however, at the top it has a monastic leadership, personified by Cheng Yen (Zhengyan, 1937–), a charismatic nun that founded the organization and still remains its undisputed leader.

The organization was founded in 1966 by Venerable Master Cheng Yen and 30 female followers. She was born into a prosperous Taiwanese family and became interested in Buddhism as a young woman.

Although lacking formal education, she officially joined a nun's order under the auspices of Yinshun (1905–2005), arguably the most respected scholar-monk in Taiwan. When Cheng Yen founded Tzu Chi in 1966, its original mission was to help the poor and educate the rich. The next year she established a convent, the Abode of Still Thoughts, which to this day remains the spiritual nucleus of Tzu Chi. She instituted a self-sustaining lifestyle for her monastic disciples, although the majority of her followers were (and still are) pious laywomen. While not known for her sophisticated understanding of Buddhist doctrines, Cheng Yen has emerged as a prominent advocate of humanistic Buddhism, whose this-worldly vision and teachings are important elements of modern Chinese Buddhism.

From early on, Tzu Chi's charitable activities involved wide-ranging involvement of the laity, who made generous donations and volunteered their time and expertise. Over the last four decades Tzu Chi has experienced extensive growth in its membership and notable expansion of its activities, first throughout Taiwan and then increasingly around the world. Currently its five million members come from 45 countries. Tzu Chi's success in mobilizing legions of volunteers and allocating large amounts of resources, dedicated to an array of welfare projects and charitable undertakings, is largely based on its effective organizational structure, which is set up hierarchically. The organization oversees many local branches, located across Taiwan and other parts of Asia, as well as in the Americas, Europe, Africa, and Australia.

Tzu Chi's public outreach and charitable work—ostensibly undertaken in the spirit of universal compassion—involve helping the poverty-stricken, delivering disaster relief, and providing free medical care. Its leaders and volunteers are also involved in educational activities and environmental protection. Tzu Chi opened its first free clinic in 1972. That was followed by the establishment of a hospital (in 1986), the creation of a bone marrow donor registry (in 1994), and the opening of nursing and medical schools (in 1989 and 1994). Tzu Chi also runs schools, a university, a television station, and publishing ventures that produce a variety of magazines and books. Its volunteers also organize youth camps and public lectures.

Tzu Chi's mission is focused on charity, medicine, education, and culture. As such, Tzu Chi is intimately involved in providing social, educational, charitable, and medical relief to the underprivileged and underserved throughout and beyond Taiwan, reaching the United States and other parts of Asia, including mainland China. Tzu Chi has been especially proficient at providing disaster relief after typhoons, floods, and earthquakes. The provision of international relief started in 1991, when the American branch of Tzu Chi in Los Angeles helped victims of a cyclone in Bangladesh. After the serious earthquake in Taiwan on September 21, 1999, Tzu Chi relief workers did most of the early rescue work as government officials dallied over who had jurisdiction. In addition, Tzu Chi has continuously provided medical and charitable relief to areas in Southeast Asia following the December 26, 2004, tsunamis and earthquake. Tzu Chi U.S.A. became a national player in relief work following the terrorist attacks of 9/11 in New York City and in the aftermath of Hurricane Katrina that shattered the Gulf Coast. In the United States alone, there are a total of 49 Tzu Chi branches, including three free clinics.

In 1994, Tzu Chi created the first bone marrow registry in Asia. The organization encouraged volunteers and members to organize blood drives in their neighborhoods throughout Taiwan. Within two years, Tzu Chi's bone marrow bank became one of the major registries in East Asia. Today, Tzu Chi Bone Marrow Bank is connected to those of other countries, making it more efficient and hence crossing national as well as potential ethnic and racial boundaries. Tzu Chi's transnational structure grows larger and more intricate day by day, and its global mission of environmentalism, health care, education, cultural pluralism, and disaster relief extends worldwide. Tzu Chi's organizational structure is transnational in scale, but its mission is global in ambition. Tzu Chi has transplanted its "just do it" socially engaged Chinese Buddhist relief work onto the global religious landscape. Compassion coupled with *upaya* (expedient means), two central teachings of Mahāyāna Buddhism, guide its relief efforts to serve clients without regard to age, sex, race, ethnicity, class, or religious affiliation. Although a religious institution, its primary goal is not evangelical, but rather, it encourages followers to emulate or to become living bodhisattvas who actualize compassion to assist others in need. As such, Tzu Chi is an important player in the development of global civil society.

Jonathan H. X. Lee

See also: Entries: Chinese American Religions; Chinese Temples in America; Hsi Lai Temple; Taiwanese American Religions

Further Reading

Huang, C. J. *Charisma and Compassion: Cheng Yen and the Buddhist Tzu Chi Movement.* Cambridge, MA: Harvard University Press, 2009.

Madsen, Richard. *Democracy's Dharma: Religious Renaissance and Political Development in Taiwan.* Berkeley: University of California Press, 2007.

U

Ullambana Assembly

The Ullambana Assembly or Yulanpan Hui (often translated into English as the Ghost Festival) takes place on the 15th day of the seventh moon according to the lunar calendar. The date coincides with the end of the rainy season retreat observed by Indian monks. Thus, it is also a time for spiritual and physical renewal. This assembly traces its source to *The Buddha Speaks the Ullambana Sūtra* or *The Yulanpan Jing* of the Mahāyāna tradition. This *sūtra* records the story of the filial act of Mulian (Ven. Mahamaudgalyayana), a disciple of the Buddha, toward his mother. This tale with variations is also found in *The Sūtra on Offering Bowls to Repay Kindness* and *The Pure Land Yulanpan Sūtra*. In brief, after realizing the sixth level of insight, Mulian wishes to repay his parents for their kindness in rearing him. With his divine eye, he sees that his mother, who has been reborn in the realm of the hungry ghosts, is unable to eat or drink. Whatever food she tries to consume transforms into burning coals before it reaches her mouth.

Deeply saddened, Mulian relates the situation to the Buddha who tells him that his mother's offenses are too great for him alone to rescue her. It will take the collective spiritual power of the assembled *sangha* from the 10 directions to liberate her. The Buddha instructs Mulian to prepare offerings with hundreds of favors and the five fruits for the monks on the 15th day of the seventh moon. Mulian follows the Buddha's instruction, liberating his mother from suffering.

The above brief summary of *The Buddha Speaks the Ullambana Sūtra* shows that the main theme of the Mulian story is filial piety toward parents, with a collateral motif of making offerings to the *sangha*.

The Beginning of the Tradition

When Mahāyāna Buddhism entered China is a matter of debate. According to the Buddhist tradition, Emperor Mingdi (r. 58–75 CE) of the Later Han Dynasty (25–220 CE) had a dream of the golden Buddha in the year 65. He immediately sent a Confucian scholar to India with the intended purpose of bringing back Buddhist *sūtras*. The scholar returned with two Indian monks and many scriptures loaded on white horses. In the year 68 the first Buddhist monastery, Baima Si (White Horse Monastery), was built in Luoyang, the capital.

However, as early as the year 65 a community of monks was active in northern Jiangsu province under the protection of the emperor's brother, a Daoist. The actual Chinese contact with Buddhism may have been as early as the second century BCE through the envoys to Central Asia. And in the year 2 BCE, a Chinese scholar traveling through one of the Central Asian kingdoms also learned about Buddhism. Buddhism did not become popular until the Southern-Northern dynasties (420–589 CE). It was said that Emperor Wudi (r. 503–548 CE) of the Liang Dynasty (503–557 CE), a devout Buddhist, established the Ullambana Assembly.

The Tang Dynasty

During the Tang Dynasty (618–907 CE), Buddhism and Daoism alternately dominated Chinese spiritual and intellectual life. But the Ullambana Assembly, perhaps influenced by the popular *The Transformation Text on Mulian Saving His Mother*, was celebrated in a combined interest of monks, householders, and ancestors by no later than mid-Tang. The assembly's popularity even reached the inner court of the imperial palace. The offerings went well beyond what transpired in *The Buddha Speaks the Ullambana Sūtra* to include endowed land, a variety of gifts from the state to the officially sponsored monasteries, seasonal delicacies, paper flowers, carvings from wood and bamboo, and so forth.

At the same time, the observance of the assembly appeared to have gone well beyond the intention of the canonical text, and it soon become a popular Chinese festival. And this left a deep impression on Ennin (794–864 CE), the Japanese monk who had come to Tang China to study Buddhism. The widespread popularity of the assembly is also recorded in the story of Cui Wei of the Tang Dynasty in *Juan* 34, in the *Taiping Guangji*, a work that consists of hagiographies and stories from the pre-Qin dynasty (221–207 BCE) to the early Northern Song Dynasty (960–1127 CE).

The Song Dynasty

The observance of the Ullambana Assembly during the Northern Song Dynasty shifted from focusing on the Buddha and the *sangha* to offering sacrifices to ancestors and conducting ceremonies to release souls from suffering in the netherworld. The state set aside places where ceremonies could be held for soldiers who died on battlefields for the purpose of releasing their souls from suffering. In addition, "paper currency" was burned for their use in the next world. Furthermore, entertainment was introduced during the observance. The most noticeable was the performance of the variety show *How Mulian Saved His Mother*.

By the time of the Southern Song Dynasty (1127–1279 CE), the assembly definitely had become part of folk custom. The author of *Suishi Zaji* observed that most of the monasteries continued the assembly in accordance with the canonical tradition, but the people used this occasion to make sacrificial offerings to their deceased parents and ancestors. They also made "Ullambana basins" by using bamboo sticks to make four-legged stands with a fifth stick in the middle. They would hang a picture of Mulian in the center and burn it along with the "paper currency" after they had offered a sacrifice to him. Moreover, by the time of Emperor Ningzong (r. 1195–1224), people began to enjoy the occasion as a three-day holiday: the day before, the day of, and the day after the Ullambana Assembly.

Even monks were swept into the popular culture. On the day of the assembly, according to the *Mengliang Lu* (The Record of Mengliang), monks from the monasteries in Hangzhou used the money and the rice donated by benefactors to make sacrifices to the dead.

The Ming and the Qing Dynasties

By the time of the Ming (1368–1644 CE) and the early Qing (1644–1911 CE) dynasties, the Ullambana Assembly had spread all over China; the observance became ever more colorful and carnival-like. This shift of focus seems to coincide with the decline of Buddhism in China and the rise of the entertainment industry. Elements of the Daoist Zhongyuan Festival, which also takes place on the 15th day of the seventh moon, had similarly infiltrated into the assembly. The Chunchang chapter in the *Dijing Jingwu Lü* tells us that the monasteries in Beijing, the capital, observed the Ullambana Assembly during the day. But at night, monks and householders and others would go to the pools in the northern or the southeastern parts of the city to set floating "river lamps" to light the way for wandering spirits; in other words, to release their souls from suffering. They also set off fireworks.

Fucha Dunmin of the Qing Dynasty in the *Yanjing Suishi Ji* reports that in addition to the traditions inherited from the previous dynasties, the Qing observance of the Ullambana Assembly even included the *yangko* dance (popular in rural areas) as well as lion dances. There were also theatrical performances of the Mulian dramas, most likely those written during the Yuan (1271–1368 CE) and Ming Dynasties, as well as the ceremony of releasing souls from suffering. Moreover, people dressed up in various ghost costumes and pretended to be ghosts while dancing in the streets.

The 20th Century

The last century witnessed even more Daoist elements being incorporated into the Ullambana Assembly. People from different locales celebrated the occasion more and more according to the local Daoist customs. For example, according to a local gazette of Fujian Province, the people designated the 15th day of the seventh month as the Burning Paper Festival. On this day families made sacrifices to the ancestors at their graves. The offerings included the provision of winter clothes made of paper.

In Shandong Province the sacrifices to the ancestors took place in the afternoon. The descendants carried bamboo to the graves to make "Ullambana basins," paper to make clothes and hats for the ancestors, incense, and vegetarian food as well as "paper currency" for the deceased to use in the next world.

In brief, the Ullambana Assembly has become progressively more and more an occasion for entertainment and merriment as well as for performing ancestral rites, rather than spiritual renewal in the Buddhist tradition.

Ullambana Assembly in the United States

Chinese Buddhist monasteries of the Mahāyāna lineage observe the Ullambana Assembly in the United States today. The ceremony may vary according to each monastic tradition. The entertainment aspect, if present at all, definitely does not rival that of the Ming and Qing dynasties. For one thing, it is hard, if not downright impossible, to find a theatrical troupe to perform the Mulian dramas.

Here is a description of the ceremony performed at the Sagely City of Ten Thousand Buddhas in Ukiah, California, and other monasteries in North America belonging to this lineage. Preparations begin two to three weeks prior to the Ullambana Assembly. A basin is placed in the middle and slightly to the front of the long table that has been put before the image of the Buddha in the Buddha Hall. Householders put their offerings into the basin, or place them on the table. In *The Buddha Speaks the Ullambana Sūtra* the offerings consist of "one hundred favors and the five fruits . . . incense, oil, lamps, beds, and bedding." Today's offerings are based on the needs of the *saṅgha*, ranging, for example, from a bar of soap to a bag of rice to whatever the *saṅgha* can use. On the day of the assembly, the householders and other community participants begin to assemble between 8:00 a.m. and 9:00 a.m. for an hour-long ceremony.

The ceremony itself consists of four parts. Part One is called "Incense Praise." The Ceremonial Master and the participants together begin the ceremony by chanting:

> Incense in the Censer now is
>   burning; all the Dharma realm
> Receives the fragrance, from afar
>   the sea vast host of Buddhas and
>   inhale its sweetness
> In every place auspicious clouds
>   appearing,

> Our sincere intention thus fulfilling,
>   as all Budhhas now show their
>   perfect body.
> Na Mo Incense Cloud Canopy
>   Bodhisattva Mahasattva

The last line is repeated three times, the participants bowing each time and ending with a half-bow.

Part Two of the ceremony consists of reciting *The Buddha Speaks the Ullambana Sūtra* or *The Yulanpan Jing* three times. Part Three is the recitation of the following mantra: *Na wo mi li dwo pe ye swo he*, "True words for repaying parents' kindness."

All participants circumambulate in single file around the Buddha Hall and around the statue of the Buddha while reciting the mantra. After an hour they return to their places for the fourth part of the ceremony.

Part Four is the "Transference of Merit" during which the following is chanted:

> I vow that this merit will adorn the
>   Buddha's Pure Land,
> Paying Four Kinds of Kindness
>   Above,
> Aiding Those Below in the Three
>   Paths Suffering,
> May those Who See and Hear All
>   Bring Forth the Bodhi Heart,
> And When This Retribution Body is
>   Done,
> Be Born Together in the Land of
>   Ultimate Bliss.

At the conclusion of the ceremony everyone is invited to share a communal meal, which is part of the Ullambana offerings. During the meal, monks and nuns share the Dharma with the people. At the conclusion of the meal, the assembly disperses.

What then is the significance of the Ullambana Assembly ceremony? To paraphrase a Dharma master: The ceremony is just an external representation, an opportunity to deeply reflect and to acknowledge the kindness of one's parents. The real significance of the ceremony lies in the sincerity of the participants in wishing to repay this kindness.

Edmond Yee

See also: Entries: Ghost Festival/Zhongyuan Festival; Qingming Festival

Further Reading

Teiser, Stephen E. *The Ghost Festival in Medieval China.* Princeton, NJ: Princeton University Press, 1996.

Unification Church (Family Federation for World Peace and Unification)

The Unification Church (UC) is an organization that emphasizes family life and peace with the goal of returning humans to the God-intended utopian state that was lost in the primal fall of Adam and Eve. Before 2010 it was called the Family Federation for World Peace and Unification— a name that is still sometimes used—and previously it was called the Holy Spirit Association for the Unification of World Christianity. The U.S. headquarters are in New York City, and there are approximately 100 churches or communities spread across most major cities and suburbs, providing a presence in all states except Mississippi. There are approximately 25,000 members and the largest community is in Clifton, New Jersey. Members have been popularly referred to as "Moonies," although this carries pejorative connotations. The UC is most widely known for its mass weddings, or Blessings. This entry will briefly survey the beliefs and practices of the UC followed by a sketch of its general history.

Beliefs and Practices

Sun Myung Moon (1920–2012) founded the UC in Korea in 1954. Moon claimed to have been visited by various religious personalities, including Jesus who "asked him to assume responsibility for the mission of establishing God's kingdom on earth" (Barker, 2005, 9466). These claimed revelations form part of the *Divine Principle*, a foundational text for the teachings of the UC. *Divine Principle* presents a particular interpretation of the Bible that views the UC, and in particular the arrival of Sun Myung Moon, as significant events that complete the message of the Bible. Especially significant is the story of Adam and Eve and original sin. "Adam and Eve were created so God could have a loving 'give-and-take' relationship with them. The original plan was that they should mature to a state of perfection when they would be blessed in marriage; their children and their children's children would populate a sinless world in complete harmony with God." However, tempted by the archangel Lucifer, Adam and Eve circumvented this plan and had a sexual relationship apart from God's blessing and then passed on sin to all subsequent humans. Human history is thus interpreted "as an attempt by God and man . . . to restore the world to the state originally intended by God."

It is this basic utopian framework that helps organize other significant beliefs and practices within the UC. With regard to belief, there is an anticipation of Messianic True Parents who will do what Adam and Eve did not. The UC teaches that Sun Myung Moon and his wife Hak Ja Han are these expected True Parents. With regard to practice, this belief informs the most significant rite for the group, Blessings. Blessings are wedding ceremonies where a male and female couple's relationship is transferred "from a Satan-centered to a God-centered lineage under Moon's messianic authority." Before receiving a Blessing, individuals are required to go through a preparatory stage of matching. Through self-study and workshops that emphasize reflection on what makes a good self and good relationships, individuals are prepared to enter a matching process that will connect them with an ideal partner and then lead to a Blessing of that partnership. However, there is a distinction between the matching processes for adult Unificationists—those who were not born to a Blessed couple—and Blessed children who are already within a Blessed lineage. In addition, there is a more restricted level of matching called Cheon Il Guk, which, according to UC resources, "is designed to represent the ideal of innocent and pure Adam and Eve, prior to the fall" and serves as a key element in bringing about the UC's utopian vision. Restricted to individuals of a certain age, purity, and physical status, among other criteria, Cheon Il Guk matching involves close supervision from the True Parents.

History

During the years after its founding in 1954, the UC faced resistance in Korea and eventually Moon moved to the United States in the 1970s, although there was a missionary presence before this. Through the 1970s and 1980s the organization experienced growth, in part, due to extensive public speaking and hosting leading academics at international conferences and local and national dignitaries at lavish dinners. The organization extended its reach through business, cultural, publishing, and educational ventures in addition to rigorous evangelistic activities. Despite the UC's Korean origins, converts within the United States early on tended to be primarily young, white, and middle-class, although the group is making efforts to foster racial diversity.

The year 1992 marked a turning point for the UC, when Moon asserted that he and his wife were the anticipated "True Parents of humankind and therefore were jointly The Lord of the Second Advent." After this, in 1997, Moon asserted that a new era had begun, the Completed Testament Age. At this point, the organization of the UC was superseded by a more outward-focused structure called the Family Federation for World Peace and Unification, which would take the UC's utopian goals to another level. The objective of the Family Federation lies in transforming families into ideal families, thereby restoring and perfecting God's ideal of creation and establishing the ideal heavenly world. Key indicators of this outward focus were extending the ritual of Blessings to non-Unification members and promoting peace initiatives, especially via the newly formed Universal Peace Federation. However, this shift in focus led to tensions within the organization over its future direction, including the anticipated transfer of leadership from Moon to his children. There has recently been a return to more of a church organization, emphasizing member growth and practical living. In support of this, the UC currently maintains a diversity of ministry and education programs. While the Blessing and family aspect remains central, there are also programs focused on college students and youth as well as peace-oriented and interreligious programs. The UC's primary education center is Unification Theological Seminary in Barrytown, New York, and its main media arm is HSA Books. Finally, while specific numbers are not readily available, current U.S. membership is approximately 25,000, and the UC has a goal of reaching 50,000 members by 2016.

Peter L. Doebler

See also: Entries: Korean American Religions

Further Reading

Barker, Eileen. "Unification Church." *Encyclopedia of Religion.* Edited by Lindsay Jones. 2nd ed. Vol. 14. Detroit: Macmillan Reference USA, 2005, pp. 9466–68.

Barker, Eileen. *The Making of a Moonie: Choice or Brainwashing?* Oxford: Blackwell, 1984.

Bromley, David G. "Financing the Millennium: The Economic Structure of the Unificationist Movement." *Journal for the Scientific Study of Religion* 24, no. 3 (September 1985): 253–74.

Bromley, David G., and Alexa Blonner. "From the Unification Church to the Unification Movement and Back." *Nova Religio: The Journal of Alternative and Emergent Religions* 16, no. 2 (November 2012): 86–95.

Bromley, David G., and Anson D. Shupe, Jr. *"Moonies" in America: Cult, Church and Crusade.* Beverly Hills, CA: Sage, 1979.

Chryssides, George D. *The Advent of Sun Myung Moon: The Origins, Beliefs, and Practices of the Unification Church.* New York: St. Martin's Press, 1991.

Family Federation for World Peace and Unification. "Cheon Il Guk Matching." http://bfm.familyfed.org/matching-2/cheon-il-guk-matching/. Accessed April 17, 2014.

Family Federation for World Peace and Unification. "Church President's Year-End Message." http://www.familyfed.org/members/index.php?option=com_content&view=article&id=4750:weekly-update-for-12312013&catid=99:national&Itemid=376. Accessed April 17, 2014.

Inglis, Michael, and Michael L. Mickler. *40 Years in America: An Intimate History of the Unification Movement 1959–1999.* New York: HSA, 2000.

Introvigne, Massimo. *The Unification Church.* Salt Lake City, UT: Signature Books, 2000.

Moon, Sun Myung, et. al. *Exposition of the Divine Principle.* New York: Holy Spirit Association for the Unification of World Christianity, 1996.

Zeller, Benjamin E. "Science as Social Identity Marker: The Case of Early Unificationism in America." *Nova Religio: The Journal of Alternative and Emergent Religions* 14, no. 4 (May 2011): 30–53.

United Church of Christ (UCC)

The American Board of Commissioners for Foreign Missions (ABCFM) began its work in Hawai'i in 1820, and in a short time Christianity flourished in Hawai'i.

The ABCFM was mainly Congregationalist in its beginnings, and there were many churches established in Hawai'i. But Hawaiians were not recognized as a group until much later. Similarly, while there were Chinese churches on the East and West Coasts and in Hawai'i, and in some cases they had their own nongeographic associations, they were not recognized by race or national origin until 1973, when at the General Synod of the United Church of Christ the Pacific Islander and Asian American Ministries of the United Church of Christ (PAAM) was born.

When it began, the leadership consisted of mainly Japanese and Chinese. PAAM advocated for Pacific Islanders and Asian American members and churches in the United Church of Christ. PAAM was and continues to be an advocate for Pacific Islanders and Asian Americans. The goal of PAAM was to have the United Church of Christ see, accept, and use the gifts and talents of Pacific Islanders and Asian Americans. While Japanese Americans and Chinese Americans made up the leadership of PAAM, now there are many Samoans and Filipinos and an increasing number of Asian Indian leaders have become members of the United Church of Christ. The mission of PAAM is stated "to promote the leadership and identities of Pacific Islanders and Asian Americans to empower them and their churches in the UCC. We persist to identify concerns of PAAM ethnic groups and advocate for developing advocacy and solutions. We are instrumental in facilitating the involvement of Asians and Pacific Islanders in covenanted ministries, conferences, associations and all other settings of the UCC.

Above all, PAAM continues to address institutional racism within the church and society, is concerned with issues of human rights and justice, and helps to support and strengthen clergy and lay leadership at the local level" (PAAM Vision and Goals).

In 1991 a "Pronouncement and Proposal for Action: A United Church of Christ Ministry with Pacific Islanders and Asian Americans" was adopted by the General Synod. In that document it was noted that there were 11 different ethnic groups: Hawaiian, Samoan, Korean, Japanese, Taiwanese, Chinese, Filipino, Asian Indian, Marshallese, Chukese, and Okinawan. Since then there are Tongan, Pohnpeian, and Kosraen ethnic groups. There are many more languages as in the Philippines where there are many languages spoken, as with the Chinese.

At one time there were eight Asian Americans in the National Setting of the United Church of Christ and at least two in the Conference Setting. Presently there are only two Asian Americans who serve in the Conference Setting and one conference minister. The notable UCC Asian American leaders include Mineo Katagiri, Teruo Kawata, and David Hirano. All three served as conference minister. Hirano also served in the National Setting of UCC.

Over the years as the United States has had major immigration from India, many from the Church of South India have started local churches related to the United Church of Christ. The congregations that are growing are from the Pacific Islands and include Samoan and Micronesian groups (Pohnpeans, Marshallese, Kosraeans, Chukese, to name a few). As some of the original Asian American churches have declined in membership, those from the Pacific Islands continue to increase in membership. Pacific Islanders have become increasingly active in the United Church of Christ.

The impact of Pacific Islanders and Asian Americans on the theologies of the United Church of Christ is yet to be seen or felt. While the *New Century Hymnal* has a few Pacific Islander and Asian American hymns, there is no major impact. At the General Synod there is an attempt to be a multicultural and multiracial denomination and the worship services reflect that diversity, but the United Church of Christ is still a predominantly European American denomination.

David Hirano

Further Reading

PAAM United Church of Christ National 2012–2014. www.uccfiles.com. Accessed July 16, 2014.

Pacific Islander and Asian American Ministries United Church of Christ. www.nationalpaarm.org. Accessed July 16, 2014.

"What Is the United Church of Christ?" www.ucc.org. Accessed July 16, 2014.

United Methodism

In North American United Methodism, Asian Americans have recently joined together in two initiatives: the National Federation of Asian American United Methodists (NFAAUM) and the Asian American Language Ministry (AALM).

The NFAAUM consists of "ten Asian sub-ethnic caucuses who are united through our faith in Jesus Christ" from Cambodian, Chinese, Filipino, Taiwanese, Hmong, Japanese, Korean, Lao, South Asian, and Vietnamese persons across generations. The NFAAUM aims to link and empower Asian American local churches by articulating the concerns, interests, and needs of Asian American constituencies at all levels of United Methodist ministry and polity. The federation also advocates for full inclusion of Asian Americans in the leadership, programs, and administration of the United Methodist Church.

The organization has a particular concern for resisting any oversimplified understandings of integration or incorporation of Asian Americans into the ministry of the United Methodist Church. It resists assimilation and blending that might lead to cultural disappearance. At the same time it acknowledges the limit of reducing Asian American identity to ancestry and perceives the increasingly complex designation of "Asian American" given the array of Asian American cultures and the diversity of what constitutes Asian American heritage, given social institutions like marriage across cultures, race, and ethnicity.

The NFAAUM originally grew out of two Asian American United Methodist organizations that formed in response to struggles of ethnic minorities on university campuses in the late 1960s—the United Methodist Japanese Americans, established in 1968, and the Western Jurisdiction of Asian American United Methodists, established in 1972. The formation of the NFAAUM followed in 1975. The NFAAUM has itself also contributed to the evolution of Asian American advocacy structuring by sponsoring the inaugural Convocation of Asian American United Methodists on August 11, 2010, in San Jose, California.

The AALM was launched in 1996 by the quadrennial national meeting of the United Methodists known as the General Conference. The AALM, now officially sponsored by the Board of Global Ministries, includes subethnic groups with 15 different languages and fortifies existing ministries with Asian American communities and fosters new ones. Four areas of concentration comprise the service of the AALM: resource development, leadership development, congregational development, and community development. From 2001 to 2006, the AALM has supported 29 church plants, 42 congregational revitalizations, and 18 partnerships with United Methodist Annual conferences. These initiatives range from the West Coast to Filipino communities in Oklahoma and Chinese Bible studies in Louisiana. Developing ministries for "Next Generation" Asian Americans born in the United States that address generational conflicts, the complexity of living in multicultural and multiracial contexts is also of principal importance for the AALM.

The AALM has also outlined in the National Plan for Ethnic/Racial Ministries of the United Methodist Church objectives to recruit and train pastoral and lay leadership and provide Asian American communities and congregations with cultural- and language-appropriate resources. The hope is to provide culturally relevant and sensitive service, literature and media for evangelism, Christian education, leadership development, stewardship, and worship. Chinese and Korean populations are of

particular interest for the AALM. The Korean American National Plan (KANP), for instance, has focused on congregational development, nurture, and revitalization, as well as leadership formation through small group ministry (where several informal and intimate gatherings of adherents such as Bible studies or prayer groups combine to start a new congregation), and work with Next Generation Ministries. New Korean-language and English-language ministries in full partnership with annual conferences (the governing bodies of regions where the United Church ministers), Korean missions, and Korean UMC congregations play a vital role in shaping the KANP as well as provide support for existing congregations toward self-sufficiency. A need has also been identified to develop and tailor leadership programs toward the needs of an increasing number of Korean American pastors serving in cross-cultural/racial appointments. For the "Next Generation," there is concern to educate parishioners born in the United States about discrimination, generational conflicts, and the need for cultural understanding relevant to living in a multicultural and multiracial society. Community programs and services that address legalities, immigration/citizenship education, ESL, ministry to the disenfranchised (housing, employment, social services), and partnership with faith-based community centers are also of especial importance. Ministering with cultural sensitivity is not limited, however, to East Asian American populations. The United Methodist Church has also undertaken studies of how to serve Pacific Islanders from Hawai'i, Fiji, Guam, Samoa, and Tonga.

In addition to initiatives led by Asian Americans to advance and enhance the ministries of the United Methodist Church, the Board of Archives and History and the United Methodist Publishing House have begun recovering forgotten and neglected histories of Asian American United Methodists to bring awareness of how Asian Americans have historically contributed to the life of the national church body. The Board of Higher Education and Ministry has dispersed Hispanic, Asian, and Native American scholarships to defray the costs of higher education for future Asian American leaders, and among the church's 50 active bishops, 5 are Asian American males.

Through social advocacy, strategic cultural ministries, and ecclesial planning, historical archiving, publications, initiatives in higher education, and election of Episcopal leaders, Asian Americans have influenced the operations of the United Methodist Church. These endeavors are of course not to the exclusion of individuals and groups working behind the scenes and in multicultural contexts that embody Asian American United Methodism.

Gerald C. Liu

Further Reading

Chung, Judy. "Ministry Reaches Out to Asian Americans." The General Board of Global Ministries. August 1, 2008. http://gbgm-umc.org/global_news/full_articlecfm?articleid=5086. Accessed July 9, 2014.

Gilbert, Kathy L. "Asian American Group Celebrates History, Elects Leaders." December 5, 2007. The United Methodist Church. http://www.umc.org/site/apps/nlnet/content2.aspx?c=lwL4KnN1LtH&b=3634679&ct=4723551. Accessed July 9, 2014.

Javier, Pong. "Convocation Looks at Asian American Involvement in United Methodist Church." The General Board of Global Ministries. August 12, 2010. http://gbgm-umc.org/global_news/full_article.cfm?articleid=5830. Accessed July 9, 2014.

Write, Elliott. "Study Set on United Methodist Ministry with U.S. Pacific Islanders." The General Board of Global Ministries. March 19, 2009. http://gbgm-umc.org/global_news/full_article.cfm?articleid=5353. Accessed July 9, 2014.

V

Vesākha (Vesak)

Vesākha (Vesak) is the most important Buddhist holiday observed in South and Southeast Asia and constitutes a national holiday in most of the countries in the region. It commemorates three major events in the life of the historical Buddha, Siddhārtha Gautama: his birth, enlightenment (*nibbāna*, at the age of 35), and passing away (*parinibbāna*, at the age of 80). According to the Theravāda tradition, as found in the *Mahāvaṃsa* (Great Chronicle), these three events all took place on the full moon (*uposatha*) day of the Vesākha month of the lunar calendar, which falls in April or May of the Gregorian calendar. It is believed to have been celebrated for almost 2,000 years. In East Asia, where Mahāyāna Buddhism is predominant, the three events of the Buddha's life are traditionally commemorated on different days. In Japan, for example, the Buddha's birthday is called Hana-matsuri, meaning the flower festival, and falls on April 8.

The activities associated with Vesākha vary from region to region. However, one common component of the observance is the Buddha *pūjā*, paying respect to the Buddha. In Thailand, where the holiday is called Vesākha Pūjā, Buddhist flags featuring the *dhammacakka* (Dharma wheel) are put up alongside the national flags across villages and cities during the week running up to the holiday. On the morning of Vesākha Day, lay Buddhists normally visit a local *wat* (temple) to offer food to the monks and to offer their respect to the Buddha. In exchange for their recommitment to the Buddha's teachings, monks administer the five precepts (to refrain from killing, stealing, sexual misconduct, false speech, and imbibing of intoxicants). Some choose to recommit themselves to the eight precepts (in addition to the five precepts, the devotee refrains from eating at forbidden times; engaging in dancing, singing, and adorning the body with cosmetics and perfumes; and sleeping on elevated and luxurious beds) by remaining at the temple until the following day, practicing meditation, and working around the monastery. Others return to the monastery in the evening to participate in chanting and to circumambulate the main Buddha hall (called *ubosot*) three times holding lighted candles, flowers, and incense, before offering them on the Buddhist altar. On this day, monks' teachings typically focus on the life story of the historical Buddha.

While Visākha is primarily a Theravāda Buddhist holiday, it has come to assume a more global status and expression for the past several decades. One of the decisive events in this process, the resolution to make Vesākha the birthday of the Buddha, was taken at the conference of World Fellowship of Buddhists held in Sri Lanka in 1950. Thus, the Buddha's birthday is now also sometimes referred to as Vesākha or

A group of Buddhists monks celebrate International Recognition of the Day of Vesak (commemorating the day of the birth of the Budha) at United Nations Headquarters, May 15, 2009. (AP Photo/David Karp)

Vesak in non-Theravāda Buddhist communities. Particularly since 1999, when the United Nations recognized the Day of Vesak as one of the internationally observed holidays, Vesākha has been celebrated more globally and collectively by followers of all strands of Buddhism, as a pan-Buddhist holiday.

Theravāda Buddhist devotees residing in the United States observe Vesākha as they once did in their homeland. In addition to attending and participating in Buddhist rituals, the event is an opportunity to showcase the culture of their respective homelands. It is mostly a festive time with cultural programs and exhibits. It is an opportunity for devotees to introduce their friends and neighbors to their traditional culture and cuisine. For the Thais and other ethnic communities, Visākha is an occasion to meet old friends and reaffirm their cultural and ethnic identities.

Kieko Obuse

See also: Entries: Songkran; Thai American Religions; Thai Buddhist Immigrant Spirituality; Thai Religious Foodways

Further Reading

Geiger, W., trans. *The Mahāvaṃsa or The Great Chronicle of Ceylon.* Reprint ed. Oxford: Pali Text Society, 2001.

Swearer, Donald. *The Buddhist World of Southeast Asia.* 2nd ed. New York: SUNY Press, 2010.

United Nations. "Resolution Adopted by the General Assembly: 54/115. International Recognition of the Day of Vesak at United

Nations Headquarters and Other United Nations offices." New York: United Nations, 2000.

Vietnamese American Buddhists

After the United States withdrew from Vietnam in 1975, more than a million refugees made their way to the United States and other parts of the world; they carried with them bitter experiences of the war, memories of their escape, and their Buddhist faith. Buddhism, however, is just one feature of the spiritual montage that animates the Vietnamese people. Other traditions include their indigenous shamanic and animistic beliefs, Confucianism, Daoism, Brahmanism, and Christianity.

History

Due to its geographical location in the Red River delta region, Vietnam hosted a confluence of Buddhist traditions that arrived via the southern maritime route from India and overland through Southeast Asia from the west, and from Central Asia and China to the north. Buddhist monks may have reached Van Lang (as Vietnam was known at the time) as early as the third or second century BCE. By the end of the second century CE, Buddhism or *Phat giao*, as it is called in Vietnamese, established a major center in Bac Ninh Province, north of the present-day capital city of Hanoi. It should be noted that Vietnamese monks took advantage of their location and traveled to India to study. Until the middle of the 10th century Vietnam was part of the Southeast Asian Buddhist cultural complex. Ironically, after the Ngo Quyen (897–944) defeated the Southern Han fleet at the Battle of Bach Dang River in 938 that secured Vietnamese independence, Chinese culture gained increasing prestige. Vietnam and China shared and still share many cultural, philosophical, and spiritual features. Vietnamese Buddhism relies on the Chinese Tripiṭika (Buddhist canon) and its doctrinal developments, including *goyi sanjiao* or *Tam Giao Dong Nguyen* (three religions have the same source)—harmony of the three teachings: Confucianism, Daoism, and Buddhism—and the integration of Tinh Du (Pure Land) devotion with Thien (Chan) meditation.

According to traditional accounts, in 589 the Indian monk Vinitaruci (Ti-ni-da-luu-chi, ca. sixth–seventh centuries) entered Vietnam after completing his studies with Jianzhi Sengcan (Tang Xan?—606; Jpn. Kanchi Sosan), the third patriarch of the Chinese Chan (Jpn. Zen) sect. Together with his disciple, Dao Tin (580–651; Ch. Daoxin, Jpn. Dōshin), he initiated the Vietnamese Thien (Chan) tradition that became quite influential with the patriarch Van Hanh (d. 1018). Other early Thien traditions were the Vo Ngon Thong and the Thao Duong. The Thao Duong tradition incorporated *nianfo* (thinking on the Buddha) chanting practices into its meditation practice. King Tran Nhan Tong (1258–1308) founded a new Thien school, Truc Lam, that was eventually eclipsed by the ascendency of Confucianism at the royal court. The 17th century saw the emergence of the Nguyen Thieu and the Lam Te (Ch. Linji, Jpn. Rinzai) schools. The Lam Te School spawned the Lieu Quan in the 18th century; it is the predominant Thien tradition today.

Buddhist clerics served as advisors to Vietnamese rulers; but their influence declined after the arrival of Catholic missions. The first Christian missionaries entered the country in the sixth century; but they did not exert much influence until Bishop Adran Pigneau de Behaine (1741–1799) became the confidant of Nguyen Anh (1762–1820). The bishop secured military supplies and European troops that enabled Nguyen to vanquish his rivals and to establish the borders of present-day Vietnam. As Emperor Gia Long, Nguyen permitted unimpeded Christian missionary activities. However, his fourth son and successor Ming Mang (1791–1841), a conservative Confucian, was not so inclined. This resulted in a power struggle with pro-Catholic officials that continued until the onset of the Vietnam War. After emerging victorious from the Tonkin campaign (1883–1886), the French gained control over the country and began to institute pro-Catholic polices; the Catholic Church was given vast tracts of royal land. Today between 5 and 7 percent of the population are Catholic.

During the 1920s and 1930s, Buddhism experienced a revival and modernization that continues today. In addition to changing the monastic life and having stricter standards for monks and nuns, reformist clerics called for the translation of documents from Chinese to integrate Buddhism more closely into the national life. After the defeat of the French in 1954, the country was partitioned into North and South Vietnam. The Communist North suppressed the faith traditions, including Buddhism. The Buddhists were also persecuted in the South. Ngo Dinh Diem (1901–1963), president of South Vietnam from 1955 to 1963, favored Catholic devotees and institutions. In May 1963, Diem prohibited Buddhists in the city of Hue, where his brother Ngo Dinh Thuc (1897–1984) was the Catholic archbishop, from hoisting the Buddhist flag during the Vesak observance that celebrates the birth, Enlightenment, and *Nirvāṇa* of Śākyamuni Buddha. A few days earlier, Catholics were encouraged to fly Vatican flags to celebrate Thuc's 25th year as bishop; government funds paid for the event. Buddhist residents were forced to contribute. These policies sparked Buddhist protests that the military promptly suppressed. Diem blamed the death of nine protestors on North Vietnam and banned further protests.

On June 11, 1963, in a seminal moment in modern Vietnamese Buddhist history, Thich Quang Duc (1897–1963), sitting in the full lotus meditation position, set himself on fire in the middle of a busy intersection on Phan-dinh-Phung Street in Saigon. In a note before the incident, he wrote:

> Before closing my eyes and moving towards the vision of the Buddha, I respectfully pleaded to President Ngo Dinh Diem to take a mind of compassion towards the people of the nation and implement religious equality to maintain the strength of the homeland eternally. I call the venerables, reverends, members of the sangha (community) and the lay Buddhists to organize in solidarity to make sacrifices to protect Buddhism.

The event led to further rallies, hunger strikes, and the distribution of pamphlets protesting Diem's anti-Buddhist policies. In an attempt to end the growing number of demonstrations, in August Diem's brother Ngo Dinh Nhu (1910–1963), head of the secret police, ordered Vietnamese special forces troops to raid Buddhist establishment throughout the country. More than 1,400 monastics were arrested; hundreds more disappeared and are presumed to have been killed. The harsh response was in part because the Diem government was aware that many of the "monks" were Communist sympathizers or agents. Later that year the military led by General Duong Van Minh (1916–2001) staged a coup d'état; Diem and his brother Nhu were assassinated on November 2. Summoned to Rome for the Second Vatican Council (1962–1965), the archbishop escaped unharmed. The post-Diem government refused Thuc's return; he died in exile in Carthage, Missouri, in 1984.

Three years after Thich Quang Duc's dramatic act of self-destruction, in 1966 Thich Nhat Hanh returned from Columbia University, where he was lecturing, to establish the Tiep Hien (Interbeing) Order; and accompanying its establishment, he refashioned and distilled the 227 traditional Buddhist precepts into the Fourteen Guidelines for Engaged Buddhism that cautions against the absolute ideological claims that polarized his country:

> Do not be idolatrous about or bound to any doctrine, theory, or ideology, even Buddhist ones. Buddhist systems of thought are guiding means; they are not absolute truth. Even meritorious teachings become a burden if one does not know when to discard them.

The ideals associated with "engaged Buddhism" first appeared in *Lotus in a Sea of Fire* (1967); they have inspired a number of social, political, environmental, and economic movements and organizations that work to end suffering and injustice in the United States and elsewhere. As a delegate to the Buddhist Peace Delegation at the Paris peace talks, Thich Nhat Hanh was prohibited from returning to Vietnam when the Paris peace accords were signed in 1973. However, from his exile in France, he led efforts to assist Vietnamese fleeing their homeland. His return to Vietnam in 2005 and 2007 generated much controversy from government officials and clerics of the Unified Church of Vietnam, each of whom believed he was being manipulated by the other. His books and lectures have had considerable impact on the U.S. public. However, the Order of Interbeing and its founder have left no impact on Vietnamese Buddhism and very little imprint on the Vietnamese émigré Buddhist community.

Beliefs and Practices

The 2010 U.S. Census Bureau counted 1.5 million Vietnamese throughout the country. Unlike Japanese Buddhist temples that are organized along sectarian lines, the Vietnamese *chua* (temple) is a self-organized and independent institution that emerges from a community's aspiration. A typical *chua* traditionally honors four Buddhist spiritual personalities. They are Thich Ca Mau Ni Phat, A Di Da Phat, Quan The Am, and Dia Tang Bo Tat, personalities that highlight compassionate aspects of the Buddhist spirit and reveal a deep yearning to be free from suffering. The devotional rituals dedicated to these spiritual personalities evince the history and nonsectarian character of the Vietnamese Buddhist experience.

Thich Ca Mau Ni Phat represents the possibility for all beings to realize enlightenment and overcome suffering. Through the cultivation of meditation, Siddhārtha Gautama penetrated the truth of *pratītyasamutpāda* (interdependence), realized enlightenment, and transitioned to *Niet-ban* (*Nirvāṇa*) at the end of his corporeal life. In some temples, Thich Ca Mau Ni Phat occupies a central place on the altar. Thich Ca Mau Ni Phat is the principal image of the Thien or Zen sect.

A Di Da Phat, the personification of compassion, has a prominent place in the *chua*. This Buddha welcomes all beings to his Tinh Do or Pure Land, where devotees dwell in a most conducive environment for receiving the Dharma and thus attain enlightenment. The *Larger Sukhāvatī Sūtra* describes the Pure Land and its establishment though the 48 vows Dharmākara Bodhisattva promises to fulfill before becoming Amitābha Buddha. Vietnamese Buddhists place great faith in the 18th vow, in which A Di Da Phat welcomes all beings who invoke his name 10 times to the Pure Land. The invocation voiced is: *Nam Mo A Di Da Phat* (Praise Amitābha Buddha). Repeating *Nam Mo A Di Da Phat* leads to inner tranquility, repentance, and excising of bad *karma*. This invocation must be rooted in a sincere faith in Amitābha Buddha's limitless compassion, the reality of the Tinh Do, and the efficacy of devotion and prayer. The simplicity of the Tinh Do method accounts for its popularity.

Besides vocalizing "A Di Da Phat," devotees can mentally invoke Amitābha Buddha's name, visualize his image, and summon him in deep concentration. These four methods designate ascending stages of the spiritual ascent. At the highest level, the practitioner identifies with Amitābha Buddha and realizes that the reality of the Pure Land resides in his or her mind-being.

Quan The Am Bo Tat and Dia Tang Bo Tat are placed to the right and left of the altar respectively; they personify the highest ideals of Buddha's compassion at work among the most needy. Quan The Am Bo Tat personifies compassion. The key to Quan The Am's great appeal is readily understood from the original Sanskrit; Avalokiteśvara literally means "one who hears the pleas of the world." Like a mother, Quan The Am is receptive and responsive to pleas of those in need and in great suffering. She is often depicted dressed in a flowing white Han Chinese–style couture holding a medicine flask in the left hand. The 1,000-armed Avalokiteśvara represents the countless ways this bodhisattva vows to help. Another of Avalokiteśvara's 32 incarnations is Quan Am Nam Hai or Goddess of the Southern Seas. In this guise, Quan Am stands on a lotus leaf afloat on the water or on a dragon coursing through the ocean. Vietnamese Buddhists who fled by boat after the fall of Saigon repeatedly invoked Quan Am Nam Hai's name for protection from storms and pirates.

According to Indian Buddhist lore, just before Śākyamuni Buddha passed into *Nirvāṇa*, he asked Dia Tang Bo Tat to remain in the world until Maitreya, the future Buddha, appears. Kṣitigarbha is Śākyamuni's spiritual equal; he had perfected all of the virtues required to achieve spiritual emancipation and could choose to enter *Nirvāṇa*. In deference to Śākyamuni's pleas, and true to his bodhisattva vows, he chose to remain. It is for this reason he continually traverses the six *gatis* or realms through which sentient beings transmigrate. He is especially active in hell, where the need for spiritual relief is the greatest. Vietnamese Buddhist tradition considers Dia Tang Bo Tat to be the king of hell. He is depicted holding an iron staff with his right hand and cradling a jewel in his left hand. The staff symbolizes his determination and the means to break down the doors of hell to free its denizens. The jewel stands for his radiant spiritual accomplishment. Dia Tang plays a prominent role in funerals and memorial services, where he is called upon to assist the spirit of the deceased pining for a better rebirth during the 49 days after death.

A third Mahāyāna tradition is Mat Tong or Mantrayāna or Tantrayāna. Tantra, a late Mahāyāna development, did not establish itself as a separate tradition in China, but its use of *mantras*, *mudras*, and *maṇḍalas* are believed to harness the forces that course through the universe. Chanting *mantras* is part of daily devotion. One of the most popular Tantric texts is *Great Compassion Minded Dhārani* (*mantra*) *of the Thousand-armed-thousand-eye One* (Avalokiteśvara) that Thich Dao Hanh (d. 1115) discovered in present-day Myanmar and brought back. When chanted with sincerity, in addition to spiritual rewards, *mantras* are believed to heal, ward off disease, and vanquish enemies.

In addition to the Mahāyāna traditions, Vietnam hosts a sizable Theravāda Buddhist presence among the Khmer (Cambodian) people living in the Mekong Delta region that was once part of the Khmer (Cambodia) empire. The region was annexed and occupied in the 18th century. The Buddhist revival in the early 20th century also sparked an interest in Theravāda Buddhism. Three centuries earlier, the Vietnamese also occupied Champa territories that are now central Vietnam. The Chams patterned their lives and society on syncretic Saiva-Mahāyāna Buddhist ideas that merged the worshiped of Shiva as embodied in the human ruler with the Buddhist idea of the *Dharmarāja* or Dharma-king.

Besides these Buddhist personalities, the Vietnamese *chua* has an ancestral hall that enshrines *paiwei* or memorial plaques that are inscribed with the names of the deceased. The *paiwei* reflects an ancient belief that the spirit of the deceased is present in them. These plaques and the ancestral hall are expressions of filiality, a prime component in Confucian spirituality. As part of their responsibilities, monks and/or nuns offer incense and chant a *sūtra* daily. Families will often visit with fruits and other offerings.

Ceremonies and Festivals

The nonsectarian character of Vietnamese Buddhism is also reflected in its devotional scripture. The service book compiled by the Sagely City of 10,000 Buddhas and translated into Vietnamese, which the Vietnamese devotees use, includes passages from three major Mahāyāna traditions: the Thien, Tinh Dou, and Mat Tong traditions. The morning recitation includes the *Shurangama Mantra*, the *Great Compassion Mantra*, the *Heart Sūtra*, and passages associated with the Thien and Mat Tong traditions. The evening recitation includes the *Amitābha Sūtra* and passages from other Tinh Do texts.

The essential purpose of these ritual texts is to harness the power of *mantras* to make real the devotees' aspirations. Mantras are efficacious because they establish a relationship between the devotee and a spiritual reality; in the case of the mantras recited in the morning and evening service, it is the compassion of Buddhas and bodhisattvas that has its being and is crystallized in these *mantras*. Through constant repetition, the compassion of the Buddhas and bodhisattvas fills the mind and being of the devotee, who then grasps the Buddhist Dharma (truth), liberating him or her from suffering and enabling him or her to share the merits that have been generated. *Mantras* can be and are practiced anywhere and everywhere by clerics and laity.

The annual ritual calendar features services that commemorate and mark important Buddhist events, as well as milestones unique to the Vietnamese. Communal services are observed on Sunday or in a few temples on Saturday, the only days of the week that most devotees can participate. The services include ritual chanting and a message. After the service, the congregation may share a vegetarian meal. Sam Nguyen/Sam Hoi (confession/repentance) services are observed on the full moon and new moon each month. On these days the devotees are expected to ob-serve the monastic rules that include chanting, meditation, and a vegetarian diet. Services observe the Buddha's and Quan Am Bo Tat's birthdays. At the Vu Lan (Ullambana) service on the 15th day of the seventh lunar month, Vietnamese honor and remember their ancestors; this expression of filiality, a prime virtue, recalls Mogallana's expression of filiality toward his mother. Services special to the Vietnamese include Tet or the Lunar New Year in late January or early February; a memorial for the Trung sisters (ca. 12–43 BCE), heroines who led a rebellion against the Chinese on the sixth day of the second lunar month; and the anniversary of the Hung kings, ancestors of the Vietnamese people, on the 10th day of the third month. The mid–Autumn Festival has special activities for the children.

Like other immigrant faith traditions, the *chua* serves as a community and social center that functions as a repository of culture and ethnic identity. It is a venue for weddings and memorial services. Funerals are held at the home of the deceased or at the cemetery, and increasingly at the funeral home. The *chua* provides a venue to offer instruction in the Vietnamese language, traditional dance and music, and the culinary arts.

Family Rituals and Practice

Devotion is an important feature in family life. The family altar is highly personal. In addition to replicating the temple altar, the family altar often includes photos and other mementos of deceased ancestors. Multiple images of Buddhas and bodhisattvas are often placed on the altar. Families make offerings of incense, fruits, and pure water. *Sūtras* are also chanted.

Hoa Hao

While approximately 80 percent of the 70 million Vietnamese claim to be Buddhist, many, especially those that inhabit the fringe rural areas, still have strong sentiments for their ancestors, nature, and communities, features of the indigenous shamanic faith. These features are evident in the Buddhist-based Phat Giao Hoa Hao or simply Hoa Hao movement that was founded by Huynh Phu So (1920–1947) in 1939 in the Mekong River Delta region. Hoa Hao is a 19th-century movement with roots in the Buu Son Ky Huong (Treasure Mountain–Mysterious Perfume) movement that emerged along the Vietnamese-Cambodian border region. Huynh tapped the enduring mythical origins of their land and aspirations of ousting the French that occupied their homeland. With the aid of the Japanese, Huynh's prophecy came true. The Hoa Hao faith stresses the lay Buddhist devotion, rather than temple worship and ritual, including clerical ordination. Aid to the poor is favored over building *chuas* and expensive rituals. Hoa Hao claims two million followers; Hoa Hao temples can be found in some U.S. cities.

Conclusion

The years immediately after fleeing their homeland were difficult for the Vietnamese Buddhist refugee community. There were few clerics and *chuas*. The community relied on Japanese and Chinese Buddhist clerics and temples for their funerals, weddings, and other spiritual and ritual needs. Despite experiencing the challenges that other older ethnic communities have faced, the Vietnamese Buddhist community increasingly engaged in their new homeland. One such example is Duc Vien Buddhist Pagoda in San Jose, California; the *chua* serves vegetarian meals to the homeless. Others participate in civic welfare on an ad hoc basis as the need arises to clean the city streets, feed the hungry, and raise funds to help the victims of natural disasters. Many *chuas* have Vietnamese Family of Buddhists (Gia Dinh Phat Tu), an organization similar to Boy/Girl Scouts of America to help Vietnamese children and youth to understand Buddhism, continue traditional family values, and engage with societal issues. Many *chuas* offer Vietnamese-language and cultural classes for the children.

Ronald Y. Nakasone

See also: Entries: Hoa Hao Buddhism; Thich Duc Niem; Thich Thien An; Vietnamese American Religions

Further Reading

Dharma Realm Buddhist Association. *Van Phat Thanh Thanh Nhat Tung Nghi Quy* [Daily Recitation Handbook in Sagely City of Ten Thousand Buddhas]. Burlingame, CA, 2008.

Kawamoto, Kunie. "Betonamu no Bukkyō [Vietnamese Buddhism]." In *Higashi ajia shochi'iki no Bukkyō* [*Buddhism of the different regions of East Asia*]. Tokyo: Kosei Shuppan, 1982, pp. 223–303.

Matthews, Bruce, ed. *Buddhism in Canada.* London: Routledge, 2006.

Moyar, Mark. "The Vietnam History You Haven't Heard." *The Christian Science*

Monitor. January 22, 2007. http://www.cs monitor.com/2007/0122/p09s01-coop .html. Accessed September 12, 2013.

Nguyen, Cuong Tu, and A. W. Barber. "Vietnamese Buddhism in North America: Tradition and Acculturation." In Charles S. Prebish and Kenneth K. Tanaka, eds. *The Faces of Buddhism in America.* Berkeley: University of California Press, 1998, pp. 129-46.

Nguyen, Cuong Tu. *Zen in Medieval Vietnam, a Study and Translation of the Tien Uyen Tap Anh.* Honolulu: University of Hawai'i Press, 1997.

Nguyen, Tai Thu, ed. *History of Buddhism in Vietnam.* Hanoi: Social Sciences, 1992.

Nhat Hanh, Thich. *Interbeing: Commentaries on the Tiep Hien Precepts.* Berkeley, CA: Parallax Press, 1987.

Nhat Hanh, Thich. *Lotus in a Sea of Fire.* New York: Hill and Wang, 1967.

Quang Minh, Thich. "Vietnamese Buddhism in America." Electronic Theses, Treatises and Dissertations. Paper 1589. 2007.

Vietnamese American Catholics

Vietnamese American Catholics are relatively new to the religious landscape of the United States. In 1975, many Vietnamese fled their war-torn country and resettled in various parts of the world with a large number coming to the United States. This first wave of refugees numbered about 130,000, and the flights of people out of Vietnam continued into the first half of the 1990s. Among the large influx of Vietnamese refugees, there was a disproportionately large number of Catholics. By the mid-1990s, about 27 percent of Vietnamese were Catholic and by the 2000 U.S. Census, that number had grown to 325,000 or 30 percent from a total population of 1.2 million. In Vietnam, only about 7 percent of the population are Catholics. Many factors contribute to this disproportionate representation, but a major aspect is the years of persecution that Catholics endured in Vietnam. As Vietnamese Catholics resettled, their faith played a major role in establishing their place in America. They brought a deeply devout and traditional practice of Catholicism combined with cultural practices. This religious and cultural mixing along with years of persecution garnered Vietnamese American Catholics a distinctive place within the American Catholic Church.

History of Vietnamese Catholicism

In the 17th century, France was a very powerful Roman Catholic nation and was active in sending missionaries to all parts of the world through the Société des Missions Étrangerès (Foreign Mission Society). French Jesuits came to Vietnam in 1615. Vietnamese at the time practiced different native spiritual beliefs and other religious traditions such as Buddhism, Taoism, and Confucianism. Alexandre de Rhodes, a French Jesuit, was instrumental in establishing a formidable French Catholic presence in Vietnam. In 1624, he landed in the southern area of Vietnam, known as Cochin China, then traveled to the central region of Annam and then to the northern kingdom of Tonkin in 1627. Through the collective hard work of his fellow Jesuits, de Rhodes used a newly adapted romanized Vietnamese script of Catholic text to teach thousands of people. This writing

Vietnamese fishermen wait in line for assistance from BP and Catholic Charities as a member of Catholic Charities registers them at a Vietnamese community center in New Orleans. The spill struck at the heart of the Vietnamese community here, posing new hardships for those who brought their fishing traditions here as refugees, helped each other rebound after Katrina, and now face another test of survival. (AP Photo/Gregory Bull)

was later adopted throughout Vietnam and called *quocngu* (national language). Gradually, *quocngu* almost entirely replaced the Chinese characters that were traditionally used in Vietnamese writing. The Jesuits' invention became the country's standard form of writing. Thus, the very beginning of Catholic contact in Vietnam contributed to one of the basic expressions of Vietnamese culture.

In the 17th and 18th centuries, missionaries spread throughout Vietnam. It was a politically tumultuous period when different imperial families fought for full control. The Nguyen ruled over the southern kingdom and the Trinh family held power over the north. The Trinh disliked Catholics and instituted laws in 1625 that prohibited any Catholic worship or evangelization. Anyone could be persecuted for violating the laws. Under a succession of different emperors more laws and edicts were implemented to suppress the growing Catholic population. This did not deter the missionaries or their new converts who paid great respect to the missionaries to the extent of pledging even to die with the missionaries. As a consequence, martyrdom became a profound historical feature of Vietnamese Catholicism.

In 1788, a peasant rebellion known as Tay Son unified the country under the rebel leader who had proclaimed himself sole emperor. This uprising caused the only surviving heir of the Nguyen family, Nguyen Anh, to seek the assistance of France with the help of Monsignor Pierre Pigneau de Behaine, who convinced Louis XVI to give French military support. The Tay Son rebels were concerned that Catholics would support the Nguyens, issued an anti-Catholic edict, and approved persecution against the missionaries and Vietnamese Catholics.

With French backing, Nguyen Anh suppressed the rebels and ultimately took control of all the regions of Vietnam by 1802. He declared himself emperor and took the imperial name of Gia Long. He initiated a policy of religious tolerance, which would only last until 1820 when his son Minh Mang inherited the throne. He revived Confucianism and the Chinese model of ruling to reestablish order in the country. Believing that Catholicism was a threat, he ordered suppression of Catholic practices in 1825. The missionaries, however, continued to be active in defiance of the imperial prohibition against Catholics.

Anti-Catholic activities intensified under Emperor Tu-Duc, who ruled from 1847 to 1883. Tu-Duc was deeply suspicious of French intentions in Vietnam, and he saw Vietnamese Catholics as part of the French strategy to colonize. The French emperor Napoleon III took up the cause of the Catholics in Vietnam and used their persecution as a reason for invading the country and seizing Saigon, including the three surrounding provinces, in 1859. Emperor Tu-Duc, preoccupied with suppressing a northern uprising, was not able to defend the south. In 1862, he ceded the southern region to France and agreed to the establishment of a French protectorate. Then in the 1880s, after France defeated China, which claimed its ancient sovereignty over Vietnam, the French extended control over all of Vietnam. They established the southern part as a colony and the central and northern regions as protectorates.

During this colonial period, Vietnamese Catholics were frequently seen as agents of a foreign power by nationalistic Vietnamese. Their suspicion effectively limited any cooperation among Vietnamese. This did not account for the fact that many Catholics were nationalists and opposed French rule. They were also generally against any political machinations, especially the disturbing rise of Communism. One of the first Catholic publications in Vietnam to address Communism was a 1927 booklet, *The Question of Communism*, which attacked the Communists as godless and violent. The Communists and many other leftists, for their part, tended to be antagonistic toward Catholicism, leading to a widespread migration of Catholics to avoid persecution. Catholics had created tight-knit communities, which helped in a smooth migration from one place to another. This experience would be instrumental when the migration occured across international borders.

In August 1945 when Japan surrendered, the Communist-dominated nationalist forces known as the Viet Minh found themselves the only power in Vietnam. The last of the French-controlled Vietnamese emperors, Bao-dai, abdicated and Ho

Chi Minh declared the independence of Vietnam, now known as the Democratic Republic of Vietnam, on September 2, 1945. Japanese forces remained in Vietnam and the Allies moved in to disarm them and then send them home. China, still under the Nationalist government of Chiang Kai-shek, was given the task of disarming the Japanese in northern Vietnam, and Britain was assigned the south. While the Chinese allowed the Viet Minh to continue to control Hanoi and the north, the British helped the French seize control of the south and reestablish French colonial power. After the British and Chinese left in 1946, Vietnam was divided into north and south once again.

The French and the new Vietnamese government accepted each other uneasily. In March 1946, Ho Chi Minh signed an agreement with France in which he accepted the deployment of French troops in the north, in return for recognition of the Democratic Republic of Vietnam. France was not interested in seeing a truly independent power in Vietnam, and the Viet Minh had no desire to see the country continue under colonial rule.

In early 1947, tensions between the two sides erupted into armed fighting and the first Vietnam War began. In the early 1950s, the growing army of the Democratic Republic of Vietnam, under the command of General Vo Nguyen Giap, began a series of offenses against the French, achieving a victory at the city of Dien Bien Phu in May 1954. This outcome pushed an international conference on Vietnam in Geneva to recognize a temporary division of the country into North and South Vietnam. In the North, the Communist-led Democratic Republic of Vietnam ruled from Hanoi. In the South, the Republic of Vietnam, under the French-supported Emperor Bao-dai, ruled from Saigon with Ngo Dinh Diem as premier. Some South Vietnamese who sympathized with Ho Chi Minh's government moved north. Likewise about one million northerners including 600,000 to 800,000 Catholics fled south on U.S. and French aircraft and naval vessels. In many cases, the Catholic refugees of the 1954 battles fled as entire villages, so that northern Catholic villages were reconstituted in the south.

During this period, Catholics strengthened their own sense of identity. Many Catholic programs and groups were formed to instruct the younger generation. Catholic associations brought together boys and girls aged 6 to 18 to engage in many activities ranging from worship, contemplation, and proselytizing to physical exercise, outdoor activities, games, retreat days, and charity work. Members were expected to attend weekly meetings, annual conferences, and other activities, all in club uniforms. Most associations had some sort of a recreation hall for study and activities, often on the grounds of a church. Although many groups such as Catholic Boy Scouts focused on mainly social and community life, others such as Catholic Youth and Eucharistic Crusades made strict religious demands of their members. They were asked to pray regularly, to say every day an Our Father, Ave Maria, and Gloria for the health of their association and for the conversion of sinners and nonbelievers. Members of nearly all youth associations were required to attend mass and take communion regularly, go to confession, and participate in religious festivals. Proselytizing was an important activity of most Catholic youth associations; their members regularly accompanied members of the clergy seeking converts and handed out religious tracts. Some of these groups have been reestablished in places where Vietnamese have resettled, for instance in the United States.

Besides the young people, Catholics also organized gatherings and groups for the adults, keeping in step with the universal Catholic Church. Papal days and worldwide Marian apparitions became part of Catholic life in Vietnam. Eucharistic Congresses began to be held regularly in the late 20th century.

It should be noted that Catholic worship was primarily oral, with prayers, songs, and stories transmitted through homilies during mass or in catechism classes. Texts circulated primarily among the clergy and elites. The rise of *quocngu* in Catholic life during the early 19th century did improve literacy rates, contributing to better lay participation. Nevertheless, printed material was still a marginal presence in the lives of many Catholics well into the 20th century.

In 1955, Diem organized and won elections that forced Bao-dai to abdicate, and Diem made himself president of Vietnam. He refused to take part in elections for national reunification of the country. This along with his Catholic background caused opposition to his presidency. The Communist North Vietnamese continued to organize their power with those disaffected by Diem. This caused great concern for the United States, which was already wary about the rise of Communism in the re-

gion. In 1963, a military coup overthrew Diem, apparently with consent of the American Embassy. The new leader of South Vietnam proved unable to maintain control and by 1965, U.S. president Johnson sent in ground troops.

Although military and political leaders believed they were winning the war, by 1968, the North Vietnamese troops launched the Tet offensive, which changed the course of the war. In 1973, the Paris peace talks ended with the United States agreeing on a timetable for withdrawing troops and turning the war over to the South Vietnamese army. The South was not prepared, thus in April 1975, Saigon fell to an invasion of North Vietnamese troops. This began one of the largest flights of refugees across international borders that the world had ever witnessed.

Since Catholics had been disproportionately involved in supporting the South Vietnamese government in opposition to Communism, they often suffered at the hands of the new authorities. Catholics were heavily represented among the refugees fleeing Vietnam, contributing to the presence of Vietnamese Catholics in different parts of the world, especially in the United States.

Vietnamese Catholics in the United States

In the latter part of 1975, the U.S. government was faced with the task of resettling thousands of Vietnamese refugees. This initial entry of refugees into the United States became known as the first wave. Those who arrived in this first wave were predominantly Catholics compared to the four subsequent waves from 1976 to the mid-1990s. The early attempts by the U.S. government to settle refugees around the nation led Vietnamese to live in Midwestern and Mountain states least populated by recent immigrants; however, through secondary migration, distinctive Vietnamese enclaves emerged. In 1980, over a fifth of Vietnamese lived in California and over a third had concentrated in nine states: Texas, Louisiana, Georgia, Massachusetts, Illinois, Michigan, Oregon, Pennsylvania, and Washington. By 1990, almost half of the Vietnamese in America had settled or relocated in California and one-third of the rapidly growing population was clustered in major metropolitan areas as well as coastal regions. Vietnamese tended to move out of the central regions of the United States to the far West, far South, and Northeast.

Vietnamese Catholics took up similar strategies learned from their home country: creating tight-knit communities, migrating, establishing organizations, and networking. The first small community of Vietnamese Catholics was established in New Orleans East in 1975 right after the resettlement process. They have now grown to be one of the largest in the United States with a mission extension into another part of the city. The first official personal parish was established in Fairfax, Virginia, in 1978, only three years after the refugee flight out of Vietnam. This is unique because personal parishes are not easily granted by church law. An explanation of parishes in the next paragraph provides a better picture.

Catholic parishes in the United States can be divided into three types: territorial, multicultural, and personal. A territorial parish includes all parishioners within a geographical area. Thus, a large concentration of Vietnamese may lead a regular territorial parish to include special services. A multicultural parish includes specific ethnic services and programs as part of a parish serving more than one ethnic group. A personal parish is a specifically Vietnamese parish that exists outside of the geographic boundaries of other parishes within a diocese. Canon law allows the creation of a personal parish whenever worshippers have special requirements dictated by rite, language, or nationality. Many dioceses have responded to the pastoral needs of the Vietnamese by creating personal parishes, of which there are now 35 in the United States. These parishes are in states such as Virginia, Louisiana, Texas, California, Illinois, Georgia, South Carolina, Kansas, and Minnesota. These parishes have reestablished organizations that they formed in Vietnam (described earlier), especially youth organizations such as Eucharistic Congresses and Boy Scouts.

In 1978, the Congregation of the Co-Redemptrix of Mary (CMC) in Carthage, Missouri, hosted the first Marian Days. These were pilgrimage days for Vietnamese refugees who resettled in the United States to give thanks to God through Mary, celebrating her Assumption on August 15. The CMC is a vowed religious community of men who fled in 1975. They were resettled in Missouri. The bishop of the diocese of Springfield–Cape Girardeau, Missouri, at that time Bernard Law, gave land in Carthage to the CMC for their community. Their first Marian Days brought together about 200 Vietnamese families from across the United States. This has grown into an annual Vietnamese Catholic gathering that attracts Vietnamese from all over the United States and other countries. Since the mid-1980s, this pilgrimage has ballooned to over 50,000 people annually.

Vietnamese Catholics continued to form networks and organizations across the nation. For instance, the Vietnamese Catholic Community of Clergy and Religious was formed in 1978, and then at the first convention of Vietnamese Catholics in 1980, the Vietnamese Catholic Federation was formed, bringing the clergy and religious under the federation. The first president elected was Father Joseph Tinh. The National Pastoral Center for Vietnamese Apostolate was established in 1989 with now Father Dominic Luong as the first director, who would later become the first Vietnamese American bishop. In 2003 along with two other Asian American priests, three bishops were ordained for dioceses in California. Bishop Luong was assigned as an auxiliary bishop of the Diocese of Orange County.

In 1993, the Vietnamese Catholic Congress, a gathering of clergy, religious, and laity, was organized and then established meetings every other year under the sponsorship of the National Pastoral Center for the Vietnamese Apostolate and the Federation of Vietnamese Catholics in collaboration with the Office for the Pastoral Care of Migrants and Refugees of the USCCB. The goal of the congress has been to establish plans and goals for the Vietnamese Catholic communities throughout the United States.

Vietnamese Catholics are supportive of encouraging vocations and forming future leaders for the church. Vocations to the priesthood and religious life are among the largest of any ethnic group in the American Catholic Church. As of 2000, there were 700 priests both secular and religious; 70 permanent deacons; 400 perpetually professed sisters; and 350 sisters in temporary vows. There were 50 religious orders or societies. Religious societies with large Vietnamese membership include the Society of Divine Word (SVD) and the Society of Jesus (SJ).

Three Characteristics of Vietnamese American Catholicism

There are three characteristics of Vietnamese American Catholicism that grounds it in Catholic tradition as well as creating a unique contribution to the Church universal: ancestor veneration as part of filial piety, Marian devotion, and martyrdom. The practice of ancestor veneration is deeply rooted in Vietnamese culture. Ancestor veneration involves the practice of living family members providing the deceased members with continuous happiness and well-being in the afterlife. The living members would make sure to have a proper funeral and burial that included burying the deceased with objects they enjoyed in this world. A picture or some other reminder of the deceased would be placed in the family home as a reminder to continually pray for their souls. On the death anniversary of the loved one, a Catholic mass is offered followed by a large gathering of family members for a banquet in memory of the deceased, along with notes, money, and food offered on the ancestor altar. The duties of remembering and maintaining the ritual usually fell to the children of the deceased.

The duties of ancestor veneration naturally required that families have children to continue the traditional practices. Naturally, ancestor veneration shaped the requirement of filial piety—children showing respect to their living and deceased parents. There were many duties involved with this that were also translated into religious obligations for the Vietnamese Catholics.

The publications of many catechetical books weaved ancestor veneration and filial piety with religious obligations and language. *Chon Dao Dan Giai* (*The True Religion Explained*) and *Hieu Kinh Cha Me* (*Filial Piety and the Respect of Parents*) enumerate believers' duties and practices toward God, authority figures, and their parents. Faithful Catholics were obligated to worship God with faith, trust, and love. The children are to show respect and gratitude toward their parents and others in authority. Filial piety is seen under three aspects: custom, things related to the body, and those related to the soul. Obeying parents gives recognition to children as representatives of God. If parents order their children to act in a way that is in opposition to God's law, they can renounce their duties. The children are to pay attention to both the material and spiritual needs of their parents. For example, when a parent is ill or unable to attend mass, the children must make sure the sacraments are taken to them. Following these duties the children will be rewarded in this life and the next. The consequence for ignoring these duties is shame placed on them and their family's reputation in this life and the next.

There is a strong devotion to Mary in Vietnamese Catholicism, especially through the accounts of her apparitions. There were two Marian apparitions, one in La Vang (more popularly known among Vietnamese) and the other at Tra Kieu. The account of Mary at La Vang in 1798 was associated with the Tay Son rebellion. The story has been passed down through several generations of Vietnamese Catholics. There are several different versions of the story told by Vietnamese Catholics and French missionaries, but all agree in reporting that Mary appeared to several people. The story describes how several Catholics chased from their village were gathered under a banyan tree to pray for protection against their attackers. As they huddled under the tree, a beautiful lady wearing a magnificent cloak appeared with the Infant Jesus in her arms. She heard their cry for help and her message was that she would always help them in time of need. She appeared several more times and news of her appearance spread throughout the villages.

The apparition did not immediately draw believers to La Vang because the harsh terrain and continual persecution made the journey quite treacherous. Nonetheless, small pilgrimages to La Vang began in 1882; then by 1901, with the dedication of a new church to Our Lady of La Vang, more pilgrims flocked there, with pilgrimages today numbering in the hundreds of thousands. It also draws Vietnamese from all over the world.

The apparition at Tra Kieu was during the time when the Vietnamese Catholic Church was afflicted with persecution by the reigning emperor Ham Nghi in 1885. A

French missionary priest, Jean Bruyere, was surrounded by the emperor's army who were attacking the whole parish community. While the young men and boys of the parish were out fighting against the attackers, Father Bruyere urged the others to place a statue of Mary on a table and recite the rosary. The larger section of the emperor's army was held off for several days. They brought cannons to shoot at the church. The cannons missed the church and a soldier reported seeing a lady dressed in white standing on top of the church. There is no way to validate these apparition stories nor has the Vatican taken up the investigations of these apparitions. But Vietnamese Catholics do not hesitate to attribute Mary's miraculous intervention to their victory over their enemies. As with La Vang, a chapel was built in Tra Kieu in 1898 and pilgrimages have been organized since then.

These apparitions contribute to the fact that Mary is supportive and protective of her children. Unlike the apparitions in Europe, especially at Lourdes and Fatima where Mary's message was of apocalyptic divine punishment, in Vietnam it was of protection and well-being. Mary's liberation of the persecuted believers creates the image of a divine mercy that speaks so powerfully to Vietnamese Catholics who have been persecuted since missionary times.

It is estimated that between 130,000 to 300,000 Vietnamese Catholics died during the persecutions from 1625 to 1886. Between 1900 and 1909, the pope beatified 92 Catholics in Vietnam who had died in communitarian violence in the 19th century. Sixteen of them were missionaries

(seven MEP and nine Spanish Dominicans), but 76 were Vietnamese; they were the first ever to receive such an honor. Twenty-five more were beatified in 1951, and Pope John Paul II in 1988 canonized 117, including some well-known catechists such as Andrew Dung Lac, Phanxico Xavier Can, Vincent Diem, Phaolo Le Bao Tinh, Phero Nguyen Khac Tu, and a woman, Agnes Le Thi Thanh. The beatifications and canonizations were the ultimate recognition of the struggles of the faithful believers. Catholics had long venerated those killed in religious violence, treating their relics as sacred objects and making the martyrs (*thanhtudao*) figures of devotion.

Catholics celebrated the canonization annually throughout Vietnam. Pastoral letters were issued from the bishops with the schedule of the celebrations, including brief biographies of the martyrs and accounts of their deaths. Before 1925, martyrs were often honored alongside Joan of Arc, usually around May 8, when she lifted the siege of Orleans, or May 30, her feast day. But in 1925, the newly appointed apostolic delegate to Vietnam decreed the first Sunday in September as a national day of mourning for Vietnam's martyrs. Today, the Vietnamese martyrs are celebrated on November 24 in the universal Catholic calendar. For Vietnamese Catholics, the traditional practice of remembering the martyrs in the home country is brought to America where large congregations gather to remember these martyrs. These celebrations have become also an occasion for Vietnamese American Catholics to remember their home country struggles.

Leaders and Future of the Vietnamese American Catholics

The establishment of parishes, national organizations, and religious vocations creates a place for Vietnamese American Catholics within the larger Catholic Church. Their presence is noted among major religious as well as secular publications. From these communal efforts, there have also emerged individuals who have become leaders among the Vietnamese American Catholics. The following three people are highlighted for their efforts to make the community more visible: Father Vien Nguyen, Sister Anna Nguyen, and Dr. Peter Phan.

Father Vien Nguyen is pastor of the Mary Queen of Vietnam Church located in New Orleans East. This was the first community of Vietnamese American Catholics, established in 1975, making it the oldest of the Vietnamese parishes in America. Father Vien had been at the parish for over three years before Hurricane Katrina hit in 2005. He was instrumental during Katrina in helping many of his parishioners escape the flooding and also relocate them after they were dispersed to other parts of the United States. There were at the time over 22,000 Vietnamese in New Orleans with approximately 14,000 of them Catholics. He was pastor of the main church as well as helping with the mission, which was an extension of the church. Father Vien and his parishioners are featured in a documentary called *A Village Called Versailles*. It describes how the tight-knit Vietnamese community rebuilt their neighborhood faster than any other in New Orleans after Katrina. They also became a strong political voice after Katrina when the city wanted to put a toxic dump site about two miles from their neighborhood. This raised much concern and under the guidance of Father Vien, the parish was able to mobilize the whole community against city leaders and helped rebuild their neighborhood into a safe community. He continues to serve the parish and has instilled a very politically conscientious church community.

Sister Anna Nguyen is a member of the Sisters of Christian Charity, the first Vietnamese religious sister to be an assistant director for the Asian Pacific Islander communities at the United States Conference of Catholic Bishop's (USCCB) Office for Cultural Diversity located in Washington, D.C. She was hired in 2011. She has worked many years with refugees and immigrants in the Washington, D.C. area. She sees her role as an animator of the various Asian and Pacific communities across the United States, and particularly she has worked in many different Vietnamese parishes in the United States. Her interest is to help the different generations in the Vietnamese American communities to work together to build a stronger Vietnamese American Catholic presence.

Peter C. Phan is a theology professor at Georgetown University. His publications range widely in theology from the patristic theology to liberation, enculturation, and interreligious dialogue. He has edited some 20 volumes including topics such as liturgy and ecumenism to the Asian church. His contribution to the Vietnamese community includes lectures given to various communities across the United States as well as in Vietnam. His book on Alexandre de Rhodes is a great addition to the history of Vietnamese Catholicism as well as Vietnamese history. He is the first Vietnamese and first non-Anglo to be elected president of the Catholic Theological Society of America (CTSA). In 2010, he was given the John Courtney Murray Award, the highest honor of the CTSA, in recognition of outstanding and distinguished achievement in theology. He works to promote future Vietnamese theologians.

This is just a small sampling of Vietnamese American Catholic leaders who have set a path for other Vietnamese Catholics to help and support the development of the wider Vietnamese American Catholic community. They continue to work hard in their respective areas to raise awareness but also contribute to the development of the larger community

The future for Vietnamese American Catholics is quite encouraging with the growing number of vocations, personal parishes, and visible leaders. They are an inspiration to the American church that has experienced a decline in vocations. But there are some concerns. As the Vietnamese Catholics continue to create a place in America, they will also face problems similar to those of previous immigrant groups. Many first-generation Vietnamese lament the fact that the second and subsequent generations do not participation in the church. Even though vocations are strong, the Vietnamese do not have a large representation among the higher leadership of the church, especially as bishops or superiors of religious communities. Another concern for the future is the type of church model that the community wants to maintain. It has been an insti-

tutional top-down model that does not leave room for younger voices to be heard or to take leadership positions. The younger generation needs to be encouraged and supported. These challenges are not impossible obstacles. As a community the Vietnamese American Catholics have demonstrated courageously that challenges become an opportunity to transform through the support of God.

Linh Hoang

See also: Essays: Catholics; *Entries:* Caodaism; Hoa Hao Buddhism; Vietnamese American Religions

Further Reading

Asian and Pacific Presence: Harmony in Faith. Washington, DC: U.S. Conference of Catholic Bishops, 2001.

Bankston, Carl L. "Vietnamese-American Catholicism: Transplanted and Flourishing." *U.S. Catholic Historian* 18, no. 1 (Winter 2000): 36–53.

Keith, Charles. *Catholic Vietnam: A Church from Empire to Nation.* Berkeley: University of California Press, 2012.

Phan, Peter C. *Vietnamese-American Catholics.* Mahway, NJ: Paulist Press, 2005.

Phan, Peter C. "Vietnamese Catholics in the United States: Christian Identity between the Old and the New." *U.S. Catholic Historian* 18, no. 1 (Winter 2000): 19–35.

VietCatholic News. www.vietcatholic.net. Accessed July 16, 2014.

Vietnamese American Religions

The religious sphere of the Vietnamese and Vietnamese American people has been shaped by several world religions: Chinese Confucianism (*Khong giao* or *Nho*), Chinese Daoism (*Lao giao* or *Laõ*), and Chinese Buddhism (*Phat giao* or *Thich*) are the result of nearly one thousand years of Chinese domination (111 BCE–938 CE); Protestantism and Catholicism were introduced with the French during the French colonial period (1859–1945 CE). Over the centuries, Confucianism, Daoism, Buddhism, and popular Chinese folk traditions have amalgamated with ancient Vietnamese animism to form what is collectively known as *Tam Giao* (Three Religions—*Nho-Thich-Laõ*), which is sometimes referred to as "Vietnamese Buddhism," but is more appropriately termed "Vietnamese popular religion." Prior to the arrival of Chinese rule, ancestral veneration profoundly influenced the religious life of the Vietnamese people.

Confucianism was introduced into Vietnam as early as the first century during Chinese rule. Confucian ethics and values have deeply penetrated the Vietnamese family structure and its emphasis on ancestral veneration and remembrance, which reinforces the Confucian virtue of filial piety. Hence, it is no surprise that the family altar is the cosmic center, the most honored place in a Vietnamese household. Daoism was also introduced into Vietnam during Chinese rule, but remained largely marginal within the *Tam Giao* tradition; nonetheless, its influence is clear in forms of divination, fortune telling, and ritual performance. The predominant religion of Vietnam is Buddhism. Vietnamese Buddhism—a combination of Chan (Zen), Pure Land, Tiantai, and popular Vajrayana—is the main tradition for the majority of Vietnamese people. Christianity has

also influenced Vietnamese spirituality. Vietnam has the highest percentage of Catholics in Asia outside of the Philippines (8 to 10 percent of the population). Portuguese, Spanish, and French missionaries introduced Christianity into Vietnam during the second half of the 16th century. Christianity was banned in Vietnam around the 17th century. Despite the proscription, Catholic missionaries continued to evangelize to the Vietnamese people, perhaps explaining why 29 to 40 percent of Vietnamese refugees in America are Roman Catholic. In addition, new Vietnamese religions have also developed and have been transplanted to Vietnamese American communities, most notably, Caodaism and Hoa Hao Buddhism.

The development of the Caodai movement in 1962 is connected to French colonialism, introducing séances and spiritism, which, blended with Chinese-style divination, resulted in the development of Caodai. Caodai can be considered a cornucopia of religions, including elements of Buddhism, Confucianism, Daoism, Protestantism, Catholicism, Hinduism, and Islam, in combination with veneration of secular personalities (e.g., French poet and writer Victor Hugo; exiled founder of the People's Republic of China Dr. Sun-Yat-sen; World War II British prime minister Sir Winston Churchill; and a Vietnamese diviner, Trang Trinh).

Hoa Hao, a reform Vietnamese Buddhist sect of the Theravāda tradition, was founded in 1930 in the village of An Giang Province. This is the religion and practice that Vietnamese refugees bring with them to America, helping them ease into their relocation as religious communities, be it

Catholic, Buddhist, or Hoa Hao, and helping them establish solidarity and a network of support to begin their new life.

In the United States many Vietnamese Americans continue to practice ancestral veneration by creating a family altar in their homes as a sacred place for the ritual performance of veneration and remembrance of their ancestors. This belief and ritual is based on a certain understanding of the soul. The *am*-soul is dense and clings to the body, and is believed to remain at the gravesite. The *duong*-soul is less dense, less malevolent, and therefore more auspicious—found around the home and the family altar. Daily ritual offerings are performed in the home altar for the *duong*-soul. Special foods are prepared during the 15th and 16th of each lunar month and during Tet Nguyen Dan (Vietnamese Lunar New Year) for the *yang*-souls on the ancestral altar.

Similar to other Southeast Asian Buddhist communities (e.g., Khmer American and Thai American), Buddhism plays a central role in the moral and social education of Vietnamese American youths. Hence, Vietnamese temples in both Vietnam and the United States are not only sites to carry out spiritual work but where traditional and cultural values are preserved and transmitted. When Vietnamese refugees first came to the United States in 1975, they brought with them the first Vietnamese Buddhist community. By 1995, there were 160 Vietnamese Buddhist temples and centers in North America.

While in Vietnam there were monks and nuns in permanent residence, not all temples in the United States have a permanent resident monk. The economic neces-sity in the United States for a monk to work outside the temple has altered the relationship between the laity and the monk. This, in turn, has modified the function of the temple in the United States. Smaller temples known as "home temples," many of which operate from private rural homes, mainly function in the performance of rituals, especially funerals, while the larger temples may function as cultural centers and language schools. The transplanted congregation would invite a monk to come and build a temple; otherwise they would build the temple and then recruit a monk.

Since the temple's primary importance is for performing rituals, Vietnamese people will visit a temple only when an occasion arises, such as a funeral, which is an important rite of passage in ancestral veneration. Memorial services are often held for family members and relatives who died during the Vietnam War. This is possible because the spirit of the deceased is considered to always remain part of the family and it accompanied the family's immigration to the United States. Some older Vietnamese Americans find the prospect of death stressful because they fear that their spirits and memories will not be given the proper traditional veneration by their Americanized children after they die.

Orange County, California, is home to the largest Vietnamese community in the United States and has come to be known as "Little Saigon." Small Vietnamese temples, "home temples," are operated throughout the United States where Vietnamese Americans live—in Denver, Colorado; Houston, Texas; New Orleans,

Louisiana; Oklahoma City, Oklahoma; Chicago, Illinois; Los Angeles, Oakland, and San Jose, California; Olympia, Washington; Portland, Oregon; and so forth.

The main characteristic of Vietnamese American communities and their religious beliefs and practices is adaptability. The communities have been able to withstand periods of colonial rule and outside influence, and hence, they will be a source of strength for new migrants rebuilding a life in America.

Jonathan H. X. Lee

See also: Entries: Caodaism; Hoa Hao Buddhism; Vietnamese American Buddhists; Vietnamese American Catholics

Further Reading

Crawford, Ann. *Customs and Culture of Vietnam*. Rutland, VT: Charles E. Tuttle, 1966.

Do, Hien Duc. *The Vietnamese Americans: The New Americans*. Westport, CT: Greenwood Press, 1999.

Henkin, Alan B., and Liem Thanh Nguyen. *Between Two Cultures: The Vietnamese in America*. Saratoga, NY: Century Twenty-One, 1981.

Wake, Lloyd K. (1922–)

Lloyd K. Wake, a native of Reedley, California, was born into a large Japanese immigrant family with eight children—two boys and six girls. His father was a farmer and Wake himself worked with him after his graduation from high school in 1939 until the forced evacuation and incarceration of his family in August 1942 (during World War II the U.S. government put more than 100,000 persons of Japanese descent in 10 different concentration camps across the United States).

For the first time in his life Wake witnessed his stoical father shedding tears. After all these years of hard work, the U.S. government took it all away. His whole family was interned in Poston III Concentration Camp in Arizona. Wake's father died in the camp. Wake kept himself busy with athletics, singing in a quartet, and being active in the ministry of Poston III Christian Church.

From 1943 to 1946 Wake attended Asbury College in Wilmore, Kentucky, and Asbury Seminary from 1946 to June 1948. He furthered his theological education at American Baptist Theological Seminary and Pacific School of Religion in Berkeley, California, from 1948 to 1950. He supported the civil rights struggles while he was studying in Berkeley and continued to be active in the movement during the 1950s and 1960s.

From September 1948 to June 1950 he served as a student pastor of Berkeley Methodist United Church and was ordained for Christian ministry in the Methodist Church in June 1950. From July 1950 to June 1967 he served as a pastor of San Francisco Pine United Methodist Church, one of the first churches ministering to Japanese Americans. During this period of his ministry he was engaged in the project to relocate the church from downtown to a new facility on 33rd Avenue. He also chaired the San Francisco County Jail Chaplaincy program of the San Francisco Council of Churches and served as a member of the Board of Trustees of Glide Foundation from 1963 till 1967.

From 1967 to December 1999 Wake served as minister of community life of Glide Memorial Church (GMC) in San Francisco. During this time he supervised 30 conscientious objectors to the Vietnam War who did alternative service at Glide and its related agencies as well as a number of the theological students who interned at GMC. Furthermore, he also served as the financial officer of GMC and the Glide Foundation. From 1980 to 1989 he was one of the first pastors to perform Covenant Service, holy union for gay, lesbian, bisexual, and transgender partners.

Throughout his ministry Wake was always involved in community concerns and theological education. For example, he supported the students and faculty during Third World strikes at San Francisco State University in San Francisco. He was an active member of the Board of San Francisco Family Service Agency advocating gay persons to become members of the board and a member of the Central City Hospitality House. He likewise served as a member of the Board of Asian Law Caucus and later as its chair from 1993 to 1997. Wake supported the redress and reparations movement for the Japanese and Japanese Americans who were incarcerated during World War II and testified at the San Francisco hearing of the Commission on Wartime Relocation and Internment of Civilians. He was the chair of the Wendy Yoshimura Fair Trial Committee from 1977 to 1980.

Wake's ministry, however, went beyond the congregations and local community involvement. For example, he was also involved with the National Agencies of the United Methodist Church, serving as a member of the General Council on Ministries, a member of the General Council of Finance and Administration, and the chair of the National Federation of Asian American United Methodists as well as the treasurer of the Council of Pacific Asian Theology.

As a theological educator, Wake contributed to the book *Out of Every Tribe and Nation: Christian Theology at the Ethnic Round Table* (1992), and he has served as an adjunct faculty member at the Pacific School of Religion since his retirement in 1990. Wake traveled extensively to attend international conferences, such as the human rights support trip to Japan, South Korea, Taiwan, and the Philippines in 1985 and the Peacemaking Seminar in Okinawa with the North American delegates in 1995.

Since his official retirement from active ministry, he continues to serve in various capacities, such as manager and chair of the Endowment Fund of the National Federation of Asian American United Methodists, and minister at large with Soko Bukai (Council of San Francisco Japanese Christ Churches). He also led the council's successful lawsuit against the San Francisco YWCA to retain ownership of the Sutter YWCA. He likewise supported the Nihonmachi Little Friends Project to upgrade the Sutter YWCA and the Lt. Ehren Watada Support Committee supporting Watada's refusal to serve in Iraq. Wake further organized and supported the empowerment of leshian, gay, bisexual, transsexual, and queer persons in the community and the church.

As a retired person he enjoys celebrating special occasions with his family of 4 children, 11 grandchildren, and 2 great-grandchildren. He and his spouse Marion are subjects of a film documentary, *Being Human, Being True.*

Paul M. Nagano

See also: Entries: Pacific and Asian American Center for Theologies and Strategies (PACTS); United Methodism

Further Reading

González, Justo L. *Out of Every Tribe and Nation: Christian Theology at the Ethnic Round Table.* Nashville: Abingdon Press, 1992.

Wangyal, Ngawang (1901–1983)

Ngawang Wangyal (1901–1983), popularly known as Geshe Wangyal, was the first major Tibetan Buddhist teacher in the

United States. A Kalmuk Mongolian born in Astrakhan Province in southeast Russia, he entered the monastery at the age of six. After the Russian Civil War, he studied at the Gelukpa-affiliated Drepung Monastic University in Lhasa, Tibet. Wary of returning to a Russia that was persecuting clerics, he secured work comparing the different editions of the *Kanjur* (Tibetan Buddhist canon) in Beijing, China, in 1935. He left China in 1937, intending to return to Tibet via India. While in Kolkata, Geshe Wangyal met the British scholar and explorer Sir Charles Bell, who hired him as a translator, and he accompanied Bell during his travels though China and Manchuria. Having earned enough money, he returned to Lhasa to complete his *geshe* degree (equivalent to a doctor of theology). When the Communist Chinese entered Tibet, he fled to India. In 1955 he left for the United States to work among the Kalmuk refugees whom the Tolstoy Foundation had resettled in the New Jersey–New York–Pennsylvania region after World War II. He founded the Lamaist Buddhist Monastery of America (Labsun Shedrug Ling), where he served as the abbot until his death in 1983. The precursor of the Tibetan Buddhist Learning Center, it was the first Tibetan monastery in the West.

Geshe Wangyal taught at Columbia University during the 1960s and 1970s. In addition to establishing other Tibetan monasteries and temples and training refugees such as scholars to work in the West, he mentored many U.S.-born scholars, including Geshe Sopa, Robert A. F. Thurman, and Jeffrey Hopkins. Geshe Wangyal translated *The Door of Liberation* and *The*

Prince Who Became a Cuckoo, popular Tibetan stories of Buddhist teachings.

Ronald Y. Nakasone

See also: Entries: Tibetan American Religions; Trungpa, Chögyam

Further Reading

Fields, Rick. *How the Swans Came to the Lake: A Narrative History of Buddhism in America.* Boston: Shambhala, 1992.

Prebish, Charles S., and Kenneth K. Tanaka, eds. *The Faces of Buddhism in America.* Berkeley: University of California Press, 1998.

Seager, Richard Hughes. *Buddhism in America.* New York: Columbia University Press, 1999.

Watt Samaki

Watt Samaki, "Unity Temple," is a Cambodian temple located in central Long Beach, California. In 2006, the city of Long Beach designated this portion of town as Cambodia Town. The blessing and dedication ceremony of the Cambodia Town sign inauguration took place at Watt Samaki on June 16, 2012. This illustrates the central role of the Theravāda Buddhist temple for many Cambodian Americans in Long Beach. Long Beach is home to diverse religious practices. The Cambodian Buddhist temple maintains an identity as a Cambodian temple through physical decorations, Khmer language, the Buddhist calendar, physical and religious rituals, gender roles, and community gatherings.

The homes that surround Watt Samaki are typical Southern California tract homes. Watt Samaki Temple sits in a bungalow home painted avocado green with white pointed trimmings. Although the temple sits within a tract home, it remains a physically distinct religious space from the neighboring homes. Watt Samaki is insulated physically from its environs through embellishments with three flags, American, Cambodian, and Buddhist, flying at high mast in the courtyard. Within the temple walls chanting, temple chime music, heavy incense, and religious and social interaction of lay and non-lay persons in making merit characterize Watt Samaki.

Inside the main worship area, flowers and candles form a personal space where the monk sits surrounded by Buddha depictions embellished with aesthetic markers in the main worship area. White roses in a vase complement the wall of the five depictions of the glittering deities sitting in meditation position. On the wall in the main worship area hang between 25 and 30 framed pictures of monks, some with orange robes while others are framed head shots; pictures are lined in rows of four or five in columns that align all the way up to the ceiling. When there are visitors, the monk sits behind four white unlit candles half a foot long; two white candles are closer together and paired off while the other two stand upright coupled off apart. The monk's seated position in front of the Bodhi tree depiction amidst freshly cut flowers, ivory-colored candles, music, and glittering depictions of deities makes him clearly visible to community visitors, the majority of whom are older women.

Upon entering the main worship area at Watt Samaki, visitors follow physical rituals. After entering the main worship area, visitors show respect by clasping both hands in front of them and bowing toward Buddha, Dhamma, and *Sangha*. It is not uncommon to see visitors walk in, kneel to the Buddha, Dhamma, and *Sangha*, then leave without saying a word. Everyone follows this ritual upon entrance into the main worship area of the temple. If visitors sit down on the floor, they must tuck their feet in so that the toes do not face the monk. Clasping the hands depends on the person being greeted. Both thumbs touch the forehead when greeting the Buddha, Dhamma, and *Sangha*. According to the monk, the thumbs touch the nose to greet parents because they are the breath that flows through the nose. The thumbs touch the mouth to greet teachers, and the hands are at the heart to greet friends and equals. Visitors may not follow the specific hand movements in showing respect but the major body movements are adhered to by everyone.

During large community events, a large triangular tent is erected in the outdoor courtyard to make shade for a long table with a thick beige tablecloth with white squiggly designs. On the table are four settings that include a glass or porcelain bowl, two bottles of water, and a can of sweet green gourd drink set out for the monks. At the end of the table is a large statue of Buddha. Gold-colored holders wrapped with yellow plastic are tied decoratively on the table. Hung above the Buddha statue is a gold-colored fabric with the texture of silk with beads sewn onto its edges. To the left of the Buddha statue is an assortment of potted flowers, including a living rose plant in a white ceramic pot. Next to the potted rose is a large glass full of unlit incense. On the edge of the tent are approximately 15 mini Buddhist flags hanging and blowing in the wind. Everything is laid out symmetrically with care, and incense is consistently lit throughout the space.

Clothing also characterizes the space at Watt Samaki. Some visitors to Watt Samaki don traditional Cambodian clothing but the majority dress in more casual clothing. On special occasions, younger Cambodian Americans are present at the temple dressed in jeans and T-shirts, as well as cargo pants. The clothing varies but is generally neatly arranged. Although the clothing worn by visitors is not necessarily traditional, because of the care involved, it seems the visitors understand that within the community on a special occasion individuals want to be seen as respectable, helping to create a sense of celebration and reverence at Watt Samaki.

Visitors may also consult the temple calendar. Each temple has its own calendar based on lunar and solar patterns. Religious days are called *sel* days. Adherents consult the calendar specific to the temple to decide which days to visit. Visitors are aware of and adhere to the Buddhist calendar, which helps maintain a religious sense of time at the temple. This concept of time helps the temple maintain a religious identity within urban Long Beach. For example, at Watt Samaki, the season of Ben Katun follows Pchum Ben as shown on the temple calendar, which notes that Ben Katun is from October 30 to November 28. People visit the temple to make offerings and chant, creating a sense of Buddhist time at Watt Samaki.

Visitors at Watt Samaki are diverse, including men and women speaking Vietnamese, in addition to the majority of visitors speaking Khmer. The large presence of women visitors at Watt Samaki is a distinct characteristic of the temple's social structure. While Watt Samaki is headed by a male, women play a significant role at the temple and make up the majority of Watt Samaki's visitors. The idea of empowerment through gender is embedded in the concepts of Buddhism and duty. Therefore, gender does not seem to exist as theoretical categories outside the cultural and religious nexus at Watt Samaki. Instead, gender is enacted by men and women at Watt Samaki, interwoven with age, the concepts of time and space, and merit. In other words, visitors create and recreate a sense of self and culture through patterns of gender, religious beliefs, and linguistic practice. This social structure helps visitors at Watt Samaki create a meaningful sense of place both externally and internally.

The monk Venerable Chancey Leung is visibly the center of the temple with the greatest social responsibilities as well as everyday labor such as washing dishes, cleaning kitchen appliances, and moving tables and chairs to clear the courtyard. He also interacts through informal conversation, partaking in the sense of social space at Watt Samaki. He is 52 years old, from Kampuchea Krom, and is fluent in both Khmer and Vietnamese. He also speaks some English and a dialect of Chinese. He spent one year in India and is learned in Pāli. He gives clear examples to make concepts easier to understand; he is a natural teacher and a clear public leader at the temple. He has practiced Buddhism for a lifetime with no salary to show that Watt Samaki is a legitimate institution dedicated to communal service.

On special occasions, a man in his 60s helps organize events at the temple, soliciting people to help move chairs and tables on Pchum Ben. On normal weekdays he has a hammer in hand. He is deeply tanned, thin, with somewhat leathery skin as if he had spent much of his life in the sun; his hair is kept short and is visibly thick. He is healthy looking, but has the fine lines of a cigarette smoker and the deep lines of the sun on his face; his eyes are somewhat light, and he has an aura of physical energy that surrounds him despite his age. On one occasion he was throwing away furniture because the city said the temple had violated some codes by adding cement to a part of the outer area. This urban space is shifted and transformed into a Buddhist temple with these physical decorations. The small courtyard is altered against Long Beach city building codes to make space for community events.

The groundskeeper is a man in his 70s who sleeps at the temple. He wears eyeglasses and has very tanned skin and short crewcut gray hair; he is pensive, talkative in a slow, low voice about the use of merit; he wears casual clothing—a blue short-sleeved striped polo shirt, black or brown pajama pants—and rides a red 10-speed bicycle. He had come from Lowell in 1990 and has four grandchildren, one of whom lives in Long Beach because it was too cold in Massachusetts. The main base of labor consists of these two men at Watt Samaki.

Men form the core of the upkeep of the temple itself in terms of fixing the chairs but the division of labor is in reality sustained by both women and men. Men are leaders in the labor and women are accepted followers but the shape of gender is nuanced, not necessarily delineated by the categories male and female but rather intertwined with the religious concept of merit. Women who no longer live the life of family and children may reside at a temple in Cambodia. However, as funding for Watt Samaki may be dependent on social reputation within its environs, two men reside at the temple. While structures of participation at Watt Samaki are comprised of a visible regular base of labor performed by two men residing at the temple, the bulk of the work is equally shared by women.

While women cannot reside at the temple, they participate by creating the temple as a second home. In Khmer Buddhist conceptions, these ideas of inequality are expressed in terms of merit, *karma*, and Dharma. Women sustain the temple through daily visits offering food and money, raising their own status through the gender hierarchy. In fact, women adherents make up 85 percent of the visitors to Watt Samaki. Nonfestive days are quiet without the large community turnout that festivals for Pchum Ben, Sihanouk's honorary homage, and Ben Katun invite. Thus, the particular time and space of regular days are unique—void of community ears and eyes, filled instead with personal religious, protective ritual and moral support. The rituals are highly personal, illustrating an emotional exchange of protective services for adherent sustenance through food and money.

During Pchum Ben the outdoor concrete courtyard at Watt Samaki temple hosts approximately 50 visitors including monks who are seated at the center of the courtyard. Four saffron-robed monks sit in the morning sun at a large wooden table eating while mostly elderly women sit in white plastic chair talking about family and reuniting with old acquaintances. Elderly women wear silk skirts in dark purples, oranges, reds, greens. The visitors catch up with old friends and share food blessed by the monk. After the food is blessed, the scene becomes lively and social with people in conversation, sharing the blessed food, and then people take the food home. The blessed food is said to be eaten for children and grandchildren as well.

Venerable Chancey Leung focuses on the future of the community with increased focus on culture, religion, and the future as evidenced by his efforts to pass on Khmer culture, language, and Buddhism to youth. Venerable Chancey Leung says that previously he had opened a school but few students showed up because the students did not know the practical purpose of learning Khmer. He says young people should know how to chant and how to meditate and treat their parents with respect. It is important to learn from a good model of Khmer culture to be Buddhist. From generation to generation youth may not understand; youth trust their peers and they lose themselves. He says that it is only when they have their own children that they begin to understand. They realize their mistakes and tell their own children, just as teachers learn from their teachers and pass on this knowledge. Venerable Chancey Leung focuses on cultural and linguistic sustainability in the Cambodian American community using terms that

give a connotation of togetherness that underlies the sense of place created at Watt Samaki.

Venerable Chancey Leung does not use the concept of *karma* to talk about trouble with youth; he says they are unpolished diamonds and does not mention the role of *karma* in their lives. He attributes their situation to patterns of poverty. Venerable Chancey Leung arrived in the United States in 1993; thus, at this point he has been here for 20 years. His interpretation of Cambodian youth may be reflective of his own awareness of U.S. norms and beliefs about justice. However, adults in dire situations are seen as carrying negative *karma*, therefore having personal responsibility. The monk upholds the Buddhist principles of merit, Dharma, and *karma*, but raises the age range of adulthood from 12 or 13 to 20 to 30 years old, thus taking away the Buddhist idea of personal responsibility to make room for the social and economic conditions that impact the lives of adherents at Watt Samaki. Therefore, the Cambodian temple remains solidly Buddhist but becomes culturally Cambodian American. The shift in age range expresses a distinct cultural shift that takes place at Watt Samaki as its identity is in flux with the Cambodian American community. Adherents seek religious, protective ritual and social and moral support at Watt Samaki. He provides religious meaning to labor at the temple; washing dishes, offering food and money become actions based on the religious Buddhist concept of merit providing solace, structure, and meaning to adherents. This religious concept of merit intertwines with the reality of the temple as a significant social space where people gossip, share international news, and console each other. This significant space of worship continues to change.

Sophea Seng

See also: Entries: Cambodian American Religions; Theravāda Buddhism

Further Reading

Harris, Ian. *Cambodian Buddhism: History and Practice*. Honolulu, Hawai'i: University of Hawai'i Press, 2005.

Ledgerwood, Judy. "Changing Khmer Conceptions of Gender: Women, Stories, and the Social Order." Ph.D. Dissertation, Cornell University, 1990.

Y

Yamato Colony

Abiko Kyūtarō, a San Francisco newspaper publisher and businessman, founded the Yamato Colony in Livingston, California. Abiko (1865–1936) was born in Suibara, Nigata Prefecture, and was baptized in 1883 at the Kyobashi (Presbyterian) Church in Tokyo. He arrived in San Francisco in 1885, enrolled at the University of California at Berkeley, and bought two newspapers that became the *Japanese American News*, the forerunner of the *Nichibei Times* (disestablished on September 30, 2009). In the meantime, a devout Christian, he joined the Fukuinkai (Gospel Society), a nondenominational and independent Japanese Christian organization, and served as its president. Abiko's desire to establish a Japanese Christian utopia was no doubt shaped by the Fukuinkai's belief in the need to continue Japanese values within a hostile cultural environment.

Abiko used the profits of his newspaper and his business connections to purchase 3,200 acres of farmland in Livingston, California, in 1907. He recruited settlers by offering to sell the land for $35 an acre, financed over five years through Nichi Bei Ginkō (Japanese American Bank), a bank in which he had an interest. In addition to Yamato Colony Number One in Livingston, Abiko established the neighboring Japanese settlements in Cressey, Yamato Colony Number Two, and Cortez, Yamato Colony Number Three. He wanted to establish an economically self-sufficient environment, where the colonists would be encouraged to develop their Japanese culture. After the 1913 Alien Land Law was passed, some of the farmers incorporated. The farmers formed the Livingston Cooperative Society in 1914, which was split into the Livingston Fruit Growers Association and the Livingston Fruit Exchange in 1917. Soon after the outbreak of WWII, and being forced off their farms, the colonists hurriedly formed a cooperation under the joint trusteeship of Ritchie, McLaughlin, and Griswold. G. A. Momberg was hired to manage the farms. This astute move enabled the colony to preserve much of their assets. At the war's end, they returned to rebuild their lives and farms amid much hostility. Subsequently, in 1956 the Livingston Fruit Growers Association and the Livingston Fruit Exchange merged to form the Livingston Farmers Association, which is still in operation. Though predominately Japanese, the cooperative is now multiethnic.

Not all of the settlers of Yamato Colony were Christians, but the church played an important role in community life. Ten years after establishing Yamato Colony, in January 1917 the Livingston Japanese Church of Christ was organized with Rev. Jiryu Fujii (served 1918–1925) as its first minister. The church joined the Methodist conference in

1929 and changed its name to Livingston Japanese Methodist Church. In 1950 the church was renamed Grace Methodist Church, and in 1969 the Grace Methodist Church merged with the Euro-American First Methodist Church of Livingston to become the Grace United Methodist Church. Livingston is possibly the only Japanese community without a Buddhist presence.

The Yamato Colony of Livingston, California, is not to be confused with other Yamato colonies in Florida and Texas. Jo Sakai, who had just graduated from New York University, purchased 1,000 acres from the Model Land Company in what is now Boca Raton, Florida in 1903; he recruited young men from his hometown of Miyazu, Kyoto Prefecture. But because of a number of difficulties, the colony never grew very large; it gradually declined and disbanded during World War II. A third Yamato colony was founded in 1917 in Texas, but it was dissolved in 1921.

Ronald Y. Nakasone

See also: Entries: Presbyterian Churches of Japanese Heritage

Further Reading

"Biography of Kyutaro Abiko" in 18 installments. *Hokubei Mainichi* (newspaper), September 3, 1980 to November 1, 1980.

Matsumoto, Valerie. *Farming the Home Place, a Japanese Community in California, 1919–1982.* Ithaca, NY: Cornell University Press, 1993.

Noda, Kesaya. *Yamato Colony: 1906–1960, Livingston, California.* Livingston, CA: Livingston-Merced JACL, 1981.

"Yamato Colony." *Five Views: An Ethnic Historic Site Survey for California.* 1988. http://www.cr.nps.gov/history/online_books/5views/5views.htm. Accessed March 26, 2014.

Yee, James J. (1968–)

James J. Yee is a third-generation Chinese American. Yee was born in New Jersey and grew up Lutheran in the small town of Springfield Township. After attending Jonathan Dayton High School, Yee enrolled at West Point and graduated in 1990. In April 1991, Yee converted from Lutheranism to Islam and took the Arabic name Yusuf Yee. In 1995, Yee went to the Abu Nour Islamic foundation in Damascus, Syria, to study the Arabic language and the traditional Islamic sciences with Muslim clerics. While in Syria, Yee met his wife Huda Suboh, a 22-year-old Palestinian. Together they have one daughter. After four years of intensive study, Yee received a Certificate of Islamic Studies, which is equivalent to a graduate degree. In January 2001, Yee took a position as U.S. Army Muslim chaplain with an endorsement from the American Muslim Armed Forces and Veterans Affairs Council.

Yee served as a U.S. Army chaplain for the U.S. prison camp at the Marine base in Guantanamo Bay, Cuba. Guantanamo Bay is a controversial prison for its treatment of detainees designated as "enemy combatants" by the U.S. government. Many critics argue it is a site of torture and goes against the founding principles of American liberty and justice. While ministering at Guantanamo Bay, Chaplain Yee advised camp commanders on Muslim religious practices and beliefs, and objected to the cruel, dehumanizing, and degrading abuses taking place there.

Army Capt. James Yee holds his daughter Sarah, 3, as he stands with his wife Huda, and listens to reporters' questions prior to his military hearing at Fort Benning in Fort Benning, Georgia, on December 9, 2003. Yee authored the book *For God and Country,* which offers the public its first glimpse into the West Point graduate's ordeal as he was arrested on suspicion of espionage and held in solitary confinement for 76 days. He was later cleared in the investigation, but says his case should be a warning to others. (AP Photo/Dave Martin)

Yee was promoted to captain for outstanding performance, but on September 10, 2013, Captain Yee was arrested while returning to the States for a two-week leave with his wife and daughter. Yee was arrested by the FBI at the Jacksonville, Florida, Naval Air Station and whisked away in shackles, blackened eye goggles, and soundproof earmuffs to an isolation cell in the U.S. Navy brig in Charleston, South Carolina, where he was kept for 76 days. Yee was charged with five offenses: sedition, spying, espionage, aiding the alleged Taliban and Al Qaeda prisoners, and failure to obey general orders. After months of government investigation, all criminal charges against Yee were dropped. Yee was then reinstated to full duty at Fort Lewis, Washington. Even though he was assured his record would be wiped clean, Yee sensed his superiors and his fellow chaplains maintained doubts about his loyalty. On January 7, 2005, Yee received an honorable discharge from the U.S. Army. Upon separation, Yee received an Army Commendation medal for "exceptionally meritorious service."

Captain Yee's defense fund was organized by Justice for New Americans, first formed during the case of Wen Ho Lee, the Taiwan-born Los Alamos National Laboratory scientist who was arrested by the FBI in 1999 and found not guilty after 10 months in solitary confinement and the ruination of his career. The FBI had initially investigated Lee as a potential Chinese spy, but never had any evidence to back up the charge.

Yee shared his account of his work at Guantanamo Bay and his arrest and incarceration in a biography entitled *For God and Country: Faith and Patriotism under Fire* (2005). Yee received the Exceptional Communicator Award from New America Media in January 2006. In June 2006, Yee earned his master's degree in international relations. He now lectures about his harrowing ordeal, Guantanamo Bay, Islam, Asian American and religious diversity issues, and the challenges of protecting both national security and civil liberties.

Jonathan H. X. Lee

See also: Essays: Islamophobia; Muslims; Religion, Race, and Orientalism

Further Reading

"Justice for Yee." http://www.justiceforyee.com. Accessed July 29, 2014.

Yee, James. *For God and Country: Faith and Patriotism under Fire, Former U.S. Army Muslim Chaplain at Guantanamo Bay.* New York: PublicAffairs Books, 2005.

Yinyang

In Chinese philosophy, the concept of *yinyang*, literally meaning "shadow and light," is used to describe the two seemingly opposite forces in the natural world and how they interact and give rise to each other. This concept lies in many different classical Chinese philosophies and science. Furthermore, it has a great influence on Chinese traditional medicine, martial arts, and divination. Many natural dualities, such as heaven and earth, female and male, dark and light, cold and hot, and so on, are regarded as manifestations of the concept of *yinyang*. The philosophy of *yinyang* has widely influenced the East Asian cultural circle for thousands of years. In the United States, cultural practices related to the philosophy of *yinyang* are also maintained in some Asian American communities.

The Concept of *Yinyang*

Origin. Originating in a prehistoric, nature-based belief system, *yinyang* referred to the two sides of a mountain or a river. According to the *Shuowen Jiezi (Analytical Dictionary of Chinese Characters)*, *yin* initially referred to the shaded north side of a mountain or south bank of a river, while yang denoted the sunny south side of a mountain or north bank of a river. Later, the two characters embraced more and more meanings.

Yi Jing and *Yinyang*. In the early ancient Chinese classics, the concept of *yinyang* first appeared in the *Xi Ci (Appended Judgments)* commentary to *Yi Jing (Book of Changes)*, which states changes are the great primal beginning. It generates the two primary forces, which in turn birth the four images. These images generate the eight trigrams. They in turn determine good and misfortune. Good and misfortune create the great field of action.

The two primary forces represent *yinyang*. Based on this concept, sometime during the Song Dynasty (960–1279), Daoism created the symbol of *taiji* and *taijitu* (the image of the concept of *taiji*). The symbol of *taiji* includes a symmetrical pattern within a circle. An S-shaped line divides the circle into two equal parts—black and white. These two parts visually represent an interdependent cosmological relationship at work between two primary and opposing forces of the world known as *yinyang*. The white area represents yang elements and is generally depicted as rising on the left, while the black (*yin*) area is shown descending on the right. Each area also contains a large dot of a differing color at its fullest point to indicate how each will transform into the other. Basically, yin is the dark, passive, weak, disintegrative, and feminine aspect, while *yang* is the light, positive, strong, integrative, and masculine aspect. However, *yinyang* are not true opposites, but rather interdependent principles that complement, define, and give rise to each other. *Yinyang* also appeared as sets of lines known as hexagrams. The solid line represents *yang*, which is the creative principle. The open line represents yin, which is the receptive principle. The six lines of each hexagram represent a changing situation of the world: when *yang* is at the top, *yin* is increasing, and vice-versa. Based on the trigrams and hexagrams, we can derive eight possible trigrams.

Wuxing and *Yinyang*. During the Eastern Zhou Dynasty (770–256 BCE),

the *yinyang* school became one of six primary schools of Chinese philosophy. This school believed there are five agents or elements associated with *yinyang* (*wu-xing*): metal, wood, water, fire, and earth. According to this theory, things succeed one another as the five agents take their turns. *Yinyang* was at first conceived as opposed to each other, succeeding each other, or complementary to each other. The five agents, too, were conceived as overcoming one another or producing one another. Eventually all alternatives are synthesized so that harmony reigns over conflict and unity exists in multiplicity. *Yinyang* and the five agents are forces, powers, and agents rather than material elements. The whole focus is on process, order, and laws of operation. Existence is viewed as a dynamic process of change obeying definite laws, following definite patterns, and based on a preestablished harmony.

Yinyang and Its Influence on Daoism, Confucianism, and Legalism

The concept of *yinyang* also influenced other significant schools of Chinese philosophy in the Eastern Zhou Dynasty, such as Daoism, Confucianism, and legalism. These schools developed their own theories based on the comprehension of *yinyang*.

The understanding of *yinyang* is central to understanding Daoism. *Xi Ci* indicated, "Dao means combination of *yinyang*." Laozi, the founder of Daoism, developed this concept and proposed it in the *Daode Jing*. In it, Laozi says that human beings take their law from the Earth;

the Earth takes its law from Heaven; Heaven in turn takes its law from the Dao. The law of the Dao is the way of the Dao and is understood as being in its natural state of being. This became the central understanding of Daoism. The way of *yinyang* should thus be followed, which brings harmony in nature, society, and all under heaven.

Confucianism indicated that disasters happen when *yinyang* are both out of control and transcend their own limitations. Therefore, the *junzi*, the superior man, embodies the course of moderation, the balance of *yinyang*.

Legalism adopted the concept of interaction and transformation of *yinyang*. The legalists pointed out that since change is inevitable, people need to understand the change and control the change. The most important part is to legislate and make use of state machinery.

During the Han Dynasty (206 BCE–220 CE), scholars led by Dong Zhongshu sought to syncretize the various schools, including Daoism and Confucianism, and *yinyang* was applied to diverse realms, including medicine. Daoism and Buddhism mutually influenced each other during the early Tang Dynasty (618–907 CE), but Daoism ultimately became the official religion.

Yinyang and Its Influence on the East Asian Cultural Circle

Yinyang is also a key concept in the metaphysical systems of other East Asian countries, including Japan (where it is called *in-yo*), Vietnam, and Korea (as evidenced by the *yinyang* symbol on the South Korean flag). The influence of *yinyang* in East Asian countries is related to the spread of *Yi Jing* and its concepts.

In 513 CE, the emperor of Japan sent doctors of the classics to China and began to learn Chinese classics. At that time, the primitive religion dominated the country, so the content of divination and the concept of *yinyang* in *Yi Jing* were accepted by the society. The mysterious part fitted the pattern of the Japanese Shintō religion. The concept also influenced the other areas of Japan, such as politics, economics, and culture. After 1883 CE, Korea began to use the symbol of *taiji* on the national flag. This idea came from the theory of *yinyang*, the balance of the two forces in the cosmos.

Belief and Practice in the United States

By using the *Yi Jing* and other concepts of *yinyang*, Asian American culture has incorporated the traditional philosophy into its manner of approaching a variety of cultural practices in the United States. For instance, in medicine, traditional Chinese medicine and treatments such as massage, acupuncture, and cupping apply the concept of *yinyang* and *wu-xing* in the therapy. Nowadays, in America, some of these treatment methods have been adopted by standard Western medicine. Some medical schools offer courses on how to use the theory of *yinyang* to understand the nature of the human body. Furthermore, the popular Eastern martial arts, such as *taiji quan*, *qigong*, *taekwondo*, and *karate*, are also influenced by the concept of *yinyang*. Another important influence of *yinyang* is in *fengshui* (geomancy). *Fengshui* surely embraces the philosophy of *yinyang* and *wuxing*. A place that is very lively and full of energy is considered *yang* and a place that is motionless and dark is considered *yin*. In short, *fengshui* is a complex body of knowledge that reveals how to balance the energies of any given space to assure the health and good fortune of the people inhabiting it.

Furthermore, the concept of *yinyang* is also used as part of the philosophy of Asian American life. In the family, the Eastern family stresses harmony and balance between male and female, older and younger. Out of the family, Asian people in American society are often described as diligent and unassertive. They believe two opposites, such as failure and success, disaster and fortune, and so on, are related to each other and can be transformed.

Certainly, the philosophy of *yinyang* has had a historical and profound influence in both Eastern and Western society. In the United States, *yinyang* has highly influenced lifestyle and philosophy within the broader mainstream culture.

Ying Li

See also: Entries: Daoism; *Fengshui*

Further Reading

Borchert, Donald M. *Encyclopedia of Philosophy*. Detroit: Thomson Gale/Macmillan Reference USA, 2006.

Cua, A. S. *Encyclopedia of Chinese Philosophy*. New York: Routledge, 2003.

Mou, Bo. *Chinese Philosophy A–Z*. Edinburgh: Edinburgh University Press, 2009.

Wilhelm, Hellmut, and Cary F. Baynes. *The I Ching or Book of Changes*. Princeton, NJ: Princeton University Press, 2010.

Yoga

Yoga, from the Sanskrit root *yuj*, to connect or yoke, has been an integral part of Indian spiritual and cultural life for over 3,000 years. The expression has been used to refer to meditative exercises, religious contemplations, states of body and mind, and to the wisdom that results from spiritual practice. From its first appearances in the Upanishads through the radical contemplative rituals of medieval Tantra, *yoga* referred primarily to meditation techniques done in stillness. As *yoga* evolved, physical practices increased in popularity,

Yoga is now a mainstream and popular form of exercise, secular meditation, and body healing art form among Americans. Here, a *yoga* instructor adjusts a student during class. (Hongqi Zhang/Dreamstime.com)

coming to prominence with the *hatha yoga* movement. The practices of *hatha yoga*, especially *asana* (postures) and *prāṇāyāma* (breath control), were supplemented by athletic standing poses influenced by European calisthenics and contortion to form the backbone of 20th-century *yoga*.

Since its revival in the 1930s, the practices of *yoga* have spread throughout the world and are practiced by people of every religion and culture. As *yoga* has spread, elements of Indian spiritual culture have accompanied it, including study of Sanskrit texts, veneration of Hindu deities, chanting, *mantra* repetition, and Indian philosophical concepts. *Yoga* as practiced in Indian culture, both in India itself and throughout Indian immigrant culture in many countries, often differs substantially from its practice among convert communities. The adoption of *yoga* by the Western middle class is central to *yoga's* current dramatic transformation and reinvention. This entry traces the historical and doctrinal development of *yoga* primarily through its canonical texts.

Beginnings

The evolution of *yoga* can be traced through a series of important texts, which are our clearest record of the practices being done in each era. Each era's practices build on earlier ones, with focused attention (*samādhi*) central to all of them. *Yoga* arises first in a period of rich spiritual invention, as the ancient ritual practices described in the four *Vedas* begin to transform into internal practices to be performed by individual seekers. *Yoga* began as a reform movement centered around *śramaṇa*

(wanderers), men who roamed the wilderness, turning away from the religious life that was controlled by hereditary Brahmin priests, who performed the *yajña* or *homa*, the ritual fire sacrifice. Rejecting the Brahmanic culture, the *śramaṇa* developed methods for cultivating the mind and body independent of the sacrifice. These seekers made the fire sacrifice a metaphor, claiming that the body itself was the altar, internal energy the fire, and the prayers and practices of the seeker the offerings. These new practices, which centered on the practitioner's relationship to the senses and to the mind and body, were first systematically described in the *Kaṭha Upanishad* (1000–500 BCE).

The Upanishads—*Yoga* as Inner Fire

The word *yoga* first appears in the *Ṛg Veda* (possibly 2000+ BCE), but the first systematic descriptions of *yoga* as a method of inner cultivation appears in the Upanishads and refers to *pratyāhāra*, or withdrawal of the practitioner's attention from the objects of the physical senses. Meditation in classical *yoga* refers to the stabilizing of the practitioner's attention on a single continuous experience like the breath or the quality of awareness itself, and through that extraordinary stillness to see clearly the nature of the self (*atman*). Because the primary practice was the stilling of the thinking mind through concentration on a single object, the practices that led to stillness were called *yoga* (to "yoke" or bring together).

The path of the *yogi* is mythologized in the *Kaṭha Upanishad* (1000+ BCE), through the story of a youth named Naciketas, who travels to the home of the Lord of Death (*Yama*) after a dispute with his father over the proper sacrifice to the gods. Death is away when he arrives, and Naciketas has to wait three days, symbolizing individual solitary practice. When Death returns, he apologizes for offending his guest by keeping him waiting without food, and offers him three wishes, or "boons." Naciketas asks first for forgiveness by his father, then for the secrets of the sacrificial fire, and finally for the secret of what happens after death. Death grants him the first two boons, but tries to dissuade him from the last, offering instead wealth, power, and long life, but Naciketas persists. Death then teaches him the practice of *yoga*: *pratyāhāra* (sense-restraint) leading to *dhāraṇā* (concentration) and union with the true self, or *purusha*. The *Kaṭha* calls this path *yoga*, "Yoga of the Deep Self."

The practices taught in the *Kaṭha* are meditative, drawing the practitioner's awareness away from engagement with the external world. This meditation practice is supported by an understanding of the nature of the self that focuses on our tendency to prefer pleasant experience over unpleasant, described by a metaphor of a fountain "in the cave of the heart" from which sweet and bitter liquid flows. The separate self prefers the sweet over the bitter, but the supreme Self drinks both without preference. This instruction to disidentify with preference both supports the renunciate *śramaṇa* through the discomforts of wilderness life and is the foundation for the inward-turning of *pratyāhāra*. Training himself to let go of preferences, the *yogi* is able to ignore the habitual demands of the body and mind for comfort, food, and entertainment, devoting himself fully to the task of meditation and inquiry.

The Buddha's Revolution—*Yoga* as Insight

Siddhārtha Gautama (possibly 563–483 BCE) lived during the fertile intellectual and spiritual period of the Upanishads and embodied its creative and passionate spiritual ethos. He was a member of the Sakyan clan, a ruling family in what is now north-central India. After experiencing distress upon seeing an old person, a sick person, and a corpse, he left home to seek the deathless. He practiced meditative concentration under two prominent *yoga* teachers, then asceticism on his own, finally realizing "The Middle Way" between sensory indulgence and self-mortification, and insight into the cause of suffering. After realization, he was called Buddha, "The Awakened One." The Buddha taught a detailed *yoga* based on cultivating focused attention (*samādhi*) and mindfulness rooted in ethical action.

The Buddha's *yoga* integrated the practices of *samādhi* that were prevalent in his day with a quality of present-moment inquiry called mindfulness (Pāli: *sati*; Skt: *smṛti*). Mindfulness is a detailed inquiry practice that uses focus and stability of attention to attend closely to the arising sensory information of each moment, revealing three fundamental characteristics of every experience, known as the Three Marks (*tilakkhana*): impermanence (*anicca*), unsatisfactoriness (*dukkha*), and not-self (*anatta/anātman*). The difficult teaching of not-self set the Buddha apart from the Hindu Vedanta, which held that there is an individual self, or soul (*atman*), even as it understood the ultimate nature of that self to be impersonal and not different from Brahman. The distinction is subtle. When asked by the seeker Vachagotta whether there is a self or not, the Buddha famously refused to answer. *Anatta* points to the insubstantiality of our habitual sense of self and how the feeling of separateness, along with the clinging that is the habit of the mind, creates suffering and stress. As Buddhist practice communities developed, they grew to include a vast array of methods, all designed to accomplish the task of uprooting the causes of suffering in the heart. These practices were impacted by local traditions as Buddhism took root in different countries.

The *Yoga Sūtra* of Patañjali—*Yoga* as Stillness

The *Yoga Sūtra* is one of the most deeply influential texts on *yoga*, and it is used in many modern *yoga* lineages as the primary philosophical text. It was written or compiled by a sage named Patañjali between 200 BCE and 200 CE, though Patañjali's historical identity is unknown. *Yoga* in the *Yoga Sūtra* refers to the stilling or "cessation" (*nirodha*) of thought patterns, sometimes translated as "fluctuations of consciousness" (*citta-vṛtti*). This stilling allows awareness (*puruṣa*) to "rest in its true nature" as a pure or unconditioned knowing, understood as separate from, and therefore not bound by, the objects of which it is aware.

The meditative process outlined in the *Yoga Sūtra* focuses on understanding the independent nature of awareness through the cultivation of profound mental stillness that uproots the practitioner's habitual identification with concepts. The *Yoga Sūtra* codified the *yoga* practices of the day into a program of practice known as the Eight Limb, or Aṣṭāṅga system, mirroring the earlier Eightfold Path of the Buddha. The *Yoga Sūtra* includes practices and quotations from Buddhist and Upanishadic sources, held within a philosophical framework borrowed from the dualist Sāṃkhya school. Patañjali's Eight Limbs chart a path of increasing subtlety of contemplative objects, beginning with ethical principles and practices for personal purification through a breath-oriented meditative practice that culminates in extraordinary unification of mind. The Eight Limbs are the following:

1. *Yama*: ethical practices that clarify the yogi's relationship with external community.

   Ahimsa: nonharming

   Satya: truthfulness

   Asteya: nonstealing

   Brahmacarya: celibacy

   Aparigraha: nonacquisitiveness

2. *Niyama*: purificatory practices that clarify the yogi's intention and practice

   Śauca: cleanliness

   Saṃtoṣa: contentment

   Tapas: discipline

   Svādhyāya: self-study, both of sacred texts and the inner self

   Īśvara-praṇidhāna: surrender to the Divine, or to the paradigm of pure awareness

3. *Asana*: the "seat" or posture of meditation

4. *Prāṇāyāma*: cultivation of the breath as a stable and spacious meditative object

5. *Pratyāhāra*: withdrawal of the senses from attachment to their objects

6. *Dhāraṇā*: the practice of concentration leading to one-pointedness of mind

7. *Dhyāna*: one-pointed meditative absorption that arises as *dhāraṇā* matures

8. *Samādhi*: "bringing together," full unification of mind in meditative stillness

Patañjali's *yoga*, like the Buddha's, is meditative, focusing on cultivating states of profound unification of mind called *saṃyama*, consisting of the combination of the last three limbs (*dhāraṇā, dhyāna,* and *samādhi*) generally in physical and mental stillness. This unification is the primary condition for the cultivation of supernatural powers (*siddhi*), and more importantly for the inquiry into the relationship of pure awareness (*puruṣa*) and nature (*prakṛti*). Patañjali's core teaching in the *Yoga Sūtra* is that we habitually confuse awareness with its objects. The mind in *saṃyama* is stable enough to see both sense objects arising and awareness of them, and through this clear-seeing deconstructs every experience to reveal pure awareness as independent (*kaivalya*) of external conditions. This independence, which was always true but veiled by ignorance (*avidyā*) and mental instability, undoes the habitual entanglement created by the clinging mind and is synonymous with *mokṣa*, or liberation.

The *Yoga Sūtra* presents the meditative path that would come to be called *raja yoga*, "The Royal Path," or classical *yoga*. Many modern *yogis* descended from the great teacher Tirumalai Krishnamacharya (1888–1989) use this text as a guide for *asana* practice and yogic life in general, blending *raja yoga* with the *hatha yoga* of postures and breath work. This blending is the source of some controversy in contemporary *yoga* circles, and Patañjali's emphasis on the distinction between *puruṣa* and *prakṛti* has led to its rejection by some Tantric schools for its dualism. Nevertheless, it is considered by many *yoga* schools to be a valuable guide to yogic life, and it is still the most commonly required source text for modern *yoga*.

The *Bhagavad Gītā*—*Yoga* as Devotion

In the *Bhagavad-Gītā*, "The Blessed Song" (ca. 200 CE), perhaps India's most beloved spiritual text, the god Krishna teaches *yoga* to the warrior Arjuna on the battlefield before the devastating battle that is the centerpiece of the epic *Mahābhārata*. Krishna is said to be an incarnation of Vishnu, who in the devotional literature manifests in the world to sustain Dharma, righteousness, or natural law. Krishna describes for Arjuna four kinds of *yoga* practice. The description of *yoga* in the Gita synthesizes Buddhist, Upanishadic, and Vedanta influences, and emphasizes the practice of devotion (*bhakti*). The four kinds of *yoga* are the following:

Karma yoga: renunciation of the fruits of action

Jñana yoga: inquiry into the nature of the self through study and investigation

Raja yoga: the unification of the mind in meditation

Bhakti yoga: union with the Divine through devotional love and surrender

These four approaches to *yoga* outline not just a personal approach to spiritual life, but weave through mainstream Hindu practice as the Gita becomes one of the primary sacred texts of the religion. *Yoga*, by the time it appears in the Bhagavad Gita, is no longer a reform tradition that resisted the Brahmanic religion, but had become central to the understanding of spirituality throughout Indian religion. *Yoga* is now understood as the pathway by which one is liberated from *karma* and the round of endless birth (*samsara*).

The *Bhagavad-Gītā* begins with the challenging renunciation teaching of *karma yoga*: letting go of attachment to the fruit of one's actions. This letting go is predicated on the same attitude toward preferences that was the centerpiece of the *Katha Upanishad* and leads to the balanced mind state of equanimity. In the Gita, this equanimity is particularly directed toward thoughts of success and failure, and is the first teaching offered to Arjuna, wrestling with the suffering that will result from war. The teachings of Krishna begin with his urging Arjuna to fight and continue into teachings on the nature of the self, its relationship to the divine, and the yogic practices that lead the seeker to realize his true nature.

Yoga in the Gita is again meditative, emphasizing the stabilization of attention through *pratyāhāra* (sense-restraint) leading to *dhāranā/dhyāna* (concentration/absorption) and *samādhi* (unification). This ancient yogic method is now held within the frame of renunciation (*vairagya*) and devotion (*bhakti*): letting go of the fruits of action, supported by insight into *karma* as the endless cycle of birth and death. Meditative concentration in the Gita is again called *raja yoga*, and the practice is similar to that in Patañjali's *Yoga Sūtra*. Study of spiritual texts and inquiry into the nature of the self is called *jñāna yoga*, the path of knowledge, understood both as "external" philosophical study and "internal" contemplative investigation.

Bhakti yoga, described in the Gita as the most accessible and powerful *yoga*, grew into a widespread reformation movement of its own. *Bhakti yoga* is praised in the Gita as easier than either meditation or study. It would become the preeminent religious practice, influencing all of the major Indian religious traditions, including Hindu, Buddhist, Jain, Sikh, and Muslim/Sufi streams of practice. The Bhagavad Gita taught a *yoga* oriented to householders that emphasized fulfilling one's caste duties and cultivating *karma yoga*, renunciation of the fruits of action, and bhakti, devotion to God. *Bhakti yoga* would become one of the foundations for the powerful Tantric revolution that transformed Indian spiritual life between the 5th and 13th centuries.

Tantra—*Yoga* as Energy

Tantra (500–1300 CE) arose as a radicalization of the classical *yoga* of inner fire, devotion, concentration, and the subtle body, replacing silent meditation with ritual, visualization, mantra, *guru yoga*, and energetic practices. Tantric texts began to appear in the fourth and fifth centuries, and spread rapidly, taking root particularly in Kashmir in the far north and in Tamil Nadu in the south. It was a householder lineage, not dependent on solitude or celibacy, and it became very widespread, with public temples, patronage, and lineages of visionary teachers. Tantra in Kashmir focused on Shiva and is known as Śaiva Tantra, which centered on the writings of the great sages Vasugupta, Abhinavagupta, and Kṣemarāja. Tantra spread throughout India into diverse schools, among them the Śrī Vidyā tradition focusing on the worship of Devī, the goddess. Tantra thrived until the Mughal conquest of India between 900 and 1300 CE, during which it was almost completely destroyed, with lineages lost, temples destroyed, and oral traditions going underground.

Tantric yoga focused on cultivation of psychophysical energy (*prāṇa* or *śakti*), and developed complex maps of the subtle (*sukṣma*) body in which *prāṇa* moves through channels (*nadi*) and swirls at energy centers called "wheels" (*cakra*). The Tantric vision of energetic movement through the body is the root of what would evolve into *hatha yoga*. *Tantric yoga* seeks to awaken *śakti*, visualized as a serpent at the base of the spine called *kundalini* ("coiled one"). Once awakened, kundalini is drawn upward through the central column of the subtle body, known as *suṣumṇā nāḍī*. Energy in Tantra is awaken through many practices: initiation, *mantra*, ritual, visualization, and energetic gestures known as *mudra*. Initiation (*dīkṣā*) comes through the grace of a *guru*, one who has

the power to awaken *śakti* in the sincere seeker. Initiation from a *guru* is the beginning of the Tantric path, followed by *spiritual disciplines such as mantra*, visualization, and ritual.

One of the most socially radical manifestations of the Tantric revelation was a reawakening of the veneration of the feminine Divine, known as Śakti, or the Goddess of Divine Energy. Like the Buddha, Krishna in the Gita, and the *śramaṇa*, Tantric sages rebelled against the Brahmin priests and the caste system. The Tantric vision is nondual (*advaita*), viewing relative and absolute reality as not separate from each other. This doctrine led to the radical vision that purity and impurity were fundamentally illusory, or *māyā*. Rebelling against the purity-oriented strictures of the caste system, Tantric practitioners (*tantrikas*) brought into their rituals five taboo substances/acts called the "Five M's" (*panchamkara*): fish (*matsya*), meat (*māṃsa*), wine (*madya*), parched grain (*mudrā*), and sexual intercourse or fluids (*maithuna*). These substances/acts, forbidden by the orthodox religious establishment, were invoked to assert the radical nonduality at the heart of the Tantric vision. Most often they were taken metaphorically, visualized in the course of Tantric ritual practice, but there are reports of *tantrika* also imbibing them literally. The literal use of forbidden substances may have been a remnant of Tantra's origin in medieval Indian alchemy.

Tantric philosophy is rich and complex, centering around the nature of supreme consciousness (Shiva) and its relationship to the universal creative force (śakti). The *tantrika* learns to perceive all forms of reality as Divine, excluding nothing from the vision of a single unified activity, felt as vibration, or *spanda*. Śaiva Tantra describes "Five Activities of the Divine" (*pañca-kṛtya*):

1. creation (*sṛṣṭi*)
2. maintenance (*sthiti*)
3. dissolution (*saṃhāra*)
4. concealing (*tirodhāna*)
5. revealing (*anugraha*)

Reality is veiled from ordinary perception through three fundamental impurities (*mala*) that describe patterns of habitual consciousness:

1. Individuality, the fundamental contraction (*āṇava-mala*) and cause of suffering (*duḥkha*)
2. Differentiation or limitation (*māyīya-mala*) that gives rise to the feeling of separateness
3. Action (*kārma-mala*), the bondage of *karma* via grasping and aversion

Tantric yoga consisted primarily of breath and energy practices within a framework of ritual visualization and mantra recitation. From the stillness-oriented meditations of classical *yoga*, Tantra evolved into dynamic imaginative practices that themselves became the seeds of the even more physically dynamic practices of *hatha yoga*. While Tantric ritual was largely sublimated into the physical practices of *hatha yoga*, the Tantric vision of the nondual nature of supreme consciousness would remain the heart of Indian metaphysics. Śaiva Tantra would enunciate this realization as "*Śivoham*," "I am Shiva, Infinite Consciousness." Though many lineages of Tantra were lost through the centuries of Muslim rule, a few survived into the 20th century. New research and translation of Tantric texts is currently contributing to a revival of both Śaiva and Śakti Tantra practice.

Hatha *Yoga*—*Yoga* as Purification

Hatha yoga arose in the 13th century as a simplification of Śaiva Tantra, omitting ritual, *mantra*, and *guru*, but retaining and developing the physical and energetic practices. The word *hatha* literally meant "forceful," but was later given the esoteric interpretation "sun-moon." Possibly originating in Tibetan Tantric exercises, *hatha yoga* used breath and posture to awaken *kundalini* and draw "her" upward through the central channel of the subtle body, called *suṣumṇā nāṃī* ("most gracious channel"). Several practice manuals from early *hatha yoga* survive, among them the *Gorakṣa Paddhāti*, *Gheranda Saṃhītā*, and *Haṭha Yoga Pradīpikā*. Svātmārāma's *Haṭha Yoga Pradīpikā* ("Light on Hatha Yoga," ca. 1350 CE) describes the practices of posture, breath, gesture, sexual energy control, and meditation that were common among his lineage, the *Natha*.

Yoga in the *Pradīpikā* begins with ethical practices and individual disciplines, clearly referencing the first two limbs of Patañjali's *yoga*, *yama* and *niyama*. The text continues with cleansing practices called *śatkarma*, intended to remove excess mucus and blockage in the respiratory and digestive systems. The cleansing practices are followed by a collection of postures (*asana*). It is in the *Pradīpikā* that the first nonseated *asana* appear, though the majority of the postures are oriented toward meditation and *prāṇāyāma*. The heart of *hatha yoga* consists of *prāṇāyāma*, emphasizing breath retention (*kumbhaka*) combined with energetic contractions in the body called *bandha*.

In early *hatha yoga*, *prāṇāyāma* and *bandha* are practiced vigorously in order to purify the body's energetic channels (*nāḍī*). Through intensive breath control, the yogi awakens and sublimates sexual energy, drawing *prāṇa* into the central column of the body. The purificatory practices are said to prepare the body to receive the powerful force of awakened *śakti* and facilitate the ascent of kundalini through *suṣumṇā* to the crown center (*sahasrāra cakra*). The accomplished yogi is known as a *siddha*, after the supernatural powers that arise with success in *yoga*, or a *jivanmukti*, one whose soul (*jiva*) is fully liberated.

Central to early *hatha yoga* are two conceptions of the movement of subtle fluids or energies in the body, both centering on the conception of *bindu*, or "drops" of vital fluid. In one model, the purpose of *yoga* is to draw upward the powerful reproductive fluids, male semen and female menstrual blood, into *suṣumṇā nāḍī*. These drops of reproductive fluid are the quintessential alchemical substances, and their uplift the cause of immortality and power (*siddha*). In a second model, the *yogi* catches *bindu* that drip down from *ajña cakra* in deep meditation using an important gesture (*mudra*) inherited from Śaiva Tantra, *khecari mudrā*.

Khecari mudrā in Tantra consists of a meditation on nondual awareness, emphasizing the turning inward of the practitioner's attention while keeping the external senses open. In *hatha yoga*, like many Tantric meditations that evolved into purely physical gestures, *khecari mudrā* became the turning back of the tongue to enter the nasal canal. To accomplish this, the *Pradīpikā* suggests gradually cutting away the frenulum at the base of the tongue until the *yogi* can touch the "third eye" (*ajña cakra*) with the tongue.

After purification through *shatkarma*, asana, and *prāṇāyāma*, the *hatha yogi* practices the three "bonds": *mūla bandha*, *uḍḍiyāna bandha*, and *jālandhara bandha*. *Mūla bandha*, the "root bond," is performed by gently engaging the musculature of the pelvic floor. It is performed during *kumbhaka* after either inhaling or exhaling. *Uḍḍiyāna bandha*, the "upward flying" bond, is performed while holding the breath after exhaling (*bahir kumbhaka*), and lifting the ribs upward to create a vacuum that draws the abdomen up into the rib cage. *Jālandhara bandha*, performed while holding the breath after inhaling (*antar kumbhaka*), consists of lifting the sternum and lowering the chin to the chest, closing off the throat. The three *bandha* are said to contain *prāṇa* in the body and channel it into *suṣumṇā nāḍī*.

The *Pradīpikā* asserts that all of its methods are for the purpose of attaining *raja yoga* and enabling the yogi to more quickly enter the meditative state of *samādhi*. The final section of the *Pradīpikā* teaches *nāda yoga*, meditation on the inner sound. Established in all the energetic practices described, with the mind quiet and energy awakened, the *yogi* enters stillness and turns awareness toward listening. *Yoga*, here interpreted as union with the

Divine (Brahman) or the Supreme Self (*atman*), arises when this *samādhi* is perfected.

Yoga in the 20th Century—*Yoga* as Embodiment

Hatha yoga was revived in the early 20th century and took root in two primary lineages, one "southern," via Tirumalai Krishnamacharya of Mysore, and one "northern," via Swami Śivananda (1887–1963) of Rishikesh. In both lineages, asana was emphasized and expanded, adapting exercises from European calisthenics and contortion. Krishnamacharya's teaching focused on the philosophy of Patañjali's *Yoga Sūtra*, while Śivananda, the *guru* of well-known teachers Satchidananda (1914–2002, founder of Integral *yoga*) and Satyananda (1923–2009, founder of Bihar *yoga*), sourced his teachings from Vedanta, the Gita, and both classical and *Tantric yoga*, with an emphasis on *bhakti*. *Yoga* as it has come to Europe and the United States is largely descended from these two lineages, with two primary students of Krishnamacharya, Pattabhi Jois (1915–2009, founder of the Ashtanga *yoga* style) and B. K. S. Iyengar (b. 1918, founder of the Iyengar *yoga* style), being most influential.

Tirumalai Krishnamacharya (1888–1989) taught in the palace of the Maharaja of Mysore in the 1930s, bringing together practices from *hatha yoga*, *Āyurveda*, and Himalayan Tantra with Patañjali's *Aṣṭānga* to create a *yoga* grounded in asana, but aspiring to *samādhi* and *raja yoga*. Krishnamacharya created a system that connected poses in movement sequences synchro-nized with breath, called *vinyasa krama*, a much more vigorous physical practice than in early *hatha yoga*. *Vinyasa krama* and the use of the Sun Salutation sequence (*surya namaskar*) as a repeated transition between sustained poses would be the centerpiece of Pattabhi Jois's Ashtanga *yoga* style and the root of modern styles of flowing asana. Krishnamacharya also greatly expanded traditional *hatha yoga* practice with the inclusion of exercises for strength and flexibility popular in the 19th century "physical culture" movement, including European calisthenics, gymnastics, and contortion.

Under Krishnamacharya's students Pattabhi Jois, B. K. S. Iyengar, and his own son T. K. V. Desikachar (b. 1938, founder of the Viniyoga style), the collection of asanas grew to include poses oriented around specific aspects of physical development such as standing, balancing, and seated poses, hip flexibility, deep back bending and forward bending, inversions, and twisting poses. In the century since this expansion of physical practice in hatha *yoga*, exercises from other systems continue to be adopted. One notable recent expansion of the *yoga* corpus is the inclusion of exercises to strengthen the abdominal musculature, influenced by the work of Joseph Pilates (1883–1967).

Krishnamacharya's style integrated multiple yogic traditions, bringing the goals of Tantra (power, *siddhi*) and Patañjali (liberation, *kaivalya*), together. While Krishnamacharya was creating modern *vinyasa yoga* through his integration of gymnastic asana with the philosophy of Patañjali's *Yoga Sūtra*, he vigorously rejected much of the historical *hatha yoga* tradition, such as *śatkarma* and the practices of sexual fluid retention that were integral to *yoga* in the era of the *Pradīpikā*. He felt that *yoga* as presented by Patañjali was the most appropriate philosophical and methodological orientation for practice. Krishnamacharya's emphasis on health and physical flexibility over the earlier *hatha yoga* goal of *kundalini* awakening became the ground of modern *yoga*.

Yoga's Continuing Evolution

As practitioners around the world dedicate themselves to *yoga*, they bring Western scientific, humanistic, and postmodern political values to the practices. One transformative recent development is the practice of *yoga* by women to a degree never before known. The current prominence of women is unique in the history of *yoga*, with women forming a substantial majority of *yoga* practitioners in the West. Women are challenging the patriarchal bias of many early *yoga* texts, creating practices that meet their needs, including perinatal and children's *yoga*, and bringing a Western feminist approach to the practice.

Karma yoga, central to the teaching of the *Bhagavad-Gītā*, was popularized by Mahatma Gandhi (1869–1948) through his *satyagraha* (truth force) movement. Inspired by Gandhi and other nonviolent leaders, politically progressive *yoga* practitioners in the West have also begun to use *yoga* as inspiration for political and social action. One current organization popularizing this approach, "Off the mat, into the world," founded by *yoga* teacher Seane Corne, uses the Sanskrit term *seva* ("self-less service") to inspire social change and global activism.

Modern and postmodern *yoga* philosophy has broadened from Krishnamacharya's focus on Patañjali to emphasize *yoga's* historical roots in Tantra. Several schools of *yoga* have arisen that source their practices to Śaiva and Śakta Tantra rather than to Patañjali, giving rise to Tantric study among *asana*-based yogis. In addition, traditional yogic philosophy has been influenced by Western psychology. The new field of *yoga* therapy uses physical and meditative practices to address both physical and emotional distress. As *asana*-based *yoga* takes root in the West, it is also encountering Buddhism in ways that it had not done previously, since Buddhism had been largely absent from India since before *hatha yoga* existed. Western practitioners of asana who are drawn to meditation now often do so through Buddhist communities, which have become widespread. Similarly, Buddhist practitioners, drawn to the physical cultivation of *yoga asana*, are integrating the two practices and perspectives.

Yoga in the 21st century is a broad collection of practices and philosophical frameworks. From its roots in ancient Indian sacrificial worship, *yoga* has been influenced by every tradition it has come into contact with, absorbing both practical exercises and conceptions of reality. It has been oriented in different eras toward both transcendent liberation and immanent worldly engagement. The word "*yoga*" continues to collect meanings and practices as it is taken up by non-Indian cultures and religions, and it evolves as it always has, through the bodies and minds of sincere practitioners in search of truth and the path to deep well-being.

Conclusion

As *yoga* has been adopted by Western culture, it has evolved far from its Indian roots. The practices of asana and *prāṇāyāma* have become central to a fitness and health–oriented *yoga* culture in Europe and the United States, creating a vast industry of *yoga* studios, training courses, teachers, and popular devotional practice. There remains a substantial divide between South Asian and white *yoga* practitioners in Western *yoga*, called Modern Postural *Yoga* (MPY) by scholars. As *yoga* evolves in the West, conversations about cultural appropriation, race, social class, and privilege in modern *yoga* are becoming more widespread. In addition, new generations of Western scholars are learning Sanskrit and other Asian classical languages, engaging with the ancient *yoga* texts in new ways, and discovering new pathways into the vast and powerful teachings of *yoga*.

While the practice of postures remains the most visible form of *yoga* in the West, the teachings on meditation, breathwork, and ethics continue to have profound effects for those who engage with them. The esoteric teachings of Tantra that seek to cultivate energy in the body through visualization, mantra, ritual, and the profound contact with a *guru* also continue to evolve as they propagate through a globalized spiritual culture. Cross-cultural study of the *hatha yoga* and Tantra teachings on subtle energy is growing, with scholars comparing *kundalini* and *prāna* as recorded in Tibetan and Indian texts with shamanic teachings from Japan, Korea, and Russia, the !Kung people of the Kalahari, Chinese Taoism, and many other indigenous traditions. And as mindfulness becomes a popular buzz word, the practices of focused attention, or *samādhi*, that are the heart of classical *yoga* and Buddhist practice are being valued and practiced more than ever. For the Western spiritual seeker, *yoga* is a rich field for exploration, spanning physical health and fitness to psychological healing and spiritual exploration. As it evolves into a global phenomenon in the 21st century, *yoga* will remain both accessible and mysterious. Seemingly simple, its riches reveal themselves in ever more complex layers as the seeker looks deeper.

Sean Feit

See also: Essays: Arts and Cultural Production; *Entries: Taiji Quan*

Further Reading

Bodhi, Bhikkhu. *In the Buddha's Words: An Anthology of Discourses from the Pali Canon. The Teachings of the Buddha.* Boston: Wisdom, 2005.

Eliade, Mircea. *Yoga: Immortality and Freedom.* New York: Princeton Bollingen, 1958.

Feuerstein, Georg. *Tantra: The Path of Ecstasy.* Boston: Shambhala, 1998.

Feuerstein, Georg. *The Yoga Tradition.* Prescott, AZ: Hohm Press, 1998.

Hartranft, Chip. *The Yoga Sūtra of Patañjali: A New Translation with Commentary.* Translated by Chip Hartranft. Boston: Shambhala, 2003.

Miller, Barbara Stoller. *The Bhagavad-Gita: Krishna's Counsel in Time of War.* New York: Bantam, 1986.

Muktibodhananda, Swami. *Hatha Yoga Pradipika*. Munger, India: *Yoga* Publications Trust, 1993.

Olivelle, Patrick. *Upaniṣads*. Oxford: Oxford University Press, 1996.

Singleton, Mark. *The Yoga Body*. New York: Oxford University Press, 2010.

Wallis, Christopher. *Tantra Illuminated*. The Woodlands, TX: Anusara, 2012.

White, David Gordon. *The Alchemical Body: Siddha Tradition in Medieval India*. Chicago: University of Chicago Press, 1996.

Zhongyuan Festival. *See* Ghost Festival/Zhongyuan Festival

Bibliography

Ādi Granth, The, or the Holy Scriptures of the Sikhs. Ernest Trumpp, trans. New Delhi: Munshiram Manoharlal, 1970.

Alpers, Antony. *Legends of the South Seas: The World of the Polynesians Seen through Their Myths and Legends, Poetry, and Art*. Oxford: Oxford University Press, 1970.

Alphen, Jan Van, and Anthony Aris, eds. *Oriental Medicine: An Illustrated Guide to the Asian Arts of Healing*. Boston: Shambhala, 1996.

Alumkal, Antony. *Asian American Evangelical Churches: Race, Ethnicity, and Assimilation in the Second Generation (New Americans)*. New York: LFB Scholarly Publishing, 2003.

Ama, Michihiro. *Immigrants to the Pure Land: The Modernization, Acculturation, and Globalization of Shin Buddhism, 1898–1941*. Honolulu: University of Hawai'i Press, 2011.

Arai, Yusei. *Shingon: Japanese Esoteric Buddhism: A Handbook for Followers*. Fresno, CA: Shingon Buddhist International Institute, 1997.

Asian American Studies, eds. *At 40: Asian American Studies at San Francisco State*. San Francisco: SFSU Asian American Studies Department, 2009.

Baffelli, Erica, Ian Reader, and Birgit Staemmler, eds. *Japanese Religions on the Internet: Innovation, Representation, and Authority*. London: Routledge, 2011.

Bailey, Jackson H., ed. *Aesthetic and Ethical Values in Japanese Culture*. Richmond, IN: Earlham College, 1990.

Barber, Stephen. *Hijikata: Revolt of the Body*. London: Creation Books, 2006.

Barker, Pat. *Dragon Boats: A Celebration*. New York: Weatherhill, 1996.

Barnes, Linda, and Inez Talamantez, eds. *Teaching Religion and Healing*. Oxford: Oxford University Press, 2006.

Basham, A.L. *The Wonder That Was India: A Survey of the Culture of the Indian Sub-Continent before the Coming of the Muslims*. New York: Grove Press, 1959.

BCA Centennial History Project Committee. *Buddhist Churches of America: A Legacy of the First 100 years*. San Francisco: Buddhist Churches of America, 1998.

Bechert, Heinz, and Richard Gombrich, eds. *The World of Buddhism: Buddhist Monks and Nuns in Society and Culture*. London: Thames and Hudson, 1984.

Beckwith, Martha Warren. *The Kumulipo: A Hawaiian Creation Chant*. Chicago: University of Chicago Press, 1951.

Beckwith, Martha Warren. *Hawaiian Mythology*. Honolulu: University of Hawai'i Press, 1970.

Berendt, Joachim-Ernst. *The World Is Sound: Nada Brahma: Music and the Landscape of Consciousness*. Rochester, VT: Destiny Books, 1983.

Berthrong, John H, and Jeffrey L. Richey. "Introduction: Teaching Confucianism as a Religious Tradition," in Jeffrey Richey, *Teaching Confucianism*. New York: Oxford University Press, 2008.

Bhikshus Heng Sure, and Heng Ch'au. *News from True Cultivators: Letters to the Venerable Abbot Hua*. 2nd ed. Burlingame, CA: Buddhist Text Translation Society, 2003.

Bhishagratna, Kaviraj Junja Lal. *An English Translation of the Sushruta Samhita, Based on the Original Sanskrit Text*. 3 vols. Kolkata: Bhaduri, 1907–1916.

Bloom, Alfred, ed. *Living in Amida's Universal Vow: Essays in Shin Buddhism*. Bloomington, IN: World Wisdom, 2004.

Bloom, Irene, "Remembering Wing-tsit Chan." *Philosophy East & West* 45, no. 4 (October 1995): 466–469.

Bocking, Brian. *A Popular Dictionary of Shintō*. Surrey, UK: Curzon Press, 1996.

Brock, Rita Nakashima, Jung Ha Kim, Kwok Pui-lan, and Seung Ai Yang, eds. *Off the Menu: Asian and Asian North American Women's Religion and Theology*. Louisville, KY: Westminster John Knox Press, 2007.

Bromley, David G., and Alexa Blonner. "From the Unification Church to the Unification Movement and Back." *Nova Religio: The Journal of Alternative and Emergent Religions* 16, no. 2 (November 2012): 86–95.

Brown, Daniel. *A New Introduction to Islam*. Oxford: Blackwell, 2004.

Brown, Kendall H. "Performing Hybridity: Wedding Rituals at Japanese-Style Gardens in Southern California." In Michel Conan, ed. *Performance and Appropriation: Profane Rituals in Gardens and Landscapes*. Washington, DC: Dumbarton Oaks, 2007, 133–52.

Buck, Elizabeth. *Paradise Remade: The Politics of Culture and History in Hawai'i*. Philadelphia: Temple University Press, 1993.

Bulosan, Carlos. *America Is in the Heart: A Personal History*. Seattle: University of Washington Press. 2014.

Burns, Jeffrey, Ellen Skerrett, and Joseph M. White, eds. *Keeping Faith: European and Asian Catholic Immigrants*. New York: Orbis Books, 2000.

Burton, Jeffery, Mary M. Farrell, Florence B. Lord, and Richard W. Lord. *Confinement and Ethnicity: An Overview of World War II Japanese American Relocation Sites*. Seattle: University of Washington Press, 2002.

Burton, John. *An Introduction to the Hadith*. Edinburgh: Edinburgh University Press, 1994.

Buswell, Robert E., ed. *Religions of Korea in Practice*. Princeton, NJ: Princeton University Press, 2007.

Cadge, Wendy. *Heartwood: The First Generation of Theravāda Buddhism in America*. Chicago: University of Chicago Press, 2004.

Canda, Edward R., and Thitiya Phaobtong. "Buddhism as a Support System for Southeast Asian Refugees." *Social Work* 37, no. 1 (January 1992).

Carnes, Tony, and Fenggeng Yang, eds. *Asian American Religions: The Making and Remaking of Borders and Boundaries*. New York: New York University Press. 2004.

Chan, Sucheng. *Asian Americans: An Interpretive History*. Boston: Twayne Publishers, 1991.

Chang, Gordon. *Asian Americans and Politics: Perspectives, Experiences, Prospects*. Washington DC: Woodrow Wilson Center Press, 2001.

Chang, Robert. "Toward an Asian American Legal Scholarship: Critical Race Theory, Post-Structuralism, and Narrative Space." *California Law Review* 81 (1993).

Cheah, Joseph. *Race and Religion in American Buddhism: White Supremacy and Immigrant Adaptation*. Oxford: Oxford University Press, 2011.

Chen, Carolyn. *Getting Saved in America: Taiwanese Immigration and Religious Experience*. Princeton, NJ: Princeton University Press, 2008.

Chen, Carolyn, and Russell Jeung. *Sustaining Faith Traditions: Race, Ethnicity, and Religion among the Latino and Asian American Second Generation*. New York: New York University Press, 2012.

Choy, Bong-Youn. *Koreans in America*. Chicago: Nelson-Hall, 1979.

Chryssides, George D. *The Advent of Sun Myung Moon: The Origins, Beliefs, and Practices of the Unification Church*. New York: St. Martin's Press, 1991.

Clarke, Peter B., ed. *Japanese New Religions in Global Perspective*. Richmond, UK: Curzon, 2000.

Clarke, Peter B., ed. *Encyclopedia of New Religious Movements*. New York: Routledge, 2006.

Clarke, Peter B., and Jeffrey Somers, eds. *Japanese New Religions in the West*. London: Routledge, 1990.

Clarke, Peter Bernard, and John Nelson, eds. *Handbook of Contemporary Japanese Religions*. Leiden: Brill, 2012.

Clarke, J. J. *The Tao of the West*. London: Routledge, 2000.

Conze, Edward. *Buddhism: Its Essence and Development*. New York: Harper and Row, 1959.

Cook, Anthony. *The Least of These: Race, Law, and Religion in American Culture*. London: Routledge, 1997.

Coomaraswamy, Ananda K. *The Dance of Śiva: Essays on Indian Art and Culture*. New York: Dover Publications, 1985. Reprint of a 1924 edition.

Cunningham, Lawrence J. *Ancient Chamoru Society*. Honolulu: The Bess Press, 1992.

Danieli, Yael, ed. *International Handbook of Multi-Generational Legacies of Trauma*. New York: Plenum Press, 1998.

Daniélou, Alain. *The Myths and Gods of India: The Classic Work on Hindu Polytheism*. Rochester: Inner Traditions International, 1985.

Daniels, Roger, Sandra C. Taylor, and Harry H. L. Kitano, eds. *Japanese Americans: From Relocation to Redress*. Seattle: University of Washington Press, 1986.

Darian-Smith, Eve. *Religion, Race, Rights: Landmarks in the History of Modern Anglo-American Law*. London: Hart, 2010.

Daschke, Dereck, and W. Michael Ashcraft. *New Religious Movements: A Documentary Reader*. New York: New York University Press, 2005.

Dobbin, Jay, and Francis X. Hezel. *Summoning the Powers Beyond: Traditional Religions in Micronesia*. Honolulu: University of Hawai'i Press, 2011.

Drinnon, Richard. *Keeper of Concentration Camps: Dillon S. Myer and American Racism*. Berkeley: University of California Press, 1989.

DuBois, Thomas A. *An Introduction to Shamanism*. Cambridge: Cambridge University Press, 2009.

Earhart, H. Byron. *Gedatsu-Kai and Religion in Contemporary Japan: Returning to the Center*. Bloomington: Indiana University Press, 1989.

Ebaugh, Helen, and Janet Chavetz, *Religion and the New Immigrants: Continuities and Adaptations in Immigrant Congregations*. Walnut Creek, CA: Altamira Press, 2000.

Eberhard, Wolfram. *Chinese Festivals, with Illustrations from the Collection of Werner Banck*. Taipei: Oriental Cultural Service, 1972.

Eck, Diana. *A New Religious America: How a "Christian Country" Has Become the World's Most Religiously Diverse Nation*. New York: Harper One, 2002.

Ecklund, Elaine Howard. *Korean American Evangelicals: New Models for Civic Life*. New York: Oxford University Press, 2006.

Edge, Peter W. *Religion and Law: An Introduction*. Burlington, VT: Ashgate, 2006.

Eliav-Feldon, Miriam Benjamin Isaac, and Joseph Ziegler. *The Origins of Racism in the West*. Cambridge: Cambridge University Press, 2009.

Ellor, J. W., and R. Y. Nakasone. "Religion and Old Age: Christianity and East Asian Buddhist Reflections." In P. McNamara and W. Wildman, eds. *Science and the World's Religions: Volume 2: Persons and Groups*. Santa Barbara, CA: ABC-CLIO, 2012.

Esposito, John. *The Oxford Dictionary of Islam*. New York: Oxford University Press, 2003.

Esterik, Penny Van. *Taking Refuge: Lao Buddhists in North America*. Tempe: Arizona State University, 1992.

Ethnic Studies Oral History Project. *Uchinanchu: A History of Okinawans in Hawai'i*. Honolulu: University of Hawai'i/United Okinawan Association of Hawai'i, 1977.

Fadiman, Anne. *The Spirit Catches You and You Fall Down: A Hmong Child, Her American Doctors, and the Collision of Two Cultures*. New York: Farrar, Straus and Giroux, 1998.

Farrell, Gerry. *Indian Music and the West*. Oxford: Oxford University Press, 1997.

Fenton, John Y. *South Asian Religions in the Americas: An Annotated Bibliography of Immigrant Religious Traditions*. Westport, CT: Greenwood Press, 1995.

Fenton, John Y. *Transplanting Religious Traditions: Asian Indians in America*. Westport, CT: Praeger, 1988.

Fernandez, Eleazar, and Fumitaka Matsuoka, eds. *Realizing the America of Our Hearts: Theological Voices of Asian Americans*. Saint Louis: Chalice Press, 2003.

Feuerstein, Georg. *The Yoga Tradition*. Prescott, AZ: Hohm Press, 1998.

Fields, Rick. *How the Swans Came to the Lake: A Narrative History of Buddhism in America*. Boston: Shambhala Press, 1992.

Fischer, Steven Roger. *A History of the Pacific Islands*. New York: Palgrave, 2002.

Flood, Gavin, ed. *The Blackwell Companion to Hinduism*. Oxford: Blackwell, 2003.

Foskett Mary F., Jeffrey Kah-Jin Kuan, and John Ahn, eds. *Ways of Being, Ways of Reading: Asian American Biblical Interpretation*. Indianapolis: Chalice Press, 2006.

Gallagher, Eugene V., and W. Michael Ashcraft, eds. *Introduction to New and Alternative Religions*. Westport, CT: Greenwood Press, 2006.

Gaston, Anne-Marie. *Bharata Natyam: From Temple to Theatre*. New Delhi: Manohar Publishers, 1996.

George, Sheba. *When Women Come First: Gender and Class in Transnational Migration*. Berkeley: University of California Press, 2005.

Gerson, Ruth. *Traditional Festivals in Thailand*. Oxford: Oxford University Press, 1996.

Giacchino-Baker, Rosalie, ed. *Stories from Laos: Folktales and Cultures of the Lao, Hmong, Khammu, and Iu-Mien*. Charlie Chue Chang-Hmong, Thomas Manokoune-Khammu, and David B. Cooke-Iu-Mien, trans. El Monte, CA: Pacific Asia Press, 1995.

Gombrich, Richard, and Gananath Obeyesekere. *Buddhism Transformed*. Princeton: Princeton University Press, 1988.

Gonzalez, Joaquin Jay III. *Filipino American Faith in Action: Immigration, Religion, and Civil Engagement*. New York: New York University Press, 2009.

Gotanda, Neil. "New Directions in Asian American Jurisprudence." *Asian American Law Journal* 17 (2010).

Gotanda, Neil. "The Racialization of Islam in American Law." *Annals of the American Academy of Political and Social Science* 637 (2011): 184–185.

Government of Guam: Political Status Education Coordinating Commission. *Hale'ta: Hestorian Taotao Tano—History of the Chomorro People*. Agana, Guam: Government Publications, 1993.

Govinda, Anagarika. *Psycho-cosmic Symbolism of the Buddhist Stūpa*. Berkeley, CA: Dharma Publishing, 1976.

Grayson, James Huntley. *Korea: A Religious History*. London: Routledge Curzon, 1989.

Groner, Paul. *Saichō: The Establishment of the Japanese Tendai School*. Berkeley: Berkeley Buddhist Studies Series, 1964.

Guillermo, Artermio R., ed. *Churches Aflame: Asian Americans and United Methodism*. Nashville: Abingdon, 1991.

Hadden, J. K. "Toward Desacralizing Secularization Theory." *Social Forces* 65 (1987): 587–611.

Hambrick, Charles H. "World Messianity: A Study in Liminality and Communitas." *Religious Studies* 15, no. 4 (December 1979): 539–553.

Hammond, Phillip, ed. *The Sacred in a Secular Age*. Berkeley: University of California Press, 1985.

Hansen, Moana. "The Loss and Transformation of the Tongan Culture and Its Effect on Tongan American Families in Utah," 2004. http://people.westminstercollege.edu/staff /mjhinsdale/Research_Journal_1/mo_paper.pdf.

Harvey, Peter. *Introduction to Buddhism: Teachings, History, and Practices*. Cambridge: Cambridge University Press, 1990.

Hashimoto, Shinnin. *A History of Shingon Buddhism in Hawai'i*. Wakayama: The Headquarters of Kōyasan Kongōbuji Temple, Department of Foreign Mission, 2006.

Hassija, Jagdish Chander. *Adi Dev: The First Man*. London: BKIS Ltd., Publication Division, 2008.

Hatamiya, Leslie T. *Righting a Wrong: Japanese Americans and the Passage of the Civil Liberties Act of 1988*. Stanford: Stanford University Press, 1993.

Hawley, John Stratton, and Gurinder Singh Mann, eds. *Studying the Sikhs: Issues for North America*. Albany: State University of New York Press, 1993.

Hayashi, Brian. *"For the Sake of Our Japanese Brethren": Assimilation, Nationalism, and Protestantism among the Japanese of Los Angeles, 1895–1942*. Stanford, CA: Stanford University Press, 1995.

Headquarters of Hawai'i Nichiren Missions. *A Century of Nichiren Buddhism in Hawai'i*. Honolulu: Obun Hawai'i Group, 2003.

Heisig, James W., Thomas P. Kasulis, and John C. Maraldo. *Japanese Philosophy: A Sourcebook*. Honolulu: University of Hawai'i Press, 2012.

Helsel, Deborah, Marilyn Mochel, and Bauer Mochel. "Shamans in a Hmong American Community." *Journal of Alternative and Complementary Medicine* (2004).

Herman, A. L. *The Bhagava Gītā: A Translation and Critical Commentary*. Springfield: Charles C. Thomas, 1973.

Hijikata, Tatsumi. *Three Decades of Butoh Experiment: A Scab and Caramel*. Tokyo: Yushi-Sha, 1993.

Hing, Bill Ong. *Defining America through Immigration Policy*. Philadelphia: Temple University Press, 2004.

Hirlekar, Hema. *Nuances of Hindustani Classical Music*. New Delhi: Unicorn Books, 2010.

Hirota, Dennis. *Wind in the Pines: Classic Writings of the Way of Tea as a Buddhist Path.* Fremont, CA: Asian Humanities Press, 1995.

Hirschman, Charles. "Problems and Prospects of Studying Immigrant Adaptation from the 1990 Population Census: From Generational Comparisons to the Process of 'Becoming American.'" *International Migration Review* 28, no. 4 (Winter 1994): 690–713. http://www.jstor.org/stable/2547154.

Hisamatsu Shin'ichi. *Zen and the Fine Arts.* Gishin Tokiwa, trans. Tokyo: Kodansha International, 1971.

Hohri, William Minoru. *Repairing America: An Account of the Movement for Japanese-American Redress.* Pullman: Washington State University Press, 1988.

Hoshino, Kazumas, ed. *Japanese and Western Bioethics: Studies in Moral Diversity.* Dordrecht: Kluwer Academic, 1997.

Hout, Michael, and Claude Fischer. "Why More Americans Have No Religious Preference: Politics and Generations." *American Sociological Review* 67, no. 2 (2002): 165–190.

Hunter, Louise H. *Buddhism in Hawai'i: Its impact on a Yankee Community.* Honolulu: University of Hawai'i Press, 1979.

Hurh, Won Moo. *The Korean Americans.* Westport, CT: Greenwood Press, 1998.

Hurst, Jane. *Nichiren Shoshu Buddhism and the Soka Gakkai in America: The Ethos of a New Religious Movement.* New York: Garland, 1992.

I'i, John P. *Fragments of Hawaiian History.* Mary Kawena Pukui, trans., Dorothy B. Barrre, ed. Honolulu: Bishop Museum Press, 1959.

Introvigne, Massimo. *The Unification Church.* Salt Lake City: Signature Books, 2000.

Ishizuka, Karen L. *Lost and Found: Reclaiming the Japanese American Incarceration.* Urbana: University of Illinois Press, 2006.

Iwamura, Jane. "Critical Faith: Japanese Americans and the Birth of a New Civil Religion." *American Quarterly* 47, no. 3 (2007): 937–968.

Iwamura, Jane Naomi. *Virtual Orientalism: Asian Religions and American Popular Culture.* Oxford: Oxford University Press, 2011.

Iwamura, Jane, and Paul Spickard, eds. *Revealing the Sacred in Asian and Pacific America.* London: Routledge, 2003.

Jalalzai, Farida. "The Politics of Muslims in America." *Politics and Religion* 2, no. 2 (August 2009): 163–199.

Jeung, Russell. *Faithful Generations: Race and New Asian American Churches.* New Brunswick, NJ: Rutgers University Press, 2005.

Jeung, Russell. *Faithful Generations: Race and New Asian American Churches.* Piscataway, NJ: Rutgers University Press, 2004.

Johnson, Rubellite Kawena. *Kumulipo: Hawaiian Hymn of Creation.* Vol. 1. Honolulu: Topgallant, 1981.

Jones, Cheslyn, Geoffrey Wainwright, and Edward Yarnold, eds. *The Study of Spirituality.* New York: Oxford University Press, 1986.

Jones, Lindsay, ed. *Encyclopedia of Religion.* Detroit: Macmillan Reference USA, 2005.

Joshi, Khyati. *New Roots in America's Sacred Ground: Religion, Race and Ethnicity in Indian America.* New Brunswick, NJ: Rutgers University Press, 2006.

Joya, Mock. *Things Japanese.* Tokyo: Tokyo News Service, 1958.

Jumsai, Sumet. *Naga: Cultural Origins in Siam and Western Pacific.* Bangkok: Chalernit Press and DD Books, 1997.

Kakar, Sudhir. *Shamans, Mystics, and Doctors: A Psychological Inquiry into India and Its Healing Traditions.* Delhi: Oxford University Press, 1982.

Karim, Jamillah. *American Muslim Women: Negotiating Race, Class, and Gender within the Ummah*. New York: New York University Press, 2009.

Kashima, Tetsuden. *Buddhism in America, the Social Organization of an Ethnic Religious Institution*. Westport, CT: Greenwood, 1977.

Kauanui, J. Kēhaulani. *Hawaiian Blood: Colonialism and the Politics of Sovereignty and Indigeneity*. Durham, NC: Duke University Press, 2008.

Kawahata, Aiyoshi. *Universal Meditation: Key to Mental and Physical Health*. Union City: Heian International, 1984.

Khan, Hazrat Inayat. *The Mysticism of Sound and Music*. Boston: Shambhala Publications, 1996.

Kim, Bock, ed. *Minjung Theology*. Singapore: The Christian Conference of Asia, 1981.

Kim, Helen K and Noah S. Leavitt. "The Newest Jews? Understanding Jewish American and Asian American Marriages." *Contemporary Jewry* 32 (2012): 135–166.

Kim, Hyung-Chan ed. *The Korean Diaspora: Historical and Sociological Studies of Korean Immigration and Assimilation in North America*. Santa Barbara, CA: ABC-CLIO, 1977.

Kim, Jung Ha. *Bridge-Makers and Cross-Bearers: Korean American Women and the Church*. Atlanta: Scholars Press. 1997.

Kim, Rebecca. *God's New Whiz Kids: Korean American Evangelicals on Campus*. New York: New York University Press, 2006.

Kitiarsa, Pattana. *Mediums, Monks, and Amulets: Thai Popular Buddhism Today*. Chiang Mai: Silkworm Books, 2012.

Klostermaier, Klaus, K. *A Survey of Hinduism*. Albany: State University of New York, 1989.

Kniss, Fred, and Paul D. Numrich. *Sacred Assemblies and Civic Engagement: How Religion Matters for America's Newest Immigrants*. New Brunswick, NJ: Rutgers University Press, 2007.

Komjathy, Louis. "Tracing the Contours of Daoism in North America." *Nova Religio* 8, no. 2 (2004): 5–27.

Komjathy, Louis. *The Daoist Tradition: An Introduction*. London: Bloomsbury Pub., 2013.

Konko Kyo's 50 Years in America. San Francisco: Konko Churches of America and Konko Missions in Hawai'i, 1976.

Korean Buddhist News USA, ed. *The Saṇgha Book of Korean Buddhism*. Fairfax: Korean Buddhist News, 2012.

Kothari, Sunil, and Bimal Mukherjee, eds. *Rasa: The Indian Performing Arts in the Last Twenty-five Years*. Calcutta: Anamika Kala Sangam Research and Publications, 1991.

Kubose, Gyomay M. *Everyday Suchness*. Raleigh, NC: Dharma House, 1987.

Kumar, Bhuvanendra. *Jainism in North America*. Mississauga, Ontario: Jain Humanities Press, 1996.

Kurien, Prema A. *A Place at the Multicultural Table: The Development of an American Hinduism*. New Brunswick, NJ: Rutgers University Press. 2007.

Kurien, Prema. "We Are Better Hindus Here: Religion and Ethnicity among Indian Americans." In Pyong Gap Min and Jung Ha Kim, eds. *Religions in Asian America: Building Faith Communities*. Walnut Creek, CA: Altamira Press, 2002.

Kuykendall, Ralph S. *The Hawaiian Kingdom, 1885–1963*. Honolulu: University of Hawai'i, 1965.

Kwan, Ho Youn, Kwang Chun Kim, and R. Stephen Warner, eds. *Korean Americans and Their Religions*. University Park: Penn State University Press, 2001.

Kyuman Kim. "Religion." In Cathy J. Schlund-Vials, Linda Trinh Vo, Kevin Scott Wong, eds. *Key Words for American Studies*. New York: New York University Press, 2015.

Latsch, Marie-Luise. *Chinese Traditional Festivals*. Beijing: New World Press, 1984.

Lavezzoli, Peter. *The Dawn of Indian Music in the West: Bhairavi*. New York: Continuum International, 2006.

Law, Bimals Chun. *The Buddhist Conception of Spirits*. Delhi: Bhartiya Publishing House, 1974.

Lawrence, Bruce. *New Faiths, Old Fears: Muslims and Other Asian Immigrants in American Religious Life*. New York: Columbia University Press, 2002.

Lebra, William P. *Okinawan Religion: Belief, Ritual, and Social Structure*. Honolulu: University of Hawai'i Press, 1966.

Lee, Deborah and Antonio Salas, eds. *Unfaithing U.S. Colonialism*. Fremont, CA: Dharma Cloud Publishers, 1998.

Lee, Jonathan H. X. "Creating a Transnational Religious Community: The Empress of Heaven, Goddess of the Sea Tianhou/Mazu, from Beigang, Taiwan to San Francisco U.S.A." In Lois Ann Lorentzen, Joaquin Jay Gonzalez III, Kevin M. Chun, and Hien Duc Do, eds. *On the Corner of Bliss and Nirvana: Politics, Identity, and Faith in New Migrant Communities*. Durham, NC: Duke University Press, 2009.

Lee, Jonathan H.X., and Kathleen Nadeau, eds. *Asian American Identities and Practices: Folkloric Expressions in Everyday Life*. New York: Lexington Books, 2014.

Lee, Jung Young. *Marginality: The Key to Multicultural Theology*. Minneapolis: Fortress Press, 1995.

Lee, Mary Paik. *Quiet Odyssey: A Pioneer Korean Woman in America*. Seattle: University of Washington Press, 1990.

Lee, Shelley Sang-Hee. *A New History of Asian America*. London: Routledge, 2014.

Lee, Timothy S. "In View of Existing Conditions: A Brief History of the North American Pacific/Asian Disciples, 1891–2010 (From the Margins to the Mainstream)." *Discipliana: A Journal of Stone-Campbell History* 71, no. 1 (Spring 2012): 6–26.

Lee, Timothy S. "From Coerced Liminality to In-Beyond the Margin: A Theological Reflection on the History of Asian-American Disciples." *Call to Unity*, Issue 9 (September 2008), Brite Divinity School (Texas Christian University). http://ccu.disciples.org /Portals/CCU/pdf/NAPAD%20paper%20-%20Tim%20Lee.pdf.

Leonard, Karen Isaksen. *Making Ethnic Choices: California's Punjabi Mexican Americans*. Philadelphia: Temple University. 1994.

Leonard, Karen Isaksen. *Muslims in the United States: The State of Research*. New York: Russell Sage Foundation, 2003.

Leonard, Karen I., Alex Stepick, Manuel A. Vasquez, and Jennifer Holdaway, eds. *Immigrant Faiths: Transforming Religious Life in America*. Walnut Creek, CA: AltaMira Press, 2005.

Levick, Melba. *Japanese-style Gardens of the Pacific West Coast*. New York: Rizzoli, 1999.

Lewis, David. *We, the Navigators: The Ancient Art of Landfinding in the Pacific*. 2nd ed. Honolulu: University of Hawai'i Press, 1994.

Lewis, Paul, and Elaine Lewis. *Peoples of the Golden Triangle: Six Tribes of Thailand*. London: Thames & Hudson, 1984.

Lien, Pei-te, Margaret Conway, and Janelle Wong. *The Politics of Asian Americans: Diversity and Community*. New York: Routledge Press, 2004.

Lim, Shirley Geok-lin, and Cheng Lok Chua, eds. *Tilting the Continent: Southeast Asian American Writing*. Minneapolis: New River Press, 2000.

Lin, Irene. "Journey to the Far West: Chinese Buddhism in America." *Amerasia Journal* 22 (1996): 106–32.

Ling, Amy, ed. *Yellow Light: The Flowering of Asian American Arts*. Philadelphia: Temple University Press, 1999.

Ling, Huping Ling, ed. *Emerging Voices: Experiences of Underrepresented Asian Americans*. New Brunswick, NJ: Rutgers University Press, 2008.

Lings, Martin, and Yasin Hamid Safadi, eds. *The Qur'an*. London: World of Islam, 1976.

Lopez, Donald. *Tibetan Buddhism and the West*. Chicago: University of Chicago Press, 1999.

Lowe, Lisa. *Immigrants Acts: On Asian American Cultural Politics*. Durham, NC: Duke University Press, 1996.

MacDonald, Jeffrey L. *Transnational Aspects of Iu-Mien Refugee Identity*. New York: Garland, 1997.

Machacek, David, and Bryan Wilson, eds. *Global Citizens: The Soka Gakkai Buddhist Movement in the World*. Oxford: Oxford University Press, 2001.

Machacek, David, and Phillip E. Hammond. *Soka Gakkai in America: Accommodation and Conversion*. Oxford: Oxford University Press, 1999.

Maki, Mitchell T., Harry H. L. Kitano, and S. Megan Berthold. *Achieving the Impossible Dream: How Japanese Americans Obtained Redress*. Urbana: University of Illinois Press, 1999.

Mann, Gurinder Singh. *The Making of Sikh Scripture*. New York: Oxford University Press, 2001.

Mann, Gurinder Singh, Paul David Numrich, and Raymond B. Williams. *Buddhists, Hindus, and Sikhs in America: A Short History*. New York: Oxford University Press. 2007.

Mansfield, Stephen. *Japan's Master Gardens: Lessons in Space and Environment*. Rutland, VT: Tuttle, 2011.

Mark, Diane Mai Lin. *Seasons of Light: The History of Chinese Christian Churches in Hawai'i*. Honolulu: Chinese Christian Association of Hawai'i, 1989.

Mason Architects. *Maui Jinsha Shrine, Historic Structure Report*. Washington, DC: United States Department of Interior, 1999.

Masuzawa, Tomoko. *The Invention of World Religions: Or, How European Universalism Was Preserved in the Language of Pluralism*. Chicago: University of Chicago Press, 2005.

Matsunaga, Alicia, and Daigan Matsunaga. *Foundation of Japanese Buddhism*. 2 vols. Los Angeles: Nembutsu Press, 1973.

Matsuoka, Fumitaka. *Out of Silence: Emerging Themes in Asian American Churches*. Cleveland: United Church, 1995.

Mazur, Eric Michael. *The Americanization of Religious Minorities: Confronting the Constitutional Order*. Baltimore: John Hopkins University Press, 1999.

McGregor, Davianna. *Nā Kua'āina: Living Hawaiian Culture*. Honolulu: University of Hawai'i Press, 2007.

McMahan, David L. *The Making of Buddhist Modernism*. Oxford: Oxford University Press, 2008.

McVeigh, Brian. *Spirits, Selves and Subjectivity in a Japanese New Religion.* New York: The Edwin Mellen Press, 1997.

Meyer, Jeffrey. "Asian American Confucianism and Children." In Don S. Browning and Bonnie J. Miller-McLemore, eds. *Children and Childhood in American Religions.* New Brunswick, NJ: Rutgers University Press, 2009.

Min, Pyong Gap. *Asian Americans: Contemporary Trends and Issues.* 2nd ed. Thousand Oaks, CA: Sage, 2005.

Min, Pyong Gap, and Jung Ha Kim, eds. *Religions in Asian America: Building Faith Communities.* Walnut Creek, CA: Altamira, 2002.

Mitchell, Donald W., and Jamese A. Wiseman, eds. *The Gethsemani Encounter: A Dialogue on the Spiritual Life by Buddhist and Christian Monastics.* London: Continuum International, 1997.

Mitter, Partha. *Indian Art.* Oxford: Oxford University Press, 2001.

Mizuno, Kōgen. *Buddhist Sūtras: Origins, Development, Transmission.* Tokyo: Kosei, 1982.

Mizuno, Kōgen. *Essentials of Buddhism: Basic Terminology and Concepts of Buddhist Philosophy and Practice.* Gaynor Sekimori, trans. Tokyo: Kosei, 1996.

Mori, Barbara L. R. *Americans Studying the Traditional Japanese Art of the Tea Ceremony: The Internationalizing of a Traditional Art.* Lewiston, NY: Edward Mellen Press, 1992.

Moriya, Tomoe. *Yemyo Imamura: Pioneer American Buddhist.* Honolulu: Buddhist Study Center Press, 2000.

Muhammad Asad, trans. and ed. *The Message of the Qur'ān.* London: The Book Foundation, 2008.

Murata, Sachiko, and William C. Chittick. *The Vision of Islam.* St. Paul, MN: Paragon House, 1994.

Murphy-Shigematsu, Stephen. *When Half Is Whole: Multiethnic Asian American Identity.* Stanford, CA: Stanford University Press. 2012.

Nakanishi, Don, and James Lai. *Asian American Politics: Law, Participation and Policy.* Lanham, MD: Rowman and Littlefield Press, 2003.

Nakashima-Brock, Rita. "Asian Protestantism." In *Encyclopedia of Women and Religion in North America.* Bloomington: Indiana University Press, 2006, pp. 498–505.

Nakasone, Ronald Y., ed. *Okinawa Diaspora.* Honolulu: University of Hawai'i Press, 2002.

Nakasone, Ronald Y. "Late Life, Mortuary, and Memorial Rituals in the Japanese Community." *Journal of Religious Gerontology* 15, no. 4 (2003): 3–14.

Nakasone, Ronald Y. "Journeying into Elderhood, Reflections on Growing Old in Asian Cultures." *Generations, Journal of the American Society on Aging* 31, no. 2 (2008).

Nakasone, Ronald Y. "Formless Form: The Aesthetics of *Sho* (Calligraphy)." *Arts in Religion and Theological Studies* 21, no. 2 (2011): 4–11.

Nakayama Miki. *Mikagura-uta, the Songs for the Service.* Tenri: Tenrikyō Church Headquarters, 1967.

Nakayama Miki. *Ofudesaki.* Tenri: Tenrikyō Church Headquarters, 1993.

Nakka-Camauf, Viji, and Tseng, Timothy. *Asian American Christianity: A Reader.* Lulu.com. 2009.

Neilsen, Reid L., Stephen C. Harper, Craig K. Manscill, and Mary Jane Woodger Goodman, eds. *Regional Studies in Latter-day Saint Church History: The Pacific Isles.* Provo, UT: Religious Studies Center, Brigham Young University, 2008.

Nguyen, Mimi Thi, and Thuy Linh Nguyen Tu, eds. *Alien Encounters: Popular Culture in Asian America.* Durham, NC: Duke University Press, 2007.

Nichiren Shōshū Temple. *Nichiren Shōshū: Basics of Practice*. Rev. ed. West Hollywood, CA: Nichiren Shōshū Temple, 2003.

Niiya, Brian ed. *Encyclopedia of Japanese American History*. New York: Facts on File, 2000.

Niwano Nikkyō. *Lifetime Beginner: An Autobiography*. Richard L. Gage, trans. Tokyo: Kosei, 1978.

Numrich, Paul David. *Old Wisdom in the New World: Americanization in Two Immigrant Theravāda Buddhist Temples*. Knoxville: The University of Tennessee Press, 1996.

Odo, Franklin, ed. *The Columbia Documentary History of the Asian American Experience*. New York: Columbia University Press, 2002.

Ogawa, Dennis M. *Kodomo no tame ni—For the Sake of the Children: The Japanese American Experience in Hawai'i*. Honolulu: University Press of Hawai'i, 1978.

Ohno, Kazuo, Yoshito Ohno, and Toshio Mizohata. *Kazuo Ohno's World: From Without and Within*. John Barret, trans. Middletown, CT: Wesleyan Press, 2004.

Okakura, Kakuzō. *The Book of Tea*. Mineola, New York: Dover, 1964.

Okihiro, Gary. *Margins and Mainstreams: Asians in American History and Culture*. Seattle: University of Washington Press, 2014.

Omi, Michael, and Howard Winant. *Racial Formation in the United States*. 3rd ed. New York: Routledge, 1986.

Osorio, Jonathan. *Dismembering Lahui: A History of the Hawaiian Nation to 1887*. Honolulu: University of Hawai'i Press, 2002.

Oster, Maggie. *Reflections of the Spirit: Japanese Gardens in America*. New York: Dutton Studio Books, 1993.

Oyama, Kōryū. *History of Hawai'i Sōtōshū 1903–1978*. Honolulu: Shōbōji Sōtō Temple, 1978.

Pacific and Asian American Center for Theology and Strategies Collection, 1972–2002. Berkeley, CA: Graduate Theological Union Library, 2003.

Paddison, Joshua. *American Heathens: Religion, Race, and Reconstruction in California*. Berkeley: University of California Press, 2012.

Park, Albert L., and David K. Yoo. *Encountering Modernity: Christianity in East Asia and Asian America (Intersections: Asian & Pacific American Transcultural Studies)*. Honolulu: University of Hawai'i Press, 2014.

Park, John, and Ed Park. *Probationary Americans: Contemporary Immigration Policies and the Shaping of Asian American Communities*. New York: Routledge, 2005.

Parrenas, Rhacel S., and Lok C. D. Siu, eds. *Asian Diasporas: New Formations, New Conceptions*. Palo Alto: Stanford University Press, 2007.

Pew Research Center. *Faith in Flux: Changes in Religious Affiliation in the United States*. Washington, DC: Pew Forum on Religion and Public Life, 2009.

Phan, Peter. *Vietnamese-American Catholics*. Mahwah, NJ: Paulist Press, 2005.

Phan, Peter C. *Christianity with an Asian Face: Asian American Theology in the Making*. New York: Orbis Books, 2003.

P'ian, Rulan Chao. "Music and the Confucian Sacrificial Ceremony." In Lawrence E. Sullivan ed. *Enchanting Powers: Music in the World's Religions*. Cambridge, MA: Harvard University Press, 1997.

Political Status Education Coordinating Commission. *Kinalamten Pulitikåt: Siñenten I Chamoru—Issues in Guam's Political Development: The Chamorro Perspective*. Hagåtña: The Political Status Education Coordinating Commission, 2003.

Prebish, Charles S., and Martin Baumann, eds. *Westward Dharma: Buddhism beyond Asia*. Berkeley: University of California Press, 2002.

Prebish, Charles, and Kenneth Tanaka, eds. *The Faces of Buddhism in America*. Berkeley: University of California Press, 1998.

Prema Kurien, *A Place at the Multicultural Table: The Development of an American Hinduism*. New Brunswick, NJ: Rutgers University Press, 2007.

Preston, David. *The Social Organization of Zen Practice: Constructing Transcultural Reality*. Cambridge: Cambridge University Press, 1988.

Pukui, Mary Kawena, E. W. Haertig, and Catherine A. Lee. *Nānā I Ke Kum: Look to the Source*. Honolulu: Hui Hanai, 1972. The original was a single edition; the reprints are in two volumes.

Putten, Jan van der, and Mary Kilcline Cody, eds. *Lost Times and Untold Tales from the Malay World*. Singapore: NUS Press, 2009.

Quang Minh, Thich. "Vietnamese Buddhism in America." Electronic Theses, Treatises and Dissertations, 2007. Paper 1589. http://diginole.lib.fsu.edu/etd/1589/.

Radhakrishnan, Sarvepalli. *The Bhagavadgītā*. New Delhi: HarperCollins India, 1993.

Radhakrishnan, Sarvepalli. *The Hindu View of Life*. New Delhi: HarperCollins India, 2009.

Rah, Soong Chan. *The Next Evangelicalism: Freeing the Church from Western Cultural Captivity*. Downers Grove, IL: IVP Books, 2009.

Rahman, Fazlur. *Islam*. London: Weidenfeld and Nicolson, 1966.

Reichl, Christopher Albert. "Transplantation of a Ryūkyūan New Religion Overseas: Hawaiian Ijun." *Japanese Religions* 30, nos. 1 &2 (2005): 55–68.

Reichl, Christopher Albert. "The Globalization of a Japanese New Religion: Ethnohistory of Seichō no Ie." *Japanese Religions* 36, nos. 1–2 (2011): 67–82.

Renard, John. *Seven Doors to Islam*. Berkeley: University of California Press, 1996.

Report of the Commission on Wartime Relocation and Internment of Civilians (CWRIC). *Personal Justice Denied*. Seattle: University of Washington Press, 1997.

Reps, Paul. *Zen Flesh, Zen Bones*. Rutland: Tuttle, 1957.

Rinehart, Robin, ed. *Contemporary Hinduism: Ritual, Culture, and Practice*. Santa Barbara, CA: ABC-CLIO, 2004.

Robinson, Richard H., and Willard L. Johnson. *The Buddhist Religion: A Historical Introduction*. Belmont, CA: Wadsworth, 1970.

Rochford, E. Burke. *Hare Krishna in America*. New Brunswick, NJ: Rutgers University Press, 1985.

Roof, Wade Clark, and William McKinney. *American Mainline Religion: Its Changing Shape and Future*. New Brunswick, NJ: Rutgers University Press, 1987.

Rudiger, Busto. "Disorienting Subjects: Reclaiming Pacific Islander/Asian American Religion." In Jane Iwamura and Paul Spickard, eds. *Revealing the Sacred in Asian and Pacific America*. New York: Routledge Press, 2003.

Russell, Scott. *Tiempon I Manmofo'na: Ancient Chamoru Culture and History of the Northern Mariana Islands*. Saipan: Division of Historic Preservation, 1998.

Sadakata, Akira. *Buddhist Cosmology: Philosophy and Origins*. Tokyo: Kosei, 1997.

Safadi, Yasin Hamid. *Islamic Calligraphy*. Boulder, CO: Shambhala, 1979.

Sakashita, Jay. "Shinnyoen and the Transmission of Japanese New Religion Abroad." Dissertation, University of Stirling, 1998. https://dspace.stir.ac.uk/handle/1893/2264.

Salyer, Lucy E. *Laws Harsh as Tigers: Chinese Immigrants and the Shaping of Modern Immigration Law*. Chapel Hill: University of North Carolina Press, 1995.

Sano, Roy, comp. *Theologies of Asian Americans and Pacific Peoples*. Berkeley, CA: Asian Center for Theologies and Strategies, 1976.

Saroglou, Vassilas. "Religious Bricolage as a Psychological Reality: Limits, Structures and Dynamics." *Social Compass* 53 (2006): 109–115.

Schimmel, Annemarie. *Calligraphy and Islamic Culture*. New York: New York University Press, 1990.

Schimmel, Annemarie. *Islam: An Introduction*. Albany: State University of New York Press, 1992.

Schipper, Kristofer Marinus, and Franciscus Verellen. *The Taoist Canon: A Historical Companion to the Daozang*. Chicago: University of Chicago Press, 2004.

Seager, Richard Hughes. *Buddhism in America*. New York: Columbia University Press, 1999.

Seager, Richard Hughes. *Encountering the Dharma: Daisaku Ikeda, Soka Gakkai, and the Globalization of Buddhist Humanism*. Berkeley: University of California Press, 2006.

Seiō (Okada Kōtama*)*. *Goseigen: The Holy Words*. Tujunga: Sekai Mahikari Bunmei Kyōdan, 1982.

Sered, Susan, and Linda Barnes, eds. *Religious Healing in Urban America*. Oxford: Oxford University Press, 2005.

Shackle, Christopher, and Arvind Mandair, eds. *Teachings of the Sikh Gurus: Selections from the Sikh Scriptures*. New York: Routledge, 2005.

Sharma, D. S. *A Primer of Hinduism*. Chennai, India: Sri Ramakrishna Math, 2010.

Shim, Jae-ryong. *Korean Buddhism: Tradition and Transformation*. Soeul: Jimoondang Publishing, 1999.

Shimizu, Celine Parrenas. *The Hypersexuality of Race: Performing Asian/American Women on Screen and Scene*. Durham, NC: Duke University Press, 2007.

Siegler, Elijah. "'Back to the Pristine': Identity Formation and Legitimation in Contemporary American Daoism." *Nova Religio* 14, no.1 (October 2010): 45–66.

Silva, Noenoe. *Aloha Betrayed: Native Hawaiian Resistance to American Colonialism*. London: Duke University Press, 2004.

Singh, Nikky-Guninder Kaur, trans. *The Name of My Beloved: Verses of the Sikh Gurus*. San Francisco: Harper San Francisco, 1995.

Singh, Shanta Serbjeet, ed. *Indian Dance: The Ultimate Metaphor*. Chicago: Arts Media, 2000.

Singleton, Mark. *The Yoga Body*. Oxford: Oxford University Press, 2010.

Smith, Christian. *American Evangelicalism: Embattled and Thriving*. Chicago: University of Chicago Press, 1998.

Smith, Jane I. *Islam in America*. New York: Colombia University Press, 1999.

Snodgrass, Adrian. *The Symbolism of the Stupa*. Ithaca, NY: Southeast Asian Program, Cornell University, 1985.

Snow, David A. *Shakubuku: A Study of the Nichiren Shōshū Buddhist Movement in America, 1960–1975*. New York: Garland, 1993.

Snow, Jennifer. *Protestant Missionaries, Asian Immigrants, and American Ideologies of Race, 1850–1924*. New York: Routledge, 2007.

Spiro, Melford E. *Buddhism and Society: A Great Tradition and Its Burmese Vicissitude*s. Berkeley: University of California Press, 1982.

Stalker, Nancy K. *Prophet Motive: Deguchi Onisaburō, Oomoto, and the Rise of New Religions in Imperial Japan*. Honolulu: University of Hawai'i Press, 2008.

Stanley, Sharon. *Bamboo, Borders, and Bricks: Theology Building for Housing Improvements with Lao Refugees in Fresno, California.* Decatur: Columbia Theological Seminary, 2008.

Stark, Rodney, Eva Hamberg, and Alan Miller. "Exploring Spirituality and Unchurched Religions in America, Sweden, and Japan." *Journal of Contemporary Religion* 20, no. 1 (2005): 3–23.

Suh, Sharon A. *Being Buddhist in a Christian World: Gender and Community in a Korean American Temple.* Seattle: University of Washington Press, 2004.

Sūkyō Mahikari. *Holy Words: Goseigen.* Rancho Santa Margarita, CA: Bishop of North American Region of Sūkyō Mahikari, 2002.

Suzuki, Daisetz Teitaro, and Richard M. Jaffe. *Zen and Japanese Culture.* Princeton, NJ: Princeton University Press, 2010.

Suzuki, Shunryū. Trudy Dixon, ed. *Zen Mind, Beginner's Mind.* New York: Weatherhill Press, 1970.

Swain, Tony, and Garry Trompf. *The Religions of Oceania.* London: Routledge, 1995.

Swatos, William, ed. *Encyclopedia of Religion and Society.* Walnut Creek, CA: Alta Mira Press, 1998.

Swatos, William and Daniel Olson. *The Secularization Debate.* Lanham, MD: Rowman and Littlefield, 2000.

Swearer, Donald K. *The Buddhist World of Southeast Asia.* Albany: State University of New York Press, 1995.

Syonzi, Michael. "Secularization Theories and the Study of Chinese Religions." *Social Compass* 56, no. 3 (2009): 312–327.

Tabrah, Ruth M. *A Grateful Past, A Promising Future: The First Hundred Years of Honpa Hongwanji in Hawai'i.* Honolulu: Honpa Hongwanji Mission of Hawai'i, 1989.

Takaki, Ronald. *Raising Cane: The World of Plantation Hawai'i (Asian American Experience).* New York: Chelsea House, 1994.

Takaki, Ronald. *Strangers from a Different Shore: A History of Asian Americans.* Revised and updated. Boston: Back Bay Books, 1998.

Takezawa, Yasuko I. *Breaking the Silence: Redress and Japanese American Ethnicity.* Ithaca, NY: Cornell University Press, 1995.

Tan, Jonathan. *Introducing Asian American Theologies.* New York: Orbis Books, 2008.

Tanabe, George, and Willa Tanabe. *Japanese Buddhist Temples in Hawai'i.* Honolulu: University of Hawai'i Press, 2013.

Tatla, Darshan Singh. *Sikhs in North America: An Annotated Bibliography.* Westport, CT: Greenwood Press, 1991.

Tatz, Mark, trans. *Buddhism and Healing: Demiéville's article "Byō" from Hōbōgirin.* Lanham, MD: University Press of America, 1985.

Tenrikyō Church Headquarters. *Mikagura-uta: The Songs for the Service.* Tenri: Tenrikyō Church Headquarters, 1967.

Tenrikyō Church Headquarters. *Ofudesaki.* Tenri: Tenrikyō Church Headquarters, 1993.

Tenrikyō Mission Headquarters of Hawai'i, ed. *Short History of Tenrikyō in Hawai'i.* Honolulu: Tenrikyō Mission Headquarters of Hawai'i, 1987.

Thompson, Laurence G. *Chinese Religion: An Introduction.* Belmont, CA: Wadsworth, 1979.

Tobu Museum of Art. *Buddha: The Spread of Buddhist Art in Asia.* Tokyo: NHK, 1998.

Trungpa, Chögyam. *Crazy Wisdom.* Boston: Shambhala, 1991.

Trungpa, Chögyam. *Cutting through Spiritual Materialism.* Boston: Shambhala, 1987.

Tu, Weiming, *Centrality and Commonality: An Essay on Confucian Religiousness* (a revised and enlarged edition of *Centrality and Commonality: An Essay on Chung-yung*). Albany: State University of New York Press, 1989.

Tuck, Donald R. *Buddhist Churches of America: Jōdo Shinshū*. Lewiston, NY: Edwin Mellon Press, 1987.

Tumang, Patricia, and Jenesha de Rivera, eds. *Homelands: Women's Journeys across Race, Place, and Time*. Emeryville, CA: Seal, 2006.

Turner, James W. "The Water of Life: *Kava* Ritual and the Logic of Sacrifice." *Ethnology* 25, no. 3 (July 1986): 203–214. http://www.jstor.org/stable/3773584.

Tweed, Thomas A., and Stephen Prothero, eds. *Asian Religions in America: A Documentary History*. New York: Oxford University Press, 1999.

Ueshiba, Kisshomaru. *Aikidō*. Tokyo: Hozansha, 1985.

Ueshiba, Morihei. *Budō Training in Aikidō*. Tokyo: Kodansha, 1999.

United States Department of State. "International Religious Freedom Report 2010: Tonga." http://www.state.gov/j/drl/rls/irf/2010/148900.htm.

Valeri, Valerio. *Kingship and Sacrifice: Ritual and Society in Ancient Hawai'i*. Paula Wissing, trans. Chicago: University of Chicago Press, 1985.

Van Esterik, Penny. *Taking Refuge: Lao Buddhists in North America*. Tempe: Program for Southeast Asian Studies, Arizona State University, 1992.

Varley, Paul. *Japanese Culture*. Honolulu: University of Hawai'i Press, 2000.

Vergara, Winfred. *Mainstreaming: Asian Americans in the Episcopal Church*. New York: Office of Asian American Ministries, 2005.

Vertovec, Steven, and Robin Cohen, eds. *Migration, Diasporas, and Transnationalism*. The International Library of Studies on Migration. Cheltenham, UK: Edward Elgar, 1999.

Vivekananda (Swami). *Complete Works of Swami Vivekananda*. 9 vols. India: Advaita Ashrama, 2001.

Volpp, Leti. "The Citizen and the Terrorist." *UCLA Law Review* 49 (2002).

Walter, Mariko Namba, and Eva Jane Neumann Fridman, eds. *Shamanism: An Encyclopedia of World Beliefs, Practices, and Culture*. Santa Barbara, CA: ABC-CLIO, 2004.

Waterhouse, John, ed. *Global Religious Movements in Regional Context*. Burlington, VT: Ashgate, 2002.

Weiler, Kathleen. "Freire and a Feminist Pedagogy of Difference." *Harvard Educational Review* 61 (1991): 449–474.

Westgeest, Helen. *Zen in the Fifties: Interaction in Art between East and West*. Amsterdam: Waanders, 1996.

Weston, Erin Leigh. "Transcultural Possessions in/of Mahikari: Religious Syncretism in Martinique." *Japanese Studies Review* 6, no.1 (2002): 45–62.

Whaling, Frank. *Understanding the Brahma Kumaris*. Edinburgh: Dunedin Academic Press, 2012.

White, James W. *The Sokagakkai and Mass Society*. Palo Alto, CA: Stanford University Press, 1970.

Williams, Duncan, and Christopher Queen, eds. *American Buddhism: Methods and Findings in Recent Scholarship*. London: Curzon Press, 1998.

Williams, Duncan Ryuken, and Tomoe Moriya, eds. *Issei Buddhism in the Americas*. Urbana: University of Illinois Press, 2010.

Williams, Raymond Brady. *Christian Pluralism in the United States: The Indian Immigrant Experience*. Cambridge Studies in Religious Traditions. New York: Cambridge University Press, 1996.

Williams, Raymond Brady. *Religions of Immigrants from India and Pakistan: New Threads in the American Tapestry*. New York: Cambridge University Press, 1988.

Williamson, Robert W. *Religious and Cosmic Beliefs in Central Polynesia*. 2 vols. Cambridge: Cambridge University Press, 1933.

Wing-tsit Chan, compiler. *A Source Book in Chinese Philosophy*. Princeton, NJ: Princeton University Press, 1969.

Winther-Tamaki, Bert. *Art in the Encounter of Nations: Japanese and American Artists in the Early Postwar Years*. Honolulu: University of Hawai'i Press, 2001.

Wong, Deborah Anne. *Speak It Louder: Asian Americans Making Music*. New York: Routledge, 2004.

Wong, Eva. *Feng-shui: The Ancient Wisdom of Harmonious Living for Modern Times*. Boston: Shambhala, 1996.

Wong, Eva. *The Shambhala Guide to Taoism*. Boston: Shambhala, 1997.

Wu, Emily S. *Traditional Chinese Medicine in the United States: In Search of Spiritual Meaning and Ultimate Health*. New York: Lexington Books, 2013.

Wu, Frank. *Yellow: Race in America beyond Black and White*. New York: Basic Books, 2002.

Wu, Jean Yu-Wen Shen, and Thomas Chen, eds. *Asian American Studies Now: A Critical Reader*. New Brunswick, NJ: Rutgers University Press, 2010.

Wu, Jyh Cherng. *Daoist Meditation: The Purification of the Heart Method of Meditation and Discourse on Sitting and Forgetting (Zuo Wang Lun)*. London: Singing Dragon, 2014.

Yanagawa, Kei'ichi, ed. *Japanese Religions in California: A Report on Research within and without the Japanese American Community*, Tokyo: University of Tokyo, 1983.

Yang, Fenggang. *Chinese Christians in America: Conversion, Assimilation, and Adhesive Identities*. University Park: Pennsylvania State University Press, 1999.

Yano, Christine Reiko. *Crowning the Nice Girl: Gender, Ethnicity, and Culture in Hawai'i's Cherry Blossom Festival*. Honolulu: University of Hawai'i Press, 2006.

Yarber, Angela. *Embodying the Feminine in the Dances of the World's Religions*. New York: Peter Lang Press, 2011.

Yee, Edmond. *The Soaring Crane: Stories of Asian Lutherans in North America*. Minneapolis: Augsburg Fortress, 2002.

Yee, James. *For God and Country: Faith and Patriotism under Fire, Former U.S. Army Muslim Chaplain at Guantanamo Bay*. New York: Public Affairs Books, 2005.

Yeh, Chiou-Ling. *Making an American Festival: Chinese New Year in San Francisco's Chinatown*. Berkeley: University of California Press, 2008.

Yoo, David K. *Growing Up Nisei: Race, Generation, and Culture among Japanese Americans of California, 1924–49*. Urbana: University of Illinois Press. 2000.

Yoo, David K., ed. *New Spiritual Homes: Religion and Asian Americans*. Honolulu: University of Hawai'i Press, 1999.

Yoo, David K., and Ruth H. Chung, eds. *Religion and Spirituality in Korean America*. Chicago: University of Illinois Press, 2008.

Young, Kanalu G. Terry. *Rethinking the Native Hawaiian Past*. New York: Garland, 1998.

Yu, Chun-fang. *Kuan-yin: The Chinese Transformation of Avalokiteśvara*. New York: Columbia University Press, 2001.

Yu, Eui-Young. "The Growth of Korean Buddhism in the United States, with Special Reference to Southern California." *Pacific World: Journal of the Institute of Buddhist Studies*, new series, 4 (1988): 82–93.

Yu, Geunhee. "Asian American Disciples." In Douglas A. Foster, et al., ed. *The Encyclopedia of the Stone-Campbell Movement*. Grand Rapids, MI: William B. Eerdmans, 2004.

Yu, Henry. *Thinking Orientals: Migration, Contact, and Exoticism in Modern America*. New York: Oxford University Press, 2001.

Zhou, Min, and James V. Gatewood. *Contemporary Asian America: A Multidisciplinary Reader*. New York: New York University Press, 2000.

Zikmund, Barbara B. *Hidden Histories in the United Church of Christ*. New York: United Church of Christ Press, 1984.

Zysk, Kenneth G. *Asceticism and Healing in Ancient India: Medicine in the Buddhist Monastery*. Delhi: Oxford University Press, 1991.

Film

Aloha Buddha Documentary. Produced by Lorraine Minatoishi and directed by Bill Ferehawk and Dylan Robertson. DVD, 72 min. West Hollywood, CA: Radiant Features, 2011.

Children of the Camps: The Documentary. Produced by Satsuki Ina. Directed and edited by Stephen Holsapple. DVD, 57 minutes. National PBS Broadcast, 1999.

Death of a Shaman. Produced by Richard Hall and Fahm Fong Saeyang. DVD, 54 min. Seattle: IndieFlix, 2000.

Moving Mountains: The Story of the Yiu Mien. Produced and directed by Elaine Velazquez. DVD, 58 min. Portland, OR: Feather & Fin Productions, 1989. Available at http://www.folkstreams.net/film,149

Redress: The JACL Campaign for Justice. Produced by Cherry Kinoshita, Carole Hayashino, and William Yoshino. VHS video, 40 min. San Francisco: JACL, 1991.

Sa-I-Gu. Kim-Gibson, Dai Sil, Christine Choy, and Elaine Kim. Produced by Dai Sil Kim-Gibson and Elaine Kim and directed by Dai Sil Kim Gibson and Christine Choy. DVD, 36 min. San Francisco: Center for Asian American Media, 1993.

The Orator (O le tulāfale). Produced by Catherine Fitzgerald. Written and directed by Tusi Tamasese. New Zealand Film Commission and Sāmoan Government. DVD, 106 min, 2011.

Editors and Contributors

Editors

Jonathan H. X. Lee, PhD, is an associate professor of Asian American studies who specializes in Southeast Asian and Sino-Southeast Asian American studies at San Francisco State University. He received his PhD in religious studies from the University of California at Santa Barbara in 2009. He is the founder and program co-chair of the Asian American Religious Studies section for the American Academy of Religion, Western Region (AAR/WR) conference. His work has been published in *Peace Review: A Journal of Social Justice*; *Nidan: International Journal for the Study of Hinduism*; *Chinese America: History & Perspective; the Journal of the Chinese Historical Society of America*; *Empty Vessel: The Journal of the Daoist Arts*; *Spotlight on Teaching/American Academy of Religion*; *Asia Pacific Perspectives*; *Pacific World: Journal of the Institute of Buddhist Studies*; *JATI: Journal of Southeast Asian Studies*; *Amerasia Journal,* and other journals and anthologies, both nationally and internationally. His works include *Cambodian American Experiences: Histories, Communities, Cultures, and Identities* (2010, second edition 2015); co-editor with Kathleen M. Nadeau of the *Encyclopedia of Asian American Folklore and Folklife* (2011) and *Asian American Identities and Practices: Folkloric Expressions in Everyday Life* (2014); co-editor with Yuk Wah Chan and David Haines of *The Age of Asian Migration: Continuity, Diversity, and Susceptibility, volume 1* (2014); and author of *History of Asian Americans: Exploring Diverse Roots* (2015). He has published extensively on Chinese, Cambodian, Vietnamese, Chinese–Southeast Asian, and Asian American histories, folklore, cultures, and religions.

Fumitaka Matsuoka, PhD, is Robert Gordon Sproul Professor of Theology Emeritus and the former Executive Director of PANA Institute (Institute for Leadership Development and the Study of Pacific and Asian American Religion) at Pacific School of Religion, Berkeley, California. An ordained minister in the Church of the Brethren,

Matsuoka served as a pastor in California, an educational missionary in Indonesia, and in campus ministries in Japan. He taught theology and Asian American ministries at PSR and served as director of the Pacific and Asian American Center for Theology and Strategies from 1984 to 1987. He was then appointed to be academic dean of Bethany Theological Seminary in Oakbrook, Illinois (1987–1992) and served as dean of the faculty and vice president for academic affairs at PSR from 1993 to 2000. Matsuoka delves into cross-cultural and cross-ethnic dimensions of ministry and theology in his books, *The Color of Faith* (1998); *Out of Silence: Emerging Theological Themes of Asian American Churches* (1995); and *Realizing the America of Our Hearts: Theological Voices of Asian Americans,* co-edited with Eleazar Fernandez (2003). His publications also include *Learning to Speak a New Tongue: Imagining a Way That Holds People Together—An Asian American Conversation* (2011) and *Asian and Oceanic Christianities in Conversation: Exploring Theological Identities at Home and in Diaspora,* co-edited with Heup Young Kim and Anri Morimoto (2011).

Ronald Y. Nakasone, PhD, is a member of the Core Doctoral Faculty at the Graduate Theological Union (GTU) in Berkeley, California, a member of the faculty of College of Religious Studies at Mahidol University, Thailand, and a longtime faculty member at the Stanford University Center for Geriatric Education (1990–2012). He has published more than 120 scholarly books and articles on Buddhist studies, ethics, and aesthetics; aging and spirituality; and Ryūkyūan (Okinawan) studies. Students and colleagues contributed essays to *Memory and Imagination, Essays and Explorations in Buddhist Thought and Culture* (Kyoto: Nagata, 2010), a festschrift that commemorated his completion of one life cycle (60 years) according to the Chinese zodiac. He received the Sarlo Excellence in Teaching Award from the Graduate Theological Union in 2011. Born and raised in Hawai'i, Professor Nakasone studied at the University of Hawai'i, Ryūkoku University (Kyoto), University of Wisconsin–Madison, and Harvard University. An accomplished *sho* (calligrapher) artist, he has exhibited in Kyoto, Tokyo, Paris, Seoul, Xian, Chiang Mai, and cities throughout the United States. His works are in the permanent collections of the Mobile Museum of Art, National Museum of Fine Arts, Havana, the Graduate Theological Union (GTU), Chiang Mai University; and in private collections in Japan, Okinawa, Thailand, Spain, and the United States. He is an ordained Jōdo Shinshū (Pure Land) priest.

Edmond Yee, PhD, is an author, editor, translator, and Professor Emeritus of Asian Studies, Pacific Lutheran Theological Seminary. He was also a member of the Core Doctoral Faculty for the Graduate Theological Union, of which Pacific Lutheran Theological Seminary is a member school. Both institutions are in Berkeley, California. Yee received his PhD degree from the University of California, Berkeley. His publications, in Chinese and English, cover the areas of Chinese literature and culture, Confucian thought, and Asian and Asian American Lutherans.

Contributors

Dean Ryuta Adachi, PhD candidate
Claremont Graduate University
Claremont, California

Ryan J. T. Adams, PhD
University of California, Santa
Barbara

Barbara A. Amodio, PhD
Housatonic Community College and
Oceania Digambara, Inc.
Norwalk, Connecticut

Shereen Bhalla, PhD candidate
University of Texas, San Antonio

Kusala Bhikshu
International Buddhist Meditation
Center

Jayanta Bhowmik, MA
Independent Scholar

Alfred Bloom, PhD
University of Hawai'i

Trikartikaningsih Byas, PhD
Queensborough Community College,
New York

Asiroh Cham, MA
University of California, Los Angeles

Sylvia Chan-Malik, PhD
Rutgers, The State University of New
Jersey

Joseph Cheah, OSM, PhD
Saint Joseph College
West Hartford, Connecticut

Carolyn E. Chen, PhD
Northwestern University
Evanston, Illinois

Patrick S. Cheng, PhD
Episcopal Divinity School
Cambridge, Massachusetts

Rueyling Chuang, PhD
California State University, San
Bernardino

James Chuck, ThD
First Chinese Baptist Church, San
Francisco
American Baptist Seminary of the
West, Berkeley

Sue Fawn Chung, PhD
University of Nevada, Las Vegas

Peter Yuichi Clark, PhD
University of California, San
Francisco
American Baptist Seminary of the
West

**Niccole Leilanionapae'āina Coggins,
PhD student**
University of California, Santa
Barbara

Sister Chandrika Desai
Brahma Kumaris World Spiritual
Organization

Sophia Dewitt, MDiv
Fresno Interdenominational Refugees
Ministries

Sonia Dhami
Sikh Foundation

**Jonathan Frank Blas Diaz, PhD
candidate**
Union Institute and University, Los
Angeles

Peter L. Doebler, PhD
Graduate Theological Union
Berkeley, California

Joanne Doi, MM, PhD
Maryknoll Sisters Integration
Program, Chicago, Illinois

Donald C. Drummond, PhD
Ryukoku University Berkeley Center

Rev. Eijun Bill Eidson
Koyasan Shingon Tenchiji Temple

Ronald Epstein, PhD
Dharma Realm Buddhist University
San Francisco State University

Brett Esaki, PhD
Georgia State University

Julia Keiko Higa Matsui Estrella, MA
Hawai'i Pacific and Asian
American Center for Theologies and
Strategies

Sean Feit
University of California, Davis

Larry Fraher, PhD
University of Mary
Tempe, Arizona

Neil Gotanda, JD
Western State College of Law
Fullerton, California

Hans Goto
Bay Marin Aikido

Maya Hara
Independent Scholar

Francis X. Hezel, SJ
Fordham University

Ikuo Higashibaba, PhD
Tenri University, Nara, Japan

Bishop Chishin Hirai
Nichiren Mission of Hawai'i

David Hirano, DMin
Central Union Church, Honolulu,
Hawai'i

Linh Hoang, PhD
Siena College, New York

Christine J. Hong, PhD
Presbyterian Mission Agency
Louisville Presbyterian Theological
Seminary

Janet Ikeda
Washington and Lee University
Lexington, Virginia

Myra Ikeda
New York Buddhist Church

Sushil Jain, PhD
University of Windsor
Ontario, Canada

Russell Jeung, PhD
San Francisco State University

Wonhee Anne Joh, PhD
Garrett-Evangelical Theological
Seminary
Evanston, Illinois

Rabia Kamal, PhD
University of San Francisco

Julius-Kei Kato, PhD
King's at Western University

Helen Jin Kim, PhD candidate
Harvard University
Cambridge, Massachusetts

Nami Kim, ThD
Spelman College
Atlanta, Georgia

Sarah Kingsbery
Lexington Theological Seminary

Prasong Kittinanthachai, PhD
Ramkhamhaeng University, Thailand

Neal Kenji Koga
Independent Scholar

Michael Kohn, BA
Journalist and author for Lonely Planet
San Francisco, California

Rev. Koyo S. Kubose, PhD
Bright Dawn Center of Oneness
Buddhism

Timothy S. Lee, PhD
Brite Divinity School, Texas Christian
University

Ying Li, PhD student
University of Texas, San Antonio

Michael J. Liberatore, Doctoral
student
Ateneo de Manila University
Quezon City, Philippines

Patricia Y. C. E. Lin, PhD
University of California, Berkeley

Rev. Gerald C. Liu, PhD
Drew Theological School, Drew
University
Madison, New Jersey

Raymond Lum, PhD
Harvard University
Cambridge, Massachusetts

Sr. Betty Ann Maheu, MM
Hong Kong Diocesan China Research
Centre

Geetha A. Mandayam, PhD
California State University, Long
Beach

Lisa Rose Mar, PhD
University of Maryland, College Park

Michael Maricio, BA
Independent Scholar

Patit Paban Mishra, PhD
Sambalpur University
Orissa, India

Scott A. Mitchell, PhD
Institute of Buddhist Studies
Graduate Theological Union
Berkeley, California

Marimas Hosan Mostiller, PhD
student
University of Hawai'i, Manoa

Kathleen Nadeau, PhD
California State University, San
Bernardino

Rev. Dr. Paul M. Nagano
American Baptist Minister

Rose S. Nakamura
Project Dana
Honolulu, Hawai'i

Heather E. Nakasone, MA
Independent Scholar

Rev. Surekha Nelavala, PhD
Evangelical Lutheran Church in
America

Thien-Huong T. Ninh, PhD
University of the West
Los Angeles, California

Kieko Obuse, PhD
Mahidol University, Thailand

Anthony Makana Paris, MA
Independent Scholar
Nānākuli, Hawai'i

Andrew Sung Park, PhD
United Theological Seminary
Dayton, Ohio

Todd LeRoy Perreira, PhD
candidate
University of California, Santa Barbara

Lori Pierce, PhD
DePaul University
Chicago, Illinois

Boonmee Poungpet, PhD candidate
Mahidol University, Thailand

Amba Raghavan
Community Elder

Victor Raj, PhD
Concordia Seminary, St. Louis,
Missouri

Sudthaporn Ratanakul
Mahidol University, Thailand

Amitava Ray, PhD candidate
University at Buffalo, the State
University of New York

Sangita Rayamajhi, PhD
Asian University for Women
Chittagong, Bangladesh

Daigaku Rummé
Zenshuji Soto Temple
Los Angeles, California

Roy I. Sano, PhD
Pacific School of Religion
Berkeley, California

Maura Helen Schmitz, MA
Graduate Theological Union
Berkeley, California

Rev. Kathryn M. Schreiber
United Church of Christ

Sophea Seng, PhD student
University of California, Riverside

Elijah Siegler, PhD
College of Charleston
Charleston, South Carolina

Jaideep Singh, PhD
Sikh American Legal Defense and
Education Fund

Jennifer Snow, PhD
Episcopal Diocese of California

Rev. Dr. Sharon Stanley-Rea, PhD
Refugee & Immigration Ministries
Christian Church (Disciples of
Christ)
Washington, DC

Stephen Suleeman, MA
Jakarta Theological Seminary

Jonathan Y. Tan, PhD
Archbishop Paul J. Hallinan Professor
of Catholic Studies
Case Western Reserve University
Cleveland, Ohio

Rev. Jodo Tanaka
Jōdo Shū North America Buddhist
Missions

Larry M. Taylor, PhD
Center for Art, Religion, and
Education
Guerneville, California

Rev. Richard Tennes, MA
Honpa Hongwanji Mission of Hawai'i

Charles M. Townsend, PhD
University of California, Riverside

Garry W. Trompf, PhD
The University of Sydney, Australia

Rev. Marma C. Urbano
United Church of Christ in the
Philippines

Rev. Dr. Winfred B. Vergara
Missioner, Asiamerica Ministries
The Episcopal Church (The Mission
Society)
New York, New York

Martin J. Verhoeven, PhD
Dharma Realm Buddhist University
Graduate Theological Union
Berkeley, California

Ofelia O. Villero, PhD
Independent Scholar

Colette L. Walker, PhD student
Graduate Theological Union
Berkeley, California

Usha Welaratna, PhD
Independent Scholar
Los Altos, California

Wayne E. Wright, PhD
University of Texas, San Antonio

Emily S. Wu, PhD
Dominican University of California

Rev. Ken Yamada
Jōdo Shinshū Ōtani ha
Berkeley, California

Yeng Yang, PhD candidate
University of San Antonio, Texas

Christina R. Yanko, MA
Jōdo Shinshū Buddhist Temples of
Canada

Angela Yarber, PhD
Graduate Theological Union
Berkeley, California

Hatice Yildiz, PhD student
Graduate Theological Union
Berkeley, California

David K. Yoo, PhD
University of California, Los
Angeles

Yu Xiaofei (Yamada Aki), PhD
Nihon University
Tokyo, Japan

Helena Zeweri, PhD student
Rice University, Houston,
Texas

Index

Essays and main entries in the book are indicated by **boldface** page numbers.